vel with Kids

Gray

For Sally,
Joseph & Eleanor

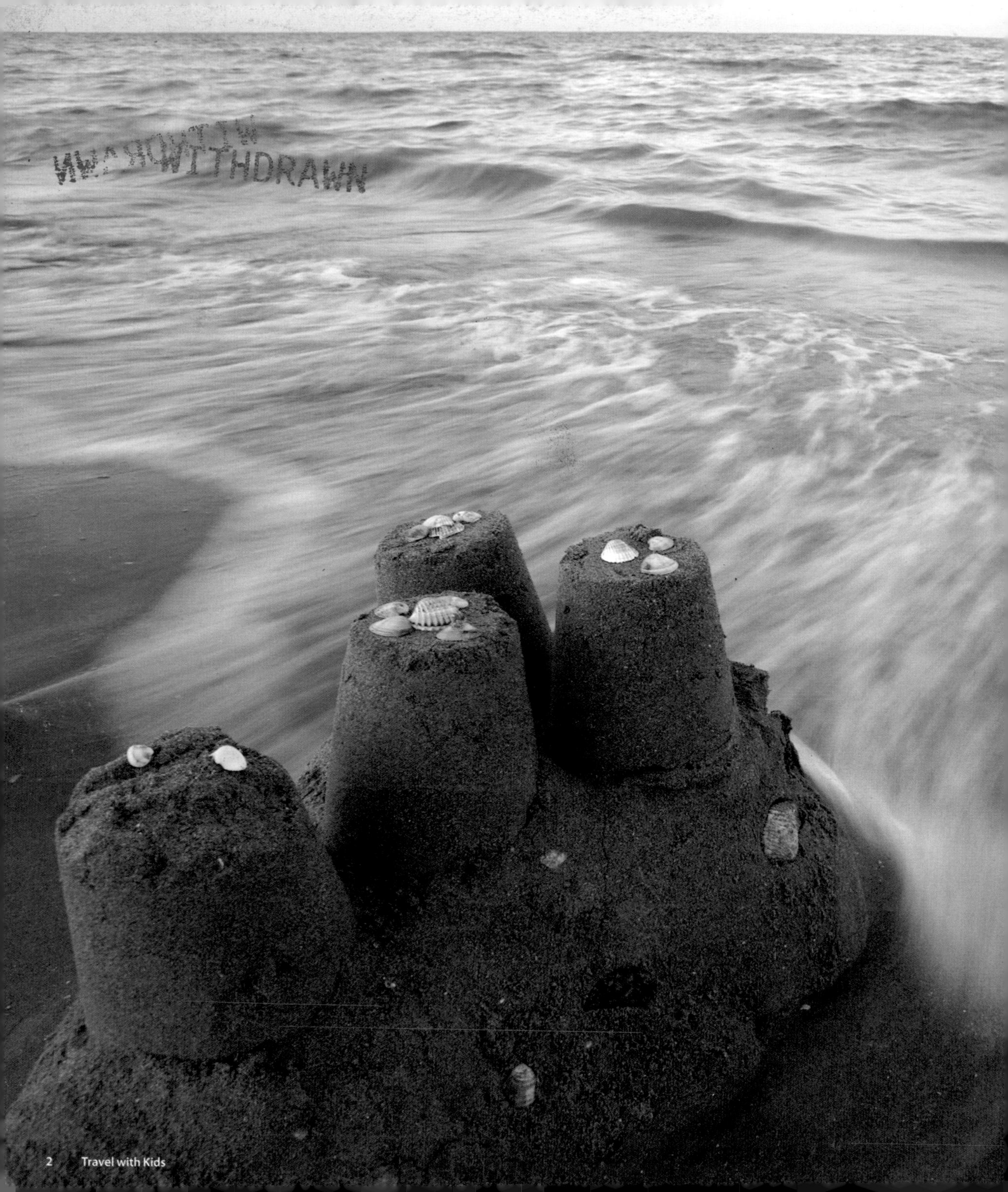

Take your kids travelling! Take them now! Children grow up fast and you'll never find a better, more rewarding opportunity to enrich their lives, minds and souls – or yours – than during a family holiday. It doesn't matter whether you skive off work for a daytrip to the seaside or embark on a three-month odyssey across Asia. From bucket-and-spade to epic escapade, family holidays create memories that will live with you long after your children have grown up. They provide quality time away from the rush and stress of everyday life; they're precious, hard-earned and over all too quickly. Yes, they can also be pricey and hard work – and occasionally they might not go to plan. But they are always money well spent, and even the bad bits inspire family jokes in years to come. So, ignore those miserable types who pour scorn on this indispensable part of life – whose blinkered, joyless view of family holidays never sees beyond travel sickness, stroppy teenagers or how parents could possibly enjoy themselves without banishing the children to a crèche or kids' club. Travelling with kids is about making compromises to meet everyone's needs. It's about sharing and bonding as a family unit. It's the pleasure of showing your children how amazing the world is; of seeing their faces light up at things you might otherwise have taken for granted. Family holidays allow you to take stock of life and appreciate what's really important. So seize them. Travel with your kids. Do it this year and every year you can.

66 99 There have been fraught moments when it hasn't been so much a holiday, as a 'hell-a-day'. But I can honestly say I don't regret a thing. Family holidays are often hard work, but the rewards are rich. Travelling with Joe and Ellie is like exploring the world afresh. I wouldn't want to leave home without them. William Gray

About the author

William Gray is one of the UK's leading travel writers and a regular contributor to the *Sunday Times Travel* and *Wanderlust* magazines. He was voted Travel Writer of the Year in 2002 and won both Travel Photographer of the Year and runner-up Travel Writer of the Year at the 2009 British Guild of Travel Writers' Awards. The following year he was voted 4th in the *Press Gazette's* Top 50 Travel Journalists. Will is also the author of Footprint's *Britain with Kids* and *Cornwall with Kids*. william-gray.co.uk

☆ **Gray family** top 12

★ Snorkelling with sea lions in the Galápagos
★ Learning to surf in New Zealand
★ Island hopping in Hong Kong
★ Driving through the interior of Iceland
★ Comparing Disney on three continents
★ Trekking in the Atlas Mountains
★ Following the Great Migration in Kenya
★ Hunting porcupine with Kalahari Bushmen
★ Horse riding in the Andes
★ Field-testing the UK's best beaches
★ Husky sledging in Finnish Lapland
★ Searching for tigers in India

Travel with Kids is unique. No other guidebook provides such detailed coverage of worldwide family travel. Over the following pages you will find inspiration, advice and ideas for taking your children on holiday pretty much anywhere. Each chapter is divided into five parts. An introduction sets the scene with a map and family-friendly highlights. Next is *Kids' stuff* – packed with ideas, resources and activities to get children interested in each destination, whether it's books to read, games to play or traditional meals to try at home – while *Tots to teens* provides a holiday planner for various age groups. This is followed by the main part of each chapter – a detailed look at the family-holiday potential of key locations. *Grown-ups' stuff* provides essential information on travel nitty-gritty, while *Family favourites* turns the spotlight on a choice selection of child-friendly accommodation. *Travel with Kids* is designed to be both inspirational and informative. You will find plenty of advice, encouragement and reassurance to plan a lifetime of family holidays throughout Europe and beyond. You won't find exhaustive directories of hotels and restaurants or laborious lists of post offices and tourist information centres. Nor will you find every country in the world featured. Those that have been selected, however, reflect a mixture of the most popular, unusual and exciting destinations to take your kids. Happy travels!

Essentials

Bucket and spade to epic escapade – family travel covers everything from seaside holidays to daring adventures

Left: Climbing the giant dunes at Sossusvlei in the Namib Desert.

The magic formula

Go on, admit it. You'd much rather not have one sitting near you on a flight. You board the plane, shuffle down the cramped aisle, coerce your hand luggage into the overhead locker, glance down and there it is – all cute and innocent on its mother's lap. But she's bound to be a hopeless parent, completely incapable of stopping it from howling, vomiting and shredding the newspaper that you try to hide behind for the nine-hour, non-stop flight.

Have baby, won't travel

It's hardly surprising that more parents shun holidays when their children are aged between one and four than at any other time. Not only do practicalities, like flying, become fraught with stress and logistical nightmares (for new parents, the journey of a thousand miles does not begin with a single step – it usually starts with trying to change a nappy in a cramped toilet before take-off), but you are constantly striving to reduce the impact of your little darlings on other, often unsympathetic, travellers. That, combined with the general fatigue that stalks new parents, does little to set the wheels of family travel in motion. We've all been there: sleep deprived, irritable, barely capable of summoning the energy (or baby paraphernalia) for a trip to the shops, let alone a holiday. However, there are at least six good reasons why it's never too early to start travelling with kids:

▸▸ Babies are easy to transport in strollers, backpacks or papooses.
▸▸ They can't dictate where you go or what you do (so make the most of it while it lasts)
▸▸ In most countries locals will make a big fuss of them which is a great morale boost for weary new parents.
▸▸ Babies often go free. The older children get, the more expensive they become, and travel is no exception.
▸▸ There are plenty of innovative baby travel products designed to make life easier.
▸▸ Choose the right hotel or resort and you get some well-deserved pampering.

Onwards, upwards and falling over

With toddlerdom come new challenges. In fact, many parents claim this to be the most demanding time to travel with children. If only toddlers had an on-off switch or some way of containing all that energy and frustration pent up in a body that won't always do what it's meant to – or, worse still, is prevented from doing so by ever-watchful parents. With this age group, you have to be especially careful over your choice of accommodation. Toddlers have an alarming tendency to wander off when something interesting catches their eye. Health and safety is not exactly foremost in the minds of these mini-explorers and you need to be particularly wary of unfenced swimming pools and balconies with squeeze-through railings. Toddlers also tend to shove a lot of unsavoury stuff into their mouths, although usually this is nothing more harmful than a bit of sand.

If there's one thing that makes travel with toddlers easier it's their increasing ability to talk – even if it's just to tell you they are about to be sick or that they object to another child walking off with their bucket and spade. In the latter case, of course, actions often speak louder than words – why struggle with newfangled speech when a tried-and-tested thump usually does the trick?

The 'why, what, when, how' years

By the time they reach school age (four or five), kids are a real pleasure to travel with. There is something wonderfully refreshing about their innocent and undisguised joy over experiencing even the most mundane aspects of travel. For example, no other age group is particularly bothered about watching the laborious task of weighing and labelling luggage at an airport check-in desk, but to a six-year-old boy it is an utterly transfixing event, punctuated by inconceivable weights, whirring sticker-producing machines and mysterious conveyor belts that whisk suitcases through trapdoors. Even airline food trays instigate goggle-eyed wonder and at least five minutes of vocal hyperactivity.

Whether it's building a dam on the beach to hold back the tide or embarking on a trek in the Andes, school-age children have seemingly limitless enthusiasm and energy. They are also at an age when they can tell you what they like and dislike, which can either be a blessing or a curse when it comes to holiday planning. Be prepared, too, for endless questions as their minds grapple to comprehend new experiences and issues.

Call it educational

A whole generation of globetrotting backpackers from the 1980s and 1990s now have young families. Rather than shred their passports and settle for the odd week with the grandparents, they also want adventure and unusual places – everything, in fact that they had before, except with youngsters in tow.

Eagerly meeting this demand are several tour operators with dedicated family programmes offering a bewildering array of adventures. Relaxed in the knowledge that a reputable tour operator has taken care of all technical and safety issues, you can take your tribe whitewater rafting in Nepal, horse riding in Iceland, canyoning in Croatia or sea kayaking in New Zealand. The world has become an enormous adventure playground where kids can sample tamed-down versions of all the things that got their parents whooping it up 20 years earlier.

The thrills and spills may be the lure of these trips, but school-age children will also absorb a huge amount of educational value from them. They'll interact with children from other cultures and learn firsthand about efforts to save endangered wildlife. They'll expand their palettes as well as their minds and they will probably pick up a new skill or two, whether it's how to speak a few words of Spanish or haggle in a Turkish bazaar.

Usually, the minimum age for family adventure trips is around five or six, but you can also find tours suitable for children as young as two. Others, meanwhile, are reserved exclusively for teenagers.

The main advantage of booking an organized trip instead of going independent is piece of mind – all travel arrangements are made for you, while the itinerary is intrinsically family friendly. You will also be with like-minded parents, many of whom are facing the same challenges of raising children as you are. The kids in the group will quickly bond and find new playmates, while the guide will provide added 'family value' by gaining the children's confidence and ensuring that mealtimes, talks and activities are tailored to their ages.

Tuning in to teenagers

It's easy to tarnish all teenagers as moody, sullen, bored and generally peeved that you've dragged them away on holiday with you. But this hackneyed image is unfair. Teenagers not only make stimulating travel companions (able to tackle physical and intellectual challenges on a par with adults), but they also simplify travel logistics by being able to stay up late or be flexible with meals. Just remember to cater for their specific needs, whether it's a few shopping trips, some adrenaline abuse or somewhere to meet socially with youngsters of their own age. Teenagers also like some personal space, so try to take this into account when planning accommodation. Give them a break too. Don't nag them about food or if they want a lie-in every morning.

Is there a magic formula for travelling with kids? No doubt you've met parents with infuriatingly well-behaved children who will tell you that family holidays are a piece of cake; that their little angel sleeps through flights, never whinges on long car journeys and always eats foreign food. For most families, however, getting holidays right is about making compromises. You won't please everyone all the time, but you can ensure that all ages have at least something going for them. Ten things that should definitely go into the equation are:

❶ **Water** Whether it's the sea, a lake or a swimming pool, most children consider swimming an intrinsic part of every holiday.

❷ **Food** Don't skip the local flavours entirely, but always ensure there's at least something on the menu that kids know and like.

❸ **Friends** Kids' clubs can be a big hit with children and allow parents some adult time.

❹ **Gear** Plan and pack with military precision to ensure you've got everything you need.

❺ **Versatility** Research your accommodation and activities to ensure they meet the needs and ages of all family members.

❻ **Challenges** Banish boredom by ensuring there are plenty of new experiences.

❼ **Money** Don't feel you have to spend a fortune to have a memorable family holiday.

❽ **Attitude** Children quickly pick up on stress or anxiety, so try to stay relaxed.

❾ **Expectations** Keep them realistic; remember that what you might find interesting might bore your children senseless.

❿ **Fun** What it's all about!

Family travel checklist

With careful research and thorough planning, independent family travel can offer freedom, flexibility and save you money. On the other hand, by arranging your holiday through a specialist travel operator, you'll receive the benefit of first-hand knowledge of your chosen area, as well as an itinerary that ensures that everything – from accommodation to activities – is suitable for families. Whichever route you choose, the following checklist will help you plan your family holiday.

The wishlist

This is the fun part of planning a family holiday. The bulk of this book delves into the extraordinary range of possibilities for taking your tribe away, from cycling through rural France to cruising in the Galápagos Islands. You could always pick a page number between 26 and 347, or get your children (blindfolded) to stick a pin in a map of the world. However, a more foolproof method for dreaming up your next holiday is to hold a conference, asking each member of the family to list five things that are important to them on holiday.

Take the plunge into the exciting world of family holidays – the operators featured on pages 24-25 can take you anywhere from Alaska to Zambia.

The reality check

Once you've compiled a wishlist, it's time to apply logistics to weed out trips that are non-feasible.

Timing is everything. With school-age children you have to plan a holiday that fits around term dates – see box, below right – while some types of holiday (such as wildlife-watching trips and winter activity holidays) are tied to specific seasons.

It's also important to consider the **length of your trip.** Trying to shoehorn a holiday into too few days can not only be impractical and stressful, but it can also mean you spend too much of your trip travelling.

Budget is likely to reap the most casualties on your wishlist. That dream trip taking the kids on safari in East Africa might become prohibitively expensive once you've added up hidden costs, like internal flights, visas and non-inclusive activities.

ⓘ Check whether a travel advisory has been issued by your government warning against visiting an unsafe country by checking fco.gov.uk/travel (for UK citizens) and travel.state.gov/travel (for US citizens).

The nitty gritty

Once you have decided where to go and what to do, and allocated an appropriate budget and time frame,

it's time to start tackling practicalities.

Decide **how you want to travel** – whether you'd prefer to join an organized group tour, ask an operator to tailor-make a trip for you or plan everything independently (see box, right). As well as cutting costs, going solo can offer the freedom to travel at your own pace. Independent travellers can also make responsible travel decisions such as staying in locally owned accommodation and hiring local guides

However, an organized tour may, in fact, offer better value once you've taken into account discounts that operators can pass on to their clients from block bookings. Remember, too, that bonded operators guarantee financial security through their membership of organizations like ATOL, IATA and AITO.

Once you've booked your trip, make sure that all of your **passports** are in date for at least six months beyond your period of travel and apply well in advance for any **visas** you might need. Check that your **vaccinations** are up to date and find out if you need to start a course of anti-malarials. Arrange **travel insurance** that is comprehensive enough to cover any activities you'll be doing. As far as **money** is concerned, traveller's cheques are the safest way to carry money, but also take a credit card and some local currency.

The school holidays – a dream wishlist

First up is February half term. Skiing in the Alps would be fun, but not nearly as exciting as an Arctic adventure in Lapland, reindeer sledging and snowmobiling.

A full two weeks off beckons during the first half of April – the perfect time to take children to North Africa or the Middle East before the sweltering heat of summer kicks in. The ancient sites of Egypt certainly have educational value (which is useful if you need to negotiate time off school with the headteacher), but Morocco offers a good balance of relaxing beach retreats and mountain escapades.

Half term in late May/early June is prime time for a multi-activity break in Europe – perfect if you need to cater to the needs of children of various ages.

The summer holidays are your best opportunity for a long-haul trip if you want to give your kids time to recover from jetlag before term starts. However, it's also high season, so look for somewhere where you can travel independently and save money on accommodation and eating out. A motorhome holiday in British Columbia would fit the bill nicely – as would a Namibian self-drive, staying in family guesthouses.

In a perfect world (and remember that this is a wishlist) October half term really ought to be spent in the Seychelles, which just leaves the Christmas holidays. You can't beat a traditional family Christmas at home, but having said that, this is also prime time for a tiger safari in India...

⑦ **Group** versus independent

✔ You're with like-minded families who share similar interests in travel.
✘ Perfect families with angelic children make you feel inadequate and tense.

✔ Children have instant holiday pals.
✘ Personality clashes lead to awkward situations.

✔ Trips have a good balance of activities and time-out.
✘ Pressure to adapt your routines to fit into other families' rules for bedtime, meals etc.

✔ Everything is organized for you, from transport to activities – and you know it's all going to be child-friendly.
✘ Schedules can be restricting; no time to linger in a place you particularly like or lie low for a day or two if children are ill.

✔ You know exactly how much you will spend and what you are going to get.
✘ You may spend more than by travelling independently.

✔ Guide provides expert knowledge, as well as local support if things go wrong.
✘ Some guides pitch talks and briefings way above children's heads.

✔ You can explore countries that you wouldn't consider visiting independently.
✘ You might still feel out of your comfort zone.

✔ Children in a group are more likely to feel motivated to try adventurous things.
✘ Frustrations may arise if some children can't keep up with the others.

✔ There are trips to suit all ages, from tots to teenagers.
✘ Some groups may have an uneven balance of ages, such as a lone teenager with half a dozen five-year-olds.

★**Online** resources

▶▶ Several websites offer inspiration and advice for family holidays, including 101familyholidays.co.uk, edited by the author of this book. Also try babygoes2.com, familytravel.co.uk and familytravel.com.

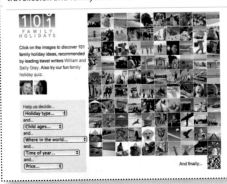

Are we there yet?

Experienced globetrotters will often tell you that it's the 'journey' not the 'getting there' that really matters; that travel is enriched by taking your time on the road, meeting people and having chance encounters. Suggest this to most parents, however, and they will either stare at you blankly, laugh out loud or start twitching uncontrollably. Whether it's the memory of dealing with a screaming baby on a flight, bickering siblings on an interminable car journey or a moping teenager who didn't want to come in the first place, every parent has good reason for treating family journeys with some trepidation.

Of course, just because you're travelling with kids doesn't automatically guarantee it's going to be a journey from hell. However, when you consider what you are putting yourselves (and them) through it's only to be expected that things occasionally go awry. Planning and packing for a family holiday require a lot of effort and you will naturally be anxious about taking your brood to unfamiliar places. Then there's all the queuing at airports, the confinement of children to cramped aircraft cabins (or cars) and the constant expectation for them to behave. It can all add up to tension, short tempers and tears. Just remember these three saving graces: even the longest long-haul flight eventually ends; you'll probably never see the people who were sitting near you again, and the worse the experience, the better the dinner-party story in years to come. And don't forget that most journeys with kids also have their fair share of relaxed moments and laughs – whether it's a sing-along in the car or the bumpy landing that, for some reason, young children always find hysterically amusing.

34-point plan for air travel

Think green
▸▸ Consider carefully whether there is a viable, more environmentally friendly alternative to flying.

At the time of booking
▸▸ Budget for children under two paying 10% of the adult fare. Remember that they have to sit on your lap and do not usually have a food or baggage allowance.
▸▸ Reserve seats so you can all sit together. If you are travelling with a baby, request bulkhead seats where bassinets can be fitted. Remember to obtain approval from the airline if you want to use your child's car seat on the flight.

Please fasten your seatbelts and prepare for mayhem...

▸▸ Pre-order children's meals.
▸▸ Check whether you can take your stroller to the boarding gate.
▸▸ Find out what other special children's facilities may be available, such as goodie bags, seat-back entertainment systems etc.
▸▸ If possible, choose a daytime flight to minimize disturbance to sleeping routines.
▸▸ Arrange a meet-and-greet service with an airport parking operator such as Purple Parking (purpleparking.com). You simply drop your car off at departures, someone parks it for you and then has it waiting at arrivals when you return.

Packing for the journey
▸▸ Take all baby essentials in your hand luggage.
▸▸ Pack a supply of healthy snacks.
▸▸ Don't forget to take sachets of infants' paracetamol.
▸▸ Pack trainer cups with non-spill lids for toddlers.
▸▸ Have a few boiled sweets handy to help ears pop during the final descent.
▸▸ Pack a familiar pillow or soft toy to comfort and help children sleep.
▸▸ Help children to pack their own inflight backpack.

The day before flying
▸▸ Try to keep things calm and normal.
▸▸ Eat light, bland meals.
▸▸ Choose loose-fitting clothes for the flight.

At the airport
▸▸ Get there in plenty of time so you're not stressed out or stuck at the back of a long check-in queue.
▸▸ Fit reins on toddlers to give them freedom – safely.
▸▸ Find out if there's a children's play area.
▸▸ Before boarding, always check the floor where you've been sitting – a favourite teddy or toy is bound to have been dropped there.
▸▸ Make use of priority boarding for families with young children.

During the flight
▸▸ Feed your baby on take-off and landing to reduce discomfort caused by changes in cabin pressure.
▸▸ Don't be afraid to ask flight attendants for help, warming baby food etc.
▸▸ Ensure your children drink little and often to ward off dehydration.
▸▸ Don't drug your child with medicines, such as Piriton, unless you've tried them before flying. Although they can help some children sleep, other side effects include irritability or short-lived deep sleep followed by hyperactivity.

▶▶ Do try natural relaxants, such as lavender oil or camomile tea.

▶▶ If the cabin's dry air causes discomfort to your child's nose, lips or sinuses, try getting them to breathe through a handkerchief soaked in water.

▶▶ Don't expect a toddler to be absorbed with one activity for the duration of the entire flight – bring lots of toys, books and snacks to distract and amuse them.

▶▶ Take kids to the toilet well before the seatbelt signs come on for the final descent.

▶▶ Respect the comfort of other passengers by dealing firmly with unacceptable behaviour (such as children kicking the seat in front), but be prepared for some people to give you the 'raised eyebrow' treatment merely at the sight of your little darlings.

▶▶ Remember, the more you tell kids not to press the attendant call button the more they will do it.

Coping with jetlag

▶▶ Trans-continental, overnight flights will leave your children flagging, but try to keep them going during your first day. Help their body clocks readjust by getting outside, doing some moderate exercise and drinking plenty of water. A few gentle hours in a local park is ideal. There's nothing wrong with them grabbing a short nap, but try to get them to bed at the same time as they would back home. Then just pray that they sleep through.

The long and whining road

It's not surprising that so many families opt for self-drive holidays, either renting a car or taking their own. With the freedom of the open road you can travel when you want and for as long as you want (although the latter is often dictated by the capacity of your children's bladders). You can schedule regular breaks at parks, beaches and other recreational areas to let children burn off energy. You can tweak your itinerary as you go along, there's more space for luggage and you can even time drives to coincide with when your baby or toddler normally has a daytime nap. Sounds like a piece of cake. So what's the catch?

Boredom. Close confinement. Sibling squabbles. Stress from coping with traffic. Stress from getting lost. Stress from rushing to catch the ferry. These, and a dozen other factors conspire to drive you to distraction. In order to endure long car journeys with the kids you need a few good tactics and plenty in the way of ICE (In-Car-Entertainment).

Tactics fall into three main categories. The first is piece of mind. Make absolutely certain, especially when renting a car, that your children will be safe. Engage child locks on the rear doors and windows, fit blinds to windows if you are travelling in a hot and sunny country and give rented child seats a thorough going-over to make sure that harnesses, buckles and head supports are not damaged in any way. It's impossible to predict the condition of child seats provided by car rental companies, so if any doubt take your own.

The second tactic involves planning. If your children are old enough get them to help you research the route, compile a schedule and pick a few options for rest breaks and side trips. Giving kids joint ownership of the drive plan offers them an incentive to look forward to journey highlights rather than lapsing into 'moan mode'. And, third, try to stay upbeat and positive. You're stuck together in the car for another two hours, so make the most of it: play travel games, sing songs or just chat.

Of course, there's no point having tactics without backing them up with some 'armour' – tangible stuff that will appeal to children either through their minds or their stomachs. Make sure you've packed a good supply of snacks and drinks. Car seats with foldout drink-cup holders help to minimize spillages, while drop-down trays that attach to the back of the front seats can be used as dinner tables, writing desks or play surfaces. Bring along colouring pads, crayons and pencils, magnetic board games, reading books, activity books, card games, dressing-up dolls… anything really that doesn't involve tiny pieces that are constantly going to end up dropped, out-of-reach, on the floor. A map or mini-atlas is a great idea for ▶▶

> ❝❞ **Helping four-year-old Ellie with her breakfast tray, I innocently peeled the lid off her yoghurt pot. She snapped. Big time. Sleep deprivation, the rush of time zones, the endless queues… all the tension and tiredness of the whole long-haul flight experience suddenly triggered a 9.5 on the temper scale. She wanted to peel that lid off and nothing I could say or do would put it right. Globules of strawberry yoghurt began to fly as the screams of an irate four-year-old bludgeoned the other passengers. Some spontaneously adopted the brace position.** William Gray

⦿ Games on the go

▸▸ **Car bingo** Give players a sheet of paper and ask them to write down 25 different numbers between one and 99. The person in the front passenger seat calls out the last one or two digits from the licence plates of passing cars. The winner is the first to cross off all their numbers.

▸▸ **Licence to thrill** Make up phrases based on the letters of licence plates. For example, 234 IFS 00 could be 'Ice-cream for Sally' or 'I feel sick!'

▸▸ **Buzz words** Pick a word, then turn on the radio or play a story tape and try to be the first to shout 'Buzz!' when the word is mentioned.

▸▸ **Alphabet animals** Starting with 'A', take it in turns to name an animal beginning with each letter of the alphabet. For an added challenge, you must repeat all the animals that have been named prior to your go.

▸▸ **Word association** Say a word; the person sitting to your left must respond with the first word that comes into their head.

▸▸ **What am I?** One player thinks of an object, animal, profession etc and can only answer 'yes' or 'no' to simple questions, such as 'Are you alive?', 'Are you small?' or 'Can I eat you?'

children who want to trace the route.

Upping the technology stakes slightly, story tapes or CDs played through the car stereo are often a good means of calming a back-seat fracas or eking out another quiet hour on the road. If your kids are of widely different ages or simply don't like listening to the same music or talking books, invest in some personal CD or tape players. Hand-held games systems, from the likes of Nintendo and Sony PSP, are guaranteed to absorb most kids, although you may find they pass the entire journey with barely a glance at the passing scenery. When it comes to in-car-entertainment, however, few things receive such universal approval from children and adults alike than a DVD player. High-spec cars often come with them ready-fitted in a ceiling-mounted unit or in the back of the front-seat headrests. Alternatively, you can buy portable DVD players or tablet computers that strap on to the headrests or can simply be held in your lap.

Coaching pros and cons

The idea of travelling by coach might initially appeal to children. They love buses. You only have to think back to their last school trip to see how much fun they can have in them. But before you get carried away and commit your family to a trans-American jaunt by Greyhound, spare a moment to consider the

All aboard the Trunki
Keep kids in tow with their very own ride-on, pull-along, pack-it-yourself hand luggage. A trunki (trunki.co.uk) is the perfect stress-reliever for parents struggling with luggage and children at airports or train stations.

realities of a long-distance coach trip with the kids. Logistically, you need to treat coach travel rather like flying – you're stuck in a confined cabin with limited legroom and your luggage is stowed out of reach in the hold. Luxury services will have an onboard toilet, TV and attendant service, but rarely approaching the standards you find on flights. Rest stops may be sporadic and too short-lived and unlike flying, of course, coach travel is slower and prone to traffic jams.

Any advantages? Well, there's no doubt that coach travel is better for both your bank balance and the environment compared to flying. You also get to see more than just clouds out of the windows. And you can often step off a coach right into the heart of your destination, rather than going through the rigmarole of baggage claim and transfers following a flight.

Coach travel also gives your itinerary huge flexibility. For example, Eurolines (eurolines.com) covers over 30 independent coach companies serving over 500 destinations across Europe, Russia and Morocco. A few specialist operators actively welcome families. Try UK-based Gemmaway Coach Tours (gemmaway.com) which offers guided itineraries throughout Britain and continental Europe.

On track with trains

There's no denying it: rail travel is definitely more family-friendly than going by coach. Not only do you get more legroom and often a table where kids can spread out their scribble pads and pens, but you can also get up and stretch your legs and visit the buffet car for a snack or meal. Trains are faster, more frequent and basically just a lot more exciting than coaches – particularly overnight sleeper services where kids love the idea of nesting in a couchette.

That's not to say train operators exactly go off the rails with making families welcome. Eurostar and French TGV trains have 'family-friendly' coaches with baby-changing facilities – but that's about it. And don't forget that train travel with kids is not without its fair share of stressful 'crunch points' – the most notorious being the short stop at your final station when you have approximately 13 seconds to disgorge luggage, infants, baby stroller and other belongings onto the platform before the train leaves again. Then there are the tight connections where you have to cajole recalcitrant toddlers and unruly suitcases from one platform to another, negotiating crowds of commuters and several flights of steps. And, yes, there are plenty of trains serving Paris (and even Disneyland Paris), but what about your holiday park in Provence or Brittany? To reach that you'll need to pile everyone and everything into a taxi at the train station.

Undeterred? Then check out The Man in Seat 61 (seat61.com), a superb online resource with detailed information, schedules, fares and advice for rail travel anywhere in the world.

Power to the pedal

Not for the fainthearted, bicycle touring with children in tow (sometimes literally) requires fitness, stamina, detailed planning and serious equipment. As well as sturdy adult bikes, you will need a child seat or trailer for young children. Child seats should fit securely onto a bike rack and have extra padding in case of a fall. Trailers are heavier, but have the advantages of accommodating two small children and even some luggage, as well as providing protection from rain and sun. Trailer bikes that attach to an adult cycle are an option for older children. With all ages, however, be realistic about daily distances and try to pick routes that are largely traffic-free.

Making waves

Ferries pop up in a lot of holiday itineraries whether it's nipping across the Channel from England to France, getting from North to South Island in New Zealand or island-hopping in the Bahamas. Not surprisingly, kids love them. There's space to move around, different decks to explore, horizons to scan and shops to peruse… some ferries even have soft play areas and games rooms.

But what about family cruises of a week or more? Are these also plain sailing? There used to be a time when cruising was considered rather dull and old-fashioned – fine for granny and the blue-rinse brigade, but anathema for parents contemplating endless days at sea with mutinous children. But now cruising is cool for kids!

Several cruise lines have children's clubs for different age groups. Carnival, for example, caters for toddlers (face painting, crafts etc), 'junior cruisers' (cookie decorating, T-shirt painting, puppet shows), nine- to 11-year-olds (dance classes, scavenger hunts, talent shows) and teenagers (games tournaments, discos, late night movies and special shore excursions.

Most cruise liners also have dedicated kids' areas, whether it's somewhere cool for teenagers to hang out or a ball pit for five-year-olds to rampage through. The Fun Factory on Celebrity's cruise liners is packed with craft activities, toys and arcade games. Of course, every ship also has a pool or three, but some operators really push the boat out when it comes to family entertainment. Royal Caribbean's onboard activities range from ice-skating and mini golf to rock-climbing and surfing on a wave simulator. On Disney cruises, of course, you get to 'feel the magic' afloat with live shows and character meetings.

Childcare, accommodation and meals are pretty much as you would expect from a good land-based family resort. On P&O's *Aurora*, *Oceana*, *Oriana* and *Ventura* ships, for example, you will find a well-qualified Youth Crew, a night nursery and an in-cabin listening service. Accommodation ranges from inter-connecting cabins to staterooms with extra beds, while children's dining arrangements usually feature a special tea, as well as a choice of meals.

66 99 When I'm travelling on my own I have to confess that I miss my children's innocent sense of wonder in all-things long-haul. They've almost become an essential part of my in-flight entertainment. It always makes me smile when I watch our two nest on the plane – disgorging their daypacks of cuddly toys, sweets, books, Nintendos etc. Next in this ritual comes the obligatory fiddling with earphone cables and seatback TV controls. Without fail, Ellie will always remove the safety card and point, grimacing theatrically, to the picture of the plane floating in the sea.

When I fly on my own I rarely, if ever, smile during takeoff. But 10-year-olds, of course, relish the sense of speed (a bumpy landing is also cause for mirth). They also have an astonishing capacity to eagerly anticipate airline food. Those plastic trays with their neat little packages and hidden 'goodies' really are the Christmas stockings of long-haul flights.

Perhaps the thing I miss most about flying without our kids, though, is sharing the views. I guess we're all kids, wide-eyed with wonder, when we're cloud-gazing or staring down at Planet Earth from 38,000 ft. William Gray

Travel light? Yeah, right!

It's a wonderful concept isn't it? Pack everything you think you're going to need for your holiday, then reduce it by half. The 'travel light' mantra of globetrotting gurus might suit backpackers with their handkerchief-sized super-absorbent towels and erratic rotation of underwear, but it's not always an easy, or necessarily desirable, option for families. Obviously, excessive luggage is a stress you can do without. However, taking enough in the way of clothes, equipment, toys and supplies, rather than skimping on things, can make the difference between making travel with kids enjoyable or just bearable.

Documents

Many countries, including the UK, USA and Australia, require children to have their own passport. Apply for these at least two months in advance of your departure date. Brace yourself for fun and games trying to get a legal passport photograph of your fidgety baby or toddler. Babies under one are allowed to have their eyes closed, children under five do not need to have a neutral expression or look directly at the camera, and photos of children under 11 can show a head size of between 21 and 34 mm instead of the adult minimum requirement of 29 mm. Otherwise, it must be a sharp, shadowless photograph – no grins, no dummies, no fingers up noses and no evidence that mum is supporting baby's head. Forget photo booths – you'll spend a fortune trying to get an acceptable image and the experience might put you off family travel for life. A professional photographer at a studio, on the other hand, will have lots of tricks for getting the perfect shot.

In addition to passports and visas, make sure you have adequate family travel insurance, certificates of any medical prescriptions or vaccinations that may need to be shown at immigration or customs controls, a print-out of your itinerary and e-tickets, as well as contact details for while you are away. Make two copies, stash one set in your hand luggage and leave the other with a friend or relative at home.

Packing

What you take will depend on several factors, such as the age of your children, the type of trip (city break, trek, beach holiday etc), the likely climate (hot, cold or wet) and whether you're going to fly somewhere or pile everything into the car and drive.

The amount of gear you take is adversely

proportional to the size of your child. Essentials for travelling with babies can include nappies, umpteen changes of clothes, feeding equipment, stroller, favourite toys, travel cot, bedding, portable highchair and car seat. For toddlers you'll still need a stroller, car seat, toys and travel potty. Once kids reach four or five, they will probably want to pack their own small daypack with a few games, some activity pads and colouring pencils, a soft toy and some sweets. Teenagers meanwhile are often content with a book or magazine, an MP3 player or games console, a supply of spare batteries and a 'do not disturb' sign.

When children (especially girls) reach a certain age, they take a determined – though not always realistic – interest in what clothes to pack. Diplomacy and supreme negotiating skills are required by parents to ensure that half your luggage isn't filled with a dozen varieties of sandals and a summer dress for each day you're away. Generally, though, clothes need to be lightweight, casual, durable, compatible with each other and easy to wash and dry.

Once you've finished deliberating over what to take you need to decide how you're going to carry it. A suitcase or holdall is fine – you can find things quickly and easily – but make sure it has wheels for those inevitable airport situations when you need to simultaneously carry a tired child and shift heavy luggage. A medium-sized case for each member of the family can be more practical than one or two colossal ones. It gives children independence, they can find their own things without turning out everyone else's and, if you're not sharing the same room in a hotel, it saves a lot of running back and forth along the corridors.

Can we take the dog?
Check out dogsaway.co.uk for details of how to get your pooch a passport and plan a doggy-friendly break in Europe.

Hand luggage

Pack spare clothes and other essentials (such as wet wipes, nappies and favourite toys) in your hand luggage in case your suitcases get lost, the flight is delayed or cancelled, or you discover that your child is airsick. Following increased security measures at airports there are now restrictions on the quantities of liquids (including all drinks, syrups, creams, lotions, oils, sprays and pastes) that can be carried in cabin baggage. You can carry small quantities of liquids, but only in separate containers that must not exceed 100 ml and are clearly visible in a single, transparent, re-sealable plastic bag ready for inspection by airport security staff. Medical equipment, such as inhalers for asthma sufferers, is permitted. Prescribed medicines, accompanied by relevant documentation, may also be allowed in quantities over the 100 ml limit, but you should check with your airline beforehand. Although

✖ **Packing** for little ones

▶▶ Reusable cloth nappies are easy to pack, environmentally friendly and can double up as towels. Coping with supply and demand, however, won't fit every parent's notion of what constitutes a holiday. If using disposable nappies, be aware that your preferred brand may not be available. One option is to stuff a holdall full of nappies and check it in – they're light, so your luggage allowance won't be affected.

▶▶ Consider taking your own travel cot for extra familiarity. Many models are lightweight and fold away neatly and compactly. They also make excellent 'holding pens' while you check out a new room for potential hazards.

▶▶ Pack a raincover, sunshade and insect net for your buggy, a non-slip bath mat, sun protectors for car windows, a waterproof undersheet for small children and a stair gate if staying in two-storey accommodation.

▶▶ If renting a car, consider taking your own child seat. The ones provided by the rental company may not meet the safety standards you're used to. Use a luggage-wrapping service at the airport to protect the seat in transit.

▶▶ With check-in times of up to three hours before long-haul flights be sure to take plenty of favourite toys and books to keep you and your toddler sane at the airport. Failing that, find a big window where they can watch the planes coming and going.

the chance, they will also find endless fascination with new and exciting objects like telephones, sugar sachets and mini bars in hotel rooms or brochure stands, fire extinguishers and waste bins with revolving lids at airports. It doesn't always work, but try diverting their attention with a surprise toy or two.

Left to their own devices, school-age children will stuff a fairly random array of their favourite knick-knacks into their hand luggage and, while Barbie, a few Hot Wheels cars, a Tamagotchi and a tube of Smarties could well be in there, you might want to make a few additional suggestions. For girls, a Polly Pocket doll set takes up little space and can be totally absorbing. Boys (and girls) can play Top Trumps card games with each other or simply study the statistics on their own. Activity books with quizzes, stickers and colouring pages are a must, as are pads (with a mixture of ruled and plain paper) and plenty of colouring pens and pencils. Sometimes the simplest, most traditional games, such as Shut the Box or magnetic travel versions of Ludo or draughts, can become utterly addictive. Inevitably, though, pride of place in any kid's personal travel kit is going to go to an electronic games console. Whatever your views on them, these high-tech gizmos are a great way of getting hyperactive or overly tired children to sit quietly for an hour or so. With all the exciting things happening on holiday, fanatical obsession is unlikely – and don't forget that some brands, like Leapfrog's Leapster, have a strong educational element.

One of the best ways to keep boredom at bay is to encourage children to keep a journal of their travels. Make it as fun and interactive as possible. Pack scissors and glue stick so they can cut and paste postcards, tickets and other souvenirs into their literary masterpiece. An envelope stuck to the inside back cover can be used to store other treasures. You may need to help younger children with cues, such as 'The journey was…', 'I like the beach because…' or 'The food was disgusting because…'. The playback function on digital cameras is also a great prompter when kids complain that they can't think of anything to write.

liquid baby food and sterilized water, sufficient for the journey, can be taken through airport security, you may be required to verify by tasting.

Boredom busters

Whether it's a rainy day, a long car journey or a delayed flight, there will be occasions during every family holiday when children – from tots to teens – simply need to have some time out and occupy themselves quietly. You can encourage these all-too-ephemeral moments by packing a few books, games, toys and activities.

Babies and toddlers need familiar, comforting playthings which smell and feel like home. But, given

❝❞ **Perhaps the most foolproof option for family holidays is to buy a bigger car, disgorge most of your house contents into it and then drive to your destination. We tried that once. I seem to remember a spectacular mobilization of colour-coded tupperware, copious toys (general, bath, cot and car), several dozen jars of assorted baby food, a double buggy, two high chairs, two travel cots, a bottle sterilizer, milk powder, sleepsuits, cot linen, at least a thousand bibs and enough nappies to plug a hole in a sinking battleship.** William Gray

Check it out before you check in

Family-friendly. Just rolls off the tongue, doesn't it? But it's a phrase that's used all too glibly by hotels, resorts and campsites keen to tap into this lucrative market. Just because they've plonked a plastic slide in the garden and scribbled chicken nuggets on the menu doesn't mean they're going to go out of their way to welcome kids or make your stay as comfortable as possible. Look beyond the superficial stuff and ask which of the following are available.

▸ Family rooms, interconnecting rooms or suites
▸ Children's menus and meal times
▸ Supervised childcare
▸ Babysitting or baby listening
▸ Family activities or kids' clubs
▸ Dedicated play areas for children
▸ Cots, high chairs and other baby gear
▸ Family pricing or discounts for children.

In addition, you should assess safety issues, such as proximity to busy roads and whether swimming pools are fenced off.

Hotel heaven and havoc

Remember those halcyon holidays before you had kids when you would casually check into your hotel room, test how bouncy the beds were, fling open the balcony doors and treat yourself to a welcome bottle of wine from the mini bar? Well, with kids yapping excitedly at your heels you will be trying, mostly in vain, to stop them doing all those things. That wonderful moment of arrival, when the holiday really starts, is a super-exuberant time when kids find joy and wonder in even the smallest things. "Wow, look mum, you've got a chocolate on your pillow – and have you seen the cool view of the building site!"

Another difference you will notice is that hotel rooms shrink once you have children. Squeeze a travel cot and a child's bed into your average double room and the floor space is reduced to roughly the area of a bath mat. Getting from one side of the room to the other is like negotiating a soft-play area – and that, of course, is exactly how your kids treat it. Then there's the en suite where the hotel staff have thoughtfully gift-wrapped all sorts of goodies for children to open – from shower caps and sewing kits to little tubes of toothpaste. And when they tire of ransacking the mini milk pots on the complimentary coffee-making tray, there are always the long hotel corridors – ideal for running relay races.

Perhaps it's not surprising that a lot families tend

Camping can be posh – as the pampered interior of this holiday yurt on the Isle of Wight shows.

to use their hotel room as a kind of base camp – a technical necessity where you sleep, wash and store your clothes, but spend as little time as possible. Of course, budget permitting, you can find sensational apartments, suites and even family chalets within the grounds of a large resort. It's probably safe to say that your hotel room is unlikely to feature in your holiday snaps, but at least you've got everything you need onsite – from restaurants, room service and babysitting to swimming pool, games room and someone making your beds.

Home from home

With space to spread out, villas and other self-catering accommodation offer a home-from-home atmosphere where you have flexibility and independence to maintain meal- and bedtime routines, do the cooking, load the dishwasher, lay the table… A big advantage over hotels and resorts is that you don't need to worry about disturbing other guests. Villas can also offer better value than hotels or resorts, particularly if you upsize to a bigger property and share with another family.

Tent pegs and tantrums

There are two types of family camping – the DIY version where dad spends most of day one grappling with multi-jointed tent poles and fiddling with an obstinate gas stove, and organized camping where you simply drive up to a ready-pitched family tent, usually on a site that has excellent facilities, such as a swimming pool and supermarket. Both are essential experiences for all families – you need to try one to appreciate the other.

Organized 'readymade' campsites are particularly popular in Europe where you also have the option of staying in well-furnished mobile homes or chalets. These have a galley kitchen and lounge area with mod cons such as LCD television, DVD player, microwave and fridge-freezer. Again, it's worth upgrading if you can – a double bed might sound fine until you discover that it's in a room the size of a double bed. Of course, these mobile homes aren't actually mobile (they're more like immobile homes), but motorhomes certainly are and make an excellent roving base for family holidays.

Homes to go

There's no better way to roam than in a motorhome. Not only do they offer flexibility and self-sufficiency, but most models offer levels of comfort undreamt of in the days of the old VW camper van. Whereas your typical VW, with its pop-up roof and flatulent exhaust, might have had little more than two coffin-sized berths and a lethal camping stove, modern motorhomes boast two or three double beds, fridge-freezer, microwave, four-ring cooker, DVD player, flat-screen TV, hot shower and a flush toilet.

If you've got kids, motorhome touring is definitely the way to go. The idea that you can have bedroom, kitchen, playroom and car rolled into one is almost too much for them to comprehend. But motorhomes also have lots of practical advantages. For example, you can stick your children in seats 6 m away from the driver's cab, so that you don't have to hear them whingeing on long journeys. And when it rains, you can keep warm and dry inside the van while you rustle up a meal. Best of all, you can explore large swathes of country without having to lug suitcases in and out of hotels all the time. You only have to unpack once. And you only have to get used to one bed. Don't forget, though, that you have to make that bed. Literally. Your motorhome may have had the latest in TV technology, but when it came to beds, it might not be cutting-edge. More like 'cut your bleedin' fingers off', in fact, as you struggle each evening with sliding plywood shelves, hinged legs and stow-away tables to build your beds. Once the bases are constructed, the real fun starts when you attempt to piece together 17 random-sized seat cushions into something vaguely resembling a mattress.

Down on the farm

You should check whether any age restrictions apply, but in general most farmstays are ideal for families. Children will love feeding the animals, collecting eggs or even helping out in the kitchen. Needless to say, on a working farm, you must be aware of your children's safety at all times – including any potential allergic reactions they may have in response to contact with animals. You usually sleep in a self-contained cottage or in the farmhouse itself. As you'd expect, most meals are based on fresh, produce and include homemade breads, cakes and soups, as well as homegrown fruit and veg. It's up to you if you want to help out on the farm. Nobody is going to drag you out of bed at dawn to muck out the cowshed or round up the sheep. If you simply want to relax and restrict your farm activities to occasionally patting the border collie then that's fine. Farm tours are often available, while some farmstays offer activities like fishing, hiking, mountain biking or horseriding. Top countries for farmstays include New Zealand, Iceland and Argentina.

Culinary culture shock

I t's a perfectly natural reaction. You arrive at your holiday destination, dump the luggage, check out the pool and then enter the intriguing, but slightly disconcerting, world of local restaurant menus and foreign supermarkets. Is that spicy? Does it come with chips? Which one is skimmed milk? Will that cheese be too strong? Will I be handed a packet of frozen fish fingers when what I thought I'd asked for was a box of ice-lollies? Some things look perfectly familiar, while others leave you flummoxed. But don't worry – culinary culture shock isn't terminal. No matter where you are there is always something to eat, no matter how fussy you or your children are.

Breastfeeding

Breastfed babies, of course, have no qualms about coping with foreign food. They have a familiar, convenient, safe and nutritious source of nourishment wherever they go. Breastfeeding mothers, however, do need to ensure that they drink lots of fluid, eat well and keep relaxed. If you are discreet, breastfeeding is acceptable in most countries. Consider packing a nursing shawl for modesty.

Bottlefeeding

Don't assume that your preferred brand of milk formula will be available in the country you are visiting. If possible take enough with you from home. Remember that you will need to use purified, bottled or boiled water to make up the formula and that it needs to be kept refrigerated if not used within 24 hours. Sterilization is also crucial. Either invest in a compact travel sterilizer (which usually holds one or two bottles, plus teats) or use boiling water or sterilizing tablets.

In-flight food and drink

It's a good idea to feed babies on take-off and landing to reduce the discomfort caused by changes in cabin pressure. Make sure toddlers have non-spill cups to sip on and give older children boiled sweets to suck. Remember that most flight attendants are pre-programmed to fill cups (even for children) right up to the rim – and they rarely supply lids. To avoid inevitable spills, bring your own bottles or cups to decant drinks into. Don't assume baby food will be available – again, the best strategy is to bring your own. Plastic bibs with scooped rims along the bottom are useful for catching fallout and minimizing mess – particularly if your baby is sick.

The one that got away – trying new food (and new ways of eating it) is all part of the travel experience – in this case, noodles in Hong Kong.

Most airlines offer children's meals if you book them in advance, although you should also bring plenty of snacks in case they turn their noses up at what lurks beneath the (often extremely hot) foil cover. Children's meals are usually served first which means you can help them negotiate all those fiddly pots and plastic bags of utensils (which invariably explode like Christmas crackers) before relaxing later with your own haute cuisine.

Travel snacks

Having a stash of goodies to nibble on is all part of the fun of travel if you're a child – and they can be a godsend if you're delayed. Leave it to them, however, and they'll stuff their hand luggage with nothing but crisps, chocolate bars, chewing gum and lurid-coloured chews encrusted with sherbet. You don't want to be a complete kill-joy (the odd packet of crisps and a chocolate bar is fine), but nor do you want your children going balmy on a 'sugar high' while you're stuck in a car or queuing at customs. Healthy travel snacks that you can buy straight off the supermarket shelf include cereal bars, string cheese, small boxes of raisins and individual boxes of (low sugar) cereal. And, of course, nothing beats a fresh apple or orange for healthy food on-the-go. With a little more time and effort you can help children prepare their own tasty, unprocessed travel snacks (see box below right).

Fussy feeders

Although some kids have more adventurous palates abroad than at home, others can be frustratingly inflexible when it comes to food. They'll love Marmite, but hate Vegemite. They'll consume Cheddar cheese by the wagonload, but run a mile from a French fondue. The tomato sauce won't be the same as it is back home and the milk will taste funny. So, how do you deal with a fussy feeder when you are on holiday? Try this list for starters:

▶▶ Self-catering gives you the flexibility to prepare food you like, when you like.

▶▶ International resorts, hotels and restaurants offer a wide selection of meals, including several that your children are bound to be familiar with.

▶▶ Fine for an occasional treat, fast-food outlets can be found everywhere nowadays.

▶▶ Take staples with you, such as soup powders, pasta, biscuits and cereals – but remember that you won't be allowed to take fresh produce across some international borders.

▶▶ Make mealtimes enjoyable and relaxed by picking restaurants with stunning views, play areas or aquariums. The novelty of room service may also get kids in the mood for eating.

▶▶ Don't fill children up on juice, milk, fizzy drinks or even water just before a meal.

▶▶ Ask for smaller portions in restaurants and let children take their time over eating.

▶▶ Keep mealtime routines as regular as possible.

▶▶ Get them involved – kids tend to eat up if they can serve themselves at buffets or help prepare the meal.

▶▶ Seeing other children eating well on a group trip might be an incentive for your picky feeder to tuck in.

▶▶ Do not force your child to eat. Be sensitive to the fact that travel – especially long-haul – can naturally affect appetites and unsettle stomachs.

▶▶ Take some children's multi-vitamins.

🍪 Do-it-yourself snacks

▶▶ **Trail mix** Combine raisins, Cheerios, dried apricot, cranberries and pineapple, banana chips and yoghurt-coated raisins in a mixing bowl. A handful of Smarties or M&Ms isn't going to harm anyone, but only add nuts if your children are over five. Give everything a good stir, then make up individual portions in small freezer bags.

▶▶ **Dippers** Add a scoop of peanut butter, hummus or whatever savoury dip appeals to your children to a small plastic food container. Clean and slice small pieces of celery, carrot, apple and cucumber and plant them in the dip. Add a lid and keep refrigerated until you are ready to go.

▶▶ **Cheese and crackers** Use a cookie cutter to stamp out fun-shaped slices of cheese. Pop them in a food storage container along with a few crackers and some grapes sliced lengthways. Kids will love crafting their own cracker creations.

> 66 99 **Our hotel room was on the third floor in the furthest corner of the building – far enough away, I hoped, to cause as little disturbance to other guests as possible. Ten-month-old Joe immediately felled a standard lamp and ate two sachets of complimentary Nescafé, while his twin sister Ellie helpfully scattered jars of baby food across the floor. I managed to sidestep three jars of spaghetti hoops, but the Moroccan chicken that was lurking under a fold of the bedspread sent me cartwheeling into the en suite.** William Gray

Bugs, bites & bowels

Family travel should be liberating. It should be spiced with excitement and tingle with new discoveries and achievements. Nobody wants to smother their family holiday with health and safety, but there are some things you need to give important consideration to – before and during your travels.

Vaccinations & malaria

Seek professional advice from a travel clinic or your doctor several months before you travel on any vaccinations you may need. In addition to their childhood immunization programme, which usually includes vaccinations for diptheria, tetanus, whooping cough, Hib, polio, meningococcus C and MMR (measles, mumps and rubella), your children may need additional inoculations, such as typhoid or yellow fever, if you're travelling to certain countries.

Your doctor or health specialist will also be able to advise on whether you need to take precautions against malaria. Young children are particularly vulnerable to this potentially fatal disease and preventative measures are crucial if you are travelling to a malaria zone. A course of malaria prophylactics does not guarantee protection against the disease. You should also try to avoid being bitten by using insect repellent and covering up at dawn and dusk when mosquitoes are more active. Malaria symptoms can be confused with flu, so be sure to tell your doctor that you have been to a malarious region if, at any time up to a year after travelling, you become ill.

Safe water

Contaminated water is the cause of several serious diseases. The best way to ensure that water is safe to drink is to boil it for several minutes. Water filters containing sterilizing chemicals such as iodine are also effective. If using bottled water, always check that the seal around the cap is unbroken before consuming. Avoid ice, washed vegetables and salads if you are in any doubt as to whether the local water is safe.

Diarrhoea

Severe diarrhoea can be life-threatening, particularly to children under-three. The biggest risk is dehydration. If your child has a bout of gastrointestinal illness be sure to keep clear fluid intake up, offering water, juices, cola and oral rehydration drinks frequently. Prevention is always better than cure, so steer clear of water from unreliable sources, avoid food that has been cooked and left to go cold and follow strict hand hygiene rules.

Footloose and fancy free – with the right preparation and attention to health and safety issues, you can take even young children on quite adventurous trips, like this trekking holiday in Morocco's Atlas Mountains.

✛ Three signs of dehydration
▸▸ Mouth and tongue are dry.
▸▸ Passing less (and darker) urine than normal.
▸▸ Skin loses elasticity; listlessness, drowsiness and unable to drink – severe dehydration, requiring hospitalisation.

Sunburn

Young children and babies are particularly susceptible to sunburn. Keep them out of the sun during the middle of the day. Always protect skin by wearing a hat, sunglasses and long-sleeved clothing (or sun-protection swimsuits) and regularly apply water-resistant high-factor suncream and lip balm.

Heatstroke

Heatstroke is life-threatening and can occur when children overdo activities when they are unacclimatized to hot conditions. In severe cases, collapse due to dehydration and over-heating can occur and urgent medical attention is required. The best precaution is to stay out of the heat during the hottest part of the day, avoid rigorous exercise until acclimatized and drink plenty. Signs of over-heating include lethargy, flushed skin and excessive sweating. If you suspect heatstroke, pour cool water over the child's head or wrap them with towels soaked in cold water. Give plenty of clear fluids and seek medical help.

✛ The ABC of resuscitation
▸▸ **Airway** Check patient's mouth and remove any obstruction. Tilt head back by lifting chin and pressing gently on forehead.
▸▸ **Breathing** Place your cheek next to patient's mouth and nose for up to 10 seconds to detect breathing. Watch for movement of chest.
▸▸ **Circulation** Check the patient's pulse. If necessary, begin artificial ventilation and/or cardiopulmonary resuscitation (CPR).

Staying safe

Sleep walking Make sure doors to balconies and low windows are securely fastened at night.
Pools and beaches Familiarize yourself with local conditions before taking the plunge. Look out for obstacles such as rocks and ledges and take note of any flag warnings. Never dive in shallow water. Swim parallel to the shore within your depth and be aware of any motorsport zones.
Roads and transport Children will need reminders that traffic may not come from the direction they are expecting. Some public transport in developing countries can be unreliable or dangerous.

✚ Health clinic Q&A

▶▶ Is it safe to fly with babies? Ideally you should wait until your baby is two or three months old and has had all the routine vaccinations, as germs tend to circulate in aircraft. However, providing your baby was full-term with no complications and has a clean bill of health, flying is usually permitted after one or two weeks (though this may vary between airlines).

▶▶ What if my child has asthma? Understand your child's symptoms and be prepared with spare inhalers, emergency steroids (if you have used them in the past) and a peak-flow meter if your child is old enough to use one. Be aware of the triggers for your child's asthma and take any necessary preventative measures.

▶▶ Can I take my child to high altitudes? Children are probably no more likely to suffer altitude sickness than adults, but the difficulty is in diagnosing the condition in very young children, as the symptoms of fractiousness and sleepiness may be attributed to travelling in general. Other symptoms such as headache and nausea are not visible and a child under the age of three may have trouble communicating this. As with adults it is safest to ascend slowly and have a plan for how to go down quickly if necessary (a rapid descent of 500 m is the best cure for mountain sickness). It would be inadvisable to plan a first trek above 3000 m with your child. Flying, driving or going by rail into areas of high altitude (such as in La Paz, Mexico City and Colorado) may cause altitude problems for adults and children alike. Avoid taking your child to high altitude if they are suffering from a cough or a cold as they will be more susceptible to high-altitude pulmonary oedema.

▶▶ What if my child is travel sick? Children between the ages of three and 12 are more susceptible to travel sickness (and girls are more likely to suffer from it than boys). Try to sit in the middle of buses or trains (where movement is less) and, if possible, get out on the open deck of a ship and focus your child on the horizon. There are various medicines available (ask a pharmacist or your GP for one that is appropriate to your child's age), wrist bands (that press on acupuncture points) or natural remedies, such as ginger or peppermint (see below).

▶▶ Can I travel when I'm pregnant? The safest time to travel when pregnant is during the second trimester, between three and six months. It is strongly advised not to travel to malarious areas or places where stomach upsets are likely. Some antimalarial prophylactics are not safe to take during pregnancy. Airlines have different policies on when it is safe to travel – generally you may not fly after the 36th week of pregnancy (or earlier if carrying twins or more). Pregnant women are more susceptible to blood clots, so wearing flight socks on long-haul flights is advisable.

▶▶ What natural remedies are available? Local people and tour guides will often enthuse about natural remedies that are used to treat various ailments. In South Africa for example, the aloe plant is referred to as a 'pharmacy on a stick'. However, even purely natural ingredients must be treated with caution, as they may cause a reaction or may not be suitable for children. Here are some tried and tested alternatives to over-the-counter medicines:

⚙ **Motion sickness** Ginger biscuits, crystallized ginger and peppermints.
⚙ **Constipation** Camomile tea and liquorice.
⚙ **Indigestion, nausea and stomach aches** Peppermint or camomile tea, ginger biscuits and crystallized ginger.
⚙ **Fever** Lemons and limes.
⚙ **Decongestant properties** Honey.
⚙ **Settling the stomach** Live yoghurt and probiotic yoghurt drinks.
⚙ **Antiseptic properties** Tea tree oil and lavender oil.
⚙ **Repelling insects** Lavender oil, tea tree oil, citronella oil.
⚙ **Soothing burns** Aloe vera cream or oil.
⚙ **Treating bites and stings** Lavender oil, Aloe vera cream or oil and Arnica cream.

▶▶ What should go in our family first-aid kit?
↘ Paracetamol syrup or dispersible tablets
↘ Child ibuprofen syrup
↘ Sore throat pastilles
↘ Thermometer
↘ Oral rehydration salts
↘ Water bottle with measure indicators
↘ Drying antiseptic, such as iodine
↘ Antiseptic wipes
↘ Antibacterial hand wash
↘ Cotton wool and cotton buds in resealable bag
↘ Sticking plasters
↘ Steristrips
↘ Non-stick dressings and micropore tape
↘ Crêpe bandage
↘ Scissors
↘ Pointed tweezers
↘ Insect repellent (natural, or low DEET concentration for children)
↘ Insect bite relief cream/calamine lotion
↘ Eye drops (antibiotic)
↘ Ear drops (antibiotic, or for trapped water)
↘ Antihistamine syrup
↘ Antimalarial medicines
↘ Travel sickness pills (or herbal alternatives)
↘ Clear plastic bags for storage
↘ Teething gel
↘ Nappy rash cream
↘ Water resistant suncream SPF 15+
↘ Water purifying tablets or filter
↘ Thermos flask

▶▶ Where can I find out more? *Your Child Abroad – A Travel Health Guide* (Bradt) by Dr Jane Wilson-Howarth contains advice on diagnosis and treatment, first-aid guidance, basic medical questions in five languages, plus a region-by-region analysis of risk.

Directory of operators

With careful research and thorough planning, independent family travel can offer freedom, flexibility and save you money. However, by arranging your family holiday through a specialist travel operator, you'll receive the benefit of first-hand knowledge of your chosen area, as well as an itinerary that ensures that everything – from accommodation to activities – is suitable for families. The operators listed here cover everything from safaris in Kenya to self-catering cottages in Cornwall.

Activity holidays
Belle France bellefrance.co.uk
▶▶ Walking and cycling holidays in France.

Crystal Holidays crystalholidays.co.uk
▶▶ Mountain activity holidays.

Equestrian Escapes equestrian-escapes.com
▶▶ Horse riding holidays, riding weekends and short breaks in the UK and Europe.

Freewheel Holidays freewheelholidays.co.uk
▶▶ European cycling holidays for families.

Headwater Holidays headwater.com
▶▶ Walking, cycling and cross-country skiing holidays in Europe, Africa and Latin America.

Inntravel inntravel.co.uk
▶▶ Walking, cycling and winter activity holidays in Europe, Morocco, India, USA and Canada.

Neilson Holidays neilson.co.uk
▶▶ Skiing, beach club, sailing and activity holidays for families throughout Europe.

PGL Adventure Holidays pgl.co.uk
▶▶ Summer camps, adventure holidays and activity breaks in the UK and Europe.

All-inclusive resorts
Beaches beachesresorts.co.uk
▶▶ Resorts in Jamaica and Turks & Caicos.

Club Med clubmed.com
▶▶ Worldwide collection of 80 all-inclusive holiday villages, from beach resorts to skiing.

▶▶ **Esprit Holidays** esprit-holidays.co.uk
Family specialist in skiing and Alpine summer holidays. Renowned childcare programme. Also arranges visits to Santa in Lapland.

Mark Warner markwarner.co.uk
▶▶ Long-established ski and beach resort operator with comprehensive kids' facilities.

Antarctica & the Arctic
Discover the World and Exodus (see Worldwide travel) both offer an extensive range of polar voyages.

Asia
Selective Asia selectiveasia.com
▶▶ Tailor-made travel in Borneo, Burma, Cambodia, Laos, Malaysia, Thailand and Vietnam.

Australia and New Zealand
Bridge & Wickers and Discover the World (see Worldwide travel) arrange family holidays to both Australia and New Zealand.

Boating & cruising holidays
Le Boat leboat.co.uk
▶▶ Boating holidays, relaxing breaks and canal and river cruises to UK, Ireland and Europe.

P&O Cruises pocruises.com
▶▶ Cruise holidays to 90 countries, including the Caribbean and Mediterranean.

Sunsail sunsail.co.uk
▶▶ Yacht charter and flotilla sailing holidays at over 30 destinations worldwide.

Camping holidays
Canopy & Stars canopyandstars.co.uk
▶▶ Luxury camping and glamping holidays in the UK and France, featuring everything from tree houses and yurts to shepherds' huts.

Feather Down Farm Days featherdown.co.uk
▶▶ Luxurious camping on working farms throughout the UK.

Caribbean
Tropical Sky tropicalsky.co.uk
▶▶ Luxury holidays to some of the Caribbean's top beach resorts. Also covers Indian Ocean.

City breaks
Kirker Holidays kirkerholidays.com
▶▶ Short breaks, cultural tours and music holidays in Europe and beyond.

SACO Apartments sacoapartments.com
▶▶ Serviced apartments in Paris, New York and other cities worldwide.

Eastern Europe
Completely Croatia completelycroatia.co.uk
▶▶ Handpicked hotels, tailor-made and family-friendly holidays in Croatia.

France
Corsican Places corsica.co.uk
▶▶ Leading specialists in family-friendly Corsican villas and hotels.

Leisure Direction leisuredirection.co.uk
▶▶ Self-drive specialist offering ferry, Eurotunnel or Eurostar packages, including Disneyland Paris.

Pierre & Vacances pv-holidays.com
▶▶ Multi-activity holiday villages in France and Spain.

Greece & Turkey
Cachet Travel cachet-travel.co.uk
▶▶ Holidays in Crete, Chios, Samos, Ikaria, Fourni, Turkey, the Canary Islands, Madeira and the Azores.

Exclusive Escapes exclusiveescapes.co.uk
▶▶ Villas, hotels and gulet cruises in Turkey.

The Villa Collection gicthevillacollection.com
▶▶ Renowned Greek Islands Club collection of family villas with swimming pools.

Holiday villages
Canvas Holidays canvasholidays.co.uk
▶▶ Luxury family camping holidays and mobile home holidays in France, Spain and throughout Europe.

Center Parcs centerparcs.com
▶▶ 20 holiday villages in the UK, Netherlands, Belgium, Germany and France with superb leisure facilities.

Eurocamp eurocamp.com
▶▶ Over 160 parcs in 12 European countries, including France, Spain, Italy, Germany, Switzerland, Austria and Croatia, plus camping holidays in the USA.

Haven haven.com
▶▶ 35 family holiday parks on the UK's coast.

Keycamp keycamp.com
▶▶ Mobile home and camping holidays in Europe and the USA.

Siblu siblu.com
▶▶ Family mobile home holidays in France.

Indian Ocean
Beachcomber Tours beachcombertours.co.uk
▶▶ Luxury holidays to family-friendly resorts in Mauritius and the Seychelles.

Elite Vacations elitevacations.com
▶▶ Tailormade holidays to the Seychelles, Mauritius and Maldives.

Italy
Real Holidays realholidays.co.uk
▶▶ Italian specialists, but also have a wider ranging family holiday portfolio.

Sardatur Holidays realholidays.co.uk
▶▶ Family holidays in Sardinia.

Latin America

Dehouche dehouche.com
▶▶ Tailor-made trips to Argentina and Brazil.

Journey Latin America
journeylatinamerica.co.uk
▶▶ Leading Latin America specialist with extensive family programme offering tailor-made trips, escorted group tours and one-stop holidays.

North America

Footloose footloose.com
▶▶ Adventures in the United States and Canada for families with children aged eight and above.

North America Travel Service
northamericatravelservice.co.uk
▶▶ Comprehensive range of holidays and accommodation in the USA, Canada and Caribbean.

Overland Adventure

Dragoman dragoman.com
▶▶ Customized trucks carry adventurous families on overland trips in Africa and Asia.

Safaris

&Beyond andbeyond.com
▶▶ Outstanding safari camps and lodges in Africa and India, with excellent guides.

Aardvark Safaris aardvarksafaris.com
▶▶ Tailor-made African safaris and family holidays to the Indian Ocean.

Bushbaby Travel bushbabytravel.com
▶▶ Malaria-free family holidays and safaris to South Africa and the Indian Ocean, plus the Middle East, Caribbean, USA and North Africa.

Expert Africa expertafrica.co.uk
▶▶ The UK's leading Africa specialist with extensive knowledge of southern and East Africa, and competitive prices for family safaris and fly-drives.

Rainbow Tours rainbowtours.co.uk
▶▶ Tailor-made safari, wildlife and beach holidays in southern and East Africa, and the Indian Ocean.

Self-catering accommodation

Big Domain thebigdomain.com
▶▶ Big holiday homes for big occasions, with properties sleeping 12 or more.

Classic Cottages classic.co.uk
▶▶ Leading provider of holiday cottages in southwest England.

CV Travel cvtravel.co.uk
▶▶ Handpicked villas and hotels in Greece.

Also cover Italy, Spain, France, the Caribbean and beyond.

Villa Select villaselect.com
▶▶ Specialists in villa holidays with private pools in the Balearic Islands, Algarve and Greek Islands.

Vintage Travel vintagetravel.co.uk
▶▶ Villas with pools in Spain, France, Greece, Italy, Portugal, Gozo, Croatia and the Canary Islands.

Spain & Portugal

Casas Cantabricas casas.co.uk
▶▶ Self-catering houses and hotels throughout the north and west of Spain as well as northern Portugal.

Volunteering

Earthwatch earthwatch.org
▶▶ Research and conservation expeditions for the whole family. No special skills are necessary.

Hands Up Holidays handsupholidays.com
▶▶ Family holidays combining sightseeing and volunteering.

Worldwide operators

Abercrombie & Kent abercrombiekent.com
▶▶ Long-established luxury holiday operator with family programme.

The Adventure Company
adventurecompany.co.uk
▶▶ Leading specialist in worldwide family adventures, including departures for single-parent families, as well as those with teenagers.

Audley Travel audleytravel.com
▶▶ Specialists in tailor-made adventure and luxury travel to over 70 countries.

Barefoot Traveller
barefoot-traveller.com
▶▶ Holidays to the Caribbean, Middle East and Asia.

Bridge & Wickers
bridgeandwickers.co.uk
▶▶ Experts in tailor-made holidays to Australia and New Zealand, Africa, Canada, Alaska, South Pacific and Middle East.

Cox & Kings coxandkings.co.uk
▶▶ Dedicated Family Explorer programme offering tailor-made journeys worldwide.

Discover the World
discover-the-world.co.uk
▶▶ Leading specialists in travel to Iceland, Lapland, the polar regions, Canada, New Zealand and Australia with several family offerings – both tailormade and group.

Explore Worldwide explore.co.uk
▶▶ Pioneers of small-group adventure holidays with walking, cycling, trekking and other activity holidays in over 130 countries worldwide, plus a comprehensive range of adventure trips for families.

Exodus exodus.co.uk
▶▶ A wide range of family adventure holidays, including small group departures, individual family trips and centre-based activity holidays.

Families Worldwide familiesworldwide.co.uk
▶▶ Worldwide experts in family adventures, with trips divided into discovery, activity, wildlife and learning categories.

The Imaginative Traveller
imaginative-traveller.com
▶▶ Small-group family adventures.

KE Adventure Travel keadventure.com
▶▶ Programme of around 40 adventurous family trips worldwide.

Kumuka kumuka.com
▶▶ Adventure specialist with range of worldwide family tours.

Peregrine Adventures
peregrineadventures.com
▶▶ Range of worldwide adventures.

Powder Byrne powderbyrne.co.uk
▶▶ A selection of the best hotels and resorts around the Mediterranean, Caribbean and the Indian Ocean, plus top ski resorts in the Alps. Superb childcare facilities.

Reef & Rainforest Tours
familytours.co.uk
▶▶ Specialists in tailor-made holidays to the world's best wildlife destinations, with several family trips.

Virgin Holidays virginholidays.co.uk
▶▶ Dedicated family holiday programme to the Caribbean, Florida, USA, Canada and Africa.

★ Also try

▶▶ **Hayes & Jarvis**
hayesandjarvis.co.uk

▶▶ **ITC Classics**
itcclassics.co.uk

▶▶ **i-escape**
i-escape.com

▶▶ **On the Go Tours**
onthegotours.com

▶▶ **Scott Dunn**
scottdunn.com

▶▶ **Sovereign**
sovereign.com

▶▶ **Tots Too**
totstoo.com

▶▶ **Travelbeam**
travelbeam.co.uk

▶▶ **Turquoise Holidays**
turquoiseholidays.co.uk

▶▶ **Western Oriental**
wandotravel.com

Rhossili Bay, Gower Peninsula

Located at the very tip of the Gower Peninsula in South Wales, Rhossili is the ultimate run-wild-and-free beach: play cricket, fly a kite, build a sandy rampart against the tide and scrawl your name in house-size letters.

★ **1** Take a spin on the London Eye
▶▶ London, page 34

★ **2** Find the perfect body-boarding beach
▶▶ Cornwall, page 39

★ **3** Explore a medieval castle
▶▶ Warwickshire, page 43

★ **4** Take a hike and paddle a canoe
▶▶ Lake District, page 44

★ **5** Spot seals, seabirds and whales
▶▶ Pembrokeshire, page 46

★ **6** Tour the Highlands & Islands
▶▶ Scotland, page 49

★ **7** Take a boat trip along the River Shannon
▶▶ Ireland, page 51

You must

★ **Catch** crabs off a harbour wall.
★ **Slurp** hot chocolate after a day's surfing.
★ **Scoff** fish and chips on the seafront.
★ **Hunt** for fossils and rock-pool critters.
★ **Paddle** a kayak to a secret cove.
★ **Pitch** a tent somewhere special.
★ **Pedal** a bike along a forest trail.
★ **Roast** marshmallows on a campfire.
★ **Spot** a dolphin on a boat trip.
★ **Storm** a castle's ramparts.

Introduction
Britain & Ireland

Many visitors to Britain and Ireland (and quite a few of the residents) love to have a good moan about the weather and how expensive everything is. The fact remains, though, that these islands are not only incredibly beautiful, but they also squeeze more child-friendly beaches, cities and family attractions into one small, accessible region than anywhere in the world. Admittedly, the weather can be temperamental (or downright frustrating) at times, and there's no denying that a British family holiday sometimes requires a fair degree of stoicism – but it doesn't rain constantly. In any case, Britain and Ireland are great family holiday destinations whatever the weather. Kids can have just as much fun exploring rock pools and building sandcastles on a wind-strafed Cornish beach during winter as they can surfing on one during a summer heatwave. As for the cost issue, some of the best family holiday highlights in Britain and Ireland don't cost a penny – cycling in Pembrokeshire, visiting London's museums and finding the perfect picnic spot in the Lake District to name just a few.

❝❞ **When I asked our seven-year-old twins what they'd like to do on holiday if they could go anywhere in the world or do anything they wanted, they barely hesitated before replying: "Go surfing, build big sandcastles, catch shrimps in rock pools and eat fish and chips by the sea." So, Cornwall it is then.** William Gray

Star rating

Wow factor
★★★
Worry factor
★
Value for money
★★
Keeping teacher happy
★★★
Family accommodation
★★★★★
Babies & toddlers
★★★★★
Cool for teenagers
★★★

Thrill rides
35 good reasons to have a growth spurt

The park	The ride	The thrill	The catch — Min height
Alton Towers Staffordshire T0871-222 3330 altontowers.com	Nemesis	Experience G-forces greater than a Space Shuttle take-off.	140 cm
	Oblivion	More bonkers than a bungee – plunge 60 m into the abyss.	140 cm
	Air	Float, swoop, soar, dive and feel you're flying.	140 cm
	Rita	She's the Queen of Speed, reaching 100 km/h in 2.5 seconds.	140 cm
	Ripsaw	Spinning is to be expected, but watch out for the water jets.	140 cm
	Submission	Wild contraption that spins and rotates in all directions.	120 cm
Blackpool Pleasure Beach T0871-222 1234 blackpoolpleasurebeach.com	Pepsi Max Big One	At 72 m, one of Europe's tallest roller coasters.	132 cm
	Infusion	Suspended coaster, five loops, plus water features.	132 cm
	Ice Blast	Get catapulted at 130 km/h up a vertical 64-m tower.	132 cm
	Bling	Imagine being strapped to a Catherine wheel...	122 cm
	Grand National	Twin track racing wooden coaster.	117 cm
	Big Dipper	Classic coaster with five big drops and dips.	117 cm
	Avalanche	Britain's only bobsled coaster, reaching speed of 80 km/h.	112 cm
Chessington World of Adventures Surrey T0871-663 4477 chessington.co.uk	Rameses Revenge	Monster machine lowers you head first over water fountains.	140 cm
	Rattlesnake	Spinning, twisting, dipping, bone-rattling ride.	140 cm
	Dragon's Fury	A fiery family spinning roller coaster.	120 cm
	Kobra	Explorers spin through the air on a 90-m track at 70 km/h.	120 cm
	Tomb Blaster	Battle with mummies to beat the curse of the tomb.	110 cm
	Vampire	Fly over Transylvanian treetops on a bloodcurdling coaster.	110 cm
Drayton Manor Staffordshire T0844-472 1950 draytonmanor.co.uk	Apocalypse	The world's first stand-up tower drop (48 m at 4 Gs).	140 cm
	Shockwave	Europe's only stand-up roller coaster.	140 cm
	G Force	Vertical ascent of 23 m followed by loops at over 70 km/h.	130 cm
	Maelstrom	Stomach-churning, outward-facing gyro-swing.	130 cm
	Stormforce 10	Plunge backwards down a 16-m water drop.	120 cm
	Pandemonium	Swing through 360 degrees, experiencing a force of 3.8 Gs.	120 cm
Legoland Windsor T0871-222 2001 legoland.co.uk	Viking Splash	Surge downstream in a fantasy Viking World.	100 cm
	Atlantis Submarine	Take the plunge for a magical underwater adventure.	None
	The Dragon	Twist and turn through the depths of a castle.	100 cm
	Pirate Falls	Mild but wild, swashbuckling water-splash ride.	100 cm
Thorpe Park Surrey T0871-663 1673 thorpepark.com	Saw	The world's first ever horror movie-themed roller coaster.	140 cm
	Samurai	Relentless, spinning stomach-churner with forces of 5 Gs.	140 cm
	Stealth	0-130 km/h in less than two seconds, and 60 m high.	140 cm
	Colossus	Swirl and corkscrew around a thundering steel track.	140 cm
	Storm Surge	Ultimate sky-high, spinning water ride.	110 cm
	Rush	Swing back and forth to 23 m at over 80 km/h, topping 4 Gs.	130 cm

Seaside safari

Can you find these six common shells? ❶ flat periwinkle; ❷ common periwinkle; ❸ limpet; ❹ dog whelk; ❺ topshell; ❻ mussel. Remember to check tide times to ensure that you do not become trapped by the rising tide. Wear shoes with good grip, take care to disturb animals and plants as little as possible – particularly when looking under rocks – and leave creatures where you find them. Check out the Seashore Code from the Marine Conservation Society (mcsuk.org).

🔍 Harry spotter

You don't need a broomstick or magic wand to visit several of the places featured in the Harry Potter movies. Platform 9¾, the mystifying departure point for the Hogwarts Express steam train, was filmed at Platform 4 of London's King's Cross Station. Harry and his fellow wannabe-wizards disembark at Hogsmeade Station, which is none other than Goathland, a village in the Yorkshire Moors, while Glenfinnan Viaduct in the Scottish Highlands featured in a spectacular action sequence in *The Chamber of Secrets*. The interior of the Hogwarts School of Witchcraft and Wizardry is based on several locations, including Lacock Abbey in Wiltshire, Gloucester Cathedral and Oxford University's Bodleian Library and the Great Hall at Christ Church. Alnwick Castle in Northumberland, meanwhile, will always be remembered as the setting for broomstick lessons and quidditch matches.

Anyone for quidditch?
Alnwick Castle, Northumberland.

Great reads
6 children's books

Early years
Katie Morag's Island Stories
Mairi Hedderwick (Red Fox)
A Hebridean community seen through the eyes of a child. Katie is always in some sort of bother, but her family and the friendly islanders keep her out of serious trouble.

The Mousehole Cat
Antonia Barber (Walker Books)
A brave fisherman and his cat battle through a storm to bring food to the children of a Cornish village.

Ages 6-12
Five on a Treasure Island
Enid Blyton (Hodder)
There's a shipwreck off Kirrin Island, but where is the treasure? The five go on the trail, but they're not alone.

Friend or Foe
Michael Morpurgo (Mammoth)
Set during the Second World War, London is under the Blitz and two friends, David and Tucky, have been evacuated to the countryside, where they are faced with a terrible dilemma when they witness a German plane crash on the moors.

Ireland, Horrible Histories
Terry Deary (Scholastic)
Find out the horrible truth about Ireland's foul famines, savage sieges and wretched rebellions, and the formidable Irish people who lived and died in them.

Teens
Tarka the Otter
Henry Williamson (Penguin Classics)
Timeless and simply beautiful, this classic tale of an otter living in the Devonshire countryside skilfully evokes life in the wild as seen through Tarka's own eyes.

Dig for glory
Make the perfect sandcastle

1 Location is crucial. Site your castle near a stream so it's easy to divert water into the moat. Also, make sure the sand is neither too dry nor too sticky.

2 A moat without a boat is no fun at all. Create a harbour on one side of your castle, using a piece of driftwood as a gate. Periodic dredging will be required.

3 Using a spade, carve steps and terraces on the flanks of the castle. Add pebbles and shells for windows and seagull feathers for medieval banners.

4 Don't overlook your outer defences. At least one tide-restraining wall will be required outside your moat. This should feature crenellations or 'dribble sand' towers.

5 Main access should always be via a bridge with pebble parapets (or a drawbridge using flat driftwood). Cobbles make ideal stepping stones across the moat.

6 Special features can include jetties to outlying towers and lighthouses, or tunnels scooped by hand through sturdy bastions of the main castle.

Taste of Wales bara brith

What you need
- 110 g sultanas
- 110 g raisins soaked overnight in 150 ml cold tea
- 110 g Demerara sugar
- 1 tbsp coarse cut marmalade
- 1 beaten egg
- 1 tsp mixed spice
- 220 g self-raising flour

What to do
- Mix ingredients together.
- Put the mixture into a greased loaf tin.
- Bake at 160-170°C for one hour.
- Cool for 20 minutes before turning out onto a wire tray.
- Cut into slices.
- Butter before serving.

Family travel in Britain is pure child's play. Nothing could be simpler. There are activities and attractions to suit every age; getting around is generally straightforward, and accommodation covers the whole gamut from campsites to luxury hotels.

Babies
The climate is gentle, baby supplies are easily found, many places are buggy-friendly and, no matter where you go, you'll usually find at least one café with highchairs or a hotel that provides cots. Seaside holidays are the natural choice – you can plonk tiny tots on the beach, swoosh them through the shallows and wheel them to sleep along the prom. The Marine Conservation Society publishes the *Good Beach Guide* (goodbeachguide.co.uk).

Toddlers/pre-school
More fun, but also more fraught, beach holidays with toddlers demand eagle-eyed surveillance by parents to ensure safety. City breaks can also work well with this age range – parks usually have excellent playgrounds, while zoos and aquariums are always a hit. Toddlers are too young to get much out of the major theme parks, although Legoland (legoland.co.uk) in Windsor will appeal, as will farm parks like Dairyland Farm World in Cornwall (dairylandfarmworld.com).

Kids/school age
Beach safety is even more paramount with this fearless age group. However, with expert tuition at surf schools, activity centres and riding stables, kids can safely start learning all kinds of new skills. They are also at an age when camping, hiking and cycling holidays start to sound feasible. As for exercising their minds, Britain is chock-a-block with interactive science museums, mysterious castles and well-interpreted nature reserves. Organizations like the National Trust (nationaltrust.org.uk), RSPB (rspb.org.uk) and The Wildlife Trusts (wildlifetrusts.org) arrange numerous child-friendly events throughout the year.

Teenagers
You really need a surf school, sailing club or some other kind of extra incentive to keep teens keen on the beach. Sandcastles and rock pools just won't do it for them. Try giving them a taste of freedom at summer camps operated by Camp Beaumont (campbeaumont.co.uk) and PGL (pgl.co.uk) where they'll not only try out cool new activities but also meet lots of people their own age. City breaks will also strike a chord with teenagers, particularly in places like London, Glasgow and Manchester, where you can combine sightseeing with great shopping and popular culture. For adventure and adrenaline, hit the theme park trail, challenge them to climb a Munro in Scotland or paddle a kayak off Pembrokeshire.

Falling head over keels for Loch Morlich, Cairngorms, Scottish Highlands

Children as young as eight can join sailing courses and taster sessions organized by the Royal Yachting Association (RYA) at watersports centres throughout Britain and Northern Ireland.

> ❝❞ **We love going to London. Don't underestimate the pleasures of simply travelling around – double-decker buses, tubes and taxis were all a rich source of entertainment for our three- and five-year-old. The highlight was a boat trip down the Thames from Westminster Pier to Greenwich. It's a great way to see lots of famous landmarks.** Alison Rippon

❶ Seven Sisters Country Park, Sussex
Follow the 2-km path alongside the meandering River Cuckmere to the famous chalk cliffs of the Seven Sisters (sevensisters.org.uk) – it leads to a shingle beach with spectacular views of Seaford Head. The path is also bike-friendly, so older children will love cycling to the beach for a picnic.

Wheely easy
Four child-friendly walks

Special needs

Holiday Care (tourismforall.org.uk) has information on transport, accommodation, visitor attractions and activity holidays for people with all kinds of disability, while Door to Door (dptac.independent.gov.uk) offers advice about travelling using various forms of transport. Disability Now (disabilitynow.org.uk) lists accessible hotels, cottages and B&Bs in the UK. Vitalise (vitalise.org.uk) has five centres where disabled or visually impaired people and their carers can enjoy themed weeks, plus various activities and excursions.

Single parents

Lone-Parents UK (lone-parents.org.uk) is a support site for single parents that provides links to a number of companies that specialize in one-parent family holidays. Single Parent Fun (singleparentfun.com) is an excellent community site where free membership enables you to meet other single parents and join organized trips and days out. Popular with single-parent families, Acorn Adventure (acornadventure.co.uk) operates activity holidays in the Lake District and Brecon Beacons.

❷ Totnes to Dartington Riverside Path, Devon
This 4-km walk follows the River Dart from Totnes Bridge to the Cider Press Centre in Dartington where you'll find a toy shop and child-friendly café.

❸ Cotswold Water Park, Gloucestershire
A 4-km walk encircles two lakes, taking in a visitor centre, lakeside café, wood sculpture trail and two adventure playgrounds. There's even a sandy beach!

❹ Durham riverbanks
Stroll down cobbled South Bailey towards Prebend's Bridge, admire Durham's magnificent cathedral, then take the woodland path back towards the city centre.

Telling tales Sarah Tucker

Author of *The Playground Mafia* | sarahtucker.info

The most important things you need to take with you on holiday are imagination, creativity, confidence and a relaxed attitude towards travel. You have a stressed out parent, you get a stressed out kid. You have a chilled out parent, you get a chilled out kid. And don't dump them on someone else when you have the benefit of their company. Children want to be with their parents – even teenagers believe it or not. It's the time you spend with your children they will remember – not the stuff that you buy them.

It's big, busy and bewildering (not to mention being one of the world's most expensive cities), but there's no denying the fact that kids love London. Just being there, in the thick of it, crawling along congested streets in a double-decker bus or rising above it all on the London Eye, gives children a huge thrill. And that's before you've hit any of the attractions. You can tailor a day out in London to suit all ages, whether it's a London Zoo/Hamleys double-whammy for six year olds or a teenage pilgrimage to the shops along Oxford Street. Whatever you decide to do, resist the temptation to cram too much into a single day. London with kids is best in small, bite-size chunks.

Two-day action plan

➤ Day 1: The South Bank

The London Eye (londoneye.com) is not only a fun (30-minute) ride, but it's also the best way for kids to grasp the scale of London and pinpoint a few landmarks. As the big wheel spins them 135 m above the Thames, they'll be able to see everything from the Houses of Parliament to Wembley Stadium. Back at ground level, take a river cruise for a different perspective of capital attractions like St Paul's Cathedral (stpauls.co.uk), HMS Belfast (hmsbelfast. iwm.org.uk), the Tower of London (hrp.org.uk) and Tower Bridge. However, if that sounds like too much sightseeing for one day, focus instead on other South Bank highlights. The London Aquarium (visitsealife. com/london) recreates a watery world of rushing streams, coral reefs, mangrove swamps and teeming rock pools. You can stroke rays in the touch pool and watch a piranha feeding-frenzy, but it's the sharks in the huge Pacific tank and the gentoo penguins in Ice Adventure that are the show-stealers. The National Theatre (nationaltheatre.org.uk) hosts a free outdoor summer festival between July and September called Watch this Space, featuring live performances, from circus acts to music and dance. The Tate Modern (tate. org.uk) has holiday activities for families, while the Unicorn Theatre (unicorntheatre.com) presents acts specifically for children. Altogether less refined, the London Dungeon (thedungeons.com) 'gorifies' the capital's less salubrious past with vivid portrayals of torture, plague and the Great Fire of London. There are even thrill rides like Extremis – Drop Ride to Doom, a simulated hanging for anyone over 120 cm tall. Located on Lambeth Road, the Imperial War Museum (iwm.org.uk) takes a more dignified approach to history with its impressive displays of weaponry and

☉ Let's go to Greenwich

Take a boat trip from central London with Thames Cruises (thamescruises.com) to reach this World Heritage Site dominated by Sir Christopher Wren's Old Royal Naval College (oldroyalnavalcollege.org). Be sure to set a course for the glorious 19th-century tea clipper, Cutty Sark (cuttysark.org.uk) and the National Maritime Museum (nmm.ac.uk). Or, if time is of the essence, head to the Royal Observatory (nmm.ac.uk/rog) which has a spectacular planetarium – not to mention zero degrees longitude at the famous Meridian Line.

sobering insights into the World Wars. Steer younger children towards the Home Front exhibit where they'll be intrigued by concepts like rationing.

➤ Day 2: Classic sights

Start at Trafalgar Square where Nelson's Column rises above a swirling torrent of taxis and buses. Flanking the famous plaza are three arty attractions. The National Gallery (nationalgallery.org.uk) offers talks and workshops for families, as well as a selection of audio tours and printed trails. There's also magic carpet storytelling for the under-fives (on Sundays). The National Portrait Gallery (npg.org.uk) provides a range of family experiences, from art workshops and storytelling to audiovisual tours using interactive touchscreen players. However, if it's good old-fashioned brass rubbing that gets your creative juices flowing, head to St Martin-in-the-Fields (smitf.org). Grab a snack lunch at the café in the crypt, before strolling down The Mall, nipping into St James's Park (royalparks.gov.uk) to see wildlife officers feeding the pelicans (daily at 1430). Continue to Buckingham Palace (royal.gov. uk) to wave at the Queen, and then take a bus to Knightsbridge where the Food Halls of Harrods (harrods.com) should distract kids for a few minutes before they drag you to the toys on the fourth floor.

South Bank – The London Eye and London Aquarium

You can easily combine either of these attractions with a visit to Greenwich (see box, above). Boats leave from piers at Charing Cross and the Houses of Parliament and take between 45 and 55 minutes to reach Greenwich.

Local favourites

★ **Battersea Park Children's Zoo** (batterseaparkzoo.co.uk) Pat a pot-bellied pig, mingle with meerkats and ruffle a lemur.

★ **The Diana, Princess of Wales Memorial Playground** Let little feet and big imaginations run wild in this Kensington Gardens' playground with its huge wooden pirate ship, sandy beach, sensory trail, mermaids' fountain and tepees.

★ **London Wetland Centre** (wwt.org.uk) Explore nature trails, stake out bird hides and discover what lurks in the reedbeds.

4 of the best museums

① British Museum
thebritishmuseum.org
Don't drift aimlessly through this vast cultural and historical treasure house – your kids will wilt. Instead, make use of the excellent children's programme – several museum trails, family activity backpacks, workshops and storytelling. Join 'Vid the Alien' and his friends for a tour of the museum's highlights using a multimedia guide. If you see just one thing, make sure it's the Egyptian mummies.

② Natural History Museum
nhm.ac.uk
A skeleton of Diplodocus has long reigned supreme in the Central Hall of this magnificent museum – although it has to be said that kids usually get more of a buzz from the new-fangled animatronic T Rex in the dinosaur gallery. Other highlights include Creepy Crawlies, Ecology, the Mammal Hall and earthquake simulator. Explorer Backpacks, complete with pith helmets, binoculars and drawing materials, are available for under-sevens; eight- to 11-year-olds can even have a sleepover with the dinosaurs, snuggle under the Diplododus and take a torch-lit T-Rex trail. Don't miss the Darwin Centre, the museum's state-of-the-art science and collections facility.

③ Science Museum
sciencemuseum.org.uk
London's best museum for hands-on fiddling and twiddling, the Science Museum has play zones targeting different age groups. The Garden helps under-fives experiment with water, light and sound, the Pattern Pod engages five- to eight-year-olds, while the Launch Pad is the museum's largest and most popular interactive gallery for school-age kids. Teenagers will find the latest science news at Antenna, while Energy challenges seven- to 14-year-olds to investigate energy demands for the future. There are also motion simulators, daily science shows and an IMAX cinema.

④ Victoria & Albert Museum
vam.ac.uk
The V&A has excellent family facilities, including various trails which take you through the galleries. Unlock your creativity by borrowing a writing or drawing kit. There are also plenty of dressing-up opportunities in the theatre and performance galleries. Activity backpacks on themes such as Chinese treasures, glass and fancy furnishings are also available for children aged five to 12. Sign up for the museum's families e-newsletter.

How to do the zoo

Most visitors make straight for Gorilla Kingdom near the entrance of London Zoo (zsl.org), so skip the crowds by walking in the opposite direction towards the wild dogs, giraffes, zebras and okapis. Next, visit the Clore Rainforest Lookout – a little piece of South American jungle which you can explore both at canopy and ground level. The adjacent Night Zone takes you into a twilight world of bats, rats and other nocturnal critters. If they're out and about, the nearby meerkats and otters are always entertaining – but walk on past the penguins to the flamingo pool and big cat enclosures. Check out the activities at BUGS! (Biodiversity Underpinning Global Survival) before backtracking to the Oasis Café for lunch. You'll then be in prime position for the penguin feeding at 1430, followed by 'Lions – built to kill' – a talk about some of nature's super-predators, held daily in the Big Cats area. Next, visit the Reptile House, the walk-through African Bird Safari, and the Komodo dragon enclosure – by which time the zoo should be less busy, leaving you to enjoy Gorilla Kingdom (main pic above) with the minimum of territorial posturing.

Covent Garden
covent-garden.co.uk
Cool cafés, street performers and plenty of shops make Covent Garden a good bet for teenagers. The London Transport Museum (ltmuseum.co.uk) has a learning zone, 'driver's-eye' simulators and a play area for under-fives.

Southeast England
The Wight stuff

Family attractions in Southeast England include everything from theme parks and castles to seaside resorts like Brighton, Eastbourne and Hastings. However, if you have to pick just one place to take the kids, it has to be the Isle of Wight with its beaches, coastal walks, cycling tracks and watersports. Take the ferry from Portsmouth and you can easily add a visit to the historic dockyard to see the *Mary Rose* and *HMS Victory*. Another great option for active families, the New Forest has miles of cycle tracks and several riding stables, while the North and South Downs offer plenty in the way of gentle walks.

Isle of Wight's Dinosaur Isle

Isle of Wight

About half of the 380-sq-km Isle of Wight is an Area of Outstanding Natural Beauty. Although there are over 800 km of footpaths, you'll probably have more luck getting kids to sample the 320 km of cycle trails. Isle Cycle (islecycle.co.uk) will deliver rental bikes to your hotel and kit you out with helmets, locks and tools. The website has suggestions for a range of routes. An easy one to start with follows the disused railway line from Yarmouth to Freshwater Bay, a good spot for swimming. Leaflets describing other cycle trails are available from tourist information centres. A mecca for 'yachties', the Isle of Wight is the perfect place to hone your sailing skills. Based in Bembridge on the eastern side of the island, X-Isle Sports (T01983-873111) offers courses in sailing, surfing, kitesurfing, windsurfing, wakeboarding and waterskiing. There are also several excellent locations for kayaking, including the sheltered beaches of Ryde and Puckpool. For swimming, the best beach is Shanklin. To any dinosaur fanatics in the family, the Isle of Wight will seem more like a pilgrimage than a holiday – nowhere else in Europe is more important for dinosaur remains. At the Dinosaur Isle (dinosaurisle.com) museum you're whisked back in time to the Cretaceous, when the Isle of Wight was prowled by the predatory *Neovenator salerii*, as well as giant lumbering sauropods and armour-plated ankylosaurs. New discoveries are made all the time – try your luck by joining one of the museum's fossil walks.

New Forest

Once a popular hunting ground for Norman kings, William the Conqueror's 'new' forest is home to peacefully grazing herds of fallow deer and New Forest ponies. For your best chance of spotting wildlife, explore the forest on foot, bicycle or horseback. Try Country Lanes Cycle Centre (countrylanes.co.uk) and New Park Manor Equestrian Centre (newparkmanorhotel.co.uk) – both in Brockenhurst. Nestled on the banks of the Beaulieu River, Buckler's Hard (bucklershard.co.uk) provides a fascinating glimpse into the past, when the forest supplied mighty oaks for Nelson's fleet.

Sussex

Spend the morning sprinting across the tidal flats at Wittering Sands and the afternoon whooping it up at Harbour Park fairground in Littlehampton. Fossil sharks' teeth litter the sands at Bracklesham Bay, while real sharks cruise the Sea Life Centre in Brighton. From donkey rides on Camber Sands to thrill rides on Brighton Pier; from sailing lessons in Hove to boat trips bound for Beachy Head, the Sussex coast is a natural magnet for families on holiday. Don't overlook the countryside though. Ashdown Forest is a must for fans of Winnie-the-Pooh. For the ultimate nostalgia rush, take a steam-train ride on the Bluebell Railway between Sheffield Park and Kingscote. Other honeypots include Arundel (with its castle and wetland centre) and Alfriston (with its tea rooms and excellent small zoo, Drusillas Park). East Sussex is also 1066 Battle Country, where the pretty village of Battle often echoes with war cries from children wielding wooden spears fresh from the battleground centre.

The Bluebell Railway's *Sir Archibald Sinclair*

Inside info

▶▶ Top attractions include Legoland (legoland.co.uk), Marwell Zoo (marwell.org.uk), Portsmouth Historic Dockyard (historicdockyard.co.uk) and Thorpe Park (thorpepark.com).
▶▶ For further information, log on to visitsoutheastengland.com, Isle of Wight Tourism (islandbreaks.co.uk) and New Forest Tourism (thenewforest.co.uk).

Bulging out between the Thames Estuary and the Wash, East Anglia may be flat, but it's far from featureless. You can hire a boat to explore 200 km of reed-fringed waterways in the Norfolk Broads or punt along the River Cam beneath the Bridge of Sighs in the magnificent university town of Cambridge. From bustling resorts, like Great Yarmouth and Southwold, to the medieval city of Norwich, this under-rated corner of Britain has lots to offer families. Pick of the crop, however, has to be Norfolk's north coast, where your kids will rediscover the pure and simple joys of kite flying, beachcombing and crabbing.

Seals at Blakeney Point

North Norfolk Coast

Before setting off, make sure you have three essentials – binoculars (Norfolk is a birdwatcher's paradise), a kite and a crab line. Driving north from King's Lynn, you pass Snettisham Park (snettishampark.co.uk) which has a deer safari, adventure playgrounds and children's farm, and Caley Mill (norfolk-lavender.co.uk) which is perfectly purple during July and August when the lavender fields are in bloom. Soon after, you reach Hunstanton, a traditional Victorian seaside resort with compulsory pier, amusement arcades and pony rides on the beach. Kids will love the seal-watching trips operated by Searles Sea Tours (seatours.co.uk) in the amphibious Wash Monster, which is equally at home trundling across the sand flats as it is bobbing in the sea beneath Hunstanton's striped cliffs. If it's raining, seek refuge at the Sea Life Sanctuary (sealsanctuary. co.uk) which rescues and rehabilitates sick or injured marine mammals found along the coast and also has permanent displays featuring penguins and otters.

Follow the coastal A149 road to Holme-next-the-Sea, where a boardwalk through the dunes provides easy buggy access to the beach. Nearby is Titchwell Marsh Nature Reserve (rspb.org.uk) where top summer ticks include avocets and marsh harriers. Three pushchair-friendly nature trails explore fen and meadow habitats where, if you're lucky, you may glimpse bearded tits, water voles or the ever-elusive reedbed-skulking bittern.

Continuing east to Brancaster, you may well find a long stretch of beach to yourself. It's a great spot to launch your kite, but not so good for swimming due to the strong tidal currents.

Beyond Burnham lies Holkham Hall (holkham. co.uk) set in a magnificent landscaped park and with access to both a nature reserve and a beautiful 6-km swathe of golden sands. Just east of Holkham, Wells-next-the-Sea is an old fishing port with a quay that's just the job for crabbing. All you need is a weighted line with some bacon tied to the end and a large bucket to store your spoils. Wait until high tide, find a gap between the moored boats and dangle away. Keep young children well away from the edge and remember to set your crabs free afterwards. Wells also has a sandy beach that can be reached by narrow-gauge railway.

A thriving port in the 13th century, Blakeney Marshes is now all silt and seals – you can see both in abundance with Bean's Boats (beansboattrips.co.uk) or Bishop's Boats (norfolksealtrips.co.uk). Nearby, Cley Windmill (which can put you up for the night) overlooks Cley Marshes where you have another chance to bag a bittern. Continue towards Salthouse for sublime seafood at Cookie's Crab Shop before reaching Sheringham and Cromer – both have sand at low tide and pebbles at high tide, and everything in between, from crazy golf to fish and chips.

Let's go to BeWILDerwood

A brilliantly conceived arboreal fantasyland, BeWILDerwood (bewilderwood.co.uk), Wroxham, near Norwich, is like Tarzan, The Hobbit and The Faraway Tree rolled into one. Based on the book, *A Boggle at BeWILDerwood* by Tom Blofeld, children follow the daring exploits of the elf-like Swampy, reliving his adventures through a beautifully crafted succession of rope bridges, tree houses, zip wires, slippery slides, mazes, obstacle courses, nature trails and den-building. Apart from a Crocklebog lurking in Sccaaaaary Lake, you don't see the characters themselves. There are glimpses of Boggle and Twiggle villages as you navigate the Broadland swamp by boat or boardwalk just beyond the entrance to BeWILDerwood – but other than that it's mostly left to children's imagination. If anything, it's almost too subtle, with kids becoming blinkered by an 'adrenaline high' as they rampage through the woods. Be sure to rein them in occasionally to help them make the connection between the action and the story.

B race yourself Brixham; look out Lyme Regis! When the summer holidays arrive, the Southwest receives a flood of families in search of quintessential British seaside. You can almost smell the factor 40 and hear the rattle of spades against buckets. Cornwall, Devon and Dorset are fringed by some of the world's most child-friendly beaches, offering everything from surf, rock pools and unrivalled sandcastle potential to great-value resorts and copious rainy-day attractions.

Devon

South Devon Linking the resort towns of Torquay, Paignton and Brixham, the English Riviera (englishriviera.co.uk) is packed with family appeal, from sandy beaches and steam-train rides to days out at Paignton Zoo (paigntonzoo.org.uk) and Quaywest Water Park (quaywest.splashdownwaterparks.co.uk). Head south along the coast and you reach the South Hams (visitsouthdevon.co.uk), an irresistible blend of glorious beaches, intriguing inlets and rolling countryside. Lying at its heart, Kingsbridge and Salcombe offer traditional seaside treats like crabbing and boat trips, while Dartmouth has its superb castle (english-heritage.org.uk) jutting out into the Dart Estuary. The beaches of the South Hams, meanwhile, are heaven on earth for kids. From east to west, take your pick from Blackpool Sands (sheltered, safe and simply idyllic), Slapton Sands (good for skimming stones), Millbay (across the estuary from Salcombe, fine sand, good for paddling), Soar Mill Cove (golden sands, streams to dam, caves to explore), Hope Cove (calm waters, small harbour at one end), Thurlestone (great rock pools, plus sand), Bantham (vast swathes of sand, shallow tidal lagoons, good surf) and Bigbury-on-Sea (natural paddling pools, views of Burgh Island).

Dartmoor If you can tear the kids away from the beach, Dartmoor (discoverdartmoor.co.uk) makes a fun day out. Hike to one of the famous granite tors, picnic beside rushing streams at Dartmeet, ride the South Devon Railway (southdevonrailway.co.uk) from Buckfastleigh to Totnes, feed lambs at Pennywell Farm (pennywellfarm.co.uk) or cuddle a pony at the Miniature Pony Centre (miniatureponycentre.com).

North Devon Just when you've set your mind on the South Hams, North Devon drops a bucket-load of golden sand and surf potential on your best-laid plans. Woolacombe Bay is the region's undisputed beach beauty, while other top surf spots include

Saunton Sands and Croyde. Cutesy, car-free Clovelly (clovelly.co.uk) with its steep cobbled lanes and 14th-century harbour is almost too picturesque to be true, while the North Devon Biosphere Reserve (encompassing part of the Taw and Torridge Estuary) includes Braunton Burrows, a huge, wildlife-rich dune system. Just inland you can saddle up at the Exmoor Pony Centre (exmoorponies.co.uk) or, if the weather turns nasty, set warp drive for The Milky Way (themilkyway.co.uk) – a farm and space-themed adventure park rolled into one.

Bath, Bristol & Somerset

The pleasures of Bath range from boating on the River Avon (bathboating.co.uk) to exploring the magnificent Roman Baths (romanbaths.co.uk) where kids can 'meet the Romans' courtesy of a special audio tour.

In Bristol, head for the harbour where the vast propeller and rudder of the dry-docked *SS Great Britain* (ssgreatbritain.org) will astound kids. Explore-at-Bristol (at-bristol.org.uk) is a hands-on science museum, while highlights at Bristol Zoo (bristolzoo.org.uk) include the Monkey Jungle, Seal & Penguin Coasts and Explorers' Creek where you can feed parrots.

In Somerset, traditional seaside fun is just a donkey ride away at Minehead, Burnham-on-Sea, Weston-super-Mare and Clevedon. At Wookey Hole Caves (wookey.co.uk) children can search for a witch that was turned to stone, while the Fleet Air Arm Museum (fleetairarm.com) features a simulated flight to *HMS Ark Royal*.

Crabbing at Lynmouth

No seaside family holiday to Devon is complete without a crabbing expedition. One of the best places is the harbour wall and slipway at Lynmouth, but you stand equally good chances of hooking a nipper at hotspots like Stoke Gabriel in the Dart Estuary, Kingsbridge and Dartmouth Quay.

Follow the Famous F

★ The Isle of Purbeck was a favoured holiday haunt of Enid Blyton, whose Famou Five adventures were inspired by the region's coves, islands and ruined castles. Kirrin Island was based on Brownsea Island (brownseaislandferries.com), while the island fictitious ruin was modelled on Corfe Castle (nationaltrust.org.uk). While you're at Corfe don't forget to call into the Ginger Pop Shop (gingerpop.co.uk) for all-things-Blyton – including lashings of ginger beer. Three cheers for Julian, Dick, Anne, George and Timmy!

Wade to go – barefoot to St Michael's Mount

North Cornwall offers a frothy cocktail of Atlantic breakers, surf schools and beach cafés, sprinkled with legends of King Arthur at Tintagel Castle. You can sea kayak from rocky coves, hike to clifftop lookouts or cycle the Camel Trail from Padstow to Bodmin – gateway to a wonderfully wild and woody side of Cornwall.

By contrast, South Cornwall is for messing about in boats and delving into gardens. The sheltered estuaries of the Fal and Fowey are ideal for launching a canoe; Falmouth has boat trips galore and the shipshape National Maritime Museum, while St Austell is the gateway to leafy gems like the Eden Project and Heligan Gardens.

Undecided? Then go for West Cornwall where you'll find the best of both worlds – surf at Whitesand Bay, smugglers' coves on the Lizard Peninsula, fine art and fine food at St Ives, boat trips on the Helford River, plus the big attractions of Land's End and St Michael's Mount.

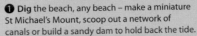

Kids' top 10 Cornwall

❶ **Dig** the beach, any beach – make a miniature St Michael's Mount, scoop out a network of canals or build a sandy dam to hold back the tide.

❷ **Venture** into the tropics at the Eden Project (edenproject.com), Cornwall's essential day-out. Find out where chocolate and vanilla come from, make crafts in the Jungle Town and operate the biggest nutcracker you've ever seen. If you thought plants were boring, think again.

❸ **Discover** how a marine rescue centre works at Gweek's National Seal Sanctuary (sealsanctuary.co.uk).

❹ **Explore** the leafy subtropical paradise of Trebah Gardens (trebahgarden.co.uk).

❺ **Learn** to surf at Whitesands Bay, a golden crescent at Sennen with a cool surf school (sennensurfingcentre.com), rock pools near the lifeboat ramp, acres of sand at low tide and great fish and chips from the café on the waterfront.

❻ **Dangle** your legs over a harbour wall, a crab line in one hand, a Roskilly's ice cream in the other.

❼ **Plan** an adventure to St Michael's Mount (stmichaelsmount.co.uk), the legendary home of the giant, Cormoran; walk across at low tide or take the boat.

❽ **Cycle** the 9-km stretch of the Camel Trail between Wadebridge and Padstow alongside the estuary.

❾ **Track** down the legend of King Arthur at Tintagel Castle (english-heritage.org.uk).

❿ **Smile** when it's raining by heading to indoor attractions like Tate St Ives (tate.org.uk/stives), Falmouth's National Maritime Museum (nmmc.co.uk) and Newquay's Blue Reef Aquarium (bluereefaquarium.co.uk).

From left to right: Camel trail, surfing lesson, Trebah Gardens

❷ Let's go to the Isles of Scilly

Lying just 45 km southwest of Land's End, the Isles of Scilly (simplyscilly.co.uk) seem to have a toehold in the tropics. Nurtured by the Gulf Stream and one of Britain's sunniest climates, the archipelago is surrounded by turquoise seas. The hub of island life, Hugh Town on St Mary's has restaurants, shops, hotels and B&Bs. The St Mary's Boatmen's Association (scillyboating.co.uk) runs a fleet of 10 inter-island launches – sailing times are chalked up daily on quayside noticeboards and include cruises to the Eastern Isles in search of shipwrecks, seals and seabirds. Island Sea Safaris (islandseasafaris.co.uk) can kit you out for snorkelling with seals, while St Mary's Riding Centre (scillyonline.co.uk) offers horse treks. If you island-hop just once, make sure it's to Tresco (tresco.co.uk) where Abbey Gardens runs riot with proteas, yuccas and other exotic plants. The island has some gorgeous sandy beaches to explore – not to mention some of the Scilly's best accommodation, including the beachfront Flying Boat Club. Smallest of the five inhabited islands, the coastline of Bryher (bryher-ios.co.uk) ranges from the calm waters of Green Bay (ideal for kayaking) to rugged Shipman Head where Hell Bay receives the brunt of westerly gales. Accommodation includes the Hell Bay Hotel, self-catering cottages and a secluded campsite. You can also pitch up at St Agnes (st-agnes-scilly.org) in the archipelago's 'wild west' where Troytown Farm Campsite (troytown.co.uk) hugs the foreshore and enjoys sensational sunsets. The island is joined to neighbouring Gugh by a sandy causeway – a favourite spot for families – while pubs, cafés and farms sell a mouthwatering range of local produce, from seafood to ice cream. If you're going to be choosy, St Martin's has the pick of the islands' beaches, with crystal-clear waters lapping sandy Great Bay. St Martin's on the Isle (stmartinshotel.co.uk) has a Michelin-starred restaurant, while Polreath Tea Rooms and Arthur Café are renowned for their home cooking. Work up an appetite with a fishing trip, farm tour or rock-pool ramble.

❶ Bantham
South Devon

It's impossible to hold your children back at Bantham. The moment you walk through the dunes to reach this beach beauty, west of Kingsbridge, they'll be off, sprinting across acres of soft, rippled sand, splashing in shallow tidal lagoons or skipping through waves clutching a surfboard. Apart from toilets in the car park, facilities are few and far between, but part of Bantham's free-spirited appeal lies in its wild, unspoilt nature. At low tide there are rock pools below the headland at the south end of the beach.

❷ Barafundle
Pembrokeshire

Tucked into the crinkle-cut coast south of Pembroke, the pristine golden sands of Barafundle Bay require a bit of an effort to reach. The 1-km walk over the cliffs from the National Trust car park at Stackpole Quay (where you'll also find the nearest toilets, a café and some good rock pools) has no doubt helped to preserve the special, secluded quality of Barafundle. Backed by dunes and woodland, this is a hidden gem with squeaky-clean sand, gorgeous swimming and all the makings of one of Britain's best beach-picnic spots.

❸ Calgary Bay
Isle of Mull, Scotland

One of the most beautiful Hebridean beaches, Calgary Bay forms a sweeping arc of silver-white sand backed by flower-speckled machair and woodland. It's the perfect location for a picnic (or overnight stay if you're prepared for self-sufficient wild camping). There are footpaths along the edge of the bay where, if you are lucky, you might glimpse an otter. On the Ross of Mull, Fidden Beach is also worth tracking down. It has a swathe of soft sand with pink-granite outcrops and pockets of pebbles, speckled like birds' eggs.

❹ Holkham Bay
Norfolk

A 24-carat-gold nugget in North Norfolk's long necklace of sandy beaches, Holkham sits pretty in one of Britain's largest nature reserves and also lies within the magnificent estate of Holkham Hall (holkham. co.uk). From wind-rippled dunes and whispering pine woods to sheltered lagoons, teeming saltmarsh and miles of pristine sand, Holkham is easily reached by footpaths from Burnham Overy, Lady Anne's Drive or Wells Beach Road. It's also accessible by bike. Take a picnic, some binoculars and a sense of adventure and go exploring.

❺ Kynance Cove
Cornwall

The rough diamond in the Lizard's crown, Kynance is the stuff of childhood fantasy. The moment you first glimpse this wild beach on the 1-km walk down from the clifftop car park, countless beach adventures surge to mind – from delving in caves and rock pools to exploring the serpentine stacks and pinnacles that rear above this extraordinarily beautiful cove. Facilities are limited to a single beach café. Aim to get there at least three hours before low tide, when sugary sand envelops the bases of the rock formations.

❻ Newton Haven
Northumberland

Sheltered by offshore reefs, this beautiful sandy bay is close to the 18th-century fishing hamlet of Low Newton. There's good rock-pooling at low tide, while a buggy-friendly trail leads to a birdwatching hide overlooking Newton Pool – a nature reserve tucked away in the dunes. Nip around the low headland and you'll get fine views of skeletal Dunstanburgh Castle presiding over the spectacular scimitar curve of Embleton Bay – a popular surf spot. The beach at Bamburgh is also superb.

❼ Rhossili
Gower Peninsula, Wales

You can walk to Worms Head from Rhossili, setting out from the National Trust visitor centre and shop for an easy, 1-km stroll to the coastguard lookout. Here you can check tide charts before venturing across the rock-pool-riddled causeway to Worms Head. Chances are, however, that once your kids have glimpsed the grand curve of Rhossili Bay from the visitor centre, they'll be dragging you down the steps to the beach where there's nothing except miles of gorgeous sand, raked by surf.

❽ Whistling Sands
Llyn Peninsula, Wales

Dry sand above the high-tide mark squeaks when you walk on it, but that's not the only reason for making a song and dance over this gorgeous bay, nestling like azure between pincer headlands. With sand the texture of fluffy cake mixture, good surf and a beach café selling everything from pizza and ice cream to buckets and spades, Whistling Sands is perfect for families. At low tide, shallow lagoons create paddling pools for toddlers, while exquisite rock pools can be found at either end of the beach.

❾ Whitesands Bay
Cornwall

Just shy of Land's End, mainland Britain's most westerly beach has child appeal by the bucket-load: a 2-km swathe of sand, turquoise sea white-ribbed by breakers and the cutesy fishing village of Sennen Cove. Learn to surf, play beach cricket or frisbee, go rock pooling near the lifeboat ramp, spot seals by the harbour, walk across the bay at low tide to Gwynver Beach (where the surf is usually at its wildest) or strike out in the opposite direction, across the cliffs, to Land's End.

❿ Woolacombe Sands
North Devon

With nearly 5 km of surf-strafed, squeaky clean sand, Woolacombe is beach heaven whether you're a bucket-toting toddler or wave-riding teen. During summer, the northern part of the beach is likely to be very crowded, but you can always find space for your picnic rug and a game of beach cricket. Wave-jumping, body boarding or full-on surfing are compulsory – as is building a sandy rampart to hold back the tide, the seawater warming as it slides in over those acres of sunbaked sand.

⓫ Charmouth
Dorset

This is what you're looking for: penny-sized, jewel-like ammonites (in shiny pyrite) plucked off the beach at Charmouth – by far the most family-friendly fossil-hunting patch on the Jurassic Coast of East Devon and Dorset. Start by visiting the excellent Charmouth Heritage Coast Centre (T01297-560772, charmouth. org, donations only) which has displays, touch tables and information on tides (a falling tide is the safest time to set out). You can sign up for a two-hour guided trip (£7/adult, £3/child) – an expert eye certainly helps, but most people go it alone.

Head east towards Golden Cap, remembering to stay clear of the cliffs. Not only are they very unstable and susceptible to landslides, but the best fossils are to be found on the beach. Keen fossil hunters should time their sorties to follow stormy weather when rain and heavy seas expose fresh fossils and wash them out. Look for shallow streams oozing from the base of the cliffs and spend some time sifting through the gritty sand where the water collects in pools further down the beach. Fossils can also get snagged between boulders.

Other nearby fossil hotspots include Monmouth Beach (west of the harbour at Lyme Regis) for giant ammonites, and Black Ven and Church Cliffs (between Lyme Regis and Charmouth) for ammonites and fragments of ichthyosaurs.

⓬ West Wittering
Sussex

One of the finest stretches of sand on the Sussex coast, West Wittering has something for everyone. Shell-seekers can sift the strandline for slipper limpets and razor shells, while kite-flyers should find plenty of air-space at low tide when vast sand flats, dimpled by shallow lagoons, are exposed. Beyond the designated zone for watersports there's a lifeguard-patrolled Blue Flag area – and behind this you'll find a café and large grassy areas that are perfect for picnics and ball games.

⓭ Porthcurno
Cornwall

The best family beaches hold secrets back, revealing them one by one as the tide ebbs and flows – and Porthcurno is a master of suspense. Stunning even by Cornish standards, it nestles beneath the stone ramparts of the clifftop Minack Theatre, brilliant turquoise waters lapping its sweep of white sand or pounding the cliffs in a magnificent procession of curling, spray-whipped breakers. Then, as the tide drops, the beach slowly creeps along the rocky coast, stranding an enticing string of coves and lagoons.

⓮ Bundoran
Northwest Ireland

This rugged coastline is a Mecca for surfers, with beautiful Bundoran and Dunfanaghy standing out as family favourites. Grab a board and embrace the swirling Alantic waters with the help of one of the local surf schools. Ireland's largest is based in Bundoran where they run a summer kids' camp as well as individual and family group lessons (donegaladventurecentre. net). The surfers' paradise extends along the beaches of Enniscrone and Mullaghmore in Sligo.

✚ Beach safe

Beach lifeguards patrol popular beaches during the main season. **Red and yellow flags** show lifeguarded areas – the safest place to swim, bodyboard and use inflatables. **Black and white chequered flags** show areas for surfboards and other non-powered craft – never swim or bodyboard here. **Orange windsocks** show offshore winds, so never use an inflatable when the sock is flying. **Red flags** mean danger! Never go in the water when the red flag is flying under any circumstances. See also page 52.

Top day out
★ **Oxford** Combine the anthropological Pitt Rivers Museum (prm.ox.ac.uk) or the interactive Science Oxford Hands-On (scienceoxford.com) with some fresh air and fun on the river. You can hire punts, rowing boats and pedalos at Magdalen Bridge Boathouse (oxfordpunting.co.uk).

With its honeystone market towns and rolling hills peppered with sheep, nowhere does traditional England better than the Cotswolds – the region that inspired a million jigsaw puzzles. Elsewhere, you will find a veritable encyclopaedia of historical sites, from ancient Stonehenge and medieval Warwick Castle to the birthplaces of Shakespeare, the Industrial Revolution and, most significantly to children, the Cadbury Creme Egg.

Amaze yourself in the Midlands

The National Forest Maize Maze is just one of the family attractions in the National Forest (nationalforest. org), a bold environmental project greening parts of Leicestershire, Staffordshire and Derbyshire.

Prairie dog, Twycross Zoo

East Midlands

Derbyshire Designated Britain's first national park in 1951, the heather-clad moors and wooded valleys of the Peak District are ideal stomping territory for active families. Two of the most popular attractions include riding the cable cars at the Heights of Abraham (heightsofabraham.com) and the trams at Crich Tramway Village (tramway.co.uk) – both near Matlock. For a forest-themed free-for-all, kids can go nuts at Conkers (visitconkers.com) with its assault course, nature trails and playgrounds.

Leicestershire Famous for its primate collection, Twycross Zoo (twycrosszoo.com) has everything from chimps and bonobos to gibbons and gorillas, while the National Space Centre (spacecentre.co.uk) challenges visitors to undertake a simulated 3D mission in Human Spaceflight: Lunar Base 2025.

Nottinghamshire With its family nature trails, cycling and horse riding opportunities, the historic royal hunting patch of Sherwood Forest (sherwoodforest. org.uk) is a great place to set free your 'inner Robin Hood'. Designed for under-10s, Sundown Adventure

Let's go to Stonehenge

Stonehenge (english-heritage.org.uk) has been luring visitors for over 5000 years. To protect this ancient wonder, a roped-off walkway keeps visitors 15 m from the giant Sarsen stones (each weighing up to 45 tonnes), so you'll have to rely on some thought-provoking questions to keep kids interested. How were those mega blocks shifted? How were the lintels placed on top? And why was it built in the first place? For light relief, Longleat (longleat.co.uk) is renowned for its drive-through safari park and Jungle Kingdom.

Park (sundownadventureland.co.uk) has gentle rides and story-book-themed attractions.

West Midlands

Birmingham Hands up who likes chocolate? Cadbury World (cadburyworld.co.uk) takes you on a mouth-watering journey through the origins and production of the sweet sensation and even goes interactive with Purple Planet where you can chase a Cadbury Creme Egg, grow your own Cocoa beans and experience chocolate rain. Birmingham's science museum, ThinkTank (thinktank.ac), has over 200 hands-on displays, plus a planetarium and IMAX cinema.

Shropshire With no fewer than 10 museums and an iron bridge (albeit the world's first) as its star attraction, you might be put off taking kids to the Ironbridge Gorge Museums (ironbridge.org.uk). Don't be. There's nothing remotely rusty about this World Heritage Site commemorating the Industrial Revolution. At Blists Hill Victorian Town costumed actors evoke a bygone era when steam engines and horses powered industry, while at the Enginuity centre children can scheme away at their own technological innovations.

Cotswold Wildlife Park

Kids' top 10 Cotswolds

1 **Fill** a long weekend or more at the Cotswold Water Park (waterpark.org) with everything from sailing, canoeing, raft-building and aerial adventures to birdwatching, angling, horse riding and water skiing.

2 **Burn** off some energy in the 850-ha park and pleasure gardens of Blenheim Palace (blenheimpalace.com) which has a maze, butterfly house and adventure playground.

3 **Spot** wolves, rhinos, zebras and lions at the Cotswold Wildlife Park (cotswoldwildlifepark.co.uk) – and don't miss the meerkats, penguins and otters in the walled garden.

4 **Play** hide-and-seek at Hidcote Manor Gardens (nationaltrust.org.uk) where neatly clipped yew hedges partition the estate into countless outdoor rooms.

5 **Feed** the trout at Bibury (biburytroutfarm.co.uk).

6 **Explore** the weird and wonderful collection of artefacts, from musical instruments to Samurai armour, at Snowshill Manor (nationaltrust.org.uk).

7 **Cycle** between chocolate-box villages like the Slaughters, Winchcombe, Northleach, Bibury and Burford on a self-guided tour with Cotswold Country Cycles (cotswoldcountrycycles.com).

8 **Hike** part of the Cotswold Way (nationaltrail.co.uk/cotswold), a 160-km walking trail between Chipping Campden and Bath.

9 **Spend** all your pocket money at the toyshop in Bourton-on-the-Water, and then beg to be taken to Birdland (birdland.co.uk).

10 **Sample** scones with strawberry jam and clotted cream at Badgers Hall Tearoom (badgershall.com) in Chipping Campden.

Woods & water

In the beautiful Forest of Dean (visitforestofdean.co.uk) you can cycle and canoe, or take to the trees at Go Ape! (goape.co.uk), a high-wire adventure with a minimum age of 10. For more sedate forest rambles, try the Dean Forest Railway (deanforestrailway.co.uk), the Dean Heritage Centre (deanheritagecentre.com) or Puzzlewood (puzzlewood.net) – where Tolkien is said to have found inspiration for Middle Earth. At Slimbridge Wetland Centre (wwt.org.uk) in the Severn Vale, you can feed geese (above), take a 4WD safari through a nature reserve and spot kingfishers from a hide.

Canoeing on the Wye

Staffordshire Taking kids to The Wedgwood Visitor Centre (wedgwoodvisitorcentre.com) might seem like, well, taking a bull into a china shop, but not only will they be fascinated by the factory tour, they'll also get a shot at the potter's wheel. For a different kind of spin, Drayton Manor (draytonmanor.co.uk) and Alton Towers (altontowers.com) are two of Britain's most popular theme parks – see page 30 to see how their rides compare with the likes of Blackpool Pleasure Beach and Thorpe Park.

Warwickshire The Shakespeare Birthplace Trust (shakespeare.org.uk) manages five properties in Stratford-upon-Avon, all linked to the life of the great bard. Two of the most interesting for children are Shakespeare's Birthplace in Henley Street and Mary

Arden's where you can experience what life was like in a 16th-century farmhouse. For a history lesson with more oomph, Warwick Castle (warwick-castle.com) delivers with a passion. Kids can lay siege to haunted towers, torture chambers and medieval banqueting halls, but it's the legendary activities they'll remember most. Jousting, archery and falconry are held throughout summer, while winter sees a skating rink installed at the 11th-century fort.

Worcestershire Chuffing 26 km between Bridgnorth and Kidderminster, the Severn Valley Railway (svr. co.uk) is a must for all Thomas and Hornby fans, while the West Midland Safari Park (wmsp.co.uk) will appeal to the wild-at-heart with its drive-through safari (spot the white lions) and daredevil amusement park.

see page 30

Inside info ⓘ

▶▶ Rutland, the UK's smallest county, is home to the largest man-made lake in Western Europe where you can windsurf, canoe and sail.

▶▶ One of the region's best cycle tracks, the 21-km Tissington Trail follows the old Buxton-to-Ashbourne railway line in the heart of the Peak District.

▶▶ For further information, log on to visitheartofengland. com, enjoyenglands eastmidlands.com.

Falling for the Lakes – Buttermere

Plan a Lake District safari

Your top ticks have to be red squirrel and osprey – and, surprisingly, neither should be too elusive. Red squirrels are found in forests throughout Cumbria (it's one of their major strongholds), but your best chance of spotting one is in Whinlatter Forest Park (forestry. gov.uk). From Oct-Apr, the visitor centre has a CCTV link to a red squirrel feeder, but if you think that's cheating, try stalking the Squirrel Scurry Trail (maps are available at the visitor centre), keeping your eyes turned skyward for that tell-tale flash of ochre-red fur. During the summer months, ospreys gain TV celebrity status at Whinlatter, courtesy of live camera footage beamed from a nest at nearby Bassenthwaite Lake. Ospreys hadn't bred in England for over 150 years when they began using this site in 2001. RSPB volunteers at the Dodd Wood Viewpoint (rspb.org.uk/ datewithnature, Apr-Aug, daily 1000-1700) will help you train telescopes on the raptors as they catch fish on the lake and carry food to their chicks.

Driving towards Cumbria you can almost hear the swish of trekking poles against Goretex. Boasting England's five tallest peaks, the Lake District is a stomping ground for the high-and-mighty, but family holidays are far more down-to-earth. Pitch a tent with a lake view, skim stones, glimpse a red squirrel, sail a stick down a gurgling beck. No trekking poles required. And if you want to raise the adventure stakes a little, rent a canoe and paddle out to a deserted island with a picnic and a copy of *Swallows and Amazons* (toddlers might prefer Beatrix Potter and a chance to feed the Jemima Puddleducks on the shores of Windermere).

England's largest national park is remarkably accommodating, whether it's teens hell-bent on conquering Helvellyn or tots who dare to dabble their toes in Rydal Water. The real challenge for families is deciding where to go. Many tend to gravitate towards Lake Windermere, where Ambleside is awash with attractions and places to eat, sleep and shop. Likewise, Keswick is a popular centre in the Northern Lakes, with Derwent Water and Borrowdale right on its doorstep, while Penrith is just minutes from Pooley Bridge at the tip of Ullswater.

It's all too tempting, though, to let fingers wander over a map of the Lakes. Before you know it, you're lost in a tangle of lanes around the sleepy old market town of Hawkshead (gateway to Tarn Hows and Grizedale Forest), or drifting west towards Coniston where the Old Man looms above Coniston Water. Then there's the stunning drive from Skelwith Bridge, past Elterwater and into the Langdale Valley. Or the great Lake District 'thoroughfare' north from Ambleside to Rydal and Grasmere, hemmed in by Helvellyn and Thirlmere, with Skiddaw looming ahead. You'll also find it hard to resist the passes of Honister, Kirkstone, Wrynose and Hardknott – each one a window to 'hidden' Lakeland gems, like Buttermere and Brothers Water. Be warned though. It's only once you've ventured west beyond Hardknott (the road unravelling through exquisite Eskdale) that you realize just how close the Cumbrian coast is. Mountains, lakes and now beaches. Deciding where to go just got a whole lot harder.

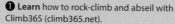

Kids' top 10 Lake District

❶ **Learn** how to rock-climb and abseil with Climb365 (climb365.net).
❷ **Sail** a yacht on Lake Windermere with Outrun Sailing (outrunsailing.co.uk).
❸ **Visit** Peter Rabbit and friends at the World of Beatrix Potter (hop-skip-jump.com).
❹ **Cruise** the lakes with Windermere Lake Cruises (windermere-lakecruises.co.uk).
❺ **Ride** a steam train on the Haverthwaite Railway (lakesiderailway.co.uk).
❻ **Wander** 'lonely as a cloud' around Grasmere before visiting William Wordsworth's house, Dove Cottage (wordsworth.org.uk).
❼ **Lose** yourself in the maze and see the owls at Muncaster Castle (muncaster.co.uk).
❽ **Find** the perfect skimming stone at Buttermere or Coniston Water.
❾ **Picnic** at Tarn Hows and then walk the buggy-friendly circuit around the lake
❿ **Conquer** Scafell Pike, the highest mountain in England at 978 m, or take on the challenge of a wilderness bushcraft course with Woodsmoke (woodsmoke.uk.com).
▶▶ Further information: lakedistrict.gov.uk

From left to right: Tarn Hows, Canoeing on Ullswater, Buttermere

Let's go to Blackpool

Dating from the 18th century, Britain's archetypal seaside resort is still a big crowd-puller – thanks in no small part to Blackpool Pleasure Beach (blackpool pleasurebeach.com). England's thrill-city-central has over 125 rides and attractions, ranging from the 140-km/h Pepsi Max Big One roller coaster (see page 30) to ice-skating, bingo and dodgems. As you'd expect there's also a water park (sandcastle-waterpark.co.uk), aquarium (sealifeeurope. com) and waxworks (madametussauds.com/ blackpool). For nostalgia mixed with fun, you can't miss the iconic, 158-m tall Blackpool Tower (theblackpooltower. co.uk) where views, ballroom dancing, circus shows and one of Europe's largest indoor adventure playgrounds will further conspire to keep you off the beach.

If you feel your warm-weather instincts tugging you southwards, dig your heels in and spare a thought for North England. The Great British family holiday was practically invented in the seaside resort of Blackpool, but the region's appeal goes way beyond donkey rides and pleasure parks. Let your kids' imaginations run riot through Roman ruins, Norman castles and cutting-edge science centres; free their spirits in wild places like the Lake District and Yorkshire Moors, and fill their days (even the rainy ones) with attractions ranging from Beatrix Potter to The Beatles.

Manchester

Footie fans will make a bee-line for Old Trafford where the Manchester United Museum and Stadium Tour (manutd.com) takes you into the hallowed heart of the world's most popular football team (controversial, but true). You can strut down the player's tunnel, admire the trophy cabinet and sit at the dressing-room peg of your favourite player. For fancy footwork on the high street, Manchester's shops will satisfy all fashion fans, while the city's mighty industrial heritage is celebrated at the Museum of Science and Industry (mosi.org.uk). For family-friendly culture, you can't beat the galleries and theatres of The Lowry (thelowry. com) at Salford Quays

Liverpool

Not to be outdone by its Mancunian rivals, Liverpool FC has the Anfield Experience (www.liverpoolfc.tv), but there's another attraction in Merseyside's great city that overshadows even football. Your kids may never have heard of The Beatles, but that's no reason why you shouldn't at least attempt to improve their music tastes. Think of it as part of their education. Of the many 'Fab Four' tours and attractions, your best bet with kids is The Beatles Story (beatlesstory.com) at Albert Dock. From rocking the world to exploring new ones, Spaceport (spaceport.org.uk) at Seacombe on the Wirral (ride the Mersey ferry to get there) takes you on a virtual journey through space. The nearby Blue Planet Aquarium (blueplanetaquarium.com) offers Bubblemaker diving courses for children aged eight to 15 – but you need to be at least 18 before they let you into the shark tank. If you continue south on the M53, you'll reach Chester Zoo (chesterzoo.org.uk). Family highlights north of Liverpool include the beaches, dunes and red squirrel reserve at Formby Point and Splash World (splashworldsouthport.com), a water park at Southport with slides and a lazy river ride.

Yorkshire

There's plenty to interest kids in York. Start with York Minster (yorkminster. org), England's largest medieval cathedral. Check out the Great East Window (a tennis-court-sized stained-glass marvel) before climbing the Central Tower for some gargoyle spotting. Back at street level, the National Railway Museum (nrm. org.uk) boasts the world's finest collection of trains, including the record-breaking *Mallard* and a replica of Stephenson's *Rocket*, while the Jorvik Viking Centre (jorvik-viking-centre.co.uk) features a ride which weaves through a diorama of houses, backyards and market stalls – complete with authentic 'Viking' aromas of manure, fish and roasting boar.

National Railway Museum

The North York Moors National Park (northyorkmoors.org.uk) offers a wonderful mixture of coast, forest and moorland. A single day could easily be divided between rock-pooling at Robin Hood's Bay and a picnic at Danby in the Esk Valley; you could hike in Dalby Forest, or ride the North Yorkshire Moors Railway (nymr.co.uk) between Pickering and Whitby.

Further south, Bempton Cliffs (rspb.org.uk) are smothered with gannets, guillemots and puffins between April and August. Other attractions nearby include The Deep (thedeep.co.uk), an impressive aquarium near Hull, and the superb children's science museum, Eureka! (eureka.org.uk) in Halifax.

The Northeast

In Newcastle, younger children will enjoy Seven Stories (sevenstories.org.uk), the centre for children's books, while the high-tech Centre for Life (life.org.uk) should appeal to most ages. The best day out from Newcastle is to explore Hadrian's Wall (hadrians-wall. org) – a 117-km long Roman fortification snaking between Wallsend and Bowness on the Solway Firth.

Further north, the spectacular Northumberland coast has long sandy beaches and a string of forts, including Bamburgh Castle (bamburghcastle.com) and Holy Island's Lindisfarne Castle (nationaltrust.org. uk). Slightly inland, Alnwick Castle (alnwickcastle.com) starred in the first two Harry Potter films, while the Farne Islands are teeming with seabirds and seals.

Inside info

▶▶ The York Pass (yorkshirepass.com) provides entry to 28 attractions.
▶▶ Hadrian's Wall Bus leaves Newcastle at 0940, arriving at Housesteads at 1106; you can take bicycles on the bus and pedal sections of Hadrian's Cycleway.
▶▶ For further info, log on to northeastengland. co.uk, visityork.org and newcastle gateshead.com.

Broad Haven South

Kids' top 10 Pembrokeshire

Beautiful beaches come naturally to this southwest tip of Wales. No other county in Britain flies more Blue Flags – or boasts a national park that is almost all coast. But it's the huge potential, from bucket-and-spade to island escapade, that makes Pembrokeshire's seaside such a 'shore thing' for kids. Pembrokeshire could almost have coined the term 'multi-activity'. If you thought a beach holiday was pretty full-on if you managed to squeeze in some surfing, a rock-pooling expedition and a sandcastle or two, try an action-packed day of kayaking and coasteering (clambering around cliffs, in and out of the sea like a lemming that can't make up its mind). Then there are Pembrokeshire's five fabulous offshore islands – each one a contender for your big holiday treat. Delve inland and most roads lead to the market town of Haverfordwest. But just because you've left the coast don't imagine you're in for a quiet time. Cycling, sailing, horse riding and dressing up as a Celtic warrior are just some of Pembrokeshire's non-beachy highlights at places like Preseli Hills, Teifi Marshes, Llys-y-Fran Country Park and Castell Henllys Iron Age Fort. **visitpembrokeshire.com**

❶ Beaches
Good family beaches include Amroth, Saundersfoot, Tenby, Dale, Broad Haven South and Whitesands. For surf, head to Whitesands, Marloes, Manorbier, Broad Haven, Caerfai and Newgale. Hire boards from Haven Sports (havensports.co.uk) and West Wales Wind Surf and Sailing (surfdale.co.uk).

❷ Boat trips
Operators include Aquaphobia (aquaphobia-ramseyisland.co.uk), Dale Sea Safari (sail-sailing.co.uk), Thousand Islands Expeditions (thousandislands.co.uk), Ramsey Island Cruises (ramseyislandcruises.co.uk), Shearwater Safaris (boatrides.co.uk) and Venture Jet (venturejet.co.uk).

❸ Seal spotting
Take a boat trip to Ramsey, Skomer, Skockholm or Caldey Island. The southwest tip of St Davids Peninsula, Cemaes Head near Cardigan and the Marloes Peninsula are also good spots. The best time to see grey seals is between September and November when they give birth to pups.

❹ Dolphin spotting
Cardigan Bay has a resident population of bottlenose dolphins, while summer witnesses the arrival of common dolphins (sometimes in pods a thousand strong). Join a boat trip with an operator adhering to the Marine Code (pembrokeshiremarinecode.org.uk).

❺ Bird islands
Reached by daily boats from Martin's Haven, Skomer is renowned for puffins, guillemots, razorbills and kittiwakes. Skokholm's petrels and puffins are best viewed from a boat trip from Dale, while Ramsey can be visited from St Davids. Further offshore, Grassholm is a nesting site for 65,000 gannets during summer.

❻ Cycle trails
Cardigan's Cycle Break Centre (cyclebreakswales.com) has set up several easy cycling routes alongside the River Teifi. Other options include St Govans Head (one of the few sections of the Coast Path that's open to cyclists), the Brunel trail from Neyland to Johnston and the 11-km circuit around Llys y Fran reservoir.

❼ Walks
Buggy-friendly paths include the 4-km jaunt from Wisemans Bridge to Saundersfoot Harbour and the 800-m circuit of Pembroke Castle's moat. For a short walk with a café, try the 10-km trail from Nolton Haven to Broad Haven. For something more ambitious, stride out on the 17-km circuit of the Dale Peninsula.

❽ Days out
Feel the adrenaline rush on the water coaster and 30 other rides at Oakwood Theme Park (oakwoodthemepark.co.uk), cheer on the knights as they battle it out at medieval Pembroke Castle (pembroke-castle.co.uk) and feed the animals at Folly Farm (folly-farm.co.uk).

❾ Activities
A mixture of climbing, swimming, scrambling along rocky shores and flinging yourself off cliff faces, coasteering is popular in Pembrokeshire. Other more orthodox pursuits include scuba diving, sea kayaking, and horse riding. Contact the Pembrokeshire Activity Centre (pembrokeshire-activity-centre.co.uk).

❿ Time travel
Reconstructed on the site of an Iron Age hill fort, Castell Henllys (castellhenllys.com) is far more than simply a cluster of thatched roundhouses – it's a time capsule where children are whisked back 2000 years to an age of chietains, Celtic myths and living off the land. Celtic Fun sessions are aimed at kids aged 6-12.

Wales is a little beauty – squat, rugged, full of character and brilliant round the edges, just like a Welsh rugby scrum half. 'An area the size of Wales' is often banded around when comparing anything from U.S. national parks to rainforest deforestation, but take a closer look at this 20,779-sq-km country and you will find plenty to shout about in its own right. Not only is Wales king of Britain's castles, but it also has some of the finest and cleanest beaches, great surf, wildlife-rich islands and rugged mountains – all in an area roughly the size of Massachusetts.

Cardiff

Masses of parkland and a beach just a stone's throw away make Cardiff a great city-break destination for families. Kids will be impressed by the Roof Garden and elaborate Banqueting Hall in quirky Cardiff Castle (cardiffcastle.com), but it's Cardiff Bay (cardiffbay. co.uk) where they'll have most fun. Just a couple of kilometres from the city centre, there's plenty to see and do here, from delving into the cafés and shops at Mermaid Quay to exploring the science centre, Techniquest (techniquest.org) and Doctor Who Up Close (doctorwhoexhibitions.com).

Swansea

The National Waterfront Museum (waterfrontmuseum. co.uk) uses the latest interactive technology to tell the story of industry and innovation in Wales over the last 300 years. Plantasia (swansea.gov.uk) brings a touch of the tropics to the city with chameleons, pythons, parrots and a colony of cotton-top tamarin monkeys housed in a giant, climate-controlled indoor garden.

Gower Peninsula

You're never far from a fabulous beach on the Gower. Blue-Flag Caswell Bay is one of the most family-friendly. You can park right behind it and there's a café, beach shop, showers and toilets, as well as a lifeguard patrol during summer. You can't visit the Gower and not go surfing. And the clifftop paths promise some exhilarating coastal walks. But how about some quad biking, windsurfing, kitesurfing, gorge walking, mountain biking, horse riding, abseiling, indoor climbing, canoeing or archery? All are available from Great Gower Outdoors (greatgoweroutdoors. co.uk). The minimum age for most activities is eight. West of Port Eynon Point, Gower gets all rugged and stand-offish, with cliffs running virtually all the way to the end of the peninsula. Gower Coast Adventures (gowercoastadventures.co.uk) operates jet-boat trips from Port Eynon along this dramatic section of coast – a great opportunity to spot seals and other wildlife around the spectacular tidal island of Worms Head.

Brecon Beacons

Covering an area of 1345 sq km of rugged moorland, limestone crags and glacial lakes, Brecon Beacons National Park (breconbeacons.org) runs a programme of children's activities including bug hunts and wilderness survival days.

Snowdonia

It's a five-hour slog up and down Snowdon, the 1085-m highpoint of Snowdonia National Park (eryri-npa. gov.uk), but families with younger children can still get spectacular views by taking the rack-and-pinion Snowdon Mountain Railway (snowdonrailway.co.uk) from Llanberis. Located in the south of the park, the Mawddach Trail is an excellent choice for families. Starting at Dolgellau, the 14-km traffic-free route follows the beautiful Mawddach Estuary to Barmouth and can either be walked or cycled. For a shorter walk try the Penmaenpool to Bont y Wern Du route. The pretty riverside town of Betws-y-Coed is another popular walking base, while the narrow-gauge Ffestiniog Railway (festrail.co.uk) takes you on a 22-km steam train journey from the slate-quarrying town of Blaenau Ffestiniog to the harbour at Porthmadog. Other family-friendly highlights in Snowdonia include Coed y Brenin Forest (forestry.gov.uk/coedybrenin) with its ecofriendly visitor centre and imaginative children's play area. Snowdonia's coast is also great for kids – particularly Llyn Peninsula with its sandy beaches and wildlife-rich Cardigan Bay.

🔍 Top 3 castles

You're never far from a great castle in Wales – and they're all just as castles should be, with rounded towers, arrow slits, drawbridges and moats. One of the most formidable is Beaumaris Castle on the island of Anglesey, although kids will be just as happy to storm the ramparts of Caernarfon (pictured), Conwy and Harlech in North Wales, and Caerphilly, Kidwelly and Pembroke in South and mid-Wales.

Inside info

▶▶ The Freedom of Wales Flexi Pass (arrivatrainswales.co.uk) provides unlimited access to mainline train services and most buses.
▶▶ There are 14 steam and narrow-gauge railways in Wales (greatlittle trainsofwales.co.uk).
▶▶ For further information log on to visitwales.co.uk.

Chances are you won't spot the Loch Ness Monster, but that won't stop your children from staring long and hard at every patch of water they come across in Scotland – and what better way for them to fall under the spell of this beautiful and diverse country. From Edinburgh's historic Royal Mile to the wild and remote Shetlands, kids will find castles to explore, Munros to conquer and deserted beaches to lay claim to. And if Nessie proves elusive, they'll be more than satisfied with sightings of whales, eagles and otters during boat trips in the Hebrides.

Edinburgh

Plenty of cities have castles, but not many have a castle perched on an extinct volcano – a double whammy for kid-friendly Edinburgh. A fun way to get an overview of this bonny World-Heritage-listed city is to take a ride through the medieval Old Town and Georgian New Town with Edinburgh Bus Tours (edinburghtour.com). Next, visit Edinburgh Castle (historic-scotland.gov.uk) to see Scotland's Crown Jewels and the Stone of Destiny. Listen out for the One O'Clock Gun and visit the dungeons to see the Prisoners of War exhibition.

Just below the castle, West Princes Street Gardens is ideal for letting youngsters burn off energy, while teenagers will prefer to exercise their wallets along adjacent Princes Street. Alternatively, head east from Castle Hill along the Royal Mile – once the main thoroughfare of medieval Edinburgh, linking the castle to the Palace of Holyroodhouse (royal.gov. uk). Flanked by impressive buildings like St Giles Cathedral and Parliament House, it's the toy-crammed Museum of Childhood (edinburghmuseums.org.uk) that will appeal most to kids. On nearby Holyrood Road, Our Dynamic Earth (dynamicearth.co.uk) has an earthquake simulator, a time machine that will whisk you back 15 billion years and a FutureDome where you decide the fate of the planet. Rearing behind this ultra-modern science centre, you can explore the ancient lava flows of Arthur's Seat, a volcano that blew its top between 350 and 400 million years ago. Rainy-day favourites for younger children include the Brass Rubbing Centre and The Ceramic Experience (theceramicexperience.com), while the excellent Edinburgh Zoo (edinburghzoo.org.uk) is a long-established favourite, whatever the weather.

Edinburgh's most notorious ghost tour, City of the Dead, is hosted nightly by Blackheart Entertainment (blackhart.uk.com) – but be warned: a possible encounter with the MacKenzie Poltergeist is not for the faint-hearted. The Secret City Tour, meanwhile, is suitable for all ages and features stories as diverse as Harry Potter, the invention of Christmas and the origin of Frankenstein's monster.

There are several fine beaches close to Edinburgh, including the popular surf spot of Gullane Bents, the wildlife-rich Longniddry Bents and Cramond where you can walk and cycle on beachside paths.

To escape the city, head east towards North Berwick, taking in the 12th-century Dirleton Castle, the long sandy beach of Yellowcraig and the Scottish Seabird Centre (seabird.org) where you can watch footage beamed live from Bass Rock, 5 km offshore and smothered in over 100,000 gannets between January and October.

Glasgow

Unlike Edinburgh, there are no iconic landmarks in Glasgow, but what this stylish, modern-thinking city lacks in the way of castles and volcanoes it more than compensates for with a buzzing cultural scene and several superb museums. By far the best for kids, the Kelvingrove Art Gallery and Museum (glasgowlife.org.uk/museums) has everything from Egyptian mummies to a Second World War Spitfire. Children under five have their own hands-on Mini Museum, while older kids can learn about wildlife, history and art at three discovery centres. Don't miss the webcam link to the Loch Ness Monster, the 4-m Ceratosaur skeleton and the impressive collection of paintings, which includes Salvador Dali's *Christ*.

Highlights at the nearby Museum of Transport include locomotives from the

Kelvingrove Art Gallery and Museum, Glasgow

Magnificent flying machines and wonders of nature adorn the museum's main hall.

Fun at Fort William

★ Fort William is the departure point for Crannog Cruises (crannog.net) – 90-minute voyages in search of seals on Loch Linnhe – and The Jacobite Steam Train (westcoastrailways.co.uk) which chuffs 68 km to the coast, crossing the 21-arch Glenfinnan viaduct of Harry Potter fame before reaching the fishing village of Mallaig where ferries run to Rum, Eigg and Muck. At Kinlochleven, Ice Factor (ice-factor.co.uk) offers family sessions on its ice-climbing wall, as well as rock-climbing, canyoning and white water rafting.

Kids' top 10 Highlands & Islands

❶ **Find** out what the real story in Balamory is by taking a ferry from Oban to Mull where the multicoloured houses along Tobermory's waterfront provided the setting for the children's TV programme.

❷ **Spot** the Loch Ness Monster – and if that fails, have a go at spying a minke whale on a boat trip from Mull with Sea Life Surveys (sealifesurveys.com) and tick off otters and eagles on a safari with Island Encounter (mullwildlife.co.uk).

❸ **Peer** into the spectacular kelp forests around Skye from the Seaprobe Atlantis (seaprobeatlantis.com), Scotland's only semi-submersible.

❹ **Play** king or queen of the castle on the Aberdeenshire Castle Trail (aberdeen-grampian.com) which links 13 forts – some rugged ruins, others posh palaces.

❺ **Walk** with a ranger through the native pinewoods of Cairngorms National Park (cairngorms.co.uk).

❻ **Discover** what it's like to climb on ice at the Glen Coe Visitor Centre (nts.org.uk), then stride outside to explore some of Scotland's most dramatic scenery – and perhaps even 'bag a Munro' (a mountain over 914 m in height).

❼ **Go** wild on the treetop trail and adventure playground of Landmark Forest Heritage Park (landmarkpark.co.uk) near Aviemore before watching ospreys at Loch Garten's RSPB Osprey Centre (rspb.org.uk).

❽ **Practise** skiing or snowboarding in the winter wonderland of the Nevis Range (nevisrange.co.uk).

❾ **Discover** the golden sands and turquoise seas of Harris and the Uists in the Outer Hebrides. Other fine beaches include Sandwood Bay and Oldshoremore on the northwest coast of mainland Scotland and the irresistible tombolo of sand linking Shetland to St Ninian's Isle.

❿ **Glimpse** marine life through an underwater camera on a Roving Eye Boat Tour (orkneyrovspecialist.co.uk), experience life in the 19th century at Corrigal Farm Museum (museumsgalleriesscotland.org.uk) and visit the Tomb of the Eagles (tomboftheeagles.co.uk) – just three of the highlights on Orkney.

The Cairngorms

What child could resist a rendezvous with a real-life Rudolf? Roaming with reindeers is just one of the family perks in Britain's largest national park, where mountain, loch, river and forest conspire to form the ultimate adventure playground. There's simply no better place for kids to experience the Highlands.

On the western fringes of the Cairngorms National Park, the A9 Pitlochry–Inverness road passes Dalwhinnie (home to Scotland's highest distillery) before dipping alongside the River Spey near Newtonmore and Kingussie where you'll find the fascinating Highland Folk Museum. Further north, near Kincraig, Loch Insh has a superb watersports centre, but it's nearby Aviemore that's the undisputed adventure capital of the Cairngorms. Although the town itself makes an ideal base for exploring the mountains, the road west to Rothiemurchus Estate, Loch Morlich and Glenmore Forest combines the very best of family-friendly accommodation and activities in the national park – from camping in the Caledonian Forest and cycling around tranquil lochs to visiting the free-roaming reindeer herd and hiking to the summit of mighty Cairn Gorm itself. Aviemore is also the western terminus of the Strathspey Steam Railway, which runs to Boat of Garten with its famous osprey centre.

Left to right: Cairngorm reindeer and mountain railway, Loch Morlich

Caledonian and Highland Railways. Nip down to the north bank of the River Clyde and you'll find the 19th-century, three-masted *SS Glenlee*, otherwise known as The Tall Ship at Glasgow Harbour (thetallship.com). On the opposite bank, Pacific Quay is the embarkation point for cruises aboard the Paddle Steamer *Waverley* (pswaverley.org.uk), as well as the location of the excellent Glasgow Science Centre (gsc.org.uk) – a technological treasure house where kids can tinker with hundreds of interactive exhibits and go goggle-eyed in the planetarium and IMAX cinema. East of the city centre, but still on the Clyde, People's Palace and Winter Gardens reveals Glasgow's social history.

Less than an hour's drive southeast of Glasgow, New Lanark World Heritage Site (newlanark.org) is a restored 18th century village where kids can discover what life was like in a Victorian cotton mill.

❷ Let's go to Loch Lomond

Just 30 km north of Glasgow, Loch Lomond & The Trossachs National Park (lochlomond-trossachs.org) is one of the most accessible chunks of the Scottish Highlands – you could easily sample it on a day-out from the city. Far better, though, to immerse yourself in this beautiful swathe of forest, loch and mountain. Start at Balloch where rangers at Loch Lomond Shores (lochlomondshores.com) can advise on activities and walks. Aberfoyle is on the fringes of Queen Elizabeth Forest Park (forestry.gov.uk/qefp) which has a play area, Go Ape high-wire adventure course and osprey nest-cam. Some of the Trossachs' best scenery can be experienced from the *SS Sir Walter Scott* (lochkatrine.com), a classic steamship that plies the waters of Loch Katrine. Make a day of it by hiring bikes at the pier, taking them on board for the morning cruise to Stronachlachar and then cycling back along the shores of the loch.

Inside info ⓘ

▸▸ The Edinburgh Pass (edinburgh.org/pass) provides free entry to over 30 attractions.
▸▸ The Daytripper Ticket (spt.co.uk) offers good value to families travelling by rail, subway, buses and some ferries throughout Glasgow and Strathclyde.
▸▸ Edinburgh's arts festival (edinburghfestivals.co.uk) takes place in August, but there's also a Children's Theatre Festival in May.
▸▸ For further information, log on to edinburgh.org and seeglasgow.com.

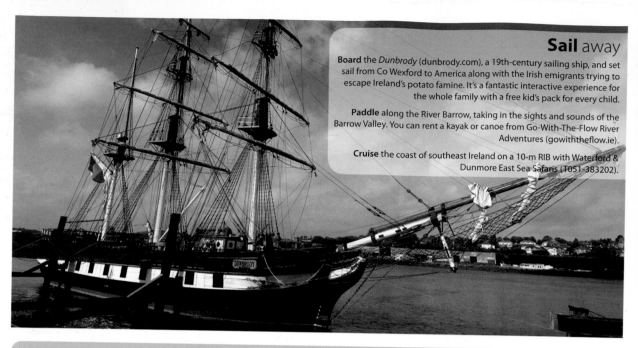

Sail away

Board the *Dunbrody* (dunbrody.com), a 19th-century sailing ship, and set sail from Co Wexford to America along with the Irish emigrants trying to escape Ireland's potato famine. It's a fantastic interactive experience for the whole family with a free kid's pack for every child.

Paddle along the River Barrow, taking in the sights and sounds of the Barrow Valley. You can rent a kayak or canoe from Go-With-The-Flow River Adventures (gowiththeflow.ie).

Cruise the coast of southeast Ireland on a 10-m RIB with Waterford & Dunmore East Sea Safaris (T051-383202).

Kids' top 10 Northern Ireland

1 Roar with the lions and parade with the penguins at Belfast Zoo (belfastzoo.co.uk).

2 Walk in the footsteps of giants at Northern Ireland's very own Eighth Wonder of the World, the Giant's Causeway (northantrim.com).

3 Step back in time with Irish settlers as they set sail for America at the Ulster American Folk Park in Omagh or sample life from a bygone era at the Ulster Folk & Transport Museum, Cultra (nmni.com).

4 Join an underground boat trip through the eerie Marble Arch Caves (marblearchcaves.net) and marvel at the stalactites and stalagmites.

5 See a real Egyptian mummy from the seventh century BC, Takabuti, in her full glory at the Ulster Museum (nmni.com/um).

6 Crack your whip and have a go at being Indiana Jones at the jaw-dropping Carrick-a-Rede rope bridge (nationaltrust.org.uk).

7 Discover what's on offer at Belfast's exciting interactive science and discovery centre, W5- WhoWhatWhereWhenWhy (w5online.co.uk).

8 Play Victorians and dress up at Castle Ward House (nationaltrust.org.uk) before mucking in down at the farm.

9 Picnic in one of the UK's top 20 picnic spots at Tollymore Forest Park at the foot of the Mourne Mountains (discovernorthernireland.com).

10 Go on a wild goose chase at Castle Espie (wwt.org.uk) where almost the entire population of light-bellied Brent geese reside during the winter.

In the last decade Northern Ireland has established itself as a must-see destination after years of political unrest. Now back on an even keel, you'll find facilities and family accommodation for families that complement the often breathtaking natural wonders already on offer. Leave the hustle and bustle of Belfast behind and head north to explore the Antrim Coast on one of Europe's most scenic drives, checking out ancient ruins en route. Alternatively, head south to sample the seaside charms of Newcastle where the Mountains of Mourne sweep down to the sea. Travelling over to the west, the Fermanagh Lakelands provide a backdrop to a host of activities from caving to cruising, while further north the rejuvenated city of Derry offers some of the country's best shopping.

Let's go to the Giant's Causeway

Over 40,000 basalt columns extending 5 km along the Antrim coast, the Giant's Causeway was created by rapidly cooling lava from volcanic eruptions 60 million years ago – but kids will prefer the legend of the two giants (one in Ireland, the other in Scotland) who built a rocky causeway across the sea so they could meet and settle their squabbles.

Cruising past Clonmacnoise

Slowly – that's the best way to experience Ireland. Take time to roam its beautiful countryside and wild, remote coasts. It's a place to share simple and spontaneous pleasures with your children – pulling off the road to explore a strange ruin or whiling away a day on a beach that was too irresistible to pass by. And whenever you feel like upping the tempo slightly, take the kids sea kayaking or horse riding, or introduce them to a spot of local Irish music and dancing.

Dublin

A fun way to become acquainted with the Irish capital, Viking Splash Tours (vikingsplash.ie) uses Second World War amphibious vehicles to cruise the city's streets and docks. Horned helmets are standard issue to all passengers, and you are encouraged by the driver (dressed, of course, as a Norseman) to utter lusty Viking war cries at every opportunity. Continuing the Viking theme (after all, Dublin was one of their strongholds), Dublinia (dublinia.ie) uses reconstructions and interactive displays to bring the city's early history to life. The National Museum of Ireland (museum.ie) not only delves into the past but also boasts a treasure trove of archaeological finds, including a fine collection of prehistoric gold artefacts. However, even these pale beside the ninth century Book of Kells, a meticulously crafted illuminated manuscript of the four Gospels, on display in Trinity College Library (tcd.ie/library). Other family highlights in the city include Dublin Zoo (dublinzoo.ie) and Lambert Puppet Theatre (lambertpuppettheatre.ie).

River Shannon

The Shannon flows 344 km through the heart of Ireland, nuzzling into a gentle landscape of floodplains and rolling hills. Travelling all or part of this waterway by river cruiser is not only great fun with children of school age, but is also one of the best ways to experience rural Ireland. Carrick Craft (cruise-ireland.com) offers an extensive fleet of two- to eight-berth, fully fitted cruisers. Rates include full tuition, a detailed Captain's Handbook and charts, plus free mooring at quays and marinas. Banagher makes a good starting base for a week-long cruise. About five hours north, you reach the sixth-century monastic ruins of Clonmacnoise (heritageireland.ie), home of the famous Cross of the Scriptures, a 4-m-tall stone cross etched with Biblical scenes. Backtracking past Banagher, navigational skills are put to the test as you negotiate Meelick Lock. Then it's plain sailing on Lough Derg, stopping at marinas and villages like Castle Harbour and Terryglass. Killaloe, a town with a 13-arch bridge, marks the southern limit of Shannon pleasure cruising.

Explore the wild west

Coach tours cajole the Ring of Kerry into a single day, but you'll see more – and stand a chance of escaping the summer crowds – if you spend at least three days probing this 179-km circuit of the Iveragh Peninsula in western Ireland. Killarney is the most popular, and somewhat touristy, gateway to the region, so consider basing yourself in Kenmare and travelling clockwise around the Ring – the opposite direction to that which most tourist buses take. On day one, get off the road altogether by joining a two-hour seal-watching cruise with Kenmare's Seafari, followed by sea kayaking, windsurfing, pony trekking or any of the other activities offered by the Star Sailing and Adventure Centre (staroutdoors.ie) – also based in Kenmare. Next day, head west on the N70, passing the colourful village of Sneem to reach Staigue Fort, an austere 2000-year-old ring fort measuring over 27 m across and with walls up to 4 m thick. You should reach Derrynane by lunchtime – the perfect excuse for a picnic and some surfing on one of Ireland's finest beaches. Spend the night at nearby Waterville, a traditional seaside resort with a variety of B&Bs. Set off early the following day to reach The Skellig Experience (skelligexperience.com) on Valentia Island before the tour groups arrive. This excellent visitor centre has displays based on the Early Christian monastery, lighthouse, seabirds and marine life of the Skellig Rocks – two offshore islands that you can visit with Casey's Boat Trips (skelligislands.com) and a variety of other operators from Portmagee. Back on the N70 later that afternoon, you should have time to visit Kells Beach overlooking Dingle Bay before checking into a guesthouse in Killorglin. The next morning, backtrack slightly to visit the Kerry Bog Village (kerrybogvillage.ie), a cluster of thatched cottages revealing what life was like in the region during the early 1800s, before continuing north to the Dingle Peninsula (dingle-peninsula.ie). You could easily spend a week on this equally beautiful finger of land, sampling activities ranging from sailing and pony trekking to watching sharks at Dingle Oceanworld (dingle-oceanworld.ie) and swimming in Dingle Bay with Fungi, a wild bottlenose dolphin that first began interacting with humans in 1984.

Inside info

▶▶ The Dublin Pass (dublinpass.ie) provides entry to over 30 attractions, including Dublin Castle and Dublin Zoo
▶▶ Irish Cycling Safaris (cyclingsafari.com) offers guided tours of the South Dublin Coastline, while Sea Safari (seasafari.ie) operates boat trips to Lambay Island and Killiney Bay (minimum age eight).
▶▶ For further information, log on to visitdublin.com.

Holiday operators

In the UK
Butlins butlinsonline.com

Camping & Caravanning Club
campingandcaravanningclub.co.uk

Center Parcs centerparcs.co.uk

Classic Cottages classic.co.uk

Coast & Country Cottages
welsh-cottages.co.uk

Coastal Cottages of Pembrokeshire
coastalcottages.co.uk

Dales Holiday Cottages
dales-holiday-cottages.com

Feather Down Farms featherdown.co.uk

Forest Holidays forestholidays.co.uk

Haven haven.com

Hoseasons hoseasons.co.uk

John Fowler Holiday Parks
johnfowlerholidays.com

Lakeland Cottage Holidays
lakelandcottages.co.uk

Luxury Family Hotels
luxuryfamilyhotels.co.uk

Norfolk Cottages norfolkcottages.co.uk

Northumbria Byways
northumbria-byways.com

PGL pgl.co.uk

Parkdean Holidays
parkdeanholidays.co.uk

Park Resorts park-resorts.com

Pontins pontins.com

Premier Holidays premierholidays.co.uk

River Deep Mountain High
riverdeepmountainhigh.co.uk

Rural Retreats ruralretreats.co.uk

Scottish Farmhouse Holidays
scotfarmhols.co.uk

The Venture Centre
adventure-centre.co.uk

Wales Holidays
wales-holidays.co.uk

Youth Hostel Association yha.org.uk

In the USA
The Backroads
backroads.com

Classic Journeys
classicjourneys.com

Luxury Vacations UK
luxuryvacationsuk.com

The Real Britain Company
realbritaincompany.com

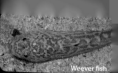

Weever fish

This hurts

Britain and Ireland's coastlines are generally very safe. Most serious accidents happen when people ignore warnings from beach lifeguards (see right), fail to check tide times or stray too near cliff edges. You should also be wary of weever fish, buried in sand at the low-water mark on some beaches with just five poisonous spines protruding from their backs. The sting can be excruciating. Submersion in very hot water is the best treatment. Better still, wear wetsuit boots when in the sea at low tide.

Go green
Three ways to skip the flight

❶ Get on your bike. In Britain and Northern Ireland, over 16,000 km of the National Cycle Network (sustrans.co.uk) are now open. A third is traffic-free, following disused railway lines and forest tracks, while the rest of the network uses quiet minor roads and traffic-calmed streets.

❷ Island hop along Scotland's West Coast and through the Hebrides with an Island Hopscotch ticket from Caledonian MacBrayne (calmac.co.uk). Bound for Ireland? Catch a ferry from mainland Britain, the Isle of Man or France, arriving into one of Ireland's ports on the north or south coasts.

❸ Take the ferry to the Isles of Scilly (ios-travel.co.uk); to the Isle of Man with Steam-Packet Ferries (steam-packet.com); to the Shetland and Orkney Islands with Northlink Ferries (northlinkferries.co.uk) and to the Channel Islands with Condor Ferries (condorferries.co.uk).

Fast facts

Country	Time	Language	Currency	Dialling code	Tourist information
England	GMT	English	GB pound (£)	+44	enjoyengland.com visitbritain.com
Scotland	GMT	English/Scottish	GB pound (£)	+44	visitscotland.com
Wales	GMT	English/Welsh	GB pound (£)	+44	visitwales.com
Northern Ireland	GMT	English	GB pound (£)	+44	discoverireland.com
Ireland	GMT	English/Gaelic	Euro (€)	+353	discoverireland.com

Grown-ups' stuff
Britain & Ireland

When to go
Britain has a mild climate with summer temperatures ranging from 14-30°C. The high season runs from April until October when most attractions are open. School holidays (most of July and August) are very busy, especially at the most popular tourist destinations such as The Lakes, Devon and Cornwall, the Scottish Highlands, Cotswolds and the Pembrokeshire coast.

Getting there
One of the busiest airports in the world, London Heathrow (heathrowairport.com) is served by most major international airports. London has three other main airports (Gatwick, Stansted and Luton), while regional airports include Edinburgh, Glasgow, Cardiff, Manchester, Belfast and Dublin. Britain's national carrier is British Airways (britishairways.com), while low-cost airlines include easyJet (easyjet.com) and Flybe (flybe.com). Aerlingus (aerlingus.com) and Ryanair (ryanair.com) serve numerous routes from Ireland. Ferries operate to several ports such as Dover, Newhaven, Portsmouth, Harwich, Hull, Liverpool, Fishguard, Holyhead, Dublin and Rosslare. Prices vary enormously according to season: check ferrycrossings-uk.co.uk or contact operators such as Brittany Ferries (brittanyferries.com). The only option that doesn't involve travel to Britain by air or sea is to use the Channel Tunnel (eurotunnel.com) from mainland Europe.

Getting around
Their compact size and excellent infrastructure make Britain and Ireland easy to get around. Self-drive is a flexible option; roads and motorways are well maintained, but bear in mind that major tourist routes can become heavily congested in peak periods and fuel is expensive. All the major car rental companies (Avis, Budget, Hertz etc) can be found at airports. For coach travel try National Express (nationalexpress.com) and Scottish Citylink (citylink.co.uk). For rail travel, Britrail (britrail.com) provides an online booking service for overseas visitors. You can also log on to nationalrail.co.uk for timetables, fares and bookings.

Accommodation
There is no shortage of places to stay in Britain and Ireland: everything from hiring your own private castle to pitching a tent is on offer. Hotels can often be expensive, with family rooms costing upwards of £150/night. Popular family choices include self-catering cottages, farm stays (farmstayuk.co.uk) and family-friendly hotels and guesthouses. Holiday villages have been popular in Britain for decades, ranging from traditional favourites like Butlins to climate-controlled Center Parcs. Another great British institution, B&Bs can be found everywhere, while the Youth Hostel Association (yha.org.uk) and Scottish Youth Hostel Association (syha.org.uk) provide excellent value accommodation at hundreds of locations throughout Britain. Bridge Street Worldwide (bridgestreet.co.uk) offers apartments in all major UK cities.

Food & drink
If you're travelling with babies and/or toddlers you may find eating out a frustrating experience, though the days of families being banished to some grubby room at the back, well out of the way of other diners, are, thankfully, a thing of the past. Smoking is banned in all restaurants and pubs. Foreign visitors may find eating times in pubs and hotels limiting (usually 1230-1400 for lunch and from around 1800 for dinner). In hotels and guesthouses the cooked breakfast (egg, bacon, sausages, tomatoes, mushrooms and beans) reigns supreme. At lunchtime, cafés serve sandwiches and jacket potatoes with various fillings, as well as pasties, paninis and salads. Gastropubs offer more ambitious lunchtime and supper menus, while traditional tearooms are the domain of the cream tea: freshly baked scones with strawberry jam and clotted cream with a pot of tea. For a cheap supper, you can't beat fish and chips.

Health & safety
No vaccinations are required for entry. Citizens of EU countries are entitled to free medical treatment at National Health Service (NHS) hospitals on production of a European Health Insurance Card (EHIC). For details see nhs.uk. Australia, New Zealand and several other non-European countries have reciprocal health-care arrangements with Britain. Citizens of other countries will have to pay for medical services, except accident and emergency care given at Accident and Emergency (A&E) Units at most (but not all) NHS hospitals. Health insurance is therefore strongly advised for citizens of non-EU countries. The RNLI (rnli.org.uk) produces a guide to beach safety summed up by the FLAGS code: find the red and yellow flags, and swim between them; look at the safety signs; ask a lifeguard for advice about where it's safe to swim; get a friend to swim with you, and stick your hand in the air and shout for help if in difficulty.

Forest Holidays

Where? Cornwall, Forest of Dean, Sherwood Forest, Yorkshire, Scotland.

Why? Forest Holidays infuses Britain's wild woods with home comforts. You'll hear tawny owls hooting – but from the comfort of your private verandah, a wood stove glowing in the lounge behind you. And your best sightings of woodpeckers will probably be in the treetops directly above your open-air hot tub. Double-storey windows flood open-plan living areas with tree-dappled sunlight. Most cabins have barbecues, flatscreen TVs and DVD players, while a few have an en-suite treehouse attached by an adventurer's bridge. You'll even find a Wii games console in Golden Oak cabins, but don't fret – children get ample opportunity to live in the real world thanks to ranger-led activities that include night-vision wildlife watching and forest survival skills. You can also buy local food and arrange activities such as mountain biking and pony trekking.

Contact Forest Holidays, T0845-130 8223, forestholidays.co.uk

Feather Down Farms

Where? England, Wales and Northern Ireland.

Why? Safari chic with wellies on, Feather Down Farm tents lead the herd when it comes to luxury camping. Lift the flap on these canvas creations and you step into a snug den complete with wood stove, oil lanterns, three bedrooms (including a secret cubbyhole for kids) and everything you need for a relaxing holiday at one of 25-plus working farms across Britain. Each farm has a clay oven for baking potatoes or pizzas, and an honesty shop stocked with local produce. A few even have field spas or the option of renting a private chicken coop. A typical day starts with children hurrying outside to collect chicken eggs while you grind fresh coffee beans and clunk the kettle on top of the stove. Breakfast is always late – it will take the kids at least an hour to check on their favourite ponies and lambs. Later in the day, the farmer may need a hand milking the cows. You might plan a picnic or cycle ride, play hide and seek or build a den.

Contact Feather Down Farms, T01420-80804, featherdown.co.uk

Luxury Family Hotels

Where? Woolley Grange, Wiltshire; Ickworth Manor, Suffolk; Fowey Hall, Cornwall; Moonfleet Manor, Dorset; The Elms, Worcestershire.

Why? Going posh with kids only works when you find a hotel devoid of pretentiousness, where staff are able to engage with life forms lower than navel height and where the term 'child friendly' doesn't in fact mean 'child friendly but we'd really rather not, thank you awfully.' Does such a place exist? Yes. In fact, there are several of them called Luxury Family Hotels. Each one is a stylish, character property set in a stunning location and offering spa treatments, gorgeous suites and interconnecting rooms, plus superb cuisine. Facilities include pools, trampolines, table football and playstations, but it's the human touches that add real value – babysitting or baby listening, OFSTED-registered dens with qualified nannies organizing activities, and staff that go out of their way to make sure your children are happy.

Contact Luxury Family Hotels, T01761-240124, luxuryfamilyhotels.com

Classic Cottages

Where? Cornwall, Devon, Somerset and Dorset.

Why? Classic Cottages have a rare knack of finding those 'X-Factor' properties with all the star qualities that discerning families look for – great location, beautifully furnished, child-friendly inside and out, plus that extra little touch – a sunny terrace or a path to the beach perhaps – that ensures everyone gives it an emphatic 'yes'. In short, they are the kind of cottages you hate to leave. Classic Cottages have specialized in the West Country holiday cottage business for over 30 years, so they've had time to build an impressive portfolio of properties (over 570 in Cornwall alone). Take your pick from stone cottages in Mousehole and Coverack, waterside apartments in Falmouth and Newquay, houses overlooking St Ives Bay and the Fowey Estuary, character barns tucked away in the Devon countryside and farms with sweeping views of Dartmoor.

Contact Classic Cottages, T01326-555555, classic.co.uk

Center Parcs

Where? Wiltshire, Suffolk, Cumbria and Nottinghamshire.

Why? The transition from the real world to a Center Parcs one requires two things: bicycle and swim gear. Everyone gets around by bike on traffic-free woodland lanes, while the indoor Subtropical Swimming Paradise will become a daily fixture in your itinerary. Activities at Center Parcs are based largely on the three W's – woodland, water and wildlife. You can choose from over a hundred things to do for all ages, from tree trekking and falconry to canoeing and sailing. There's more than a nod towards conservation, too, with birdwatching, nature trails and ranger activities, while indoors you can sign up for dance and craft classes, ten-pin bowling, plus an Olympian range of sports. Each parc has comfortable self-catering accommodation and a range of restaurants for eating out, while the Aqua Sana Spa provides a retreat for grown-ups in need of pampering.

Contact Center Parcs, T08448-267723, centerparcs.co.uk

Boating holidays

'Believe me, my young friend, there is nothing – absolutely nothing – half so much worth doing as simply messing about in boats.' Of course, Ratty was absolutey right when he shared this nugget of wisdom with Mole in *The Wind in the Willows*. Moments later their boat struck the bank, but that didn't dent their enthusiasm for a jolly day out on the river.

You're bound to have the odd scrape or gunwale-grabbing moment if you take your kids on a boating holiday – safety obviously has to be paramount – but there's no denying the simple pleasures or sense of adventure that accompanies a journey by narrowboat or cruiser. Think it's all a bit too fuddy-duddy? Try telling that to children who love the idea of nesting in cosy cabins, taking turns at the helm, working lock gates, feeding swans, spotting kingfishers and tying up for riverside picnics. The leisurely pace of a boating holiday also makes it one of the best opportunities busy families will ever get to simply wind down, share a good book or just chat. And don't imagine you'll be cramped or skimping on comforts. Most boats are cleverly equipped with kitchens, bathrooms and saloons, with many boasting mod-cons like flat-screen televisions.

Where to get afloat? The simple answer is 'Somewhere near you.' Britain's waterways range from the Norfolk Broads to Scotland's Caledonian Canal – with an intriguing tangle of canals and rivers stretching between Basingstoke and Skipton. Short breaks are available for testing the water, or you could embark on a two-week odyssey, perhaps sharing an eight-berth cruiser with another family.

Contact Hoseasons, T0844-499 0088, hoseasons.co.uk/uk-boating

France

Natural cycle

There are endless
opportunities
for cycling on
holiday in France
– from mountain
biking in the Pyrenees
to pedalling along a
section of the Loire à
Vélo (see page 69).

metres
3000
2000
1000
500
200
0

N

50 km
50 miles

LONDON

Calais

BRUSSELS

Lille

English Channel

Cherbourg

Le Havre

Rouen

1

Caen

Channel Islands (UK)

Seine

Nancy

Strasbourg

Roscoff

St Malo

Mont St-Michel

2

PARIS

Brest

Pointe de Raz

3

Rennes

Highest mountain
Mont Blanc
4807 m

Orléans

Belle Isle

Loire

Nantes

5

FRANCE

Dijon

Longest river
Loire
1020 km

Geneva

Mont Blanc

6

Ile de Ré

Ile d'Oléron

Atlantic Ocean

Lyon

Grenoble

Tur

Bordeaux

A l p s

L a n d e s

Massif Central

Garonne

Rhône

Avignon

Nice

Biarritz

4

Toulouse

Montpellier

Camargue

Cannes

Côte d'Azur

San Sebastián

Marseilles

7

Pic du Midi

P y r e n e e s

Highest waterfall
Grande Cascade
de Gavarnie
423 m

Mediterranean Sea

Bastia

Corsica

Ajaccio

Bonifacio

1 ★ Climb the Eiffel Tower

»» Paris, page 64

2 ★ Conquer Mont St Michel

»» Normandy, page 68

3 ★ Sail a dinghy or windsurfer

»» Brittany, page 68

4 ★ Learn to surf or bodyboard

»» Atlantic coast, page 70

5 ★ Cycle to a château

»» Loire Valley, page 69

6 ★ Ski in the French Alps

»» French Alps, page 72

7 ★ Spot a flamingo

»» The Camargue, page 75

◉ Did you know?

★ The world record for spitting a prune stone is held by Serge Fougère who managed an impressive 17.81 m at the 1996 championship at Sainte Livrade sur Lot.

★ The French consume around a million tonnes of cheese a year.

★ In 1925 the Eiffel Tower was sold not once but twice by Victor Lustig to gullible scrap dealers.

★ In 2002 Didier Bovard became the first person to cross the Atlantic by Pedalo.

Introduction
France

France is one of the world's most popular holiday destinations. Even the French choose overwhelmingly to stay put en vacance and, for that reason, you'll find most places have an intrinsic child-friendliness. The biggest problem you'll face is deciding where to go and what to do. A big city like Paris, for example, might be the last thing on your mind, but even in a world without Disney, you'd still find a city brimming with child-friendly attractions, from scaling the Eiffel Tower to getting down to some serious fun in the interactive science museum at Parc de la Villette. The real boon for families, though, is the ease with which you can combine two or three regions. Sandwiched by a few days on the Normandy coast and an interlude in the Loire, that Paris city break begins to look even more enticing. Likewise, you could make a tasty combo of walking and rafting in the Pyrenees with beach fun on either the Atlantic or Mediterranean coasts. You may decide that some regions deserve your undivided attention: Provence and Brittany spring to mind. Both have idyllic coastlines, loads of activities, medieval castles and Roman ruins. Not forgetting the fine cuisine and cheap wine. France is *très bon* for parents too.

❝❞ **One of my best holidays was at Côte de Vermeille in the South of France. I loved being able to swim in the sea and see the snow-capped mountains at the same time.** India Seely, age 14

Star rating

Wow factor
★★★★

Worry factor
★

Value for money
★★★

Keeping teacher happy
★★★

Family accommodation
★★★★★

Babies & toddlers
★★★★★

Cool for teenagers
★★★★

How to play

➤ Form two teams of up to three players each. Share out the boules.
➤ Toss a coin to decide which team goes first.
➤ Choose a starting point and draw a circle on the ground in which to stand; both feet must remain in the circle until the boule lands.
➤ The first player throws the cochonnet 6-10 m away and then throws the first boule, trying to get it as near as possible to the cochonnet.
➤ A player from the other team tries to throw his or her boule closer to the cochonnet (or to knock away the leading boule).
➤ The team that is farthest from the cochonnet continues to throw.
➤ When a team has no boules left the players of the other team take turns to throw theirs and place them as close as possible to the cochonnet.
➤ The winning team scores a point for each of its boules that has landed nearer to the cochonnet than the closest boule of the other team.
➤ A member of the winning team throws the cochonnet in the opposite direction from the previous end and play continues until one team reaches 13 points.

⊘ Game plan pétanque

What you need
➤ A coin
➤ 12 metal or hard plastic boules
➤ 1 cochonnet (small marker ball)
➤ An area of open ground; the beach is ideal
➤ A measure and scoring cards, paper and pens

★ Make a Monet

With a bit of artistic flair and a dash of technology you can create your own Monet-style masterpiece. You will need a digital camera, a computer and Adobe Photoshop Elements software.

➤ Look at some books or prints showing Monet's work, noticing the colours, light and compositions that he used
➤ Choose your own subject matter, perhaps flowers, fields or countryside, and either take a digital picture or scan an image from a book or magazine
➤ Open your picture in Photoshop Elements. Make sure it's in RGB format.
➤ Go to Filter > Artistic > Paint Daubs and set Brush Size and Sharpness to 10 and Brush Style to Simple.
➤ Go to Filter > Artistic > Dry Brush and set Brush Size and Brush detail to 5 and texture to 2.
➤ Go to Filter > Artistic > Palette Knife and set Stroke Size to 10, Stroke Detail to 2 and Softness to 5.
Voila! Your masterpiece is finished! Now try altering the settings to obtain different effects. If you make a mistake go to Edit > Step Backward.

Great reads ◄
5 books for kids

Early years
Katie Meets the Impressionists
James Mayhew (Scholastic)
Find out what happens when Katie visits
an art gallery with her grandmother and
five famous Impressionist paintings come
to life.

All ages
Perrault's Fairy Tales
Laurence Anholt (Houghton Mifflin)
This classic collection of fairy tales from
the French founder of the fairytale genre
includes favourites such as Cinderella, Little
Red Riding Hood and Sleeping Beauty.

Ages 5+
Degas and the Little Dancer
Perrault (Frances Lincoln)
The fascinating story behind Degas'
renowned bronze of Marie the ballet
dancer is brought to life in this beautifully
presented book.

Ages 7+
The Three Musketeers
Alexandre Dumas (Puffin Classics)
The world-famous tale has been told in
films, television series and all manner
of books. But have you actually read it
yet? This version is specially abridged for
younger readers.

Ages 8+
Horrible Histories: France
Terry Deary (Scholastic)
Everything from gruesome guillotines
and foul famines to a horrible host of
kings, queens and emperors. Find out
lots of revolting facts about the French
Revolution and how to play hopscotch like
a highwayman.

Taste of France perfect crêpes

Deliciously light and thin, crêpes are tasty with a little sugar,
but douse them in chocolate and ice cream and we're talking
seriously scrumptious. Here's how to do it at home.

What you need
➤ 150 g plain flour
➤ 2 eggs
➤ 140 ml milk
➤ 140 ml water
➤ ¼ tsp salt
➤ 2 tbsp butter, melted
➤ oil for cooking

➤ Cook for about two minutes
until the bottom is light brown;
loosen with a spatula, turn and
cook the other side.
➤ Slide on to a plate, add your
choice of yummy topping
(such as chocolate, ice cream or
honey) and fold into a handy-
sized snack.

What to do
➤ Whisk together the flour and
eggs; slowly add the milk and
water, stirring to combine.
➤ Add the salt and butter;
beat until smooth.
➤ Heat a lightly oiled
griddle or frying pan
over medium-high
heat; pour on the
batter using around
a quarter of a cup for
each crêpe.
➤ Tilt the pan with
a circular motion so
that the batter coats the
surface evenly.

The Young Chef's French Cookbook
(Crabtree Publishing)
Have fun with 15 easy-to-prepare
French traditional dishes with step-
by-step instructions. Bon appetit!

Smell the flowers

A walk or cycle ride on the Plateau de Valensole packs a perfumed
punch between June and early September when the famous
lavender fields of Provence reach their purple prime. Grasse,
meanwhile, is the capital of the world's perfume
industry. Join a tour around one of its many perfume
houses or visit during mid-May for the Fête de la Rose.

To the uninitiated, France might appear rather too sophisticated and aloof for carefree family holidays. But once you see beyond the manicured image of nouvelle cuisine, chic boutiques and immaculate vineyards you'll soon encounter a more down-to-earth, *laissez faire* approach to life. The French understand the needs of families probably better than any other country in Europe. Children's facilities and attractions abound, while the opportunities for camping and self-catering – the two most popular forms of family accommodation in France – are almost endless. For holidaymakers from the UK, it's also straightforward and cheap to nip across the Channel, with or without your car.

Babies

With lots going on around them, buggy-bound babies can be wheeled happily around Paris for hours while their parents soak up the sights, take in a museum or two and indulge in a spot of pavement café culture. As yet unaware of Disneyland, babies will get their kicks from a crawl about in one of the city's parks. Although public transport between Paris and its suburbs is good, you can avoid the hassle of a daily commute by staying in a centrally located self-catering apartment or hotel with babysitting services. With babies there's a lot to be said for piling everything you need into a car (from bottle sterilizers

Sailing boats in Jardin des Tuileries, Paris

The French capital has several wonderful parks with plenty of open space for kids to run free.

to bales of nappies) and setting off on your own *tour de France*. Travelling outside school holidays means you can get better deals on accommodation and explore the Mediterranean either side of the fiercely hot months of July and August.

Toddlers/pre-school

Long, meandering car journeys across France don't have quite the same appeal when you've got fractious toddlers strapped in the back who have just discovered the liberating joys of walking.

Fortunately, France has an extensive network of holiday parcs that you can link together in a kind of self-drive dot-to-dot. Many have waterparks and numerous activities for young children, including supervised clubs. You can even find parcs within easy striking range of cities, including Paris.

As for Disneyland, Europe's number one tourist attraction, many parents claim toddlers are too young to get much out of it. Certainly, the big rides, with their height restrictions, will continue to elude them until they are five or six, but that's not to say you won't be able to keep a one- or two-year-old happy for a calmer, more gently paced day with Mickey and pals.

Kids/school age

Adventure beckons for this age range. They'll be up for anything, whether it's a maiden ride on the Goudurix loop-the-loop roller coaster at Parc Astérix,

Special needs

The French ministry of tourism has initiated a campaign to improve access for disabled people travelling in France. Reliable and up-to-date information can be obtained from L'Association des Paralysés de France (www.apf. asso.fr), while *Access in Paris* (accessinparis.org), provides excellent advice for wheelchair users visiting the city. Crystal Ski (crystalski.co.uk) has a programme for disabled skiers – Crystal Adaptive is available in the French Alps resort of La Plagne and offers a complete package to ensure a fully accessible skiing holiday.

Single parents

Acorn Adventure (families.acornadventure.co.uk) provides an infrastructure for supporting single parents on their trips to the Ardeche and Normandy. Eurocamp (eurocamp.co.uk) offers discounts for lone-parent families and will even help with unpacking on arrival.

> ❝ ❞ **We've been to Antibes in the South of France by train which was a really exciting experience. It's great to wake up to blue skies and blue seas, and if you're willing to lug your suitcases along endless platforms it's a good way to travel. It's quite expensive, but I think as long as you think of the journey as being part of the holiday it's OK.** Caroline Mewes

a cycle through the backroads of the Loire Valley or a race to conquer the Eiffel Tower sans élévateur.

As with younger children, holiday parcs make an ideal base. However, now that they've reached an age when they can begin to appreciate local culture, you might also want to consider a self-catering gîte or villa that's more in touch with rural life.

A visit to the local shops or market is a great way to get kids speaking French. If it's food for thought you're after, then France will stimulate even the most inquiring young minds. In fact, you may decide to sidestep certain aspects of the country's tumultuous history (such as the terrible legacy of the Second World War in Normandy) until your children have studied it at school. Less harrowing historical hotspots include Mont St-Michel, the Loire châteaux, Lascaux's prehistoric cave paintings and, of course, the wonderful museums and landmarks of Paris. For education with a wild twist, you can't beat Brittany with its teeming rock pools or the Alps with their flower- and insect-filled summer meadows.

Teenagers

Paris is cool. So is the French Riviera. Fashion-conscious teenagers will enjoy browsing the shops, seeing the sights and joining the trendy café crowds.

The appeal of camping in France might be ebbing for this age group (although many parcs hold special activities for teenagers, like discos). A villa is a good alternative – plenty of space for independent-minded, occasionally moody, teenagers. You could even consider renting one that had enough space for them to bring along a friend or share with another family. All-inclusive resorts should also meet with approval.

For adrenaline-fired adventure, France has numerous possibilities, from surfing on the Atlantic coast to parapenting in the Alps. However, the Côte d'Azur/Provence region scores highest from a teenage perspective – nowhere else combines such an impeccably stylish coastline with a rugged hinterland of gorges and mountains bristling with adventure activities. Operators such as Explore Worldwide (explore.co.uk) and Exodus (exodus.co.uk) offer teenage-only trips to France.

Telling tales Charlotte Hindle
Travel journalist

One of my top family travel experiences in France is to get up early with the children and visit the local boulangerie to buy croissants and baguettes for breakfast. Encourage your child to breathe in the warming smell of freshly baked dough and pastries; allow them to ask in French for what you need and let them buy one extra baguette so that on the way back they can nibble both ends (and usually much more) before you reach the breakfast table.

From Disney to Da Vinci, Paris bridges a cultural chasm that will leave you and your kids reeling. Imagine one day staring at the world's most famous painting and the next coming face to face with a tall mouse dressed in a dinner jacket and bow tie. Whether you're looking to stimulate a spot of art appreciation or simply opting to escape into a land of make-believe, Paris makes a supremely child-friendly city break. In another life (*sans famille*), you may remember Paris as a stylish, romantic place where you wafted between cafés, delved in designer boutiques and lingered in the Louvre. With kids in tow, its going to be different. Once you accept that fact, you'll begin to see the French capital in a whole new light – and enjoy it no less.

Visit Versaill

Built in the mid-17th century the enormous Château de Versailles provides a glimpse into the opulent tastes of the French monarchy during the reign of Louis XIV. Located 21 km southwest of Paris, the château has no fewer than 700 rooms and 6300 paintings. Pace yourself and be selective. Highlights include the Queen's Apartment and Hall of Mirrors – 73 m long and shimmering with 357 mirrors. Outside you'll find the largest palace grounds in Europe – 100 ha of elaborate flower beds, symmetrical paths, the 1.6-km-long Grand Canal and Versailles' famous fountains.

Eiffel Tower

Champs de Mars, eiffel-tower.com. Year round, daily from 0930 (or 0900 mid-Jun to Aug) ⤷ Trocadéro Métro, RER Champs de Mars/Tour Eiffel

A riveting romp up this Parisian landmark has to be top of your must-do list. You can take the lift or climb 1665 steps to the second level, from where another elevator is the only way to reach the viewing gallery at 274 m. Just 50 m shy of the tower's flagpole, this often-crowded platform provides superhero views reaching 80 km on a clear day. Apart from giving their parents palpitations (don't worry, its like an iron cage up there), kids will love gazing down on the ant-like columns of traffic and trying to spot other city landmarks. A route has been marked out to the first floor to engage six- to 10-year-olds on the history of the Eiffel Tower – look out for the bright yellow footprints. If they start to tire on the climb up (or down), arm yourself with these inspiring and diversionary facts about Gustave Eiffel's engineering wonder: The Eiffel Tower has over 18,000 metal parts and 2.5 million rivets; it expands up to 15 cm on hot days and took more than two years to build; over 220 million people have visited since it opened in 1889 and it weighs 10,100 tonnes (that's like 2020 elephants standing on top of each other).

Musée du Louvre

99 Rue de Rivoli, louvre.fr. Year round, Wed-Mon 0900-1800 ⤷ Palais Royal Musée du Louvre Métro

You've got to see it, but where do you begin in a gallery displaying over 35,000 works of art? There are several ways families can crack this mighty treasure chest. If you want to remain independent, focus on

Top: Versailles; above: Eiffel Tower; below: gargoyle on Notre Dame Cathedral

just a few major exhibits, such as the *Mona Lisa*, *Venus de Milo*, *Winged Victory* and *Grand Sphinx*. Alternatively, download a trail from the museum's website (where you'll also find a virtual museum guide for children), book a workshop or sign up for a guided family tour with Paris Muse Clues (parismuse.com) – an educational treasure hunt that takes kids (aged six to 12) from Ancient Egypt to Renaissance Italy, testing their detective skills to lead them to a prize hidden somewhere beneath the Louvre's glass pyramid.

Cathédrale Notre Dame de Paris

Parvis Notre-Dame, T01-4234 5610, notredamedeparis.fr. Cathedral entrance open year round, Mon-Fri 0800-1845, Sat-Sun 0800-1915, tower entrance Apr-Sep, daily 1000-1830, Oct-Mar, daily 1000-1730 ⤷ Cité Métro

This beautiful Gothic cathedral will be familiar to many children through Disney's *Hunchback of Notre Dame*. Climb the South Tower to the Galerie des Chimères to pull faces at gruesome gargoyles lurking between the towers to ward off evil. There are 387 steps and no elevator.

Artist in Montmartre

Kids' top 10 Best of the rest: Paris

❶ Catacombes de Paris
A dark side to the City of Light, this macabre museum is piled with the bones of six million Parisians exhumed from the city's overcrowded cemeteries during the late 1700s. Maximum gross factor for teenagers; maximum nightmare potential for littl'uns. Also be warned that there are 130 steps going down into the catacombs and 83 climbing back out again.

❷ Centre Georges Pompidou Wacky contemporary arts centre with a vibrant spattering of visual and performance art. Don't miss the buskers, 'living statues' and surreal Stravinsky Fountain. Then ride the external escalator and get arty in the Children's Gallery (for six- to 12-year-olds).

❸ Champs Élysées
The city's most famous avenue, dominated by the Arc de Triomphe and Grand Palais. Look out for the Punch and Judy show at Théâtre du Vrai Guignolet. The dialogue is in French, but the gratuitous violence will be all too familiar.

❹ Muséum National d'Histoire Naturelle (Ménagerie du Jardin des Plantes) As well as galleries showcasing geology, palaeontology and evolution, this large museum (located next to the Seine) is home to the Ménagerie – one of the world's oldest zoos. The 5-ha park has 240 mammals, 500 birds and 130 reptiles.

❺ Jardin d'Acclimatation
Quirky amusement park with traditional attractions such as a carousel, hall of mirrors, narrow-gauge train, puppet theatre and pony rides.

❻ Jardin du Luxembourg
Puppet shows, donkey rides, boating pond, children's playground and vintage carousel.

❼ Jardin des Tuileries
Elm-lined avenues lead to famous landmarks such as the Arc de Triomphe and Louvre pyramid. Soak up the atmosphere while the kids sail wooden yachts on the pond.

❽ Montmartre
Hilltop district crowned by the Sacré Cœur basilica. Children will enjoy watching the street artists at work in Place du Tertre.

❾ Musée de la Magie
Dingy 16th-century cellars provide a creepy setting for magic shows, optical illusions and other tricks of the mind.

❿ Musée d'Orsay
One for older children who have perhaps studied the Impressionists at school and will be entranced by this exquisite collection, which includes Monet's *Blue Waterlilies* and Renoir's *Ball at the Moulin de la Galette*, as well as masterpieces by Cezanne, Degas and Manet.

Parc de la Villete

Ave Corentin-Cariou, T01-4005 7000, cite-sciences.fr. Year round, Tue-Sat 0930-1800, Sun 0930-1900 ➡ Porte de la Villette Métro

This enormous park contains the Cité des Sciences et de l'Industrie, a high-tech, hands-on science museum where kids can tinker with physics and biology. Head straight for the captivating Cité des Enfants. A section for children aged two to seven is divided into themed areas designed to challenge, inspire and inform. Another area for five- to 12-year-olds is crammed with hundreds of interactive challenges for enquiring young minds. Once your children have finished splitting the atom, operating robots, running the European space programme or playing at being Archimedes, spend some time exploring the *Argonaute* submarine (once the pride of the French navy) or Expositions d'Explora (showcasing the latest developments in the world of science), then take in a movie at La Géode (a giant hemispherical IMAX cinema) or go starry-eyed at the new 3D planetarium.

Inside info

➡ Visit anytime. It can be hot during August. Christmas lights give the Champs Elysées and the Eiffel Tower extra sparkle.
➡ Crêperies make great energy-boosting stops for children – or, for a real treat, take your pick of 70 ice cream flavours from Berthillon (across the bridge from Notre Dame).
➡ The Métro is a good way to get around, but backpack babies rather than buggy them as there are few lifts. Alternatively, use the River Seine's hop-on, hop-off Batobus boats.

Parc Astérix Let's hear it for the Gauls

Never mind the Romans. Astérix and Obélix are fighting their greatest battle against Mickey and his pals. It's no surprise that Disneyland reigns supreme as Europe's top theme park attraction, but don't write off Parc Astérix. To get the most out of this eclectic park it helps if you are familiar with the comic strip. Follow these five steps to get well and truly addicted to the antics of those indomitable Gauls.

❶ Read the books
"The year is 50 BC. Gaul is entirely occupied by Romans. Well, not entirely... one small village of indomitable Gauls still holds out against the invaders." So the scene is set for the adventures of Astérix, created by René Goscinny and Albert Uderzo in 1959 and now translated into 107 languages with over 320 million copies sold worldwide. Orion (orionbooks.co.uk) has relaunched 24 re-inked, re-coloured and re-designed titles in the series, including *Astérix and the Falling Sky*, *Astérix and the Soothsayer*, *Astérix in Corsica*, *Astérix and the Normans*, *Astérix the Legionary*, *Astérix the Gaul*, *Astérix and Cleopatra* and *Astérix the Gladiator*.

❷ Know the characters
A cunning little warrior who never passes up the chance of a perilous mission, **Astérix** gets his superhuman strength from the magic potion brewed by village druid **Getafix**. Astérix's inseparable companion **Obélix** fell into the potion when he was a baby. Addicted to wild boar, the menhir delivery man is followed everywhere by **Dogmatix**, who howls whenever a tree is cut down. Meanwhile, **Vitalstatistix**, the village chief, is constantly afraid that, one day, the sky will fall on his head.

❸ Watch the film
Astérix and the Vikings (2007).

❹ Visit the official website
asterix.com.

❺ Visit the theme park
Parc Asterix
Plailly, T02-8792-9715, parcasterix.fr (French only). Apr-Oct, times and days vary ⇢ RER B3 from Paris to Roissy Charles de Gaulle, then Parc Asterix bus
By Toutatis, let the fun begin! Tucked into forest 30 km north of Paris, Parc Astérix is divided into five lands – Gaul, Roman, Greek, Viking and Travel through Time. There's an authentic Gaulish Village where you can meet characters from the comic strip, a Roman Arena and numerous adrenaline-charged rides. For top thrills, don't miss Tonnerre de Zeus (minimum height: 120 cm) – Europe's biggest wooden roller coaster reaching speeds of 80 km/h along its 1.2 km length. Goudurix (minimum height: 140 cm) is a 950-m loop-the-loop roller coaster which sends you upside down no less than seven times; La Trace du Hourra (minimum height: 120 cm) is a 60-km/h Gaulish bobsled, while the Menhir Express water ride has a 13-m splash drop.

Paris How to do Disneyland

Disneyland Resort Paris
Marne-la-Vallée, disneylandparis.com. Year round, daily from 1000 (check website for 'extra magic hours')
⇢ RER to Marne-la-Vallée/Chessy

If you're thinking of taking the kids to Paris and not spending at least one day at Europe's most popular family attraction, forget it. At best, they'll never speak to you again; at worst they'll do something spiteful in the Louvre when you drag them there instead. In any case, Disneyland, for all its zigzag queues and rictus smiles, is great fun whether you're a Cinderella-doting five-year-old, an adrenaline-hungry teenager or the 40-something paying for it all.

When to go
Well, it sure isn't Florida, so be prepared for an invigorating range of unpredictable European weather. The upside of visiting in winter, of course, is that queues are shorter and you can get special deals.

How to get there
The train is the easiest and most relaxed option. If you're staying in Paris take the RER (40 minutes from the city centre) or, if you're travelling from further afield, hop on Eurostar. Either way you'll arrive at Marne-la-Vallée/Chessy station right outside the park entrance.

Where to stay
It depends on whether you want to spend a day at Disney or make a long weekend (or more) out of it. If it's the latter, pick one of the hotels near Disneyland – several are run by Disney so you'll be able to live the magic (breakfast with Chip 'n' Dale, etc) even after the parks have closed. For a Paris holiday that simply includes a day trip to Disney you'll get better value by staying in a mid-range city hotel or a suburban holiday park, such as Camping International in Maison-Laffitte.

What to do
There are two parks: Disneyland and Walt Disney Studios. If it's your first time, focus on **Disneyland** where you will find five distinct zones.

The entrance leads straight to **Main Street USA**, a nostalgic evocation of small-town America in the early 1900s, complete with ice-cream parlours, horse-drawn streetcars

and the chuff-chuff Disney Railroad. Autograph hunters will find Mickey, Minnie and the Disney Princesses here, while the Discovery Arcade takes you on a journey through the Golden Age of 20th-century inventions.

Walk through Sleeping Beauty Castle to **Fantasyland** where Peter Pan's Flight, It's a Small World, Mad Hatter's Tea Cups, Lancelot's Carousel, Alice's Curious Labyrinth and the Flying Dumbos are all big fairytale-themed hits with children.

Discoveryland features several big rides, including the Space Mountain: Mission 2 roller coaster (minimum height: 132 cm), Buzz Lightyear Laser Blast (where you score points by zapping Zurg and other nasties) and Star Tours (a simulator flight to the Moon of Endor). Children can test their driving skills on the Autopia track (minimum height: 132 cm), descend 20,000 leagues under the sea in Captain Nemo's Submarine and pilot a rocket ship through the planets and constellations of the Orbitron.

Frontierland has the runaway roller coaster, Big Thunder Mountain (minimum height: 102 cm), the spooky Phantom Manor, Pocahontas Indian Village, paddle steamer rides on the *Mark Twain* and *Molly Brown* and live shows at the Chaparral Theatre. Swagger through the wooden gates of Fort Comstock for Legends of the Wild West and take aim at the Rustler Roundup Shootin' Gallery.

Adventureland has Pirates of the Caribbean (a rollicking ride through secret caverns and rowdy taverns), the secret pirate hideout of Adventure Isle, Captain Cook's Pirate Ship and another wayward roller coaster, Indiana Jones and the Temple of Peril (minimum height: 140 cm).

Remember to intersperse the big rides with some of the smaller, queue-free attractions, such as Le Passage Enchanté d'Aladdin with its exquisite scenes of Agrabah – and be sure to stake out a good spot on Main Street to wave to your favourite characters in the daily parade.

Right next door to Disneyland Park, **Walt Disney Studios Park** puts you centre-stage in a world of a special effects, animation and big-screen drama. Each of the park's four studio lots (Front Lot, Back Lot, Toon Studios and Courtyard Production) has its own mix of attractions and rides.

Big rides at Walt Disney Studios include the Twilight Zone Tower of Terror (an elevator ride from hell, with random drops of up to 13 floors; minimum height: 103 cm), Stitch Live! (an interactive encounter with the animated alien) and Moteurs... Action! (a stunt show spectacular with high-speed car chases). Based on *Finding Nemo*, Crush's Coaster (minimum height: 107 cm) is an indoor/outdoor spinning roller coaster

ride, in which you explore real-life underwater scenes, meet Bruce the veggie great white shark and battle against the East Australian Current. Cars Race Rally takes you for a spin along Route 66, while Rock 'n' Roller Coaster (minimum height: 120 cm) inflicts Aerosmith music and high-speed loops and turns.

At park closing time, nearby **Disney Village** continues to buzz with its plethora of shops, restaurants and entertainment. Street artists, live shows and concerts vie for your attention, and there's also a 15-screen multiplex and 3D IMAX cinema complex.

How to save time

‣ Before you visit, check out the Disneyland website (see left) where you'll find suggestions for customized visits for families with under-fives to those in search of big thrills.

‣ Use FastPass – a polite way of queue jumping. Just insert your entrance ticket into a FastPass machine and you'll receive a designated time when you can board the ride by a special, often queue-free, entrance. The catch, of course, is that you can only FastPass one ride at a time. FastPass is available for the following rides: Indiana Jones and the Temple of Peril, Space Mountain: Mission 2, Buzz Lightyear Laser Blast, Big Thunder Mountain, Peter Pan's Flight, Star Tours, Rock 'n' Roller Coaster, The Twilight Zone Tower of Terror and Flying Carpets over Agrabah.

‣ Parent Switch allows parents with young children to take turns on adult rides, without queuing twice.

‣ Take a picnic into the park with plenty of drinks.

‣ Leave the park well before closing time if you want to eat in Disney Village – otherwise the queues are huge. Alternatively book a table at one of the Disney hotels as you arrive in the morning.

⊕ Let's go to Puy du Fou

Les Epesses, nr Cholet, T02-5157 3547, puydufou.com. Apr-Sep, times vary.

A theme park for wannabe time travellers, Puy du Fou allows you to witness rampaging Vikings, gladiator battles, knights in shining armour and the exploits of the Three Musketeers in breathtaking live shows with special effects and stunts. There are also reconstructions of historical villages to explore and, during summer, the Cinéscénie evening show spectacular.

Northern France
En vacances sur la mer

A seaside holiday. That's what lures most families to Northern France. And who can blame them. From the vast sandy beaches of Normandy to the Atlantic-gnawed cliffs and sheltered coves of Brittany, this varied stretch of coastline is paradise for anyone armed with a bucket, a spade and a shrimping net. History, too, comes alive along this shore – from megalithic standing stones at Carnac to the D-Day beaches of the Second World War. And to crown it all you've got Mont St-Michel, an excuse for a Famous Five-style adventure if ever there was one.

Normandy & the northeast

For many families arriving from the UK by cross-Channel ferry, Normandy and Pas de Calais are simply gateways to a wider-reaching *tour de France*. However, don't overlook the regions' mixture of family-friendly beaches and evocative historical sites.

Best beaches The coastal strip between Calais and the Somme Estuary is basically one long beach. Look out for resorts with Kid Station status, indicating children's facilities and high standards of safety and cleanliness. They include Wissant (a vast expanse of sand and a good spot for land-yachting), Wimereux (with its gently shelving beach and shallow sea, ideal for children learning to windsurf) and Hardelot (a sheltered beach backed by sand dunes).

Le Touquet-Paris-Plage is another popular resort with everything from waterparks to carousels. Further west, near Le Havre, Trouville is one of Normandy's favourite family beaches (quieter and more relaxed than its chic neighbour, Deauville). Meanwhile, the Péninsule de Cotentin has some excellent beaches south of Granville, with a long promenade for walking or cycling. And if all that sand starts to drive you crazy, retreat to the Somme Estuary and spend a day birdwatching at La Parc Ornithologique du Marquenterre, a prime site for spotting seabirds and migrants.

Battleground tour The D-Day landings endowed Normandy with one of the most poignant legacies of the Second World War. Starting at Caen drive north to Ouistreham and Pegasus Bridge where troop-laden gliders landed just after midnight on 6 June 1944, spearheading the huge allied invasion codenamed Operation Overlord. At Arromanches a museum and 360-degree cinema describe how an artificial port (known as the Mulberry Harbour) was built here in just 12 days to secure Allied supply routes. Further along

the D514, you reach Omaha Beach where American troops met fierce German resistance. On the clifftop at Colleville-sur-Mer the 9387 graves at the American Cemetery provide a stark reminder of the heroism and sacrifices of D-Day.

Bayeux If your kids are studying William the Conqueror at school, then seeing the 11th-century Bayeux Tapestry will bring 1066 and the Battle of Hastings into vivid relief (and just think how impressed their history teacher will be). The embroidered linen measures 70 m in length and took nuns 10 years to stitch.

Kids' top 10 Brittany & beyond

❶ **Conquer** Mont St-Michel (ot-montsaintmichel.com), a 1000-year-old fortified abbey perched on a rock in the middle of a bay and guarded by lethal tides and whiffy mudflats. Climb through a steep warren of streets, hemmed in by wonky half-timbered houses, to reach the Gothic abbey – a major pilgrimage site in the Middle Ages and still hugely popular.

❷ **Taste** delicious local delicacies, from chocolate-smeared crêpes to smoked sausages (or just stick with the crêpes), at one of Brittany's numerous markets.

❸ **Walk** to Pointe du Raz, the Land's End of France, and strike an epic pose as you gaze across the Atlantic towards America.

❹ **Count** (or rather lose count) of the 3000-odd menhirs and other megalithic shenanigans at Carnac, a prehistoric conundrum dating from 4500 to 1800 BC. Resist the temptation to 'do an Obélix'.

❺ **Cruise** to the Sept-Îles, home to 20,000 pairs of seabirds (don't even attempt to count these), including a raucous gannet colony. Departures from Perros-Guirec.

❻ **Learn** to sail a windsurfer, catamaran or sand yacht at the St-Malo Surf School (surfschool.org).

❼ **Discover** the secret life of a rock pool, from lightning-fast blennies to bumbling hermit crabs. Beware of tide times and those razor-sharp oyster-encrusted rocks.

❽ **Cycle** 35 km of biking trails on La Belle Île.

❾ **Vote** for your favourite beach, but sample lots first, including the sand sensations at Audierne, La Baule, Carnac, St Cast, Dinard, Douarnenez, Perros-Guirec, Trégastel-Plage and La Trinité-sur-Mer.

❿ **Explore** Océanopolis (oceanopolis.com). Brest's mega-aquarium is divided into polar, tropical and temperate seas and has Europe's largest penguin colony, seven species of shark, a 13-m coral reef and a boardwalk through tropical rainforest. A touchpool and a seal rescue centre add a splash of local sea life.

Inside info ⓘ

▸▸ Self-drive touring is the easiest and most popular way to go.
▸▸ The Channel can be chilly, so consider wetsuits for the kids.
▸▸ For coastal diversions, try the famous lily pond at Giverny (home of Impressionist artist Claude Monet) or go canoeing in Parc Naturel Régional Normandie-Maine to the south of Caen.

Forget your traditional touring holiday: it might be time to ditch the car. The Loire Valley presents too good an opportunity for a family-friendly, eco-friendly alternative. It's called La Loire à Vélo, a signposted itinerary made up of minor roads and cycling tracks that allows you to pedal through the gently undulating, châteaux-speckled countryside of one of Europe's most beautiful river valleys. Easy to plan and easy to pedal, La Loire à Vélo forms part of a grand plan to link Nantes with Budapest via a 2400-km cycle route. But first things first – hand over the car keys and reach for your helmets…

La Loire à Vélo

Relax. No one is expecting you to cycle the entire Loire à Vélo route (a total of 800 km from Cuffy in the Cher region to St-Brévin-les-Pins in Loire-Atlantique). And, if your thighs cramp at the mere thought of two-wheel, leg-powered transport, all of the Loire highlights on the following cycle trails can easily be visited in the comfort of your car.

Châteaux Trail
Lestiou – Candé-sur-Beuvron, 51 km
Following riverbanks as far as St-Dyé, this route visits the ancient port of Chambord with its long stone quayside, as well as the majestic 400-room Château de Chambord – the largest in the Loire with a famous double-turn spiral staircase and great views from the roof terrace. Small roads then lead you to the Château Royal de Blois before continuing on tree-lined routes to the peaceful town of Candésur-Beuvron.

River Cher
Tours – Langeais, 32 km
Must-see sights in Tours include the cathedral and the timber-framed buildings of the medieval quarter. Then it's off along the banks of the River Cher, cycling to Château de Villandry, one of the most family-friendly in the Loire with spectacular gardens to explore and even a maze and children's playground.

Riverbank Trail
Langeais – Chinon, 40 km
Château d'Ussé on the willow-swept River Indre is another favourite with kids. Charles Perrault is said to have been inspired to write the tale of *Sleeping Beauty* after visiting this fairytale castle of turrets and spires (and Walt Disney found inspiration here too). Cycling through vineyards, the route continues to Chinon, overlooked by a medieval fortress.

Château d'Ussé

Confluence and Caves Trail
Chinon – Saumur, 41 km
More vineyards line this route as it meanders towards the beautiful village of Candes-St-Martin and the Royal Abbey of Fontevraud, Europe's largest monastic complex. To get to Saumur and its castle, the trail follows a hillside riddled with ancient troglodyte dwellings that are now used as wine cellars or mushroom-growing beds.

Other châteaux

Château d'Angers
Château d'Angers is renowned for its Apocalypse Tapestries, but kids are more likely to enjoy running riot on the ramparts that link its 17 impressive towers.

Château de Brézé
Perfect for a rainy day, Château de Brézé has an incredible system of underground tunnels to explore.

Château de Chenonceau
Château de Chenonceau has a 16th-century farm and a waxwork museum. Children will love paddling a boat under the château's arches.

🛶 **Float** away

You can rent kayaks (with or without a guide) by the hour, half-day or full-day at towns such as Amboise, Angers and Saumur. **Loire Aventure** (Île d'Or, Amboise, T02-4723 2652, loire-aventure.fr) can kit you out with two- or three-seater Canadian canoes and drive you upriver for a gentle 10-km paddle downstream. Rates are usually around €15/person for a half-day trip.

There's plenty to keep families occupied in this corner of France, from surfing on the Atlantic coast and hiking in the Pyrenees to canoeing, cycling and horse riding in the Dordogne. Combine all three regions and you will probably need another holiday to recover. But you will also have experienced something of the extraordinary diversity of landscapes that France is renowned for – from serpentine rivers snug in gorges to wide sandy beaches ravaged by Atlantic breakers.

Atlantic coast

The southwest coast of France is one long, wild, wave-swept beach – give or take a sheltered bay or two. For a surfing holiday you won't find anywhere better in Europe. There are surf schools scattered along the length of the coast with a concentration around Biarritz in the south. You'll find no shortage of waves to suit all ages and abilities, but choose beaches that are supervised by lifeguards. Families with younger children will appreciate more tranquil spots, like Bassin d'Arcachon – a huge bay protected from the Biscay bruisers and a popular spot for gentler watersports like sailing and kayaking. You can also visit the nearby Dune du Pyla (or Pilat), Europe's largest sand dune at 110 m high, from where there are great views and a brilliant excuse for a roly-poly. Boat trips in the bay, meanwhile, are often rewarded with sightings of dolphins and seabirds. Take your pick of numerous campsites and holiday parks, as well as family-friendly resorts like Biscarosse, Mimizan and Moliets.

The Dordogne

Caves, castles, clifftop villages – it's small wonder the Dordogne is such a magnet for holidaymakers – and that's before you've cajoled canoeing, horse riding and cycling into your itinerary. No visit is complete without a stroll around Domme – a fortified town (or *bastide*) with narrow streets, a market square and stomach-lurching views from a terrace perched atop a precipitous cliff. Below the village you can explore a large stalactite-filled cave. West of Domme, medieval masonry at Château de Castelnaud is brought to life through a wonderful range of workshops where kids can learn how to fire a crossbow and devise the perfect strategy for laying siege to a castle – not necessarily the kinds of skills you might want your little darlings to acquire, but great fun nonetheless. Hugging the base of a steep cliff looming above the river, La Roque-Gageac is a fascinating place

that's been inhabited since prehistoric times. You can climb to cave forts bored in the cliffs and visit a garden of subtropical plants that thrive in the warm microclimate. The honey-stone town of Sarlat is also worth visiting, particularly during the Saturday market where you can see, and try, local delicacies such as foie gras, chestnuts, walnuts, mushrooms and truffles.

Biarritz on the Atlantic coast

French Pyrenees

They may not be as high or as grand as the Alps, and you might struggle to name any actual peaks, but what the Pyrenees lack in size and notoriety they more than compensate for with spectacular scenery, abundant wildlife and a wide range of activities. For families, the French Pyrenees also score highly for their accessibility to both the Atlantic and Mediterranean coasts, making it a cinch to combine some huff and puff in the mountains with a week relaxing on the beach.

Mountain trains These are ideal if you are lugging around a baby in a papoose or have small children. Just south of Biarritz, Le Petit Train de la Rhune rattles its way to 905 m above Basque Country, while Le Petit Train d'Artouste, accessible by cable car from Lac

Dordogne

Cirque de Gavarnie, Pyrenees

de Fabrèges, climbs high into the central Pyrenees. Admire views of Lurien (2826 m) and Palas (2974 m) before walking the short distance to Lac d'Artouste.

Cable car rides Another easy way up and down the mountains is to take the cable car to the top of Pic du Midi. In just 15 minutes you'll be whisked from La Mongie to the summit (2877 m), where there's an interesting observatory and museum.

Walks This is what it's all about! Pack a picnic and some warm, waterproof clothes and hit the trails. If you only have the time (or energy) for one hike, make sure it's in the Cirque de Gavarnie – about 50 km south of Lourdes. If the children seem reluctant to walk, plonk them on a donkey (you can hire one at the village of Gavarnie), then follow the path into the vast natural amphitheatre of the cirque. You can't miss the 400-m Grande Cascade, but also keep an eye out for alpine flowers, such as edelweiss, and mountain birds like the chough and wallcreeper. Bonus points if you spot a golden eagle or lammergeier. Bonus points with bells on if you spot a brown bear (there's only a handful of them left around these parts).

Caves Going underground may seem like an odd thing to do with all the gorgeous scenery available topside. But the Pyrenees is a great spot for caves, and chances are you're going to get at least one rainy day anyway. When you do, make a dash for either Grottes de Bétharram (near Lourdes) or Grotte de Lombrives (near Tarascon-sur-Ariège). Both are positively dripping with stalactites and bristling with stalagmites; there are guided tours and even underground train rides.

Other activities For children around 11 and up, the Pyrenees offers plenty of activities guaranteed to get the pulse racing, including whitewater rafting, river boarding, potholing, rock climbing, abseiling, canyoning and *via ferrata*. Some you might not have heard of – others you may wish you'd never heard of when you see your loved ones grappling with ropes and ladders on a precipitous mountain route that is part-hike, part-scramble (that's *via ferrata*) or disappearing over the lip of a waterfall wearing a wetsuit, a crash helmet and a devilish grin (one of the thrills of canyoning).

🔍 Top 3 birds to spot

Wallcreeper does what it says on the label – creeps around walls, rocks and cliffs; look out for bright red wing patches, high whistling call and long thin bill.

Lammergeier huge vulture mostly seen circling around peaks or patrolling a mountainside on the lookout for carcasses; look out for the long, wedge-shaped tail.

Golden eagle smaller than the lammergeier and holds its wings in a flat V when soaring; look out for the white wing patches.

Inside info

▸▸ Barèges and La Mongie share one of the largest ski areas, while other winter resorts include Font Romeu and Les Angles.
▸▸ Summer activities like walking can be adapted to suit most ages, while rafting, rock climbing and canyoning are better suited to older children.
▸▸ Nearby towns worth visiting include Foix, where you can row a boat along an underground river, and the famous pilgrimage site of Lourdes.

French Alps
Peak perfection

Le Mer de Glace

The snow has melted, the ski lifts are closed and the pistes are smothered in alpine flowers. Summer is coming and it's time to head to the mountains. Several alpine resorts alternate effortlessly between winter ski Mecca and action-packed summer destination, making them a perfect alternative to the traditional family seaside holiday. Just think of all that invigorating alpine air, comfortable temperatures, healthy outdoor activities and beautiful scenery. Your kids may never want to see a bucket and spade again.

Chamonix

If you can't do it in Chamonix, it probably doesn't exist. From river rafting and rock climbing to parapenting and summer tobogganing, Chamonix has got to be your top choice for non-stop activities. Just don't expect a cutesy alpine village. This bustling Savoy town has 10,000 hotel and guesthouse beds, dozens of restaurants, a casino and sports centre. But what Chamonix lacks in intimacy it more than compensates for with breathtaking views of Mont Blanc, 330 km of footpaths and an extensive network of cable cars and mountain railways.

Kids' activities Don't miss the summer luge (chamonixparc.com) – a 1820-m concrete bobsleigh run that's suitable for all ages (although young children must be accompanied by a parent). Bikes can also be hired and then, of course, there's good old-fashioned walking. Take your pick from gentle forest ambles to high-altitude hikes. Two favourite starting points are the Aiguille du Midi cable-car

station at 3842 m and Le Brévent, with its famous views across the valley towards the seven summits of the Mont Blanc massif – each one rising to over 4000 m. At Vallorcine, a gentle trail weaves through summer meadows of bistort, studding the ground like a massed array of pink ice-lollies. The track culminates at the Bérard waterfall, where you can scramble through a cleft to stand behind the cascade – quite an adventure for littl'uns.

Rock climbing (minimum age six) and ice-climbing (minimum age 12) are also available. Then there's whitewater rafting (for children aged 10 and up), horse riding and, if it rains, swimming and bowling in the large indoor sports complex.

Best family day out Board the rack-and-pinion railway for an alpine journey to Le Mer de Glace. Expect to pay around €55 for a family ticket (compagniedumontblanc.com), which includes return train fares, cablecar rides and entrance to the Grotte de Glace.

One for the grown-ups Take a leap of faith on a tandem parapente flight. Strapped to a pilot, you'll get airborne from either Brévent or the Aiguille du Midi and spend 30 minutes riding thermals and swooping over forested slopes.

Tignes-Le-Lac

Built around a natural lake and surrounded by snow-capped peaks, Tignes is around three hours' drive from Geneva or 1½ hours from Chamonix.

Kids' activities For maximum thrills try whitewater rafting near Centron and Gothard, or a 4WD safari on the high alpine trails in Vanoise National Park. Then there's horse riding, mountain biking, canyoning, quad biking, *via ferrata* and the adventure assault course in Tignes-les-Brevières. Pony riding is available for children as young as three, while slightly older kids can learn to sail on the lake.

Best family day out From Tignes-Val-Claret take the funicular and connecting cable car to reach the glacier beneath the mighty 3656-m Grand Motte. Here you will find the best summer skiing in France (with access to about 20 km of runs), not to mention stupendous views.

One for the grown-ups Europe's highest golf course can be found at Tignes-le-Lac. During high the season be sure to book a tee-off time.

Inside info

▶▶ Allow 90 minutes to drive from Geneva or nine hours from Calais.
▶▶ Nip through the Mont Blanc tunnel into Italy or take the scenic route via Aiguille du Midi and Pointe Heilbronner, using three different cable cars.

Alps ski guide

How to choose the perfect family resort

1 Does it meet everyone's needs? Do you have a baby who will need crèche facilities, or teenagers who will be bored senseless without a snowboarding half-pipe to practise their eggflips and corkscrew 540s?

2 Does it have other activities available? A resort that offers extras like husky sledding, ice skating, bowling or an indoor swimming pool can be a godsend in bad weather or if – shock, horror – you discover that your child just doesn't like skiing.

3 Does it have easy access to ski lifts and a diverse range of runs to suit everyone in the family, from infant novices to adult powder-carvers? Short legs quickly get tired when walking in ski boots, so compact resorts with well-linked slopes are a bonus.

4 Does it have ski classes for children of different ages and abilities? Do the instructors speak English?

5 Does it offer chalet or hotel accommodation that's suitable for children? Exclusive occupancy of a chalet means you don't have to worry about your kids disturbing other guests – or being kept awake after bedtime.

6 Does it involve a long journey from home? What are the options for self-drive, flying or taking the train?

7 Does it have a good reputation for being family-friendly? Saas Fee in Switzerland, for example, is a car-free resort, which instantly gives it family appeal. Other resorts, however, are exclusive and expensive.

Snow business

Specialist operator Esprit Ski (espritski.com) provides nursery care, children's ski classes and clubs, plus a whole range of other incentives to get you and your family on the pistes.

Key to table

* Figures cover the Three Valleys area (can also be skied from Méribel)

** Figures cover the Espace Killy area (can also be skied from Val d'Isère)

B	Bowling
HR	Horse riding
HS	Husky sledding
IC	Ice-climbing
IS	Ice skating
S	Swimming
SM	Snowmobiling
SR	Sleigh rides
SS	Snowshoe walks
T	Tobogganing

Resort	Country	Altitude (m)	Distance to airport (km)	Nursery areas	Pistes			Snow-boarding		Lifts					Activities
					Beginners	Intermediate	Advanced	Parks	Pipes	Funiculars	Cable cars	Gondolas	Chairlifts	Drag lifts	
Arinsal	AND	1500	172	2	19	18	5	1	2	0	1	1	11	13	S·T·SM
Obergurgl	AUS	1930	97	2	12	15	8	1	1	0	0	4	12	7	IS·SS
St Anton	AUS	1300	100	3	48	71	31	2	2	1	6	3	36	36	S·T·IS·SR
Kaprun	AUS	800	80	2	55	50	25	1	0	0	4	7	15	28	S·IS·B·T·HR
Neustift	AUS	1000	220	2	21	23	10	1	2	0	0	5	8	19	S·IS·T·SR·SS·IC
Les Arcs	FRA	2000	135	6	144	66	29	5	1	1	3	12	66	58	IS·SM·B·IC·SR
Avoriaz	FRA	1800	88	3	150	110	28	10	3	0	3	11	82	110	SR·B·IS·SS
Courcheval *	FRA	1850	128	12	183	119	33	5	3	3	3	34	69	71	IS·S·HS·SM·T
Chamonix	FRA	1035	100	4	41	25	13	0	0	0	6	6	17	12	S·IS·SR·SS·HS·T
La Plagne	FRA	2100	149	6	144	66	29	5	1	1	3	12	66	58	IS·B·S·SR·HS
La Rosière	FRA	1850	170	3	32	29	12	1	0	0	1	0	17	19	SS
Tignes **	FRA	2100	165	3	80	35	16	2	1	2	4	4	45	36	HR·HS·B·SM·SS
Cervinia	ITA	2050	140	8	18	33	16	7	0	0	0	7	13	13	B·IC·IS·S·SS
La Thuile	ITA	1441	150	3	32	29	12	1	0	0	1	0	17	19	S·SS
Grindelwald	SUI	1050	195	3	15	28	8	1	1	2	1	2	11	7	S·IS·B·SS·T
Saas Fee	SUI	1800	230	2	13	14	7	2	2	1	4	3	1	13	S·T·IS·HS·IC·SS

South of France
Coast with the most

The Cannes Film Festival, Monte Carlo Grand Prix, Châteauneuf-du-Pape… the South of France is where legends are created and stars are born. It's where the world's mega-rich park their palatial launches and strut their stuff along the promenades of glitzy resorts. So not much on offer for families then? Don't you believe it! This venerated strip of Mediterranean coastline may be très posh in places, but it's also irresistibly kid-friendly. Not only is the Côte d'Azur and Languedoc-Rousillon coastline star-studded with coves and beaches, but you won't have to go far inland to find action-packed gorges, wonderful wildlife and a good spattering of Roman ruins and medieval hilltop villages.

Provence-Alpes-Côte d'Azur

The region of Provence-Alpes-Côte d'Azur is one of France's most popular destinations and it's easy to see why. Family holiday staples, like sandy beaches, warm sea and sunshine come in bucket-loads along the French Riviera, but with its head in the Alps and its toes dabbling in the Camargue, adventure is never far away.

Best beaches You're spoilt for choice. The stretch of coast between St Tropez and St Raphael has wonderful coves and beaches – just don't expect to have one all to yourself. Not only does beach towel space become a precious commodity during peak season, but parking can be a challenge too. Your best bet is to arrive early. Family favourites include Plage d'Agay, Cannes Plage, Cassis Plage and Fréjus Plage. All but Plage d'Agay have good sand for building castles. There are also several Aqualand waterparks along the Côte d'Azur, each one with a spaghetti tangle of daredevil waterslides.

Aix-en-Provence There are more than 100 fountains in this elegant town, where you can visit Cézanne's studio, explore the market (Tuesday, Thursday and Saturday) and enjoy a drink in one of the cafés along tree-shaded Cours Mirabeau. The perfect place to introduce kids to a spot of Provençal culture.

Arles A Roman treasure hunt awaits children in this market town on the banks of the Rhône. Corinthian columns and fragments of ancient temples seem to sprout from every street corner. You can't miss the well-preserved amphitheatre (Les Arénes) or the Théâtre Antique, but will you find the remains of the Roman circus where chariots once raced side by side?

Côte d'Azur

Avignon The fortress-like façade of the Palais des Papes dominates this walled city. Explore the maze of medieval streets, take a spin on an antique carousel in Place de l'Horloge, then visit Le Pont d'Avignon for a good old nursery rhyme singalong.

Monaco The tiny principality that thinks big. Teenagers will love ogling the launches gleaming in the harbour, while younger children will enjoy the aquarium at the Musée Océanographique and the glass-bottom boat trips from Quai des États-Unis.

Le Pont du Gard Part of an ambitious Roman scheme to convey water to the city of Nîmes via a 50-km-long aqueduct, Le Pont du Gard is now a World Heritage Site (kids may prefer to think of it as an early attempt to create the ultimate waterslide). The visitor centre has an interactive programme for children aged five to 12 where they can experience life as Gallo-Roman pupils, devise ways of controlling water and become archaeologists and naturalists.during high season.

Languedoc-Rousillon

Best known for the bucket-and-spade appeal of its fine Mediterranean coastline, the Languedoc-Roussillon region has a fascinating hinterland dotted with hilltop castles and impressive abbeys.

Pick of the beaches goes to Argèles-sur-Mer and Cap d'Agde, both with long sandy stretches and the added attractions of waterparks, aquaria, mini-golf and the like.

Inland, you'll find the Cathar castles of Quéribus, Peyrepertuse and Puilaurens – each one perched atop a seemingly unassailable cliff. Young children may find it hard to conquer these largely ruined

Inside info

▶▶ Fly to Nice or take the TGV train from Paris to Avignon.
▶▶ July-August can be stifling, beaches and roads are crammed and prices take a hike; try to visit in cooler, less crowded months.
▶▶ Accommodation ranges from hotels and apartments to campsites and gîtes; consider travelling with another family and renting out a large villa with pool.

♻ **Active** Provence

The Camargue Saddle up and ride a pony or bicycle into the watery wilderness where the Rhône meets the sea. Famous for its white horses, black bulls and pink flamingos, the Camargue is a like a breath of salt-laden fresh air after the flashy resorts along the Côte d'Azur. You can hire your trusty mount at Ste-Maries-de-la-Mer. Pony treks are suitable even for beginners, while the Digue à la Mer is designed for walkers and cyclists. Allow at least half a day to pedal to the lighthouse and the flamingo-nesting site at Étang du Fangassier. Remember to take a pair of binoculars – the Camargue is also home to some 400 other bird species, including ducks, egrets, herons and kingfishers.

Gorges du Verdon Don wetsuits and helmets for a splash through mainland Europe's deepest river gorge. Canyoning (minimum age eight) in France's so-called Grand Canyon provides an epic perspective of sheer cliffs towering 700 m overhead as you negotiate a tortuous river by swimming, abseiling, jumping off waterfalls and sliding down natural water chutes. Other excellent spots for watersports are Gorges de l'Ardèche near Vallon Pont d'Arc and Gorges du Tarn near Parc National des Cévennes.

Parc National du Mercantour An idyllic spot in the Alpes-Maritimes, Mercantour is a refuge for a unique blend of alpine and Mediterranean flora and fauna. It's also prime walking country with opportunities for both short ambles and adventurous hikes.

Camargue flamingos

Corsica Island of adventure (and great beaches)

Corsica seems a world away from the rampant resorts and crowded beaches that stereotype much of the Mediterranean. Although it receives its fair share of summer holidaymakers, this enigmatic island remains one of the truly wild and unspoiled gems of the region. An island of contrasts, Corsica has a kaleidoscope of busy ports and impenetrable pine forests, ancient citadels and plummeting sea cliffs, jagged mountains and sandy beaches. If you're after a family holiday that combines adventure and fun by the sea, then look no further.

In the northwest, the gently shelving bay at Calvi has sunbeds, restaurants and watersports. Nearby Algajola, Île Rousse and Lozari are also popular with families. St Florent has some of the best beaches in the northeast, while Campomoro, Propriano and the coves at Cappiciola are worth checking out in the southwest. With fine white sand and brilliant turquoise water, Palombaggia in the far south is stunning, but can get very busy during the height of summer.

Bonifacio A medieval town perched on 60-m-high limestone cliffs near the southernmost tip of Corsica, Bonifacio rears above a marina packed with gleaming yachts and launches and lined with outdoor restaurants – a far cry from the ninth and 10th centuries when the town thrived on fishing and piracy. Explore the old town, have lunch by the marina, then take a boat trip to gaze up at the lofty citadel.

Les Calanques de Piana Children will enjoy spotting faces and shapes in these weird granite formations on the west coast between Ajaccio and Calvi.

Col de Bavella The long-distance GR20 path traverses Col de Bavella, but for those with less stamina several short walks are also available, including a two-hour jaunt to the Trou de la Bombe, a peculiar 9-m-wide hole that has been eroded through a rock face.

▸▸ You can fly direct from the UK to Bastia or take a ferry (corsica-ferries.fr) from the French or Italian mainland. Crossings take between two and 5½ hours.
▸▸ Daytime temperatures during July and August can exceed 35ºC.
▸▸ A homage to the wind, Festival du Vent (lefestivalduvent.com) takes place in Calvi during October with everything from kite flying to parades.
▸▸ Further information: visit-corsica.com

forts (and parents will want to keep them on a short rein when they see some of the unguarded drops). Adventurous kids, however, will love the challenge (and counting the steps).

For something less crumbly, visit the restored fortress city of Carcassonne (carcassonne-tourisme. com). Guarded by 52 towers and 3 km of battlements, it's an exciting place to roam, despite the crowds and inevitable rash of souvenir shops. Beyond the main entrance (Port Narbonnaise) lies a medieval mishmash of narrow streets. The 12th-century Château Comtal is worth exploring, as is the Gothic St-Nazaire basilica. In the lower town, an interactive museum called Im@ginarium brings the Middle Ages to life. A short distance outside Carcassonne, Lac de la Cavayère provides light relief in the form of swimming and pedal boats.

Fortified city of Carcassone

Normandy beach in summer

Go green
Four ways to skip the flight

❶ Sail across the Channel with P&O Ferries (poferries. com) from Dover to Calais (70-90 minutes) or with Brittany Ferries (brittanyferries.com) from Portsmouth to Caen (six hours), Portsmouth to St-Malo (8½ hours), Poole or Portsmouth to Cherbourg (three-four hours); Fastcraft 2¼ hours) or Plymouth to Roscoff (five hours). Speed Ferries (speed.ferries.org) has a 50-minute Dover-Boulogne service, while Transmanche Ferries (transmancheferries. com) operates from Newhaven to Dieppe and Portsmouth to Le Havre.

❷ Take your car through the Eurotunnel (eurotunnel. com) from Folkestone to Calais in just 35 minutes. Shuttle trains depart up to four times an hour.

❸ Hop on Eurostar (eurostar.com) from St Pancras International for high-speed trains direct to Paris, Lille, Avignon, Disneyland Paris and the French Alps.

❹ Catch a bus with Eurolines (eurolines.co.uk) from London's Victoria Coach Station to Paris, via Eurotunnel or ferry.

When to go
Spring is an ideal time to visit **Paris** – the days are getting longer and temperatures haven't reached the muggy extremes of high summer. In fact, many Parisians flee the city during August to escape the heat. The capital has plenty of festive sparkle during December, which is also a good time to visit **Strasbourg**'s Christmas market. Skiing in the **Alps** is best from January to March, although summer is also a wonderful time to visit the mountains, with alpine meadows in full bloom, plenty of warmth and sunshine and no shortage of lakes to swim in. The **South of France** has hot, dry Mediterranean summers – too hot for some families who might prefer the milder **Atlantic coast** (albeit with its less predictable sunshine). The best time to visit **Corsica** is from May to early July and September to October. Weather forecasts for various French regions can be found at france.meteofrance.com.

Getting there
Through its SkyTeam Alliance network, Air France (airfrance.com) connects destinations in 85 countries via its hub at Paris Charles de Gaulle (CDG) airport. The national carrier also serves 25 cities in France. British Airways (britishairways.com) has flights to Bordeaux, Chambery (winter only), Lyon, Marseille, Nice, Paris and Toulouse. Low-cost airlines operating between the UK and France include easyJet (easyjet.com), Ryanair (ryanair.com), Flybe (flybe.com) and BmiBaby (bmibaby.com).

Getting around
Driving in France is a pleasure thanks to its comprehensive road network, although venturing by car into Paris is not recommended. The autoroute system has service stations at approximately 40-km intervals and *aires* (rest areas with toilets and recreation areas but no food or fuel services) every 10 km. Car rental companies include Avis (avis.fr), Europcar (europcar.fr) and Hertz (hertz.fr).

France has a modern and fast **rail** system. Take Eurostar to Paris, connect with TGV (tgv.com), France's high-speed train service, and you could be in Marseille or Bordeaux just three hours later. Regional express trains, known as TER, connect smaller towns. You can book an InterRail pass, allowing unlimited travel on three, four, six or eight days in one month from Rail Europe (raileurope.co.uk).

Getting around in cities is usually very straightforward and economical thanks to efficient Métro, bus and tram systems.

Accommodation

The most popular family options are either to rent a **gîte** (a self-catering cottage or house) or to stay at a **holiday park** in a mobile home or pre-pitched tent. A directory of accredited gîtes is administered by Gîtes de France (gites-de-france.fr). Available during the school holidays, a carefully selected range of children's *gîtes* organizes special activities for kids aged four to 15. Companies specializing in cottage and villa rental in France include Allez France (allezfrance.com), Dominiques Villas (dominiquesvillas.co.uk), Rentals France (rentalsfrance.com) and VFB Holidays (vfbholidays.co.uk). For something really special, try Simply Château (simplychateau.co.uk) which has over 200 French châteaux and castles for rent – many of them with swimming pools.

Camping France (campingfrance.com) has an online reservation system for over 10,000 campsites. As well as searching by region, you can select various criteria, such as sites with kids' clubs or beach access or waterparks. Many of the most popular holiday parks have superb facilities, including well-equipped mobile homes, swimming pools and waterslides, entertainment programmes and sports. Try Canvas Holidays (canvasholidays.com), Eurocamp (eurocamp.com), Keycamp (keycamp.ie) and Siblu (siblu.com). Treehouses with one double and three single beds are Keycamp's new twist at the International parc in Paris.

Center Parcs (centerparcs.com) has four villages in France, while organized adventure holidays are available with Acorn Venture Holidays (acorn-venture.com) and PGL (pgl.co.uk). Esprit (esprit-holidays.co.uk) and Mark Warner (markwarner.co.uk) are two of the leading family specialists in winter and summer holidays in the French Alps, while Club Med (clubmed.com) has an all-inclusive resort with children's facilities in Provence, as well as a new ski resort in Valmorel.

Food & drink

The French love their food and you'll find everything from informal brasseries and family-run bistros cooking local dishes to Michelin-starred restaurants serving nouvelle cuisine. To save money, have your main meal at lunchtime when many restaurants serve a *menu du jour* for around half what it might cost in the evening. Be brave and introduce your kids to a few regional specialities. Along the **Brittany** and **Normandy** coasts, *assiette de fruits de mer* is a seafood platter of crayfish, oysters, prawns, mussels, crab and whelks which kids will enjoy dissecting even if they don't eat much. A sure hit from this region, though, are crêpes and galettes

– pancakes with either sweet or savoury fillings. *Tarte tatin*, upside-down apple tart, should also go down a treat. **Mediterranean** dishes are some of the tastiest of all. Anything '*á la provençale*' promises a delicious concoction of olive oil, garlic, tomatoes, onions and herbs. Duck and goose dishes feature prominently in **southwest France** and the **Pyrenees** – too rich for many kids, but as with anywhere in France, you'll always find standard fare like steak-frites. In the **Alps**, cheese fondues and *gratin dauphinois* (sliced potatoes baked in cream) are always popular with children, while traditional lamb stew and *fiadone* (lemon cheesecake) should tempt them in **Corsica**.

Health & safety

The sun can be strong in France during midsummer, so pack plenty of high-factor suncream and make sure children get some shade during the middle of the day. Mosquitoes can be irritating in some areas, so it's also a good idea to take insect repellent.

Holiday operators

The Adventure Company
adventurecompany.co.uk

Belle France
bellefrance.co.uk

The Big Domain
thebigdomain.com

CV Travel cvtravel.co.uk

Canvas Holidays
canvasholidays.co.uk

Center Parcs
centerparcs.com

Club Med clubmed.com

Corsican Places
corsica.co.uk

Crystal Holidays
crystalholidays.co.uk

Esprit Holidays
esprit-holidays.co.uk

Eurocamp
eurocamp.co.uk

Exodus exodus.co.uk

Explore explore.co.uk

Families Worldwide
familiesworldwide.co.uk

Headwater
headwater.com

Inntravel inntravel.co.uk

Keycamp
keycamp.co.uk

Kirker Holidays
kirkerholidays.com

The Kids and Me
thekidsandme.co.uk

Leisure Direction
leisuredirection.co.uk

Mark Warner
markwarner.co.uk

Neilson Active Holidays
neilson.co.uk

PGL pgl.co.uk

Peak Retreats
peakretreats.co.uk

Pierre Vacances
pv-holidays.com

Powder Byrne
powderbyrne.co.uk

Scott Dunn
scottdunn.com

Siblu siblu.com

Simply Château
simplychateau.co.uk

Sovereign sovereign.com

Travelbeam
travelbeam.co.uk

Vintage Travel
vintagetravel.co.uk

Wake up in France
wakeupinfrance.co.uk

Fast facts

Time GMT+1
Language French
Currency Euro (€)
Dialling code +33
Tourist information france.guide.com

Château des Ormes
Where? Dol-de-Bretagne, Brittany.
Why? Lively holiday park set in 100 ha of château parkland with 18-hole golf course, waterpark with four-lane waterslide, indoor pool complex and all-weather football pitch. Children's clubs are available for toddlers through to teenagers and there is an extensive activity programme.
Contact Keycamp Holidays, T+44 (0)844-406 0200, keycamp.co.uk
Also try... other Keycamp sites in Brittany, such as Les Menhirs at Carnac Plage or De la Baie at La Trinité-sur-Mer.

La Baume
Where? Fréjus, French Riviera.
Why? Well-equipped parc with every amenity imaginable, from Fun Stations for kids aged four and above to a soundproof disco for over-16s. On-site activities include tennis, archery and cycling and there are lovely beaches nearby if you can tear yourself away from the parc's two pool complexes.
Contact Eurocamp, T+44 (0)844-406 0402, eurocamp.co.uk
Also try... Eurocamp's Esterel site at St Raphael.

Domaine de Dugny
Where? Blois, Loire Valley.
Why? Four-star parc in the heart of the Loire Valley with indoor and outdoor pools, children's play areas, archery, bike hire, boules, crazy golf, fishing, pedalos, table tennis, volleyball and free football tournaments for all age groups. Holiday extras include baby packs and free children's clubs for kids aged one to 14.
Contact Siblu, T+44 (0)871-911 2288, siblu.com
Also try... Siblu's Domaine de Litteau site in Normandy or La Carabasse in Languedoc.

Disneyland Hotel
Where? Disneyland Paris.
Why? Ultimate Disneyland hotel right in the heart of the Magic Kingdom. Facilities include an indoor pool, spa and Club Minnie playroom. Guests receive a FastPass and have plenty of opportunities for meet 'n' greet sessions with Disney characters.
Contact Disneyland Paris, hotels.disneylandparis.co.uk
Also try... Disney's Hotel New York, Newport Bay Club, Sequoia Lodge, Hotel Cheyenne, Hotel Santa Fe and Davy Crockett Ranch.

Country Kids
Where? Herault, near Montpelier.
Why? With its drop-in crèche, splash-pool, play area and petting farm this stylish self-catering accommodation also has a huge range of nursery and play equipment on hand. The grounds include a tennis court, heated swimming pool and a farm shop fully stocked with homemade meals. Two free activities are included per guest.
Contact Baby Friendly Boltholes, T+44 (0)845-489 0140, babyfriendlyboltholes.co.uk

" The Vendée region of France boasts over 200 sunshine-filled days a year, endless stretches of safe, sandy beach and an excellent range of family accommodation. It's also an easy drive from channel ports, so the kids can be building sandcastles and getting stuck into water sports from day one. 101familyholidays.co.uk

Villa du Lac
Where? Lac de Cazaux, Atlantic coast.
Why? Located close to surfing beaches and the famous Dune du Pyla, this comfortable family base has four bedrooms, a fitted kitchen, living/dining room and 10-m swimming pool. Shops and restaurants are an easy walk away.
Contact French Affair, T+44 (0)207-616 9990, affairtravel.com
Also try... French Affair's Villa Larros, a magnificent villa near Gujan-Mestras and the harbour of Larros.

Les Hauts de Bruyères
Where? Loir et Cher.
Why? Special features include the Experience Factory (with mini golf, play areas, crêperie etc), subtropical waterpark, Aqua Sana spa and a forest assault course using a network of suspended bridges, beams and lianas.
Contact Center Parcs, T+31 (0)10-498 9754, centerparcs.com
Also try... Center Parcs' Le Lac d'Ailette, located close to Paris and Disneyland and with Canadian-style villas and a lakeside setting.

Opio en Provence
Where? Nice, Provence.
Why? Tucked into olive groves and pine forests, this all-inclusive resort boasts luxurious accommodation and a wide range of facilities, including four swimming pools, Turkish and Roman baths, golf course, kids' clubs, Circus School, and teen-only spaces.
Contact Club Med, T+44 (0)871-424 4044, clubmed.co.uk
Also try... other Club Med resorts, such as La Palmyre Atlantique on the Arvi Peninsula or Cargèse, Corsica.

Villa Chavaz
Where? Cappiciolo, Corsica.
Why? This beautifully situated beachside villa (sleeping up to six) overlooks Valinco Gulf and has a path leading through its garden to a secluded sandy beach. The resort of Propriano is just a 20-minute drive away.
Contact Corsican Places, T+44 (0)845-330 2059, corsica.co.uk
Also try... Coriscan Places' other villas, like Bergerie Murtetu, perched on a mountainside near Olmeto with its own pool.

The beach beckons

Praia de Odeceixe on the
Algarve's Atlantic coast.

Spain & Portugal

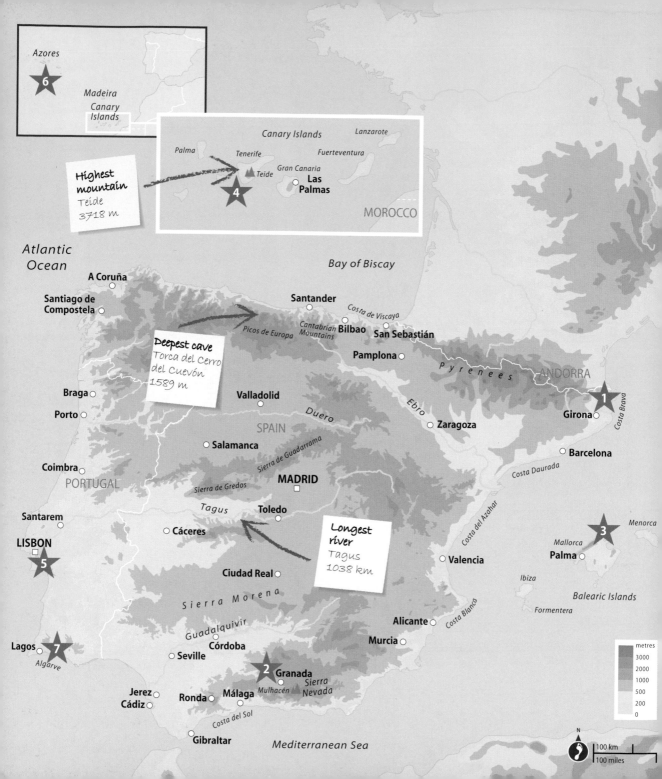

Azores

6

Madeira

Canary
Islands

Canary Islands

Lanzarote

Palma

Tenerife

Fuerteventura

Gran Canaria

Teide

**Las
Palmas**

4

MOROCCO

**Highest
mountain**
Teide
3718 m

Atlantic
Ocean

Bay of Biscay

A Coruña

**Santiago de
Compostela**

Santander

Costa de Viscaya

Bilbao

Picos de Europa

Cantabrian
Mountains

San Sebastián

Pamplona

Pyrenees

ANDORRA

Deepest cave
Torca del Cerro
del Cuevón
1589 m

Braga

Valladolid

Duero

Ebro

Zaragoza

1

Girona

Costa Brava

Porto

SPAIN

Salamanca

Barcelona

Coimbra

Sierra de Guadarrama

Costa Daurada

PORTUGAL

Sierra de Gredos

MADRID

3

Menorca

Santarem

Tagus

Toledo

Costa del Azahar

Mallorca

LISBON

Cáceres

**Longest
river**
Tagus
1038 km

Palma

5

Valencia

Ibiza

Balearic Islands

Ciudad Real

Formentera

Sierra Morena

Alicante

Costa Blanca

Guadalquivir

Murcia

Lagos

7

Córdoba

Algarve

Seville

2

Granada

Jerez

Ronda

Málaga

Mulhacén

Sierra
Nevada

Cádiz

Costa del Sol

Gibraltar

Mediterranean Sea

metres

3000
2000
1000
500
200
0

N

100 km
100 miles

Introduction
Spain & Portugal

With its stunning beaches, almost-guaranteed sunshine and excellent value for money, it's not hard to see why Spain is such a popular family holiday destination. And while Portugal has less in the way of beach resorts and nightlife than its Iberian neighbour, it's still a friendly, fun place to take kids. Don't be put off by the reputation of certain Costas and islands for crowded beaches and rowdy nightlife. You can always find smaller, quieter resorts or travel in the low season – particularly to year-round destinations like the Canary Islands. There are also plenty of opportunities for getting off the beaten track, from roaming the Spanish steppes of Extremadura to island-hopping through the mid-Atlantic archipelago of the Azores. And if that sounds too taxing (or too far from the beach) there is always scope for adding an adventurous twist to a traditional seaside holiday – whether you combine northern Spain's coast with some action-packed days in the mountains of the Picos de Europa or head inland from the Costa del Sol on a cultural quest to Granada and Seville.

> **Up in the foothills of the Sierra Nevada, the tracks linking the villages and pastures provided ideal avenues of exploration for our children. We passed men leading donkeys and working threshing machines, while just 40 minutes away were the busy resorts of the Costa del Sol.** Mike Wynne

○ Did you know?

★ La Tomatina, the world's biggest, stickiest food fight, originated in 1944 when irreverent bystanders pelted a civic procession with tomatoes. This fruity climax to Buñol's annual festival gets larger and messier each year.

★ Spain produces over a million tonnes of olives every year – more than any other country. Most of it is pulped for olive oil.

★ The Iberian Peninsula has Europe's two highest capitals – Andorra la Vella (1300 m) and Madrid (650 m).

Star rating

Wow factor	★★
Worry factor	★
Value for money	★★★★★
Keeping teacher happy	★★
Family accommodation	★★★★★
Babies & toddlers	★★★★★
Cool for teenagers	★★★★

How to be a super snorkeller

The coasts and islands of Spain are great places to learn how to snorkel, particularly sheltered rocky coves teeming with fish and other marine life. Before you take the plunge, however, follow these simple steps to happy, safe and leakproof snorkelling.

❶ Get gear that fits
Hold the mask up to your face and breathe in through your nose. If it sticks to your face when you take your hands away, it fits. Choose a snorkel with a mouthpiece that isn't so big it hurts your gums. Fins should be snug, not tight.

❷ A bit of spit
To stop the inside of your mask misting over, rub a little spit, a dab of toothpaste or a drop of baby shampoo over the glass, then rinse thoroughly.

❸ Practise in the bath
Much more fun than plastic ducks or bubble mixture, a snorkel lesson in the bath will help you get used to breathing through a snorkel. Make sure the mask strap is high on the back of your head and not too tight. Put the snorkel mouthpiece all the way in your mouth and close your lips around it.

❹ Ready for the sea
Start in a calm, shallow area. Lie face down and relax. For extra buoyancy wear a lifejacket or wetsuit. Make sure you're happy with everything before you swim out of your depth.

❺ Clearing water
If water seeps into your mask, tread water and pull the lower edge of the mask away from your face to allow it to drain out. A burst of air should shoot any water out of your snorkel.

❻ Fin like a mermaid
Use a relaxed, 'fluttering' kick with your flippers. If you're doing it right, there should not be too much splashing.

❼ Don't overdo it
Every few minutes lift your head above the surface to check that currents haven't taken you too far from the shore. Always be aware of boats in the area and stay well clear of breaking waves. Remember, it's far more rewarding to fin gently over one small area, observing the life below you, than to fin madly, see nothing and risk leg cramps.

❽ Be sun smart
Wear a surf vest with built-in sun protection, smother the back of your neck and legs with waterproof sunblock and avoid snorkelling during the middle of the day.

Kids' top 7
tapas nibbles

❶ Almendras Fried and salted almonds.

❷ Calamares fritos Fried squid rings and tentacles.

❸ Chorizo Sausage with paprika and garlic.

❹ Costillas Spare ribs.

❺ Croquetas Fried ham, chicken or fish croquettes.

❻ Diabolitos picantes Spicy mini hamburgers.

❼ Soldaditos de Pavia Cod fingers fried in batter.

Craft like Picasso

▸ Take a look at some of Picasso's famous paintings. Notice the way that he sometimes painted pictures of faces with lots of different views. The book *Draw with Pablo Picasso* (Frances Lincoln) is a good source of inspiration.
▸ Take a piece of modelling clay (the kind that doesn't need to be kiln-dried) about the size of a tennis ball. Flatten and roll it to make a circle, around 4 cm thick.

▸ Use clay tools to draw a line from the top to the bottom of the circle that shows a side view (or profile) of a face.
▸ On the other side of the line, draw one eye facing forward.
▸ Add raised features such as lips, eyebrows and a nose also facing forward on that side.
▸ Score, or make little marks, with your clay tool and then use a wet finger to help seal the

features in place.
▸ At the top of the face make 10 holes for adding hair later.
▸ Allow the clay to dry completely before painting; then insert pipe cleaners into the holes to create wacky hair.

Great reads
6 books for kids

Ages 5+
Prince of the Birds
(Frances Lincoln)
Ahmed, Prince of Granada, lives in a high
tower. Through his ability to communicate
with birds he finds true love in the form of
a princess locked in a faraway tower. To win
her hand he must conquer his fears before
they finally escape on a flying carpet.

The Life and Work of Salvador Dalí
(Heinemann)
Delve into the surreal world of Spanish
painter, Salvador Dalí – well known for his
weird and wonderful paintings.

The Story of Ferdinand
(Penguin)
The endearing tale of a bull who would
much rather sit under a cork tree smelling
the flowers than enter the bullfighting ring.

Ages 7+
**Ferdinand Magellan and the First
Voyage around the World**
(Chelsea House)
A biography of the daring Portuguese
sea captain who commanded the first
expedition that sailed around the world.

With Love from Spain, Melanie Martin
(Yearling)
In this diary of her holiday in Spain, 11-year-
old Melanie dances flamenco, tries Spanish
food, visits museums and falls in love.

Asterix in Spain
(Orion)
When Pepe, the kidnapped son of a
Spanish chief, escapes from his Roman
captors, who should find him but those
indomitable Gauls, Astérix and Obélix.

Kids' stuff
Spain & Portugal

Taste of Spain gazpacho

What you need
» 1 kg plum tomatoes
» 1 small onion
» 1 small green pepper
» 1 small chubby cucumber
» 1 small cup olive oil
» 4 tsp vinegar
» 200 g white bread soaked
in water
» salt and pepper
» glass of water (optional)
» garlic cloves, peeled and
crushed
» bowl of diced tomatoes, red
and green peppers, cucumber,
onion and croutons to garnish

What to do
» Blend the tomatoes, onion, pepper, cucumber, vinegar, bread
and oil in a food mixer.
» Add the water and garlic to suit your own taste; the water will
make it less strong, while the garlic will make it stronger.
» Add salt and pepper to taste and put the mixture in a bowl.
Chill for at least an hour, the colder the better (you can add ice
cubes if you like).
» Serve in bowls with side dishes of the diced vegetables and
croutons for people to add themselves.

🐾 Puppy power

A living sculpture sustained by an internal irrigation
system, the Puppy sits obediently outside Bilbao's
extraordinary Guggenheim Museum (guggenheim-
bilbao.es) in northern Spain, where it contrasts with the
museum's titanium-clad façade. Inside, you'll find cutting-edge
art and design exhibitions. Check the website for details of
children's workshops where you can use fun artistic techniques
and a wide range of materials to create your own sculptures.

> ❝ ❞ As soon as I got in the water and put my head under, there were dolphins everywhere, making clicking noises and moving around a lot. I saw six in front of me playing. It was really good. The sea was very deep!
> Henry (age 10)

Planning a family holiday to Spain, Portugal or any of their islands is not only straightforward but can also offer excellent value for money. Accommodation ranges from self-catering apartments and resort hotels to holiday villages with tents and mobile homes, while food covers everything from burgers and pizzas to tapas bars where children can try lots of small traditional dishes. Although you will usually find a friendly welcome wherever you go, the Portuguese have a special weakness for children – particularly babies and toddlers. Children in Spain and Portugal are treated like mini-adults and it's not unusual to see them in restaurants with their parents late at night.

Babies

Avoid the hot and crowded summer season – it will still be warm enough in spring and autumn to enjoy Spain's Mediterranean resorts. The main resort beaches have play areas, while babysitting is usually available in the larger hotels. High chairs are not always common, so consider bringing a collapsible travel seat that attaches to a chair.

Toddlers/pre-school

The quietest resorts include Llafranc on the Costa Brava, San Pedro de Alcántara on the Costa del Sol and

Swim with wild dolphins

The Dolphin Connection (dolphinconnectionexperience. com) offers holidays swimming with wild dolphins in the Azores, where it is not uncommon to meet pods of up to 200 individuals. Each seven-day trip (Apr-Oct) includes five three-hour boat trips. The recommended minimum age is seven years old and all children (and adults) are given snorkel training in a pool prior to venturing into the open ocean. Professionally trained guides (with RLSS Aquatic Rescue certification) are always on hand to help children develop snorkelling confidence, while local experts provide talks on the biology and conservation of the archipelago's renowned whales and dolphins.

Dénia on the Costa Blanca. In the Balearics, Menorca is the most laid-back island for young families. There are some excellent beaches on the Algarve, although some are strafed by strong Atlantic currents and winds – fine for beachcombing and playing chicken with the waves, but dangerous for swimming.

If you are unfazed by the longer flight, the Canary Islands are an ideal choice for toddlers. With warm, sunny weather year-round, you can travel outside the busy school-holiday season and still enjoy good beach weather. For ultimate flexibility, opt for a self-catering apartment and hire car; for onsite facilities choose a family resort.

Kids/school age

Although you are restricted to busier school-holiday periods with this age group, crowded beaches at least provide guaranteed playmates for your children. They will also be able to enjoy a wide range of beach-based activities, from snorkelling to trips in glass-bottom boats. Popular tourist spots always have a waterpark (Siam Park in Tenerife being one of the largest and most spectacular) and there are also several excellent theme parks, such as PortAventura on the Costa Daurada.

Rather than restricting yourselves entirely to the beach, however, consider a trip that combines the

Special needs

Most tourist offices can provide information on accessible accommodation. Disabled holiday specialists Can be Done (canbedone.co.uk) list several properties in Spain and Portugal that offer facilities such as wheel-in showers and pool hoists. Also try Accessible Travel & Leisure (accessibletravel.co.uk).

Single parents

One-parent family holiday specialists Single Parents on Holiday (singleparentsonholiday.co.uk) offer trips to mainland Spain and the Canary Islands, while Mango (mangokids.co.uk) runs single-parent holidays in Mallorca and Andorra. Try Eurocamp (eurocamp.co.uk) for single-parent discounts on holidays to the Costa Brava, Costa del Sol, northern Spain and the Algarve.

> " " **I love Spain because it's always hot. I love walking along the sandy beaches collecting seashells. And I also love eating swordfish.** Lottie Gale (age 6)

coast with the mountains. In northern Spain, for example, a week or so relaxing on Cantabria's lovely sandy bays can easily be followed by a multi-activity adventure in the mountains of the Picos de Europa, while southern Spain's Costa del Sol combines well with walking or horse-riding trips in the Sierra Nevada. If you just want a taster of the high ground, try Tenerife where a day or two clambering about on the volcanic slopes in Teide National Park will give kids a real sense of achievement.

Educationally, Spain's premier museums and galleries are in Madrid – quite a sophisticated destination for kids until you factor the Warner Bros theme park into the equation. For an insight into the country's history and culture you could also combine the Spanish capital with Extremadura, but you'll need an itinerary that's short and sweet to keep kids interested. Valencia's super-modern City of Arts and Sciences is a guaranteed hit with children, as is Lisbon's Parque das Nações with its superb oceanarium.

Teenagers

If it's lively beach resorts you're after, Spain has them in bucket loads – although you should steer clear of the rowdiest fleshpots on Ibiza or along the Costa Blanca. As well as buzzing nightlife and a similarly aged,

like-minded crowd to hang out with, most teenagers are up for a sporty challenge whether it's learning how to sail, windsurf or waterski. And when the beaches begin to pall, there are always the waterparks, theme parks and shops – particularly in cities like Barcelona, which teenagers will love for its trendy vibe and wacky art scene.

For multi-activity breaks, Explore Worldwide (explore.co.uk) has dedicated teenage departures to the Spanish Pyrenees.

Telling tales Dan Linstead

Editor, *Wanderlust* | wanderlust.co.uk

The best beach I know for young families is the Praio do Barril near Tavira in Portugal's Eastern Algarve. It's a great long stretch of vanilla sand, with thatched umbrellas for hire, clean showers and toilets, and a big, shady outdoor restaurant where you can always get a table. But its trump card for kids is simple and overwhelming: you reach it by taking a five-minute miniature train ride across the lagoon. Toot toot!

Central Spain may be a long way from the beach, but there is still enough in this region to keep children happy on holiday. At first glance, Madrid's reputation for fine art doesn't exactly make it an easy sell to kids. If you're desperate to see the capital's famous Prado, Thyssen or Reina Sofía galleries, you'll need to dangle a pretty tempting carrot under your children's noses – preferably in the form of the Warner Bros Park south of the city. Once you've seen some of Madrid's traditional (and not so traditional) highlights head west to Extremadura, an unspoilt region with fascinating birdlife and history (but alas, still no Costas).

Madrid

City highlights If you have time to visit just one of Madrid's three world-class art museums, the Museo del Prado (museodelprado.es) should be top of your list. Inside you'll find a wealth of paintings by Spanish masters Goya and Velázquez, as well as an impressive collection of Italian and Flemish works. Highlights for children include *Las Meninas* by Velázquez, in which the infant Margarita is fussed over by her ladies-in-waiting. Goya's so-called Black Paintings may be too harrowing for young children – although some teenagers will probably delight in the gross-factor of *Saturn Devouring his Son*. Also worth tracking down is Caravaggio's *David Victorious over Goliath*, an exquisite study in light and shadow.

For more art appreciation, head to the Museo Nacional Centro de Arte Reina Sofía (museoreinasofia.es) to see Picasso's anti-war masterpiece *Guernica*, or to the Museo Thyssen-Bornemisza (museothyssen.org) to study paintings by Rembrandt, Raphael and others.

A short walk from the galleries, the Parque del Retiro has plenty of space to run around, as well as boats to hire on the lake and a Sunday afternoon puppet show. On the opposite side of central Madrid, you'll find Palacio Real (patrimonionacional.es), Madrid's extravagant Royal Palace with its lavishly decorated dining hall and throne room.

From central Madrid, take the metro west to Batán to reach Casa de Campo, a former royal hunting ground that's home to Parque de Atracciones (parquedeatracciones.es), an amusement park with

Museo del Prado

hanging roller coasters, free-fall rides and water chutes. The Tranquillity Zone offers more relaxing activities such as a jungle boat cruise, while younger children have their own special area with roller coasters, water rides and puppet theatres.

Also in Casa de Campo, Parque Zoológico (zoomadrid.com) has everything from koalas and tigers to dolphins and sharks, while Faunia Madrid (reached by taking the metro east to Valdebernardo) recreates various ecosystems, from polar to tropical.

For waterparks with slides, try Aquópolis de Villanueva de la Canada or Aquópolis de San Fernando de Henares (aquopolis.es).

Warner Bros Park
San Martín de la Vega, T902-024100, parquewarner.com. Mar-Nov, from 1100 (days and times vary) ▶▶ A short bus or train ride south of Madrid city centre
Warner Bros Park is divided into five themed areas. Peruse the shops, cafés and cinemas along Hollywood Boulevard before witnessing a spectacular stunt show at Movie World Studios. Some of the biggest rides can be found in Superheroes World, including The Vengeance of the Enigma – a 100-m vertical tower drop (minimum height: 130 cm) and the 90-km/h Superman roller coaster (minimum height: 132 cm). Old West Territory keeps the adrenaline pumping with a giant wooden roller coaster and various water rides. Cartoon Village, meanwhile, is where you can meet Tweety, Bugs Bunny and other Looney Tunes characters, and ride the Correcaminous Bip Bip – a roller coaster based on the Roadrunner (minimum height: 130 cm). Gentle rides for little ones include Scooby-Doo spinning cups, while the park's loudest screams are usually generated by the 106-km/h Stunt Fall coaster (minimum height: 137 cm).

Spot storks
White storks nest on church towers and rooftops throughout Extremadura – a remote and little-visited region of central Spain. In Parque Natural de Monfragüe, the Peña Falcón provides a suitably precipitous nesting site for griffon, Egyptian and rare black vultures which you can observe from viewpoints along the road opposite. Elsewhere in the park, easy walking trails probe the bird-rich oak woods and grasslands of the *dehesa*.

Stretching from the Pyrenean foothills to the crinkle-cut shoreline of Galicia, the Atlantic coast of northern Spain has everything from rugged cliffs to sandy bays, fishing villages and holiday resorts. What it doesn't have, though, is the almost guaranteed heat and sunshine of the Mediterranean Costas: a small price to pay, perhaps, for less crowded beaches and quieter resorts. But northern Spain appeals to families in search of more than sun, sand and sea. Lush broadleaf forests sweep up the flanks of the Cantabrian Mountains, with adventure-rich national parks like Picos de Europa just a short distance inland. There are also caves to be explored – many with prehistoric paintings – while a wonderful procession of cathedrals, churches and monuments mark the pilgrimage route to Santiago de Compostela.

Langre beach in Cantabria

Vizcayan Coast

Stretching east from the busy commercial port of Bilbao, the rugged Basque coastline has a long history of fishing, and at the Museo del Pescador in Bermeo you can catch the whole story, from whales to anchovies. Just beyond Bermeo the coastal road diverts inland following a scenic route along the west bank of the Oka River estuary to Gernika. It was here in 1937 that German and Italian planes unleashed a devastating bombing raid, killing over 1600 people – an outrage vividly portrayed in Picasso's powerful *Guernica* painting on display in Madrid (see opposite).

A few kilometres north, the Cuevas de Santimamiñe are worth a visit, although the chamber with the prehistoric cave drawings of bison is closed to the public. Cantabria's caves (see right) might be more satisfying. Following the west bank of the estuary back to the coast, you reach Mundaka, an attractive old harbour town renowned for its long surf break. Continuing east, Lekeitio has a couple of good beaches, but for the ultimate Basque holiday resort look no further than San Sebastián (sansebastianturismo.com). Surrounded by hills and overlooking the beautiful horseshoe bay of La Concha, San Sebastián has loads for kids to do – from swimming and sailing to ogling sharks in the aquarium near the town's old quarter.

Cantabria

A region blessed with a heady mixture of golden-sand beaches (particularly at Laredo and Santander) and a spectacular mountainous hinterland, Cantabria not only has the best of northern Spain's scenery, but it also has the added attraction of some fascinating prehistoric caves. The most famous of these are the Cuevas de Altamira (museodealtamira.mcu.es) where charcoal and ochre images of bison, deer and horses festoon a rock face. In order to protect the original drawings (created by Cro-Magnon communities up to 14,000 years ago) a replica of the cave is open to visitors. For a glimpse of the real thing head to Cuevas del Castillo, a des-res for cave dwellers from as early as 130,000 years ago. Here you can see animal drawings as well as some 50 hand prints. Kids will also enjoy the nearby Cabárceno Wildlife Park where African elephants, rhinos and other exotic beasts roam a 750-ha swathe of the Peña Cabarga Nature Reserve.

For a proper taste of northern Spain's great outdoors, though, you need to set your sights on the Parque Nacional de los Picos de Europa. Easily accessed from either Santander or the Asturian town of Oviedo, this dramatic chunk of the Cordillera Cantábrica is home to vultures, eagles, chamois, wolves and bears, as well as a dazzling array of butterflies and orchids. The riverside village of Potes makes a good base. You will find several adventure operators here (offering activities ranging from mountain biking, whitewater rafting and horse riding to paragliding and 4WD tours), while nearby Fuente Dé is the setting for a dramatic cable-car ride.

Galicia

The coast to the north of this westernmost province of Spain, especially the Costa da Morte, is wild and windswept – fine for a scenic drive and an invigorating picnic on a headland, but not exactly what you'd call child-friendly. Instead, head for the Rías Baixas on Galicia's southwest coast. This series of deep inlets has a milder climate and safer beaches, especially at the resort of Panxón. There are good watersports facilities at Vilagarcia de Arousa, while the tiny island of A Toxa is worth a visit to see its church, which is covered in scallop shells.

Northern Spain
Caves, costas & mountains

Inside info

▶▶ Sail to Bilbao or Santander with Brittany Ferries (brittany-ferries.com) and you stand a chance of spotting whales and dolphins in the Bay of Biscay.
▶▶ Inland from Bilbao, Pamplona is renowned for its annual fiesta, Los Sanfermines (July), in which bulls stampede through the frenzied, crowded streets of the city.
▶▶ For further information, visit euskadi.net, infoasturias.com, turismodecantabria.com and turgalicia.es.

A superb family holiday destination, Catalonia caters for all ages, whether you have 10-year-olds in search of mountain adventure, teenagers in search of city chic or toddlers in search of sand and sea. Rivalling Madrid for cultural importance, child-friendly Barcelona is the vibrant capital of this diverse region which stretches from the 3000-m peaks of the Pyrenees to the sandy bays of the Costa Daurada. One of Europe's original package-holiday destinations, Catalonia's rugged Costa Brava continues to draw the crowds, while inland attractions include the mesmerizing Monastery of Montserrat.

Barcelona

Day 1 Start at Plaça de Catalunya, a large square at the heart of the city, and walk down La Rambla, a 1-km-long pedestrian thoroughfare adorned with colourful pavement mosaics and thronging with cafés, bird and flower stalls, buskers, street artists and spray-painted human statues. About halfway down you can detour to the left to see Barcelona's magnificent Gothic Cathedral. At the end of La Rambla, take the lift up the Monument a Colom where Christopher Columbus stands atop an 80-m column. The views are spectacular. You'll be able to see the dramatic and otherworldly spires of Gaudí's Sagrada Família (although you should schedule time for a close-up visit to this extraordinary church).

From the Monument a Colom, stroll a little way along Avinguda de les Drassanes to Museu Marítim (mmb.cat) where Barcelona's seafaring tradition is brought to life with imaginative exhibits and special effects. Nearby at Port Vell, admire the beautiful schooner, *Santa Eulàlia*, before walking across the pontoon of Rambla de Mar to visit L'Aquarium (aquariumbcn.com) – one of Europe's largest, with a walk-through shark tank.

Other attractions in Port Vell include an IMAX cinema, the submarine *Ictíneo II* and the Museu d'Història de Catalunya (en.mhcat.net), a child-friendly museum that allows children to experience Catalan history through dressing up and role-play. Boat trips are available with Las Golondrinas (lasgolondrinas. com) and on the catamaran *Orsom* (barcelona-orsom. com), while sandy beaches with play areas and cafés can be found at both Port Vell and Port Olímpic.

For something more peaceful, make for the green oasis of Parc de la Ciutadella just to the east of Port Vell. Here you'll find a boating lake, a fountain and shady paths to explore, as well as the Parc Zoològic

with its dolphin shows, pony rides, adventure playground and children's farm.

Day 2 Take the metro to Paral.lel from where a funicular connects with the cable-car station on Avinguda de Miramar. A thrilling ride up Montjuïc Hill leads to Castell de Montjuïc with its far-reaching views of the city. There's a military museum inside the castle, although most kids will be happy enough exploring the gardens, which are littered with ancient cannon.

On the opposite side of Parc de Montjuïc, the majestic Palau Nacional houses the Museu Nacional d'Art de Catalunya (mnac.es), renowned for its Romanesque church frescos. Admittedly, children will be more captivated by the cascades and fountains outside, but if you're determined to instil some cultural appreciation there's always the nearby Poble Espanyol (poble-espanyol.com), an open-air museum with streets, squares, buildings and monuments from around Spain. It's a bit touristy, but children will enjoy the handicraft workshops, street entertainers and puppet shows.

Day 3 From Plaça de Catalunya take the open-topped Bus Turístic to Parc Güell, a colourful and wacky mishmash of pavilions, benches, archways and other architectural shenanigans hatched from the playful mind of Antoni Gaudí.

Continue north to Avinguda del Tibidabo and take the funicular up 517-m-high Tibidabo Hill where colour-coded paths and nature trails probe the woodlands of Parc de Collserola. Round off the day at the 100-year-old Parc d'Atraccions del Tibidabo (barcelonaturisme.com) which has traditional funfair rides and amusements as well as some more modern, white-knuckle embellishments.

Parc Güell

Originally commissioned as a stylish park for Barcelona aristocracy, Gaudí's Parc Güell is adorned with extraordinary stone structures and intricate tiling, and offers wonderful views across the city.

🔍 **High** spirits

Built into a mountainside 40 km northwest of Barcelona, the **Monestir de Monserrat** is the spiritual heart of Catalonia and was built on the spot where La Moreneta – a statue of the Virgin Mary – was hidden from the Moors. Reach the monastery by car or train, then take the cable car or rack railway up the mountain. The Montserrat Visita Card (montserratvisita.com) includes tickets for the rack railway or cable car, Montserrat Museum, and lunch in the café.

Costa Brava

The 200-km 'Wild Coast' of Catalonia is an enticing mixture of golden beaches, rocky cliffs and bustling resorts. At its northern end, Roses has sheltered beaches and makes a good base for visiting the fishing village of Cadaqués and the Dalí museum in Figueres. Further south, the small resorts of L'Escala and L'Estartit have a thriving sardine fishery and are close to the Greco-Roman ruins of Empúries. Don't miss a snorkelling or kayaking trip to the offshore Medes Isles, available through Medaqua (medaqua. com). Palafrugell has three of the Costa Brava's finest beaches (Calella de Palafrugell, Llafranc and Tamariu), while the popular resort of Platja d'Aro has a 2-km stretch of lifeguard-patrolled beach and lively nightlife. A beautiful old fortified town above the sheltered sweep of Platja Gran beach, Tossa de Mar has a watersports centre at Cala Llevadó. The busiest and liveliest stretch of the coast, Lloret de Mar suits families with teenagers in search of watersports and a buzzing nightlife. The catamaran *Sensation* (catamaransensation.com) operates sailing trips between Blanes and Lloret de Mar, while the Jardí Botànic Mar I Murta gardens makes a pleasant retreat from the coast. Waterparks along the Costa Brava include Aquabrava (aquabrava.com) in Roses, WaterWorld (waterworld.es) in Lloret de Mar and Marineland (marineland.es) south of Blanes.

Costa Daurada

Stretching south of Barcelona the 'Golden Coast' is renowned for its long sandy beaches. Sitges is a long-established and trendy resort, but not as popular as Salou – one of Spain's prime Mediterranean hot spots. Here you will find the gently shelving beaches of Platja de Ponent and Platja de Llevant, with smaller, less crowded coves towards Cap Salou. Beyond this lies Le Pineda with more beaches and the waterpark Aquopolis (aquopolis.com). Just inland, kids will be desperate to visit Costa Daurada's legendary theme park, PortAventura (portaventura.com). With no less than eight loop-the-loops, the Dragon Khan roller coaster used to be the ultimate thrill ride at PortAventura. Then along came Furius Baco, which accelerates its passengers from 0 to 135 km/h in three seconds. Europe's highest roller coaster arrives in 2012. More stomach-clutching moments are available on Hurakan Condor, a 42-storey free-fall tower. Families with younger children will find plenty of softer options, including the Sea Odyssey submarine ride and spinning Armadillos. In addition to three on-site hotels, PortAventura also boasts the Caribe Aquatic waterpark, so it looks like you'll be spending at least two days here.

Costa del Azahar, Costa Blanca & Costa Cálida

The sun-drenched beaches of the Costa del Azahar, Costa Blanca and Costa Cálida attract millions of holidaymakers each year. In the north of Valencia, the main resorts of Costa del Azahar include Benicassim, Oropesa and Peñíscola, which has a fortified old town enclosing a maze of narrow streets. There's an Aquarama (aquarama.net) waterpark in Benicassim, while inland attractions include the ruined medieval castle of Morella. Further south, boats carry visitors through the flooded subterranean passages of the Coves de Sant Joseph, while Sagunt has the remains of an ancient fortress dating back to Roman times. Aside from being a departure point for ferries to the Balearic Islands, the regional capital of Valencia is home to the futuristic Ciudad de las Artes y de las Ciencias (cac.es) which contains a hands-on science museum, IMAX cinema, planetarium and aquarium. Following the coastal road south, you reach L'Albufera, a freshwater lake that supports over 250 bird species. The Cap de la Nau marks the transition to the Costa Blanca, with the resort of Dénia offering a mixture of sandy and rocky beaches. The Costa Blanca's most dramatic landmark, the 332-m-high limestone bluff of Peñón de Ifach, rises above the harbour town of Calp from where you can take a boat trip to admire the impressive coastline. A short distance inland, the mountain village of Castell de Guadalest is a popular day trip from resorts along this stretch of coast.

Spanish Pyrenees

The Parc Nacional d'Aigüestortes is a beautiful tapestry of peaks, forests, lakes and streams offering wonderful walking trails, particularly around Lake Sant Maurici. Further west lies Baqueira-Beret (baqueira. es), a popular ski resort with over 40 pistes. During summer, children aged six and above can take part in an excellent activity programme including team games, horse riding, archery, craft workshops and picnics in the mountains. For older children and teens there's canyoning, whitewater rafting, climbing and hiking. Nearby Vall d'Aran is the perfect place to spot butterflies and perhaps even glimpse a golden eagle or bearded vulture. Further west still, in the province of Aragón, the Pyrenees reach their most dramatic in Parque Nacional de Ordesa – a rugged melange of peaks, canyons and densely wooded valleys.

Inside info

▶▶ Barcelona divides nicely into three family-friendly sections: La Rambla and Port Vell, Parc de Montjuïc and Tibidabo.
▶▶ The Barcelona Card (available from the tourist office – see below) allows free travel on public transport as well as discounts at various museums and attractions.
▶▶ For further information, visit barcelonaturisme.com.

Costa de la Luz

Kids' top 10 Costa del Sol

❶ **Find** the best beaches. **Torremolinos** has several kilometres of golden sand backed by a modern promenade; Blue-Flag **Benalmadena** is another long stretch of sand and offers plenty of watersports as well as shade; **Los Boliches** and **Fuengirola** also have European Blue Flag status and a wide range of facilities, from showers and sunbeds to beach lifeguards; **La Cala de Mijas** (between Fuengirola and Marbella) is a semi-urban beach with lots of cafés and restaurants on the promenade; **Cabopino** is sandy, sheltered and gently sloping, making it ideal for younger children; **Calahonda** is over 4 km long and a great all-round family beach; Marbella's **Nikki Beach** is where the rich and famous hang out; **Playa el Saladillo** (near Costalita) is another long, sandy beach, **La Rada** (Estepona) has a 2.5-km sandy beach with an attractive promenade, gardens and children's play areas; **El Cristo** (also at Estepona) is a sheltered cove with plenty in the way of watersports and places to eat; **Sabinillas** is a sandy beach popular with locals and fishermen; **Costa de la Luz** (between Cadiz and Tarifa) has gorgeous sandy beaches backed by dunes and is a popular spot for kite surfers.

❷ **Escape** into the mountains of the Sierra Nevada for cool air, cool views and cool activities. Spanish Highs (spanishhighs.co.uk) offers family-friendly activity holidays in the Sierra Nevada, with summer activities that include walking, camping, rock climbing, navigation and survival, horse riding, mountain biking, 4WD adventures and quad bike safaris. In winter (Dec-May), you can choose from snowshoeing, winter skills (using ice axe and crampons), tobogganing and skiing.

❸ **Spot** film stars and celebrities in Marbella (marbella.com). Ogle their luxury yachts in the marina, browse stylish shops in the old town and then hit the beach at Playa de Don Carlos.

❹ **Conquer** the 450-m-tall Rock of Gibraltar (gibraltar. gi) and meet the famous Barbary macaques, Europe's only wild primates. Then take to the sea on a Dolphin Safari (dolphinsafari.gi) in search of whales, dolphins and porpoises in the Straits of Gibraltar.

❺ **Delve** underground into the Cuevas de Nerja (cuevadenerja.es), a spectacular cave system where a 32-m-tall limestone column in the Hall of the Cataclysm is recognized as the world's largest.

❻ **Learn** about sea turtle conservation at the Sea Life Centre (sealifeeurope.com) in Benalmádena.

❼ **Discover** the unspoilt beaches of Cabo de Gata, a nature reserve in Almería province that can be visited from the resort of San José.

❽ **Reach** new speeds on the waterslides at Aqualand (aqualand.es) in Torremolinos where highlights include the 100-m-long Black Hole, the 22-m free-fall Kamikaze, an artificial surf beach and river rapids, the rubber ring Boomerang ride and an eight-lane racing slide.

❾ **Enjoy** the fun of the fair at Benalmádena's Tivoli World (tivoli.es) where you'll find a mixture of rides, shows and places to eat.

❿ **Go** east to find the Wild West at Almería's Mini Hollywood (unique-almeria.com), where Oasys Theme Park recreates a spaghetti western movie set where you can watch staged shoot-outs and Cancan dancing.

ⓗ Look for
Iberian lynx

One of Europe's most endangered mammals, about 265 Iberian lynx survive in the cork oak forests of Sierra Morena and the scrublands of the Coto Doñana – an important wetland reserve south of Seville. To increase your chances of spotting one of these elusive predators, you will need to be out and about at dawn and dusk when they are more likely to be active. Other rarities in the Coto Doñana include the imperial eagle and purple gallinule, while migratory birds, like the greater flamingo, flock to the reserve's wetlands. Access is strictly by guided tour, although several visitor centres on the park's outskirts provide birdwatching opportunities and nature trails. At the Centro de Visitantes El Acebuche there's an exhibition, café and shop, as well as a rehabilitation centre for injured birds.

For sheer variety, Andalucía is hard to beat. Even if you opt for a beach holiday on the Costa del Sol, that still puts you within range of excursions to the lofty wilderness of the Sierra Nevada and the cultural gems of Ronda and the Alhambra. Further west, Seville and the Parque Nacional del Coto Doñana make a great city break/safari combo, while the Costa del Sol itself has several options for beach-free days, from the caves at Nerja to the Rock of Gibraltar.

Alhambra

Seville

Andalucía's beautiful capital is rich in heritage and most of its historical highlights are within easy walking distance of each other. Just how much you see in the way of Moorish and Renaissance architecture, however, will depend on your children. You can always use Isla Mágica (islamagica.es) as a bargaining tool – an outing to this theme park with its roller coasters, waterslides and free-fall towers on Isla de la Cartuja is easily worth a day of sightseeing in return. Start with Seville Cathedral (catedraldesevilla. es), a vast Gothic creation built on the site of a great mosque. Originally constructed as a minaret in 1198, La Giralda now serves as the cathedral's belltower. Designed to accommodate a man on horseback, 35 ramps help smooth the climb to the top. Back at street level, explore the maze of narrow streets in Seville's historic centre (on foot or by horse-drawn carriage). Pause to admire the exotic royal palace, Real Alcázar (patronato-alcazarsevilla.es), before finding a tapas bar to sample some traditional Andalucían fare. Next, head west to Torre del Oro in the adjacent district of El Arenal. This Moorish tower contains a small maritime museum and is also the starting point for cruises on the Guadalquivir. If your kids need to burn off some energy, make instead for Parque de María Luisa.

Ronda

Just half an hour's drive from the Costa del Sol (see opposite), Ronda is the most visited of Andalucía's *pueblos blancos* (white towns). However, it's worth contending with the crowds of day trippers simply to see Ronda's spectacular clifftop setting, with the Puente Nuevo bridge spanning a 100-m-deep cleft to link the old town with the new.

Granada

Although young children won't necessarily appreciate the Romanticism or subtle beauty of the Alhambra,

this incredible medieval Arab palace is something you simply have to show your kids. A large complex of palaces, pools and patios with gardens at one end and a ruined fortress at the other, the Alhambra demands at least a full morning or afternoon. Your tickets will show an allocated time when you are allowed to enter the most famous section known as the Palacios Nazaríes. Highlights here include the Salón de Embajadores, a sumptuously decorated throne room, and the Patio de Arrayanes, a peaceful courtyard with a long rectangular pool reflecting the graceful arches of surrounding arcades. At the western end of the Alhambra, children will relish the chance to explore the more rugged 13th-century Alcazaba fortress where they can climb the Torre de la Vela for stunning views of the Sierra Nevada.

Sierra Nevada

Home to mainland Spain's highest mountain, Mulhacén (3482 m), and a haven for various endemic plants and rare butterflies, the Sierra Nevada has been protected as a national park since 1999. It also boasts Europe's southernmost ski resort – Solynieve (Pradollano), at 2100 m – which has a good range of pistes and a half-pipe. Las Alpujarras, a region of fertile valleys dotted with almond orchards, vineyards and olive groves on the range's southern flanks, is an ideal place to introduce children to a rural and non-commercialized part of Spain. Based in one of the region's Moorish-style villages you can explore the mountains on foot, horseback or bike.

Las Alpujarras

Inside info

▶▶ Stretching from Málaga to Gibraltar, the Costa del Sol receives on average around 300 days of sunshine a year.
▶▶ Avoid queues at the Alhambra by booking tickets in advance at alhambratickets.com.
▶▶ For further information, log on to andalucia.org.

Balearic beach beauties (from top, left to right): Cala Pregonda (Menorca), Port de Benirras (Ibiza), Formentera, Macarella (Menorca) and Formentor (Mallorca)

Renowned for inexpensive package holidays, fine beaches and lively nightlife, the Balearic Islands are well-established family favourites. However, there's more to this Mediterranean archipelago than crowded beaches and wild nightclubs. The islands of Mallorca, Menorca, Ibiza and Formentera have a diversity to suit all tastes – from the cultural sights of Mallorca's capital to the quiet, unspoilt beaches of Menorca and Formentera. Accommodation ranges from boisterous resorts to rustic farmhouses, while children will find no shortage of activities – both on and off the beach.

Mallorca

Best beaches Mallorca's coastline is dimpled with countless coves including those at Cala d'Or, Illetes and along the rugged west coast. The island also has several longer stretches of beach, the most desirable being on the dramatic northern peninsula where Platja de Formentor is lapped by calm turquoise water.

Best activities Snorkelling is excellent from any of the island's rocky coves, while birdwatching is rewarding during spring and autumn when migrant species use the S'Albufera wetlands as a stopover. Illa Dragonera, a tiny island off the west coast, is a lovely spot for a picnic and a walk; for more challenging hikes look to the mountains of the Serra de Tramuntana.

Best parks For wild and wacky water rides choose from Western Park (westernpark.com) in Magaluf, Aqualand (aqualand.es) in El Arenal or Hidropark (hidropark.com) at Puerto de Alcudia. Just west of Palma, Marineland (marineland.es) has dolphin and sea lion shows, while the Auto-Safari Park near Portocristo provides close encounters with giraffes, rhinos and monkeys.

Best days out Mallorca's capital, Palma has an excellent aquarium (palmaaquarium.com) which combines well with a visit to the city's cathedral and the 14th-century Castell de Bellver. A series of spectacular caverns on the east coast, the Coves del Drac can be explored by boat and on foot, while further north the Coves d'Artà exit dramatically onto the open sea.

Menorca

Best beaches Many of the north coast beaches, like Cala Pregonda, are deserted gems, accessible only by boat or on foot. One of the most popular resorts, Cala Santa Galdana overlooks a beautiful crescent-shaped cove on the south coast, while just to the west, Cala en Turqeta has aquamarine water, sea caves and shady pines.

Best activities Don't expect as much in the way of watersports and beach facilities as you find on Mallorca and Ibiza. Boat trips are an ideal way of exploring Menorca's beautiful and unspoilt coastline, while pony trekking along the island's rural tracks is available from horse-riding centres at Maó, Ferreries and Ciutadella.

Best parks The Los Delfines Aquapark (aquacenter-menorca.com) is located at Ciutadella.

Best days out Bronze Age ruins are scattered throughout the interior of Menorca. Some of the larger, more impressive ones, like Trepucó and Torre d'en Gaumes are worth visiting with children, but not in the heat of midday. Combine them with a beach visit or a trip to Ciutadella or Maó – both of which have interesting harbours and café-lined squares.

Ibiza & Formentera

Best beaches A busy resort, with a sandy beach, safe swimming and plenty of watersports, Es Canar is a family favourite on Ibiza. With fine sand and sparklingly clear water, the sheltered bay of Cala Vadella promises excellent swimming and snorkelling, as well as boat trips. On Formentera, the large, sandy sweep of Platja de Migjorn boasts excellent facilities.

Best activities Glass-bottom boat trips operate from several beaches on Ibiza, including lively Sant Antoni where Club Náutico de Sant Antoni also offers sea kayaking and sailing tuition. For birdwatching, head to Estiny Pudent, a saltwater lagoon on Formentera where flamingos mingle with herons, stints and other water birds during late summer and autumn.

Best parks Water parks on Ibiza include Aqualandia at Cap Martinet and Aguamar at Platja d'en Bossa.

Best days out Cycling is possible on both islands (leaflets describing various 'green routes' are available from tourist offices), while child-friendly horse riding is offered by Ibiza's numerous stables. For a cool escape underground, head to the 14-m-high caves of Can Marçà in the north of Ibiza, or to the Cap Blanc Aquarium, located in a natural cave near Sant Antoni.

Balearic Islands
Holiday heaven in the Med

Inside info

▶▶ The main ports in the Balearics are Palma de Mallorca and Alcúdia (Mallorca), Maó (Menorca), Ciutadella de Menorca, Ibiza and La Savina (Formentera).
▶▶ Acciona Trasmediterránea (trasmediterranea.es) operate fast ferries from Barcelona and Valencia.
▶▶ For further info, log on to illesbalears.es and ibiza.travel.

The Canaries have a split personality. At one extreme you could bake yourself on a beach for two weeks, eat English food and restrict your sightseeing to discos and waterparks, while at the other you could go truly wild, whale watching, climbing volcanoes, learning to scuba-dive and hiking through ancient forests. There's a huge range of things to see and do in the archipelago, but the three characteristics that all four major islands share in abundance are sun, sand and sea. Quite simply, there is nowhere better in Europe to plan a winter beach escape with the kids.

Gran Canaria

Third largest of the Canary Islands (after Tenerife and Fuerteventura), Gran Canaria receives over three million holidaymakers each year. Most zip down the motorway on the island's east coast to resorts like Playa del Inglés, Maspalomas and Puerto Rico where apartment blocks and high-rise hotels crowd golden-sand beaches. Activities in the sunny south range from windsurfing (steady breezes at Playa del Inglés and Pozo Izquierdo) to camel riding. Just north of Maspalomas, Aqua Sur (aqualand.es/grancanaria) is one of the biggest waterparks in the Canary Islands with no fewer than 33 waterslides. You'll find a roller coaster and other jollities at nearby Holiday World, while go-karting (for children as young as five) is available at San Agustíns Gran Karting Club. For a triple whammy of themed days out you can witness a Wild West shoot-out at Sioux City, performing parrots at Palmitos Parque and crocodile shows at Agüimes' Crocodilo Park.

After that lot you'll either need a week recovering on the beach or else you will be yearning to see a more natural side to the island. If it's the latter, *Spirit of the Sea* (dolphin-whale.com) sets out from the harbour in Puerto Rico on two- or three-hour boat trips in search of some of the 29 species of whales and dolphins found in the Canary Islands. Alternatively, you could make tracks across the Dunas de Maspalomas, a spectacular swathe of dunes between Playa del Inglés and Maspalomas.

However, the two areas where Gran Canaria really shakes off its package-holiday image are along the cliff-strewn west coast and in the central highlands. Allow at least a full day to explore the rugged volcanic interior of the island. Not only are there several traditional mountain villages to visit, but there are also numerous possibilities for walks, including a moderate 6.5-km hike to the base of Roque Nublo –

a dramatic basalt spire. In the north of the island, you'll find plantations of orange, mango and papaya trees in the valleys around Agaete and exotic plants at the botanical garden in Tarifa.

Las Palmas, Gran Canaria's capital, is also worth a visit. In addition to Museo Elder (an interactive science museum and IMAX theatre), kids will be intrigued by the Guanches mummies on display in Museo Canario and the exploits of Christopher Columbus depicted in Casa de Colón. That's assuming, of course, you can drag them away from the city's beach – a 3-km curve of enticing sand.

Lanzarote

Arid, barren and windswept, Lanzarote's volcanic interior has a stark and haunting beauty. Children probably won't notice the lack of trees on the island – they'll be too mesmerized by the volcanic carnage wrought by the Montañas del Fuego in Parque Nacional de Timanfaya. Can you imagine their faces when your guide demonstrates how the volcano is dormant, not extinct, by shoving sticks into a crevice where they instantly ignite?

Footprints in the sand

The giant Maspalomas sand dunes on Gran Canaria.

Let's go to Siam Park
★ One of Europe's largest waterparks, t thrills at Siam Park (siampark.net) include the Dragon and Volcano raft rides, Tower Power (a 28-m vertical drop slide), a six-lan racing slide and rapids galore. Wave Palace boasts artificial waves up to 3 m in height, while more placid waters can be found on the Mai Thai lazy river ride. Young children will love The Lost City, an adventure pool with a fortress, bridges and waterfalls. Siam Park also has aquariums, restaurants, a sea lion cove and even a floating market.

Mt Teide

Kids' top 10 Tenerife

① **Burrow** through tunnels of *laurisilva* (ancient forests of laurel and myrtle) that festoon the slopes of the Anaga Massif in the east of Tenerife.

② **Spot** pilot whales and dolphins on a boat trip out of Las Américas (choose an operator that follows guidelines for minimizing disturbance to the whales).

③ **Experience** the thrill of scuba-diving at Los Gigantes Diving Centre (divingtenerife.co.uk), which offers two-hour Discover Scuba adventures (minimum age 14 if accompanied by a parent or guardian).

④ **Talk** to the animals at Loro Parque (loroparque.com) in Puerto de la Cruz, where you'll find the world's largest collection of parrots, as well as gorillas, chimpanzees, tigers, orcas, sea lions and a breeding colony of penguins.

⑤ **Track** down a dragon tree at Parque del Drago (parquedeldrago.es) in Icod de los Vinos.

⑥ **Splash** out at the waterpark Aqualand Costa Adeje (aqualand.es/tenerife) or take a dip in the natural saltwater pools along the coastline of Puerto de la Cruz.

⑦ **Ride** a camel at El Tanques Camello Center (camellocenter.com) or a pony at the Oasis del Valle (oasisdelvalle.com) in the Oratava Valley.

⑧ **Climb** Mount Teide, the highest point in the Canary Islands at 3718 m – or at least have a good scramble on its volcanic slopes. Keep an eye out for Teide Eggs – magma boulders created by the same principles that make snowballs grow when rolled downhill. Families with young children can opt for the eight-minute cable-car ride to within 160 m of Teide's summit.

⑨ **Sample** as many beaches as possible. Some of the island's most family-friendly include Playa de las Teresitas (1.5 km of imported Sahara sand, close to Santa Cruz de Tenerife and sheltered by a breakwater), El Médano (2-km stretch of golden sand fringed by calm, shallow waters, perfect for windsurfing) and Playa Fanabé (Blue Flag beach with lots of watersports).

⑩ **Visit** Siam Park – see below left.

And that's after you've ridden camels up the cinder-strewn slopes for spectacular views across the park's ochre-red volcanic cones.

Timanfaya is an essential day trip on Lanzarote, but you will spend most of your time on the coast. The majority of visitors stay in Puerto del Carmen, a sprawling resort with hotels, bars, restaurants and discos, but none of the high-rise brashness that has blighted parts of Tenerife and Gran Canaria. Another good family option is Playa Blanca at the southern tip of Lanzarote, where you'll find hidden coves and gorgeous stretches of golden sand. The north of the island is also worth exploring. Visit the old capital of Teguise on Sundays to buy handicrafts at the weekly market, before continuing on to Cueva de los Verdes, a 6-km-long lava tube that you can explore on guided tours. The nearby Jameos del Agua lava caves have

been cleverly landscaped to incorporate a restaurant and swimming pool.

Fuerteventura

Compared with the other main islands in the Canaries, tourism is still in its infancy on Fuerteventura. The two most popular resorts are in the south at Península de Jandía and in the north at Corralejo. Both have spectacular beaches, although Corralejo has the added attraction of a massive belt of sand dunes. The former fishing village also boasts the Baku Water Park (bakufuerteventura.com), glass-bottom boat trips to the tiny offshore Isla de los Lobos and a 40-minute ferry service to Lanzarote. A popular day trip in the south, Oasis Park (lajitaoasispark.com) in La Lajita combines an animal park, garden and camel farm.

F ew families look further than the Algarve when it comes to holidaying in Portugal, and who can blame them? Not only is it largely sheltered from cool Atlantic winds and ocean currents, but its coastline is notched with a glorious succession of sandy coves and beaches, some of which have smugglers' den written all over them. There's also an endless variety of boat trips to choose from, as well as a good range of family-friendly accommodation. So why even consider going to Lisbon? Well, for starters, the Portuguese capital has plenty to appeal to youngsters, particularly at the Parque das Nações. However, it's only when you start contemplating a few days in Lisbon as the prelude to an island odyssey in Madeira or the Azores that the Algarve begins to seem less of a foregone conclusion.

Lisbon

City highlights There are three main areas in Lisbon worth visiting with children. The most central is the city's hilltop citadel, Castelo de São Jorge. This huge walled compound contains the tiny neighbourhood of Santa Cruz do Castelo as well as the Inner Battlements – a kind of castle-within-a-castle where children can scamper between watchtowers and gaze across the rooftops of the city below. Originally a Moorish fort (but captured by Afonso Henriques in 1147), the castle is believed to be the site of Lisbon's earliest settlement, dating as far back as the 6th century BC. However, the period of Portuguese history that is most likely to capture the imagination of kids is the Age of Discovery.

Belém, Lisbon's westernmost suburb, reached by tram 15 from the city-centre square of Praça da Figueira, is home to the 52-m-tall Pradrão dos Descobrimentos monument depicting famous Portuguese mariners, such as Vasco da Gama and Magellan. Standing at the prow of the sculpture, with a caravel in hand, is Henry the Navigator, while on the pavement nearby a huge world map is etched with the routes taken by the explorers during the 15th and 16th centuries. A monument to the wealth of the Age of Discovery, the beautiful Mosteiro dos Jerónimos, set a little way back from the waterfront at Belém, contains the tombs of Vasco da Gama and Henry the Navigator. Two museums in the monastery's west wing cover archaeology, shipbuilding and navigation but be sure to leave time to visit the nearby Torre de Belém, a wonderful 16th-century defensive tower on the River Tagus with battlements, watchtowers and a dungeon.

To boldly go...

Portugal's famous mariners are immortalised in Lisbon's Pradrão dos Descobrimentos monument, while ragged-tooth sharks cruise Oceanário at the Parque das Nações.

Parque das Nações Lisbon's leisure hot spot, Parque das Nações (portaldasnacoes.pt) is a guaranteed hit with children. Built on the site of the city's Expo 98 world fair, the park boasts gardens, restaurants, shops, the impressive canopied Portugal Pavilion and even a cable car running along its length to the 145-m-tall Vasco da Gama Tower where you can get great views over Lisbon, the River Tagus and Vasco de Gama Bridge – Europe's largest bridge at 17.2 km long.

The science centre Ciência Viva (pavconhecimento. pt) will captivate kids; however, the highlight is Oceanário (oceanario.pt), one of the world's largest and most imaginatively designed aquariums. Based on a Global Ocean theme, its central exhibit comprises a giant 7-m-deep aquarium from which four distinct zones radiate. These cover the North Atlantic, Antarctica, temperate Pacific and tropical Indian Ocean – from both above and below the surface. One moment you are watching sea otters frolicking on a rocky shore; the next you're peering through the swaying fronds of a kelp forest. Look out for star appearances from penguins, sea dragons, wolf eels, cuttlefish, manta rays and blacktip sharks.

Madeira

A dot in the Atlantic, 608 km from Morocco and almost 1000 km from Lisbon, Madeira is a subtropical gem with year-round appeal.

In Funchal, the island's capital, children will enjoy setting sail on a replica of Columbus' *Santa Maria*. Whale watching off the coast is also rewarding with almost guaranteed sightings of fin, sei, sperm or pilot whales during summer months – try Madeira Wind Birds (madeirawindbirds.com) or Madeira Island Tours (madeira-island-tours.com). Don't miss the cable-car ride to Monte or the famous street toboggan ride back down again. Swimming is possible along Funchal's Lido Promenade or you could head east to Santa Cruz where the Praia das Palmeiras has a children's play area and pedal boats for hire.

Highlights on Madeira's north coast include the natural rock pools at Porto Moniz and the São Vicente Caves where you can explore 700 m of lava tunnels. At Santana there's a theme park devoted to the history, science and traditions of Madeira, while hardy walkers will find plenty of challenging trails in the island's rugged interior. For a 30-minute taster, try the straightforward trail between Rabaçal and the Risco Waterfall. If even that sounds too much like hard work, nip over to Porto Santo, a small island lying 37 km to the northeast of Madeira and boasting a superb 9-km beach.

Funchal

Kids' top 10 The Algarve

1 **Discover** beach heaven at Lagos, exploring the small, sheltered bay of Praia de Dona Ana, hemmed in by cinnamon-coloured sandstone cliffs, or revel in the space of 4-km-long Meia Praia, the Algarve's longest beach. A short distance to the east of Lagos, the combination of golden beach and lively nightlife at Portimão's Praia da Rocha will appeal to teenagers.

2 **Cruise** through the myriad waterways of the Parque Natural da Ria Formosa (ilha-deserta.com), spotting birds and collecting shells on a deserted island; or explore the reserve on foot by walking the 3.2-km São Lourenço nature trail across saltwater marshes and lagoons.

3 **Snorkel** in the shallows off Albufeira's Praia da São Rafael, a beautiful sandy bay surrounded by cliffs and rock formations riddled with caves. Located in front of the old quarter of Albufeira, Praia dos Barcos is renowned for its fleet of colourful fishing boats.

4 **Surf** on the Atlantic coast at Praia do Armado, Carrapateira, or explore the rock pools at low tide.

5 **Paddle** a canoe on the Alvor Estuary (outdoor-tours. net), hauling out on a tidal sandbank for a game of beach volleyball and a swim.

6 **Ride** a high-speed RIB (rigid inflatable boat) out of the marina at either Lagos or Portimão in search of dolphins, orcas and sharks. Dolphin Seafaris (dolphinseafaris.com) offer daily 90-minute trips.

7 **Stalk** the battlements of Silves Castle, a Moorish stronghold built on the site of a Roman fort, and then visit the excellent Museu Arqueológico in the town below.

8 **Sail** in search of smugglers' caves aboard the *Santa Bernarda* (santa-bernarda.com), a replica of a 500-year-old Portuguese *caravela*.

9 **Plan** a day at the park, taking your pick from theme parks like Zoomarine (zoomarine.com), A Cova dos Mouros (minacovamouros.sitepac.pt) and Krazy World (krazyworld. com) or waterparks such as Aqualand Algarve (aqualand.pt) near Alcantarilha.

10 **Escape** the crowds by heading north to Praia de Odeceixe, a stunning Atlantic beach that's perfect for sandcastle-building, body boarding or a walk at low tide. Curling behind the beach, the River Seixe is ideal for canoeing and there are cafés and a beach shop nearby.

The Azores

Scattered some 1300 km west of Lisbon, this isolated archipelago will appeal to adventurous families who enjoy walking and island hopping. Each island has its own character and special appeal.

Starting in the west, Flores is one of the most beautiful, with hydrangea hedgerows lacing the island in bright cerulean each July. Graciosa is renowned for the Furnas do Enxofre, a sulphur lake located in a cave beneath the island's caldera. On Faial, the historic port of Horta is worth a day of exploration, as is Capelinhos, where an eruption in 1957 added 2 sq km to the island. With its dramatic sea cliffs and deep valleys covered in lush vegetation, São Jorge is a magnet to walkers, as is Pico with its challenging ascent of Ponta do Pico. Whale watching (particularly for sperm whales) is also excellent from Pico, with three-hour boat trips from Lajes available from Espaco Talassa (espacotalassa.com) – see also page 86. On Terceira, highlights include the World Heritage Site of Angra do Heroísmo, a town that once formed the hub of Atlantic trading routes. The twin volcanic lakes of Sete Cidades – one blue, one green – can be found on São Miguel, the largest and most diverse of the islands. However, be sure to also visit Gorreana, the site of Europe's only tea estate, and the spa town of Furnas where you can see bubbling mud pools and hissing vents. Nearby Terra Nostra Gardens is a haven of exotic flora, while a drive out to Nordeste on the east coast provides wonderful clifftop views. Dramatic scenery is also a drawcard for Santa Maria. This peaceful island has terraced vineyards at Maia and a white sandy beach at Praia Formosa.

Inside info

▸▸ The Lisboa Card (askmelisboa. com) includes free public transport and admission to museums and monuments.
▸▸ Save money at the Parque das Nações by purchasing a Cartão do Parque, which provides free entry to the Oceanarium and Knowledge Pavilion, a return ride on the cable car and a discount on bike rental.
▸▸ For further information, log on to visitlisboa. com, madeiratourism. org or visitazores.org.

When to go

If possible, try to visit Spain and Portugal during May, June or September to avoid the blistering heat and tourist crush of midsummer. In the south, you can often rely on decent weather as early as April or as late as October – although the sea will be warmer, especially around the **Balearic Islands**, during the latter period. If you have no choice but to visit southern Spain in the peak summer season, remember that you can retreat to the mountains to escape excessive heat. The Atlantic-facing Costa de la Luz in **Andalucía** receives cooling breezes, as do parts of the **Algarve**.

Despite the **Canary Islands'** celebrated year-round sunshine, their geography does create local variations. For example, between late autumn and early spring you can experience frost in Tenerife's El Teide National Park during the morning and be sunbathing on Playa de las Américas by the afternoon. The south of the island is sunnier than the north where trade winds bring more cloud and rain. Generally speaking, though, the archipelago has enviable weather with ample sunshine, little rain and an average annual temperature of 23°C.

In the **Azores**, locals will tell you to expect all four seasons in one day. In general, however, expect warm temperatures (up to 27°C in summer, dropping to around 13°C in winter) and a chance of rain in any month. Visit between May and September if you are keen to go whale-watching, sailing or fishing. Walking is good year-round, but to witness the island's famous azaleas and hydrangeas in flower, June and July are the best months.

Getting there

One of the most inexpensive ways of reaching Spain or Portugal is by charter flight, although departure and arrival times are not always ideal. For **scheduled flights**, Iberia (iberia.com) has the most extensive network in the region and flies from various airports in the UK, as well as Dublin and the United States. British Airways (britishairways.com) serves several destinations on the Iberian peninsula. SATA Air Açores (sata.pt) operates from London to Ponta Delgada, Horta and Terceira in the Azores and Funchal on Madeira, and also has flights from Lisbon, Faro, Porto and several other cities in Europe, USA and Canada. For **budget flights** to Spain and Portugal you're spoilt for choice, with a wide range of UK regional airports covering the region. easyJet (easyjet.com) serves Madrid (from Bristol, Edinburgh, Gatwick, Liverpool and Luton), Bilbao (Stansted), Barcelona (Bristol, Gatwick, Luton, Liverpool, Newcastle and

All sunny smiles
Beach life on the Algarve.

Stansted), Lisbon (Bristol, Gatwick, Liverpool and Luton), Faro (Bristol, East Midlands, Gatwick, Liverpool, Luton and Newcastle) and Funchal (Bristol and Stansted) in addition to various routes to Alicante, Almeria, Ibiza, Mahon, Malaga, Murcia and Palma. Ryanair (ryanair.com) has an equally comprehensive network with flights to numerous destinations, including Alicante, Barcelona, Faro, Gran Canaria, Jerez, Lanzarote, Madrid, Malaga, Murcia, Palma, Santander, Tenerife and Valencia. Air Berlin (airberlin.com) also covers the Iberian Peninsula, Balearic Islands, Canaries Madeira and the Azores, while Thomsonfly (thomsonfly.com) has many flights to the Balearic Islands and Canaries, as well as to Alicante, Barcelona, Faro and Malaga.

Getting around

Trains operated by RENFE (renfe.es) provide a high-speed service between Madrid and other cities such as Seville and Barcelona. **Buses** also provide a relatively efficient service between major towns in both Spain and Portugal, but you will need to hire a **car** to explore off the main routes. Major car-hire companies are represented in most cities and airports, including Avis (avis.com), Europcar (europcar.com) and Hertz (hertz.com). Unless you take organized coach trips, car hire is also essential for getting around the Balearics, Canaries and Azores. In the Balearics, inter-island **ferry** services are operated by Trasmediterrínea (see right). Island hopping in the Canaries is possible with connections by plane, ferry and jetfoil. All of the islands in the Azores are linked by the domestic airline SATA (see left) and Transmaçor ferries (transmacor.pt).

Accommodation

You can choose from a vast range of accommodation in Spain and Portugal, from family hotels, luxury resorts and villas to apartments, farmstays and holiday villages. One of the most economical options for families is to rent a **rural house** (*casa rurale*) where you can expect to pay around €400 per week for a simple village property to €1000-plus for something more luxurious with a pool and garden. Try Colours of Spain (coloursofspain.com) for an online directory, or book through regional associations such as RAAR (raar.es) in Andalucía; Ruralia (ruralia.com) in Asturias; and Ruralverd (ruralverd.com) in Catalonia. Casas Cantabricas (casas.co.uk) offers self-catering properties and small, family-run hotels in northern Spain, Pyrenees Accommodation (pyreneesaccommodation.com) has a selection of family hotels in the Spanish Pyrenees and Inns of Spain (innsofspain.com) has a portfolio of character properties on Spain's mainland and islands.

For **city breaks**, try Madrid B&B (madridbandb. com) for two- and three-bedroom apartments in Spain's capital, Loving Barcelona (lovingbarcelona. com) for apartments in Catalonia's trendy urban hot spot and the luxurious Hotel Real Palácio (realpalaciohotel.com) for a central location and good children's facilities in Lisbon.

For **seaside villas** with pools, try James Villa Holidays (jamesvillas.co.uk), which offers properties in Mallorca and the Algarve. Meon Villas (meonvillas. co.uk) and Simply Travel (simplytravel.co.uk) also have a good selection. To make your money go further, book a package with an operator like First Choice (firstchoice.co.uk) or Thomson (thomson.co.uk).

Camping is another excellent option for the budget-conscious. Canvas Holidays (canvasholidays. co.uk), Eurocamp (eurocamp.com), Keycamp (keycamp.com) and Siblu (siblu.com) represent all the region's best sites.

Food & drink
Eating out is a family affair in Spain and Portugal and it's not unusual to see children in restaurants late at night. Some highly salted dishes are not advisable for babies and toddlers, but that still leaves plenty of choice, particularly if you pick and mix from a tapas menu with its breads, dips and other goodies. Some regional specialities to tempt adventurous children include *botifarra amb mongetes* (Catalan sausages and white beans), *gazpacho* (chilled tomato soup), *tortilla Española* (a thick potato and onion omelette), *frango assado com piri-piri* (a spicy chicken dish from the Algarve), *leitão à bairrada* (roasted suckling pig, popular in Portugal) and *empanadas* (pastry parcels stuffed with tuna or ham). Don't forget to try *paella*, Spain's famous rice dish with beans, tomato, paprika and either meat or seafood. In the Azores, try to get hold of a bowl of *pudim nao sei*, which translates as 'pudding with no name' and resembles something that one of Pico's earthquakes might do to a load of chocolate, mousse, sponge cake, peaches and cream.

Health & safety
Spain and Portugal are generally safe countries to visit. The European Health Insurance Card (EHIC) entitles you to emergency medical treatment. Drinking water is safe and standards of food hygiene are generally good. Be wary, however, of tapas dishes that may have been left out for a while or reheated.

Go green
Three ways to skip the flight

1 **Catch a ferry** from Spain to the Balearics with Iscomar (iscomar. com) with departures from Barcelona, Valencia and Dénia. Trasmediterránea (trasmediterranea.es) operates ferries to both the Balearic and Canary Islands. Fast catamarans are used for the shorter routes, while on longer journeys the ferries have many of the facilities you'd expect on a cruise liner, such as a swimming pool, restaurants and cinema.

2 **Sail across the Bay** of Biscay from the UK to northern Spain. Brittany Ferries (brittany-ferries. co.uk) runs services (lasting around 20 hours) from Plymouth and Portsmouth to Bilbao and Santander.

3 **Take the train** from London to Madrid or Barcelona, using Eurostar (eurostar.com) to Paris and then changing to a sleeper service to Spain. Bookings can be made online at Rail Europe (raileurope.co.uk).

Holiday operators

The Adventure Company adventurecompany.co.uk

Club Med clubmed.com

Eurocamp eurocamp.com

Families Worldwide familiesworldwide.co.uk

First Choice Holidays firstchoice.co.uk

Freewheel Holidays freewheelholidays.com

Headwater headwater.com

i-escape i-escape.com

Individual Travellers individualtravellers.com

Inntravel inntravel.co.uk

Keycamp keycamp.com

Mark Warner markwarner.co.uk

Portuguese Affair portugueseaffair.com

Powder Byrne powderbyrne.com

Scott Dunn scottdunn.com

Siblu siblu.com

Sovereign sovereign.com

Spanish Affair spanishaffair.com

Sunvil sunvil.co.uk

Thomson Holidays thomson.co.uk

Travelbeam travelbeam.co.uk

Villa Select villaselect.com

Vintage Travel vintagetravel.co.uk

In the USA
Abercrombie and Kent abercrombiekent.com

Adventures by Disney abd.disney.go.com

Tauck Bridges tauck.com

Fast facts

Country	Time	Language	Currency	Dialling code	Tourist information
Spain	GMT+1	Spanish	Euro (€)	+34	spain.info
Portugal	GMT	Portuguese	Euro (€)	+351	visitportugal.com

Canary Islands: GMT; Azores: GMT-1

Casa Olea
Where? Priego de Córdoba, Andalucía.
Why? Tucked into the heart of Andalucía, halfway between Córdoba and Granada, this luxurious six-room guesthouse is surrounded by ancient olive groves and provides an authentic experience of rural Spain. The nearby woodland is teeming with wildlife, including wild boar. Casa Olea is perfect for a walking or mountain-biking holiday exploring local villages, while home comforts include stylish bedrooms, a swimming pool and sun terrace and delicious locally sourced food.
Contact Casa Olea, T+34 696-748209, casaolea.com

Cambrils Park
Where? Costa Daurada.
Why? This lively park is close to the beach and has a fantastic pool complex with waterslides and squirting elephants! Facilities include tennis, football and minigolf. Self-catering is a piece of cake thanks to the park's bakery and supermarket, and there's also a restaurant and takeaway for eating out.
Contact Keycamp, T+44 (0)844-406 0200, keycamp.com

Cal Rei Petit
Where? Puerto Pollenca, Mallorca.
Why? Just five minutes' drive to sandy beaches, this three-bedroom villa has mountain views and is surrounded by beautiful gardens with olive and fig trees. As well as a swimming pool, family-friendly touches include stair gates and air-conditioning.
Contact Mallorca Farmhouses, T+44 (0)118-947 3001, mallorca.co.uk/res

Sheraton Algarve
Where? Albufeira, Algarve.
Why? They say location is everything – and the Sheraton is certainly sitting pretty above one of the Algarve's best stretches of golden-sand beach. But it also gets gold stars for its family-friendly accommodation and activities which include top-notch sports facilities, with academies for tennis and golf.
Contact Sheraton, T+351 (0)289-500100, sheratonalgarve.com

Finca el Almendrillo
Where? Andalucía.
Why? Set in lovely countryside, this property sleeps up to 20 and is well placed for visiting Granada and the coast. Parents will find everything from high chairs to bottle sterilizers. There's also a fenced-off pool, a courtyard for riding bikes, a local goat farm and horse riding.
Contact Finca el Almendrillo, T+34 620-525739, granada-farmhouse.com

La Manga Club
Where? Costa Calida.
Why? One of the world's best holiday destinations for active families, La Manga runs junior sports academies in golf, tennis, football, dance, rugby, karate and cricket. Other activities include scuba-diving, waterskiing, horse riding, sailing, quad-biking and kayaking – and for those in search of slower pulse rates, there are also pools, beaches and a spa. Accommodation ranges from a five-star hotel to self-catering villas.
Contact La Manga Club, T+34 (0)968-331234, lamangaclub.com

66 99 **Looking for sun, sand and sport? La Manga Club is just the ticket. Its range of activities is nothing short of Olympian with three championship golf courses, a 28-court tennis centre and junior academies in golf, tennis, cricket, football and dance. If you've got a budding Beckham or a wannabee Wozniacki, this could be their ultimate holiday destination.** 101familyholidays.co.uk

The Abama Golf & Spa Resort
Where? Algarve.
Why? Luxurious rooms, spa, Michelin-starred restaurant and 18-hole golf course aside, the Abama takes childcare and kids' facilities to new heights with everything from family pools and sports academies to kids' clubs and cinema nights on the beach.
Contact Abama Golf & Spa Resort, T+34 902 105 600, abamahotelresort. com or travelbeam.co.uk

Princesa Yaiza Resort
Where? Lanzarote.
Why? Winter sun isn't the only treat on offer here. Basking in luxury, you'll also enjoy fabulous suites (some with PlayStation and free babysitting), a choice of restaurants and pools and a golden-sand beach. Children get all-singing, all-dancing kids' clubs, while parents can relax at the Thalasso Spa.
Contact Princesa Yaiza, T+34 928-519300, princesayaiza.com or sovereign.com

Trails with a donkey
Where? Castile.
Why? Take a beautiful patch of Spain, a self-guided walking trail and a succession of comfy hotels; add a donkey and you've got all the essentials for a relaxed family walking holiday. Your four-legged friend is always there to respond to cries of 'Carry me!', while an equally helpful person transports your luggage.
Contact Inntravel, T+44 (0)1643 617009, inntravel.co.uk

Hotel Presidente
Where? Portinatx, Ibiza.
Why? Located in a quiet, family-friendly part of Ibiza, away from the nightclubs, Hotel Presidente is surrounded by pine trees and overlooks a sheltered bay. Some of the hotel's 270 rooms sleep four and there's also a kids' club for three- to 12-year-olds. Activities include snorkelling and archery.
Contact Hotel Presidente, T+34 971-320576, hotelpresidenteibiza.com.

Italy

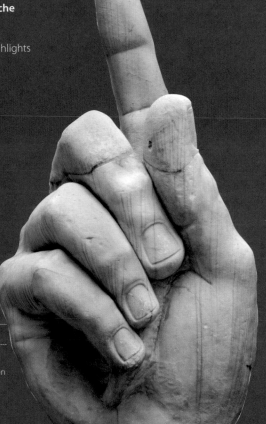

Pigeons in the piazza

Flights of fancy in St Mark's Square, Venice. Right: the giant hand of Constantine, on display in Rome.

Largest lake
Garda
370 sq km

Highest mountain
Mont Blanc
4807 m

Longest river
Po 650km

metre
3000
2000
1000
500
200
0

N

100 km
100 miles

Mont Blanc

Lake Maggiore

Lake Como

Turin

Milan

Lake Garda

Verona

Padua

Venice

Po

Parma

Genoa

Bologna

Ligurian Sea

A p e n n i n e

Lucca

Pisa

Florence

SAN MARINO

Conero Peninsula

Siena

Lake Trasimeno

Perugia

Assisi

Adriatic Sea

Elba

ITALY

Tiber

5

Corsica (France)

ROME □ 1

M o u n t a i n s

Tremiti Islands

Gargano Peninsula

6

Naples

Vesuvius

Bari

Sardinia

Lecce

Tyrrhenian Sea

Cagliari

Aeolian Islands

Stromboli

Ionian Sea

Palermo

Taormina

Mt Etna

Sicily

7

Catania

Syracuse

Mediterranean Sea

1 Find out how ancient Romans lived

▸ Rome, page 112

2 See the Leaning Tower of Pisa

▸ Tuscany, page 114

3 Explore the canals of Venice

▸ Venice, page 116

4 Swim and sail on Lake Garda

▸ The Lakes, page 118

5 Go medieval in a hill town

▸ Umbria & Le Marche, page 120

6 Relive the days of Pompeii

▸ Naples, page 122

7 Stand on an active volcano

▸ Sicily, page 123

Did you know?

★ At least 5000 animals and gladiators were killed during the Colosseum's 123-day inaugural games in AD 90

★ Venice has 116 islands and 409 bridges.

★ You can walk around the Vatican, the world's smallest country, in less than an hour.

★ The world record holder of the fastest time to eat a 12-inch pizza is not Italian, but a Belgian called Tom Waes who took two minutes 19.91 seconds.

Italy

Introduction

It's one of those places you have to visit at least once in a lifetime – but should you leave Italy until the kids are older and more likely to appreciate its cultural and historical treasures? Of course not! Kids love Italy, and Italians love kids. Not only are the locals barmy about bambinos, but they also know a trick or two when it comes to feeding them. With a staple diet of pizza, pasta and pastries (supplemented, of course, with copious *gelato*), your children should have more than enough energy for at least a taster of Rome, Florence or Venice (Italy's triumphant trio of World Heritage cities). Don't be bamboozled into thinking you've got to see all the museums and ancient sites, and pay homage to every Michelangelo masterpiece – experiencing Italy has just as much to do with spending an afternoon in a piazza, lingering over lunch, playing around the fountain and, you guessed it, pillaging the local *gelato* parlour. Beyond the cities, Italy's beautiful countryside encompasses rolling hills, mountains and lakes – perfect for a relaxed break in a villa with a pool. There's no shortage of beaches for more traditional family holidays, while locations like Naples and Sicily add a bit of spark to sightseeing days, courtesy of Vesuvius and Mount Etna.

❝❞ We managed to balance our need to soak up the atmosphere in some medieval towns (aided by the customary bribe of *gelati*) with swimming, tennis and football for the children. Alison Rippon

Star rating

Wow factor	★★★
Worry factor	★
Value for money	★★★
Keeping teacher happy	★★★★★
Family accommodation	★★★★★
Babies & toddlers	★★★★
Cool for teenagers	★★★★

Make a mosaic

» Study examples of Roman mosaics in books and on websites.
» Decide on the picture or pattern you want to create. Roman mosaics often featured animals or geometric designs.
» Draw your design on card.
» Cut up small pieces of coloured paper, magazines or comics. Sort them into colour groups.
» Stick them on to your design, thinking carefully about where you place the colours to highlight the details of your design.

Taste of Italy perfect pizza

What you need

» 1 tsp dried yeast
» 1 tsp sugar
» 150 ml warm water
» 225 g plain flour
» Tomato sauce such as passata or tomato paste
» Grated cheese
» Favourite toppings such as tuna, ham, mushrooms, sweetcorn and olives

» Roll out to make your pizza base.
» Leave dough to rise.
» Spread the tomato sauce over the base and then add the grated cheese and other toppings.
» Bake for 10-15 minutes at 180°C depending on the thickness of the pizza base.

What to do

» Mix the yeast, sugar and water. Leave to rest in a warm place for about 10 minutes (until the yeast and sugar has dissolved).
» Add flour and mix to make a firm dough, adding extra flour if required.

How to play camicia

You can play this Italian card game with a normal set of 52 cards, or use an Italian pack (often 40 cards). This is a game of pure luck for two players. The aces, twos and threes are the attack cards (suits are ignored).

» Deal out the cards evenly.
» Players take turns to place their top card face-up in a pile on the table. If the card is normal, no action is taken and play passes to the other player.
» When an attack card is played by one of the players, the other player has to add to the exposed pile the number of cards corresponding to the face value of the attack card – that is one card for an ace, two cards for a two, and three cards for a three.
» If all the cards played in response to an attack are normal, the attacking player takes the pile of played cards and adds them to his or her hand. If one of the cards played in response to an attack is an attack card itself, the former attack is finished, and the new attack takes place.
» The player who runs out of cards is the loser.

Great reads
5 children's books

Ages 4+
Mr Benn – Gladiator
David McKee (Andersen Press)
Mr Benn visits a costume shop and turns gladiator. But can the gentle character steel himself to join in with such violent games?

Ages 6+
Zoe Sophia: An Adventure in Venice
Elisa Smalley (Chronicle Books)
Zoe and her dog Mickey visit great aunt Dorothy in Venice. Zoe's scrapbook brings the enchantment of the city to life, but then Mickey gets lost in the maze of canals.

Ages 8+
I am Spartapuss
Robin Price (Mogzilla)
This humorous series is set in Rome AD 36, when the mighty Feline Empire ruled the world! Spartapuss, a ginger cat, becomes imprisoned by the evil emperor Catligula. Spartapuss must fight and win his freedom in the Arena – before his opponents make dog food out of him!

Pompeii – The Day A City Was Buried
Chris Rice (Dorling Kindersley)
A beautifully illustrated account of the life and people of Pompeii, a city in southern Italy destroyed during the eruption of Mount Vesuvius in AD 79. Includes information on life in Roman Pompeii, as well as the destruction of the city and its subsequent rediscovery.

Ages 9+
Leonardo da Vinci
Andrew Langley (Dorling Kindersley)
A detailed look at the Renaissance period, revealing fascinating facts about the great artist as well as giving an in-depth view of everyday life in an Italian city-state.

Gelato flavours in Italian

Know your *ananas* from your bananas with this guide to popular *gelato* flavours. When you're ordering an ice cream, try saying the following in Italian:
'Vorrei un gelato per favore.' I'd like an ice cream please.
'Quanti gusti posso prendere?' How many flavours can I have?
'Cono grazie.' Cone please.
'Mi può mettere anche un po' di panna?' And could I have a bit of cream on top too?

- ★ *Albiocca* apricot
- ★ *Ananas* pineapple
- ★ *Bacio* chocolate and hazelnut
- ★ *Banana* banana
- ★ *Caffe* coffee
- ★ *Ciliega* cherry
- ★ *Cioccolato* chocolate
- ★ *Cocco* coconut
- ★ *Cocomero* watermelon
- ★ *Crema* egg-yolk custard
- ★ *Fragola* strawberry
- ★ *Frutti di bosco* wild berries
- ★ *Lampone* raspberry
- ★ *Limone* lemon
- ★ *Macedonia* fruit salad
- ★ *Malaga* raisin
- ★ *Mandarino* tangerine
- ★ *Mela* apple
- ★ *Menta* mint
- ★ *Mirtillo* blueberry
- ★ *Nocciola* hazelnut
- ★ *Panna* whipped cream
- ★ *Pera* pear
- ★ *Pesca* peach
- ★ *Pistacchio* pistachio
- ★ *Pompelmo* grapefruit
- ★ *Stracciatella* chocolate chip
- ★ *Tarocchio* blood orange
- ★ *Tiramisu* tiramisu
- ★ *Vaniglia* vanilla

Kids are welcome everywhere in Italy. You will have no problem getting them to adapt to the local cuisine (assuming, of course, they like pizza, pasta and ice cream), while accommodation ranges across the entire family-friendly spectrum, from campsites and holiday villages to beach resorts and self-catering villas. If there's one potential fly in the *gelato* it's that major tourist attractions can become very crowded and unbearably hot during the summer – so try not to overdo the sightseeing.

Babies

Italy promises a well-earned rest for new parents. Most hotels offer babysitting if you arrange it in advance, but a far more relaxing alternative is to rent a villa. Self-catering might not sound like much of a rest, but it suits a lot of new parents desperate to maintain feeding and sleeping routines. If renting a car, check that the safety standards of any children's seats provided are up to scratch or, better still, consider bringing your own. Don't forget sunshades for car windows. With a baby in tow you're unlikely to want to embark on an ambitious sightseeing tour of Rome (in fact, you'd be wise to avoid all Italian cities during the fierce heat of midsummer). However, even a modest medieval town in Tuscany can reduce you to a gibbering wreck trying to cajole a pushchair along its cobbled streets and pavements. To preserve sanity, take an all-terrain three-wheeler buggy or a backpack-style baby carrier.

Toddlers/pre-school

That villa with a pool still sounds very tempting with children of this age. However, you do need to be extra vigilant about pool safety: holiday villages may well have fenced-off pools and lifeguards on duty; private villas may well not. For a seaside holiday, Italy has no end of lovely beaches to choose from, especially in Sicily, while the northern Lakes offer a freshwater alternative (just remember to pack jelly shoes for the kids so they can negotiate the often pebbly beaches).

Historical and cultural sights are always a challenge with children of this age. The concepts of queuing, keeping quiet in cathedrals and art galleries, staying behind security barriers and not mauling priceless works of art are all completely alien to them. This doesn't necessarily mean that your Italian sojourn need be culturally bereft. Car-free city piazzas can provide toddlers with (supervised) freedom while you admire the façades of the *duomo* (cathedral) or the *palazzo*. And you can always take it in turns to sightsee – one parent entertains the kids while the

Decisions, decisions...

See page 109 for a guide to gelato flavours and how to order an ice cream in Italian.

Special needs

An increasing number of hotels, restaurants, monuments and galleries are installing facilities, such as ramps and lifts, to assist wheelchair users. CO IN Sociale (coinsociale.it) provides information and assistance for disabled travellers in Rome. For excellent advice on accessible travel around Venice, try Informahandicap Venezi (comune.venezia.it) which provides several ideas for 'itineraries without barriers'.

Single parents

Eurocamp (eurocamp.co.uk) and Keycamp (keycamp.ie) offer special deals for single parents at their holiday camps in Italy. Most also have babysitting services or activity clubs (for toddlers to teens) where you can sit back and relax while the kids are entertained. Try the Adventure Company (adventurecompany.co.uk) for single-parent departures on some of its Italy trips.

> **Italian piazzas are great places to go with kids. They're lined with restaurants, and a lot are car-free so the kids can run around in safety – and in view – while parents enjoy a drink or a meal. We always found waiters happy to make space for high chairs, which most restaurants had.**
> Jason Hobbins

other snatches an hour or two of Bernini browsing.

Kids/school age

In Italy, vast swathes of the school curriculum come to life. Few places are more synonymous with famous artists, brilliant minds and ancient cultures. The food is an education in itself; the language is fun to learn; and to top it all, Italy scores top marks on the geography front, with everything from volcanoes to vast limestone caverns.

There is a downside though. Few museums and galleries have the special children's facilities or activities that you find in northern Europe. Nor is there much in the way of hands-on science centres. At this age they at least have the potential to enjoy a full day's sightseeing; and if not then you can always resort to bribery (a double scoop of *gelato* for the *duomo* and we'll throw in a waterpark for the Renaissance exhibition).

Don't forget, though, that there is far more to Italy's heritage than shuffling around daunting museums and galleries. Most kids will leap at the challenge of climbing the steps to the top of a medieval bell tower, while sites like Pompeii and the Colosseum instantly ignite a child's imagination. And then, of course, there's all the purely fun stuff, from theme-park rides at Gardaland in northern Italy to snorkelling in the crystal-clear coves of Sicily.

Teenagers

Although sometimes a little too far off the beaten track for their liking, villas (with chill-out pools) are still a good option for teens – particularly if they bring along a friend or two. Holiday parks and resorts, with their clubs and activities, are also a good bet. Pick a location that provides a couple of teen mainstays, such as a city for shopping and nightlife and a beach or lake for watersports and hanging out with mates.

As for sightseeing, you might find that some teenagers are more in tune with their iPods than the Italian Renaissance – although just as many will be blown away by the country's spectacular art and architecture. If it's wow factor they need, concentrate on the big sights in Venice and Rome. Explore (explore.co.uk) offers an activity holiday in Tuscany for families with teenagers.

How to make museums fun

▸▸ Head straight for the gift shop, buy some postcards showing the exhibits and then challenge children to find the actual paintings and sculptures.
▸▸ Check at the ticket office whether it's okay for kids to take a sketchbook and pencil into the museum with them.
▸▸ Pick a couple of straightforward themes (such as horses and angels) and challenge kids to spot five or 10 of each before moving on to the next gallery.

Those about to sightsee, we salute you! Touring Rome with kids requires a gladiatorial effort. It's a hot, sprawling, chaotic city packed with ancient monuments, museums, churches and galleries. Throw in the Vatican and it will feel like two city breaks rolled into one. But before you sidestep Italy's vibrant capital, just think what you will be missing: Michelangelo's Sistine Chapel ceiling, the Pantheon, the Roman Forum, the Colosseum... kids will feel like time travellers as they explore these historical icons. Just make sure you don't enslave them in a non-stop history lesson – Rome's lighter side (*gelato*, fountains, parks, shopping, etc) will help to ensure your conquest of the city is enjoyable as well as informative.

City highlights

» **Day 1** Start with the Colosseum. It opens at 0900 and can be reached by Metro Line B to Colosseo station, as well as by bus or tram. It's not only big and impressive, but it's the one sight in Rome that children are most likely to relate to – especially teenagers who have watched Russell Crowe strut his stuff in *Gladiator*. You can join an organized tour or explore the ruins on your own. Be sure to stand centre stage where warriors, slaves and wild beasts engaged in deadly combat nearly 2000 years ago. Try to imagine the roar of the 70,000-strong crowd, and don't miss the maze of tunnels and pens where lions, tigers and other animals were held prior to the slaughter. About 200 cats still prowl the Colosseum – challenge your kids to see how many they can spot.

Now that your children are fired up about ancient Rome, take them to see the adjacent Roman Forum (Foro Romano), a patchwork of ruined triumphal arches, basilicas and temples that once formed the city's civic and ceremonial heart. You can access it from Via dei Fori Imperiali, but kids will grasp the layout better if you walk up the small hill behind the Colosseum and enter the Forum by the Arch of Titus on Via Sacra – the street along which victorious commanders paraded their spoils of war. Don't even attempt to see everything in the Forum. By now it will be approaching midday and you'll be getting hot and hungry. Make a beeline for the House of the Vestal Virgins and the vaulted Basilica of Constantine and Maxentius, then hop in a taxi or bus (or walk if you have the energy) to Piazza Navona. Built around three flamboyant Baroque fountains, this beautiful square is lined with palaces and pavement cafés, and is usually bustling with street performers and artists.

Let the games begin...

Imagine the roar of the crowd as you stride into the arena at the Colosseum.

It's a great place to boost your children's energy levels aided, no doubt, by *tartufo*, a chocolate ice cream, fudge and cherry concoction served at Tre Scalini. From Piazza Navona, it's a short walk to the Pantheon, the best-preserved ancient building in Rome, where kids will be intrigued to discover an 8.3-m-wide hole (or *oculus*) in the dome. From the Pantheon, take bus route 116 to Villa Borghese, a large park where kids can rent bikes and boats or ride ponies – just rewards for all that sightseeing earlier in the day.

» **Day 2** By now, the Vatican City will seem irresistible, but you're risking cultural overload (and rebellion) by taking kids to the city state straight after a day hotfooting it around ancient Rome. Save the Vatican for your third day and keep day two relatively laid-back. Teenagers may want to check out the big names in *haute couture* along Via Conditti or scour Via del Corso for anything from CDs to shoes.

Nearby is the famous Trevi Fountain which is particularly beautiful when floodlit at night. Don't forget to toss a coin into the fountain, throwing it over your shoulder to ensure a safe return visit to the Eternal City. A little further north, the Rococo monument of the Spanish Steps (ablaze with azaleas in

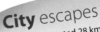

City escapes

★ **Tivoli** Located 28 km east of the city, this country escape for ancient Romans (pictured above) has temples and gardens, but is best known for nearby Hadrian's Villa, a lovely place to picnic or explore.
★ **Aquapiper** Cool relief from city sightseeing, Aquapiper waterpark (aquapiper.it) is located on the road to Tivo
★ **Lake Bracciano** This large crater lake set in beautiful countryside to the northwest of Rome is ideal for a refreshin swim during summer.

Best of the rest

1 Galleria Borghese
galleriaborghese.it.
This small museum in the Villa
Borghese gardens contains an
exceptional collection of Bernini
sculptures, as well as paintings by
Raphael and Caravaggio.

2 Museo Nazionale Romano
Split into three sites, the National Museum of Rome
houses one of the world's most important archaeological
collections, including the mosaics in the Baths of
Diocletian and classical statues in Palazzo Massimo.

3 Musei Capitolini
Located on Capitoline Hill, these
two fine museums contain some
of Rome's greatest treasures. In
Palazzo Nuovo, look out for the
famous sculpture of the *Dying
Galatian* and the original second-
century, bronze statue of Emperor Marcus Aurelius
astride his horse (a replica is in the piazza between the
two museums). In the Palazzo dei Conservatori kids will
be wowed by the outsize body parts from the Colossus
of Constantine and intrigued by the bronze, *Lo Spinario*,
showing a boy trying to remove a thorn from his foot.

St Peter's Square, Vatican

Trevi Fountain, Rome

May) is another popular spot from which to soak
up the city's atmosphere. The best *gelato* in the
Trevi neighbourhood is at San Crispino on Via della
Panettaria, while pick of the pizzas can be found at
Pizzeria da Ricci on Via Genova.

Afterwards, assuming you can stomach it, wander
over to the Capuchin Crypt on Via Veneto where the
bones of dead monks adorn the walls. Alternatively,
for something equally macabre, head south along Via
Appia Antica to visit the Catacombs – a labyrinth of
cemeteries where roughly hewn, dimly lit corridors
are lined with tomb niches. Some, like the Catacombs
of San Domitilla, still contain human bones.

▶▶ **Day 3** The Vatican might only cover 43 ha, but what
the world's smallest state lacks in size it more than
makes up for with historical, cultural and religious
esteem. The quickest way to get there is by Metro
Line A to Ottaviano San Pietro, from where it's a short
walk to St Peter's Square. This vast papal-audience
ground is flanked by the 284 columns of Bernini's
Colonnade (great for hide and seek) and punctuated
at its centre by an obelisk brought from Egypt in
AD 37. But inevitably you will be drawn towards
the massive façade of St Peter's Basilica, the world's
largest church. Doors open daily at 0700, but you
won't be allowed inside wearing sleeveless tops,

shorts or above-knee-length skirts. Suitably attired,
steer your children towards the first nave on the right
where Michelangelo's exquisite marble carving, *Pietà*,
depicts a grief-stricken Mary cradling the crucified
body of Jesus. For children, one of the highlights of a
visit to the Vatican is to climb St Peter's 136.5-m-high
dome from where there are superb views across the
rooftops of Rome. You can take a lift part of the way,
but that still leaves you with some 330 steps.

By now your kids will be developing a healthy
respect for Michelangelo (St Peter's dome was his
design), but if there's one Michelangelo masterstroke
that you've simply got to show them, it has to be
the ceiling art of the Sistine Chapel. To reach it you
need to navigate the immense art treasury of the
Vatican Museums. It's a 20-minute walk from the
entrance of the museum complex to the Sistine
Chapel without even pausing to admire the wealth of
Roman antiquities and Renaissance paintings. What,
if anything, you decide to linger over will depend on
how your children are bearing up and how much
queuing you've had to endure. Ultimately, though,
those nine colourful scenes from *Genesis* (which took
Michelangelo four painstaking years to complete,
mostly while lying on his back at the top of a scaffold)
are usually enough to lift the eyes and the spirits of
even the most jaded child.

Inside info

▶▶ The three-day Roma
Pass (romapass.it) offers
free admission to the
first two museums and/
or archaeological sites
visited and full access to
public transport.
▶▶ Bring binoculars so
kids can see the details
on the ceiling of the
Sistine Chapel.
▶▶ For further
information, visit
turismoroma.it, and
vatican.va.

A beautiful Tuscan villa set amongst cypress trees and vineyards, a day or two marvelling at the art treasures of Florence and a lazy tour between historic hilltop towns like San Gimignano. No wonder Tuscany is one of Italy's best-loved destinations. But won't kids find it a bit boring? Not if the villa has a pool and you transform your cultural forays into an adventure trail of medieval streets to be explored, bell towers to be conquered and *gelato* to be sampled.

Siena

At 102 m in height, the Torre del Mangia is one of the tallest medieval towers in Italy. Challenge your kids to climb the 505 steps to the top from where there are superb views across Siena's medieval maze of lanes and *piazzas*. Afterwards, relax with a picnic on the Piazza del Campo – you can get supplies from the grocery store down Via di Salicotto. One of Europe's greatest public squares, the fan-shaped Campo has been used for everything from bullfights to executions, but it is now famed for its Palio, a fiercely contested bareback horse race that takes place twice a year. Nearby, the Piazza del Duomo is dominated by Siena's magnificent Gothic cathedral, which contains sculptures by Michelangelo.

Leaning Tower of Pisa

Piazza Duomo, opapisa.it. Apr-Sep, daily 0830-2000, Oct-Mar. Italy's most recognizable landmark, the Leaning Tower of Pisa has immense appeal to children. The ultimate stack of building blocks teetering on the brink of collapse, there's something intrinsically childlike about the eight-storey belfry. Recent engineering work stabilized the 12th-century wonky wonder, reducing its lean to around 5 m from the vertical. It's now safe to climb the 294 steps to the top, but only as part of a 30-minute guided tour (minimum age eight). Most people contemplate the tower (and the splendid *duomo* and baptistry) from the lawns of the Campo dei Miracoli – a lovely spot for a picnic. If your kids are crestfallen because they're too young to climb the tower, try to placate them with the medieval alternative in the northwest corner of the Campo – it's free and there's no age limit.

Lucca

Founded by the Romans in 180 BC, Lucca's crowning glory is the 11th-century cathedral of San Martino – unless, of course, you're an opera fan in which case you will want to call in at Puccini's birthplace on Via di Poggio. Children, on the other hand, will be drawn to Lucca's massive 16th-century ramparts which encircle the town and are wide enough for you to walk or cycle on – a popular elevated circuit shaded by overhanging trees. To the northeast of Lucca, Collodi has a Pinocchio theme park (pinocchio.it) in recognition of the fact that Carlo Lorenzini penned the story of the wooden puppet here in 1881.

Best hill towns

Children will feel like they've walked into a fairy tale in San Gimignano (sangimignano.com). No fewer than 14 weather-beaten stone towers (originally there were 72) rear above a skyline that has remained largely unchanged since the Middle Ages. For the best views, scramble up the ramparts of the Rocca, a ruined 14th-century fortress tucked into the eastern side of the town. Torre della Diavola (She-Devil's Tower) houses the Museo della Tortura, containing enough gruesome torture instruments to make children squirm with delight.

In the far east of the region, Cortona has all the sweeping views, medieval alleyways and Renaissance art that you'd expect from a Tuscan hill town. What sets it apart from the others, though, is its rich Etruscan heritage, evident in the many ancient tombs dotting the surrounding countryside. You can see artefacts from this early civilization, including an oil lamp dating back to the 5th century BC, in the Museo dell'Accademia Etrusca. Follow Via S Margherita to the Fortezza Medicae – the views towards Lake Trasimeno make it worth the steep climb. Other hill towns worth visiting include Montepulciano and Montalcino.

Best beaches

Not far from Pisa or Lucca, the sandy beach resort of Viareggio has a promenade lined with cafés and shops. There's more sand to the north at Forte dei Marmi, while the best beaches on the island of Elba – reached by ferry from Piombino – are on the west coast.

Towering glories

The Torre del Mangia rises above the streets of Siena (above), while Pisa's famous Leaning Tower (below) continues to defy gravity.

Kids' top 10 Florence

1 Rise above it all by climbing the orange-tiled dome of the *duomo* (or adjacent *campanile*) for stupendous views and then, back at ground level, marvel at the famous bronze doors of the baptistry and the colourful Byzantine mosaics that decorate the ceiling above the cathedral's font.

2 Plan a treasure hunt in the Uffizi (uffizi.firenze.it), ticking off at least one painting by each of the following masters: Leonardo da Vinci, Michelangelo, Botticelli, Bellini, Raphael, Rembrandt, Rubens, Van Dyck and Caravaggio. An extra scoop of *gelato* afterwards if you correctly identify *The Birth of Venus* by Botticelli.

3 Grapple with science at the Museo Galileo (museogalileo.it), which not only features two of Galileo's telescopes, but also has demonstrations of his experiments on motion. Look out, too, for early maps and globes, and a gruesome collection of 19th-century surgical instruments.

4 Meet Michelangelo's *David*, a 5.2-m statue of the biblical hero who slew Goliath. The original sculpture is in the Galleria dell'Accademia (where you'll have to pay and queue), so you might want to settle instead for the copy in Piazza della Signoria.

5 Reward yourself with *gelato* for every museum, art gallery, cathedral and church that mum or dad drag you into. One of the best *gelato* parlours in the city is Vivoli (vivoli.it) on Via Isole delle Stinche, where only a triple scoop will do.

6 Indulge in a spot of window-shopping along Ponte Vecchio, the oldest surviving bridge in Florence (built in 1345) and famous for its antiques and jewellery shops.

7 Escape to Boboli Gardens for a game of hide-and-seek amongst the statues, box hedges and cypress trees – or find a shady spot for a picnic.

8 Browse the colourful stalls at Mercato Centrale for fruit, vegetables and flowers, as well as local Tuscan fare, like wild mushrooms, truffles and *porchetta* (roast suckling pig).

9 March over to the Museo Stibbert (museostibbert.it) where a spectacular column of armour-clad knights rides on horseback through a grand hall.

10 Don't stop at *gelato* when there are all kinds of other Florentine sweets and pastries to sample, such as *ricciarelli* (honey and almond cakes dusted with sugar).

Inside info

▶▶ Trains are quick and efficient, but a hire car offers a more flexible way to explore Tuscany's backroads and hill towns.
▶▶ The compact city centre of Florence is easily explored on foot.
▶▶ Siena's Palio horse race takes place on 2 July and 16 August.
▶▶ For further information, log on to firenzeturismo.it, terresiena.it, pisaturismo.it, and luccaturismo.it.

66 99 It's mid-August and we're on a ferry that's more crowded than a Ganges Delta riverboat during rush hour. We're making slow progress to the world's most adult, romantic, couply city. And it's hot – the kind of heat that usually makes kids whingy and clingy. But the voices around me are hushed because the Campanile is coming into view, rising like a giant exclamation mark above a sun-spangled sea.

"Is it really floating on the water?" chime Joe and Ellie, adding a touch of innocent wonder to this most magnificent of city approaches. The six-year-old twins look shocked when I tell them it's actually sinking. As soon as we disembark, Joe stamps on the pavement and Ellie seems reassured.

The queues for the Campanile and Palazzo Ducale are Disneyesque. Not that it matters – all Joe and Ellie want to do is feed the pigeons, which allows their parents ample time to gawp at the head-spinning façades of Piazza San Marco. It's only when an overgenerous handful of birdfood leads to Ellie being mobbed that we tear ourselves away and search for something cooling and calming.

Unfortunately, the gondoliers are charging €150 for a 40-minute punt – €200 if you want to include Rialto Bridge. So instead we delve into the wonderful maze of narrow streets beyond St Mark's Square and feign interest in Gucci handbag shops for quick doses of air-con before the staff get wise and evict us.

The shops selling masks and little glass ornaments captivate the twins – as does the spectacle of Rialto Bridge where day trippers are scrumming down on the parapet, five or six deep, for a glimpse of the Grand Canal. There is something surreal about being wedged in this mêlée of pixel-popping humanity while below you people glide serenely past in gondolas, trailing their fingers in the water... but Joe and Ellie seem genuinely entranced by the graceful curve of palazzos and the non-stop bustle of boats.

We extract ourselves from the crowds, buy ice creams and catch a waterbus back to St Mark's Square. There's just time to feed the pigeons again (which are now so bloated they have almost lost the ability of flight) before catching our ferry back to Cavallino.

So is it worth taking young kids to Venice? Of course! Just don't expect a romantic meal at a pavement café or a lingering look inside St Mark's Basilica. Instead, you'll experience the innocent fun of exploring a labyrinthine city floating on water. You'll also introduce your children to one of the world's cultural icons. And you'll spend a lot of money on pigeon food. William Gray

City escapes

★ **Museo Storico Navale** (Campo S Biagio) A shrine to ships of every kind, from Chinese junks to a replica of the Doge's ceremonial barge.

★ **Museo di Storia Naturale** (Salizzada del Fondaco dei Turchi) Contains an aquarium and a 4-m-tall dinosaur skeleton of *Ouranosauris nigeriensis* from the Sahara.

★ **Glassblowing** Take a ferry to the island Murano where skilled craftsmen have en forging Venetian glass for

It's going to be busy and expensive – and oppressively hot if you go in summer. And there might be the occasional fraught moment, cajoling your buggy up and down countless bridge steps, restraining your toddler from nose-diving into yet another canal or preventing teenagers from playing havoc with your holiday budget in all the fancy boutiques. But will any of this stop you from going? Of course not. Venice is irresistible – an exciting watery maze, a fantasy city of palaces and churches slowly sinking beneath the waves. Go there soon while it manages to keep its head above water.

One-day action plan

. The moment you stroll into Piazza San Marco (St Mark's Square) your children are likely to say one of three things:

➤ Can we feed the pigeons? No problem. Vendors sell bags of sweetcorn for €1.

➤ Can we climb up there? Yes. The views from the top of the 98.5-m Campanile are exhilarating, but be prepared to queue. Help kids pass the time by challenging them to count the arches in the Palazzo Ducale (Doge's Palace).

➤ Can we go on a gondola? Maybe. There's a gondola mooring at the edge of Piazza San Marco, but you'll pay a premium rate. For a quicker, cheaper, but less romantic option, *traghetto* gondolas shuttle back and forth across the Grand Canal.

Once you've fed the pigeons and conquered the Campanile, explore the warren of alleyways and canals between Piazza San Marco and Ponte di Rialto (Rialto Bridge), delving into shops along the way. There's a Disney Store near Ponte di Rialto, but if it's fantasy you're after, nothing beats the views of the Grand Canal from the most graceful and famous bridge in Venice. Nearby, you can board a *vaporetto* for a cruise along the Grand Canal, passing elegant old *palazzos* and famous landmarks like the Accademia (a treasure trove of Venetian paintings) and the fine Baroque church of Santa Maria della Salute. Vaporetto routes 1 and 82 will take you back to Piazza San Marco. Spend some time admiring the exquisite façade of the Basilica San Marco. Five mosaics adorn each of the doorways to this Byzantine beauty, while the four Horses of St Mark (replicas of the bronze originals kept inside) prance above the main entrance. You may well feel compelled to enter this great building – kids will be entranced by the mosaic floor and the dazzling

Gliding along in a gondola

Ascension Dome – but leave time for the Palazzo Ducale where highlights include a torture chamber.

Cavallino Peninsula

You could splash out on a converted palace or luxury hotel in Venice, but most budget-conscious families opt to stay outside the city. Curling out from the mainland towards the east of Venice, the Cavallino Peninsula – also known as the Litorale del Cavallino – makes an ideal family base. Not only is it packed with holiday resorts, but it also boasts a 15-km stretch of sandy beach and one of Italy's top water parks, known as Aqualandia (aqualandia.it). While water slides and crazy golf might seem a million miles from your dreamy-eyed vision of Venice, don't underestimate their usefulness as a negotiating tool. The kids get a day at Aqualandia, but only after you've perused the art collections in the Doge's Palace or Accademia. As for reaching Venice, Cavallino is perfectly placed, with regular boats departing from Punta Sabbioni and taking around 30 minutes to cruise to Ca' di Dio – a 10-minute walk from St Mark's Square.

Inside info

➤ Valid for a week, the Venice Card (venicecard.com) offers free admission to the Doge's Palace, various museums and churches, and use of toilets and nursery facilities.
➤ Venice is joined to the mainland by a causeway, but the best way to arrive is by *vaporetto* (actv.it), a waterbus network linking the city to Marco Polo Airport, Punta Sabbioni (Cavallino), Santa Maria Elisabetta (Lido) and other islands.
➤ For further info, visit turismovenezia.it.

Lake Como is peaceful and relaxed, Lake Maggiore is romantic and sophisticated and Lake Garda is a bustling summer playground. That may be oversimplifying the allure of northern Italy's three major lakes (all share stunning scenery, elegant lakeside towns, a rich historic and artistic heritage and plenty of beaches and watersports), but there's no denying the obvious family appeal of Lake Garda. Largest of the trio, it has over 120 beaches and a wide range of places to stay, from villas to campsites. The medieval fortress town of Sirmione makes a great day out, but the real clincher as far as kids are concerned is Gardaland, Italy's answer to Disney World.

Lake Garda

Located at the tip of a narrow peninsula protruding from the southern shore of Lake Garda, Sirmione is dominated by the 13th-century castle, Rocca Scaligera. Children will enjoy marching across the drawbridge and storming the towers and battlements, which are almost totally surrounded by water. When they've finished raining imaginary arrows on the tour boats below, lead them down the narrow lane along one side of the ramparts to a string of small beaches – all with good stone-skimming potential. Looping back into the heart of Sirmione you'll find streets and squares lined with galleries, craft shops, pizzerias and *gelato* parlours. Buy an ice cream and sit on the jetty wall, feeding the ducks and watching the ferries come and go. At the tip of the peninsula (which you can reach by following the Passeggiata Panoramica along the eastern shore) are the remains of a vast, sprawling Roman villa known as Grotte di Catullo – a lovely spot to contemplate the lake views.

Another child-friendly highlight in the south of Lake Garda is Gardaland (see right), but it's also worth spending a day or two exploring further north – either by ferry or by driving along the lakeside road. Heading up the west coast, you pass several towns and villages well endowed with medieval churches and castles, neoclassical mansions and idyllic waterfronts bristling with yachts and launches. Stop at Gardone Riviera to see the fine collection of alpine, Mediterranean and subtropical plants in the Giardino Botanico Hruska before pushing on up to the lake's northern tip where the approach to Riva del Garda is hemmed in by towering cliffs. With its lifeguard-patrolled swimming area and shady lakeside park, Riva is popular with families, while nearby Tobole gets the thumbs up from windsurfing and sailing aficionados. Pretty much

All aboard the water taxi

Public transport on Lake Garda beneath the towers and battlements of Sirmione.

Cinque Terre

Italian Riviera

❶ The Cinque Terre
Explore by foot, boat or train the five remarkable villages that cling to this stretch of rocky coastline on the Riviera di Levante.

❷ Aquarium of Genoa
One of Europe's largest aquariums (acquariodigenova. it) where imaginative displays including an 18-m long Caribbean coral reef and a recreation of a 15th-century wharf from the Port of Genoa.

❸ Grotte di Toirano
Venture into Italy's most beautiful caves (located in the Val Varatella) where a 90-minute tour leads you past subterranean pools and through caverns festooned with stalactites (toiranogrotte.it).

Milan action plan

Start by taking the elevator up the dome of the *duomo*. The Roof Terraces are bristling with spires adorned with some 3500 statues depicting saints, animals and monsters. Descend to Piazza del Duomo, bearing right towards the vast iron and glass-domed arcade of the Galleria Vittorio Emanuele II. Inside you'll pass shops and cafés before emerging at the other side facing Milan's famous opera house, Teatro alla Scala (teatroallascala.org). A short walk from the northwest of Milan's historic centre, Castello Sforzesco houses a large art collection, while the adjacent Sempione Park is an appealing green space with a lake.

Nearby Santa Maria delle Grazie is famous for Leonardo da Vinci's masterpiece, *The Last Supper*. Measuring 8.5 m wide and 4.6 m tall, the famous scene can be found above the doorway in what was once the convent's refectory. Reservations are required and a maximum of 25 people are admitted at a time – and only then for 15 minutes viewing. Is it worth it? The painting is in a fragile condition, so see it while you can is one argument. But far more interesting to kids is the Museo Nazionale della Scienza e della Tecnologia (museoscienza.org) on Via San Vittore, where a gallery is devoted to wooden models of inventions based on Leonardo sketches. The museum also has a wide range of interactive science exhibits covering topics as diverse as

acoustics and astronomy. There's not much in the way of English interpretation, but kids will figure out what to do.

Other child-friendly museums include the Museo di Storia Naturale and the Planetarium. Both are on Giardini Pubblici – a large city park. If the city gets too much, take the Metro Line 1 to Primaticcio, followed by bus route 64 which passes Aquatica (parcoaquatica.com), a waterpark in Milan operated by Gardaland. Teenage girls, however, will more likely want to stay central in Milan's fiendishly fashionable *quadrilatero*, where all the top Italian and international designer labels can be found, from Gucci to Prada.

everywhere you go, however, you'll find watersports galore, from luxury speedboat cruises to banana-boat rides. If it floats, you'll find it on Lake Garda.

Gardaland

Near Peschiera, T045-644 9777, gardaland.it. Apr-Sep, daily from 1000, Oct, weekends, plus Christmas.

Italy's largest theme park, Gardaland is like Disney, SeaWorld and Universal Studios rolled into one. The park has five themes – fantasy, adventure, energy, live shows and a SeaLife Aquarium – but anything goes at Gardaland. One moment you could be floating past jungle-clad ruins on a river rapids ride and the next you're hanging on for dear life riding the monstrous 90 km/h Raptor roller coaster. From exploring a pirate ship to delving into the myth of Atlantis, Gardaland will leave your head spinning. As well as the floorless roller coaster, Blue Tornado (above), big rides include Space Vertigo (a 40-m tower drop), Magic Mountain (a loop-the-loop roller coaster) and Sequoia Adventure (a bizarre ride where you spin round and upside down as if you were the chain on a chainsaw). For hot summer visits, there are plenty of water rides with potential for cooling splashes, like Colorado Boat.

And there is also plenty to keep little ones happy in Fantasy Kingdom with its train ride, tree house and animal farm. Don't miss 4D Adventure or the live theatre shows, which include everything from Broadway spectaculars to Gardaland on Ice. More themed fun can be found just up the road towards Lazise, where Caneva World (canevaworld.it) pushes the boundaries of reality even further with its triple whammy of Movieland Studios (full of stunt shows and simulators), waterpark and Medieval Times arena complete with jousting knights in armour and rowdy banquets.

🔍 Romeo Romeo

Base yourself on the southeast shore of Lake Garda and you are only around 40 km from Verona. Not to be missed are the spectacular Roman Arena and the market in Piazza Erbe which sells a mouth-watering range of local produce. Love-struck teenagers, meanwhile, will no doubt want to swoon over Casa di Giulietta where Romeo is said to have climbed to Juliet's balcony.

Umbria & Le Marche
Escaping the crowds

Unlike many of Italy's more visited regions, Umbria and Le Marche have little in the way of gold-star family attractions. There are no must-see Roman arenas, leaning towers or volcanoes – but what you will find is a gentle, rural and unspoilt part of Italy with rolling countryside dotted with medieval castles and hilltop towns, fine stretches of sandy beaches along the Adriatic coast and spectacular national parks in the Apennine Mountains. It's the perfect place to relax and experience a less hectic side to Italian life with plenty of the cultural and scenic highlights you'd expect from somewhere like Tuscany, but without the crowds.

Assisi

If there's one must-see in Umbria, it's this medieval hill town. The magnificent Basilica di San Francesco is renowned for its frescos depicting the life of St Francis, who is buried here. See if your kids can spot the beautiful *Sermon to the Birds*, one of the remarkable Giotto frescos that, like many works of art in the basilica, were carefully restored after the 1997 earthquake. From the basilica, walk to Assisi's main square, Piazza del Comune, for *gelati* on the steps of the fountain. From Assisi, a scenic route climbs the slopes of Monte Subiaso before descending to Spello where the church of Santa Maria Maggiore has frescos depicting scenes from the New Testament.

Perugia

Umbria's old capital is riddled with narrow medieval streets and there's also a museum containing prehistoric, Etruscan and Roman artefacts. It won't take long, however, before your kids latch on to the fact that Perugia is home to Italy's most famous confectionary. Italian for 'kisses', *baci* are creamy dark chocolates with rich hazelnut centres, wrapped in poetic love notes. Shops along pedestrianized Corso Vannucci are laden with the stuff, but for the ultimate sweet treat you can tour the Baci factory in Perugia's San Sisto suburb. Make arrangements at the tourist information office near the *duomo*. Just 2 km to the west, Città della Domenica (cittadelladomenica.com) is an animal park with various rides and attractions.

Other Umbrian highlights

In the north, Gubbio is a medieval hill town with terracotta-tiled houses and pink-stone palaces set against the thickly wooded slopes of the Apennines.

Castelluccio di Norcia, Umbria

Lake Trasimeno in the west has small sandy beaches and clear warm water, perfect for swimming and watersports, while lakeside towns like Castiglione del Lago offer trips to Isola Maggiore, an island known for its lace-making. Highlights in southern Umbria include the 80-m-high 14th-century aqueduct, Ponte delle Torri, in Spoleto, and the elaborate façade of the *duomo* in Orvieto. To escape into the wilds of the Apennine Mountains, head for Monti Sibillini (sibillini.net), a national park with great potential for hiking and horse riding.

Le Marche

To the east of Umbria, Le Marche has the added attraction of almost continuous sandy beaches running the length of its Adriatic coastline. The most picturesque section is the Conero Peninsula, a dramatic seascape of limestone cliffs, sandy coves and turquoise waters. The three resorts in the area, Portonovo, Sirolo and Numana, can get busy in summer, so consider taking a boat trip to one of the quieter coves along the coast. Head inland from Ancona (Le Marche's main town) and you enter the foothills of the Apennines, dotted with medieval towns like Urbino and Ascoli Piceno. Visit the spectacular cave system of Grotte di Frasassi (frasassi.com), the mighty fortress at San Leo and the tiny republic of San Marino (visitsanmarino.com).
In the south of Le Marche there are wonderful scenic drives through the Monti Sibillini.

Inside info ⓘ

▸▸ The A1 motorway between Florence and Rome skirts western Umbria, and there are also good rail and bus links.
▸▸ The A14-E55 and a good rail service link the coastal resorts of Le Marche.
▸▸ For further information, log on to regioneumbria.eu, and turismo.marche.it.

Tucked into the heel of Italy, this little-visited province may not have the cultural clout of Rome, Florence or Venice, but what it lacks in notoriety it more than compensates for with a quirky range of monuments – from Neolithic tombs and Gothic cathedrals to the curious *trulli* houses. And even if you are not a culture vulture, Puglia has plenty of rich pickings. Natural highlights include the lovely beaches and forests of the Gargano Peninsula, the spur on Italy's heel, while 20 km offshore lie the Tremiti Islands, an unspoilt cluster of limestone islands.

Trani

Bari & Trani

Most tourists arrive at the busy Adriatic port of Bari to catch a ferry to Greece or Croatia. However, if you find yourself with a few hours to spare in Bari, head to the old district of Città Vecchia to explore the castle. Also worth a look, Bari's Basilica di San Nicola is one of Puglia's earliest churches (begun in 1087), while further north along the coast, Trani's Norman *duomo* (San Nicola Pellegrino) rises above a harbour filled with blue-hulled fishing boats. One of the most striking of Puglia's monuments can be found inland from Trani on the central limestone plateau known as Le Murge. Built around 1240, Frederick II's Castel del Monte is a perfect octagon in shape, with a hefty tower at each corner.

Alberobello

A large swathe of this town is pimpled with over 1000 *trulli* – tiny, conical-roofed houses sprouting from narrow streets like stone toadstools. Constructed entirely of local limestone, each circular dwelling is no larger than a garden gazebo; most are whitewashed while a few are daubed with strange pagan symbols. Kids will love exploring this World Heritage Site, particularly since many *trulli* are now used as craft or souvenir shops.

Lecce

Dubbed the Florence of the Baroque, Lecce is renowned for its elaborate architecture. The imposing façade of the 16th-century Santa Croce church is dominated by a large rose window surrounded by intricately sculpted columns and friezes where saints, dragons and gargoyles crouch in niches like seabirds on a crowded cliff. Lecce is also famed for papier-mâché (known as *cartapesta* in Italian), and figures can be purchased in several shops.

Otranto

Pleasure boats and fishing trawlers form orderly rows across the turquoise shallows of Otranto's harbour where, 3500 years ago, Mycenaean traders beached their ships. These Bronze Age forays were a precursor to the first Greek colonies in Italy. A scenic route hugs the coast south of Otranto, weaving past medieval watchtowers, limestone caves and seaside villages.

Alberobello – *trulli*, madly steeply

🔍 **Best** beaches

Dotted with sandy coves and beaches, the rugged Gargano Peninsula (parcogargano.it) is popular with holidaymakers, as are the Tremiti Islands, accessible by boat from Termoli.

🔍 **Best** local buys

Finely sculpted papier-mâché figures (often depicting nativity characters) can be found in Lecce. Alberobello is renowned for its rugs and fabrics, and the *trulli* district is also a good place to purchase local pasta and olive oil.

Inside info

▶▶ The historic centres of most towns are compact and easily explored on foot.
▶▶ Buses and trains serve many destinations, but for ultimate flexibility rent a car at one of the region's airports.
▶▶ From Naples, allow three hours to drive to Bari.
▶▶ For further information, log on to pugliaturismo.com.

Bay of Naples
In the shadow of Vesuvius

Italy's third largest city, Naples is hot, crowded and chaotic. Not only are its pavements as congested as its roads, but scooters often fail to distinguish between the two. So why bring kids here? First and foremost, Naples is the jumping-off point for excursions to Pompeii – the most enigmatic ruins you'll find anywhere. And then there's the Amalfi Coast – a bit on the posh side, but nevertheless a fine excuse for beach hopping and a breathtaking coastal drive. But even Naples itself is worth a day or two of sightseeing. If the castles and archaeology museum don't do it for your kids, at least you can introduce them to some of Italy's most authentic pizza and ice cream.

Castel Nuovo, Naples

Naples

An ideal place to start is Castel Nuovo. Not only does this striking fortress lie at the city's heart, but its ramparts afford views towards Mount Vesuvius brooding across the Bay of Naples. Nearby, in striking contrast, is the Galleria Umberto I with its glass-domed roof built in the late 1800s. Continue walking around Piazza Trieste e Trento to Caffè Gambrinus – the city's prime spot for pastries and ice cream. Kids can then run off their sugar high in the paved expanse of Piazza del Plebiscito while parents admire the magnificent façade of the Palazzo Reale – once one of the Mediterranean's most important royal courts. A short walk along the seafront leads to Castel dell'Ovo, the oldest castle in Naples, parts of which date from the ninth century. It now shelters a small marina and several popular restaurants.

Located in the heart of central Naples, Spaccanapoli threads a tourist lifeline between numerous churches, statues and historic buildings. A narrow canyon-like street, it is one of the most vibrant parts of the city. Street vendors crowd the cobbles, while shops are crammed with everything from pasta and pastries to Neapolitan masks and clay nativity scenes. Cafés overflow with locals sipping coffee, while open-air restaurants serve delicious pizza Margherita. One church definitely worth visiting on Spaccanapoli is Santa Chiara – if only to relax in its garden-framed cloister, which is beautifully decorated with hand-painted tiles. At the end of Spaccanapoli, turn right on Via Toledo (Naples' main shopping street) and continue walking up the hill until you reach the Museo Archeologico Nazionale. Must-sees include *Hercules* and other famous statues from the Farnese Collection. Many relics from Pompeii and Herculaneum have also found sanctuary here, including some wonderfully intricate mosaics. There

is also a fascinating scale model of the Pompeii excavations – the perfect primer before visiting the actual ruins.

Pompeii

T081-857 5331, pompeiisites.org. Nov-Mar, daily 0830-1700, Apr-Oct, daily 0830-1930 ⏩Train Circumvesuviana, stopping at Pompei Scari or Pompeii Santuario.

Set the scene for your kids: It's August in the year AD 79. For several days, small earthquakes have shaken Pompeii, but otherwise life in the thriving Roman city continues as normal. Then, on the afternoon of the 24th, Vesuvius suddenly erupts, shooting a column of ash over 30 km into the atmosphere. Fearful of Vulcan, the Roman god of fire, the people of Pompeii cower at the sight. Then terror and blind panic seizes them as a cloud of superheated, poisonous fumes and volcanic debris sweeps down the volcano killing everything in its path. The eruption lasts 19 hours, by which time Pompeii lies buried beneath 6 m of pumice and ash, while nearby Herculaneum has vanished beneath a deep layer of mud and lava.

Such was the ferocity of the eruption that both settlements were petrified in time. At the excavated ruins of Pompeii, look for cart tracks along Via dell'Abbondanza and visit Modesto's bakery where several loaves of carbonized bread were found. Perhaps too haunting for youngsters, the Garden of the Fugitives contains over a dozen plaster casts of human victims – adults and children – frozen

Inside info

⏩ Calm sanctuaries for frayed nerves include the cavernous nave of the *duomo* and the cloisters of Santa Chiara; for somewhere to let kids run around in traffic-free safety, try Piazza del Plebiscito.
⏩ Circumvesuviana train services connect Naples with Pompeii and Sorrento.
⏩ For further info, log on to inaples.it, theamalficoastline.com, and guidevesuvio.it.

Positano, Amalfi Coast

in anguished postures as they succumbed to the onslaught of ash and lethal fumes. There are other areas of Pompeii that you might wish to steer kids away from – particularly the brothels where frescos depict the services of prostitutes in graphic detail. Otherwise, must-sees include the well-preserved temples, baths and theatres, as well as the House of the Vettii with its colourful friezes.

Sorrento & the Amalfi Coast

A dramatic coastline of white limestone cliffs along the southern boundary of the Bay of Naples, the Sorrento Peninsula is not your typical family seaside destination. Villages cling to its precipitous slopes, beaches are few and far between, and much of the accommodation tends to be quite up-market. Nevertheless, Sorrento makes a good base for exploring the surrounding area (including Pompeii and Herculaneum). The town has a range of shops and restaurants, and you can take a boat trip to the island of Capri (35 minutes). Continue around the peninsula and state road 163 begins to twist and turn along the spectacular Amalfi Coast. The fishing village of Praiano and the pastel-tinted houses of Positano, stacked like Lego blocks against the cliffside, are just some of the highlights.

The ruins of Pompeii with Vesuvius in the background; left: a victim of the eruption

Just 3 km from the toe of Italy, Sicily is an island of contrasts where rolling wheatfields, olive groves, vineyards and citrus plantations hold sway beneath the brooding hulk of Europe's largest volcano. While Etna puffs away in the east, holidaymakers seek out Sicily's sandy beaches or explore its wealth of archaeological sites – a rich legacy of the many civilizations that have left their mark on this fiery and fascinating island.

Volcanoes

Constantly simmering and regularly boiling over in spectacular pyrotechnic displays of bright red sparks and molten lava, 3370-m Mount Etna is one of Italy's most impressive (and unexpected) sights. Not only is it Europe's largest volcano, but it is also one of its most active. Parents might be a little alarmed to discover that it's possible to set foot on the slopes of Etna. Few volcanoes, however, are more closely monitored and, as long as you arrange a guided tour, you should be safe. Take the Circumetnea Train (circumetnea.it) from Catania to Nicolosi and Zafferana for walks on old lava flows. Remember to bring warm clothing, sturdy shoes and sunglasses to protect your eyes from windblown grit. Jeep tours start from the Rifugio Sapienza Etna Sud and follow the line of the cable car that was destroyed in the 2001 eruption. For a less intimidating volcanic escapade, take a boat trip from Milazzo on Sicily's north coast to the Aeolian Islands, a volcanic archipelago where you can swim and snorkel from black-sand beaches, collect fragments of pumice floating in the sea and delve back in time at the museum in Lipari. To the north of the main group of islands lies Stromboli – a feisty little volcano that has been active for more than two millennia.

Temples & castles

Sicily's top historical sites include the ancient Greek theatre at Taormina (Sicily's first resort), the Roman hunting lodge of Villa Romana del Casa, the lavish mosaics inside the Norman cathedral at Monreale and the magnificent Greek temple ruins at Agrigento (pictured right) and Selinunte. Among Sicily's numerous castles ripe for rampart-romping and dungeon-delving, try Castello di Eurialo, Castello di Lombardia and Castello di Venere.

Inside info

▸▸ A city with diverse architecture, from Arabic to Art Nouveau, Palermo (palermo tourism. com) is Sicily's regional capital.
▸▸ You will find most types of accommodation on Sicily, from resorts, hotels and self-catering villas to farmstays and campsites.
▸▸ For further info, log on to regione.sicilia.it/ turismo, and parcoetna.ct.it.

Go green
Three ways to skip the flight

❶ Take your car by train to Italy. Dutch company Auto Slaaptrein (autoslaaptrein. nl) operates a weekly motorail service from June to September between s'Hertogenbosch (a short drive from the Channel ports of Hoek van Holland or Rotterdam) to Bologna. The train runs overnight with couchettes and sleepers southbound on Friday nights, northbound on Saturday nights.

❷ Get a coach pass with Eurolines (eurolines-pass. com) linking classic cities such as Venice, Florence, Milan, Rome and Naples.

❸ Travel by train from London to Rome. Book a ticket with Eurostar (eurostar.com) to Paris. Cross Paris by Métro to the Gare de Bercy and connect with the Palatino sleeper train to Rome. Bookings online at raileurope.co.uk.

How to keep a budding archaeologist happy

Bare Bones Tours (andantetravels.co.uk) takes adventurous and inquisitive people to some of the world's most exciting archaeological sites. You travel with a specialist guide who brings even the oldest, driest and dustiest ruins to life. Suitable for families with children aged nine and over, tours include Pompeii, Rome and Sicily.

Holiday operators

The Adventure Company adventurecompany.co.uk

Club Med clubmed.com

Eurocamp eurocamp.com

Exodus exodus.co.uk

Families Worldwide familiesworldwide.co.uk

First Choice Holidays firstchoice.co.uk

Headwater headwater.com

i-escape i-escape.com

Inntravel inntravel.co.uk

Keycamp keycamp.com

Kirker Holidays kirkerholidays.com

Thomson Lakes & Mountains thomsonlakes.co.uk

Mark Warner markwarner.co.uk

Powder Byrne powderbyrne.com

Real Holidays realholidays.co.uk

Sardatur Holidays sardatur-holidays.co.uk

Scott Dunn scottdunn.com

Sovereign sovereign.com

Spanish Affair spanishaffair.com

Sunvil sunvil.co.uk

Thomson Holidays thomson.co.uk

Travelbeam travelbeam.co.uk

Vintage Travel vintagetravel.co.uk

In the USA
Abercrombie and Kent abercrombiekent.com

Adventures by Disney abd.disney.go.com

Tauck Bridges tauck.com

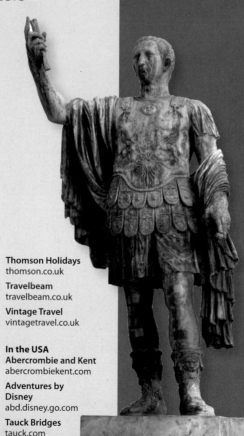

When to go
Italy has a varied climate, based on its distinct geographical regions. In the north, expect cold Alpine winters and warm, wet summers; in the **Po Valley** the summers are hot and dry and the winters are cold and damp; the rest of Italy has a wonderful climate of long hot summers (with temperatures consistently over 25°C) and mild winters, with cooler weather and a chance of winter snow in the **Appenines**.

Italy's historic sites and cities are busy and crowded from spring to October and the heat can be oppressive during the midsummer months of July and August. Remember, though, that you can always escape into the cooler hill towns when the heat gets too much. Be aware that **Rome** and the Vatican City will be packed with pilgrims at Christmas and Easter, and that **Venice** triples its population during Carnevale in February. Consider visiting Venice in the low season (October to March) – everything stays open and gondola rides will be cheaper!

Getting there
Milan, Verona and Bologna are the key transport hubs in northern Italy; Rome and Naples in the south. The national carrier, Alitalia (alitalia.com), flies from Europe and the United States to all major cities in Italy. British Airways (britishairways.com) flies to 17 Italian destinations, including Rome, Naples, Milan, Pisa and Bologna.

For **budget flights** to Italy, BMI British Midland (flybmi.com) serves Bologna, Milan, Naples, Rome and Venice; easyJet (easyjet.com) flies to Bari, Brindisi, Lamezia, Milan, Naples, Pisa, Rimini, Rome, Sardinia, Sicily, Turin, Venice and Verona; and Ryanair (ryanair. com) also covers numerous Italian destinations including Bari, Bologna, Brindisi, Milan, Pisa and Rome.

Getting around
Travelling within Italy usually poses few problems, particularly in the north of the country, where the road, bus and rail networks are modern and efficient. Alitalia (alitalia.com) operates an extensive network of **internal flights** as does low-cost Club Air (clubair.it).

Fly-drive deals are often the cheapest way to arrange **car hire**. Most rental agencies are located at major Italian airports. Motorways, although generally good, can become heavily congested at weekends and during peak periods. One way to avoid the busy routes is to take the **train**, which provides good value and is especially useful if you want to link two or more cities (where you'd be crazy to attempt to drive yourself). Trenitalia (trenitalia.com) has an online reservation system.

Italy also has a large and well-developed network of **ferries** that ply routes between offshore islands, as well as making international crossings. SNAV Collegamenti Marittimi (snav.it) operates ferries between Civitavecchia and Olbia (Sardinia) and Palermo, and from Naples to Palermo, Capri and Ischia. Also try Grand Navi Veloci (gnv.it).

The best way to get around Italian cities varies from place to place. For example in Venice, waterbuses or *vaporetti* are abundant; in Rome, buses are most useful, and in Milan there is an efficient metro. You will often find that walking is quicker than taking a taxi or bus through congested streets.

Accommodation

Families are spoilt for choice when it comes to places to stay in Italy – you will find everything from beachside campsites and rural farmstays to resorts, hotels and converted *palazzos*.

Most **hotels** welcome children, even if they have no special facilities. Some of the cheaper hotels may not be able to supply cots, but most hotels will provide an extra child's bed if required. Many of the big international hotel chains have a presence in Italy, including Best Western (bestwestern.com) and Starwood Westin (starwoodhotels.com).

Most of Itay's **self-catering** accommodation is generally of a high standard, and is often in wonderful locations. The Associazione Nazionale per l'Agriturismo (agriturist.it) represents more than 2000 farms, villas and mountain chalets and offers reasonably priced accommodation. For something unusual, contact Apulia Bella (apuliabella.com) to arrange a stay in a converted *trullo* in the Puglia region.

For an online directory of Italian **campsites** and resorts, log on to camping.it. For **holiday villages** offering accommodation in well-equipped chalets and tents, try Eurocamp (eurocamp.com), Keycamp (keycamp.com) and Vacansoleil (vacansoleil.co.uk).

Food & drink

Food is an obsession in Italy and a quintessential part of Italian lifestyle. If your children enjoy pizza, pasta and ice cream they won't go hungry. However, encourage them to try some of the regional specialities in the table, below, if only to supplement their diet of pizza Margherita, spaghetti bolognese and *gelato*.

Health & safety

It is strongly recommended that you have good medical and travel insurance prior to visiting Italy. EU citizens should ensure they have a European Health Insurance Card (EHIC), which entitles the holder to emergency medical treatment. It does not cover you for medical repatriation, on-going medical treatment or treatment of a non-urgent nature.

Italy is generally a safe place to visit, with few health and safety risks. There is a small risk of contracting Leishmaniasis from an infected sand fly bite or Lyme disease from a tick bite.

Crime levels in Italy are generally low. The biggest risk to tourists is petty crime such as bag snatching – particularly in major tourist spots. Try to keep valuables hidden from view.

Regional specialities

★ **Rome**   *Spaghetti alla Carbonara*   Spaghetti cooked with raw egg, Parmesan cheese, cracked black pepper and pancetta (bacon)

★ **Tuscany**   *Panforte*   Fruit cake made with chewy nougat, fruits and spices
Donzelle   Fried dough balls
Crostini   Rounds of bread toasted and brushed with olive oil with a number of toppings such as chunks of tomato or spread with chicken liver paté

★ **Venice**   *Tiramisu*   Dessert with a creamy sauce of mascarpone and eggs between layers of sponge cake drenched in coffee or liqueur – pictured below
Pasta e fagioli   Bean soup with homemade pasta

★ **Umbria**   *Schiacciata*   Similar to pizza crust, bread baked with olive oil and sometimes with cooked greens and onions

★ **Sicily**   *Cassata*   Sponge cake, ricotta cream, marzipan and candied fruits
Granita   Fruity iced drink

Fast facts

Time GMT+1
Languages Italian
Currency Euro (€)
Dialling code +39
Tourist information enit.it

Tuscan View Apartments

Where? Montaione, Tuscany.

Why? A perfect base from which to explore the hill town of San Gimignano, this working estate has lots to keep families happy, from tennis to horse riding. There is even a bar, restaurant and mini-market selling the estate's honey and olive oil. Equipped with living rooms and kitchenettes, the apartments are located in attractively restored farmhouses.

Contact Inntravel, T+44 (0)1653-617004, inntravel.co.uk

Villa Pia

Where? Lippiano, Tuscany.

Why? Stylish, yet relaxed and homely, this 18th-century manor is within easy reach of Florence and Siena. In addition to four family suites, with interconnecting bedrooms, there is a living room and kitchen with help-yourself fridge. Boasting wonderful views, the villa has two swimming pools, a sandpit, trampoline, adventure play areas and tennis court.

Contact Villa Pia, T+39 (0)75-850 2027, villapia.com

Club Med Kamarina

Where? Ragusa, on the southwest coast of Sicily.

Why? This 96-ha beachside holiday village has something for all ages, from catamaran sailing, rollerblading and tennis to swimming in one of three pools. Kids' clubs include a Mini Club Med for children aged four to 10 and Club Med Passworld for youngsters up to 17. For grown-ups there's a Club Med Spa, Turkish bath and aqua fitness classes.

Contact Club Med, T+44 (0)871-424 4044, clubmed.co.uk

Europa Silvella

Where? Lake Garda.

Why? With its own lakeside beach, this well-equipped holiday park is ideal for watersports. It also has its own swimming pool, along with a range of other facilities, including shop, takeaway and restaurant. Accommodation is available in six-berth tents or mobile homes – all scattered through shady woodland. The Gardaland theme park is just 33 km away.

Contact Eurocamp, T+44 (0)844-406 0402, eurocamp.com

Ca'Savio Campsite

Where? Cavallino, Venice.

Why? Venice is just a bus and boat ride away from this lively holiday camp with its vast swimming pool complex and nearby sandy beach. Accommodation ranges from five-person tents to well-equipped mobile homes sleeping up to seven. Facilities include a supermarket, restaurant and pizzeria, while activities range from minigolf to cycling, canoeing and archery.

Contact Keycamp Holidays, T+44 (0)844-844 1000, keycamp.com

Hermitage Hotel
Where? La Bidola, Elba.
Why? With a variety of interconnecting rooms, the Hermitage makes a great bolt hole for families. There's plenty to keep kids occupied, with windsurfing, waterskiing, jet-skiing and boat hire available from the private beach. As well as three saltwater swimming pools (including a children's pool), the hotel offers tennis, golf, mountain biking, volleyball, football and pétanque. For adults there's a wellness centre.
Contact Powder Byrne, T44 (0)208-246 5300, powderbyrne.com

Escape to the country, Italian style. Agriturismi – rural holidays in the heart of Italy's unspoiled countryside – are just the tonic for families in search of relaxation mingled with some gentle adventure and exploration. Real Holidays has some beautiful properties, from Umbrian villas to farms in Puglia and Sicily. Some are close to sandy beaches, while others offer countryside activities like horse riding and mountain biking.

realholidays.co.uk, 101familyholidays.co.uk

Sardinia highlights

A beautiful island with a rugged interior smothered in herb-scented *macchia* (scrubland) and a shoreline alternating between isolated coves and long sandy beaches, Sardinia makes a superb family-holiday destination – whether you like to hike and bike or flop on a beach. There's plenty of family accommodation available, from country villas to outstanding family resorts like Forte Village (fortevillageresort.com) and Chia Laguna (chialagunaresort.com), where kids can be kept happily occupied without you ever needing to leave the resort. It would be a shame, however, not to track down at least

one of Sardinia's quirky *nuraghe* (ancient stone structures dating from 1800 to 300 BC) that you will find dotted around the island. The Museo Archeologico Nazionale in Sardinia's capital, Cagliari, provides an insight into the people who created them. As for the best beaches, they are not just confined to the exclusive Costa Smeralda in the northeast. Look to the northwest and to the east near Cala Gonone for equally enticing coves and aquamarine waters. At the latter don't forget to take a boat trip to the famous sea caves, Grotte del Bue Marino.
sardegnaturismo.it

Central Europe

Swishing down a Swiss slippery slope

Tobogganing in the Alps. Right: castle tower in Germany.

Introduction
Central Europe

t first glance, the problem with Central Europe is that everywhere surrounding it looks more exciting. Head north to Scandinavia, south to the Mediterranean, east to Poland and the Baltics and west to France. But keep focused, keep staring straight ahead, because Central Europe not only offers an excellent range of family-holiday options, but it's also less crowded (and sometimes better value) than its higher-profile neighbours. Belgium, the Netherlands and Germany all have sandy beaches along the North Sea coast, while Austria and Switzerland have countless lakes that are perfect for swimming and watersports. The region has plenty of family-friendly hotels, guesthouses and holiday villages; public transport is super-efficient, and the cuisine features chocolate, chips, cheese and waffles. As for adventure, you will find every kind of action sport available in the Austrian and Swiss Alps, from rock climbing to whitewater rafting, while the Low Countries promise more in the way of gentle touring and cycle routes. In Germany you can follow in the fairy-tale footsteps of the Brothers Grimm, in Austria you can take your cue from *The Sound of Music* and in Switzerland you can ride on some of the world's most spectacular mountain railways.

❝ ❞ Amsterdam is like one big children's playground. We found loads to do, so don't let its red light reputation put you off. William Gray

◉ Did you know?

★ Amsterdam has 1281 bridges, 2000 houseboats and 600,000 bicycles.
★ Belgium produces 172,000 tonnes of chocolate each year, which is equivalent to 1000 solid chocolate blue whales.
★ The Manneken Pis in Brussels has over 700 costumes in the City Museum, including an Elvis jumpsuit.
★ Leichtenstein is the world's largest exporter of false teeth.
★ Mountains cover over 70% of Switzerland.

Star rating

Wow factor	★★★★
Worry factor	★
Value for money	★★★
Keeping teacher happy	★★★
Family accommodation	★★★★
Babies & toddlers	★★★★
Cool for teenagers	★★★

How to do a backside 360 spin

This is one of the easiest and safest advanced tricks to learn.
▸▸ Make sure you start the spin on the kicker before you take off.
▸▸ Drive your front shoulder towards your back foot and wind your arms in front of you, before unwinding them towards your back just as you approach the jump.
▸▸ After leaving the kicker you'll be flying backwards; keep turning your upper body, and you should still be travelling upwards, spinning blind until you're at your highest point in the jump.
▸▸ Keep turning those shoulders in the direction of the spin as you get ready to land. Don't forget, the board needs to travel 360 degrees, so keep that board turning.
▸▸ Using your arms for balance, prepare for the oncoming landing. Bring the board to the ground and meet the floor with a fully extended body, your board pointing perfectly forwards and your weight centred over the board.

Grow a tulip

Did you know that over nine billion flower bulbs are produced in the Netherlands every year? Tulips are some of the easiest to grow. Just follow these simple steps:

▸▸ Decide on a colour scheme or pattern.

▸▸ Purchase your bulbs; generally the bigger the bulb, the bigger the bloom.

▸▸ Prepare the soil by removing rocks and adding compost and bone meal.

▸▸ Plant the bulbs any time during autumn, placing them around 15-20 cm apart, and at a depth that's roughly twice the width of the bulb.

▸▸ After flowering, let the plant continue to grow until it dies back naturally.

🔍 Toblerone bite-size facts

▸▸ The famous Swiss chocolate is named after creator, Theodor Tobler, and *torrone*, a type of Italian nougat.
▸▸ The first Toblerone was sold way back in 1908.
▸▸ Toblerone's unique shape is based on Switzerland's famous Matterhorn mountain.

Great reads
5 children's books

Ages 3+
Play, Mozart, Play!
Peter Sis (Greenwillow)
Artist Peter Sís introduces the child genius, Wolfgang Amadeus Mozart.

The Complete Brothers Grimm Fairy Tales
Edited by Lily Owens (Random House)
With over 700 pages, this illustrated volume contains every published story by the Brothers Grimm, including well-known classics like Cinderella, The Frog Prince, Hansel and Gretel, Little Red Riding Hood, Rapunzel, Rumpelstiltskin and Snow White.

Ages 6+
The Adventures of Tintin
Herge (Egmont)
Read three classic Tintin adventures – *The Castafiore Emerald*, *Flight 714 to Sydney* and *Tintin and the Picaros* – by Belgian cartoon-strip supremo, Hergé, in volume 8 of this latest series of compilations.

Ages 8-11
Heidi
Johanna Spyri (Puffin)
The classic tale of a little Swiss girl who is sent to live with her grandfather in a mountain hut high in the Alps – an idyllic life that's shattered one day when Heidi is brought back to Frankfurt by her aunt Dete.

Ages 12+
Diary of Anne Frank
Anne Frank (Longman)
The tragic, deeply moving and inspiring story of a Jewish girl living in Amsterdam who is forced into hiding during the Holocaust.

Taste of Germany
perfect pretzels

Hailing from southern Germany in the 12th century, the humble pretzel is now a popular snack worldwide. This recipe shows you how to make soft pretzels, traditionally served in Bavaria for breakfast and accompanied by *weisswurst* (white sausage) and sweet mustard.

What you need
- 775 g flour
- 2 tsp salt
- 2 tbsp baking soda
- 4 tbsp brown sugar
- 1 tbsp yeast dissolved in water
- 1 egg

What to do
- Mix 300 ml of warm water with the yeast, brown sugar and salt.
- Gradually add the flour and mix to form a smooth dough.
- Chill the dough for an hour and then divide it into six pieces.
- Roll out each piece until it is slightly thicker than a pencil.
- Arrange each dough string into an upside-down U-shape.
- Hold the ends of each string and twist them together.
- Flatten the ends with your fingers, then bring them to the top of the pretzel pressing them into the dough.
- Place the pretzels on a greased baking tray and leave them to rise for about 30 minutes. Meanwhile, preheat the oven to 230°C.
- Boil 600 ml of water, add the baking soda, then dip each pretzel in the solution for about 10 seconds before placing them back on the baking tray.
- Beat the egg with one teaspoon of water, then brush it over the pretzels.
- Sprinkle the pretzels with salt, sesame seeds, cheese or cinnamon.
- Bake for around 15 minutes until golden brown.

☠ One to ride

Europe's biggest and highest roller coaster, Silver Star, can be found at Germany's Europa-Park (page 139).

Yodel like a local

- Find a remote mountain pasture with plenty of echo potential.
- Take a deep breath, open your mouth wide and sing, 'Hodl oh-ooh-dee'.
- Try it again, going high-pitched on the 'ooh'.
- Now practise 'Hodl-ay-ee-dee', going up a note on the 'ee'.
- Put the two lines together, and you're yodelling.
- Optional: finish with a 'heh-ee-dee-ho-ooh-dee-yo'.

On a mountain high

Family trek in the Swiss Alps.

Travelling with kids in Central Europe is a breeze. The Dutch in particular are relaxed and friendly, but you'll find families are generally welcome wherever you go. Children receive discounts on admission to most major sights, and often travel free on the slick public transport systems that operate across the region. You'll also have no problem finding family-oriented accommodation and places to eat.

Babies

Take the low ground or the high ground. Buggy-friendly Amsterdam is ideal for a relaxed city break, just as Austria or Switzerland are perfect for an Alpine jaunt or two while your baby is still light enough to be lugged around in a carrier or papoose.

Flying from the UK to anywhere in Central Europe is quick and simple, but with a baby in tow you might feel happier piling everything you need into your car and taking a ferry to Belgium or the Netherlands.

Don't forget that several hotel brands in the region, such as Kinderhotels and KidsHotels, offer all-inclusive packages with outstanding childcare for the tiniest of tots – not to mention some pampering incentives for their parents.

Toddlers/pre-school

Amsterdam's reputation for being family-friendly might not strike a chord with parents of hyperactive toddlers. One glance at a city map and all those canals is enough to give any parent instant palpitations. The same could be said for the Alps with their mountain paths and precipitous drops. In both cases, toddler reins are essential.

The big boon with this age group, of course, is that you can sidestep the busy school-holiday periods and take advantage of cheaper travel deals and less crowded cities, beaches or ski slopes. Just watch the weather though. Central Europe's climate can be unpredictable at the best of times – stray too far either side of midsummer and that balmy beach holiday on the North Sea coast could be decidedly damp and chilly. Still, there's always Center Parcs, where it's permanently subtropical thanks to their dome-covered water worlds. You'll find them in Belgium, the Netherlands and Germany.

Kids/school age

Holiday villages, such as Center Parcs and Eurocamp, are a great option for children of this age who often have limitless energy and require constant stimulation. Active holidays in Central Europe can

Special needs

In Belgium, Toegankelijk Reizen (toegankelijkreizen.be) has information on accommodation and transportation for people with disabilities. Log on to holland.com/uk/ Tourism/Transport/Disabled-Travelers for details of fully accessible tourist attractions in Holland. In Germany, NatKo (natko.de) promotes tourism for all, while in Austria, IBFT (urlaubfueralle.at) has information on barrier-free tourism. Mobility International Switzerland (mis-ch.ch) has information on wheelchair-accessible travel, accommodation and attractions in Switzerland.

Single parents

Single Parents on Holiday (singleparentsonholiday.co.uk) offers both winter and summer holidays in Austria, while Crystal (crystalski.co.uk) offers discounts for one-parent families on a selection of its skiing holidays. Special lone-parent deals are also available with Eurocamp (eurocamp. co.uk) and other camping operators.

> 66 99 **There were the inevitable stress points when the hills seemed to be alive with the sound of whingeing children. How come none of the Von Trapp family ever seemed to get mauled by horseflies, brush against stinging nettles or scrape their knees on gravelly mountain paths?**
>
> William Gray

include anything from cycling in the Low Countries to learning how to rock climb in the Alps. You can also satisfy many a childhood passion by touring one of Germany's themed routes, such as the Castle Road or Fairy Tale Route, and spending time at world-class theme parks like Europa-Park and Legoland.

From an educational point of view, Central Europe has plenty of lessons in store for children, from Van Gogh's strokes of genius to Salzburg's intriguing brush with salt.

Teenagers

When children begin learning about the World Wars at school, Central Europe will inevitably loom large in their minds. The tragic, thought-provoking story of Anne Frank, the Jewish teenager who hid from the Germans for over two years in a tiny annexe that is now a museum in Amsterdam, will grip many teenagers. So too will the rise and fall of the Berlin Wall – again, meaty stuff, but something that teenagers can at least begin to grasp the magnitude and meaning of.

Of course, you probably won't get teenagers within a hundred miles of either Amsterdam or Berlin unless you tempt them with something slightly less bitter.

Fortunately, both cities carry the sweet promise of retail heaven, as well as a suitably trendy café and arts scene. For teenagers who prefer the sound of thrills over tills, head for the mountains for year-round adventure and action sports.

Telling tales Simon Calder
Travel editor, The Independent | independent.co.uk

We are not a skiing family, but we decided to give it a go this year. Our children are six and three. To our complete astonishment, our week's skiing holiday was one of the most successful ever. Why? Firstly, we skied at Easter which meant the weather was warm (warm kids equals happy kids). Secondly, both Daisy and Poppy had gone ice-skating a couple of times in the UK and developed a taste for balance and ice, which I am sure helped them stay upright on skis. Thirdly, we punctuated the skiing day with breaks for delicious, hot chocolate which both children looked forward to when they were getting tired.

Belgium, Netherlands and Luxembourg might not cause the biggest blips on family-holiday-planning radars, but there's more to this diminutive trio than chocolate, windmills and a dismal reputation in the Eurovision Song Contest. They tend to be the kinds of places you drive through on the way to your family holiday, but linger in Luxembourg, for example, and you will discover some beautiful countryside and one of Europe's most spectacularly situated capitals. Belgium and the Netherlands, on the other hand, not only share a long stretch of sandy coastline but possess a liberal scattering of theme parks, cycling routes and other family attractions. Amsterdam emerges as the region's most child-friendly city with its 'green light' district of museums and parks.

Walibi theme park

Brussels

Belgium's capital is nothing if not diverse. At one extreme you have the bureaucratic edifice of the European Union headquarters, at the other a statue of a little boy peeing into a fountain. An obligatory first stop on any family sightseeing tour of the city, the Manneken Pis has been eliciting sniggers from children since it was unveiled in 1619 on the corner of Rue de l'Etuve and Stoofstraat. The city's most significant historical landmark, however, is the Grand Place, a beautiful square surrounded by ornate buildings dating from the 13th century. It's in complete contrast to Atomium (atomium.be) – a massive molecule of nine escalator-linked spheres rearing above Bruparck in northern Brussels. Not far from the mighty atoms you'll find Mini-Europe (minieurope.com), a quirky collection of 300 pint-sized monuments, plus an interactive Spirit of Europe exhibition. Other attractions include the Musée des Enfants (museedesenfants.be), Musée des Sciences Naturelles de Belgique (sciencesnaturelles.be) and the hands-on exhibits at Scientastic (scientastic.be). The Centre Belge de la Bande Dessinée (comicscenter.net) showcases Belgium's comic-strip heroes, including Hergé of Tintin fame. Several cartoon-adorned buildings around the city form part of an outdoor exhibition known as the Comic Strip Route.

Wallonia

Occupying the southern half of Belgium, Wallonia's big crowd-puller is Walibi Belgium (walibi.be), a theme/water park combo boasting over 50 rides, including seven roller coasters and a 140-m river run through rapids and waterfalls. For more natural thrills, go underground at the Grottoes of Han (grotte-de-han.be) or kayak along the River Lesse (lessekayaks.be). To give your brain a buzz, head for the Euro Space Center (eurospacecenter.be) or Pass (pass.be), an interactive science adventure park.

Flanders

Deeply moving lessons in the mindless brutality of two World Wars can be found in cemeteries and museums throughout northern Belgium, including the Memorial Museum Passchendaele 1917 (passchendaele.be) near Ypres, where, in 1917, casualties exceeded 500,000 in 100 days for a gain in territory of just 8 km. On a lighter note, the North Sea coast has sandy beaches, while Ghent and Bruges have canals to explore and chocolate shops to peruse.

Battle plan

★ Located 20 minutes' drive south of Brussels, the site of the Battle of Waterloo (waterloo1815.be) has an excellent visitor centre, battlefield tours and a puzzle book to help children aged seven to 12 decipher the strategies that led to Napoleon's defeat. Don't miss the re-enactments of cavalry and artillery manoeuvres at Lion Mound Hamlet every weekend in July and August.

✪ Let's go to Luxembourg

The Grand Duchy may be little more than a dot on the map, but it crams in everything from a World Heritage-listed capital to the forested hills of the Ardennes and the wine region of the Moselle Valley. Perched on a rocky promontory, Luxembourg city offers fine views over the Pétrusse Valley, particularly from the Place de la Constitution. Walk along the Chemin de la Corniche up to the Bock – a cliff where Count Sigefroi laid the foundations for a fortress more than 1000 years ago. All that remains is a honeycomb of underground passages known as the Bock Casemates. These, and other highlights, can be visited on a City Safari Tour for families that leaves from the tourist office at Place Guillaume. Heading north towards the Ardennes, Bourschied Castle is worth a detour, as is the National Military Museum in Diekirch with its displays of the 1944 Battle of the Bulge. The Ardennes is ideal for exploration by bike. Well-signed routes vary in length from 10 km to 40 km and there are some specifically for kids.

Kids' top 10 Amsterdam

❶ **Pedal** a four-seater canal bike around the waterways.
❷ **Ogle** a Van Gogh (or revere a Rembrandt) at either the Van Gogh Museum (vangoghmuseum.nl) or Rijksmuseum (rijksmuseum.nl).
❸ **Climb** the 85-m-tall tower of Westerkerk church for a pigeon's-eye view of the city.
❹ **Find** out what makes your brain tick, discover how to purify water and uncover the science behind adolescence at the hands-on technology museum, NEMO (e-nemo.nl). Designed in the shape of a ship's prow, Amsterdam's largest science museum (pictured right) contains five floors of interactive exhibits, with themes ranging from 'The search for life' and 'Codename DNA' to 'Amazing constructions', 'Teen facts' and 'Future Fuel'.
❺ **Travel** back in time as you board the replica Dutch East Indiaman *Amsterdam* and discover other maritime treasures at the Scheepvaart Museum (scheepvaartmuseum.nl).
❻ **Cycle** out of town to Amstelpark to see the well-preserved De Rieker windmill, built in 1636 and a favourite subject for Rembrandt.
❼ **Marvel** at the tragic, yet inspiring, story of Anne Frank at Anne Frankhuis (annefrank.org), the secret annexe in which the Jewish teenager and her family hid from the Nazis for 25 months during the early 1940s.

NEMO science museum

❽ **Discover** what it was like to live on a houseboat in the old days at the Houseboat Museum (houseboatmuseum.nl).
❾ **Cook** up a feast at KinderkookKafé (kinderkookkafe.nl), where kids get to prepare, cook and serve meals.
❿ **Run** wild at TunFun (tunfun.nl), a subway-turned-adventure playground for one- to 12-year-olds.

Houseboat Museum

Amsterdam

The Dutch capital may have something of a steamy image, but it gets an emphatic green light when it comes to travelling with kids (see box, above). This is largely due to its spider's web of 13th-century canals – a great excuse to transform boring old city sightseeing into something far more exciting. You can get afloat on a pedal boat, but you'll see more on a canal tour boat (canal.nl). Keep an eye out for De Pozenboot, a houseboat moored on the Singel that has become a refuge for stray cats. You can also hire bikes at several locations in the city (Vondelpark has safe paths, as well as a café, paddling pool and puppet theatre). Alternatively, hop on a tram (museumtram-amsterdam.nl) at Centraal Station for the 20-minute ride to Amsterdamse Bos, a woodland park with space to run around.

3 of the best cycle routes

❶ **Flower Bulb Route**
Petal power meets pedal power. This 30-km route between Haarlem and Sassenheim (near Leiden) passes through the dazzling bulb fields of southern Holland – at least, they will be when the daffodils and tulips are in bloom during April and May. Purchase a route guide at the tourist office in Lisse.

❷ **North Sea Route**
Stretching from Den Helder to Boulogne-sur-Mer, the Dutch part of this coastal epic is still 300 km long – so be sure to do it in a northerly direction to make the most of tailwinds. Apart from beaches, dunes and seaside resorts like Scheveningen, highlights on the ride include the Oosterschelde storm-surge barrier in Zeeland.

❸ **Windmill Route**
A 43-km spin through the Alblasserwaard area in southern Holland. Start near Kinderdijk (which has a row of 19 beautifully preserved windmills), then it's plain sailing as you follow the signposts through a typical Dutch polder landscape of rivers, reedbeds and lush meadows.

4 of the best touring routes

❶ Castle Road

burgenstrasse.de

Mannheim to Prague: 1000 km

Tales of witches, knights and dragons add zest to this long-established scenic tour of castles and palaces in Germany and the Czech Republic. In Heidelberg Castle, for example, children can discover the 'witch's bite' – a crack in an iron door ring where a witch tried to force entry to the castle using her teeth. Several castles organize costumed festivals, ghost tours and medieval banquets. You'll also encounter medieval games in towns like Bad Wimpfen, while others, such as Ansbach and Schwetzingen, run special guided tours for children. Other highlights include the impressive fortifications of Auerbach, the medieval imperial city of Nürnberg and the ancient towns of Bamberg, Coburg, Kronach, Kulmbach and Bayreuth. The Castle Road is a designated cycle route and there are also coach tours and train stations along its length. Other child-friendly highlights include Sea Life Speyer (sealifeeurope.com) near Heidelberg – a series of aquariums evoking the various habitats of the Rhine from Alpine source to Rotterdam harbour – and Zirndorf's Playmobil Fun Park (playmobil.de) where the knight's castle stands alongside a pirate ship, gold mine and jungle ruins.

❷ The Toy Road

spielzeugstrasse.de

Nurnberg to Waltershausen: 300 km

Site of an international toy fair (toyfair.de), Nürnberg is an appropriate place to start this trail through a land of dolls, teddies and model railways – although don't forget that Legoland (legoland.de) lies well to the south of the route near Gunzberg. A short distance from Nürnberg is the Playmobil Fun Park (see above), while the town of Fürth is home to several major toy manufacturers and a puppet festival in May. Coburg dotes on dolls, Weidhausen tends towards teddies, while Neustadt not only has copious amounts of both (in the Museum of the German Toy Industry), but also has a doll and teddy bear doctor. Educational toys are on display at Friedrich Froebel's memorial museum in Oberweissbach; Lauscha is the birthplace of Christmas tree baubles, while Ohrdruf's claim to fame is the rocking horse and porcelain doll. Don't miss the massed display of gnomes at Trusetal Gnome Park (note that sledgehammers and golf clubs must be left at the entrance).

❸ Fairy Tale Route

deutsche-maerchenstrasse.com

Bremen to Hanau: 600 km

The road to enchantment starts in Bremen, birthplace of the Brothers Grimm, whose timeless fairy tales come to life as you travel north. There's a chance you might meet Snow White and the Seven Dwarves in the Weserbergland hills. Schwalmstadt, meanwhile, is Little Red Riding Hood country, while Mother Goose waddled about in the Werra Valley. Sleeping Beauty nodded off in Sababurg Castle, Cinderella had a ball at Polle Castle, Rapunzel let her hair down in Trendelburg and, of course, Hamlyn is where the Pied Piper (pictured right) led his rats on a merry dance. In just about every town you will find fairy-tale tours, theatre shows, museums, and picture-perfect half-timbered buildings. At the heart of the Fairy Tale Route, Kassel is home to the Brothers Grimm Museum and also hosts a summer folklore festival and fairy-tale Christmas market. Don't miss the Bremen Town Musicians, on stage every Sunday between May and September.

❹ German Alpine Road

germany-tourism.de

Lindau to Berchtesgaden: 450 km

Stretching between Lakes Constance and Königssee, the German Alpine Road links a healthy succession of forests, meadows, lakes and farming villages – all set against the backdrop of the Bavarian Alps. No less than 20 lakes and some 25 castles, abbeys and palaces can be found along the historic route. Don't miss the island town of Lindau on Lake Constance, the Linderhof Palace at Ettal or the fairy-tale castles of Füssen. Many lakes offer watersports and, if you're feeling really energetic, you can cycle the German Alpine Road using a special track that runs along part of its length. Cable cars and chairlifts, meanwhile, whisk you into the mountains where there's no shortage of walking trails and skiing areas.

N ice cars, good beer, fine composers – but surely not that great for family holidays? Well, actually, yes. Germany might lack the charisma of the Spanish Costas or the magnetism of Disneyland Paris, but what it lacks in big names and notoriety it more than compensates for with a veritable cheer-fest of family attractions, ranging from island retreats in the Baltic Sea to roller-coaster mayhem at Europa-Park. What's more, Germany is easy to reach and a piece of (Black Forest) cake to get around, whether you're cruising the autobahn towards Berlin or dawdling along the Fairy Tale Route on the lookout for the seven dwarves.

Berlin

Germany's happening capital doesn't exactly buzz with family appeal, but don't overlook it as drab or uninviting. There's plenty to keep families interested for a day or two – although older children will definitely get more from the city. In addition to iconic landmarks like the Brandenburg Gate, Berlin's defining moments of post-war history are best revealed at Haus am Checkpoint Charlie (mauermuseum.de), a small museum documenting the rise and fall of the Berlin Wall and the numerous, often fatal, attempts made to flee East Germany.

If you visit just one other museum in Berlin, make sure it's the Pergamon Museum (smb.spk-berlin. de) – one of the collection of museums on Museum Island where pride of place goes to the Hellenistic masterpiece, the *Pergamon Altar*, a frieze of sparring gods and giants that dates from the second century BC. Continue into the Museum of the Ancient Near East and you will find other amazing artefacts, including the truly monumental reconstructions of brilliantly coloured Babylonian monuments – the Processional Way, the Ishtar Gate and the façade of the throne hall of King Nebuchadnezzar II.

Berlin may be heavy on history, but light relief for kids is available in the form of the excellent Berlin Zoo (zoo-berlin.de) with its famous sculptured Elephant Gate and extensive animal collection. Don't miss the Hippopotamus House where you can view the lumbering 'river horses' from both above and below water. The aquarium is also worth a visit, particularly for its walk-in Crocodile Hall, black-tip reef sharks and breeding jellyfish. Take the U5 underground or M17 tram to the city's outskirts and you'll discover Tierpark (tierpark-berlin.de), a 160-ha landscape zoo with spacious open-air enclosures for everything from pachyderms to primates.

Black Forest

Coast & islands

Germany's North Sea coast has no shortage of sandy beaches, including the 12-km-long St Peter-Ording. Avid naturalists should head to the Elbe Estuary off Cuxhaven where the islands of the Hamburg Wattenmeer National Park are popular with terns and seals. Just to the north, Schleswig-Holstein Wattenmeer National Park provides a memorable, if messy, opportunity to venture into the world's largest contiguous area of mudflats – a rich wildlife habitat that, for safety reasons, should only be explored on a guided tour. On Germany's Baltic coast, the island of Rugen (ruegen.de) makes a superb family-holiday base, with everything from sea promenades and sandy beaches to boat trips.

Black Forest

Home of the cuckoo clock, the Black Forest in southwest Germany can easily be toured by road, but you'll feel much better walking – especially after indulging in a slice or two of ubiquitous cherry-filled chocolate cake. A guided trail lasting from one to 10 days starts at Triberg (triberg.de) where you can also take a day hike to the 160-m Wasserfaelle Gutach, the highest cascade in Germany. St Märgen also makes a good base for walks, while Furtwangen's cuckoo clock museum is worth a quick visit.

Europa-Park

Rust, T01805-776 688, europapark.de. Apr-Oct, daily 0900-1800, Nov-Dec 1100-1900.

Reaching speeds of 130 km/h and centrifugal forces of 4 G, Silver Star (the biggest and highest roller coaster in Europe, minimum height: 140 cm) is just one of the 100-plus rides and attractions at this outstanding theme park. Other highlights include fjord rafting through Scandinavia, gondola rides through Venice and an interactive Atlantis Adventure where you explore a sunken citadel armed with laser harpoons. But it's the themed streetscapes of 12 European countries, from Greece to Russia, which may well leave the most lasting impression.

Germany
Fast rides & fairy tales

Inside info

▸▸ Several cities, including Berlin and Hamburg, have super-saver cards, offering free travel on public transport and free or discounted admission to major attractions.
▸▸ Satisfy sweet-tooth cravings at the Chocolate Museum in Cologne (Köln) and the Haribo factory in Bonn.
▸▸ Germany has an extensive cycle route network (adfc.de) and over 5000 'bike-friendly' places to stay (bettundbike.de).

Going with the flow...

Hydrospeeding and white-water rafting on the Vorder Rhine Gorge (swisstrails.ch).

Kids' top 10 Swiss treats

❶ **Race** down the Churwalden toboggan run (pradaschier.ch) at speeds of up to 40 km/h.

❷ **Hoof** up the Binn Valley on a mule trek (bergland.ch).

❸ **Sleep** in a fairy-tale castle at Mariastein-Rotberg (youthhostel.ch).

❹ **Spot** ibex and marmots (pictured right) in Swiss National Park (nationalpark.ch).

❺ **Strike** it lucky at Grabenmühle (grabenmuehle.ch), trout fishing or panning for gold.

❻ **Swing** like Tarzan at Pilatus Rope Park (pilatus.ch), a suspension rope park in central Switzerland suitable for kids aged eight and above.

❼ **Ride** Switzerland's oldest steam cog railway up 1678-m Rothorn Kulm (brienz-rothorn-bahn.ch).

❽ **Discover** sweet sensations on the Chocolate Train from Montreux to the Nestlé factory in Broc, or visit Schoggi Land in Flawil (schoggi-land.ch).

❾ **Ride** a cool scooter-bike from Belalp to Blatten along 7 km of mountain paths and tracks (brig-belalp.ch).

❿ **Live** like a shepherd for the day at Alpine Museum Riederalp (riederalp.ch or myswitzerland.com/en/alpine-museum-riederalp).

Top resort Saas Fee

★ **Kids' activities** For those with energy, try horse riding, mountain biking and hiking some of the 350 km of marked footpaths; for those who want an easier way up and down the mountains take the cable car to the start of the Feeblitz summer toboggan run.

★ **Best family day out** A 40-minute drive away, Zermatt and the Matterhorn are well worth a visit. Closer at hand is the 3500-m Mittelallalin, reached by cable car and underground railway. Here, you can find out about glaciers in the Ice Pavilion.

The great Swiss outdoors has more family-friendly attractions than you can shake a ski stick at. From nature trails and mountain railways to gold panning and whitewater rafting, boredom is easily banished in the squeaky-clean, rosy-cheeked land of Heidi and Peter the Goatherd. Public transport runs with typical Swiss precision and there are even 30-odd resorts and around 50 hotels that have been cited as particularly family friendly. Any downsides? Well, Switzerland can be pricey, but you'll find family travel passes (plus some Toblerone therapy) will help to sweeten the pill. See page 73 for a round-up of winter ski resorts.

Lake Lucerne steamer

Bernese Oberland

Eiger, Mönch and Jungfrau reign supreme above the Bernese Oberland (berneroberland.ch), Switzerland's ultimate outdoor playground and the setting for such classic Alpine destinations as Interlaken and Gstaad. For peak perfection, set your sights on Jungfraujoch (jungfraubahnen.ch), a breathtaking visitor centre perched on a mountaintop with giddy views of summits and glaciers. You reach the top of Europe using three rack-and-pinion trains and, once there, you can visit the Ice Palace and go hiking, dog sledging and summer skiing.

Another summit that's easily bagged is 2190-m Stockhorn (stockhorn.ch), reached by cable car from Erlenbach in just 20 minutes. The views from the top take in everything from distant Mont Blanc to the lakes of Thun and Brienz.

More down-to-earth adventures include Aldeboden Flower Trail (adelboden.ch), a gentle 3-km amble from the Hahnenmoos Pass to Sillerenbühl with drawings and information to help you identify alpine flora. If you prefer something more cute and fluffy, try the Marmot Trail on Betelberg Mountain. Kids aged four to 10 will also enjoy the 5-km Dwarf Trail. Upping adrenaline levels slightly, the Bernese Oberland is riddled with hiking and biking opportunities, and there's also whitewater rafting on the Saane (swissraft.ch).

Graubunden

Family highlights in this eastern canton include luggage-free hiking holidays in the Engadine, Val Bregalia, Val Poschiavo and Swiss National Park (nationalpark.ch), where your bags are transported from hotel to hotel leaving you to carry little more than a packed lunch and a stash of cable-car tickets.

For hiking with a literary twist, skip along the Heidi Adventure Path above Maienfeld. Gold panning (goldrush.ch) is available on the Rhine at Disentis, while those who splash about on the Inn River at Scuol will be rewarded with some gold-star whitewater rafting (engadin-adventure.ch).

Valais

With the Matterhorn and numerous other 4000-m giants straddling the French and Italian borders, it's little wonder that Valais is a magnet to rock climbers. Children can get to grips with ropes and carabiners on the Aletsch Fixed-Rope Trail (alpincenterbelalp.ch), a four-hour scramble around Gibidum Reservoir. Also on offer are two-day adventures, combining *via ferrata* and a glacier hike or rafting on the Rhône and canyoning through the Massa Gorge. Slightly more contrived, but no less fun, is Aquaparc (aquaparc.ch) at Le Bouveret on the shores of Lake Geneva where you can experience 3 Gs of acceleration on the Booster Loop water chute (minimum age 14).

Lucerne

Highlights in Lucerne include the 14th-century Chapel Bridge and Weinmarkt – an old city square surrounded by buildings adorned with elaborate frescoes, while the *Dying Lion of Lucerne* is a rock sculpture described by Mark Twain as "the most mournful and moving piece of stone in the world". The Lake Lucerne Navigation Company (lakelucerne.ch) operates five vintage paddle steamers and 15 modern cruisers. The most interesting section of the lake is the Urnersee where you can intersperse ferry travel with walks along the 35-km lakeside Swiss Path.

Inside info

▶▶ The Swiss Pass (swisstravelsystem.ch) permits unlimited free travel by train, bus and boat (including scenic routes like the Glacier Express), plus free entry to 400 museums.
▶▶ Swiss holiday resorts that have a range of services geared specifically to the needs of children and parents are awarded a Families Welcome label (swisstourfed.ch).
▶▶ Zurich Airport (zurich-airport.com) has a children's playground with a trampoline and Alouette helicopter, as well as 75-minute tours of the apron, runways and nature reserve.

Altogether now: "Doe, a deer, a female deer; ray, a drop of golden sun..." Welcome to the land of the family singalong. Resistance is utterly futile. If you're not singing it, you'll be humming it. And if it's not a ditty from *The Sound of Music* it will be Falco's *Rock Me Amadeus* or, worse still, an impromptu yodelling session. Depending on their age, your children will either join in with gusto or shrink away in disgust. Salzburg, Austria's musical maestro-piece, is great fun for kids, while Vienna, with its Lipizzaner stallions, is somewhat more refined. But it's only out on the mountain paths, the bike trails and the sparkling lakes that you'll tune in to the some of the best sounds in Austria – the rarefied silence of Alpine wilderness.

Vienna

Horse-lovers will be enchanted by Vienna's Spanish Riding School (srs.at) where the famous Lipizzaner stallions strut their stuff. You can book tickets online for the limited performances that take place, usually on Sundays, throughout the year. However, there's a stampede to get them, so you may have to settle for the Morning Exercises (daily, except Mondays) when the white beauties are put through their paces.

Take the high road

Drive along the Grossglockner High Alpine Road (grossglockner.com) into the heart of the Hohe Tauern National Park for views of Austria's highest mountain, the 3798-m Grossglockner, soaring above the Pasterze glacier. There are four themed children's playgrounds along the way, as well as an Alpine Nature Show Museum.

Lipizzaner horse

Rarer, but more accessible, creatures can be viewed at Schönbrunn Zoo (zoovienna.at), which not only has giant pandas, a Borneo rainforest habitat and a polarium, but also does its bit for the less fortunate equines of this world – namely the endangered Turkmenian donkey and Mongolia's Przewalski horse. To escape horses altogether, take a spin on the 65-m-tall Riesenrad (wienerriesenrad.com), Vienna's iconic Ferris wheel which first cranked into life in 1897. For a more hands-on view of the past, the Schönbrunn Palace (schoenbrunn.at) has a kids' museum where you can learn how to lay a royal table and dress up as a prince or princess.

Salzburg

There's something you should know before visiting Salzburg: most of the locals have never seen *The Sound of Music*. They don't wander around singing *Edelweiss* and they haven't erected a statue of Julie Andrews in the city centre. They do, however, appreciate its tourism potential, so if you want to see movie locations, like the Mirabell Gardens where Maria and the Von Trapps sang *Do-Re-Mi* or the Leopoldskron Castle that was used as a backdrop for the Von Trapp family home, simply sign up to one of the many Sound of Music Tours (panoramatours.com).

Salzburg

Try to spare some time, though, for Mozart. You can see his memorial in Mozartplatz Square in the heart of the old town. Of the two Mozart museums in Salzburg, the house at Getreidegasse 9 (containing his concert violin, clavichord and other memorabilia) is probably of more interest to children.

Salzburg's Baroque splendour was financed largely through sales of salt mined from the Durrnberg. At Salzwelten Hallstatt (salzwelten.at) you can explore the ancient mines, descending into their depths on thrilling wooden slides (reaching over 60 m in length) to an underground lake where salt was dissolved from the surrounding rock. To add a pinch of creepiness to the experience, you'll also learn of the remarkable discovery in 1734 of a miner who, having died during a tunnel collapse centuries earlier, became naturally embalmed in the salt.

Salzburg's white gold brought immense wealth to its prince archbishops and one of them, Markus Sittikus, indulged in a summer palace, known as Hellbrunn (hellbrunn.at). Sittikus, who evidently loved a good laugh, designed his pleasure gardens (between 1613 and 1616) with all sorts of push-button pranks, from trick fountains and spurting grottoes to a stone dining table where all but one of the seats is rigged with a water jet. Bring a sense of humour and change of clothes.

Carinthia

Austria's southernmost province has some 1270 lakes, 200 of which are suitable for swimming. Other summer activities include hiking and cycling, while winter snows create over 800 km of pistes. One of the region's most popular family attractions is Minimundus (minimundus.at) where you can see the world in miniature.

Styria

Located in southeast Austria, Styria's forest-draped hills are perfect for biking (there are over 5000 km of cycle trails), while lakes and rivers offer boating, fishing and whitewater rafting.

Tyrol

This magnificent Alpine region in western Austria is the country's adventure playground, with everything from mountain biking and marmot-spotting (in Hohe Tauern National Park, hohetauern.at) to climbing and year-round skiing. Prepare to be dazzled at Swarovski Crystal World (kristallwelten.swarovski.com) in Wattens, and to be spooked at Hexenwasser Hochsöll (hexenwasser.at), a land of witchcraft in Hohe Salve.

Inside info

▶▶ The Vienna Card allows unlimited free travel by underground, bus and tram for 72 hours, plus discounts at over 200 attractions, shops and restaurants.
▶▶ Allow a week to pedal along the easy, level Danube Cycle Path from Passau to Vienna.
▶▶ A drive of about one hour from Vienna, the Sonnentherme Lutzmannsburg (sonnentherme.com) has a spa and adventure waterpark.

When to go

The most popular time is summer – unless, of course, you're going for the winter sports. Snow cover lasts from December to March in the Alpine valleys of **Austria** and **Switzerland**, although in higher regions you can often eke out a skiing holiday as late as April or May (some resorts, like Kaprun, offer summer skiing). In the **Netherlands**, April is the best month for seeing daffodils in bloom; May for tulips. In **Germany**, the forests are golden-hued in autumn, a time when resorts are less crowded and the weather less settled.

Getting there

Several airports in the region are major international hubs, particularly Schipol (Amsterdam) and Frankfurt. National carriers include Austrian Airlines (austrian.com), KLM (klm.com), Lufthansa (lufthansa.com) and Swiss Air (swiss.com). The Dutch carrier operates an extensive European and global network, linking up with Northwest Airlines to serve numerous cities in the United States. Low-cost airlines serving Central Europe from the UK and Ireland include easyJet (easyjet.com), with flights to Amsterdam, Berlin and Zurich, and Ryanair (ryanair.com), which flies to Brussels, Frankfurt, Karlsruhe-Baden and Salzburg. Air Berlin (airberlin.com) also has an extensive network.

Getting around

Public transport is excellent throughout the region. If you arrive in **Brussels** by Eurostar your ticket includes travel to any other Belgian station within 24 hours (b-rail.be). Bus services are operated throughout Belgium by TEC (infotec.be).

In the **Netherlands**, a slick rail network (ns.nl) can whisk you from Schiphol Airport to Amsterdam in just 16 minutes. Once in the capital you can rent a bicycle or explore the city by Canal Bus (canal.nl).

In **Luxembourg**, the Luxembourg Card (ont.lu) provides free travel on trains and buses, plus free admission to over 50 attractions in the Grand Duchy.

Germany's rail network is operated by Deutsche Bahn (bahn.de), with InterCityExpress (ICE) trains capable of reaching speeds of 320 km/h. Some ICE trains have a Kleinkindabteil (or toddler compartment) reserved for families with small children. Most major German cities boast an underground, bus and tram system, and in many you'll find Welcome Cards offering discounted admission to tourist attractions, as well as unlimited travel on local public transport.

As you might expect, super-efficient, integrated public transport systems reach their

Mountain railway

Trading hiking boots, map and compass for a public transport pass and a pair of sensible shoes places a whole new perspective on travel in Switzerland. It takes the 'puff' out of the views, makes more sense if you have very young children and puts you in touch with more of the country's cultural highlights.
William Gray

peak in **Switzerland**. The Swiss Travel System (swisstravelsystem.com) offers a variety of travel passes for making use of the country's network of over 20,000 km of rail, bus and boat routes. The Swiss Pass allows unlimited free travel on the entire network, including scenic routes like the famous Glacier Express (glacierexpress.ch), city trams and buses, a 50% discount on several mountain railways and cableways and free entry to 400 museums. Children aged between six and 15 travel free if accompanied by a parent. Coaches in Switzerland are operated by PostBus (postauto.ch) and trains are run by Swiss Federal Railways (sbb.ch). RailAway (railaway.ch) offers winter and summer excursions combining discounted fares and admission to various attractions.

Austrian Federal Railways (oebb.at) connect major towns and cities in **Austria**, while various cruise operators offer excursions on the River Danube (ddsg-blue-danube.at).

Accommodation

There are Center Parcs (centerparcs.com) in Belgium, Netherlands and Germany, each one with its own special attractions (see page 147). Camping holidays are available throughout Central Europe with Canvas Holidays (canvasholidays.com), Eurocamp (eurocamp.com) and Keycamp (keycamp.com). Also try Select Sites (select-site.com). Ski specialists offering all-inclusive family packages to Austria, Switzerland or both countries include Esprit (esprit-holidays.co.uk), Mark Warner (markwarner.co.uk) and Powder Byrne (powderbyrne.com).

In **Belgium**, the Belgian Tourist Office (belgiumtheplaceto.be) has an online search facility for hotels and guest houses. Also try Gîtes de Wallonie (gitesdewallonie.net) and Logis de Belgique (logis.be).

Germany has more than 2500 campsites, most of which are open from April to October. There are also 600 youth hostels (djh.de) and a huge choice of self-catering properties and B&Bs (bed-and-breakfast.de). For farm holidays, browse the selection at landtourismus.de. Hotels that cater specifically for families include Dorfhotels (dorfhotel.com), Familotel (familotel.de) and Kinderland (kinderland.by). Europa-Park (see page 139) also has great themed hotels.

Switzerland offers a range of family-friendly accommodation, from igloos (iglu-dorf.com) to mountain huts. Over 40 KidsHotels (kidshotel.ch) offer quality family accommodation, with well-equipped play areas, children's menus and baby essentials if you need them. Some even provide free childcare during the high season, as well as a weekly programme of activities. Another long-established family favourite,

Reka (reka.ch), operates several holiday villages around Switzerland, each one with a relaxed mixture of self-catering cottages, playgrounds, swimming pools and even a wellbeing centre for the grown-ups. Farm holidays are available from Swiss Holiday Farms (agrotourismus.ch). Swiss Youth Hostels (youthhostel.ch) have good-value family rooms and self-catering kitchen facilities, while Bed and Breakfast Switzerland (bnb.ch) has an online directory.

Austria's all-inclusive, full-board Kinderhotels (kinderhotels.com) are well known for their outstanding childcare. English-speaking childminders are provided free of charge (even for babies as young as seven days old) for up to 60 hours a week. Baby and toddler equipment is provided free of charge, and all food is organic.

Food & drink

Although you will find a cosmopolitan range of restaurants, cafés and fast-food outlets everywhere you go, be sure to try one or two regional specialities. In **Belgium**, kids will love getting to grips with *gauffres* – thick waffles dripping with chocolate, strawberry or raspberry sauce and doused with whipped cream. The **Netherlands** has *poffertjes*, small pancakes dusted in sugar; **Germany** has the formidable Black Forest cake; **Austria** has strudels and **Switzerland** and **Belgium**, of course, are magnets to chocoholics. On the savoury front, **Germany** is renowned for its sausages – but be warned: they are not always your typical barbecue bangers. In **Switzerland**, fondues, raclettes and rosti should all go down a treat with children – as long as they haven't overdosed on Toblerone beforehand.

Health & safety

Apart from a small risk, during spring, of contracting illnesses from tick bites in forested parts of Germany, no special health precautions are necessary for travel in Central Europe. Remember that strong currents affect the North Sea coast, so always check whether it's safe to swim.

Belgian waffles

Go green
Four ways to skip the flight

① **Take Eurostar** (eurostar.com) from London St Pancras to Brussels, with connections to Amsterdam by high-speed Thalys (thalys.com) or Germany by Deutsche Bahn (bahn.de). Switzerland is also served by inter-European rail services.

② **Catch a bus** Eurolines (eurolines.com) has an extensive service across Central Europe.

③ **Take the ferry** from the UK to France (see page 76), Belgium or the Netherlands. P&O Ferries (poferries.com) has 14-hour services from Hull to Zeebrugge and Rotterdam; Stena Line (stenaline.com) sails from Harwich to Hook of Holland.

④ **Use Eurotunnel** (eurotunnel.com) to reach mainland Europe and access the motorway network.

Holiday operators

The Adventure Company
adventurecompany.co.uk

Bents Tours
bentstours.com

Canvas Holidays
canvasholidays.com

Crystal Holidays
crystalholidays.co.uk

Esprit
esprit-holidays.co.uk

Eurocamp
eurocamp.com

Families Worldwide
familiesworldwide.co.uk

Inntravel
inntravel.co.uk

Keycamp Holidays
keycamp.com

Lakes & Mountains Holidays
thomsonlakes.co.uk

Mark Warner
markwarner.co.uk

Powder Byrne
powderbyrne.com

In the USA
The Backroads
backroads.com

Classic Journeys
classicjourneys.com

Ski Europe
ski-europe.com

Fast facts

Country	Time	Language	Currency	Dialling code	Tourist information
Belgium	GMT+1	French Dutch	Euro €	+32	belgiumtheplaceto.be
Netherlands	GMT+1	Dutch	Euro €	+31	holland.com
Luxembourg	GMT+1	French German	Euro €	+352	visitluxembourg.com
Germany	GMT+2	German	Euro €	+49	germany.travel
Switzerland	GMT+1	German French Italian	Swiss Franc	+41	myswitzerland.com
Austria	GMT+1	German	Euro €	+43	austria.info

Duinrell Parc
Where? Wasssenaar, Netherlands
Why? With the Duinrell Theme Park and Tiki Water Park nearby, there's no chance of boredom at this popular holiday park, located within a nature reserve and close to the Dutch bulb fields. Older children and teenagers will love Tiki's splash-happy array of whirlpools, wave machines and giant water slides. Accommodation ranges from six-berth tents to well-equipped three-bedroom holiday homes. **Contact** Eurocamp, T+44 (0)844-406 0402, eurocamp.com

Chalet Pepi Gabl
Where? St Anton, Austria
Why? Located right next to the Nasserein gondola for quick access to the slopes, this cosy and traditional Austrian chalet is a great family choice when combined with Esprit's legendary childcare, Snow Club and children's ski classes.
Contact Esprit Ski, T+44 (0)1252-618300, espritski.com

Hotel Edelweiss
Where? Engelberg, Switzerland
Why? A friendly hotel in the relaxed village of Engelberg, the Edelweiss makes a great base for exploring the Swiss Alps during summer. Activities range from boat and train rides to glacier walks and mountain biking.
Contact Inntravel, T+44 (0)1653-617009, inntravel.co.uk

Tirolerhof
Where? Tyrol, Austria
Why? Boasting spacious, luxurious family suites and a wealth of children's extras – from baby gear to horsedrawn carriage rides and skiing lessons – this beautiful Tyrolean hotel also caters for adults with its spa and nine-hole golf course.
Contact Kinderhotels, T+43 (0)4254-4411, kinderhotels.com

" " Grimentz is a beautiful Swiss village that's perfect for a skiing holiday with young children. There's a crèche at the top of the gondola and you can hire baby equipment (prams, sledges etc) in the village. The tourist office has a list of babysitters, and the ski school has a baby slope with travelator and snowpark.
Alison Williams, valetdanniviers.com

Flims, Swiss Alps

" " From nature trails and mountain biking to rock climbing and white-water rafting, boredom is easily banished in rosy-cheeked Flims – one of the best summer holiday bases for active families in the Swiss Alps. For peak perfection, add Powder Byrne's kids' programmes and their pick of Flims' finest family hotels. Powder Byrne have been refining the art of luxury family holidays for over twenty years. Their childcare is second to none. powderbyrne.com, 101familyholidays.co.uk

Center Parcs at a glance

Country	Parc	Highlights
Belgium	Erperheide	▸▸ Aqua Mundo in an Asian fishing village setting, indoor play world.
	De Vossemeren	▸▸ Aqua Sana wellbeing centre, Discovery Bay in jungle setting, indoor skate arena.
Netherlands	De Kempervennen	▸▸ Montana Snowcentre, outdoor high adventure experience, waterskiing and dive college.
	Het Meerdal	▸▸ Aqua Mundo with 101-m water slide, Mini Baluba indoor playworld.
	Het Heijderbos	▸▸ Aqua Mundo with wild-water rapids, horse-riding school, tropical dome with jungle expedition.
	De Eemhof	▸▸ Aqua Mundo with body-boarding Flow Rider, magnetic climbing in Action factory, watersports centre.
	Port Zélande	▸▸ Sail and dive college, Adventure Factory, close to Zeeland coast.
Germany	Bispinger Heide	▸▸ Aqua Mundo with Dragon Rock water spout, Aqua Sana spa.
	Park Hochsauerland	▸▸ Aqua Mundo, crazy river.
	Park Heibachsee	▸▸ Indoor play world, watersports.
	Butjadinger Kuste	▸▸ Aqua Mundo with crazy river.

Eastern Europe

Sizzling Slovenia

Lightning strikes at the old Adriatic port of Piran. Right: a dragon stands guard in Slovenia's capital, Ljubljana.

Baltic
Sea

LITHUANIA

VILNIUS

Largest city
Warsaw,
population
2.2 million

Vistula

□ **WARSAW**

BERLIN
□

Oder

POLAND

Elbe

★1 □ **PRAGUE**

Kraków ○ ★3

CZECH REPUBLIC

Danube

Tatra
Mountains

Bieszczady
Mountains

★2

SLOVAKIA

VIENNA □

□ **BRATISLAVA**

Carpathian
Mountains

Lake
Balaton

□ **BUDAPEST**

HUNGARY

ROMANIA

★5 SLOVENIA

□ **LJUBLJANA**

□ **ZAGREB**

Venice ○

★6

CROATIA

Transylvanian Alps

★4

□ **BUCHAREST**

Danube

Adriatic
Sea

**Longest
river**
Danube
2850 km

BULGARIA

Blac
Sea

Dalmatian Coast

Korčula

Mljet ○ **Dubrovnik**

★7

□ **SOFIA**

Musala

Balkan Peninsula

Rhodope Mountains

**Highest
mountain**
Musala,
Bulgaria
2925 m

metres
3000
2000
1000
500
200
0

N

100 km
100 miles

Mediterranean
Sea

Introduction
Eastern Europe

When it comes to carefree holidays in Europe with the kids, traditional favourites like France and Spain will always reap the most beach towels. However, an increasing number of families are looking to the east for a holiday that not only gives them excellent value for money, but also has many of the facilities offered by resorts further west. Following the turbulent 1990s, Croatia's tourism is back in top gear with excellent hotels and holiday camps along the Adriatic coast. Adventurous families can kayak through the Dalmatian archipelago or explore inland national parks like Plitvice Lakes. Making a quieter splash, Croatia's northern neighbour, Slovenia, is slowly gaining popularity. It's small (about the size of Wales), but has everything from mountains and castles to Alpine lakes and a dash of Adriatic coastline. Prague and Kraków are well-established city-break destinations, but families in the know will be able to find plenty to please children, from Prague Castle to the Wieliczka Salt Mine near Kraków. A cultural sojourn in either city combines well with an adventure- or wildlife-focused break in the Carpathian Mountains. There are wolves and bears to be spotted in Romania's wildwoods and if that doesn't have enough bite, try Dracula's Castle.

Did you know?

★ The 13th-century traveller, Marco Polo was born on the Croatian island of Korčula.
★ Born in 1810, Polish composer Frédéric Chopin gave his first public piano concert at the age of eight.
★ Weighing 1.31 kg, the world's largest truffle was found in Istria, Croatia, in 1999 by Giancarlo Zigante and his dog, Diana.
★ *King Ottokar's Sceptre*, one of the Adventures of Tintin, is based on the Czech Crown Jewels that are kept under lock and ~~Prague Castle.~~

Star rating

Wow factor	★★★
Worry factor	★★★
Value for money	★★★★
Keeping teacher happy	★★★★
Family accommodation	★★★
Babies & toddlers	★★
Cool for teenagers	★★★

⚽ Cool kayaking

Croatia's island-spattered Adriatic coastline is crying out for some serious sea kayaking. You must wear a lifejacket and be able to swim. Sea kayaks are quite stable, but try to avoid rough water. If you're a beginner it's a good idea to share a two-person kayak with an adult. Here's how to perfect your paddling:

1 Adjust your seat and foot pedals so that your knees are touching the inside of the hull. This will help your balance.

2 Sit upright and space your hands on the paddle about 50 cm apart.

3 Grip the paddle lightly, otherwise your forearms will quickly feel tired.

4 Don't dip the paddle too deeply into the water.

5 Imagine tracing a figure-of-eight with your hands as you paddle. Keep a smooth and steady rhythm.

6 Use the rudder only when necessary – oversteering will slow the kayak and make paddling much harder work.

All sounds too complicated? Try a sit-on kayak instead. They are generally more stable, simpler to paddle and easier to fall off.

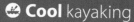

Enter if you dare ☠

Bran Castle in Romania is home to the vilest vampire of them all – Count Dracula (see page 159).

🔍 How to decorate an egg

It is traditional to paint and decorate eggs in many parts of Eastern Europe. Here's how to create your own *pysanka*, or Ukranian Easter egg, using the written-wax batik method. It's fiddly but fun.

What you need
- ▸ smooth fresh eggs
- ▸ long straight pins stuck into corks (your writing tools)
- ▸ wax (equal amounts of beeswax and paraffin)
- ▸ wax warmer (candle-heated container)
- ▸ egg dyes in containers large enough to submerge eggs
- ▸ paper tissues
- ▸ candle
- ▸ varnish

What you need
- ▸ Ask an adult to help you blow your egg. Use a long pin to make a tiny hole at each end (slightly larger at the bottom). Pierce and break the yolk with the pin, shake to mix the contents. Blow gently through the smaller hole to empty the contents into a bowl. Rinse carefully and leave it to dry.
- ▸ Practise your design on paper.
- ▸ Dip your pinhead into melted wax and use it to draw your design on the egg.
- ▸ When you are happy with the design, place the egg in the lightest-colour dye for 10 to 30 minutes. Blot dry with tissues.
- ▸ When completely dry add further designs with wax before submerging in the next colour of dye. Repeat with one more colour.
- ▸ An adult can complete the design by holding the egg, a small section at a time, against the side of a candle flame for no more than five seconds to remove the wax (by blotting with a tissue).
- ▸ Preserve the egg with two light coats of clear varnish.

Great reads
6 children's books

Ages 4-6
Little Dracula's First Bite
Martin Waddell (Walker Books)
The inhabitants of Castle Dracula are a
colourful bunch – not least Little Dracula
who is small, bald and green. In this story
Little Dracula tries to be just like Dad and
has a 'fangtastic' time!

Ages 8-12
Stories of Dragons
Gill Doherty (Usborne Books)
There's a dragon to match every mood in
these myths and folklore tales gathered
from around the world. Some are friendly,
some fierce and there's even one which
loves to dance.

All ages
Hidden Tales from Eastern Europe
Antonia Barber (Frances Lincoln)
A collection of elegantly told and
beautifully illustrated folk tales from
Poland, Slovakia, Russia, Croatia, Serbia,
Slovenia and Romania.

Ages 9+
Dracula
Bram Stoker (Usborne Classics retold)
Can eccentric Professor Van Helsing and
his brave young friends take on the world's
vilest vampire? A modern retelling of the
classic Bram Stoker horror novel.

Ages 12+
Chopin and Romantic Music
Carlo Cavelletti (Barrons Educational Series)
Discover the accomplishments of Polish-
born Frédéric Chopin, including his
influence on the Romantic movement
of music.

Ages 14+
Surviving Auschwitz:
Children of the Shoah
Milton Nieuwsma (ibooks)
The harrowing story of three young girls
who survived Hitler's most notorious death
camp. Intensely moving, these children's
stories provide a remarkable insight into
the Holocaust years and its implications.

Taste of poland apple baba

A popular dessert in Poland, apple
baba is a light and delicious cake
made with tart apples and plenty
of sugar.

What you need
▸ 4 tart apples (such as Granny
Smiths), peeled, cored, quartered
and thinly sliced crosswise
▸ 500 g granulated sugar
▸ 1 tsp cinnamon
▸ 4 large eggs
▸ 150 ml vegetable oil
▸ 75 ml fresh orange juice
▸ 2 tsp vanilla extract
▸ 900 g plain flour
▸ 1 tsp baking powder
▸ Icing sugar
for sprinkling

What to do
▸ Heat oven to 175ºC
and grease a 25-cm
loaf tin.
▸ Place the apples in a
bowl and sprinkle with 60 g
sugar and the cinnamon.
▸ In another bowl, beat the eggs
and the rest of the sugar until

pale yellow and thick.
▸ Gradually beat in the oil,
orange juice and vanilla extract.
▸ Sift the flour and baking
powder and slowly add it to
the egg mixture until it is like
thick honey.
▸ Fold the apples evenly into
the batter and pour into the tin.
▸ Bake for around 1½ hours
until the top is well browned
and splitting.
▸ Invert on to a wire rack to cool
and sprinkle with icing sugar just
before serving.

ⓗ Spot a bear
★ Bears still roam the dense forests of
Eastern Europe, but they can be very
elusive. One of the best places to catch a
glimpse is Kingstone Mountain National
Park in Slovenia. Poland's Bieszczady
Mountains are still roamed by Europe's Big
Five: wolf, bison, bear, lynx and red deer,
while Croatia's Plitvice Lakes National Park
is home to bears and wolves.

When it comes to family holidays there's no doubt that some parts of Eastern Europe, particularly rural areas, can be more of a challenge than elsewhere on the continent. You won't, for example, find as many theme parks here as you do in Scandinavia or France. And on more remote forays in Eastern Europe you might occasionally find yourself wondering whether you've strayed too far off the beaten track. However, all of the countries covered in this chapter have not only popular resort areas and fascinating cities but also a good range of family-friendly accommodation, activities and facilities.

from, including self-catering villas, holiday camps with crèches and hotels with paddling pools.

Now is also the time to snatch a weekend break in cities like Prague or Kraków while your little darling is still buggy-bound and hasn't yet found the voice to offer unwanted suggestions to your sightseeing plan. Avoid the crazy midsummer months, though, when you'll spend half your time apologizing for running your buggy over the feet of endless streams of other tourists.

Exploring the wild woods

Footloose in Slovenia's Triglav National Park.

Babies

Lake Bled

If you've tried a Mediterranean holiday in France, Italy or Spain with tiny tots, you'll find that Croatia's Adriatic coast is just as warm, comfortable and friendly. True, it's further to fly – and there can't be many new parents willing to summon the energy required to drive 1600 km from the UK to Split. However, once you reach Croatia, there's a wide range of baby-friendly accommodation to choose

Toddlers/pre-school

As with babies, travelling to Croatia with pre-school children means you can avoid the blisteringly hot month of August. It's cooler and less crowded in June and September. Be aware that many beaches along this stretch of the Adriatic coast are either rocky or pebbly – a godsend to parents who abhor the prospect of sand finding its way into every nook and cranny, but a tad frustrating for a budding sandcastle-building three-year-old. It's worth remembering to pack jelly shoes or wetsuit boots to help littl'uns negotiate pebbly coves with the minimum of fuss and scraped knees.

With its shallow waters and gently shelving shores, Lake Balaton in Hungary (page 157) is another good beach option for young children – and excellent value if you're on a tight budget. So too are the Baltic states (see box opposite).

Special needs

Certain attractions in Eastern Europe, such as Slovenia's Skocjan Caves, present obvious difficulties to wheelchair users. However, although facilities for the disabled are still somewhat limited throughout the region, most countries are making strong moves to improve access for all. Wheelchair-accessible monuments in Prague include St Vitus Cathedral, Old Royal Palace, St George's Basilica, Ballgame Hall and Prague Castle Gardens, while Wawel Royal Castle in Kraków can be reached (albeit with some effort) by its ramp-like approach road. Thanks to a million-dollar accessibility project, disabled travellers can tour most parts of the Wieliczka Salt Mine.

Single parents

Mango (mangokids.co.uk) specializes in group holidays for single-parent families and runs trips to both Slovenia and Croatia. For a holiday on the Adriatic, Small Families (smallfamilies.co.uk) operates single-parent holidays to Croatia, staying in the resort of Cavtat.

> **Little Slovenia not only proved to be big on boredom-busting, but it enabled our children to experience something new, from whitewater kayaking to sipping water straight from a mountain spring. It was less crowded and better value for money than its more popular European rivals, but ultimately its main draw was that it was somewhere just that little bit different.** William Gray

Kids/school age

The Czech Republic, Slovakia, Romania and Slovenia all start to have more appeal around this age. Slovenia is a doddle to travel around and its compact size means you can give youngsters a taster of all things Eastern European, from spooky castles and mysterious forests to action-packed mountain resorts.

Usually, you will find that the minimum age for things like river rafting (with gentle rapids) is five or six. It's around this age (possibly earlier if they have older siblings) that kids start nurturing a fascination with all things gruesome – vampires included. Romania's Bran Castle, the legendary home of Dracula, will either titillate or terrify them. If it's likely to be the latter, opt instead for Kraków where the Royal Castle has an altogether less sinister dragon's lair.

The history of Eastern Europe doesn't feature as much on the school curriculum as other parts of the continent, but that's no reason to sidestep the beautiful Czech capital, Prague. Forget its reputation as a couples-only city break destination. With a little forward planning you can easily adapt it to suit children and adults alike.

Teenagers

One aspect of Eastern European history that older children will encounter in their studies is the rise and fall of Nazi Germany. However, prepare yourself for some difficult questions before taking teenagers to Auschwitz in Poland. Reading about it in school textbooks is one thing, but to actually visit the site of this notorious death camp is a harsh lesson for young minds.

Elsewhere in the region, teenagers will love the mix of nightlife and water-based activities along the Croatian coast. Plan a sea-kayaking expedition among the Dalmatian islands or opt for a centre-based holiday in which youngsters can dabble in a range of activities, from sailing to scuba diving.

The Adventure Company (adventurecompany.co.uk), Explore Worldwide (explore.co.uk) and Exodus (exodus.co.uk) offer dedicated teenage departures on many of their trips to various Eastern European countries, including Croatia, the Czech Republic, Poland, Romania, Slovakia and Slovenia.

Baltic break

Easily overlooked, but bursting with ideas for a family holiday, the Baltic states of Estonia, Latvia and Lithuania promise exceptional value for money. English is widely spoken, it's easy to get around and accommodation includes child-friendly guesthouses, farms and cottages.

Lithuania family holiday Start by exploring the narrow lanes and secret courtyards of Vilnius' Old Town, then delve into the countryside by kayak or cycle. Visit the island castle of Trakai on Lake Galvè, then relax on the Amber Coast.

Czech Republic
Prague for kids

The beautiful medieval capital of the Czech Republic, Prague has become one of Europe's most trendy city-break destinations – a magnet for couples in search of café culture, a spot of shopping and a lazy trawl around the historical sights. However, before you ship your brood off to the grandparents, you might want to know that Prague is also quite child-friendly. One or two carefully planned days will mean you can still see many of the city's highlights and keep the kids happy in the process. Of course, it would help if you promise them a week of fun activities in Slovakia's Tatra Mountains afterwards…

Prague

▶ Day 1 Take the funicular railway up 318-m Petrín Hill where you'll find an imitation Eiffel Tower built for the Jubilee Exhibition of 1891. Although it's only a quarter the height of the Parisian version, the 299 steps lead to a viewing platform with far-reaching views of the city and distant mountains.

Next, head to the nearby maze, which has walls lined with distorting mirrors, so you can get lost and laugh about it at the same time. Inside this bizarre labyrinth is a huge painting depicting the 1648 battle that ended the Thirty Years' War. On the way down from Petrín Hill, stop for a snack at the Nebozizek restaurant, which has an outdoor patio, fine views and a varied menu.

In the afternoon, tram route 22 or 23 will take you to Prague Castle (hrad.cz). Founded in the ninth century, the city's crowning glory contains churches, palaces, towers and convents within its fortified walls. As you enter, look out for the statue of the fighting giants above the castle gates. Beyond the president's office looms Prague's richly decorated Gothic icon, St Vitus's Cathedral. See if you can spot the gargoyles on the western façade. Inside, you'll find the tomb of Good King Wenceslas, who founded a chapel here around AD 925, only to be murdered by his brother a few years later. A relief depicting the brutal act can be seen on the west door.

If cultural fatigue starts to take its toll on your children, give them a quick boost at the Toy Museum. This quirky collection has everything from tin soldiers, model aeroplanes and wooden farm animals to clockwork robots, teddy bears and several hundred Barbie dolls. While you're at this end of Prague Castle, take a wander down Golden Lane with its quaint 16th-century artisans' cottages, then backtrack towards the cathedral for one last cultural biggie.

The Vltava River

It's a difficult decision between the Royal Palace, with its massive vaulted halls and coats of arms, and St George's Convent with its national collection of Renaissance and Baroque art.

▶ Day 2 Start in the Little Quarter where kids can play in the park on Kampa Island and feed the swans on Vltava River. Then cross Charles Bridge, admiring the famous statues of various saints, and walk the short distance to the Old Town Square. Traffic-free (unless you count the horse-drawn carriages) this wonderful public space, with cafés spilling out on to the cobbles, is framed by beautiful churches, palaces, town houses and arcades. The most eye-catching building is the Old Town Hall. Make sure you get a good position in front of its astronomical clock, which strikes the hour accompanied by an elaborate charade of clockwork Apostles and other moving figures.

In the afternoon, catch a tram to the Prístaviste Parníku landing stage (located between Palackého and Jiráskuv bridges) for a boat ride on the Vltava. Heading north, you'll pass riverside landmarks, like the National Theatre, before reaching Stromovka Park and the Výstaviste fairgrounds – site of a dancing fountain and the Sea World aquarium (morsky-svet.cz). On the opposite bank, Prague Zoo (zoopraha.cz) is renowned for its captive breeding programmes of endangered species, such as Przewalski's horse.

> ## ⊘ Cool castles
>
> **Karlstein** (25 km southwest of Prague) Rises above woodland that has changed little since Charles IV hunted there in the 14th century.
> **Konopiste** (40 km southeast of Prague) Striking for its displays of stags' heads and other hunting trophies.
> **Krivoklát** (45 km west of Prague) Dominated by a massive Great Tower, Krivoklát has a vaulted Gothic hall reminiscent of the one in Prague's Royal Palace.

Hiking in the Tatra Mountains

Orava Castle

Malá Fatra National Park

Cloaked in beech forests and home to bear, lynx and golden eagle, this beautiful mountain reserve (80 km from Zuberec) is also renowned for its whitewater rafting. Trips depart from Parnica, swooping you through grade 2-3 rapids in the Vratna Valley.

Oravice

More gentle float trips are possible here – drifting downstream on traditional wooden rafts to Orava Castle (oravamuzeum.sk), perched on a rocky bluff 100 m above the river. Oravice also has a thermal pool complex which doubles as a ski park in winter.

Zuberec

As well as being the starting point for hiking trails to nearby lakes and waterfalls, Zuberec is within cycling distance (around 18 km) of Brestova's open-air museum (museum.sk) where traditional buildings – from sawmills to churches – evoke rural Slovakian life from the late 19th century. Hands-on activities allow children to take part in crafts, games and folk dancing. In winter, Zuberec is an ideal place for learning to ski or snowboard, with easy access to around 4 km of pistes. Cross-country trails, snowshoeing and dog sledging are also available.

Bulgaria break

★ There's more to Bulgaria than Black Sea resorts and cheap skiing packages. Head for the Rhodope Mountains in summer for hiking, caving, rock-climbing and horse riding. If a winter visit appeals, base yourself in one of the quieter resorts, like Chepelare, which offer dog sledging and snowmobiling as well as skiing.
Further info Bulgaria Tourism (bulgariatravel.org).

🔍 Hungary for a holiday

Lake Balaton is the place to go. Central Europe's largest lake has an average depth of just 2-3 m. It warms quickly in the sun and has gently shelving beaches, making it ideal for young children. Sailing, windsurfing, canoeing and other watersports can be found on the southern shore, while the north has rugged scenery that will appeal to hikers, cyclists and horse riders. Thermal springs and spas, meanwhile, offer a spot of relaxation.
Get a package Vacansoleil (vacansoleil.co.uk) offers holidays on the shores of Lake Balaton in fully equipped six-berth tents. The campsite offers excursions to Budapest where kids will love exploring the 10-km labyrinth of passageways beneath Buda Castle (labirintus.com). Ryanair (ryanair.com) has flights to Budapest.
Further info Hungarian National Tourist Office (hungary.com).

Inside info ⓘ

▶▶ Take the overnight sleeper train from Prague to the Slovakian town of Liptovsky Mikulas, which is within easy striking distance of the Tatra Mountains.
▶▶ Nestled beneath the Roháče range, the small village of Zuberec (zuberec.sk) has become a thriving centre for winter and summer activities.
▶▶ Other popular resorts in the Tatras include Štrbské Pleso, Starý Smokovec and Tatranská Lomnica.

Like Prague in the Czech Republic (see page 156), Kraków in southern Poland is one of Eastern Europe's essential city-break destinations. Spared the ravages of the Second World War, its Old Town is a medieval marvel that could almost have been lifted straight from the pages of a child's storybook (there's even a dragon's den under the castle). Combine a day or two in Kraków with a visit to the nearby Wieliczka Salt Mine (not as dry and dull as you might imagine), then head south to the mountains.

Kraków

Heart and soul of the city, Kraków's central square (Rynek Glowny) is a great place to start your sightseeing. Young children will be obsessed with feeding the pigeons, while teenagers can practise being cool at the pavement cafés. Either way, parents will be able to snatch admiring glances at the square's impressive buildings, including the Cloth Hall and the 14th-century St Mary's Church.

Kraków's Old Town is only 800 m wide by 1200 m in length, so it won't take you long to walk to the Czartoryski Museum (muzeum-czartoryskich.krakow.pl) with its exquisite portrait, *Lady with an Ermine*, by none other than Leonardo da Vinci. Next, it's off to Wawel Hill (wawel.krakow.pl), where Kraków's greatest urban myth lurks beneath the Royal Castle. Once upon a time there was a powerful prince called Krak who built a castle on a hill above the Vistula River. He founded a town named after himself and everyone lived happily ever after – or at least they would have done had it not been for the dastardly dragon living in the cave under the castle. This monstrous beast was a perfect nuisance, gobbling up cattle, sheep and people (it was particularly partial to pretty maidens). But wise Prince Krak had a cunning plan. One day, he ordered a sheep's hide to be stuffed with sulphur and tossed into the dragon's den. Of course, the repulsive reptile swallowed it in one gulp, only then feeling the sulphur burning its stomach. Rushing down to the river, the dragon drank and drank… until it exploded. The end. Well, not quite – you can visit the Dragon's Cave for yourself by clambering down the steps inside one of the castle's towers, but be sure to explore the fine treasures in the fort beforehand.

🎿 Ski poles

Located in the Tatra Mountains about 100 km south of Kraków, Zakopane (zakopane.pl) is Poland's premier ski resort, with access to over 50 lifts and runs for all abilities.

Kraków Castle

Wieliczka Salt Mine

Wieliczka, T012-278 7302, kopalnia.pl. Apr-Oct, daily 0730-1930, Nov-Mar, daily 0800-1700 ▸▸Mainline train Kraków – Wieliczka Rynek.

Caves made of salt? You may well have to pinch yourself when venturing into this extraordinary subterranean labyrinth, carved entirely from salt and extending to some 300 km of passages and more than 2000 caverns. Mined since the Middle Ages, when salt was as valuable a commodity as oil is today, the Wieliczka Salt Mine is just 10 km from the city centre. Although excavations reach a depth of 327 m, the section accessible to visitors only goes down as far as 135 m. The 2-km tour takes you through a surreal, almost fairy-tale, world of vast floodlit chambers – some with underground lakes, others with salt carvings and murals left by Wieliczka's miners. There are chapels illuminated by chandeliers, great wooden stairways, displays of old mining gear and even a subterranean restaurant and souvenir shop.

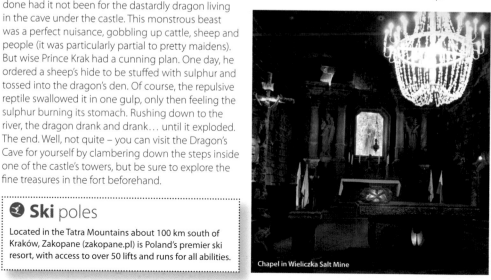

Chapel in Wieliczka Salt Mine

Bran Castle

The Carpathian Mountains sweep through Romania in a broad swathe of densely forested peaks, peppered with small villages and farming communities, while the River Danube scrawls a lazy outline along the country's southern border. Rural Romania feels remote and unspoilt – locals will tell you the country has more brown bears than British Columbia. But despite this image of tranquil wilderness, there's always something gnawing away at your mind – or rather your neck – when you contemplate Romania. Just the mere mention of the words 'Dracula's castle' will have your kids more riveted than any amount of spiel about the adventure, wildlife and cultural highlights in this land of Transylvanian vampires!

Bran Castle

Nr Brasov, T0268-237 700, bran-castle.com. Year round, Mon 1200-1900, Tue-Sun 0900-1900.

Creepy courtyards, dingy passageways and an underground network of secret tunnels – if this austere, forbidding Gothic stronghold, perched on a rocky outcrop in the village of Bran, doesn't give you goose pimples, nothing will. After all, this was the lair of Dracula, wasn't it?

Before you dash off to buy garlic cloves, wooden crosses and any other vampire repellents, let's be absolutely (and historically) clear about Bran Castle and its Dracula association. Dracula never existed. He was a character in Bram Stoker's 1897 classic novel. Vlad Tepes, on the other hand, did exist. Born in 1431, he was the son of a Transylvanian governor who happened to be a member of an anti-Turk secret society known as the Order of the Dragon. In folklore, the dragon was associated with the devil, so Vlad's father was known as Dracul ('Devil'), while Vlad himself became Dracula ('Son of the Devil').

What's this got to do with vampires? Well, that's where fact and fiction begin to blur. Tepes grew up to be a ruthless warlord, battling the hated Turks and picking up a few of their less salubrious habits, such as impaling prisoners on long stakes (earning him the jolly title of 'Vlad the Impaler').

So, more of a blood-letter than a bloodsucker, but the whole Dracula vampire myth has somehow stuck to Bran Castle where Tepes briefly sought refuge in 1462. When it comes to the crunch, though, no kid is going to let a bit of history spoil a juicy excuse for a vampire hunt.

Carpathian Mountains

A three-hour drive north of Bucharest, Kingstone Mountain National Park has one of Europe's largest concentrations of brown bears, wolves and lynxes. Based in nearby Zarnesti, you can make forays into the reserve's primeval woods, tracking these elusive predators or even seeing them up-close from a hide. Elsewhere in the Carpathians there are plenty of opportunities for activities, including mountain biking and whitewater rafting in summer, and cross-country skiing and horse-sleigh rides in winter. The village of Lunca Bradului will lull you into a gentle pace of life, where you can experience rural traditions while indulging in a spot of hiking, horse riding or fishing.

Painted churches

Located in Bucovina, northern Romania, an extraordinary cluster of picture book medieval churches are painted, inside and out, with elaborate murals depicting Biblical stories, ranging from *Genesis* to the *Last Judgement*.

Danube Delta

Sprawling over 5700 sq km, Europe's largest wetland is a watery wilderness of lakes, channels, reed beds, meadows and islands that's home to lively nesting colonies of great white pelicans (pictured below), herons and terns, plus huge flocks of overwintering ducks, geese and waders. You can feast your eyes on this avian spectacle by taking the train to Tulcea and then hopping on a tour boat.

Inside info

▸▸ Rail travel is inexpensive, although a hire car will give you more freedom and flexibility to roam.
▸▸ As well as the highlights on this page, try to fit in a visit to the medieval town of Sighisoara.
▸▸ Beach resorts are located along the Black Sea coast between Mangalia and Mamaia.

Slovenia
A little bit of what you fancy

S mall, but perfectly formed, Slovenia is a medley of dramatic Alpine peaks, beguiling lakes and bear-filled forests tucked away at the top of the Adriatic. It is often hailed as one of Europe's last genuinely unspoilt destinations. But if that translates in your mind as wild and uninviting, then think again. Slovenia is not only emerging as prime adventure territory, but its compact size, extraordinary diversity and well-established infrastructure makes it ideal for family holidays. With its modest 46-km coastline, there's not much in the way of sun-soaked beaches, but at least you can paddle your toes in the Adriatic at the lovely old town of Piran.

Ljubljana

Slovenia's capital (visitljubljana.si) won't blow your mind, but it's pleasant enough for a day or two at either end of your holiday. Climb up to the castle for views over the city's terracotta-tiled rooftops, and wander the old quarter's tangle of cobbled streets and squares. Tivoli Park has a children's playground, and there's a waterpark (atlantis-vodnomesto.si) on the city's outskirts. With its lovely town squares, riverside setting and hilltop castle, the nearby medieval town of Škofja Loka (skofjaloka.si) makes a lovely day trip.

Lake Bled

With paved lakeside paths, picture-perfect Lake Bled is a godsend if you've got a baby or toddler in a stroller. There are also horse-and-cart rides, boat trips to the island and an excellent swimming area with waterslide and shady trees. Treat the kids to a cream cake at the Park Hotel.

Lake Bohinj

Far less manicured than Bled, Lake Bohinj is wild and woody. Pick up a map from the tourist office, pack a picnic and set off to explore Triglav National Park. Right on your doorstep there are easy, level trails around Lake Bohinj – or you could hire a bike, canoe or rowing boat. Mount Vogel cable car has stunning views over the lake and Julian Alps, while a 90-minute hike through beautiful beech woodland leads to the impressive 78-m-high Savica Falls. Children will love horse riding at Ranch Mrcina where the ponies are small and docile. For adrenaline addicts there is canyoning, tandem paragliding, rock climbing, quad-biking and gentle whitewater rafting on the Sava Bohinjka. Swimming is also popular – but bring

Hiking in Triglav National Park

Rafting the Sava Bohinjka

Predjama Castle

something for the kids' feet because the lakeside beaches are quite gritty and stony.

Caves & castles

A combo ticket will allow you to explore Postojna Caves (postojnska-jama.si) and lay siege to the nearby 700-year-old Predjama Castle, wedged dramatically in a 123-m-high cliff face. But if you go underground just once in Slovenia, make sure it's into the mighty Skocjan Caves (park-skocjanske-jame.si). You'll need jackets, torches and a head for heights. It's pitch black (surprise, surprise), so don't take kids who are afraid of the dark – or bats for that matter. After several smallish caverns that are drizzled with stalagmites and stalactites, you enter a vast chamber with plunging cliffs, a subterranean river and Indiana Jones-style bridge. The guided tour lasts 90 minutes; there are hundreds of steps (slippery in places), but kids will emerge wide-eyed with wonder.

Adriatic Coast

With its cutesy harbour, Venetian architecture and restaurant-lined waterfront, Piran (piran.si) is a perfect little seaside retreat. Try to get Room 40A in Hotel Tartini – it's a family apartment with great views over the town square and harbour. For sandy beaches, nip around the coast to Portoroz (portoroz.si).

Dubrovnik

Of all the countries in Eastern Europe, Croatia is the one that cries out 'family holiday'. Not only is its beautiful coast bathed in crystal-clear waters and warm sunshine, but it is also endowed with enough islands and cultural nuggets to turn a seaside holiday into an Adriatic adventure. Base yourself in Dubrovnik, for example, and the kids could be scaling the ramparts of the old city one day and paddling a sea kayak to a deserted cove the next. Rocked by war in the early 1990s, Croatia's tourism industry is back in top gear, whether you want to island hop along the Dalmatian coast or head inland to explore the freshwater wonder of the Plitvice Lakes National Park.

Dubrovnik

Built between the 13th and 16th centuries, Dubrovnik's fortified walls encircle the Old Town in a curtain of stone 6 m thick and 25 m high, punctuated by 16 towers. You can walk right around the walls – an epic 2-km amble which offers spectacular views across Dubrovnik's terracotta-tiled rooftops and the Adriatic beyond. The access point for the one-hour circuit is at Pile Gate; head clockwise to get the uphill bits over with first. Down at street level, most of the highlights are concentrated around the Old Port, including the Dominican Monastery and Rector's Palace. There's also an aquarium, but better to don mask and snorkel and head to one of the city's offshore islands.

Best islands

Just a stone's throw from the city walls, tiny Lokrum is a beauty, with its own subtropical gardens, an 11th-century monastery and a small lake linked to the open sea. You can join a half- or full-day sea-kayaking trip here, or take the less strenuous option of a boat tour. Lying further afield are the three, equally verdant isles of the Elaphite archipelago: Kolocep, Lopud and Šipan. All have small, picturesque villages with options for staying overnight, making them an excellent proposition for a multi-day, island-hopping adventure, either by kayak or ferry. If you take the former option, you should be prepared to paddle up to 14 km a day, although in a double kayak you can at least share the workload. Be sure to visit Lopud's sandy Šunj Bay and explore the sea caves on Kolocep. Further north lies the large island of Mljet (mljet.hr) – possibly the most beautiful in the Adriatic, with emerald forests, turquoise seas and saltwater lakes. That said, however, Korcula (korculainfo.com), further along the coast, is also pretty special – not to mention the hundreds of other islands dotted along the Dalmatian coast.

Plitvice Lakes

A beautiful mosaic of 16 lakes connected by waterfalls, the densely forested Plitvice Lakes National Park (np-plitvicka-jezera.hr) lies 140 km from Zagreb. You can take boat trips on the larger lakes or explore walking trails in the woods and along boardwalks.

Plitvice Lakes National Park

Inside info ⓘ

▶▶ There's a small beach next to Dubrovnik's Old Town (tzdubrovnik.hr), with pebbly coves around the Lapad headland.
▶▶ The Elaphite Islands are connected by ferries, while old-timer motor cruisers can be chartered for voyages lasting a few days to a week or more.
▶▶ Sea-kayaking is available from Adriatic Kayak Tours (adriatickayaktours.com) and Adria Adventure (adriaadventure.hr).

When to go

The climate varies widely across Eastern Europe. **Croatia**'s long hot Mediterranean summers, for example, might allow you to eke out a beach holiday in late October – a time when the Carpathian Mountains of **Poland**, **Slovakia** and **Romania** are bracing themselves for their first winter snowfalls. As you might expect, anywhere in the region away from the Adriatic coast can be bitterly cold during winter. The skiing season lasts from December to mid-April, while the peak summer months are July and August. Avoid the crowds (and the prospect of irritable, overheated children) by visiting popular cities like Prague and Kraków during spring or autumn.

Getting there

Numerous airlines serve the region, including national carriers Adria (adria.si), Croatia Airlines (croatiaairlines.hr), Czech Airlines (czechairlines.com), LOT Polish Airlines (lot.com), and Tarom (tarom.ro). Also try easyJet (easyjet.com), Ryanair (ryanair.com), Flybe (flybe.com), BmiBaby (bmibaby.com) and Jet2 (jet2.com).

Getting around

Trains and buses probe most corners of the **Czech Republic**, although you will find that buses have a reduced service at the weekends.

Information on rail travel in **Poland** is available from PKP Intercity (intercity.com.pl), while international coach lines connect cities like Warsaw, Kraków and Gdansk. LOT Polish Airlines will whisk you from Warsaw to Kraków in just 55 minutes.

In **Slovakia**, Lod (lod.sk) upholds the long tradition of river travel on the Danube with regular cruises departing from Bratislava, while major rail routes (slovakrail.sk) connect the capital with Kúty, Zilina, Košice and Štúrovo.

In **Romania**, domestic flights are operated by Tarom (see above) and Carpatair (carpatair.com). Getting around by bus and train is also straightforward and inexpensive. For details of rail services, log on to infofer.ro.

Small in size, but with an excellent road network, **Slovenia** is perfect for self-drive and you will find all the main car-rental companies in Ljubljana. For details of bus services in Slovenia, contact Avtobusna Postaja Ljubljana (ap-ljubljana.si). For trains, contact Slovenske zeleznice (slo-zeleznice.si).

In **Croatia**, buses operated by Autotrans (autotrans.hr) connect main towns and cities, while Hrvatske zeljeznice (hznet.hr) runs trains to most major centres. If you have the time, rent a car and drive the scenic Adriatic Highway from Rijeka to Dubrovnik. Car and passenger ferries are operated by Jadrolinija (jadrolinija.hr) between islands as well as ports along the mainland.

Accommodation

You can pitch a tent in one of the **Czech Republic**'s 500 or so campsites for as little as €5 a night. At the other end of the scale, a room in a five-star hotel in Prague will easily relieve you of €250 or more. Cloister Inn (cloister-inn.com) is a good mid-range option in Prague's Old Town, just a few minutes' walk from Charles Bridge. An increasingly popular alternative for families is to rent a self-catering apartment. Apartments.cz (apartments.cz) offers more than 80 furnished apartments in Prague, with rates starting at just €25 per person per night.

A family apartment in Kraków's Old Town costs from around €85 per night with Stay Poland (staypoland.com), which also offers hotels in Warsaw and Kraków. For rural holiday accommodation (or *agroturystyka*) in **Poland**, try agroturystyka.pl.

Apartments and hotels in **Slovakia**'s capital, Bratislava, are available from Bratislava Hotels (bratislavahotels.com), while ABC Slovakia (abcslovensko.sk) has links to a wide range of rural properties, from cottages and pensions to horse ranches. For information on where to stay in the Tatra Mountains, try tatry.sk.

In **Romania**, there are several hotels in Suceava – a good base for exploring Bran Castle and the Carpathian Mountains.

Accommodation in **Slovenia** ranges from campsites, farmstays and pensions to lakeside hotels.

With its alluring Adriatic coastline, **Croatia** has the cream of Eastern Europe's family-friendly accommodation. Holiday camp operators, such as Keycamp, feature northern Croatia, while villa and apartment specialists like Croatian Affair have properties throughout the country.

Food & drink

Hearty and non-spicy (though occasionally on the stodgy side), traditional Eastern European cuisine should appeal to most children. In the **Czech Republic** and **Slovakia**, expect plenty of fried or roast meat, usually pork or beef, accompanied by dumplings, potatoes or rice. Pot-roasted beef in a rich creamy sauce with cranberries and vegetables is delicious, as are fruit dumplings, strudels and pancakes. In the cities, you will find everything from pizzas to Chinese.

Prague Old Town

Go green
Three ways to skip the flight

❶ **Skim across the Adriatic** from Venice to Piran (Slovenia) aboard a high-speed catamaran operated by Venezia Lines (venezialines.com).
❷ **River-cruise companies** based in Austria ply the Danube River to Hungary. DDSG Blue Danube Shipping (ddsg-blue-danube.at) offers return trips by hydrofoil between Vienna and Budapest

(with 50% discounts for children aged two to 14). Alternatively, take the boat one way and return by night train.
❸ **Travelling by coach** to Eastern Europe inevitably means long journeys, but if you're feeling up to it Eurolines (eurolines.com) has services to Poland, Czech Republic, Hungary and Romania.

A typical meal in **Poland** consists of noodle soup followed by pork cutlet with red cabbage and potatoes and rounded off with cheesecake.

Traditional dishes in **Romania** include *ciorba de perisoare* (meatball soup), *scrumbie la gratar* (grilled herring), *sarmale* (pickled cabbage leaves stuffed with minced meat and rice) and *papanasi* (cottage cheese doughnuts). Parents will no doubt want to sample *tuica*, a potent plum brandy, as well as a few of Romania's best wines, such as Murfatlar and Jidvei.

In **Slovenia**, dishes range from Hungarian goulash, Austrian strudels and Italian risotto to more local fare, such as fresh lake trout and sweet pastries. Expect lots of cabbage and potatoes with everything and don't forget to try *potica*, a roll stuffed with walnuts, poppy seeds, raisins, herbs, cottage cheese or honey.

Not surprisingly, **Croatia** has excellent seafood, ranging from universal favourites like scampi to Dalmatian *brodet*, a mixed fish stew served with rice. You'll also find no shortage of Italian-inspired food along the coast.

Health & safety
No special inoculations are required for Eastern Europe. However, if you plan on walking in thickly forested areas, take precautions against tick-borne encephalitis by avoiding tick-infested areas from May to August, using insect repellent, tucking long trousers into socks and wearing a hat. On the whole, tap water is completely safe to drink. If in doubt, err on the cautious side and buy bottled water. Sunburn and dehydration can be a threat during summer, particularly along the Adriatic coast where you should also keep an eye out for spiny black sea urchins.

Holiday operators

The Adventure Company
adventurecompany.co.uk

Completely Croatia
completelycroatia.co.uk

Croatian Affair
affairtravel.com/croatia

Crystal Holidays
crystalholidays.co.uk

Eurocamp
eurocamp.com

Explore
explore.co.uk

Exodus
exodus.co.uk

Families Worldwide
familiesworldwide.co.uk

Just Slovenia
justslovenia.co.uk

KE Adventure Travel
keadventure.com

Keycamp Holidays
keycamp.com

In the USA
Adriatic Tours
adriatictours.com

Croatia Travel
croatiatravel.com

Slovenia Travel
sloveniatravel.com

Fast facts

Country	Time	Language	Currency	Dialling code	Tourist information
Czech Rep	GMT+1	Czech	Koruna	+420	czechtourism.com
Poland	GMT+1	Polish	New Zloty	+48	poland-tourism.pl
Slovakia	GMT+1	Slovak	Euro €	+421	slovakia.travel
Romania	GMT+2	Romanian	New Leu	+40	romaniatourism.com
Slovenia	GMT+1	Slovenian	Euro €	+386	slovenia.info
Croatia	GMT+1	Croatian	Kuna	+385	croatia.hr

Kayaking is one of our favourite holiday activities, so I admit to being slightly biased when it comes to Croatia. With its turquoise shallows and emerald isles, the Dalmation Coast is a paddle made in heaven. But you don't have to look far to find other family-friendly adventures – from scaling the walls of Dubrovnik's Old Town and exploring Plitvice Lakes National Park to sailing in the Adriatic.

William Gray, 101familyholidays.co.uk

Radisson Blu
Where? Dubrovnik, Croatia.
Why? Located just 12 km from historic Dubrovnik, this five-star resort has spectacular panoramic views of the Dalmation coast. Facilities include two family pools, a rock-climbing wall, kids' club, babysitting service, teenagers' bar and the largest spa on the Riviera. The two-bedroom villas (available as self-catering, B&B or half board) sleep up to five.
Contact Completely Croatia, T+44 (0)800-970 9149, completelycroatia.co.uk

Camping Lanterna
Where? Porec, Croatia.
Why? Good value for money and excellent facilities, including three fabulous swimming pools, supermarket, pizzeria and watersports such as sailing and canoeing, make this large holiday park a safe bet for families. The resort of Porec is just 10 km away, while Brijuni Safari Park, Cave Baredine and Plitvice Lakes National Park are also within easy striking distance.
Contact Keycamp Holidays, T+44 (0)844-406 0200, keycamp.com

Greece & Turkey

Under the Aegean

Learning to scuba
dive in Greece.
Right: statue of the
goddess Athena.

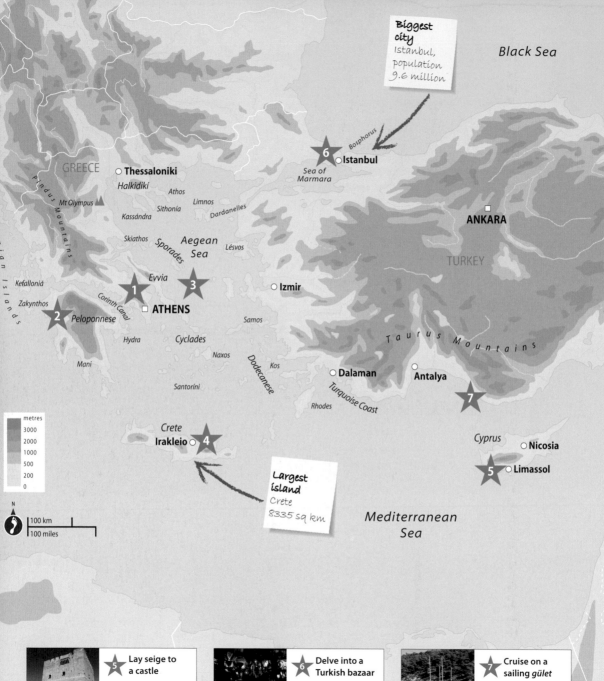

Biggest city
Istanbul, population 9.6 million

Black Sea

Bosphorus

6 ○**Istanbul**

Sea of Marmara

GREECE

○ **Thessaloniki**

Halkidiki

Athos

Pindus Mountains

Mt Olympus ▲

Sithonia

Limnos

Kassándra

Dardanelles

Skiathos

ANKARA □

Sporades

Aegean Sea

Lésvos

TURKEY

Kefanloniá

Evvia

3

1

Zakynthos

2

□ **ATHENS**

Peloponnese

Corinth Canal

● **Izmir**

Samos

Taurus Mountains

Hydra

Cyclades

Mani

Naxos

Kos

Dodecanese

● **Dalaman**

○ **Antalya**

Santorini

Turquoise Coast

Rhodes

7

Crete **4**

Irakleio ○

Cyprus

○ **Nicosia**

5 ○ **Limassol**

Largest island
Crete 8335 sq km

Mediterranean Sea

metres	
	3000
	2000
	1000
	500
	200
	0

N

100 km
100 miles

Lay seige to a castle

▸▸ Cyprus, page 181

Delve into a Turkish bazaar

▸▸ Istanbul, page 182

Cruise on a sailing *gület*

▸▸ Turkey, page 185

Introduction
Greece & Turkey

The people are friendly, the sea is warm, the sunshine is guaranteed and the accommodation and food won't upset the contents of your wallet or your children's stomachs. No wonder Greece and Turkey are such popular family holiday destinations. You probably went there as a kid yourself and know just the place with that perfect beach or laid-back taverna. The Greek Islands are the undisputed stars of the region, spattering the azure Aegean with over 2000 irresistible reasons to pack your bags and go Greek. Only a few dozen islands are holiday hotspots, but such is their diversity that you could easily spend a lifetime sampling them. Well-established favourites include Corfu, Rhodes and Crete. Then there's Cyprus and the coasts of Turkey and the Peloponnese – all with enough sandy beaches, ice-cream kiosks and banana-boat rides to satisfy most kids. There's also a lot to be said for combining beach bliss with a little culture. The Greeks practically invented the stuff, so it would seem rude not to spend a day or two exploring the historical wonders of Athens or strutting your stuff in Ancient Olympia. Istanbul, meanwhile, carries more shock with its culture, but its hectic bazaars and flamboyant architecture will leave most children wide-eyed with wonder.

" Youngsters love playing hide and seek at ancient ruins, collecting stones or chasing grasshoppers, while older children will enjoy the detective challenge of working out what's what. William Gray

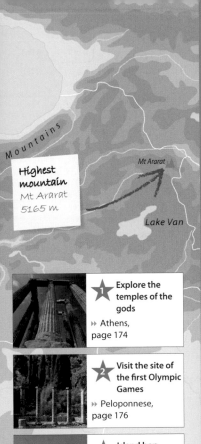

Highest mountain
Mt Ararat
5165 m

Mountains

Mt Ararat

Lake Van

★1 Explore the temples of the gods
▶▶ Athens, page 174

★2 Visit the site of the first Olympic Games
▶▶ Peloponnese, page 176

★3 Island hop through ghe Aegean Sea
▶▶ Greek Islands, page 178

★4 Uncover the myth of the Minotaur
▶▶ Crete, page 180

Did you know?
★ When a child loses a tooth in Greece it is thrown on the roof for good luck.
★ Two of the Seven Wonders of the Ancient World stood in Turkey – the Temple of Artemis at Ephesus and the Mausoleum of Halicarnassus in Bodrum.
★ The word 'astronaut' is derived from the Greek words *ástron* (star) and *nautes* (sailor).
★ Pausanias, a Greek geographer who lived in the 2nd century BC, is credited with writing the first ever travel guide, *Description of Greece*.

Star rating

Wow factor
★★★

Worry factor
★★

Value for money
★★★★★

Keeping teacher happy
★★★★★

Family accommodation
★★★★★

Babies & toddlers
★★★★

Cool for teenagers
★★★★

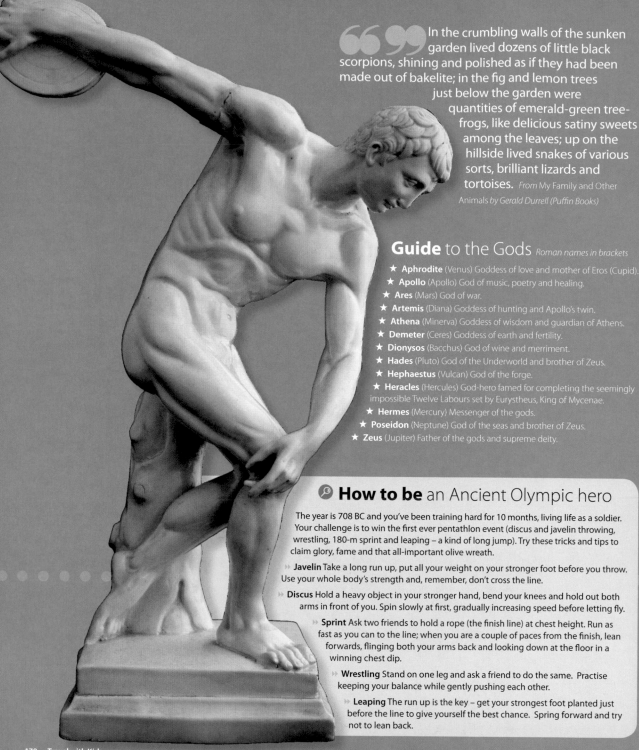

> In the crumbling walls of the sunken garden lived dozens of little black scorpions, shining and polished as if they had been made out of bakelite; in the fig and lemon trees just below the garden were quantities of emerald-green tree-frogs, like delicious satiny sweets among the leaves; up on the hillside lived snakes of various sorts, brilliant lizards and tortoises. *From My Family and Other Animals by Gerald Durrell (Puffin Books)*

Guide to the Gods *Roman names in brackets*

★ **Aphrodite** (Venus) Goddess of love and mother of Eros (Cupid).
★ **Apollo** (Apollo) God of music, poetry and healing.
★ **Ares** (Mars) God of war.
★ **Artemis** (Diana) Goddess of hunting and Apollo's twin.
★ **Athena** (Minerva) Goddess of wisdom and guardian of Athens.
★ **Demeter** (Ceres) Goddess of earth and fertility.
★ **Dionysos** (Bacchus) God of wine and merriment.
★ **Hades** (Pluto) God of the Underworld and brother of Zeus.
★ **Hephaestus** (Vulcan) God of the forge.
★ **Heracles** (Hercules) God-hero famed for completing the seemingly impossible Twelve Labours set by Eurystheus, King of Mycenae.
★ **Hermes** (Mercury) Messenger of the gods.
★ **Poseidon** (Neptune) God of the seas and brother of Zeus.
★ **Zeus** (Jupiter) Father of the gods and supreme deity.

How to be an Ancient Olympic hero

The year is 708 BC and you've been training hard for 10 months, living life as a soldier. Your challenge is to win the first ever pentathlon event (discus and javelin throwing, wrestling, 180-m sprint and leaping – a kind of long jump). Try these tricks and tips to claim glory, fame and that all-important olive wreath.

» **Javelin** Take a long run up, put all your weight on your stronger foot before you throw. Use your whole body's strength and, remember, don't cross the line.

» **Discus** Hold a heavy object in your stronger hand, bend your knees and hold out both arms in front of you. Spin slowly at first, gradually increasing speed before letting fly.

» **Sprint** Ask two friends to hold a rope (the finish line) at chest height. Run as fast as you can to the line; when you are a couple of paces from the finish, lean forwards, flinging both your arms back and looking down at the floor in a winning chest dip.

» **Wrestling** Stand on one leg and ask a friend to do the same. Practise keeping your balance while gently pushing each other.

» **Leaping** The run up is the key – get your strongest foot planted just before the line to give yourself the best chance. Spring forward and try not to lean back.

Great reads ◄ ⋯⋯⋯⋯⋯
5 children's books

Ages 5+
Aesop's Fables
Carol Watson (Usborne)
Book/CD of famous tales, like *The Hare and the Tortoise* and *The Thirsty Crow* from the most moral-minded of Greek storytellers.

Greek Myths for Young Children
Heather Amery (Usborne)
Pandora's Box, *Theseus and the Minotaur* and *Jason and the Golden Fleece* are just three of the classic tales in this beautifully illustrated collection.

Ages 7+
The Wooden Horse of Troy
John Malam (Book House)
Trojan prince, Paris, abducts Helen, the beautiful wife of King Menelaus, in a crime that unites Greek armies against Troy. Featuring cartoon-style illustrations, this book also has a who's who section and pronunciation guide.

Ages 8+
The Groovy Greeks
Terry Deary (Scholastic)
Gods who ate their own children, doctors who tasted their patients' earwax… it's all here, along with other revolting facts about food, war and sport in Ancient Greece.

Ages 10+
My Family and Other Animals
Gerald Durrell (Puffin)
Durrell's classic account of how his family moved to Corfu in the 1930s is humorous and insightful. Share Durrell's passion for creatures great and small and gain an insight into Greek culture and family life.

✎ How to be an archaeologist

What you need
▸ Large terracotta dish or pot (from a garden centre)
▸ Black and white acrylic paint
▸ Paintbrushes
▸ Mallet
▸ Safety goggles
▸ Gardening gloves
▸ Gardening trowel

What to do
▸ Paint pictures that symbolize an aspect of your life onto the dish and leave to dry. Consider what the pictures would tell archaeologists if they dug it up.
▸ Ask an adult to break the dish into several pieces (using a mallet and safety goggles).
▸ Use gardening gloves and a trowel to bury your pottery pieces.
▸ Challenge a friend to discover the pottery pieces.
▸ Help your friend put it together. Can they guess what the pictures were trying to say?

Taste of Turkey baklava

A sticky and irresistible pastry that's impressive to look at and easy to make.

What you need
▸ 400 g ground almonds
▸ 250 g butter, melted
▸ 2 tsp ground cinnamon
▸ 1 pinch ground cloves
▸ 500 g filo pastry
▸ lemon juice
▸ 250 ml thyme honey
▸ 2 tsp vanilla extract
▸ 450 ml water

What to do
▸ Mix together the almonds, cinnamon and cloves.
▸ Butter four sheets of pastry and place in a deep pan or dish.
▸ Spread a thin layer of nuts and spices on top of the pastry sheets, then add two more sheets of pastry.
▸ Repeat the process, using the last four sheets for the top layer.
▸ Cut the baklava into squares, making sure you cut all the way through the pastry.
▸ Top with the remaining butter and bake in a medium-hot oven for 45 minutes.
▸ Mix the sugar, honey, vanilla, lemon and water and boil in a saucepan for five minutes.
▸ Pour over the baklava and serve cold.

A quiet corner of Greece

Voidokiliá, near Pylos on the Peloponnese peninsula of the Greek mainland, with the lagoon of Giálova in the background.

Turks and Greeks love children. They dote on them and are usually very forgiving of their moods. Don't be surprised, for example, if your irritable, scowling, post-tantrum toddler receives a squidge on the cheeks and some affectionate hair ruffling rather than a disapproving glance from the locals. While shopping you might find storekeepers spontaneously lavishing balloons, sweets and other freebies on your little darlings, while waiters will often go out of their way to cater for children at restaurants and cafés. Accommodation, meanwhile, covers the entire family-friendly spectrum, from activity-packed all-inclusive resorts to self-catering rural villas.

Babies

Should you really even consider Athens with a baby? What would possess you to drag him, her or, heaven forbid, them around one of the hottest, busiest cities in Europe? After all, most things you will want to see, like the Acropolis and Ancient Agora, are about as buggy-friendly as an SAS assault course. City pavements are either narrow, wonky or non-existent and can you imagine the havoc you'd create pushing your Mamas and Papas three-wheeler into a curio shop crammed with imitation Greek vases? Still determined to go?

Well, the good news is that, during the run-up to the Athens 2004 Paralympics, access for wheelchair users in the city was greatly improved. This doesn't mean families with prams can use the wheelchair lift to scale the Acropolis, but it does mean that they can take advantage of the fully accessible metro and other improved access facilities around the city.

Of course, you could ditch the wheels altogether and carry your baby around in a papoose or sling. Just be extremely wary of doing this during summer when it becomes insanely hot. If you're determined to feast your eyes on propylaea, stoas and the like, it will be far more relaxing to base yourself at a beachside hotel or apartment in the Peloponnese and make brief forays to Corinth, Epidaurus or ancient Mycenae.

Plenty of Greek islands also have ancient ruins, so you can combine the odd day's sightseeing with a predominantly beach-based holiday. The same applies to the Turkish coast. As for Istanbul, it could well be as hot and challenging as Athens. Hygiene may be more of a concern, but one thing is certain: locals will fall over themselves to help you, your baby and your buggy.

Toddlers/pre-school

This could possibly be an even worse age to take children to Athens or Istanbul than when they were babies. Not only are they still largely buggy-dependent (for naps or when they get tired of toddling), but they are heavier to push and more prone to accidents when you set them free. Having

Special needs

Greece is slowly addressing access issues, helped in no small part by the 2004 Paralympics which spearheaded the need to improve facilities for the disabled. There is now a wheelchair elevator on the Acropolis, although once at the top the ground is irregular and littered with fragments of marble. Athens airport and the metro both have good access, while the larger catamarans are usually the best option for getting to islands. The city's National Archaeological Museum is accessible, as is the main floor of Irákleio's museum on Crete. Many parts of Knosós are also wheelchair-friendly, but watch out for sudden unprotected drops. Visit greecetravel.com/handicapped for further information on accessible sites, hotels and tours, including Greek sailing tours for the disabled.

Single parents

The Kids and Me (thekidsandme.co.uk) offers a single-parent holiday on Corfu; Mango (mangokids.co.uk) runs group holidays for single-parent families to Cyprus and the Turkish coast.

"" Our favourite destination is Turkey; we love the people, food, culture, history, climate, scenery – in fact, there isn't much we don't like about it, except perhaps the driving and the odd earthquake. We've had several sailing holidays there, which the kids loved.

Maxine Browning

said that, this is a great time for taking them to the Peloponnese, Halkidikí, Greek Islands or Turkish coast. You might need to ask yourself whether these destinations are worth flying the extra distance when you could have a similar Mediterranean beach holiday in Italy, France or Spain. Ultimately, of course, it all comes down to personal preference. But for sheer variety and value, Greece and Turkey are hard to beat.

Kids/school age

Ancient Greece storms onto the school curriculum around the age of seven – a time when your mini Greek warrior (or goddess) will be thrilled at the prospect of a family odyssey. They are better able to cope with bewildering cities like Athens at this age, although it's still crucial to take precautions against heat and sun exposure. Don't forget to help fire their imagination when visiting ancient ruins (see box right for some tips). As with all ages, there are plenty of kids' clubs at excellent resorts throughout Greece, but don't assume this type of accommodation is the only one that will meet with approval. A villa tucked into a forested mountainside on Corfu, for example, might be just the kind of thing to unleash the budding Gerald Durrell in your child.

Teenagers

Mass tourism in parts of Greece and Turkey have spawned the kind of nightlife that might well appeal to your teenager, but most parents of this age group will be happier in a more controlled resort environment where there are special activities and social areas provided for teens. This style of resort is also an excellent opportunity for teenagers to learn a new sport, such as kitesurfing, sailing or scuba-diving.

How to make ruins riveting

What comes to mind when you look at the tumbled pillars of Ancient Olympia's Temple of Zeus? A classic example of Doric-style columns dating from the fifth century BC? Giant slices of chocolate Swiss roll? Rocks, rocks and more rocks? Let's face it – the average parent's grasp of ancient Greek history is going to be limited to distant recollections from the 1963 movie, *Jason & the Argonauts*. That's fine for starters, but you're going to need additional tactics if you want to avoid a mutiny from the kids at every ruin you visit. Try these tips for starters:

▸▸ Try to view a model reconstruction beforehand so your kids have an idea of what the site looked like in its heyday.
▸▸ Give them a leaflet with an artist's impression of the reconstruction and let them play detectives – matching the drawing to the remains.
▸▸ Swat up on a few epic tales of Greek mythology.
▸▸ Play hide-and-seek – although make sure it's safe and that children are aware of roped-off no-go areas.
▸▸ Quiz them on what was good and what was bad about living in ancient Greek times.
▸▸ Role-play a Greek tragedy or a sporting event.
▸▸ Strike a deal – one ruin equals a boat trip or special treat.

You don't need to be Athena (goddess of wisdom) to fathom why Greece is such a popular holiday destination for families. Boasting fantastic beaches, warm, sheltered seas and an easy-going atmosphere, the Greek Islands are legendary. With holiday bliss scattered so liberally across the Aegean Sea, the Greek capital is always going to have a hard time vying for attention. But spare a thought, and a day or two in your itinerary, for Athens. It's a hot and chaotic city, but the ancient sites truly are amazing. And then there's the Peloponnese, that large, spiky peninsula clinging to the mainland like a stubborn maple leaf. There are more crumbly old wonders here (so that'll impress your history teacher), but the Peloponnese, like Halkidikí in the north, is also blessed with an enticing coastline of beaches and laid-back tavernas.

The Acropolis

T210-321 4172, acropolisofathens.gr. Year round, daily from 0800. Acropolis Museum: Dionysiou Areopagitou St, T210-900 0900, theacropolismuseum.gr. Year round, Tue-Sun
» Red line metro to Acropoli.

Caryatids

Still rising supreme above Athens, this 90-m-high global icon is the crowning glory of ancient Greece. But as with any ruin you will need to bring it to life for kids. So, picture the scene as you walk through the grand temple gateway of the Propylaea: you are following in the footsteps of the Panathenaic Procession when, 2500 years ago, the people of Athens marched through the city to the Acropolis bearing a special robe to honour their patron goddess, Athena. Beyond the Propylaea, towering bronze statues would have reared either side of you – one of Athena Promachos (so dazzling she could be seen by ships sailing towards Athens) and the other of a Trojan horse. But it was the Parthenon that drew the crowds on. Inside this magnificent temple, with its 46 columns and 13,400 blocks of marble, stood another statue of Athena – a 12-m beauty, clad in gold and ivory and bearing a huge shield.

The exterior of the temple was lavishly adorned with sculptures and brightly coloured friezes – most of these have succumbed to erosion, wars or theft, but you can still imagine something of the fine detail of the Acropolis temples by seeking out the Porch of the Caryatids. You'll find it on a building called the Erechtheion (a sacred site where Poseidon and Athena are said to have fought for control of the city) where, instead of columns, exquisitely carved priestesses support the roof.

Spend some time admiring the views of the surrounding city, then visit the Theatre of Herodes Atticus, added to the Acropolis by the Romans in the second century AD and still used for cultural performances during the summer Festival of Athens (greekfestival.gr).

By now you'll probably need some shade and a rest, so head for the pine-clad hills to the west of the Acropolis for a picnic. Philopáppou Hill is the classic vantage point from which to admire the Parthenon. Imagine the scene in 1687 when Turks ruled Athens and used the temple as a gunpowder store. You're in the Venetian army trying to wrestle control of the city; you aim your cannon towards the Parthenon, light the fuse and… kaboom! It's a wonder archaeologists were able to piece any of it together again. You'll find more mind-blowing stuff at the sensational new Acropolis Museum with its state-of-the-art displays.

Ancient Agora

odysseus.culture.gr. Year round, daily from 0800
» Green line metro to Monastiráki.

If anything, kids will be able to relate more to the Agora than the Acropolis. This was where the nitty-gritty of daily mortal life was carried out in ancient Athens. You'll be able to find the

Crowning glory – Acropolis

To sightsee in Athens is to romp through the ages. With a little bit of planning, a modest itinerary, sun hats and a healthy dose of imagination you'll be able to fill your children's minds with riveting tales of gods, heroes, villains and geniuses.

City escapes

★ Catch a ferry from Piraeus to one of the islands in the Saronic Gulf. Aegina has beaches at Perdika and Agia Marina, Hydra (above) has a harbour lined with tavernas and shops and Spétses has beaches at Agioi Anárgyri and Agia Paraskeví.
★ Hop on a bus for the two-hour drive south to Cape Soúnion and watch the sun set behind the Temple of Poseidon.
★ Visit Delphi – a spectacular ruin on Mt Parnassós where ancient Greeks commun with gods through the mysterious oracle

Best museums

1 National Archaeological Museum
namuseum.gr

School-age children studying the ancient Greeks will find more than enough inspiration at this extraordinary and recently renovated museum. Star exhibits include the Mask of Agamemnon (a gold death mask discovered at Ancient Mycenae – see page 176) and a collection of bronze statues (*Poseidon*, *Horse with the Little Jockey*, and *Youth of Antikythira*) salvaged from ancient shipwrecks. It's a huge collection, so prioritize some highlights or devise a treasure hunt for your children to find their favourite characters from Greek mythology.

2 Benáki Museum
benaki.gr

The Benáki Museum houses an exceptional collection of Greek treasures, including simple but striking Cycladic figurines (dating from 2600-2500 BC), El Fayum portraits (dating from the third century AD) and a magnificent 17th-century map of Greece. Of particular interest to kids, however, is the wonderful display of toys dating from antiquity to 1970 and ranging from costumed dolls to intriguing board games.

Other museums worth an hour or two include the **Acropolis Museum**, **Museum of Greek Popular Musical Instruments** (bouzoukis and lutes galore), the **Hellenic Children's Museum** (interactive displays and activities), the **Museum of Greek Children's Art** (paintings inspired by an annual children's competition), the **Museum of Greek Folk Art** (costumes and shadow puppet theatre) and the **War Museum** (weapons and strategies from Mycenean battles to the Second World War).

remains of everything from law courts and markets to schools and a prison. The most obvious building is the replica of the Stoa of Attalos – a two-storey shopping arcade. The original version, opened in 138 BC, would have housed 42 shops, but the modern one contains the Agora Museum. Inside, see if you can find the children's toys and an ancient potty.

Pláka & Monastiráki

Lying to the north of the Acropolis, these historic districts are chock-a-block with ancient ruins, as well as some more modern goodies. Among the contemporary highlights are the curio shops along the pedestrianized streets of Pandrósou and Adrianoú and the flea market at Platéia Avissynías. There are also dozens of cafés, tavernas and restaurants.

If your kids are game for more old stuff, however, start with the Roman Agora where you can challenge them to spot all eight winds depicted on the 12-m-tall Tower of the Winds (right) – a multi-purpose sundial, water clock, weather vane and compass devised by Andronikos around 150 BC. Nearby Anafiótika is a tangle of narrow streets hemmed in by whitewashed houses nuzzled up against the Acropolis.

Syntagma

Ermoú Street links Monastiráki with this city-hub district centred on Platéia Syntágmatos. However, it's more fun to ride the metro – the underground station at Syntagma is a veritable museum of Athenian history with displays of relics uncovered during its excavation.

Above ground, take a minute to watch the traditionally attired soldiers high-stepping in slow motion by the Monument to the Unknown Soldier, then seek refuge in the National Gardens. There are children's play areas here, as well as shady benches, a duck pond and a café. Walk through the gardens and you'll emerge opposite the Temple of Olympian Zeus. It's a whopper, although only 15 of the original 104 17-m-tall columns remain.

Lykavitós Hill

Departing every 10 minutes from Ploutárchou Street a funicular railway scales 277-m Lykavitós Hill. At the top you'll find cafés and an observation deck with Olympian views of the Acropolis and other landmarks.

Inside info

▸▸ The Acropolis and Ancient Agora are within easy walking distance of each other.
▸▸ The metro (ametro. gr) links archaeological sites, as well as the port of Piraeus, from where ferries serve the islands.
▸▸ The tram (tramsa. gr) links central Athens with the city's southern suburbs and the coast.
▸▸ Many sites and state museums (culture.gr) close early afternoon.
▸▸ Cool off by getting a day pass to the Athens Hilton pool or seeking shade in the forests at Moní Kaisarianí.

Peloponnese
Where myth meets history

Cross over the Corinth Canal to the Peloponnese and watch your children's faces light up as you explain that this was the birthplace of winged wonder-horse Pegasus and the evil snake-headed Hydra. Tell them about Greek hero, Heracles (or Hercules to the Romans) who battled here to complete the daunting Twelve Labours. It's all myth, of course, but that won't stop your kids' imaginations running riot when you explore the ancient sites of this enigmatic peninsula.

Ancient Mycenae

Rearing from a rugged mêlée of mountains and ravines, this 3300-year-old Bronze Age citadel leapt to fame in 1867 when archaeologist Heinrich Schliemann discovered what he thought was the grave of a legendary king. "I have gazed upon the face of Agamemnon!" he proclaimed – moments before it crumbled to dust as he lifted the gold death mask (now on display in the National Archaeological Museum, page 175).

You can still see the grave circles where Schliemann toiled, but far more exciting are Ancient Mycenae's Cyclopean walls, so-called because later generations, who had lost the ability to move such massive rocks (weighing an average of six tonnes), believed that the giant, Cyclops, must have had a hand in it. In places they still tower 15 m above you.

Even more mind-blowing is the Lion Gate at the citadel's main entrance, where a 12-tonne lintel has been raised 3 m off the ground. An unsurpassable feat? Don't you believe it. The nearby Treasury of Atreus has a 9-m-long lintel weighing 120 tonnes – twice the weight of the heaviest rock at Stonehenge.

Epidaurus

Snug in a cluster of hills clad in pines and oleanders, Epidaurus boasts the best-preserved theatre in Greece. Try to visit before the tour buses arrive so that you can demonstrate its near-flawless acoustics. Get the kids to sit 55 rows up in the spectacular scoop of tiered seats while you stand on the stage and whisper something. They should be able to hear every word.

Ancient Olympia

For sporting fans these incredible ruins are a must-see. Inhabited as early as 4000 BC, Ancient Olympia only achieved esteem as a religious and athletics centre in 776 BC when the first Olympic Games were

The Lion Gate at Ancient Mycenae

held there. Many of its treasures are displayed in the Olympia Archaeological Museum, including fine statues, temple reliefs and various sporting artefacts. Check out the Stone of Bybon, a 144-kg rock with the inscription, "Bybon, son of Phorys, threw me above his head with one hand". An Olympian feat if ever there was one.

Exploring the ruins themselves, you can almost imagine the roar of the crowd as you walk beneath the archway leading to the stadium where running races were held. You can still see the starting line, marked in stone with grooves for athletes' toes.

Challenge your kids to a race and then have them in fits of giggles (or disbelief) when you explain that ancient Greek athletes competed naked. Other essentials at Olympia include the remains of the Temple of Zeus and the reconstructed colonnade of pillars surrounding the Palaestra (a training centre for boxers, wrestlers and jumpers).

Nafplio

An elegant city with airy squares and narrow streets choked with bougainvillea and geraniums spilling from wrought-iron balconies, Nafplio is perfect for a spot of curio browsing and a relaxed meal at a pavement café.

Best beaches

Head to the south and west coasts. You'll find sandy bays and clean, warm seas near Methoni, Pylos and at Porto Kayio on the Mani Peninsula. Stamped like a disc of turquoise in the rocky shoreline, Voidokiliá near Pylos is a sheltered, shallow-water gem.

Further north, top beaches include Kalogria, a 6-km stretch of sand bordered by pine trees. On the east coast, Tolon is a popular resort offering watersports and boat trips.

Dangling into the northern Aegean like a cow's udder, Halkidikí has three peninsulas. Two of them – Kassándra and Sithonía – have some of the best sandy beaches in Greece and a good choice of resorts to go with them, while the third – Athos – is an autonomous republic ruled by monks.

Kids' top 10 Greece ★

❶ **Cruise** on a traditional Greek sailing or fishing boat for the day – island hopping through the Cyclades, dropping anchor in deserted bays to swim and snorkel.

❷ **Hunt** for brilliantly tacky souvenirs, like painted wooden donkeys and miniature Greek statues and vases, among the streets and flea markets of Pláka and Monastiráki in Athens.

❸ **Challenge** mum or dad to a sprint in the 2700-year-old stadium at Ancient Olympia – and win.

❹ **Search** for chameleons in the dunes near Giálova Lagoon (near Pylos in the Peloponnese) – one of the only places in Europe where you can find African chameleons.

❺ **See** a Mediterranean monk seal before they become extinct. They're one of Europe's most endangered mammals (only around 500 are left), but you might be lucky enough to glimpse one in the seas around Alónissos – there are boat trips to Sporades Marine Park.

❻ **Ogle** the gold treasures discovered at Ancient Mycenae (page 176) and now on display in the National Archaeological Museum in Athens (page 175).

❼ **Explore** the ruins of the Palace of Knosós on Crete (page 180), pretending it's the legendary labyrinth of the Minotaur – a fearsome beast, half-bull and half-man, that devoured young victims lost in the maze.

❽ **Learn** to sail a yacht around the Greek Islands (see page 185).

❾ **Make** lots of new friends on the beach, in the resort or at the kids' club.

❿ **Imagine** what happened to the legendary city of Atlantis when the Santorini volcano erupted some 3500 years ago (see page 179).

Regional highlights

You have to be male and obtain special permission to visit the hallowed ground of Mount Athos, although boat trips from Ouranoúpoli offer views of the 20 Orthodox monasteries that lie beneath it.

Be sure to tear yourself away from the beach for at least a day or two in order to explore the northern part of Halkidikí. Here you'll find the prehistoric troglodyte dwelling of Petrálona Caves where a human skull believed to be 700,000 years old was found. Marvel at the cave interior with its impressive stalactites and stalagmites, then check out the various fossil bones on display in the museum. Keen birdwatchers should schedule a stop at nearby Lake Korónia where you might spot pygmy cormorants, night herons and black kites.

Further afield, there are Macedonian treasures to peruse in the Thessaloníki Archaeological Museum (museumsofmacedonia.gr) and walking trails to pound on the slopes of Mount Olympus. The lofty abode of the gods of Greek mythology, the 2917-m-high peak can be scaled from the village of Litochoro, although the final section to the Mitikas summit is a tough scramble that only experienced rock climbers should undertake.

Finally, if you're craving an ancient ruin, head for Stágeira – birthplace of the great philosopher Aristotle – where you will find the remains of a Classical conurbation that includes an acropolis, fortifications and a Hellenistic temple.

 Inside info

▶▶ Greece's second city, Thessaloníki is the international gateway to the region.
▶▶ Although the best family holiday resorts are located in Halkidikí, other options can be found further east at Alexandroúpoli.
▶▶ Take a ferry from Kavála to visit the northern Aegean islands or from Thessaloníki to reach the Sporades.

Palaiokastritsa Bay, Corfú

Look at a map of Greece and it's almost as if someone has shaken a pepper pot over the Aegean Sea, such is the abundance of islands and islets scattered between Turkey and mainland Greece. Some, like Corfu, attract hundreds of thousands of tourists each summer, while others remain quieter and less developed. Somewhere in this archipelagic constellation you're bound to find a particularly bright star – an island that's made in beach-holiday heaven. But how to find it, that's the trick. Start by asking yourself the questions shown below right – although chances are you'll end up visiting the Greek Islands over and over again, sampling a different one each time.

Corfu

Family appeal One of the greenest and most beautiful of the Greek Islands, Corfu's hilly interior is draped with forests of olive and cypress trees. Gerald Durrell based *My Family and Other Animals* here, and you can still stumble upon wild, unspoilt corners of Corfu that inspired the author. There are resorts like Benítses where nightclubs, not cicadas, reverberate through the night, but there are also plenty of bolt-holes where you'll find a more sympathetic balance between traditional Greek charm and tourist facilities.

Best beaches Most of the mass-market resorts are concentrated in the southeast. For something quieter look to the southwest (for sandy Maltas backed by thickly wooded hills), the northwest (for Palaiokastrítsa with its three coves clustered around a forested headland), the north (for long sweeping bays and interesting rock formations at Sidári) and the northeast (for sandy Almíros or the resort at Kassiópi).

Best days out Older children will appreciate the elegant Venetian architecture, pavement cafés and shops of Corfu Town, and even littl'uns will enjoy exploring the maze of narrow streets in the old quarter – especially if you plonk them in a horse-drawn carriage. Also worthwhile is a day (or two) of island touring. Hire a car and dawdle inland, stopping for Durrell-style nature hunts (or more strenuous jaunts on Mount Pantokrátor). Alternatively, hire a motorboat and potter along the coast in search of hidden coves. And if you're seized by wanderlust, don't forget that Albania is just a ferry ride away.

Kefalloniá

Family appeal Kefalloniá has it in bucket loads. From mountains and caves to beach resorts and fishing villages, this large island is ideal for families seeking a bit more than just a beach holiday.

Best beaches The liveliest resorts are at Lássi and nearby stretches of coast. Elsewhere you'll find a mixture of pebbly and sandy beaches, usually with a striking backdrop of mountains. Lourdas and Skála in the far south both have long stretches of white sand with safe swimming, while the north of Kefalloniá has mainly white-pebble beaches. Myrtou Bay, south of Asos, is considered the island's most beautiful.

Best days out Bus services are limited, so it's essential to hire a car. Allow plenty of time for getting around this large, rugged island. Highlights include Asos (with its nearby Venetian fortress), Fiskárdo (Kefalloniá's prettiest village), Mount Aínos (home to wild horses and native fir trees), Drogkaráti Caves (the size of a large concert hall) and the Melissaní Cave-Lake (a mysterious subterranean azure-blue lake). The island of Ithaca – fabled as the home of Odysseus – is also worth a visit. Join a tour with a good guide who will bring to life the legends of Homer's epic, the *Odyssey*.

Kos

The sandy beaches in the southeast of Kos, as well as north-coast resorts like Tigkáki, make this a popular family destination. Inland, you'll find the remains of the Asklepieion, a fourth-century BC sanctuary dedicated to the god of healing. Kos Town, meanwhile, is the jumping-off point for boat trips to Kalymnos, renowned for its sponge-fishing industry.

Lésvos

Family appeal Once a favoured holiday haunt of the Romans, Lésvos still has what it takes to draw the crowds. A large island with a good scattering of sandy

Pick the right island

▶▶ **What do we want to do?**
Relax on a beach, swim in the sea, sample a few tavernas… these are all Greek-island staples and won't help much in whittling down your shortlist. Instead, think of specifics. Do you want lots to do away from the beach? The larger islands – such as Crete, Evvia, Rhodes and Lésvos – have plenty to tempt you inland. Do you want to split your time between two or more islands? The Cyclades, are well suited to island hopping by ferry, cruise ship or chartered yacht. What about activities? Do you need somewhere that offers walking (Corfu, Crete, Lésvos and Samos) or scuba-diving (Corfu and Zákynthos)?

▶▶ **How do we get there?**
Some islands have direct international flights (ideal for younger kids who will want to hit the beach as soon as possible), while others require a ferry transfer, which older children might see as part of the adventure.

▶▶ **What accommodation do we need?**
You'll find something to suit most budgets, from luxury hotels and villas to self-catering apartments. Consider sharing a larger, pricier villa (which might have extra facilities) with the grandparents or another family. Lively resorts (like those on Kos and Corfu) will suit families with teenagers.

Santorini

to spark their imagination. Inside, challenge them to find the mosaic of the mythical Gorgon Medusa, with hair of writhing serpents. The nearby Street of the Knights, with its austere gateways and impressive coats of arms, is also worth a look. In the new town you can arrange diving and boat trips at Mandráki harbour where the 40-m statue of the Colossus of Rhodes is believed to have once stood. A popular boat excursion is to Líndos where an ancient acropolis looms over a village of whitewashed houses and cobbled streets. If you want shade and tranquillity, visit Petaloúdes, a wooded valley where thousands of Jersey tiger moths gather between June and September (get there before the tour buses arrive).

Santorini

This famous island blew its top around 1450 BC, spewing clouds of molten debris over 30 km and unleashing a tsunami that devastated Minoan Crete. The volcanic eruption left a giant caldera, which subsequently flooded with seawater and inspired the legend of Atlantis. With whitewashed buildings perched on volcanic cliffs, the town of Firá is a port of call on just about every cruise ship operating in the Aegean Sea. Although there are black-sand beaches on Santorini, families will find more inviting stretches of sand on other islands in the Cyclades, such as Náxos and Páros. For independent-minded (ferry- or yacht-bound) families, this beautiful archipelago is ideal for island hopping.

Skiathos

Just 13 km long and with more than 50 sandy beaches, it's small wonder that package tourists overrun Skiathos during July and August. This exquisite little island is buzzing with resorts, watersports and nightlife, but combines well with much quieter Alónissos to the east.

Zákynthos

Although blighted in places by new development, Laganás Bay has fine sandy beaches. Certain stretches are off-limits to tourists to enable endangered loggerhead turtles to lay their eggs in relative peace between May and August. The resorts of Tsiliví and Alykes are further north, along with the island's most popular boat-trip destinations – Shipwreck Beach and the Blue Caves. Meanwhile, at the tip of Vasilikós peninsula, Gerakí beach has clean, white sand and is gently shelving, making it ideal for kids.

beaches and resorts, the so-called Garden of the Aegean has a rugged landscape rich in tradition.
Best beaches Skála Kallonis, a fishing village at the head of the Kallonis Gulf, has a gently shelving beach and warm shallow water that's ideal for small children. To the west, Skála Eresoú boasts one of the island's finest beaches – a 3-km stretch of dark sand.
Best days out There's a petrified forest and 12th-century monastery at Mount Ordymnous – an extinct volcano in the west of the island. Birdwatchers should stake out the lagoons along the western coast, while culture vultures should descend on the atmospheric harbour town of Sykaminiá.

Límnos

Perfect for families in search of a traditional island with few other visitors, Límnos has plenty of sandy beaches for children, although teenagers may find it a little too quiet. The west coast has the pick of the beaches – try Avlónas, just to the north of Myrina with its cobbled streets, bazaar and Ottoman houses.

Rhodes

Family appeal Deservedly popular, this large sunny island has some excellent beaches, a fascinating historic town and a certain buzz that will appeal to families with teenagers.
Best beaches The east coast has a string of beaches: from boisterous resorts like Faliráki, with watersports and nightlife, to quieter coves further south.
Best days out Base yourself on the east coast and it's a straightforward bus ride into Rhodes town. Kids will love exploring the walled Old Town where the Palace of the Grand Masters, a medieval citadel built by the Knights of St John in the 1300s, is guaranteed

This gnarled island of mountains and gorges, stubbled with olive groves and orchards, and fringed with superb sandy beaches, may lack the cutesy, intimate feel of smaller Greek islands, but you'll never be bored. As well as delving into ancient Minoan ruins, there are gorges to trek through, caves to visit and rare birds and flowers to spot.

Irákleio

Like Chania in the west, Irákleio's instant appeal for kids is the old harbour and Venetian fortifications. Lure them beyond the uninspiring façade of the city's archaeological museum, however, and they will discover a treasure trove of Minoan artefacts. Star exhibits include the Phaestos Disc (a clay tablet inscribed with mysterious symbols), the black-stone Bull's Head (used for pouring ritual wines) and a pair of figurines depicting snake goddesses (serpents symbolized immortality for the Minoans). The museum provides a vivid insight into the highly sophisticated Minoan civilization that thrived on Crete some 3000 years ago – but don't overdo it; spend an hour or two checking out the highlights, then head out of town to Knosós.

Palace of Knosós

Many of the exhibits displayed in the Irákleio Archaeological Museum were found at these extraordinary ruins. The first palace was levelled during an earthquake in 1700 BC, so the Minoans knocked up a swanky new one – multi-storied and with grand courtyards, over 1000 rooms and an elaborate drainage system. The Royal Apartments even had an ensuite bathroom with what is believed to be the first-ever flush toilet (water was poured down by hand). The palace and some of its colourful frescoes were partially restored in the early 1900s, so they're not quite as baffling as many other Greek ruins. And, of course, Knosós has the big advantage of a really juicy myth – there never was a labyrinth beneath the palace, but that won't stop kids pretending they're in the lair of the Minotaur.

Samariá Gorge

It's a long way (18 km to the coastal village of Agía Rouméli), but older kids and teens may well be up to the challenge of hiking through this dramatic gorge in western Crete. The well-trodden route takes at least five hours; it's mostly downhill, but take plenty

Samariá Gorge

of water and snacks, wear good walking shoes and set off early in the morning. Keep an eye out for wild goats. You don't need to hike back up – boats depart from Agía Rouméli to Sfakií and Paleochora until around 1700.

Best beaches

Crete has no shortage of good family beaches, although some (particularly in the north where there is more development) tend to get very crowded at weekends and during peak summer months. The west-coast beaches are more remote and have fewer facilities. Elafonisi is a pink-sand beauty. Separated from an islet by a sheltered tidal lagoon of knee-deep water it's perfect for small children. Nearby, the laid-back resort of Paleochora also has a fine beach and is just a 90-minute bus ride to Chaniá with its old Venetian quarter, covered market and taverna-lined harbour.

Knosós

Inside info

▶▶ Crete is the largest, most southerly and most spectacular of the Greek Islands.
▶▶ For flexibility (and somewhere for the kids to cool down) hire a car with air conditioning.
▶▶ Buses ply the north-coast highway, while ferries link villages along the southwest coast.
▶▶ Crete has ferry connections with Piraeus, the Peloponnese, Rhodes and the Cyclades.

Kyrenia, North Cyprus

Splash zones

Fasouri Watermania (fasouri-watermania.com) Waterpark at Limassol with a kamikaze slide and wave pool.

Waterworld (waterworldwaterpark.com) Ayia Napa's splash zone, boasting the hair-raising waterslide, Fall of Icarus, and Poseidon's Wave Pool.

Aphrodite (aphroditewaterpark.com) Waterpark at Paphos with 26 rides, including a pirate ship slide.

Fabled as the birthplace of Aphrodite, goddess of beauty and love, Cyprus has legions of holidaymakers well and truly smitten by its beaches, climate and scenery. The southern part of Cyprus is by far the more developed with the kind of all-singing, all-dancing resorts that most teenagers will rave about. However, if you prefer something quieter and more off the beaten track, then North Cyprus (occupied by Turkey since 1974) couldn't be more of a contrast to its Greek Cypriot neighbour. Here, you will find sleepy harbour towns and rural villages, castles perched in the Kyrenia Mountains and beaches where turtles still dare to nest.

South Cyprus

The fine sandy beaches along the south coast are what most families come here for. However, a few days in a rental car will put you in touch with the quieter, more authentic hinterland. It will also enable you to escape the heat by driving into the Troödos Massif (high and cold enough for skiing in winter). Walking in the mountains is superb, especially during spring when wild flowers are in bloom. A few kilometres outside Limassol, Kolossi Castle stands as testament to the rule of the Knights of St John in the 13th century, while the ancient port of Paphos in the southwest is famous both for its Roman mosaics and as the mythical birthplace of Aphrodite. If you want to find out more about the mysteries of the sea, check out the Museum of Marine Life and the Thalassa Municipal Museum of the Sea in Ayia Napa. Other favourites include the donkey sanctuary near Limassol and the Mazotos Camel Park. If go-karts are preferred, you'll find circuits at Erimi, Polis and Ayia Napa.

North Cyprus

Although divided by the UN's Green Line, Nicosia remains a friendly, laid-back place. However, kids will be far more interested in the harbour town of Kyrenia (Girne). Not only is there a great castle to explore, but inside you'll find the Shipwreck Museum where a 2300-year-old Greek trading vessel is on display, along with its cargo of wine amphorae and some 9000 almonds that were salvaged from the seabed. Perched on a rocky crag in the mountains behind Kyrenia, St Hilarion Castle is a fairy-tale ruin of crenellated walls and watchtowers. A little further inland, visit Bellapais Abbey, then strike out along the Karpas Peninsula where you can run wild on long sandy beaches.

Inside info

The antithesis to the large resorts of Limassol, consider renting a traditional Cypriot house in the countryside (agrotourism.com.cy).

You'll bake in July and August, so try to visit Cyprus either side of this period; it often stays fine through to October.

Travel between the Greek and Turkish Cypriot regions is legal and straightforward.

Istanbul
Where Europe meets Asia

With one foot in Europe and the other in Asia, Turkey is just that little bit more exciting and off the beaten track than Greece. Istanbul provides a distinctively Turkish workout for the senses, but don't feel bewildered. Istanbul is certainly crowded and noisy, but it's also a relatively straightforward place to explore. And what's more, you'll find that the Turks dote on children just as much as their Greek neighbours.

Two-day action plan

▶ **Day 1** Save the history lesson until later. On day one your main priority is to get to Aya Sofya early when morning light filters through the upper windows of this magnificent basilica. Any child who has ever attempted to create a design from tiny pieces of coloured paper will be enthralled by the exquisite artistry of Aya Sofya's mosaics. When Emperor Justinian opened his grand Byzantine design in AD 532, the interior was adorned with some 30 million gold mosaic tiles. But when the city fell to Islam in 1453, the great dome was converted to a mosque, four minarets were added and the iconic mosaics (unacceptable to Muslim beliefs) were plastered over – inadvertently preserving them. Now a museum, with many of the mosaics restored, Aya Sofya is regarded as one of the world's most important artistic treasure troves. Take a long, close look at the Deësis (Prayer) mosaics depicting Jesus, Mary and John the Baptist, and it's not hard to see why.

A short stroll from Aya Sofya, the Blue Mosque was constructed over 1000 years later as a rival to its Byzantine neighbour – and its six minarets and colossal 43-m-high dome still dominate the Sultanahmet district. The interior is decorated with some 20,000 exquisitely painted tiles, shimmering in the light pouring through 260 windows. Each of the elephant foot pillars supporting the dome is 5 m wide.

With all the head spinning, neck craning and hushed reverence that goes on at Aya Sofya and the Blue Mosque, you would be asking a lot of your kids to take in the Topkapi Palace in the same day. Save this historical gem for your second day and instead head for the spooky (and blissfully cool) Basilica Cistern – a vast underground chamber with pillars supported by carved Medusa heads.

A few hundred metres away, you'll find the 650-year-old Grand Bazaar. A vaulted labyrinth of 4000 shops, this is the world's original shopping mall where you'll be able to buy anything from a gold trinket to a belly-dancing costume. Be prepared to haggle, to enter into friendly banter with stallholders and to get

Interior of Aya Sofya

lost – it's all part of the fun. If your children are tired and fractious, however, the Grand Bazaar is almost guaranteed misery.

▶ **Day 2** Start with a boat trip on the Bosphorus, arriving at least an hour before departure to get a good seat. A typical four-hour tour takes you north along the famous straits that link the Sea of Marmara with the Black Sea. On your left is Europe, on your right is Asia. How cool is that! You'll pass the extravagant Dolmabahçe Palace, where Ottoman sultans were enthroned in rooms of gold leaf and alabaster. Then you'll sail under the Bosphorus Bridge and continue to the fortress of Rumeli Hisari before returning to the Eminönü waterfront in Istanbul.

From there it's a short walk to the Topkapi Palace – once the powerhouse of the sultans and now a fine museum. Don't miss the treasury, which displays riches from the Ottoman Empire, including gold thrones, the emerald-encrusted Topkapi Dagger and the 86-carat Kasikdi Diamond. The rooms in the palace are lavishly decorated with painted tiles and gold leaf, particularly in the harem, which functioned as a glorified prison for the sultans' wives, concubines and children.

Inside info ⓘ

▶▶ Most major sites (kultur.gov.tr) are found in the small district of Sultanahmet; the Grand Bazaar is just a 15-minute walk away, while the ferry dock for trips on the Bosphorus is at the nearby Eminönü waterfront (departures daily at 1035).
▶▶ Take binoculars to help kids see the detail in the high domes.
▶▶ Mosques are closed Friday, from around 1300-1500.

There are plenty of family resorts and enticing beaches along Turkey's 8300-km coastline. On the Aegean Coast, ancient ruins like Ephesus are some of the finest in the Mediterranean, while the unspoilt Turquoise Coast (hemmed in by pine-covered mountains and stretching from Marmaris in the west to Antalya in the east) offers a wide range of activities – particularly if you like boat trips. Beach-lovers will find no shortage of long sandy bays and warm, sheltered sea on the Mediterranean Coast – and adventure addicts can take to the Taurus Mountains in search of hiking and rafting opportunities.

Library of Celsus, Ephesus

Northern Aegean

Think hard before visiting the legendary city of Troy in the far north – it's a patchy, largely uninspiring ruin that children might struggle to marry with Homer's epic tale of the Trojan War. Having said that, the site does have a large wooden horse that children will enjoy clambering inside, just as Greek soldiers are said to have done when they besieged the city thousands of years ago. A better all-round family destination in the northern Aegean is the popular spa resort of Cesme. Explore the 14th-century Genoese fortress overlooking the harbour, and take a trip on a *gület* (traditional schooner) to Donkey Island – a sanctuary for abandoned beasts of burden.

Southern Aegean

Ephesus In complete contrast to Troy, above, Ephesus fires the imagination with its incredibly well-preserved gateways, columns and streets. The most complete ancient city in the eastern Mediterranean, the former Roman capital of Asia Minor began life in the 11th century BC as a centre of worship to Artemis, goddess of fertility. Ephesus only floundered in the sixth century AD when its port silted up, effectively severing the city's lifeblood. Try to reach Ephesus early – there's little shade. The site also gets very crowded, but if anything that will help to recreate the atmosphere of this once-bustling city – especially when you stroll down Curetes Street. This colonnaded thoroughfare was the equivalent of London's Oxford Street or New York's Fifth Avenue. Get the kids to imagine they're Romans out for a morning's shopping. At the end of Curetes Street looms the grand, two-storey façade of the Library of Celsus, built as a grand tomb in 117 AD, while the Marble Way (its surface etched with ancient cartwheel tracks) leads to a vast

Roman theatre capable of seating 24,000 people.

To put Ephesus into even greater focus, visit the museum at nearby Selçuk where a multi-breasted statue of mother goddess Artemis will either bemuse or amuse your children, depending on their age. If the heat and dust begin to take their toll, retreat to the resort of Kusadasi where kids will find cool relief in the form of the Adaland Aquapark (adaland.com). The best beach, meanwhile, is Kadinlar Plaji.

Bodrum Further south, Bodrum and its satellite resorts of Bitez and Gümbet are magnets to the bronze-and-booze crowd. However, the old part of Bodrum is definitely worth visiting for its medieval castle. When kids tire of firing imaginary arrows from the ramparts onto the yachts moored in the harbour below, entice them into the castle's fascinating Museum of Underwater Archaeology (bodrum-museum.com). As well as finding out about Roman shipwrecks and crusading knights they can venture into the dungeons and learn about ancient medicine in the spooky-sounding Snake Tower.

Cool pools

★ Limestone deposits from a mineral-rich spring have created the travertine waterfall at **Pamukkale** in the southern Aegean, 220 km east of Kusadasi. The best viewpoint of these mysterious pools is from the north gate, but beware of steep, unfenced drops.

Inside info

▶▶ Tourism is more established in the southern Aegean with a more resorts.
▶▶ Handy for visiting Ephesus, Kusadasi is a major cruise port, while boisterous Bodrum is a popular sailing and watersports centre.
▶▶ To reach the southern Aegean from Istanbul, one option is to take the overnight express train to Pamukkale, then head west to the coast.

Turkish coast
Turquoise

Action stations

▸ Paraglide from the 1969-m summit of Mount Baba to the beach at Olüdeniz (skysports-turkey.com).
▸ Go canyoning through Saklikent Gorge (bougainville-turkey.com).
▸ Scuba-dive or sea kayak in the waters near Kas (bougainville-turkey.com).

Highlights

Dalyan River One of the region's most popular excursions, tour boats depart at 1030 and return to Dalyan around 1600. At the start of the cruise you'll see some of the perplexing Lycian tombs for which the Turquoise Coast is renowned. How stonemasons from the fourth century BC managed to chisel these elaborate graves in the middle of a cliff face is still something of a mystery. Remember to pack binoculars – you'll need them for scanning the tombs and spotting birds, terrapins and other river wildlife. After a stop at the ancient Roman trading centre of Kaunos (where you may also glimpse herons and storks in the nearby reed beds) you continue to Istuzu Beach, a 7-km sandy strip which is frequented by nesting turtles between May and July. Then it's back through the marshy waterways to Ilica for the tour's gooey highlight – a frolic in the natural mud pools.

Fethiye For a sweet treat, stop at one of Fethiye's Turkish delight stores where you can see the sticky stuff being made and sample the bewildering range of flavours.

Kekova Island Most boat trips to uninhabited Kekova leave from Andriake and involve a 40-minute boat journey across open water. A better option for families is to drive to the fishing village of Uçagiz from where it's only a 15-minute crossing. That way, you get more time for swimming, snorkelling and viewing the strange Sunken City – a Lycian town off the island's northern shore that was inundated by rising sea levels.

Myra If the cliff tombs at Dalyan, left, sound intriguing, then the extraordinary Sea Necropolis at Myra will give you an opportunity to study more of these vertiginous graveyards. Get there early, though, because the site can feel like an oven by mid-morning.

Best beaches Spectacular, some say overdeveloped, the teardrop beach and azure lagoon of Olüdeniz graces almost every other postcard along the Turquoise Coast. The shallow, sheltered waters are perfect for tots, while older children will enjoy the wide range of watersports. Further east, Patara is a complete contrast – a 19-km swathe of sand that has been spared the curse of the concrete mixer thanks to its popularity with nesting loggerhead turtles. Apart from a drinks and ice-cream stall, there are no facilities here, but it's still a beach made in sandcastle-building heaven. Just inland there are some atmospheric Roman ruins, while canoe trips on the nearby Xanthos River include gentle rapids as well as wallowing in some natural mud pools.

Original Santa

At Demre, near Myra, you'll find a small church containing the tomb of Nicholas I, a local fourth-century bishop who was canonized after his death for performing miracles and for his generous habit of dropping bags of gold down the chimneys of the poor. In the 17th century, Dutch immigrants brought tales of St Nicholas (or *Sinterklaas*) to America where the name was eventually corrupted to Santa Claus. The feast day of the Turkish saint was in December, so people began to envisage him in winter attire, riding a sleigh.

Inside info

▸ There are several family resorts at centres such as Kas and Olüdeniz.
▸ Rent a car to explore the coast and the rugged hinterland.
▸ Rhodes (see page 179) is an easy day trip from Marmaris.

Antalya harbour

Best ruins Crowned by a vaulted walkway, the magnificent Roman theatre at Aspendos is so well preserved that it's still used for opera, ballet and folk concerts during June and July. Perge, meanwhile, showcases more second-century remains, including a stadium measuring 234 m by 34 m that could hold 12,000 spectators. Statues found at the site are on display at Antalya Archaeological Museum.

Best adventures Sloshing its way through a canyon in the Taurus Mountains, the Köprülü River is a popular rafting destination between May and October. For something drier (but no less bouncy) book a 4WD safari into the mountains with a tour operator in Antalya, Side or Alanya. A typical tour climbs through forests on the slopes of the Taurus Mountains, visiting remote villages and picnicking beside a river.

⛵ Sail away

Just imagine sailing through the Greek Islands or along the Turkish coast, dropping anchor off a deserted beach, paddling a kayak ashore or taking a dip with a mask and snorkel. In Turkey, you can join a crewed sailing *gület* – one of the country's traditional sailing boats, elegantly converted with good-size cabins and plenty of deck space for sunbathing or stargazing. *Gület* day-trip cruises are available from resorts along Turkey's coast, or try Exclusive Escapes (exclusiveescapes.co.uk) for overnight voyages aboard the beautiful *Aleyna* or *Seyhan Hanna*.

For yachties, Families Worldwide (familiesworldwide. co.uk) offers eight-day family sailing holidays in the Greek Islands, suitable for all ages, while Sunsail (sunsail.co.uk) has a range of charter and flotilla sailing holidays. You and your children can learn the skills of dinghy sailing or take the first steps at being master and commander of your own yacht at Sunsail's sailing school at Club Vounaki in Greece. On a flotilla sailing trip, a lead boat provides all the support and back up you need. And if you're new to sailing, you can start off with a week of instruction.

Inside info

▶▶ With its cafés, shops and marina, Antalya would suit teenagers.
▶▶ The popular resort of Alanya has 11 km of sandy beaches and a 13th-century citadel.
▶▶ The town of Side combines Roman ruins with a thriving holiday centre.

Go green
Four ways to skip the flight

❶ **Take a ferry** from the Italian port of Bari to Patras in the Peloponnese with Blue Star Ferries (bluestarferries.com). Alternatively, sail from Venice to Corfu and Patras with Minoan Lines (minoan.gr).

❷ **Join a family-friendly cruise** in the eastern Mediterranean.

❸ **Travel by train** using Europe's international rail network. You can travel from London to Greece in just 48 hours, either by train and ferry via Italy or solely by train via Budapest.

❹ **Link mainland Greece and Turkey** by travelling on the air-conditioned Thessaloníki–Istanbul sleeper train.

Holiday operators

The Adventure Company
adventurecompany.co.uk

Anatolian Sky
anatolian-sky.co.uk

Cachet Travel
cachet-travel.co.uk

ClubMed
clubmed.com

Cretan Ambience
islandambience.com

CV Travel
cvtravel.co.uk

Exclusive Escapes
exclusiveescapes.co.uk

Exodus exodus.co.uk

Families Worldwide
familiesworldwide.co.uk

First Choice Holidays
firstchoice.co.uk

GIC The Villa Collection
gicthevillacollection.com

Greek Options
greekoptions.co.uk

Greek Sun Holidays
greeksun.co.uk

Headwater
headwater.com

i-escape
i-escape.com

Ionian Island Holidays
ionianislandholidays.com

Islands of Greece
islands-of-greece.co.uk

Inntravel inntravel.co.uk

Kirker Holidays
kirkerholidays.com

Mark Warner
markwarner.co.uk

Neilson Active Holidays
neilson.co.uk

Powder Byrne
powderbyrne.com

Scott Dunn scottdunn.com

Sovereign sovereign.com

Sunsail sunsail.co.uk

Sunvil sunvil.co.uk

Thomson Holidays
thomson.co.uk

Travelbeam
travelbeam.co.uk

Vintage Travel
vintagetravel.co.uk

Western & oriental
wandotravel.com

In the USA
Abercrombie and Kent
abercrombiekent.com

> 66 99
> **Our favourite destination has to be northeast Corfu in a decent CV Travel villa, plus a rented motor boat. If you've got teenagers, go for something near Kassiópi because then they can go to the (safe) discos.** David Wickers, Journalist

When to go
Spring and autumn are ideal times to visit **Athens**. The weather is not usually too hot and the city's attractions are less crowded. Summer lingers in this corner of the Mediterranean, so you might find decent weather as late as November. Temperatures in January reach an annual low of around 12°C, while summer highs soar above 30°C.

The tourist season in the **Greek Islands** begins during April and May, when you can expect few other tourists, warm sunny days and cool nights; the spring flowers are out, but not all facilities, shops and tavernas will be open. In June and early July temperatures start to reach 25°C and, although resorts remain uncrowded, most facilities will be open. Mid-July to late August is peak season (with prices to match). It's hot and busy with everything up and running. Crete, the Dodecanese and the Cyclades may be windy during this period. The weather in September is still good, although you can expect a few thunderstorms; tourist facilities start to close down towards the end of the month. October sees changeable weather, but it's often sunny, especially on southern islands like Crete.

In **Turkey**, the weather and tourist season follow a broadly similar pattern, with Istanbul becoming unbearably hot (35°C+) during July and August – a time when locals and holidaymakers make for the coast. Try to visit in spring or autumn when it's cooler.

Getting there
The majority of holidaymakers to Greece arrive by **charter flight** arranged through a package tour company. However, there are also numerous **scheduled flights** operated by airlines such as Olympic Air (olympicair.com), British Airways (britishairways.com), Cyprus Airways (cyprusairways.com) and Turkish Airlines (turkishairlines.com).

Low-cost flights are available with easyJet (easyjet.com), with direct services from Luton and Gatwick to Athens. Thomson (flights.thomson.co.uk) has flights from over 20 UK airports to numerous destinations in the region.

Getting around
The Athens metro (ametro.gr) has three main lines converging on the city centre, while the Athens tram system (tramsa.gr) provides a fast link between Syntagma and the southern (coastal) suburbs. The suburban railway connects Elefthérios Venizélos International Airport to central Athens, Corinth and Piraeus. Rent a car from one of the numerous agencies based at the airport and you

Fast facts

Country	Time	Language	Currency	Dialling code	Tourist information
Greece	GMT+2	Greek	Euro (€)	+30	visitgreece.gr
Cyprus	GMT+2	Greek Turkish	Euro (€)	+357	visitcyprus.com
Turkey	GMT+2	Turkish	Turkish Lira	+90	goturkey.com

can easily drive to western Attica via the Attiki Odos motorway and onwards to the Peloponnese across the Rio-Andirrio Bridge. There are also numerous tour operators in Athens, such as Hop In Sightseeing (hopin.com) offering excursions to Cape Soúnion, Corinth, the Saronic Gulf Islands and further afield.

Most major towns and cities in **Greece** are connected by coach services operated by KTEL (ktel. org), while the Hellenic Railways Organization (ose. gr) offers another reasonably priced means of getting around. Companies operating domestic flights in Greece include Olympic Air and Aegean Airlines (aegeanair.com). Not surprisingly, Greece has an extensive domestic ferry network, with the port of Piraeus acting as the main hub. There are numerous operators, offering everything from high-speed catamarans and hydrofoils to slower and cheaper ferries. Schedules, timetables and online bookings are available at ferries.gr. Also try Hellenic Seaways (hellenicseaways.gr).

Like Athens, **Istanbul** has an excellent public transport system. To save money, time and stress at ticket booths get hold of a daily Akbil travel pass or the more up-to-date Istanbulkart. You can charge either with as much Turkish Lira as you like, then it's simply a case of pressing the card into the fare machine on a bus, ferry, train or tram and the correct amount is deducted.

Turkish Airlines operate flights from Istanbul to Izmir, Antalya, Bodrum and Dalaman. If you have the time, a cheaper alternative is to catch a long-distance bus. You won't need to drive in Istanbul, but hiring a car is the most relaxing way of touring the coast.

Accommodation
In a country so heavily dependent on tourism, **Greece** has abundant accommodation – and much of it is good value compared with other European countries. Numerous package-holiday companies and specialist tour operators offer a bewildering range of hotels, resorts, villas and self-catering apartments. The Hellenic Chamber of Hotels (grhotels.gr) has an online search facility for 9000 properties, while a campsite directory is available from the Panhellenic Camping Association (panhellenic-camping-union.gr).

Like Greece, **Cyprus** and coastal parts of Turkey have a great choice of family-friendly villas, hotels and resorts. In **Istanbul** there are dozens of hotels to choose from, but an excellent alternative for families are the Istanbul Holiday Apartments (istanbulholidayapartments.com) located near the tourist sights of Sultanahmet.

Food & drink
In **Greece**, a traditional meal starts with a selection of *méze* dishes. These nibbles and tidbits are a great way to introduce your kids to a range of Greek cuisine, from bread dipped in *tzatzíki* or *taramosaláta* to fat, juicy Kalamátas olives. Other must-try *méze* snacks include *souvláki* (grilled pork kebabs), *melitzanosaláta* (grilled aubergine purée), *melitzánes* (aubergines stuffed with onions and tomatoes) and *choriátiki saláta* (Greek salad made with feta cheese, tomatoes, cucumbers and onions).

The main course is usually a meat or fish dish. For visual impact, order *psária plakí*, a whole fish baked with potatoes and vegetables. Other seafood worth trying is grilled swordfish, fried calamari and, for the more adventurous, whitebait and octopus. For the carnivore in your family, order *stifádo* (braised beef and onion stew) or *keftédes* (pork mince balls).

When it comes to dessert, *giaoúrti kai méli* (Greek yoghurt and honey) always slips down a treat, or you could go the whole hog and order a platter of *loukoúmia* (doughnuts drenched in syrup).

Food in **Cyprus** is a similarly daunting, yet pleasurable, affair with plenty of *méze* dishes to try, as well as lamb or fish cooked with tomato and herbs.

In **Turkey**, the *méze* is more of a social event than merely a meal course – something to be lingered over with friends and *raki* (a raisin and aniseed spirit). Dishes include garlic yoghurt, mashed broad bean salad, salted fish, olives, hummus and flat bread.

For a basic main course, few children will turn their noses up at a grilled meat kebab or *lahmacun* (Turkish pizza topped with ground meat or sausage). You'll also find many Greek-influenced foods, such as fried calamari and aubergine, while the more adventurous can grapple with local specialities like *hülüklü dügün çorbasi* (a thick soup of chopped tripe and meatballs). Those with a sweet tooth will find salvation in *lokum* (Turkish delight) and *baklava* (a layered pastry).

Health & safety
Greece is generally a safe country with a low crime rate compared to other European nations. Tap water is usually safe to drink in Greece and Cyprus. The most obvious precaution to take on holiday is to avoid overexposure to the sun. Other potential dangers include road accidents – Greece has one of the highest crash rates in Europe. Make sure that any children's seats you may have rented with your hire car are fit for the job. To avoid travellers' diarrhoea steer clear of street food (particularly meat or fish snacks in Istanbul) and be wary of reheated *méze* dishes.

Grown-ups' stuff
Greece & Turkey

Villa Argiro
Where? Kassiopi, Corfu.
Why? Sleeping up to 10, this gorgeous villa has sweeping views across the azure bays and forested mountains of northeast Corfu. Rent a small motor boat for your holiday and moor it at Soukia Bay, just a short stroll from the villa's elegant terrace and swimming pool. Villa Argiro is impeccably furnished and is within easy reach of the amenities at Kassiopi.
Contact CV Travel, T+44 (0)20-7401 1026, cvtravel.co.uk

Tamarisk Beach Hotel
Where? Bodrum, Turkey
Why? A great find for families in search of a low-key, no-frills bolthole on the Turkish coast, the Tamarisk has all the essentials for a relaxed beach holiday – swimming pool, dining terrace, beachfront location – but with a few special extras, like the spacious family suites and the watersports centre where you can get afloat in anything from a sailing dinghy to a canoe.
Contact Cachet Travel, T+44 (0)20-8847 8700, cachet-travel.co.uk

Sea Garden Beach Resort
Where? Bodrum, Turkey.
Why? Mark Warner is renowned for its comprehensive children's facilities and this all-singing, all-dancing, all-inclusive resort is no exception, offering non-stop sports action for kids – big and small. Grown-ups get free sailing and windsurfing tuition, while children aged 2 to 17 can try their hand at a variety of watersports, tennis and other activities.
Contact Mark Warner, T+44 (0)844-273 5398, markwarner.co.uk

Daios Cove
Where? Crete.
Why? The sleek, sensational and shiny new Daios Cove resort on Crete has an exclusive Scott Dunn children's club, making it one of the most desirable luxury family boltholes in the entire Mediterranean. Catering for children aged from four months to 13 years, the children's club (run by qualified nannies) features a huge range of activities, from archery to treasure hunts.
Contact Scott Dunn, T+44 (0)20-8682 5099, scottdunn.com

Sani Resort
Where? Halkidiki, Greece.
Why? The Halkidiki peninsula has some of the best sandy beaches in Greece. Stay at the Sani Resort and you also get a superb watersports centre. But that's just the tip of the iceberg when it comes to family facilities at this luxury resort. There are also children's clubs for tots to teens, a crèche and some very stylish family accommodation to choose from.
Contact Western & Oriental, T44 (0)20-7666 1230, WandOtravel.com/families

Aphrodite Hills Resort
Where? Cyprus.
Why? Fabled as the birthplace of Aphrodite, goddess of beauty and love, Cyprus has holidaymakers well and truly smitten by its beaches, climate and scenery. Where better place to unwind than the luxurious Aphrodite Hills Resort? As well as a wonderful range of children's activities, it offers family accommodation ranging from suites to villas.
Contact Sovereign, T44 (0)844-415 1984, sovereign.com

" " You can rely on Greek Islands Club to find some of the most intimate villa retreats in the star-studded Aegean and Ionian, and with Villa Eleni we think they may have hit the jackpot. A supremely family-friendly property on the unspoilt island of Meganissi, Eleni has wonderful views and a great pool, and is just a short walk from the beach.

gicthevillacollection.com, 101familyholidays.co.uk

Palmiye
Where? Antalya, Turkey.
Why? This excellent resort offers a fantastic family package with sports galore (sailing, waterskiing, wakeboarding, circus school, kayaking, football etc), two childrens pools, dedicated clubs for babes to teens, plus a spa and hammam (Turkish bath) for the grown-ups.
Contact Club Med, T+44 (0)8453-670 670, clubmed.co.uk

**Snow doubt about it – kids love
a winter Lapland**

Finnish Lapland in December

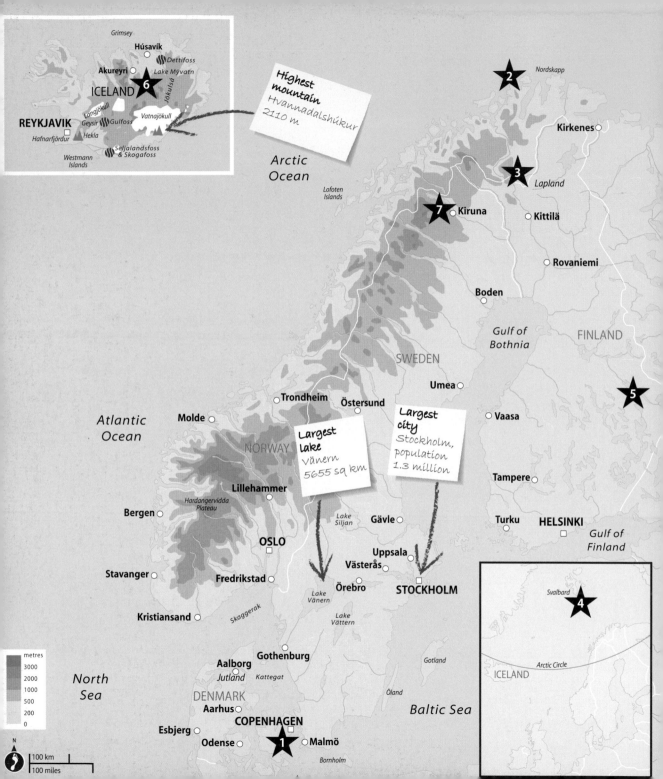

Grimsey

Húsavík

Dettifoss

Akureyri

Lake Mývatn

ICELAND **6**

Jökulsá

REYKJAVIK

Langjökull

Vatnajökull

Geysir Gulfoss

Hafnarfjörður

Hekla

Seljalandsfoss
& Skogafoss

Westmann
Islands

**Highest
mountain**
Hvannadalshúkur
2110 m

Nordskapp

2

*Arctic
Ocean*

Kirkenes

3

Lapland

Lofoten
Islands

7 Kiruna

Kittilä

Rovaniemi

Boden

*Gulf of
Bothnia*

FINLAND

SWEDEN

Umea

*Atlantic
Ocean*

Trondheim

Östersund

Vaasa

Molde

5

NORWAY

**Largest
lake**
Vänern
5655 sq km

**Largest
city**
Stockholm,
population
1.3 million

Tampere

Lillehammer

Hardangervidda
Plateau

Lake
Siljan

Gävle

Turku

HELSINKI

*Gulf of
Finland*

Bergen

OSLO

Uppsala

Stavanger

Fredrikstad

Lake
Vänern

Örebro

Västerås

STOCKHOLM

Kristiansand

Skaggerak

Lake
Vättern

Svalbard

4

Gothenburg

Gotland

Arctic Circle

Aalborg

*North
Sea*

Jutland

Kattegat

DENMARK

ICELAND

Aarhus

COPENHAGEN

Baltic Sea

Esbjerg

Odense

1

Malmö

Öland

Bornholm

metres
3000
2000
1000
500
200
0

N

100 km

100 miles

★1 **Board a Viking ship**

▸▸ Denmark, page 198

★2 **See the midnight sun**

▸▸ Lapland, pages 200 & 205

★3 **Go husky sledging**

▸▸ Lapland, page 200

★4 **Sail to the Arctic**

▸▸ Spitsbergen, page 202

★5 **Learn how to cross-country ski**

▸▸ Finland, page 204

★6 **Visit the land of ice & fire**

▸▸ Iceland, page 206

★7 **Stay in a hotel made of ice**

▸▸ Swedish Lapland, page 210

Did you know?

★ There are around 60,000 lakes in Finland.
★ Icelandic horses have a fifth gait, known as the tolt, which allows them to move easily over rough terrain.
★ In 1911, Norwegian Roald Amundsen was the first person to reach the South Pole.
★ Swedish pop sensation Abba have sold over 370 million albums.
★ Legoland in Denmark is built with 60 million bricks.

Introduction
Scandinavia

When it comes to family holidays, there's more to Scandinavia than Santa Claus and Legoland – although both will probably get a vigorous chorus of approval from your children. Cities like Copenhagen, Stockholm and Oslo may be on the pricey side, but they are also supremely child-friendly with plenty of attractions, ranging from theme parks and gardens to museums and castles. Further afield you'll discover nature's very own theme park – a wilderness of lakes, forests and mountains where thrills and spills come in the form of rafting trips, husky sledging and copious other activities, depending on when you visit. Scandinavia is also an easily accessible place to introduce your children to some of the world's most extraordinary phenomena. Lapland has the northern lights and midnight sun, Iceland has volcanoes and ice caps and Finland has the Moomins. If those endearing white hippo-like characters don't do it for your kids, however, Denmark's Viking legacy is sure to fire their imagination. Lapland's reindeer-herding Sami culture will also captivate most children, while the home of the big man himself, Mr S Claus, can be visited year round.

❝❞ **Iceland is not a hard sell to children. We lined up a veritable smorgasbord of family-friendly activities during our 12-day trip, including whale watching, horse riding, glacier hiking and white-water rafting.** William Gray

Star rating

Wow factor
★★★★★
Worry factor
★★
Value for money
★★
Keeping teacher happy
★★★★
Family accommodation
★★★★
Babies & toddlers
★★★
Cool for teenagers
★★★★★

How to build an igloo

What you need
▸▸ Saw
▸▸ Spade
▸▸ Several short sticks
▸▸ Hard snow

What to do
❶ Use the sticks to mark out a circle measuring no more than 2 m wide.
❷ Cut out blocks of snow around 20-30 cm thick.
❸ Arrange the first row of blocks, making sure they are angled slightly inwards (otherwise you will end up with a tower instead of a dome shape). Don't worry about any gaps between the blocks at this stage.
❹ Use vertically placed blocks for each side of the entrance with a solid block on top to form a small porch at the front of your igloo.
❺ Continue adding snow blocks to the igloo, removing any snow that piles up inside. You can also dig out the floor at this stage, increasing headroom.
❻ Slide the last few blocks through the entrance and push them up into the remaining gap in the roof to close the igloo.
❼ Fill in any cracks with snow.
❽ Smooth the inside of the igloo using your gloved hand.

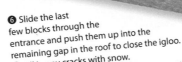

See Santa

▸▸ Write a letter to Santa Claus a few weeks before your journey.
▸▸ Fly to Ivalo airport in Finnish Lapland where you will be met by one of Santa's elves and a reindeer with its Sami handler.
▸▸ Get kitted out in thermal bodysuits, boots, gloves and hats.
▸▸ Make a snowman, go tobogganing and try your hand (and feet) at snowshoeing.
▸▸ Take a reindeer sleigh ride, then learn how to mush a team of huskies.
▸▸ Receive a certificate celebrating your crossing of the Arctic Circle and listen to stories from a Sami guide.
▸▸ Ride a snowmobile through snowy forests, keeping an eye out for wild reindeer and a glimpse of Santa's cabin.
▸▸ Meet Santa in his secret hideaway and tell him how good you've been all year.

🔍 Search for the Hidden People

Up to 80% of Icelanders admit to believing in elves. In 2006, machinery failure interrupted an extension project at the Blue Lagoon when it became clear that the work was disturbing local elves. Staff lit 12 candles to make peace with the Hidden People and avoid further mishaps. Your best chance for spotting an **elf** is at Hafnarfjodur, near Reykjavík. Also look out for **dwarves** (moodier than elves), **light-fairies** (think Tinkerbell) and **trolls** (who live solitary lives inside mountains and glaciers and don't like being disturbed).

✴ Big six

How many of Sweden's 'big six' will you spot on a Scandinavian wildlife safari?

Moose	**Lynx**
Wolverine	**Wolf**
Brown bear	**Musk ox**

Great reads
6 books for kids

Ages 2-6
Children of the Forest
Elsa Beskow (Floris Books)
This exquisitely illustrated story explores the lives of the little folk who live deep in the roots of an old pine tree.

Ages 4+
Hans Christian Andersen's Fairy Tales
Martin Waddell (Orchard Books)
A beautifully illustrated collection of nine captivating stories, including *The Little Mermaid*, *The Princess and the Pea*, *The Ugly Duckling* and *The Emperor's New Clothes*.

Ages 8+
Viking
Susan Margeson (Dorling Kindersley)
Vivid photography and at-a-glance captions transport young readers into the world of the Vikings.

Pippi Longstocking
Astrid Lindgren (Oxford University Press)
A classic tale about the feisty, unconventional nine-year-old who lives at Villa Villekulla with a horse, a monkey and a suitcase full of gold coins.

The Vicious Vikings
Terry Deary (Scholastic Hippo)
Find out how to build a longboat and why some Vikings had names like Fat Thighs and Stinking.

Ages 12+
Troll Blood
Katherine Langrish (HarperCollins)
The action-packed conclusion to Katherine Langrish's acclaimed trilogy describes a perilous journey to Vinland (or North America).

Taste of Scandinavia madekeitto

A popular winter dish in Finland, *madekeitto* is a delicious creamy soup of fish and potatoes traditionally made using burbot, but salmon works just as well.

What you need
- 1 kg burbot or salmon
- 6 potatoes
- 2 onions
- ¼ tsp ground allspice
- 500 ml water
- 500 ml milk
- 250 ml double cream
- 2 tbsp flour
- Chopped dill and a pinch of salt

What to do
- Peel and dice the potatoes and onions; add to boiling water with salt and allspice and simmer for 10-15 minutes.
- Cut the fish into large chunks and add to the vegetables.
- Whisk the milk and flour together and pour into the soup; simmer for a further five minutes.
- Add the cream, sprinkle with chopped dill and serve with crusty bread.

Stay up late

Head to northern Scandinavia to witness the midnight sun. A celebration of the longest day, midsummer here is as popular as Christmas. Flower-wreathed women dance around maypoles in Sweden, while in Finland and Norway bonfires are lit to ward off evil spirits.

⚽ Wacky sports

World Wife-Carrying Championships Sonkajarvi, July.
World Cell Phone Throwing Championships Riihisaari, August.
Swamp Football World Championships Hyrynsalmi, July.
Other eccentric Finnish contests include snowshoe football, cattle calling, milking stool throwing, mosquito swatting and sitting on ants' nests.

🔍 How to make snow angels

 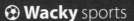 

Scandinavia, as you might expect, is generally a very straightforward place to take children on holiday. It's the Volvo of the family travel world; safe, reliable and efficient. Everywhere you go you will find copious and clean facilities, whether you're looking for a city park playground, family accommodation or somewhere to change a nappy. The only potential downside is that travelling *en famille* in Scandinavia can wallop your wallet. Iceland, Norway, Sweden, Finland and Denmark are some of the world's most expensive travel destinations. But when you weigh this up against a reassuring level of child-friendliness and unique attractions (Santa Claus and Hans Christian Andersen to name a couple), the extra expense is usually more than justified.

Babies

Stick to the cities and you'll find supermarkets stocked with baby food, parks with playgrounds and restaurants with high chairs. Most Scandinavian cities are also compact (especially Copenhagen) with excellent public transport that is gentle on both your stroller and your nerves. Most people speak English and in summer there's a relaxed outdoor café culture that new parents will relish. If you're feeling slightly more adventurous, head for the countryside or

Falling for Iceland

A superb destination for adventurous families, Iceland's easily accessible highlights include the waterfall Seljalandsfoss.

coast where you'll find plenty of options for renting cottages or staying at a holiday park. Just be wary of the fact that the further north you go, the more severe the landscape and climate become, and the less you'll find in the way of facilities.

Toddlers/pre-school

It's every child's dream to visit the home of Santa Claus high above the Arctic Circle in Finnish Lapland and it's surprisingly easy to make it come true (see page 205). Arrange a package trip through a reputable operator and you can avoid the slightly tacky, over-commercialized aspects of a Santa pilgrimage and instead experience something far more intimate and magical. Santa is at home all year (except during a certain night in December, of course) so you can pop up and see him during the long balmy days of summer if you like. However, it's much more fun when Lapland is transformed into a winter wonderland and you can ride in a reindeer-pulled sleigh and perhaps even glimpse the northern lights. Remember that Jack Frost will definitely be nipping at the toes, nose and other extremities of your toddler at this time of year (temperatures can plunge to -30°C during a Lapland winter). Be sure to pack plenty of warm clothing, including spare sets of essential items like gloves, hats and goggles. It's amazing how these things tend to go

Special needs

Tourist boards can advise on hotels, restaurants and attractions that are wheelchair-friendly, while many forms of public transport have facilities for travellers with mobility, sight or hearing impairment. In Denmark, many restaurants, hotels, campsites and attractions provide facilities for the disabled; ferries have special cabins and wide elevators for wheelchair users and intercity trains have toilets for the disabled as well as special lifts and ramps. Sweden has launched Tourism For All – Accessible Equality (turismforalla.se), which features an online database of accessible facilities. In Finland check out travel4all.fi). In Iceland, several hotels in Reykjavik and Akureyri have rooms specially designed for guests with disabilities. A list of fully accessible tourist attractions can be found at sjalfsbjorg.is. One of the best options for disabled travellers in Norway is to book a voyage on a wheelchair-friendly cruise ship. Try Accessible Travel & Leisure (accessibletravel.co.uk).

Single parents

Small Families (smallfamilies.co.uk) offer single-parent holidays in Lapland, while The Kids and Me (thekidsandme.co.uk) offer action-packed wilderness experiences in Sweden – both summer and winter.

missing when your children are this age.

Another obsession for pre-schoolers is Lego, and the original home of building-block heaven can be found at Legoland in Denmark. Piece together a day in the theme park with a couple of days in Copenhagen and a few more at the coast and you'll make most three- and four-year-olds very happy indeed. Denmark is also ideal for family cycling.

Kids/school age

Legoland and Santa Claus still appeal to this age range, as do many Scandinavian cities. All seem to have more than their fair share of theme parks and child-friendly museums, with enough attractions to satisfy toddlers through to teenagers. Visit Santa with a three-year-old, for example, and they will probably be content with a sleigh ride; take kids aged seven or eight, however, and they'll want to ride a team of huskies to St Nick's door. Similarly, Legoland and other theme parks are more than capable of meeting the hyped-up adrenaline demands of older children. Just don't let the slick marketing of these contrived pleasurelands divert you from Scandinavia's real adventure hotspot – its wilderness.

The woody, watery hinterland of countries like Sweden and Finland is prime territory for hiking and canoeing in summer, and snowmobiling, cross-country skiing, ice fishing and husky sledging in winter. Iceland, too, offers plenty in the way of outdoor activities, from scouring the north Atlantic for minke whales to riding Icelandic ponies across glacial valleys. Several family tour operators offer winter or summer multi-activity packages to Scandinavia where, in just a week, you can sample a variety of adventure pursuits, all under expert guidance and in the company of other families. Alternatively, strike out alone on a self-drive tour. With its coastal ring road and laid-back farmstays, Iceland is particularly well suited to this form of travel.

Educationally, Scandinavia scores highly on the national curriculum. When your children start to learn about Vikings at school, plan a visit to Denmark where they will be able to witness this vibrant culture through restored longships, hands-on museums and even themed parks where actors role-play characters from the period.

Another aspect of Scandinavian culture that will appeal to school-age children (and impress their teachers) is the Sami culture. You can visit these reindeer-herding people in the remote reaches of Lapland or get a taster of their lifestyle at the open-air museum of Skansen in Stockholm.

Animal lovers should focus on coastal critters, like puffins, whales and dolphins, which can often be seen on ferry trips and cruises in Norway and Iceland. That said, a quiet rafting or canoeing trip along a river in Sweden or Finland may reward you with sightings of beaver, otter or moose.

Scandinavia's strong literary tradition is a great excuse to get your kids' noses in some excellent books. Hans Christian Andersen's *Little Mermaid*, Tove Jansson's *Moominland* and Astrid Lindgren's *Pippi Longstocking* are all from here – and chances are you'll also find a theme park or hands-on museum where they can see the characters brought to life.

Teenagers

Image-conscious teenagers will find suitably trendy shops and cafés in cities like Copenhagen, Bergen, Stockholm and Oslo, though prices may hamper their style somewhat. Big thrill rides can be found at amusement parks like Liseberg near Gothenburg and Oslo's Tusenfryd. For adventure, Iceland has horse riding and whitewater rafting, while Sweden and Finland offer all kinds of epic undertakings from week-long husky-sledging expeditions to wilderness survival and multi-activity breaks. Various family adventure tour operators offer teenage departures on their Scandinavian itineraries, including The Adventure Company, Explore, Exodus and Families Worldwide.

Kids' top 10 Viking Denmark

1 Dress like a Viking warlord and board a 7-m replica longboat at the Children's Museum in Copenhagen's Nationalmuseet (natmus.dk).

2 Imagine what daily Viking life was like inside the reconstructed house at Fyrkat Viking Fortress in Hobro.

3 Sail a replica longboat (or man one of the oars) at Roskilde where five Viking ships have been reconstructed from wrecks dragged from the fiord at Vikingeskibsmuseet (vikingeskibsmuseet.dk).

4 Imagine the formidable Harold Bluetooth presiding over Trelleborg, a Viking fortress built around AD 980 and excavated near Slagelse.

5 Discover the treasures found at Ladbyskibet, the burial ground of a Viking chief unearthed near Kerteminde on the island of Funen.

6 Learn how Vikings lived at Ribe Viking Centre (ribevikingecenter.dk) where costumed actors bring the period to life. Join in with activities, from baking and pottery to archery and warrior training.

7 Marvel at Jelling's runic stones (standing stones with ancient inscriptions) – one erected more than 1000 years ago by King Gorm the Old and containing the first written mention of Denmark; the other erected by Harold Bluetooth recording the arrival of Christianity and the end of the Vikings.

8 Celebrate the ancient feast day of St Olaf at the Viking Moot held during the last weekend in July at Moesgård Museum (moesmus.dk) near Århus. As well as traditional craft stalls and spit-roasts galore, faux-Vikings stage ferocious battles on foot and horseback. While you're at the museum don't forget to gawp at Grauballe Man – a 2000-year-old body found almost perfectly preserved in a peat bog.

9 Investigate the mysterious Viking graveyard at Lindholm Høje near Nørresundby where stone circles are arranged in the outline of longboats.

10 Ride the Vikings River Splash at Legoland. Located in Billund, central Jutland, Legoland (legoland.dk) has nine main lands, including the signature Miniland – a miniature masterpiece of famous world locations constructed from over 20 million Lego bricks. In Adventure Land, you will find the X-Treme Racers roller coaster (minimum height 120 cm) and The Temple where you shoot your way through a giant archaeological dig. Smaller kids will get a buzz from the Jungle Racer water scooters and the Falck Fire Brigade where you race other teams to douse a burning building. Don't miss the 4D movie in the Imagination Zone where you will be clutching at the characters that appear to leap from the screen. New for 2012 is Polar Land, featuring a rollercoaster with a 5-m free-fall and a Polar Pilot School.

Cycle paths

You can cycle just about anywhere in Denmark. The country has a 4000-km cycle network linking most major towns. Routes follow traffic-scarce roads, forest tracks, cycle lanes and disused railway lines. There are 11 long-distance routes, or you can simply pedal about in Copenhagen on the well-marked cycle paths.

D enmark might not strike you as an obvious choice for a family holiday, but few European countries can match its combination of compact size, efficient, family-friendly infrastructure and range of attractions. You've probably heard of Legoland and Tivoli Gardens – two of the country's family favourites, but there's a lot more to Denmark than roller coasters and brightly coloured bits of plastic. Copenhagen is a laid-back city endowed with parks, museums, palaces and the rich legacy of storyteller-supreme, Hans Christian Andersen. Further afield, you will find long sandy beaches, holiday centres and a veritable treasure trail of Viking sites. Denmark's real trump card – particularly with young families – is that it just seems that little bit less remote than other parts of Scandinavia.

Nyhavn

Copenhagen

The Little Mermaid If your four- to seven-year-old daughter has any say in the matter, a pilgrimage to The Little Mermaid statue will top your sightseeing list. Hans Christian Andersen's 1837 fairy tale about the mermaid who falls in love with a prince she saves from drowning has enchanted just about every girl who has seen the feature cartoon and bought the Disney merchandise. Break it to them gently, but a 165-cm-tall bronze figure perched on the edge of Copenhagen's harbour might be a bit of an anticlimax.

Rosenborg Slot Ample compensation for any disappointment over The Little Mermaid, this 17th-century castle (dkks.dk) not only has a fairy-tale moat and gardens, but holds glittering displays of the crown jewels.

Amalienborg Slot Although Queen Margrethe II lives here, visitors can peek into a wing of her palace where rooms have been reconstructed to show what royal life was like from 1863 to 1947.

Christiansborg Slot The Royal Reception Rooms (ses. dk) in this impressive palace (home to the Parliament) contain colourful tapestries depicting the history of Denmark and the world.

Rundetårn A spiral staircase leads to the top of the Round Tower (rundetaarn.dk), from where there are great views across Copenhagen's red-tiled rooftops.

Nyhavn Lined by colourful townhouses and trendy

cafés and filled with wooden sailing ships, historic Nyhavn canal is an atmospheric place for a drink or ice cream. Boat trips are also available.

Strøget Thronging with street performers this pedestrianized shopping strip is essential stomping ground for anyone in search of retail therapy.

Tivoli Gardens Easily worth a day on its own, Tivoli Gardens (tivoli.dk) combines simple pleasures with high-octane thrills. Dating from 1843, it is a nostalgic mishmash of flower gardens, amusement park rides, open-air stage shows, restaurants, cafés and a boating lake. The rides range from a train journey through a land of pixies to the Demon roller coaster with its triple loop-the-loop. Not to be missed is The Flying Trunk, where you are transported into puppet scenes from Hans Christian Andersen stories.

Best museums Pick of the bunch is the interactive Experimentarium (experimentarium.dk), a science museum with over 260 hands-on exhibits ranging from an earthquake simulator to a special area for three- to six-year-olds. Also highly recommended are the Guinness World of Records Museum and the Louis Tussauds Wax Museum.

Best parks Most of Copenhagen's parks have playgrounds. During summer there are puppet shows in Kongens Have.

Inside info

▶▶ A CPH Card includes entry to 60 museums and sites throughout Copenhagen, as well as unlimited transport by train, bus and metro.
▶▶ Copenhagen is compact and pedestrian- friendly, baby-changing facilities are widespread and there are numerous parks with children's play areas.
▶▶ Tivoli Gardens are open April to September and for a few weeks prior to Christmas when there is ice-skating on the lake and a festive market.
▶▶ Another popular amusement park is Bakken (bakken.dk), to the north of the city.

Camping out under the northern lights

Swedish Lapland midnight sun or northern lights?

With its positively balmy temperatures and 24-hour daylight, summer might seem the obvious time to take your kids to Lapland. Unleash them on Europe's Great Outdoors and they'll be more than happy fishing, kayaking, hiking and getting away with later bedtimes thanks to the midnight sun. The big question is whether winter is even more fun. Yes, the days are ridiculously short and you'll have to wear snowsuits that feel like wraparound duvets, but the fact remains that a week of winter activities in Lapland makes a superb break at Christmas, Easter or the February half term. Several family adventure operators offer guided activity breaks to either Finnish or Swedish Lapland. Typically, they include a mixture of dog sledging, snowmobiling, snowshoeing, cross-country skiing, ice fishing and reindeer sleigh rides. More of a polar pot-pourri than a full-blown Arctic expedition, these trips are designed to give you a gentle introduction to everything – which means they're suitable for children as young as five. And, of course, the added bonus of a winter visit to Lapland is that you may glimpse the northern lights – two of the best places in the world (Abisko National Park and the Icehotel) are found in Swedish Lapland. Contact a specialist operator like Discover the World (discover-the-world.co.uk) for further details. See page 204 for a first-hand account of a winter activity break in Finland.

Six really cool things to do at the Icehotel

❶ Snowmobiling Guided tours range from 90-minute flits through the forests surrounding Jukkasjarvi to a three-hour or overnight adventure in the wilderness.

❷ Reindeer sledging Learn how to drive a reindeer sledge (the preferred mode of transport for the indigenous Sami people), then enjoy a traditional meal in a *lavvu* tent.

❸ Moose safari There are mose loose about these woods. Hop on a horse or a snowmobile for a snow safari in search of one of Scandinavia's most impressive animals.

❹ Ice sculpting Inspired by the sculptures in the Icehotel? This is a chance to create your own piece of frozen art, with the help of an expert.

❺ Husky sledging You can transfer to and from the airport and the Icehotel by husky sledge or join a 90-minute mush through the forests with a skilled driver, stopping for drinks and cake by a campfire.

❻ Aurora gazing The aurora borealis or northern lights can appear anytime from 5pm, September to March.

❷ To mush or not to mush

In addition to Lapland, you can mush in Greenland, Iceland and Alaska. Arctic specialists, Discover the World (discover-the-world.co.uk) cover all four destinations. Don't worry if the closest you've come to dog sledging is grappling with a trolley down the frozen foods section of your local supermarket. With expert tuition you'll quickly get the hang of it and don't forget that the sledges do have brakes. Older children can join dedicated husky safaris, controlling their own sledge, looking after their team of dogs and staying overnight in cosy wilderness cabins. Young children can ride in the sledge, but make sure they are very well wrapped up, with goggles to protect their eyes from bits of ice kicked up by the huskies. Remember that huskies are excitable, bouncy and noisy, and a lot of them look like they've stepped straight from the local wolf pack. If your children are the slightest bit nervous of dogs, take them to see Santa instead. He's a lot less frisky.

Parents in Sweden get some of Europe's best deals in maternity and paternity rights, so you can expect no shortage of child-friendly facilities when you head there on holiday. The two major cities, Stockholm and Gothenburg, have plenty to keep all ages entertained during a short break, but sooner or later you'll feel the lure of the Arctic Circle. Head north in winter for a fairy-tale night at the Icehotel and to learn the art of husky mushing, or enjoy long summer days in Sweden's great outdoors.

Stockholm

Sweden
Call of the Arctic

Stockholm

The Venice of the North, Stockholm is a beautiful city spread over 14 islands. Get your bearings by taking a boat trip through the capital's waterways, then focus your attention on the parkland island of Kungliga Djurgården. You'll find several family-friendly attractions here, including Skansen (skansen.se), the oldest open-air museum in the world. Children will love stepping back in time as they explore Skansen's 150 historic buildings, ranging from a traditional Swedish farmstead to a Sami camp – each one inhabited by staff in period costumes. There's even a zoo where you can learn about Scandinavian wildlife, such as wolves, brown bears and lynx. Djurgården is also the home of Junibacken (junibacken.se), a treat for anyone who has enjoyed Astrid Lindgren's children's books. This indoor attraction (perfect for a rainy day) brings the adventures of Pippi Longstocking to life through theatre shows, craft activities, a playhouse based on Villa Villekulla and a fantasy train ride through some of Lindgren's best-loved stories. Other children's highlights on Djurgården include the shark tunnel at Aquaria (aquaria.se) and the National Maritime Museum (vasamuseet.com).

Stockholm Archipelago

A liberal scattering of 24,000 or so islands fringing the Gulf of Bothnia, the Stockholm Archipelago is a popular playground for urbanites. For a taster you can simply join a cruise from the capital, but you'll find it far more satisfying to spend a few days staying on one or more of the islands. The best ones for kids are Vaxholm with its historic fortress, Sandhamn, a popular seaside resort with lots of watersports, and Utö – a three-hour ferry ride from Stockholm, but well worth the trip for its beautiful walking trails and fine swimming. You'll find shops, restaurants, and accommodation (including family-friendly cabins and camping) on many of the islands. Operators on Utö,

Grinda and Sandön can arrange sailing trips with an experienced skipper or rent kayaks.

Gothenburg

Though not as pretty as Stockholm, Sweden's second biggest city still has plenty to offer children. Top of their list will be Liseberg (liseberg.com), Scandinavia's largest amusement park. With 35 rides there's everything from a pony carousel to the hair-raising Balder, a mighty wooden roller coaster that inflicts passengers with no less than 10 doses of negative G-force. The Uppswinget, meanwhile, does just that – swings you up and around at 80 km/h, while the gut-wrenching Atmosfear claims to be Europe's tallest free-fall attraction. Replenish your children's brain cells at Gothenburg's interactive science museum, Universeum (universeum.se) before striking out north along Sweden's dramatic, rocky west coast. There are plenty of simple pleasures to be found here, such as crab-fishing from jetties or exploring the offshore islands on a boat trip. Other natural diversions include Havets Hus aquarium (havetshus.se) at Lysekil and Nordens Ark (nordensark.se), a captive-breeding programme for endangered species like snow leopard and great grey owl.

Let's go to Skane

★ Fancy unleashing your 'inner Viking'? Then head to Foteviken, an intriguing Viking time capsule complete with wild-bearded men. Elsewhere in Skane (Sweden's most southerly province) you'll find glorious sandy beaches (it's warmer here than anywhere else in Sweden), a buzzing café culture in Malmö and beautiful rolling countryside that's crying out for a laid-back summer touring holiday.

Inside info ⓘ

▶▶ A Stockholm Card (available online at visitstockholm.com) entitles you to free admission to 75 museums and sites, unlimited travel on buses and trains, plus a sightseeing boat trip.
▶▶ A ferry network (waxholmsbolaget.se) links the Stockholm Archipelago.
▶▶ If you need to get from Gothenburg to Stockholm, break the journey at the Sommarland theme park (sommarland.se) near Skara or take a longer loop via Lake Siljan (siljan.se), a popular holiday centre.

Hurtigruten ferry arriving in the Vesteralen Islands at dawn

Coastal *voyage*

★ The Hurtigruten Coastal Voyage (hurtigruten.com) operates a fleet of stylish ferries calling at 34 ports along Norway's coast, between Bergen and Kirkenes.

★ Spare time in Bergen before your cruise? Visit the aquarium (akvariet.no), ride the Fløibanen funicular railway (floibanen.no) or explore the fish market and the old wooden buildings alongside Bryggen Wharf.

★ To reach Bergen from Oslo (or vice versa) take the spectacular train journey (nsb.no) across the Hardangervidda plateau.

🔍 Let's go to Spitsbergen

Despite being squashed by converging lines of longitude and barely clinging to the top of a world map, Spitsbergen (svalbard.net) is served by scheduled flights from Norway, making it the most accessible High Arctic region in the world. Visit between June and September when retreating pack ice frees the spectacular coastline of this mountainous archipelago. Expedition ships range from icebreakers capable of holding 100 passengers to the 20-berth, steel-hulled schooner, *Nooderlicht*. Arctic cruises to Spitsbergen specially designed for families are available from Discover the World (discover-the-world.co.uk) and Exodus (exodus. co.uk). The gently-paced, seven-night voyage includes photography lessons, zodiac rides, tundra hikes and, of course, wildlife watching. Seeing polar bears in the wild is a highlight of any Spitsbergen trip, but on this family cruise kids will also find out how to identify animals by their tracks and droppings. Other onboard activities include learning about navigation and early explorers.

Walruses basking under the midnight sun in Spitsbergen

A maritime theme quickly emerges when you contemplate a family holiday to Norway. The fjords are perfect for a voyage on a child-friendly cruise liner, while Oslo's trio of nautical museums showcases a wonderful array of historical ships. More adventurous families can set sail for the Arctic wilderness of Svalbard, while adrenaline addicts can experience the watery thrills and spills of theme parks like Bø Sommarland.

Kontiki

Oslo

Bygdøynes Peninsula With a coastline as famous as Norway's, it's hardly surprising that the nation has a strong seafaring tradition, and nowhere is this more vividly portrayed than in the four nautically themed museums on Oslo's Bygdøynes Peninsula. Start with Vikingskiphuset (khm.uio.no), where three Viking funerary ships are displayed, along with treasures and practical objects that accompanied the deceased into the afterlife.

The *Oseberg* is the most exquisite of the trio. Built in 820 AD and measuring around 22 m in length, this richly ornamented oak vessel was exhumed from a large burial mound in 1904. Two skeletons were discovered on board, one of whom may have been a queen or priestess – study the grave goods on display and decide for yourself.

The Norsk Maritimt or Norwegian Maritime Museum (marmuseum.no) chronicles the entire history of Norwegian seafaring, from a 2200-year-old Bronze Age log boat to a panoramic film depicting a cruise through the fjords. Next door, Frammuseet (frammuseum.no) contains the famous exploration ship, *Fram*, and recounts the epic voyages of Roald Amundsen and other great polar explorers.

Finally, the Kon-Tiki Museum (kon-tiki.no) houses the original 14-m-long balsa raft that Norwegian scientist Thor Heyerdahl sailed 6880 km across the Pacific in 1947 – a voyage that lasted an incredible 101 days.

Norwegian fjords

If you thought Norwegian cruising was the kind of thing only the grandparents would be interested in, think again. Just imagine the thrill your kids would get from living on a ship bound for the Arctic! Calling at remote fishing communities to drop off cargo or to collect local passengers, Hurtigruten Coastal Voyage vessels are more entwined with daily life than your average cruise ship. There will also be times when you feel you can almost stretch out your arms and touch both walls of a fjord; youll be able to spot dolphins, orca whales, puffins and sea eagles from on deck and notch up a few geographical milestones – crossing the Arctic Circle, visiting Honingsvåg (the world's northernmost village) and witnessing the midnight sun. Not bad for a week's comfortable cruising.

Other highlights include stopovers at Trondheim (Norway's first capital with its well-preserved medieval district), Geiranger (nuzzled in the head-spinning grandeur of Geirangerfjord) and the Lofoten Islands (a fascinating, weather-beaten archipelago of jagged mountains, U-shaped glacial valleys and brightly coloured fishing settlements dotted with wooden cod-drying racks).

Ultimately, though, your compass is set for Honingsvåg where the Midnight Sun Road dips and turns across the Nordskapp plateau to reach the top of Europe and an unforgettable view over the Arctic Ocean.

Theme parks

Tusenfryd
Around 20 km from Oslo, Tusenfryd (tusenfryd.no) is home to one of Scandinavia's most extreme rides, Speed Monster, which takes you to 90 km/h in two seconds and inflicts seven bouts of weightlessness.

Hunderfossen
Located 13 km from Lillehammer, Hunderfossen (hunderfossen.no) is a fairy-tale land with 50 attractions, including a troll park, high ropes course, 4D films, white-water rafting ride and an adventure ship that swings through 70° to a height of 14 m.

Bø Sommarland
Norway's biggest waterpark, Bø Sommarland (sommarland.no) has one of the world's largest artificial waves for surfing, as well as Europe's first roller-coaster flume – an enormous water chute with tight bends and stomach-churning drops.

❝ ❞ In Finland there's no better place for a winter activity holiday than Pielinen, a 900-sq-km lake in the province of North Koraelia. Our first morning was bright and chilly, sunlight sparking through the fresh powder snow that had fallen overnight. Due to the unusually mild winter, however, the lake hadn't frozen sufficiently to safely support the weight of seven hyperactive children (aged five to eleven), so the ice fishing would have to wait.

Instead, we drove to a nearby farm where wild boar and reindeer looked on bemused as our children cavorted through the snow like a pack of highly wired wolf cubs. There were calming moments, like the wonderful views over pine-stubbled hills to the Russian border, and the traditional lunch huddled around an open fire clutching steaming bowls of salmon and potato broth.

Next up was cross-country skiing where the children were briefly reduced to penguin-shuffling mode. However, with their low centres of gravity and amply padded snowsuits, they quickly learnt not to be afraid of falling over. Inevitably, the first session deteriorated into a hysterical tangle of limbs, skis and poles, but they quickly picked up the technique over the following days. Like all the activities on this week-long trip, it was best done in quick bursts before tiredness or cold set in.

Talking of speed, nothing could match the pace of our next icy pursuit. No sooner had we stepped from our minibus into a forest clearing somewhere near Russia than we were assailed by the canine cacophony of dozens of huskies. They whipped themselves into a frenzy of leaping, slavering, wild-eyed excitement that was only unleashed when they were allowed to run. Each child sat huddled on a reindeer skin in the sledge, while a parent stood on the back runners, operating the spiky foot brake, leaning into corners and generally keeping things running smoothly. That, at least, was the theory. In fact, once the dogs started bounding though the forest it was more a case of hang on and try not to let your shoulders become dislocated.

After the exhilaration of husky sledging, there were more high-speed thrills with a snowmobiling safari and an adrenaline-charged tobogganing session in the mountains of Koli National Park. The lake never did freeze sufficiently for ice fishing, but it hardly mattered. Besides, the children would probably have been far too busy making snow angels, cross-country skiing or pelting each other with snowballs. William Gray

Finland has plenty to keep kids entertained, whatever time of year you visit. Give them a choice of where and when to go, however, and they will invariably choose Lapland in winter. And who can blame them? Whether it's a sleigh ride in search of Santa or a white-knuckle ride with a team of boisterous huskies, Finland's northern extremity is the ultimate winter wonderland.

Helsinki

Suomenlinna Constructed in the 1700s and now a UNESCO World Heritage Site, Suomenlinna (suomenlinna.fi) is one of the world's largest maritime fortresses. Built on several islands off the coast of Helsinki, it's a fun place to explore by boat and on foot. There are several museums and cafés, plus special events during the summer.

Heureka Helsinki's interactive science centre, Heureka (heureka.fi) challenges young minds with a smorgasbord of high-tech activities. The adjacent outdoor Galilei Science Park (open May to September) has water-themed experiments and contraptions – a kind of waterpark for budding Einsteins.

Linnanmäki A perennial summer favourite for Finnish children, Linnanmäki (linnanmaki.fi) has been providing thrills and squeals since 1950. In addition to old favourites like the wooden roller coaster, there are numerous modern rides, as well as an aquarium where you can get dizzy by walking inside a ring-shaped aquarium full of shoaling herring.

Further afield To the west of Helsinki, the cities of Tampere and Turku have no shortage of quirky family attractions. For example, there's Moominworld (muumimaailma.fi), a theme park 16 km from Turku dedicated to those loveable, white hippo-looking creatures created by Finnish author Tove Jansson. Yes, that's right – you can actually meet Moominmamma, Moominpappa, Sniff, Snufkin and the Snork Maiden. Older children (though not necessarily their parents) will prefer Tampere's Spy Museum (vakoilumuseo.fi) where aspiring secret agents can learn how to decipher hidden messages, change their voice and conceal a sword inside a walking stick.

Let's visit Santa

★ For the most authentic, least tacky and commercialized Santa experience, book a package with Esprit (SantasLapland.com) to Saariselkä, north of the Arctic Circle and within 30 minutes of Ivalo international airport. On arrival, you're greeted by elves and a reindeer led by a traditionally dressed Lapp. Mr Claus guarantees a private meeting for every family in his secret woodland cabin. And the magic doesn't end there. You also spend a day ice-fishing, kick-sledding, tandem skiing, tobogganing and riding mini-skidoos, reindeer sleighs and husky sleds.

Inside info ⓘ

▶▶ Get a feel for the city by hopping on the T3 tram.
▶▶ Helsinki has several parks, while the islands are perfect for a picnic and a swim. In winter you can skate on dozens of ice rinks throughout the city.
▶▶ A Helsinki Card gives unlimited travel on public transport and free entry to major sights and over 50 museums, including Suomenlinna fortress and Helsinki Zoo.

Iceland puts the wild in wilderness. It's an austere land riddled with suppurating mud pits, sulphurous steam vents and lava flows that resemble vast swathes of burnt apple crumble. Waterfalls bloated with glacial silt retch into canyons, while fully grown trees cower close to the ground to shelter from scything Arctic winds. It's hardly your typical image of a family holiday paradise and yet Iceland, for all its austerity, is a superb destination for kids who have a sense of adventure. More back of beyond than back to the beach, the Land of Ice and Fire is Europe's ultimate – though admittedly quite pricey – adventure playground, where you can search for whales one day and skidoo across an ice cap the next.

Southwest Iceland

Reykjavík Chances are you'll be out and about most of the time, but Reykjavík (visitreykjavik.is) has enough to keep you occupied for any spare mornings or afternoons. Young children will enjoy feeding the ducks at the city's central lake, while Reykjavík Zoo & Family Park (mu.is) makes a fun outing to see reindeer and seals. There's also an aquarium here, plus a park for pony rides. For a dose of culture, head to the Saga Museum (sagamuseum.is) where your kids can go Viking, or the open-air Reykjavík City Museum (minjasafnreykjavikur.is) with its nostalgic village and farm recreations.

The Blue Lagoon Located between the airport and Reykjavík, The Blue Lagoon (bluelagoon.com) is about as weird and wonderful as swimming pools get. Surrounded by a barren lava landscape, the milky-blue, geothermal waters of this open-air pool steam away at 35-40°C. Wading into the waist-deep water your toes squidge into a layer of silica sludge that you can slap on your face for a therapeutic mud mask. Gently poaching yourself in The Blue Lagoon is without doubt Iceland's balmiest – and most barmy – pastime. If you're heading to North Iceland (see opposite), be sure to take a dip in the equally magical Nature Baths, near Lake Myvatn.

The Golden Circle Iceland's definitive day trip, this geologically supercharged tour visits Thingvellir (a UNESCO World Heritage Site of lava flows, deep ravines and the site of Iceland's original parliament), Geysir (a hotspot of geothermal vents, including the Stokkur geyser, which erupts 20 m every five minutes) and the double-tiered cascade of Gullfoss.

Cool for kids

Fully equipped with crampons and ice axes, glacier hiking on Sólheimajökull is possible for children as young as eight.

The highlight of our week had to be our Highlands expedition – an epic all-day drive through lunar-like desolation to the heart of Iceland, fording rivers and crunching over lava flows and pumice-scattered plains to reach an explosion crater called Hell.
William Gray

Seljalandsfoss & Skogafoss This gushing duo is accessible from Road 1. Be prepared for a good soaking from the falls' spray, and watch your step on the slippery, uneven terrain.

Hekla & Eyjafjallajokull You can take a 4WD jeep tour to these active volcanoes. It's a long and bumpy ride, but the scenery is amazing.

Westman Islands Unless it's dead calm (in which case the three-hour ferry trip is just about bearable), hop on a flight to this cluster of 15 volcanic islands off the south coast – made famous in 1973 when a volcano on Heimaey erupted and destroyed much of the main town. From May to early August you'll be able to see thousands of puffins.

🌀 Great outdoors

Horse riding
Just 10 minutes' drive from Reykjavik, Ishestar Riding Tours (ishestar.is) offers horse-riding (for first-timers to experts) using sure-footed Icelandic ponies.

Whale watching
Summer boat trips from Reykjavík are often rewarded with sightings of dolphins and whales. Head north to Grundarfjordur in February or March for orcas.

Whitewater rafting
For gentle to moderate rapids, paddle on the Hvítá River, about an hour from Reykjavík. The River Fun trip offered by Arctic Rafting (arcticrafting.com) is suitable for children aged 10 and above.

4WD self-drive adventure to Askja in the Central Highlands

North Iceland

Lake Myvatn Nowhere is Iceland's volatile character more evident than near Lake Myvatn. At Hverarönd, for example, kids will be captivated by (and no doubt keen to impersonate) the belching, foul-smelling mud pits, while at Krafla they can scurry across lava fields contorted into swirls, coils and honeycombs. Hverfjall, meanwhile, is a squat, kilometre-wide crater with a rough path stamped in its flank of loose rock. The scramble to the rim at 312 m provides dramatic views of Lake Myvatn. At Dimmuborgir, a walking trail probes a bizarre maze of tortured basalt, sculpted into spires, caves, arches and a disconcerting number of trolls. Driving (or cycling) around the lake, you will also encounter pseudocraters (mini-volcanoes created by steam exploding from water trapped beneath lava) and lava pillars (formed during a fissure eruption). Don't worry if the technical interpretations are beyond you or your kids; the gawp factor of the scenery far outweighs the need to grapple with too much in the way of geophysics.

Dettifoss The central highlands of Iceland are smothered in ice caps. Thousands of years ago, volcanic activity under one of the largest, Vatnajökull, unleashed a catastrophic flood that chiselled out the Jökulsá Canyon (an hour's drive east of Lake Myvatn and a lovely location for easy walks), and laid the foundation for a series of impressive waterfalls. Dettifoss is one of Europe's most powerful – a bloated cataract spewing between terraced cliffs of lava. Every second, 200 cu m of dirty water is hurled 45 m to the canyon floor where it roars and froths like a gigantic cappuccino machine.

Húsavík Setting out several times a day into Skjátfandi Bay from the fishing town of Húsavík, a small fleet of beautifully restored, oak-hulled herring trawlers (northsailing.is) have found a new lease of life as whale-watching boats. Fulmars and Arctic terns swirling above the surface are often your best clues as to the cetaceans' whereabouts. Minke whales are seen on well over 90% of outings, while harbour porpoises and pods of leaping white-beaked dolphins are also fairly common. Humpback whales and orcas are regular visitors and there have even been close encounters with blue whales.

Superjeep safari

With their giant tyres, 4WD and raised suspension, superjeeps are, quite simply, unstoppable. Join a safari from Reykjavík or the Lake Myvatn region to explore Iceland's interior in one of these monster machines and you'll spend the day driving up and down mountains, pummelling snowdrifts and treating glacial rivers like car washes.

Inside info

▶▶ Car hire is available, but you'll need 4WD if you want to venture into the interior.

▶▶ Several companies offer tours, including Iceland Adventure Tours (icelandadventuretours.co.uk).

▶▶ **Warning!** Iceland's waterfalls and geothermal attractions have few safety fences – keep small children strapped in strollers or firmly tethered on reins.

▶▶ It's a 45-minute flight from Reykjavík to Akureyri, followed by a 90-minute scenic drive to Lake Myvatn.

▶▶ In Húsavík don't miss the superb Whale Museum (icewhale.is), open May-September.

When to go

Milder than other parts of Scandinavia, **Denmark** has a climate more like that of London or Amsterdam. July and August are the busiest months for heading to the beach or countryside. Expect snow in the Lapland region of **Sweden** and **Finland** from November to April, with temperatures plunging to -30°C. This is the best time of year to witness the aurora borealis. Further south, cities like Stockholm and Helsinki don't get so cold or dark, and everywhere warms and brightens up in summer. Bring mozzie repellent if venturing into the wilds between June and August. The lowest temperature recorded in **Norway** is -51°C in Kárásjohka-Karasjok in the far north. However, average annual temperatures along the western coast are around 8°C with the warmest month being July. Norway's mountains protect much of the eastern part of the country from precipitation, with as little as 300 mm falling annually in some areas. Expect up to ten times this along parts of the coast. Despite its lofty latitude, **Iceland** benefits from the Gulf Stream to enjoy a temperate climate with cool summers and fairly mild winters. Average January temperatures in Reykjavík are actually higher than those in New York. Come prepared, however, for changeable weather.

Getting there

The most extensive flight network in the region is from Scandinavian Airlines (flysas. com), which has flights to numerous destinations, including Copenhagen, Stockholm, Gothenburg, Oslo, Bergen and Stavanger. Other airlines include Finnair (finnair.com), Icelandair (icelandair.com) and British Airways (britishairways.com). For low-cost flights, try Ryanair (ryanair.com), Bmi (flybmi.com), easyJet (easyjet.com), Iceland Express (icelandexpress.com) and Norwegian (norwegian.no).

Getting around

In Denmark, the national train network is operated by Danish Rail (dsb.dk), coach services are offered by Abildskous Busser (abildskou. dk) and ferries are run by Scandlines (scandlines.dk). In Sweden, a sophisticated rail network covers all major routes, including Stockholm-Malmö-Copenhagen (via the Öresund bridge) and Stockholm-Gothenburg. Some train services in Sweden offer family carriages with children's play corners. Express coach service is provided by Swebus (swebusexpress.se). The Norwegian State Railway (nsb.no) has a well-developed network stretching from the southwest coast to Nordland. Norway Bus Express (nor-way.no)

also covers most of the country. Numerous ferries ply the fjords, including the long-established Hurtigruten Coastal Voyage (hurtigruten.com) which sails between Bergen and Kirkenes. The trip takes around 11 days with frequent stops along the coast. There are daily departures and the ships can carry cars.

For travel in Finland, try the comprehensive coach network (matkahuolto.fi) and high-speed trains (vr. fi). Finland's maze of interconnected lakes can be navigated on ferries operated by companies such as Karelia Lines (karelialines.fi). Silja Line (silja.com) and Viking Line (vikingline.fi) offer cruises between Helsinki and Stockholm with activities and entertainment laid on for kids and teenagers. In Iceland, bus tours are operated by Trex (trex.is), Reykjavik Excursions (re.is) and SBK (sbk.is), while cars and campervans can be rented through several agencies.

Accommodation

Check out tourist board websites for online booking facilities. In Denmark, popular family choices include rental cottages, holiday villages, farmstays, campsites and hostels. Novasol Cottages (novasol.co.uk) offer weekly rentals throughout the country. Also try Dansommer (dansommer.com). Denmark's holiday villages are well equipped for self-catering holidays. Lalandia (lalandia.com) near Rødby has its own waterpark; Strandhotellerne (dayz.dk) has several beachside resorts around Denmark; Skallerup Klit (skallerup.dk) has an indoor Atlantis Waterland and Silkeborg (danparcs.com) boasts an artificial ski slope. You can book farmstays in Denmark at bondegaardsferie.dk and ecoholiday.dk, while family hostels are available through Danhostels (danhostel. dk). Denmark's campsites have excellent facilities and are very popular with Danish families.

In Sweden, SCR (camping.se) publishes an extensive directory of campsites, as well as some 12,000 rental cottages. Also offering excellent facilities for inexpensive self-catering holidays, the Swedish Tourist Association (svenskaturistforeningen.se) has a network of about 300 youth hostels (known as vandrarhem). Hotel accommodation in Stockholm is expensive, but you can save money by staying in a holiday cottage on the coast, 30 minutes' drive from the city. Destination Stockholms Skärgård (dess.se) lists properties throughout the region (including the Stockholm Archipelago). Two hours north of Gothenburg, TanumStrand (tanumstrand. se) is a family-friendly resort with waterslides and a mini-zoo, while Isaberg (isaberg.com), 120 km east of Gothenburg, has 70 chalets in a holiday village setting, plus year-round activities, from canoeing to skiing.

Norway's Fjord Pass (fjord-pass.com) offers discounts on accommodation at 150 hotels, guesthouses and cabins throughout the country. Also good value, Hostelling International (vandrerhjem.no) operates 110 youth and family hostels.

In Finland you will find a wide range of cottages and farmstays at Lomarengas (lomarengas.fi), while Destination Lapland (destinationlapland.com) specializes in log cabins in Lapland. Camping in Finland (camping.fi) provides access to 330 campsites across the country.

Iceland has a wide range of hotels and guesthouses, many of which offer children's discounts. For hands-on rural stays, try Icelandic Farm Holidays (farmholidays.is). There are also 26 hostels around Iceland which can be booked through Hostelling International (hostel.is). Campsites in Iceland are usually open from the beginning of June until the end of August and are free of charge for children under 16.

Food & drink

Seafood features predominantly in Scandinavian cuisine. Local specialities like pickled fish and black bread may demand an acquired taste, but you will also find basics like meat and potatoes. The *smörgåsbord* buffet-style of dining will appeal to picky children, while fast-food outlets are widespread. In Denmark try herring (raw and pickled or cooked in a cream sauce). *Smørrebrød*, the Danish open sandwich, is available in umpteen varieties. Fresh, pickled and smoked seafood (particularly herring, crayfish and salmon) are popular dishes in Sweden, but you should also try game dishes such as reindeer. In northern Norway there is a long tradition of drying cod on wooden racks. Other specialities include roast pork ribs, cured mutton and sheep's heads, with ears, eyes and all. In Finland, summer menus are dominated by salmon, whitefish and Baltic herring, with crayfish in season from late July to September. Game meats, mushrooms, cloudberries, blueberries and lingonberries figure prominently in the autumn, while fish, such as burbot, are hauled from ice-covered lakes during winter. The seafood in Iceland is of outstanding quality. Try Icelandic fish and chips in the old harbour area of Reykjavík.

Health & safety

Scandinavia is generally very safe with no need for any special vaccinations. Mosquitoes can be a nuisance during summer months. Potentially more dangerous are severe winter temperatures in the far north. Be especially alert to the threat of frostbite or hypothermia in young children.

Go green
Five ways to skip the flight

❶ Drive or take the train across the 16-km Öresund Bridge linking Denmark's capital, Copenhagen, with Malmö in Sweden.

❷ Catch a ferry with DFDS Seaways (dfdsseaways.co.uk) from Harwich to Esbjerg in Denmark. The crossing time is 17 hours and the service operates every other day.

❸ Cruise with Smyril Line (smyril-line.com) which operates a weekly passenger/car-ferry service between Bergen (Norway), Hanstholm (Denmark), Lerwick (Shetland Islands), the Faroe Islands and Seyðsfjörður (Iceland).

❹ Hop on a Eurolines (eurolines.com) coach bound for Denmark, Sweden or Norway.

❺ Travel by Eurostar (eurostar.com) from London St Pancras International to Brussels, with connecting trains to major cities in Denmark via Cologne and Hamburg.

Holiday operators

The Adventure Company
adventurecompany.co.uk

Discover the World
discover-the-world.co.uk

Esprit Holidays
santaslapland.com

Exodus
exodus.co.uk

Explore
explore.co.uk

Families Worldwide
familiesworldwide.co.uk

First Choice Holidays
firstchoice.co.uk

Headwater
headwater.com

Inntravel inntravel.co.uk

KE Adventure Travel
keadventure.com

Nature Travels
naturetravels.co.uk

Neilson
neilson.co.uk

Nordic Experience
nordicexperience.co.uk

Specialised Tours
specialisedtours.com

Sunvil sunvil.co.uk

Fast facts

Country	Time	Language	Currency	Dialling code	Tourist information
Denmark	GMT+1	Danish	Krone	+45	visitdenmark.com
Sweden	GMT+1	Swedish	Krona	+46	visitsweden.com
Norway	GMT+1	Norwegian	Krone	+47	visitnorway.com
Finland	GMT+2	Finnish	Euro €	+358	visitfinland.com
Iceland	GMT	Icelandic	Krona	+354	visiticeland.com

Icehotel

Where? Jukkasjarvi, Swedish Lapland.

Why? Expect a frosty reception at the Icehotel (icehotel.com). The thermometer at the check-in desk usually reads around -6°C. It's made of ice, along with everything else in this fairy-tale hotel, newly created each year some 200 km north of the Arctic Circle. From the outside, the hotel resembles a giant, featureless igloo. But inside there are ice chandeliers sparkling with fibre optics, candles burning in carved recesses, intricately chiselled pillars and stunning suites designed by the world's leading ice sculptors. It feels like you've arrived on Planet Krypton. Each room has its own ice bed strewn with reindeer furs, but guests are also given Arctic-grade sleeping bags. A few family rooms sleep four. Hotel staff provide a full briefing on what to wear (thermal everything) and how to breathe (preferably through your nose). In the morning you're awoken with a hot cup of lingonberry juice. There's a fabulous range of winter activites at the Icehotel (see page 200) which melts back into the Torne River each spring.

Contact Icehotel, icehotel.com or Discover the World, T+44 (0)1737-218812, discover-the-world.co.uk

Vatnsholt Farm

Where? Selfoss, Iceland.

Why? The cosy cottages and large dining/play barn are perfect for families, while children love the resident menagerie of dogs, cats, horses, rabbits, cows and ducks. Within easy reach of Iceland's Golden Circle, the farm also has views of Eyjafjallajökull volcano and the Westman Islands.

Contact Discover the World, T+44 (0)1737-218812, discover-the-world.co.uk

Iso-Syöte

Where? Syöte National Park, Finnish Lapland.

Why? Take your pick from a traditional log cabin with its own fireplace and sauna, or stay at the comfortable Iso-Syöte Hotel with its restaurant, swimming pool and stunning views across the surrounding fells and valleys. Lots of winter activities are available, including snowmobiling.

Contact Iso-Syöte, T+358 (0)201-476400, syote.fi

Kongsfjord Guesthouse

Where? Finnmark, northern Norway.

Why? Just a 30-minute drive from Berlevag and enjoying sweeping views over the fjord, this lovingly restored farm affords a high standard of accommodation with cosy, tastefully furnished rooms and a restaurant which specializes in hearty local dishes.

Contact Kongsfjord Guesthouse, T+47 (0)78-981000, kongsfjord-gjestehus.no

Kakslauttanen

Where? Finnish Lapland.

Why? Imagine sleeping in a glass igloo (perfect for watching the northern lights) deep in the wintry heart of Lapland. Hotel Kakslauttanen also has log cabins equipped with fireplace, toilet, shower, sauna and kitchenette. A wide range of activities are available, both in winter and summer.

Contact Hotel Kakslauttanen, T+358 (0)16-667100, kakslauttanen.fi

Lava House
Where? Near Lake Myvatn, northern Iceland.
Why? A beautifully converted 12-bed schoolhouse in a rural hamlet between Lake Myvatn and Húsavík, the Lava House is ideal for large family gatherings or groups of friends. The Scandinavian-style, five-bedroom property has a large deck with a hot tub – perfect for soaking up the views across the Adaldalur Valley. Lake Myvatn, with its volcanic attractions, is just a 40-minute drive away, while Húsavík, to the north, is one of Europe's premier whale-watching destinations.
Contact Discover the World, T+44 (0)1737-218812, discover-the-world.co.uk

66 99 **Iceland is traditionally a touring destination, but there are plenty of single-centre options for families. Basing ourselves in the Lava House meant that we could not only save money by self-catering, but we could also relax and explore the local area at our own pace. There's loads to do nearby – from horse riding and whale watching to poaching yourselves in the geothermal Nature Baths.** William Gray

Hotel Ullensvang
Where? Sorfjorden, Norwegian Fjords.
Why? Located on the sunny side of Sorfjorden (a branch of the mighty Hardangerfjord), this well-equipped hotel has an indoor swimming pool, and tennis court, table tennis and golf simulator. Rowing boats are available during the summer and there's also a children's playroom.
Contact Hotel Ullensvang, T+47 (0)53-670000, hotel-ullensvang.no

Lyngen Lodge
Where? Lyngen Alps, northern Norway.
Why? A fjordside retreat in the Lyngen Alps of Arctic Norway, this turf-roofed lodge sleeps 18 guests and is the ideal base for wilderness activities in either summer or winter. Boat tours, fishing, trekking, horse riding, snowshoeing and dog sledding are all on offer.
Contact Lyngen Lodge, T+47 (0)47-627853, lyngenlodge.com

Akademik Sergey Vavilov
Where? Spitsbergen, Svalbard.
Why? Equipped with an ice-strengthened hull, the stable and quiet, 107-berth *Vavilov* is perfect for summer voyages to the Arctic archipelago of Svalbard. Discover the World offer special family cruises aboard the ship (see page 202). Onboard facilities include a range of twin and triple cabins, dining room, lounge, bar, library, doctor's clinic, sauna and plunge pool.
Contact Discover the World, T+44 (0)1737-218812, discover-the-world.co.uk or Quark Expeditions, quarkexpeditions.com

Africa

It's all a big game

On safari at Satao Elerai Camp near Kenya's Amboseli National Park.

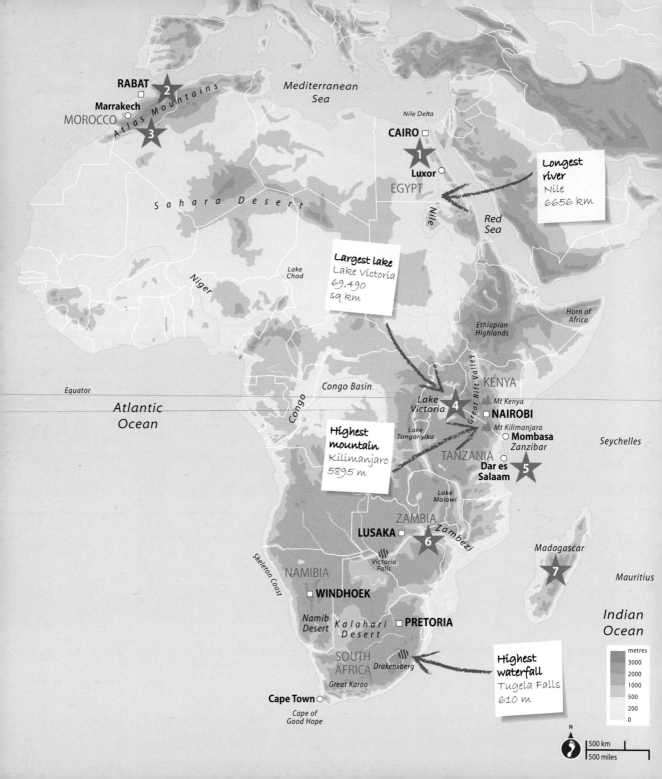

RABAT
□
2

Marrakech ○

MOROCCO

Atlas Mountains

Mediterranean Sea

3

Nile Delta

CAIRO □

Longest river
Nile
6656 km

Luxor ○

1

EGYPT

Red Sea

S a h a r a   D e s e r t

Nile

Niger

Lake Chad

Largest lake
Lake Victoria
69,490
sq km

Ethiopian Highlands

Horn of Africa

Equator

Atlantic Ocean

Congo Basin

Congo

Lake Victoria

4

Great Rift Valley

Mt Kenya

KENYA

□ **NAIROBI**

Seychelles

Highest mountain
Kilimanjaro
5895 m

Lake Tanganyika

Mt Kilimanjaro

Mombasa ○
Zanzibar ○

TANZANIA

Dar es Salaam

5

Lake Malawi

ZAMBIA

Madagascar

LUSAKA □

6

Zambezi

Mauritius

Victoria Falls

NAMIBIA

7

Skeleton Coast

WINDHOEK □

Indian Ocean

Namib Desert

K a l a h a r i   D e s e r t

□ **PRETORIA**

SOUTH AFRICA

Drakensberg

Highest waterfall
Tugela Falls
610 m

Great Karoo

Cape Town ○

Cape of Good Hope

metres
3000
2000
1000
500
200
0

N

500 km
500 miles

1 Sail through the land of the Pharaohs
» Egypt, page 220

2 Ride a camel through the desert
» Egypt & Morocco, pages 220 & 221

3 Trek in the Atlas Mountains
» Morocco, page 221

4 Track down the big five
» Kenya & Tanzania, pages 222 & 224

5 Learn to snorkel or scuba dive on a coral reef
» Indian Ocean, page 228

6 Canoe on the River Zambezi
» Zambia, page 226

7 Discover the land of lemurs
» Madagascar, page 229

Did you know?

★ The Sahara Desert is expanding southwards an average of 800 m a month.

★ Two continental plates in East Africa are slowly moving apart to form the Great Rift Valley which will eventually split Africa in two and create a new ocean when water floods in.

★ 70% of Africa's population survives on less than US$2 a day each.

★ The word for 'crossword' in Kiswahili is chemshebongo which means 'boil brains'.

If there's one thing guaranteed to get the grandparents tutting and clucking it's the mere mention of the words 'kids', 'holiday' and 'Africa' in the same sentence. "Is it safe? What about malaria? The local zoo has lions – why don't you go there instead?" You can't blame them for being concerned. Africa has its fair share of challenges when it comes to travel. But, equally, it has plenty of destinations that are ideal for families. South Africa's Cape region, for example, has everything from wonderful beaches to malaria-free game reserves, while East Africa is perfect for a safari/beach combo. There's more to Africa, though, than these well-established family favourites. Ever wondered what it would be like to do a roly-poly down one of the world's highest sand dunes? Or paddle in the wake of famous explorers like Dr David Livingstone? These and countless other adventures are up for grabs in Namibia and Zambia. And let's not forget North Africa. In Morocco, mule-supported treks can transport your tribe into the heart of the Atlas Mountains, while you might opt for camels or sailing feluccas to introduce your kids to the wonders of ancient Egypt.

66 99 **Over 40 lions, five leopards, five cheetahs, 23 hyenas, 18 jackals, five bat-eared foxes and 60-plus mongooses. Numbers dominated the thoughts of nine-year-old Joe on our Kenyan safari. In fact, Joe himself discovered that he was worth two cattle or 10 goats, although we never got round to sealing the deal with our Maasai guide.** William Gray

Star rating

Wow factor
★★★★★

Worry factor
★★★

Value for money
★★★

Keeping teacher happy
★★★★★

Family accommodation
★★★★

Babies & toddlers
★★

Cool for teenagers
★★★★

🔍 Game plan mancala

There are lots of variations on how to play this ancient board game. All you need are 36 stones, a mancala board with two rows of six holes (an empty egg carton will do) and a 'store', such a small bowl, for each player.

How to play

» Place three stones in each hole.
» One player starts by picking up all of the pieces in any one of the holes on his side of the board.
» Moving anti-clockwise, the player places one of the stones in each hole until they run out.
» If you reach your own store, deposit a stone in it – but skip your opponent's store.
» If the last stone you drop is in your own store, take another turn. If it lands in an empty hole on your side, you capture any stones in the hole directly opposite and place them in your store.
» The game is over when all six spaces on one side of the board are empty. The winner is the player with the most pieces in his or her store.

📷 Photo tips on safari

Joe and Ellie Gray, 11, share their snap-happy tips for wildlife photography.

» Always try to focus on the animal's eyes.
» Taking great pictures isn't all about the camera; it's what you put in front of it and where you point it!
» Getting used to your camera before going away is a really good idea.
» Resting your camera on a steady solid object like a fencepost or tree dramatically improves your pictures.
» If possible, crouch down to the animal's level to keep the background uncluttered and draw attention to the main subject.

👁 Spot the small five

» Elephant shrew   » Leopard tortoise
» Rhinoceros beetle » Ant lion
» Buffalo weaverbird

☠ Fish for baboon spiders

On safari it is generally not a good idea to go poking around in holes. Many are home to harmless creatures, such as mice, gerbils and lizards, but others might harbour less endearing critters like snakes and bees. Even an innocent looking mouse hole may not be all that it seems. Shine a torch down one and you may find eight eyes staring back. What you may not realize is that all eight eyes belong to one, large hairy spider. Check out the sides of the hole: the presence of a silk lining should confirm that you've found the lair of a baboon spider – common in dry grassland across much of East and southern Africa. Using a long grass stem your Maasai guide will show you how to tempt the arachnid out by singing to it while gently scratching around the entrance to its burrow, imitating the patter of passing prey, such as grasshoppers and beetles. This elicits the spider's ambush response, luring the palm-sized tarantula into the open. Count all eight eyes – two large ones facing forwards, four small ones in a row below them and another two on the sides of the spider's domed head. And check out those enormous orange fangs – more than capable of seizing prey and dragging it down that old mouse hole.

Great reads
6 books for kids

Ages 3-8

Crafty Chameleon
Mwenye Hadithi (Hodder Headline)
Beautifully illustrated, this is the story of
how clever little Chameleon got the better
of Leopard and Crocodile.

**Ebele's Favourite: A Book of African
Games** *Ifeoma Onyefulu* (Frances Lincoln)
Ebele loves games. But when her friend
comes to stay she finds herself wondering
which is her favourite. Ten traditional
Nigerian games are described.

Ages 6-11

Fly, Eagle, Fly: An African Tale
Christopher Gregorowski (Frances Lincoln)
An engaging parable of an eagle chick
raised amongst chickens. Despite being
assured by the farmer that the eagle will
never fly, a man teaches it how to soar.

The Girl who Married a Lion
Alexander McCall Smith (Cannongate)
A collection of traditional folktales from
Botswana. Includes the stories *Sister of
Bones* and *Hare Fools the Baboons*.

Ages 8+

The Awesome Egyptians
Terry Deary (Scholastic)
History with all the nasty bits left in. Funny
and gruesome, it covers everything from
making a mummy to revolting recipes for
3000-year-old sweets.

Ages 12+

Chain of Fire
Beverley Naidoo (Puffin)
The apartheid government is forcibly
removing black South African people from
their villages. Schoolchildren, Naledi and
Tiro decide to get involved in a student
protest march.

Taste of Morocco tagine

A delicious slow-cooked stew, tagine is also the name given to
the clay pot that it is cooked in. Tagines can be meat, fish or vegetarian
dishes, cooked with aromatic spices, vegetables and dried fruits.

What you need
- 1 tbsp olive oil
- 1 kg lean lamb, chopped into 4 cm cubes
- 4 pears, peeled and cubed
- 2 large onions, peeled and sliced
- 500 g sultanas
- 500 g flaked almonds
- 1 tbsp each of ground cumin, ground cinnamon, ground ginger, chopped coriander leaves and black pepper

What to do
- Fry the onion in the oil and transfer to the tagine.
- Add the meat. When browned, add the spices.
- Add enough water to cover the meat.
- Cover and simmer on a low heat for around two hours until the meat is tender and infused with the spices.
- In the last five minutes, add the pears, almonds and sultanas, along with the chopped coriander leaves.

🔍 How to make
a Bushman snare

- Extract the fibres of Kalahari sisal by dragging your digging stick across the leaves.
- Twine the fibres together across your thigh.
- Tie one end to a 'bendy' sapling and anchor the other end in the ground with a half-buried twig.
- Attach a loop to the free end of twine and stake it in a circle using sticks.
- Attach a trigger stick baited with wild raisins.
- Scatter leaves around snare, then wait for a guinea fowl to peck at the raisins...

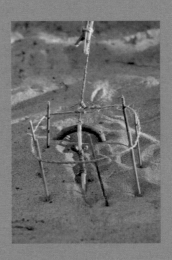

Whatever age your children, health risks are likely to be the main factor in deciding where you go in Africa – or even whether to go at all. Malaria, of course, is the single biggest worry. Force-feed your children with Malarone, douse them with insect repellent and insist they wear long clothes and you may still find yourself lashing out at every winged insect that passes anywhere near them. Paranoid? Perhaps. There are numerous parents who are quite happy to take even young children paddling down the Zambezi, riding camels through the Sahara or spotting big game on an East African safari. Ultimately, it all boils down to your individual assessment of the risks, the precautions you are prepared to take and the age limits imposed by tour operators, camps and lodges.

Babies

Think very hard before taking children aged four and under to malarious parts of Africa. If they have older siblings who are desperate to go on safari, remember that parts of South Africa have malaria-free game reserves where you can spot big game. The safest, most relaxing and affordable way to visit South Africa with babies is to split your time between Cape Town and the Garden Route, staying in comfortable hotels or guesthouses with babysitting services. If you are set on something more adventurous, consider a guided,

Playing with fire

Maasai warriors teach children how to make fire by rubbing sticks together.

mule-supported trek in Morocco. A pre-crawling-stage baby in a papoose is a wonderfully portable thing, while breast-fed babies have a safe and readily available food, even in remote places like the Atlas Mountains. However, be sure to take every precaution to protect your infant from the sun, and visit during autumn or spring to avoid the worst of the heat.

Toddlers/pre-school

Sub-Saharan Africa is one of the world's highest-risk areas for malaria, so most families restrict their travels to South Africa's Cape provinces and parts of North Africa. As babies evolve from nappy-bound blobs to mobile mini-explorers they inevitably encounter more in the way of germs and accidents. With hygiene and safety coming to the fore you may be further put off from visiting Africa. Don't be. In addition to the Cape and Morocco, other non-malarial places you should consider are Namibia and the Seychelles. Following the initial shock and stress of early parenthood, a self-drive campervan tour of Namibia is a great holiday choice for families with toddlers. Not only does your campervan function as a self-contained bedroom, playroom and kitchen, but the Namib Desert will seem like one giant sandpit. For something a little more indulgent, the Seychelles and Mauritius boast numerous fabulous beach resorts with supervised children's clubs and great facilities, allowing adults some much-needed 'me-time'.

Special needs

Mobility impairment needn't rule out an African adventure. Specialist tour operators in South Africa and Kenya offer family-friendly, wheelchair-accessible holidays where everything from vehicles and accommodation to the pace of the itinerary are designed to suit physically disabled travellers. One or two also offer trips for people reliant on oxygen or kidney dialysis. Try Epic Enabled (epic-enabled.com), Endeavour Safaris (endeavour-safaris.com) and Able Travel (able-travel.com).

Single parents

Group safaris, Nile cruises and treks in the Atlas Mountains lend themselves particularly well to single parents. Your children will quickly bond with others in the group, while the tour leader will remove all the logistical headaches you might otherwise encounter if travelling alone. However, if you do crave independence, try a self-drive tour in South Africa, prebooking each night's accommodation in guesthouses where you'll get to know locals faster than by staying in big, impersonal hotels.

> **" " Our guide commanded instant awe in our six-year-old twins simply by probing the contents of a hyena pellet, scooping up a handful of giraffe faeces as if they were raisins and breaking open and sniffing an elephantine offering as if it was a freshly baked loaf of bread.** William Gray

Kids/school age

At this age, Africa starts to sound really exciting. Most four-year-olds will have seen *The Lion King* and you may already have taken them to see Timon and Pumba at Disneyland. Now is the time to bring the wilds of Africa to life – warthogs and all! You have two main options when it comes to family safaris – lodge-based or camping. For safety reasons, children usually need to be near the upper end of this age category for camping safaris, while many of the more exclusive lodges also have strict minimum age limits (some as high as 12 years). That's not to say you won't find family-friendly safari accommodation. Far from it. Both East and southern Africa have several excellent camps and lodges where children are specially catered for with activities ranging from guided bush tracking to poo identification (always a hit with youngsters). Egypt is another excellent family destination for children who have reached school age. Ancient Egypt usually features on the curriculum around the age of seven or eight, so this is an ideal time for a tour of the Nile Valley using a combination of traditional sailing felucca, sleeper train and camel. Other cultural hotspots to aim for include Zanzibar and Lamu on the East African coast.

Teenagers

Africa has several adventure 'capitals' with more than enough adrenaline-charged activities to please teenagers. Top of the list has to be Victoria Falls, where you can bungee jump, ride elephants and raft some of the world's wildest water. Other adventure hotspots include Swakopmund in Namibia (for desert sandboarding, kayaking with seals and 4WD tours along the Skeleton Coast), Cape Town (for great white shark encounters, surfing and abseiling off Table Mountain) and South Africa's Drakensberg Mountains (for hiking, horse riding, rafting and paragliding). Alternatively, why not set your teenager a single, big challenge, such as learning how to scuba dive in the Red Sea, catch a tiger fish on Lake Malawi or joining a Young Rangers' Club in Kenya. There are also plenty of opportunities for getting off-the-beaten-track in places like Zambia's South Luangwa Valley.

Telling tales Sir Steve Redgrave
British rower and five times Olympic gold medallist

I convinced our kids they weren't going to see much, that the wildlife would be a long way away and that they would be extremely lucky to see a leopard. As it turned out we saw so many leopards they began saying "Big deal, Dad". We also went kayaking at Simon's Town. At first the children weren't keen. Natalie was absolutely paranoid that she was going to get attacked by a shark. But by the time we got round into Boulders they thought it was brilliant. They didn't want to come in.

Egypt
Unlocking the treasure chest

Got yourself an infant Indiana Jones or little Lara Croft? If your kids are into adventure and hidden treasure, Egypt makes an exciting and educational destination where you can combine the mysteries of the Pharaohs with some beach time on the Red Sea coast. Obviously, school-age children who have covered Ancient Egypt in the classroom will be blown away by seeing the real thing, but that doesn't mean younger travellers will find it boring. The secret is to combine fact with fun. Don't make your trip an endless procession of museums and adult-focused tours – instead, build itineraries around mini-adventures, like sailing on a felucca or riding a camel.

Cairo

Divide your time between the Pyramids of Giza and the Egyptian Museum (egyptianmuseumcairo.org). At the latter, don't expect much in the way of interactive exhibits or English interpretation. However, what you do get are the dazzling treasures of teenage Pharaoh, Tutankhamun, including his famous gold funerary mask. Another must-see is the grizzly and engrossing Royal Mummy Room, displaying the remains of 11 Egyptian queens and rulers.

The last surviving Ancient Wonder of the World, the Pyramids of Giza are often bemoaned by adult visitors as being 'swamped by Cairo's suburbs' or 'spoilt by over-zealous touts'. Most children, however, will simply be struck by innocent wonder at the sheer size of these extraordinary monuments – especially the Great Pyramid of Khufu (Cheops) which rises to 137 m and is thought to have been constructed using more than two million limestone blocks, each one weighing over two tonnes. Most kids' initial impulse is to climb the thing. However, this is a definite 'no-no', so quash any disappointment by exploring the pyramid's long, cramped 'secret' passages that lead to mysterious subterranean chambers.

Aswan

An exciting way to reach Egypt's southernmost city is to take the overnight sleeper train from Cairo. After the hustle of the capital, Aswan appears positively tranquil, so take time to relax by strolling through the Nubian villages of Koti and Siou on Elephantine Island where you can learn about local culture (older girls, and possibly their mums, will no doubt want a henna tattoo). Later, catch a ferry to the west bank of the Nile where you can arrange a camel ride through the

Great Pyramid and Sphinx

desert to the seventh-century Monastery of St Simeon. Aswan is also the starting point for trips to Abu Simbel and the Great Temple of Ramses II. However, it's a 560 km round trip and you'll be stuck in a minibus for much of the day (unless you have the budget to fly). Instead, set your sights on Luxor and the Valley of the Kings – or a sailing trip on the Nile aboard a small traditional felucca or larger, modern motor cruiser.

Luxor

With Karnak a short distance north of the city and the Valley of the Kings just across the Nile, Luxor has the potential to both amaze and daze. Don't be tempted to try and squeeze in dynasty after dynasty of tomb sightseeing, but focus instead on a few of the most enigmatic sites. Highlights of the West Bank include the elegantly colonnaded Temple of Hatshepsut and the tombs of Ramses I and Ramses VI – both of which have burial chambers with elaborately painted scenes of animal-headed gods. Older children may enjoy the challenge of reaching the tomb of Tuthmosis III with its steep shafts and challenging passageways that were designed in an (unsuccessful) attempt to thwart tomb robbers.

You'll find that a series of early morning excursions to the West Bank has less 'whinge potential' than a single, long, hot daytrip. Spend the afternoons relaxing by a pool and then set off again when it's cooler to visit local Luxor beauties like the Great Hypostyle Hall – a forest of 134 towering pillars that forms part of the Amun Temple enclosure at Karnak. A great way to reach this spectacular complex is to take one of the local horse-drawn carriages.

Inside info

▸▸ Avoid excessive heat by travelling during autumn and spring.
▸▸ At historic sites, keep children interested for longer by setting them challenges like hieroglyphic code-busting.
▸▸ Top kids' foods include *shish tawouq* kebabs, *fiteer* pizzas and *kushari* noodles. Let fussy feeders choose from a range of mezze dishes.

☁ Atlas trekking

★ Don't try and go it alone. Not only will a good local guide smooth out logistics (such as hiring mule teams), but you'll also glean fascinating insights into the region's geology, wildlife and Berber culture, and contribute directly to the local economy.

★ Several Moroccan and foreign operators offer guided treks in the Atlas Mountains, but one of the most experienced family specialists is UK-based Families Worldwide (familiesworldwide.co.uk).

If you want a family trip that's big on adventure, culture and scenery, but only feel like dipping a toe outside the 'comfort zone' of Europe, then Morocco is the place for you. Nip across the 13-km-wide Straits of Gibraltar and you will find yourself transported into a world of exotic new sights, sounds, smells and tastes. Don't feel intimidated. The souks of Marrakech and Fès may well leave you reeling, but Morocco has plenty of other less frantic highlights – from family-friendly mule-supported trekking in the Atlas Mountains to surfing on the Atlantic coast.

Marrakech

Brace yourself. It's going to be crowded, noisy and intense. You're going to run a gauntlet of hard-sell tactics the likes of which you've probably never experienced before. You may feel bewildered – nervous even. But you'll emerge from the medina of Marrakech with a tingling sense of having felt the very pulse of Morocco. Delving into crowded souks you might expect children to recoil with culture shock. If anything, however, it is their enthusiasm and lack of inhibition that helps the parents adjust. Youngsters will spontaneously attract the cheek-squidging attention of stallholders, drawing grown-ups into contact with locals far more swiftly than if they were lone adult tourists.

Djemaa el-Fna This huge square is the setting for one of the world's greatest cultural spectacles – a seething mêlée of musicians, snake-charmers, storytellers, water sellers, jugglers, acrobats, henna artists, fortune-tellers, market traders, potion mixers and food vendors (selling everything from cinnamon tea to stewed sheep heads). This truly bizarre bazaar (which gets particularly lively from around dusk) will hold your kids completely spellbound.

The souks Glistening pyramids of olives, smooth mounds of saffron, racks of multicoloured slippers… the souks (located on the north side of Djemaa el-Fna) are like a giant marketplace and maze rolled into one. You'll witness artisans at work, from blacksmiths and carpenters to tailors and jewellers. Hire an official guide at the tourist office or stick to main streets and follow the flow of people. Be prepared to bargain hard and enter protracted negotiations. Alternatively, just keep walking and soak up the atmosphere.

The Sahara

Erg Chebbi, Morocco's only genuine Saharan *erg* (a large expanse of sand dunes) can be found near the village of Merzouga, about 50 km south of Erfoud. Camel treks, ranging from sunset strolls to overnight expeditions, can be booked through local hotels. Auberge Kasbah Derkaoua (aubergederkaoua.com) also offers desert escapades by horseback and 4WD.

🏖 Atlantic coast

Morrocco's Atlantic hotspot, Essaouira (with its fortified old town and bustling harbour) is big on surfing and you can also ride camels on the beach. Better suited to families with young children, Agadir has a good range of seafront hotels with pools and kids' activities. Larache has a clean sandy beach, but be wary of strong currents.

Inside info ⓘ

▸▸ In Marrakech, hone in on the medina's main square, Djemaa el-Fna, and the nearby labyrinth of souks. Hold hands – this is not a place you want to lose someone! When kids start to tire, flag down a horse-drawn calèche or retreat to a rooftop terrace.

▸▸ For something similar on a smaller, less bewildering scale, visit Taroudant, a walled city in southern Morocco that resembles a 'mini Marrakech'. Fès also has a wonderfully chaotic medina.

Safari. If ever there was a word to inspire wanderlust in a child this is the one. Not only does it conjure images of lions, elephants, zebras and all the other childhood animal favourites, but it simply oozes with the promise of adventure. Safaris are the ultimate I-Spy. Yes, there will be dust, heat, pre-dawn wake-up calls and even the occasional frustrating game drive when all you see is the retreating posterior of a lone warthog, its tail held aloft like a defiant flag of victory. But Kenyans have been refining the safari for long enough to ensure that the needs of families are well catered for – this was, after all, where safaris were invented (the word means 'journey' in Swahili). Combine animal magic with beach bliss by dividing your holiday between a safari and a sojourn on Kenya's reef-fringed coastline.

Great Rift Valley

Choosing a Kenyan safari can leave you wallowing in logistics like a proverbial hippo. Operators offer everything from specialist birdwatching tours to budget camping expeditions to Lake Turkana. When it comes to family safaris, however, there is one circuit that's hard to beat. It combines the country's best wildlife-watching areas with child-friendly lodges and as few long days on the road as possible.

Nairobi Few capitals have national parks right on their doorstep, but Nairobi is one of them. Check into your hotel, dump your luggage and, ten minutes later, you could be watching lions or black rhinos in the wonderful, underrated Nairobi National Park. Be sure to visit the David Sheldrick Wildlife Sanctuary (sheldrickwildlifetrust.org) where orphaned elephants and rhinos are cared for.

Mount Kenya Nestled in forest on the western slopes of 5200-m Mount Kenya, Naro Moru makes a relaxing base for walks, horse riding and fishing. Nearby Ol Pejeta Conservancy (olpejetaconservancy.org) is unique in being the only place in Africa where you can see the big five as well as chimpanzees. Although the chimps are not indigenous to Kenya (orphans are brought here from other countries), Ol Pejeta's Chimpanzee Sanctuary offers a privileged insight into the plight of these endearing primates.

Nakuru From Mount Kenya it's a five-hour drive to this alkaline lake renowned for its flamingos. Changes in water levels mean you're unlikely to see the

concentrations of up to two million birds that were common in past decades. However, this is still a world-class spectacle – and when you tire of gawking at the flamingos there are buffaloes and rhinos to be spotted in the woodland surrounding the lake.

Naivasha This beautiful lake to the south of Nakuru is an altogether different kettle of fish – and birds. Freshwater Naivasha is fringed with papyrus bursting with over 350 species of birds, including herons, kingfishers and ducks – but not a single flamingo. Find out about the lake's ecology at the Elsamere Conservation Centre (elsatrust.org), once the home of the late Joy Adamson of *Born Free* fame. Older children who need to burn off energy might be tempted by the two-hour hike up nearby Mount Longonot.

Masai Mara Time your trip right (Jul-Oct) and your arrival in Kenya's finest wildlife reserve may coincide with the Great Migration when some 1.5 million wildebeest and several hundred thousand zebra and Thompson's gazelle head north from their breeding grounds in Tanzania's Serengeti. Even without the migration, however, the Mara offers superb game viewing, excellent accommodation and a chance to mingle with the Maasai.

The coast

The perfect place to unwind after a safari and wash the dust from your ears, Kenya's Indian Ocean shoreline is a beguiling blend of coral sand beaches and turquoise

Wildlife close up

Vehicle safaris allow you to get close to wildlife without putting you, or the animals, in danger.

Ghost crab hunting, Diani Beach

Elephants in Tsavo National Park

lagoons. It's also within easy striking distance of some excellent wildlife reserves which means that families short on time can base themselves at the coast and still get a safari fix.

South of Mombasa Diani and Tiwi beaches have every imaginable watersport available, from scuba diving and snorkelling to kitesurfing and banana boat rides. There's also no shortage of accommodation. With their swimming pools and children's facilities, the large seafront resorts are an obvious choice for families, but also consider the wide range of more intimate beach cottages. Just inland is Shimba Hills National Reserve – a protected fragment of coastal forest that is home to sable antelope and colobus monkey. Adjoining the reserve is the community-run Mwalugange Elephant Sanctuary where you can not only see jumbos, but also buy postcards made from their recycled dung!

North of Mombasa Head to Watamu where the Local Ocean Trust (watamuturtles.com) has set up a turtle conservation project. Several species lay their eggs on the beaches here between January and April. Malindi is the most popular resort along this stretch of coast and offers snorkelling and glass-bottom boat tours in Malindi Marine National Park. Inland, you can take a guided walk to spot some of the several hundred bird and butterfly species in Arabuko Sokoke Forest Reserve and visit Gedi – the remains of a 13th-century Swahili trading centre. It is well worth making the effort to continue north to the charming and friendly Lamu archipelago. Lose yourself in the winding alleyways that riddle the World Heritage Site of Lamu Town, spend a day cruising the islands on a traditional sailing dhow, then kick back on Shela Beach.

☸ **Best** of the rest

Amboseli National Park Amboseli's 1500 elephants (studied by Cynthia Moss and her team since 1972) are the highlight of this iconic park. Matriarchal herds and lone 'big tusker' bulls roam its typically dry plains where dust-devils swirl against the hazy backdrop of Mount Kilimanjaro. Far outnumbering lions, spotted hyenas are the dominant hunters in Amboseli. You can observe a den on one of the safari circuits where, curiously, the hyenas share with warthogs. Climb Observation Hill for panoramic views across Amboseli Lake where closer inspection (by vehicle) reveals hippo, mud-wallowing buffalo and elephant, plus numerous waterbirds.

Tsavo National Park A vast arid wilderness, Tsavo supports at least 6000 elephant. Stake out a waterhole and you will see an almost endless procession of red-dust-coated herds arriving to drink. Lion thrive in the reserve and there are also two black rhino sanctuaries. Drought-tolerant species include gerenuk and oryx.

Samburu National Reserve Acacia scrub studded with rust-coloured termite mounds and rocky ridges sprouting spears of euphorbia and aloe characterize this trio of reserves. Grevy's zebra, reticulated giraffe, gerenuk, beisa oryx and Somali ostrich are indicators of their semi-arid environments, but more widespread species are also found here, such as lion, cheetah and elephant. The Ewaso Nyiro River is a favourite spot for drinking – and springing an ambush.

Wildebeest on the move

Little king of the swingers

A juvenile mountain gorilla in Volcanoes National Park, Rwanda.

Kids' top 10 African safari wishlist

1 Stroll out with the Samburu in Kenya's Laikipia Plateau. Camel trekking with Samburu warriors provides an intimate, low-impact way to explore this arid frontier land – home to Grevy's zebra, reticulated giraffe, black rhino and gerenuk.

2 Rise above it all in a hot-air balloon. Dawn balloon flights are available from camps in the Masai Mara and Serengeti, as well as Loisaba in northern Kenya. You can also get aloft above the Namib Desert and several locations in South Africa.

3 Experience nature's greatest show. The perpetual pilgrimage of 1.5 million wildebeest, 500,000 Thomson's gazelle and 200,000 plains zebra is punctuated by the dramatic crossings of the Grumeti and Mara Rivers in Tanzania's Serengeti and Kenya's Masai Mara.

4 Fly-camp in the wilderness of Tanzania's Selous Game reserve. Walk in one of Africa's greatest wildlife reserves, sleeping out in the bush at small, temporary camps where dinner is cooked over an open fire, the sounds of the African night all around.

5 Follow in Livingstone's footsteps. North of the Luangwa Valley in Zambia, the little-visited papyrus swamps, floodplains and moist forests of Kasanka National Park and the Bangweulu Wetlands are rich in big game and birdlife.

6 Walk on the wild side. Zambia's South Luangwa National Park has long been renowned as *the* place in Africa for walking safaris. Its lavish spread of dappled woodlands, rivers and lily-covered lagoons is perfect for exploring on foot.

7 Canoe along the Zambezi. Launch a canoe on the River Zambezi, paddle silently past hippos and herds of browsing elephant, drift within a few metres of bee-eater colonies and camp out on remote islands.

8 Explore the Delta. The extraordinary wetland of Botswana's Okavango is home to an amazing variety of wildlife, from frogs and fish eagles to elephant and wild dog. Drift along the channels in a *mokoro* (dugout canoe).

9 Track wildlife with Bushmen. No one knows the Kalahari better than the Bushmen. Joining Ju/'hoansi hunters in Bushmanland as they track game, set traps and gather wild food is a unique privilege.

10 Meet mountain gorillas in Rwanda's Volcanoes National Park, trekking through thick montane forest for an unforgettable encounter with your distant hairy cousins. The minimum age for gorilla trekking is 15.

ⓤ Flamingo free-for-all

Great Rift Valley, Kenya & Tanzania
Even a lone flamingo is a head-turner. Just imagine over a million of them strutting their stuff, flushing pink the soda lakes of Bogoria, Nakuru, Magadi and Natron. The hubbub is extraordinary, the smell unforgettable. Breeding occurs on Natron Oct-Dec.

In many ways Tanzania is like a bigger version of Kenya. It has perhaps slightly less in the way of family-friendly accommodation (particularly for children under eight), but you can still easily combine a safari with a beach holiday. Three places that are likely to spring to mind when contemplating a trip to Tanzania are Kilimanjaro, the Serengeti and Zanzibar. Although trekking on Africa's highest peak is a considerable undertaking for adults and children alike (see below), a safari to the Serengeti and Ngorongoro Crater, followed by some snorkelling on Zanzibar's coral reefs, has all the ingredients for Africa's ultimate wildlife experience.

Zebras, Ngorongoro Crater

Northern Circuit

From Arusha, a typical safari includes Lake Manyara National Park, the Serengeti and Ngorongoro Crater. Distances are great (for example, it's a full day's drive between the Serengeti and Arusha), so allow at least a week to do the region justice.

Lake Manyara National Park encapsulates everything that is wild and wonderful about this corner of Africa. Not only does it have a magnificent setting, cowering beneath the western escarpment of the Great Rift Valley, but it's also home to an intriguing cast of wildlife, from tiptoeing flamingos to tree-climbing lions. Some safaris also loop through Tarangire National Park, which has high concentrations of elephant, zebra and wildebeest between August and October.

But it's Serengeti National Park that really gets the pulse racing. Nowhere else in Africa is more synonymous with big horizons, big skies and big game. The Great Migration between the Serengeti and Kenya's Masai Mara (see page 222) is one of the world's greatest natural spectacles, involving 1.5 million wildebeest, plus several hundred thousand zebras and Thompson's gazelles. Keeping a keen eye on proceedings are lions, cheetahs, leopards and other predators. The great animal-watching bonanza climaxes at Ngorongoro Crater, a 19-km-wide caldera with one of Africa's greatest concentrations of wildlife.

Zanzibar

The gem of Tanzania's coast, Zanzibar Island's highlights include setting out on foot in ancient Stone Town where a maze of streets threads between buildings like paths in a narrow, twisting canyon; sniffing exotic spices like nutmeg, cinnamon and cardamom at one of the island's plantations, and snorkelling off any of the east-coast beaches, which are all protected by coral reefs.

✪ Best of the rest

Selous Game Reserve Lying at the heart of Tanzania's less-trodden southern safari circuit, Selous covers 45,000 sq km of plains, forests and hills – plenty of space for you to immerse yourself in the solitude of a true African wilderness. The handful of camps in the Selous are found mainly along the Rufiji River – the reserve's wildlife artery, pulsing with birds, hippo and crocodiles. Boat trips and walking safaris are a highlight of any visit.

Mahale Mountains National Park Tracking chimps in lush forest along the far-flung eastern shore of Lake Tanganyika is the highlight of a visit to this beautiful park. Members of the habituated Mimikire group are relaxed near human visitors, often enabling you to view them from close quarters. Minimum age for chimp tracking is 12.

☁ High ideals

★ It might look tempting, rising serenely above the savannah, but the 5895-m summit of Kilimanjaro is not something to set your sights on with young children in tow. Although non-technical, the return trek to the summit is a five-to-seven-day slog, fraught with possible fatigue, dehydration and mountain sickness. Fair enough if teenagers feel up to the challenge, but parents with determined younger children should stick to a two-day taster – hiking the lower stages of the Marangu Trail.

Zambia might not immediately strike you as being particularly family-friendly. However, don't let its reputation for posh lodges, private air charters and pricey five-star pampering put you off. There are some great options for family safaris in South Luangwa National Park ranging from reasonably priced self-catering camps to seriously expensive private safari houses. And then, of course, there's Victoria Falls. Over 100 m high, 1700 m wide and disgorging up to 550 million litres of water every minute, this World Heritage Site has become Africa's undisputed adventure capital.

Victoria Falls

Knife Edge Bridge leads to a spectacular viewpoint of the Eastern Cataracts, but be prepared to get soaked by spray. Victoria Falls National Park on the Zimbabwean side has more viewpoints, including Danger Point and Devil's Cataract.

Flight of the angels Getting airborne is the best way to fully appreciate the scale of this natural wonder. Choose from helicopters and fixed-wing Cessnas for flights with all the family, or microlights and ultralights for one lucky passenger (livingstonesadventure.com).

Whitewater rafting Downstream of the Falls, Terminator, Devil's Toilet Bowl, Gnashing Jaws of Death and other grade five rapids conspire to form the world's wildest one-day whitewater rafting experience. You get lifejackets, helmets, wetsuits and the reassurance that safety kayakers shoot the rapids first – so they're always waiting to help rafters who inadvertently find themselves taking a swim. Be prepared for the steep trek in and out of the gorge to the put-in and take-out points. The minimum age is 15. Operators include Bundu Adventures (bunduadventures.com) and Safari Par Excellence (safpar.net).

Bungee jumping Take a 111-m leap of faith from Victoria Falls Bridge for the ultimate adrenaline rush. If it's any comfort, the cord tied around your ankles has a breaking strain of 2000 kg. Bungee jumps can be booked through any of the adventure operators in Livingstone. Minimum age is 14. Abseiling (thezambeziswing.com) is also available.

Canoeing Gliding silently past herds of drinking elephants, pausing to study a colony of rainbow-hued bee-eaters and hauling out on uninhabited islands

for a well-earned picnic – paddling a canoe along the Upper Zambezi is one of those classic African adventures that perfectly combines the thrill of exploration with unrivalled wildlife viewing. Two-person, Canadian-style canoes or inflatable 'crocodile' canoes are stable and easy to manoeuvre, and you can choose either daytrips or overnight camping tours. The minimum age is 12.

Train rides The Victoria Falls Safari Express trundles back and forth between Livingstone and the bridge – a mini steam adventure for all ages.

Safaris Game drives in Mosi oa Tunya National Park often lead to close encounters with white rhino and other game, while elephant-back safaris from Thorntree River Lodge (minimum age 10) provide a unique perspective of the bush and a chance to learn about elephant behaviour and conservation. Horse riding (children under seven must have had at least one year of riding lessons) and quad biking (for 16-year-olds and over) are also available.

The Smoke that Thunders

Mosi-oa-Tunya, 'The Smoke that Thunders', was how the local Makololo people described Victoria Falls and explorers were equally spellbound. "Scenes so lovely must have been gazed upon by angels in their flight," wrote Dr David Livingstone when, in 1855, he became the first European to explore the area around the Falls.

Elephants dust bathing; below: leopard dropping (with undigested hooves of puku fawn); jackal print

66 99 **Every few minutes, our guide revealed a nugget of bushlore or identified a bird from the cacophony of calls. The graffiti of animal prints on the trails we followed were as clear to him as entries in a visitors' book.** William Gray

South Luangwa

Ranking alongside Africa's great wildlife wonders, like the Serengeti, Okavango and Etosha, South Luangwa National Park covers 9050 sq km of woodland, grassland and wetland – a veritable Eden, teeming with over 60 species of mammals, including around 15,000 elephant and one of Africa's densest leopard populations. Lion and hyena are also abundant, while antelopes (14 species in total) range from bushbuck and waterbuck to sable and roan.

Although traditional game drives are available here, it's the walking safari that has become synonymous with a visit to South Luangwa. Some lodges offer short morning or afternoon strolls, while others operate multi-day trails, linking rustic bush camps. Always accompanied by an expert guide and armed scout, these footloose forays into the bush fine-tune your senses to every crackle of leaf, whiff of dung or slightest movement. There is no better way to wise up on bushlore, hone your tracking skills or learn about the traditional uses of plants.

⊗ **Best** of the rest

Kafue National Park From the 'mini Serengeti' of Busanga Plains in the north to dense miombo woodland further south, Kafue has a wide range of bush camps and safari lodges. The Kafue River is a good place to look for hippo.

Kasanka National Park With its water-repellent fur, splayed hooves and ability to dive underwater when threatened, the sitatunga is a truly amphibious antelope – and there is no better place in Africa to see one than Kasanka, particularly if you spend time in the park's Fibwe Hide. Perched 18 m off the ground in a mahogany tree, the hide also offers spellbinding views of the mass exodus of a million straw-coloured fruit bats as they leave their roost in the swamp forest on nightly feeding forays (Nov-Dec).

Lower Zambezi National Park The gull-like cry of the African fish eagle is quintessential Lower Zambezi. You can often see the raptors perched on dead trees near the water's edge. Also look out for bee-eaters, kingfishers, egrets and storks, plus large herds of elephant wading in the river – preferably from the seat of a Canadian canoe being paddled gently along a backwater.

Inside info (i)

▶▶ **Warning!** At Victoria Falls there are few if any fences between you and the gorge.
▶▶ The Falls are impressive year-round, however spray during peak flood (Mar-Apr) can obscure views.
▶▶ Choose from accommodation in Livingstone or along the banks of the Zambezi upstream from the Falls.
▶▶ Most hotels can book any of the plethora of activities.

66 99 The sea was as smooth and blue as a royal sash – not the slightest breeze ruffled its surface. When flying fish began scattering before our wake they left glittering trails, like silver sparks from firework rockets. "Five!" shouted Ellie. "No way! That was easily a nine," countered her brother, Joe. Our seven-year-old twins were leaning over the railings of the *Cat Cocos* ferry, timing the airborne efforts of the flighty fish. By the time we reached Baie St Anne on the southern tip of Praslin (an hour's crossing from Mahé) they had unanimously declared a 15-second glide the outright winner.

Later that day, Joe and Ellie practised their snorkelling, floating over waist-deep seagrass meadows where bright yellow cowfish pirouetted amongst the swaying fronds. During our second day on Praslin, we decided to venture further offshore, snorkelling hand-in-hand around Chauvre Souris, a tiny island a few hundred metres from the beach. As the water deepened (and handholds tightened), seagrass gave way to jumbled boulders of granite encrusted with coral. The sea began to chatter with the clicking sounds of a myriad fish nibbling away at the reef. It was like floating in a giant bowl of Rice Krispies.

We went even further the next day, joining a boat trip to the isolated granite islets of St Pierre Marine Park where an eagle-spotted ray briefly joined the technicoloured procession of angelfish, surgeonfish and parrotfish. It was all going swimmingly until Ellie got zapped by a stinger. It only left a mild rash, but it was enough to put her off snorkelling for a day or two.

Fortunately, the Seychelles have several 'dry diversions', the foremost of which is the Vallée de Mai, a World Heritage-listed palm forest that's home to the indigenous coco de mer. Famous for its suggestive bi-lobed nut and metre-long stamen, the sexual connotations of the coco de mer are lost on children – especially when they learn that the Vallée de Mai is a remnant of the prehistoric forests that grew on Gondwanaland at the time of the dinosaurs. Joe and Ellie spent a rapt couple of hours exploring the forest trails, spotting geckos (the nearest thing you'll find to dinosaurs) and discussing whether a 30-kg coco de mer nut could poleaxe a T Rex.

Inevitably, we found ourselves back at the beach later that afternoon. Still wary of jellyfish, Ellie focused on building 'dribble castles', the cookie-mixture texture of Anse Lazio's legendary sands perfect for creating fairy-tale fortresses. William Gray

In a toddler's mind the difference, say between the beach at Lyme Regis in the UK and Beau Vallon in the Seychelles is probably minimal – both have sea to splash in and all the basic ingredients for building sandcastles. So, why bother hauling them all the way to the Indian Ocean? Well, for starters, the beaches of the Seychelles and Mauritius are some of the most idyllic and desirable in the world – something only parents might appreciate (but, hey, it's their holiday too). Beach bliss aside, though, these islands offer plenty in the way of gentle activities, from forest ambles to island hopping. And, if you have older kids with adventure on their minds, why not go lemur spotting in Madagascar?

Grand Anse, La Digue, Seychelles

The Seychelles

Never mind the private islands, posh resorts and swanky spas. Through the eyes of a child, the Seychelles promise the ultimate tropical island adventure. You'll find less in the way of kids' clubs, crèches and watersports here than on Mauritius, the default all-inclusive choice for family holidays in the Indian Ocean. But that's exactly what makes the Seychelles so appealing – the emphasis is on getting out and exploring rather than being based in a resort where days become mapped out by the schedules of onsite clubs. With over 100 irresistible islands to choose from, the Seychelles are almost too much of a good thing. However, unless you have serious cash to splash, focus on Mahé, Praslin and La Digue, with an excursion to either Aride or Cousin Island.

Mahé The best family beach is Beau Vallon, a long curving scimitar of sand that's sheltered from the May-Sep trade winds and has no strong currents. Spend a day in the Baie Ternay Marine National Park where even toddlers can get a glimpse of the corals and fishes on a glass-bottom boat trip. Away from the coast, hike the Trois Frères trail through cool montane forest in Morne Seychellois National Park.

Praslin For beach perfection head to Anse Lazio. Then go nuts at Vallée de Mai, famed for its rare coco de mer palms that can produce nuts weighing 30 kg. Keep an eye out for black parrots, unique to Praslin. For the ultimate avian encounter, join a tour to either Aride or Cousin Island. Hundreds of thousands of seabirds nest on these specks of land, along with rare endemic species like the Seychelles warbler and magpie robin. Neither island has a jetty, so be prepared to carry youngsters ashore.

La Digue Backed by rounded pink boulders and lapped by emerald waters, Anse Source d'Argent consistently ranks in the world's top 10 beaches. But tear yourself away for at least one afternoon of exploring La Digue by bicycle (hire them at the pier when you arrive) or ox cart – and pedal over the island to the equally sensational Grand Anse.

Mauritius

If you want nothing more than a comfortable resort (complete with kids' club), a sandy beach and safe, shallow seas, then Mauritius is hard to beat – especially if you're travelling with tots. However, if all-inclusive resort packages sound too pricey, there are plenty of guesthouses and apartments for independent-minded families.

Madagascar

For a typical two week trip, your best bet is to focus on the north of the island where you can combine some of the most accessible wildlife reserves with time out on the beach. From the capital, Antananarivo (or 'Tana'), it's a three-hour drive to Andasibe where it's eyes (and ears) open for the indri. The eerie wailing call of this large black and white lemur with its teddy bear face can carry for over 3 km – so you'll probably hear one before you see it. From Tana, fly north to Diego Suarez from where it's a short drive to Ankarana reserve – home to no fewer than 10 species of lemur, including the shy, nocturnal aye-aye. Nearby Nosy Be is Madagascar's most popular beach destination and the starting point for boat trips to Nosy Tanikely (for snorkelling) and Nosy Komba (for black lemurs).

Inside info

▶▶ In the Seychelles July and August are the driest, busiest and most expensive months. Try Mar-Apr and Oct-Nov when it's quieter.
▶▶ Accommodation ranges from top-end resorts to self-catering guesthouses.
▶▶ Save money by using the ferry to island hop between Mahé, Praslin and La Digue.
▶▶ In Madagascar, your best chance of spotting lemurs is on foot – walking trails can take 3 hours. Avoid Jan-Mar when heavy rain makes travel difficult; May-Oct is coolest. Unlike the Seychelles and Mauritius, Madagascar is a malaria area.

When it comes to family holidays in southern Africa, the Cape will always have the lion's share. It's got everything from charismatic Cape Town to malaria-free game reserves in the Eastern Cape. So why take your kids to Namibia instead? Well, for starters it has lots in common with its southern neighbour – direct flights from Europe, guaranteed sunshine, good infrastructure and loads to do for all ages. But add to the equation Namibia's haunting emptiness, fantasy landscapes and a sandpit the size of a desert and you have a family adventure that leaves the Cape looking rather tame. What's more, planning a family trip to Namibia is a piece of cake – just slice your itinerary into three chunks: desert, coast and safari.

The Namib Desert

Windhoek is pleasant enough, but there's little in Namibia's capital that's going to rivet your kids – unless, that is, they have a leaning towards German colonial architecture. And besides, you've come this far, so why not make straight for the desert.

Fly or drive Namibia is perfect for self-drive – distances are great, but roads are well-maintained and traffic is light. You don't need 4WD, but always think twice about passing a fuel station without stopping to fill up. It may be some time before you pass another! Allow five hours to drive from Windhoek to Sesriem, the gateway to the classic desert scenery of Sossusvlei. If you're short on time (but not cash) hop straight on to a chartered six-seater Cessna bound for the NamibRand Nature Reserve (namibrand.com) – a 1800-sq-km swathe of mountains, dunes and grass-gilded plains to the south of Sesriem. The spectacular flight from Windhoek takes just over an hour.

Desert activities Guides can tailor outings to suit children aged five and up. Bring 16-year-olds here and they'll be off on the quad bikes before you can blink the sand from your eyes. Hot-air balloon flights (namibsky.com) are also a guaranteed hit with older children (minimum height 130 cm). Even with much younger kids, you can explore springbok-dotted plains and study porcupine droppings and the S-bend tracks of horned adders. There are skittish beetles and 'sand-swimming' lizards to chase, strange outcrops (or kopjes) of granite boulders to conquer and, best of all, the sheer, unabashed exhilaration of running barefoot through the Namib Desert with a kite in tow.

Don't miss a day trip to Sossusvlei for quintessential

Picnic on the Skeleton Coast

Turnstone Tours tame Namibia's notorious coast on their superb 4WD safaris.

desert scenery in the heart of the vast Namib Naukluft National Park. Youngsters probably won't stand in awe of the record-breaking 380-m-high dunes for long – or appreciate the subtle play of light and shadow across their scalloped flanks. To your average kid (grown-up or otherwise), Sossusvlei means one thing: roly-poly heaven. It might take them a good half-hour to walk, crawl and stagger to the crest of one of the giant dunes – but barely 30 seconds to somersault, slide and tumble down again. For days afterwards they'll be picking sand from their pockets, ears, hair, noses...

Skeleton Coast

Namibia's surf-ravaged Skeleton Coast calms down at Swakopmund (a two-hour flight from the NamibRand). Instead of rusting shipwrecks, whale carcasses and the kind of desolate wilderness that nearly forced British explorer Benedict Allen to eat his camels, you'll find a quirky seaside resort with everything from sandcastles to fish and chips. True, it's not as pretty as Plettenberg Bay on South Africa's Garden Route, and the water definitely feels like it's come straight from Antarctica, courtesy of the Benguela Current – but that won't stop children shrieking with joy for an afternoon or two as they play chicken with the waves.

Things to do in town Swakopmund Museum (swakopmund-museum.de) may well be your best chance in Namibia to see, albeit stuffed, examples of nocturnal critters like the porcupine and aardvark, while Kristall Galerie has some whopping great quartz clusters and a scratch pit where you can search for semi-precious stones.

Sossusvlei roly-poly

Giant dunes at Sossusvlei

Adventure activities Once you've relaxed in Swakopmund for a day or two, you'll be wanting to hit the adventure trail again. Activities include everything from sky diving and paragliding to sandboarding and kayaking. If you book just one activity, however, make sure it's a 4WD outing to Sandwich Harbour with Turnstone Tours (turnstone-tours.com). Their guides not only know the ecology and history of the Skeleton Coast intimately (and are great at engaging children of all ages), but their driving skills will transform your daytrip into one long thrill ride.

Hemmed in by towering dunes on one side and ocean breakers on the other, you'll find yourself racing the incoming tide along a beach riddled with quicksand and the occasional corpse of a turtle or seabird. As well as tracking jackals and spotting seals, the undisputed highlight of the trip is the 'singing dunes'. Riding the roller coaster of the desert, your guide will cut the engine and let the Land Rover slide down the scarp slope of a particularly huge dune. As sand starts to avalanche and resonate beneath its wheels the desert hums. It's a magical, surreal experience. Don't forget to get out of the vehicle and try it on your bottom!

Namibia safari

Etosha National Park Home to large numbers of big game (including lion, leopard, elephant, black and white rhino, giraffe and zebra), Etosha is designed for visitors to drive themselves around. Independent-minded families will find inexpensive restcamps with good facilities, such as bungalows with small kitchens, a shop for basic supplies and a swimming pool.

Caprivi Strip This is the least travelled safari option and involves the greatest distance – not ideal if your kids get fractious on long car journeys. However, by striking eastwards to the Caprivi Strip, you not only experience a green and verdant side to Namibia that's a wonderful contrast to the desert, but you can also round off your trip with a few days at Victoria Falls. Be aware, though, that malaria is present in northern and eastern parts of Namibia, particularly from November to June. Some lodges, like Lianshulu in Mundulu National Park, have a minimum age limit of 12.

Waterberg Plateau About half way between Windhoek and Etosha, the Waterberg has malaria-free game reserves. Safaris here are gentle, subtle affairs where you might stake out a waterhole, waiting for the resident rhinos to appear, or join a game drive to spot regional rarities, such as sable antelope.

Okonjima An option for families with children aged 12 or over, Okonjima guest farm (okonjima.com) is home to the Africat Foundation – renowned for its work to safeguard Namibia's cheetahs, leopards, lions and caracals. As well as its main camp, Okonjima has a luxurious family villa with its own chef, guide, 4WD vehicle and pool. Activities range from cheetah tracking to learning about Bushmen traditions.

Mundulea Nature Reserve For more adventurous families, this 120-sq-km private reserve in the Otavi Mountains offers wonderful four-day walking trails, spending nights in tented camps with bucket showers. It's a superb opportunity to gain an intimate insight into Namibian wildlife and bushlore with Bruno Nebe – one of the most knowledgeable and enthusiastic guides in the business.

☺ More adventure

★ **Damaraland** Rugged scenery and a great location for overland camping trips. Track black rhinos and rare desert elephant, see Bushmen rock art sites, hunt for gems and visit a fossilized forest. Camps like Etendeka have expert guides who will take you on wildlife walks and drives.

★ **Fish River Canyon** (pictured) Are you up for the challenge of a five-day trek through the world's second largest canyon? Arrange a guide and book permits for May-Sep when it's coolest. Or just admire the views.

G ive Africa a good shake, leave to stand a while and let all the best bits settle at the bottom. It's almost as if South Africa has distilled everything that is thrilling and remarkable about the continent. You might find wilder national parks in Zambia, the wildebeest migration in Tanzania or emptier roads in Namibia, but the Rainbow Nation's irresistible lure lies in its sheer diversity. You've got Cape Town – right up there with other urban beauties like Sydney and Vancouver. You've got vast swathes of wilderness, stunning wildlife, superb food, great places to stay, and, best of all for families, you've got plenty to keep you busy. Boredom simply is not an option – not in a country where, in the same day, you can stand on top of Table Mountain, swim with wild penguins and then tuck into a plate of good old-fashioned fish and chips.

Cape Town

Day one First, take a peek at Table Mountain. If you can see the top, go for it. A frothy layer of cloud (known locally as the 'tablecloth') can obscure the 1073-m high icon for days on end, so you should aim to get up there at the first clear opportunity. The Cableway (tablemountain.net) features a revolving floor – ensuring everyone can enjoy the spectacular views of Cape Town and Table Bay. At the top, allow two hours to walk to all 11 viewpoints (the paths are stroller-friendly). Keep an eye out for dassies.

Day two Head for the Victoria & Alfred Waterfront (waterfront.co.za) where you can explore a restored historic dockland and spot fur seals hauled out on the boardwalks. Next, take a ferry to Robben Island (robben-island.org.za). The three-hour trip includes a fascinating tour of the prison by past inmates. You'll be able to peek into Nelson Mandela's cell and see the lime quarry where he, and other prisoners, toiled during their incarceration at the hands of South Africa's brutal apartheid regime. It's all serious, hard-hitting stuff, so if you have young children, stick to the Waterfront and visit the impressive Two Oceans Aquarium (aquarium.co.za) instead. Here you can get nose-to-nose with ragged-tooth sharks in the two-million-litre predator tank and stroke crabs in the touch pool. In the afternoon, take your pick of Cape Town's excellent beaches – the best ones are at Clifton and Camp's Bay, but be warned: the water's chilly! Children aged four or more will enjoy the interactive exhibits at the Telkom Exploratorium, while the SA Museum and Planetarium (museums.org.za), with

its four-storey whale hall and dinosaur displays, will appeal to all ages.

Day three Get an early start for a spectacular tour of the Cape Peninsula. First, drive south to Simon's Town where the African penguins at Boulders (sanparks. org) will keep you spellbound for hours. A boardwalk leads to the heart of the 3000-strong colony at Foxy Beach – a wonderful spectacle, but a beach that is strictly for the birds. You'll find a less frustrating option for children at adjacent Boulders Beach where they can build sandcastles and if they're lucky, swim with a penguin or two. Continue south to Cape Point and the Cape of Good Hope where from August to December you can spot southern right whales in the sea 200 m below. Head north back towards Cape Town along Chapman's Peak Drive (a breathtaking 10 km route etched into sea cliffs). Detour to Kirstenbosch Botanical Gardens (sanbi.org) where children can burn energy in the ample open spaces, then dawdle back to the city, stopping for fish and chips at Camps Bay.

The Garden Route

With its sandy beaches, family resorts and countless tourist attractions, the Garden Route is unashamedly the Cape's holiday hotspot. From west to east, these are the highlights that should feature on your itinerary:

Mossel Bay If you've driven straight from Cape Town along the N2 you will be more than ready for a break at this gateway town to the Garden Route. Head to Santos Beach for swimming or take a one-hour boat trip to Seal Island to view the whales, dolphins, seals

Conquering Table Mountain

You can climb Cape Town's iconic mountain, but the Aerial Cableway is a somewhat easier route to the summit.

Two Oceans Aquarium

Bottlenose dolphins leaping through the backs of breakers at Plettenberg Bay

and seabirds that inhabit Mossel Bay. The Bartholomeu Dias Maritime Museum contains a replica of the ship used by the Portuguese navigator when he stopped here in 1488 to take on fresh water.

Wilderness National Park A network of rivers, lakes and estuaries, Wilderness supports 79 of South Africa's 95 species of water bird. Hire a canoe at Ebb & Flow South Camp and paddle through this watery maze for a spot of twitching. Easy ticks include yellow-billed ducks and redknobbed coots cruising open water, weaverbirds fussing about in reedbeds and the neat 'plop' as a pied kingfisher dives for fish. Extra points for a fish eagle or the dazzling malachite kingfisher.

Knysna Protected by pincer headlands, the large lagoon at Knysna was originally developed as a shipbuilding and timber port. Today, it is the epicentre of Garden Route tourism, offering everything from scuba-diving to oyster-slurping. The Outeniqua Choo-Tjoe steam train runs between here and George and there are also cruises on the lagoon and good family dining at Knysna Quays. However, two of the most popular kids' attractions lie between Knysna and Plettenberg Bay. At Monkeyland (monkeyland. co.za) you can explore a 23-ha sanctuary and cross a 120-m-long rope bridge in search of no less than 14 species of free-swinging primates. Almost as much fun are the squirty water bottles provided at the open-air restaurant to deter mischievous marmosets from making off with your lunch. Nearby, the Elephant Sanctuary (elephantsanctuary.co.za) and Knysna Elephant Park (knysnaelephantpark.co.za) offer walking tours with jumbos and a chance to learn about Africa's

most southerly pachyderm population. The wooded hinterland of the Garden Route was once a stronghold for elephants, but now only a few survive in the wild.

Plettenberg Bay Plett's marine life is legendary and although you can catch tantalizing glimpses from headlands and beaches, you need to get afloat to really appreciate it. Cleaving the surf in a dramatic beach launching, a boat trip (oceanadventures. co.za) will get you up-close and personal with seals lolling around Robberg Peninsula and pods of 150+ bottlenose dolphins leaping through the curling, turquoise walls of huge rollers. Horse riding, sea kayaking and skydiving are also available, while a surf school caters to all abilities.

Nature's Valley Heaven for shell-seekers, this quiet hamlet nestles behind a beach strewn with all sorts of tidal goodies. Pink and mauve urchins stud rock pools like designer pincushions, while a dense forest dripping with old man's beard runs riot behind the beach. Pack a picnic and go exploring.

Tsitsikamma National Park Watch surf bloom four storeys high before hiking the easy 1-km boardwalk to the suspension bridge over Storms River Mouth. You can learn about the native plants from interpretation boards along the way.

Jeffrey's Bay Famed for Supertubes (once described as 'the most perfect wave in the world'), J-Bay is South Africa's surfing Mecca. Teenagers, in particular, will love its 'happening' vibe and there's no better place in the country to hone your surf style (infojeffreysbay.com).

Inside info

▸▸ Flights from Europe to Cape Town take 10-11 hours, but most are direct, you'll arrive early morning and only have to adjust to GMT+2.
▸▸ Good roads make touring a breeze.
▸▸ Seek local advice before swimming – several beaches have strong riptides or surf.
▸▸ For malaria-free safaris, stick to the game reserves of Madikwe, Pilanesberg and the Eastern Cape; for nature on a grander scale head to Kruger – but be prepared to take malaria protection.

To put it bluntly, money and malaria are the main deciding factors when it comes to choosing a family safari in South Africa. Stick to malaria-free zones and your choice is limited mainly to the Eastern Cape and a handful of game reserves northwest of Johannesburg, such as Madikwe. Feels a bit like drawing the short straw? Don't believe it. Kruger National Park may be big and famous, but that doesn't mean you'll see less or have a 'tamer' experience in smaller, malaria-free reserves like Shamwari and Kwandwe. These, and other Eastern Cape reserves, not only boast the big five – elephant, rhino, lion, buffalo and leopard – but a wide range of other large mammals, such as giraffe, cheetah and zebra.

However, don't get too obsessed with ticking off the cast of *The Lion King*. A safari has as much to do with small wonders. A good guide will have a knack for intriguing and informing children – drip-feeding them nuggets of bushlore, like the reason woodpeckers don't get headaches, why warthogs run with their tails in the air and how termites protect themselves from sunburn. You'll study animal tracks around waterholes, decipher the calls of birds and discover extraordinary treasures like a shed cobra skin turned inside out or the egg cocoon of a praying mantis which the female fashions from her spit. The secret to a successful family safari is to take your time and encourage children to tune into the subtleties of the bush.

Addo Elephant National Park Just 72 km north of Port Elizabeth, this is an excellent option for families on a budget (and makes a great extension to the Garden Route). You can drive yourself around the 120,000-ha reserve, but for added value, pick up a 'hop-on ranger' at the gate. He'll be able to show you the best spots and advise on 'ele-etiquette' in the likely event of a close encounter with one of Addo's 300 or so jumbos. Walking is prohibited except at designated points.

Kwandwe Game Reserve A 20,000-ha wilderness just north of Grahamstown, Kwandwe's Uplands Homestead offers private family accommodation with a dedicated chef, safari vehicle and guide. Just as wonderfully decadent is the reserve's Ecca Lodge with its contemporary and minimalist styling – perfect for parents who might be stressed-out by more traditional safari lodges with their baskets of ostrich egg shells and vases of porcupine quills.

Shamwari Game Reserve Another top-end reserve, Shamwari is famous for its work with the Born

Free Foundation to rehabilitate big cats. Long Lee Manor, with its family suites, is your best option for somewhere to stay.

Madikwe Game Reserve A three-hour drive northwest of Johannesburg, malaria-free Madikwe is home to the supremely family-friendly Jaci's Safari Lodge. Not only do Jaci's welcome kids of all ages, but they also organize special children's safaris for 3-12 year-olds with activities such as detective trails, animal tracking, touch tables and river safaris. Infants under two even get taken on their own 'jungle drives' – shorter than your typical game drive and specially tailored to suit their interest levels.

Kruger National Park There are several magnificent, all-inclusive camps in game reserves along Kruger's western boundary, but many won't accept children under 12. Those that do, such as Sabi Sabi, restrict game drives to children over six unless the family can arrange exclusive use of a safari vehicle. Many families find a more free-spirited (and cheaper) option is to drive themselves around Kruger, staying in the park's many self-catering restcamps. Many, like Olifants, have a restaurant, swimming pool and guided game-viewing.

On the game trail

A late afternoon game drive in Madikwe Game Reserve.

🏖 Beach guide

★ KwaZulu Natal has miles of sandy beaches, but take time to pick one that suits the age of your children. South of Durban, Marina Beach is good for younger children since the surf is usually restrained and there are plenty of tidal pools. North of Durban, Willard Beach is also popular with families. For surfing your best bet is shark-netted Umhlanga Rocks where you can also go whale watching and kite surfing. If you want lots to do off the beach, base yourself in Durban itself, which has a Sea World park.

Drakensberg

⊗ **Best** of the rest

Drakensberg You can abseil off Table Mountain and ride an ostrich in the Karoo, but for South Africa's greatest concentration of adventure activities head for the Drakensberg. Merely sighting the 700-m-high rampart of the Amphitheatre in Royal Natal National Park is enough to get the adrenaline pumping. Hike the Sentinel Trail, then raft the Tugela River as it pounds its way along a 22-km stretch of rapids with enticing names like Horrible Horace and Whiplash Smile. Mountain biking and horse riding allow you to probe hidden corners of the Drakensberg and, for a vulture's eye-view, nothing beats a spot of tandem paragliding. Get airborne at Arthur's Seat in the Central Berg.

Whale watching Africa's most family-friendly whale watching can be found at Hermanus just over an hour's drive east from Cape Town. You don't even need to get in a boat to view southern right whales which come close inshore between Nov-Mar. However, boat trips from Kleinbaai with Dyer Island Cruises (dyer-island-cruises. co.za) have the added advantage of potential great white shark sightings and the wonderfully smelly spectacle of 60,000 fur seals at Dyer Island.

Elephant-back safaris Ride atop a jumbo in Letsatsing Game Reserve (Pilanesberg National Park) near Sun City, swaying in a padded saddle 3 m above ground, pausing occasionally to outstare giraffe, zebra and rhino.

Horse riding safaris Saddle up at Ant's Nest, a 1,500-ha private game reserve in the malaria-free Waterberg, north of Johannesburg, stocked with white rhino, giraffe, zebra and a variety of antelope.

Elephant safaris, Pilanesberg National Park

Horse riding at Ant's Nest

When to go

The most comfortable periods to visit **North Africa** are March to May and September to November. In mid-summer it can be unbearably hot, even for flopping at a Red Sea resort. Don't be tempted by cheap deals in July and August – your kids will fry – and remember that during Ramadan many restaurants and cafés close.

In **East Africa** there's no bad time to visit Kenya or Tanzania, although if possible try to avoid the rainy season from late March to June when some camps and lodges close. It gets busy between December and February, so consider a trip in the quieter and cooler shoulder season, July to October.

Most people visit **Zambia** during the dry season from May to November – although both the Zambezi and Luangwa Valley can become swelteringly hot towards the end of this period. Victoria Falls are impressive year-round, although thick spray can obscure views during peak flood, March to April.

Apart from avoiding the cyclone season (December to March), the **Indian Ocean** islands are pleasant to visit anytime. Likewise, **Namibia** has an idyllic climate – warm and dry with plenty of sunshine. You may want to avoid the summer months (December to March), when temperatures can rocket to over 40°C. The best time to enjoy the Cape beaches of **South Africa** is during the warm summer months, December to April, while the drier winter period (June to September) offers the best wildlife viewing and lowest malaria risk in Kruger National Park.

Getting there

With international airline hubs at cities like Cairo, Nairobi, Johannesburg and Cape Town, reaching Africa is straightforward. From America, flights are usually routed through Europe, while Australian flights have connections in the Middle East. Charter flights operate between Europe and popular African destinations during peak seasons. African airlines include Egyptair (egyptair.com), Royal Air Maroc (royalairmaroc.com), Kenya Airways (kenya-airways.com), Air Namibia (airnamibia.com.na) and South African Airways (flysaa.com).

Getting around

You'll find everything from charter flights, private 4WD vehicles and luxury trains to horse-drawn carts, camels and overcrowded, accident-prone minibuses. For independence in southern Africa a **self-drive** is the way to go. Major car and campervan rental companies can be found in cities like Cape Town and Windhoek. Be sure to factor in the additional costs of a one-way rental. Roads in South Africa and Namibia are uncrowded and well maintained – note that your insurance may not cover you on gravel tracks. Long-distance bus touring is a more economical, but less flexible, way of covering a lot of ground. Reputable operators include Intercape Mainliner and Greyhound.

In East and North Africa, **organized tours** and **safaris** fall into two main categories: package and tailor-made. The latter are obviously more expensive, but they do allow you full control of your plans. If you opt for a package, be sure to find out what's included. A 'bargain' may conceal hidden extras, such as national park fees. On cheap tours you could also be fighting for window seats in a crowded vehicle or be frustrated by a driver-guide who is more 'driver' than 'guide'.

Accommodation

You will find international hotel chains in **Egypt** – all offering high quality accommodation and swimming pools. On the Red Sea coast there is no shortage of resorts and hotels geared towards families. The Hilton Dahab Resort (hilton.com), for example, has a kids' club for 3-17 year-olds, a crèche and activities ranging from camel treks to learning to dive at the PADI Gold Palm Centre.

In **Morocco**, try to spend at least one night in a riad – a traditional house surrounding a central courtyard. In Marrakech, for example, Les Jardins de la Medina (lesjardinsdelamedina.com) is a short walk from Djemmaa el Fna and has a swimming pool for relaxing in after a morning at the souks.

Tanzania's best family-friendly accommodation is on Zanzibar where you'll find everything from the resort-style Breezes Beach Club (breezes-zanzibar.com) to the educational, eco-sensitive Chumbe Island (chumbeisland.com). A few safari camps, such as Sand Rivers (nomad-tanzania.com) in Tanzania's Selous Game Reserve, welcome children over eight.

Kenya's Heritage camps and lodges (heritage-eastafrica.com) are also renowned for their children's programmes. Another name to look out for is Cheli & Peacock (chelipeacock.com) which has properties like Elsa's Kopje (with its family cottage, swimming pool and guided walks with the Maasai) and Loisaba (nestled in the rugged Laikipia Plateau and famed for its Starbeds which can be rolled out into the open. The classic and luxurious Governors' Camps (governorscamp.com) in the Masai Mara welcome families, as do Kicheche Camps (kicheche.com). On the Kenyan coast you will find numerous resorts, including Turtle Bay Beach Club (turtlebay.co.ke) and Leopard Beach Resort (leopardbeachresort.com).

Wilderness Safaris (wilderness-safaris.com) has numerous properties in southern and East Africa, some with interlinking family rooms and tents. Generally, the minimum age is eight.

Formerly known as CC Africa, &Beyond (andbeyond.com) may be renowned for luxurious safari camps and lodges, but that doesn't mean kids are taboo. In fact, several of their properties, including Madikwe Safari Lodge in South Africa and Kichwa Tembo in Kenya, offer special environmental programmes for children. Activities can range from bug collecting to fishing and bark rubbing.

For beach bliss in the **Seychelles** and **Mauritius**, just about every resort has a kids' club, swimming pool and copious watersports. Two that should receive emphatic thumbs up are Iles des Palmes (beachbungalow.sc) on Praslin and the impeccable Le Saint Géran (oneandonlyresorts.com) on the east coast of Mauritius. For ultimate style, however, the incomparable North Island (north-island.com) in the Seychelles offers tailor-made family activities, such as private picnics, treasure hunts, and fishing trips.

In **Zambia**, the Zambezi Sun (suninternational. co.za) is within earshot of the Falls and has a superb family pool, plus loads to keep kids entertained. Elsewhere in Zambia, relatively few safari camps and lodges are genuinely child-friendly. One of the, albeit expensive, exceptions is Safari Houses (safarihouses. com), a portfolio of sensational private properties with their own safari vehicle, guide and chef.

In **Namibia**, most lodges and guestfarms welcome children. There is also a good choice of guesthouses at Swakopmund, such as Sam's Giardino (giardinonamibia.com).

With its thriving domestic tourism, **South Africa** has a huge range of accommodation options. For an overview, check out The Portfolio Collection (portfoliocollection.co.za) which lists everything from city hotels to guesthouses.

Food & drink

If you're staying at a major hotel, resort or safari lodge there should be enough familiar foods available to satisfy even fussy feeders. But no visit to Africa is complete without sampling some local delicacies. Browse any North African market, for example, and you'll find plenty of nuts, dried fruits and other high-energy snacks. Hearty traditional dishes range from South African *potjiekos* to Moroccan tagines (both variations on a meat and vegetable stew). Then there's the wonderful seafood, from fish and chips in Cape Town to prawn coconut curry on the East African coast. Meat-eaters meanwhile can munch their way through half the mammal kingdom in East and southern Africa – try biltong (chewy strips of spicy, cured game meat), ostrich steaks and Kenya's *nyama choma* (roast goat or chicken). Fresh fruits, including countless varieties of banana, are commonplace, as is the African staple mash made from maize meal, water and salt. If you get the chance, try termites – the large winged varieties are tasty sautéd with a pinch of salt.

Health & safety

Malaria is endemic to most of sub-Saharan Africa and it is crucial that you take precautions against this potentially fatal disease. Discuss malaria prevention with your doctor well before you travel. You should also plan an appropriate course of vaccinations.

Tap **water** is generally not safe for drinking except in South Africa and Namibia. If in doubt always assume the worst and take appropriate measures.

Wildlife is often perceived as the most obvious threat to travellers in Africa. Few safari camps and lodges have fences, which means potentially dangerous animals are free to come and go. Stay calm and keep a respectful distance and you should be perfectly safe. Young children, however, who can be unpredictable and easily excitable, might alarm some animals (or arouse the predatory instinct in others) and that is when danger can arise. For this reason, camps generally have a minimum age limit.

In terms of personal **safety**, most visits to wildlife reserves and other tourist areas are trouble-free, but as with anywhere in the world, you should be particularly vigilant in cities. In addition to taking normal security precautions to deter opportunistic criminals, you should check with your hotel if you are in any doubt as to the safety of an area.

Fast facts					
Country	Time	Language*	Currency	Code	Tourist information
Egypt	GMT+2	Arabic	Egyptian pound	+20	touregypt.net
Morocco	GMT	Arabic	Dirham	+212	visitmorocco.org
Kenya	GMT+3	Swahili	Kenyan shilling	+254	magicalkenya.com
Tanzania	GMT+3	Swahili	Tanzanian shilling	+255	tanzaniatouristboard.com
Zambia	GMT+2	Bemba	Kwacha	+260	zambiatourism.com
Seychelles	GMT+4	French	Seychelles rupee	+248	seychelles.travel
Mauritius	GMT+4	French	Mauritius rupee	+230	mauritius.net
Namibia	GMT+1	English	Namibian dollar	+264	namibiatourism.com
South Africa	GMT+2	Afrikaans, Ndebele	Rand	+27	southafrica.net
* English also widely spoken					

Sossusvlei Desert Lodge

Where? NamibRand Nature Reserve, Namibia.
Why? Located near the spectacular Sossusvlei dunes and offering nature drives, desert picnics and quad biking, this stylish stone and glass lodge even has its own stargazing observatory. Inside each chic suite, skylights provide a mesmerizing alternative to bedtime stories, while a small pool offers welcome respite from the heat.
Contact &Beyond, T+27 (0)11-809 4300, andbeyondafrica.com

Zambezi Sun

Where? Livingstone, Zambia.
Why? Sister property to the upmarket Royal Livingstone Hotel, the 212-room Zambezi Sun has a fun and lively atmosphere with plenty of activities for children (nature walks, crafts etc) and a wonderful landscaped swimming and outdoor restaurant. Victoria Falls is just a short walk away and there's an adventure shop for arranging activities.
Contact Sun International, T+27 (0)11-780 7810, suninternational.com

Jaci's Safari Lodge

Where? Madikwe Game Reserve, South Africa.
Why? A suspended walkway leads to the entrance of this rustic concoction of canvas, stone and thatch where spacious family tents have a monkey's-eye view through a dense grove of tamboti trees. Kids love the rope swing, swimming pool and riverside walk to a wildlife-viewing hide. Special game drives are available for youngsters.
Contact Jaci's Lodges, T+27 (0)83-700 2071, madikwe.com

Cape Grace Hotel

Where? Cape Town, South Africa.
Why? A boutique hotel with a great location on the V&A Waterfront, the Cape Grace has luxurious two- and three-bedroom family apartments (with kitchens). Kids receive welcome baskets stuffed with goodies and there's also African story telling, gingerbread decorating, and a children's menu. A spa, fine dining and luxury private yacht are some of the adult perks.
Contact Cape Grace, T+27 (0)21-410 7100, capegrace.com

Mara Intrepids

Where? Masai Mara National Reserve, Kenya.
Why? With two-bedroom family tents and a spacious lounge overlooking the Mara's Talek River, this superb camp boasts the highly acclaimed Adventurers' Club for kids aged 4-12 and Young Rangers' Club for teenagers. Both offer fantastic cultural and wilderness-based activities, from bush survival to making casts of big cat tracks.
Contact Heritage Hotels, T+254 (0)20-444 6651, heritage-eastafrica.com

Tangala House

Where? Near Livingstone, Upper Zambezi, Zambia.
Why? One of Zambia's sensational Safari Houses, riverside Tangala comes with its own 4WD vehicle, guide and chef. Other properties in the portfolio include Luangwa Safari House in South Luangwa National Park.
Contact Safari Houses, T+265 (0)17 70540, safarihouses.com

66 99 **When it comes to blissful beach holidays, Mauritius is a no-brainer (great weather, warm seas, no jet lag), but choosing the perfect resort is not so easy. To make life simpler, Beachcomber (pioneers of the island's hotel industry) have a family holiday section featuring the choicest properties.** beachcombertours.co.uk, 101familyholidays.co.uk

Kurland Hotel

Where? Garden Route, South Africa.
Why? This Cape Dutch-style hotel is set in its own polo estate. Kids are spoilt rotten with free access to the kitchen for cookies and ice creams, a walled play area with jungle gym and pool, a huge playroom with pool table and home cinema, plus activities such as horse riding and tennis. Cottages have loft rooms specially designed for children.
Contact Kurland, T+27 (0)44-534 8082, kurland.co.za

Ant's Nest

Where? Waterberg, Limpopo, South Africa.
Why? Where once there was little more than a dilapidated tin-roofed farm shack, the eight-bed thatched masterpiece of this stunning bush home rises above landscaped lawns and a large outdoor heated swimming pool. Located in a private game reserve, Ant's Nest offers delicious home cooking and child-friendly horse riding and game drives.
Contact The Ant Collection, T+27 (0)81-572 2624, waterberg.net

Leopard Beach Resort

Where? Diani Beach, Kenya.
Why? Perched right above the white sands and turquoise lagoon of Diani Beach, south of Mombasa, the 155-room Leopard Beach Resort and Spa has excellent family facilities, including a fabulous pool, beach-side pizzeria, watersports centre, glass-bottom boat and snorkelling trips and a lively programme of evening entertainment.
Contact Leopard Beach Resort and Spa, T+254 (0)40-320 2721, leopardbeachresort.com

A Tent with a View

Where? Saadani National Park, Tanzania.
Why? Scattered along a pristine stretch of Indian Ocean shoreline, this unique camp combines a safari and beach holiday. Its six suites and nine bandas peek through coconut palms to the sea. Elephants roam the beach, while nearby Madete Marine Reserve is a turtle nesting site. Heading inland on foot, by boat or 4WD, you can see a variety of big game.
Contact A Tent with a View, T+255 (0)22-211 0507, saadani.com

Asia

Top tips

Plucking tea leaves on a plantation in southern India. Right: Colourful carving of a Thai dragon.

1 Float in the Dead Sea
➤ Jordan, page 248

3 Track a wild tiger
➤ India & Nepal, pages 251 & 255

5 Walk the Great Wall of China
➤ China, page 256

2 Be transfixed by the Taj Mahal
➤ India, page 250

4 Trek in the Himalaya
➤ Nepal, page 254

6 See the big city lights
➤ Hong Kong & Singapore, pages 258 & 259

Caucasus

Aral Sea

MONGOLIA

Caspian Sea

Gobi Desert

Highest mountain
Mt Everest
8850 m

Yangshuo

Tigris

1 ■ **AMMAN**
JORDAN

Euphrates

CHINA

Xi'an

The Gulf

Plateau of Tibet

Yangtze

Red Sea

Dubai ○

Indus

H
i
m
a
l
a
y
a

Mt Everest

DELHI □

Agra ○

NEPAL

3

4

□ **MUSCAT**
OMAN

2 ★ **KATHMANDU**

Ganga

Brahmaputra

HANOI □

Kolkata ○

Arabian Sea

INDIA

Mekong

Chiang Mai ○

Mumbai ○

Bay of Bengal

THAILAND

BANGKOK □

PHNOM PENH

CAMBODIA

Malabar Coast

○ Chennai

◉ **Did** you know?
★ Ice cream was invented in China around 2000 BC.
★ Arulanantham Suresh Joachim from Sri Lanka holds the world record for standing on one foot – 76 hours and 40 minutes.
★ With no less than 170 letters, Bangkok's full ceremonial title is the world's longest place name.
★ The world's largest underground chamber, the Sarawak Chamber in Gunung Mulu National Park, Borneo, could easily hold 40 jumbo jets.

SRI LANKA

KUALA LUMPUR

COLOMBO □

Indian Ocean

Equator

SINGAPORE □

metres
3000
2000
1000
500
200
0

Sumatra

N

500 km
500 miles

JAKARTA

Explore the heart of Borneo

▸▸ Malaysia,
page 262

Hokkaido

gest city
nghai,
lation
5 million

JAPAN

Sea of
Japan

Honshu

Mt Fuji
☐ TOKYO

Kyoto ○ Osaka

Kyushu

○ Shanghai

Longest
river
Yangtze
6299 km

Pacific
Ocean

ina Sea

Kong

ity
Mt Kinabalu
Sabah

k 7

rneo
Sulawesi
antan

Asia can send you reeling. Even the most travel-hardened adult is not immune to the multi-sensory onslaught of its hot, over-crowded cities and chaotic transport systems. From fervent religious festivals and feisty cuisine to unavoidable encounters with abject poverty, Asia is a master of the cultural body blow – so why even contemplate taking your kids? Perhaps, it's the continent's very exuberance, its colours, tastes, smells and experiences that appeal. After all, nowhere fills a young, enquiring mind faster than Asia. And don't forget that there is a great deal more to the place than swarming bazaars, relentless touts and traffic-clogged streets. Cities like Dubai, Kuala Lumpur, Hong Kong and Singapore are some of the most modern and sophisticated in the world, while child-friendly beach resorts can be found everywhere from Jordan's Red Sea coast to the islands of Malaysia. But even when you venture beyond these pampered enclaves to experience Asia's iconic highlights you'll usually find a spontaneous warmth and affection, no matter how hectic the journey. Ultimately, though, Asia's allure as a family destination boils down to one simple truth: your kids will never forget it. Whether it's trying to outstare a terracotta warrior in China or meeting the smouldering gaze of a tigress in India; from trekking in the Himalayas and riding elephants in Thailand to exploring caves in Borneo and riding a ferry beneath Hong Kong's skyscrapers, Asia makes big impressions on little travellers.

Star rating

Wow factor
★★★★★

Worry factor
★★★★

Value for money
★★★★

Keeping teacher happy
★★★★★

Family accommodation
★★★

Babies & toddlers
★★

Cool for teenagers
★★★★

🤿 Learn to scuba

Imagine swooping like an aquatic Peter Pan through surreal citadels of corals and giant anemones, gazing with goggle-eyed wonder at shoals of fish flickering around you like pulses of electricity and maybe even glimpsing a shark or a turtle.

Learning to scuba dive opens your eyes to a whole new world and there are some great places to learn in Asia. Look out for operators that are accredited to PADI (padi.com). PADI scuba courses put lots of emphasis on diver safety.

If you are at least eight, you can take the plunge with a PADI Bubblemaker try-dive (in a swimming pool and to a maximum depth of 2 m). Seal Team courses (also for children eight and above) include exciting scuba AquaMissions where divers are introduced to underwater photography, navigation and environmental awareness.

Children aged 10-14 can enrol in a Junior Open Water Diver qualification course, during which you will learn the fundamentals of scuba diving, reaching depths of up to 12 m. The Junior Advanced Open Water Diver course (for 12- to 14-year-olds) builds on your scuba skills and includes five Adventure Dives.

Junior Rescue Diver teaches children (12-14) to master essential safety and first-aid techniques, while the Junior Master Scuba Diver course gives you experience of exploring a whole range of underwater environments.

🔍 Paint a brighter future for wildlife

★ Become a Friend of the David Shepherd Wildlife Foundation (davidshepherd.org). Since the 1960s, international wildlife artist, David Shepherd, has been campaigning and raising funds to help save tigers, elephants, rhinos and other critically endangered mammals in the wild.

★ Adopt an animal. The DSWF offers adoption schemes for African and Asian mammals. Lyuti, an Amur tiger, was found, severely injured, deep in the Siberian forest after poachers had killed his mother. Unable to survive alone in the wild he was taken to the Utyos Rehabilitation Centre. Now fully recovered he lives in a protected area of natural forest where he will remain safely for the rest of his life. When you adopt Lyuti you will help fund anti-poaching operations to protect this region of the Russian Far East, where fewer than 500 of Lyuti's wild cousins survive.

★ Paint a picture. Follow David Shepherd's top three tips for budding wildlife artists:

▸▸ Study the animal you are painting very carefully.

▸▸ If you can't see animals in the wild, then a safari park is the best alternative.

▸▸ The landscape around the animal or bird is just as important – there are huge numbers of books and television programmes which will provide you with reference material.

★ Chinese new years

▸▸ Dragon (2012)
▸▸ Snake (2013)
▸▸ Horse (2014)
▸▸ Sheep (2015)
▸▸ Monkey (2016)
▸▸ Chicken (2017)
▸▸ Dog (2018)
▸▸ Pig (2019)
▸▸ Rat (2020)

🐾 How to track tigers

Prime time for tiger spotting in India and Nepal is from February to April when vegetation withers and trees lose their leaves at the end of the dry season. Boost your chances of a tiger encounter by following these five tips:

▸▸ Set off in the early morning or late afternoon when tigers are more likely to be active.

▸▸ Their camouflaged coats can make them almost invisible, so look and listen for telltale clues, such as fresh tracks or alarm calls from nearby wildlife.

▸▸ Try to blend in with your surroundings by wearing clothes that are dull in colour.

▸▸ Tigers are very wary of human voices. Instead of talking, use hand signals that you have practised before setting off on safari.

▸▸ Tigers have an exceptional sense of smell so, if possible, stay downwind of them or you may give yourself away.

Great reads ◄
5 books for kids

Ages 4-8
**The Great Race: The Story
of the Chinese Zodiac**
Dawn Casey (Barefoot Books)
Find out how the Jade Emperor sets up
a race to decide the order of years in
the Chinese calendar in this well-paced
retelling of an ancient oriental legend.

The Tiger and the Wise Man
Andrew Fusek Peters (Child's Play)
How will the wise man escape being
eaten by the tiger when it seems that all
the other animals are against him too?
The jackal appears to help, but is it simply
another trick?

Ages 5-11
Malaysian Children's Favourite Stories
Kay Lyons (Tuttle Publishing)
The traditional culture and rich tropical
environment of Malaysia are revealed in
this collection of beautifully illustrated
legends, including *How the Tapir Got its
Colours* and *The Dragon of Kinabalu*.

Ages 6+
The Jungle Book
Rudyard Kipling (Templar Publishing)
Wonderful artwork accompanies this
edition of Kipling's enduring classic. Few
other tales evoke the atmosphere of the
Indian jungle quite like this one.

Ages 6-10
Panda in the Park
Lucy Daniels (Hodder Children's Books)
Mandy and James visit China in the
school holidays to help with a wildlife
conservation project. Can they help to
reunite a panda cub with its mother before
it's too late?

Taste of Asia moon cakes

Traditionally eaten during the Chinese Moon Festival, these
round fruity pastries are good for feasting on at any time of the year.

What you need
➤ 500 g self-raising flour
➤ 3 eggs
➤ 3 tbsp vegetable oil
➤ 100 g sugar
➤ 500 g dried figs
➤ 20 dried apricots
➤ 1 egg yolk

What to do
➤ Pre-heat the oven to 200°C.
➤ Mix the flour, oil, eggs, sugar
and water together in a bowl to
make pastry.
➤ Let the pastry rest in a
refrigerator for about 30
minutes.
➤ Cut the figs into
small pieces, then
purée them in a food
processor.
➤ Roll the apricots in
the fig purée to make
small balls.
➤ Divide the pastry
into 20 equal portions
and flatten them into
10-cm wide discs.
➤ Wrap each pastry disc around
a ball of fig and apricot and press
the edges of the pastry together
to make a muffin shape.
➤ Turn the cakes over so that the
sealed sides are underneath, prick
them with a fork and place them
on a greased baking tray.
➤ Brush the cakes with beaten
egg yolk and bake for around 30
minutes or until golden brown.

🔍 How to make
a Chinese lantern

What you need
➤ Coloured paper or gift-wrap
➤ Scissors
➤ Glue, tape, or stapler

What to do
➤ Fold a piece of paper in half,
making a long, thin rectangle.
➤ Make at least 12 cuts along the
fold line.
➤ Unfold the paper and glue or
staple the short edges together.
➤ Cut out a thin strip of paper and
attach to the lantern for a handle.
➤ Make lots more, string them
together and hang them up.

Upset tummy, Delhi belly, the trots, the squits, exploding poo… no matter what delightful terminology you or your children use to refer to it, the one aspect of travelling in Asia that's likely to be foremost in your minds is the threat of diarrhoea. Basic hygiene issues become paramount, especially when travelling with babies and young children who are more susceptible to dehydration following a bout of gastrointestinal illness. Malaria prevention also needs to be given serious consideration. Now the good news: travelling with kids of any age in Asia will bring out the best of local hospitality, while getting around will almost certainly be easier than when you backpacked there 15 or 20 years ago. You will also find that Asia is generally very affordable – the exceptions, of course, being cities like Singapore and Hong Kong where even a few days of high living can haemorrhage your bank balance.

Babies

Give high-risk malaria zones a wide berth. For parents with babies, two of the best malaria-free options are Dubai and Singapore – modern, squeaky-clean cities that will not only give you a taste of traditional Asian culture when you step beyond the air-con, but will also provide quick access to baby supplies and medical care should you need them. Singapore has even launched a system of 'Businesses for Families'

Local transport

A cycle rickshaw ride is a great way to experience the colourful chaos of life in an Indian city, like here in Madurai, Tamil Nadu. Other top spots for hopping in a rickshaw are Chandni Chowk Bazaar (Old Delhi) and Agra (to the entrance of the Taj Mahal).

branding (bfc.sg), so you know which shops and companies will pay extra attention to your needs. In Thailand and Malaysia the risk of malaria is mainly confined to remote, rural areas, so you might feel tempted by a stint on a tropical island paradise, complete with childcare facilities and parent-pampering spa. If you're travelling from Europe or North America, however, you may need to ask yourself whether a resort in the Caribbean or Mediterranean might make more sense. Jordan's Red Sea coast, or even the Maldives, would also make good 'shorter haul' alternatives, particularly for parents who are keen divers. Just be sure to avoid the blisteringly hot summer months.

Toddlers/pre-school

They are still too young at this age to appreciate much in the way of Asia's cultural kaleidoscope, but that doesn't mean you can't have fun with a toddler at a beach resort or in the zoos and theme parks of cities like Dubai, Hong Kong and Singapore. The deciding factor with this age group is more likely to revolve around the journey than the destination. Are you really sure you want to spend 13 hours with a fidgety four-year-old on a flight from London to Singapore? On the other hand, children in this age category are still compact and highly portable which means you could contemplate something really quite adventurous – such as a gentle, fully-supported trek

Special needs

Singapore is probably Asia's most accessible destination for the physically challenged. The MaxiCab airport shuttle, all MRT train stations and several SBS Transit buses are wheelchair-friendly. Published by the Disabled People's Association of Singapore (dpa.org.sg), *Access Singapore* is a comprehensive guide to accessible places. Hong Kong also provides excellent facilities for disabled travellers. An access guide is available from the Hong Kong Council of Social Services (hkcss.org.hk), while Easy Access Travel (easyaccesstravelhk.com) can arrange tours.

Single parents

The prospect of a family trip to Asia can be daunting to single parents. However, some family operators, such as The Adventure Company (adventurecompany.co.uk), offer special departures for single parent families on their trips to Sri Lanka and Thailand.

"" The procession seemed to arrive from nowhere. One moment we were gazing up at the temple's spectacular gopuras – 50-m-tall gateway towers adorned with colourful carvings of deities and supernatural beasts – the next we were swept away like leaves on an irresistible current of people, all of whom were shouting, laughing, dancing and singing. William Gray

in the Himalayas, staying in comfortable lodges and carrying your child – or hiring a porter to do so. A few adventure operators offer this kind of trip for families with children as young as two, but generally the minimum age for any organized Asian itinerary is five or six.

Kids/school age

This is a wonderful age range to take kids to Asia. Not only are they more robust when it comes to health and safety, but they are also both physically and intellectually more equipped to cope with adventure activities and cultural issues. Jordan and Sri Lanka both make excellent introductions to Asia. They are not as far-flung as eastern China or Southeast Asia, so flying there is usually cheaper and you can also justify going for a shorter period of time. This is just as well with Jordan since it's best to visit in the cooler spring and autumn over half term or Easter holiday periods. Both countries are also quite compact which means you can see and do lots without having to endure long overland journeys or internal flights.

From an educational point of view, most Asian destinations rate highly. Two of the most culturally and historically saturated itineraries are India's Golden Triangle (Delhi, Agra and Jaipur) and China's northeast (Beijing, Great Wall and Xi'an). Both would require a minimum of 12 days.

For adventure, Nepal and Thailand offer non-stop thrills, including trekking, rafting and riding elephants. Again, 12 days, or preferably two weeks, is the minimum time you should consider – particularly if you are heading to Nepal and need to factor in acclimatization days to a trekking schedule.

Teenagers

Asia is an ideal destination for teens. In particular, Southeast Asian destinations like Thailand and Malaysia offer a perfect 'teen combo' of cool modern cities, chilled beach resorts and full-on adventure activities. If your teenagers are more into retail therapy than adrenaline abuse, take them to Dubai, Singapore or Hong Kong. If adventure rules, get their pulses racing on a multi-activity break in Nepal where you can combine whitewater rafting and mountain biking with a Himalayan trek and a jungle safari.

Washing elephants at Kodanad, Kerala

Jordan
A desert adventure

It won't be the magical desert city of Petra that first springs to mind when you contemplate a family holiday to Jordan. Nor will it be the hypnotic spattering of stars that fills a desert night in Wadi Rum. Nor even the perplexing and titillating sensation of bobbing like a cork in the Dead Sea. Inevitably, all these highlights are likely to be overshadowed by one nagging doubt: 'Is Jordan safe?' Nowadays, it makes sense to seriously consider the security situation in any country you're planning to visit, but don't let Jordan's Middle East location overly prejudice your decision of whether or not to go.

Petra

Country highlights

Jerash An hour's drive north of Amman, the well-preserved ruins of Jerash evoke the glory days of the Roman Empire. You'll discover paved streets and plazas, imposing temples and all the other trimmings of a 2000-year-old Roman city. Head for the Hippodrome at 1100 or 1500 when the Jerash Heritage Company (jerashchariots.com) stages a fantastic display of battle manoeuvres and chariot racing. You can also cheer on your favourite gladiator as four pairs of warriors slog it out using traditional weapons, the ancient arena ringing with their cries of "*Ave, imperator, morituri te salutant!*" – "Hail Caesar, we who are about to die salute you!"

Dead Sea After the gratuitous violence at Jerash, there's nothing better than a calming dip in the ever-so-salty Dead Sea. Kids love the sensation of floating in the super-buoyant water ("Look Mum, no armbands!"). Good luck trying to explain to them that this is the lowest place on earth and that they've just swum at more than 400 m below sea level. Parents and their teenage daughters will no doubt appreciate the pampering treatments available at the various luxury resorts and hotels.

King's Highway Heading south from Amman, you pass several attractions, including Mount Nebo (the holy summit where Moses is believed to have been buried), Madaba (famed for its sixth-century Byzantine mosaic map) and Karak (a crusader castle with enough corridors and dungeons to keep your medieval-minded little monsters happy for hours).

Petra You know this place, even if you've never been. Harrison Ford seared Petra onto our minds when he galloped through a canyon to emerge in front of the rock-hewn Treasury in the finale to *Indiana Jones and the Last Crusade*. Such is the 'wow' factor of Jordan's premier attraction, that you could be forgiven for thinking it was all Hollywood hype. In fact, this Nabataean city dates from 400 BC and is riddled with elaborately carved tombs, as well as temples, shrines and a fort. For centuries, it was lost to all but a few Bedouin families – only to be 'rediscovered' by Johann Ludwig Burkhardt in 1812. Nowadays, despite its popularity, it's still a thrill to walk through the narrow Siq canyon, stealing yourself for the first glimpse of the Treasury. Get the Indiana Jones theme tune out of your head by experiencing the all-absorbing sound-and-light show (Mondays, Wednesdays and Thursdays at 2030) or joining a traditional cookery lesson at the Petra Kitchen (petramoon.com).

Wadi Rum "Vast, echoing and God-like." T E Lawrence wasn't exaggerating when he used these words to describe the glorious desolation of Wadi Rum's heat-shattered mountains, canyons and sand dunes. Venturing into such a hostile environment might seem an epic undertaking, but relax in the knowledge that you'll travel by 4WD vehicle and spend the nights in comfortable camps. In addition to striking Lawrence of Arabia poses at every opportunity, activities at Wadi Rum include walks, camel rides and some of the best stargazing in the world.

Dive the Red Sea

★ Scuba dive on the reefs at Aqaba for a colourful window on the psychedelic coral reefs of the Red Sea. Glass-bottom boat rides and snorkelling are also possible.

Jumeirah Beach Hotel

Barely a century ago Dubai was little more than a pearl-fishing village where camels outnumbered people. Now it's Arabia's premier playground and one of the most child-friendly destinations on earth. Through a number of audacious development projects, Dubai has taken the sting out of the Arabian desert and created a sensational, some say contrived, holiday destination. As well as beaches, watersports and modern hotels, you'll find theme parks, a ski dome and the ultimate 'super-resort' of Dubailand.

Country highlights

See the sights Explore the atmospheric old quarter of Bastakia, then visit the nearby Dubai Museum which has a series of realistic dioramas evoking the city's past. Continue walking along the Creek to the Waterfront Heritage Area. Don't miss the beautifully restored Sheikh Saeed Al Maktoum House with its wind towers (an early and ingenious form of air-conditioning). Backtrack to the Bur Dubai abra station for a ride across the Creek before delving into the spice, gold and perfume souks.

Make a splash Wild Wadi (wildwadi.com), Dubai's famous water park, is awash with no fewer than 30 attractions, including Breakers Bay with its non-stop surf and the 33-m-high Jumeirah Sceirah slide – the ultimate slippery slope which will accelerate you to speeds approaching 80 km/h. Young children who prefer their water more horizontal will find no shortage of swimming holes and tidal pools.

Explore the desert Take a 4WD safari (arabian-adventures.com) into the meringue-whip of dunes beyond Dubai City, hurtling up and down their slopes like something out of a *Mad Max* movie. Dune bashing (as well as sandboarding) is restricted to

an approved area of desert, but if it still strikes you as environmentally dubious, take to the dunes on a camel instead. Afterwards, you'll retire to a Bedouin-style camp for a barbecue feast. When the evening entertainment begins you will no doubt embarrass your children with some impromptu belly dancing and they probably won't speak to you again until you give in to their pleas for a henna tattoo.

Go skiing Using 6000 tons of snow to create five different runs measuring up to 400 m in length, Ski Dubai (skidbx.com) is one of the world's largest indoor ski centres. There are beginner slopes, a black run, a snowboarder's stunt zone and a snow park where kids can mess about on toboggans.

Have fun learning Children's City (childrencity.ae) takes youngsters on a hands-on educational journey through themed zones covering computers and communication, space and flight exploration, the human body, nature and international culture.

Have fun shopping Dubai is retail heaven, with giant malls like and Wafi City (waficity.com) and The Mall of the Emirates fusing shopping and entertainment.

> ❝❞ **Walking from the Creek, you burrow into alleyways where sacks of spices pack a heady blow in the sultry heat. Shopkeepers proffering boxes of plump dates lure you into Dubai's spice souk where you peruse mounds of cardamom and cloves while chewing frankincense-flavoured chewing gum.** William Gray

Inside info

▶▶ Temperatures frequently soar to over 40°C between April and October, so aim to visit during winter when the weather is sunny but not searing .
▶▶ Forget about hiring a car – it's a 30-minute transfer from the airport to most hotels.
▶▶ Explore souks on foot, and cruise the Creek by water taxi.
▶▶ Jumeirah's Burj al-Arab (jumeirah.com) is Dubai's iconic hotel of choice, but there are plenty of other high quality (and cheaper) alternatives.

A cow wandering amongst a traffic jam; a fresh dollop of elephant poo in the road; a bullock hauling a cart; an exhilarating ride in a cycle rickshaw; people staring; people spitting… Children have an insatiable curiosity, and everything about India's chaotic street life will hold them rapt. And that's before they've seen the country's romantic palaces, explored its rugged deserts or encountered its *Jungle Book* wildlife. Of course, India can also be hot, dusty and crowded. And you might find that your kids refuse to eat anything except boiled rice and chapattis. But with careful planning, an adventurous spirit and the odd day at the pool or beach, a family trip to India can be incredibly rewarding.

Delhi

Venturing with kids into the hurly burly of Delhi may fill you with trepidation, but take a deep breath, hail an auto rickshaw or taxi and get stuck in. New Delhi has tree-lined avenues, swanky embassies and imposing monuments like India Gate, while Old Delhi has the labyrinthine bazaar of Chandni Chowk where you can buy anything from chess sets and silver jewellery to handmade paper and toy rickshaws. You can explore a mighty relic of the Mughal Empire at the Red Fort, while the nearby Jama Masjid (or Friday Mosque) offers eye-popping views of Old Delhi from its soaring minarets. The Rail Transport Museum (Chanakyapuri) has mighty steam engines like the 1855 *Fairy Queen*, plush saloon carriages used by royalty and even the skull of an elephant that charged a mail train in 1894 and lost. Shankar's International Dolls Museum (Bahadur Shah Zafar Marg) showcases 6000 costumed dolls from over 85 countries, while the National Children's Museum (Kotla Road) has craft workshops. If your kids need some space to burn off energy, take them to the park next to India Gate or to the stone observatory of Jantar Mantar which has several intriguing stairways to explore.

Agra

A symbol of undying love crafted in white marble, Agra's Taj Mahal was commissioned in 1641 by grieving Mughal emperor, Shah Jahan, in memory of his favourite wife, Mumtaz Mahal. Adults and children alike cannot fail to be overwhelmed by the exquisite beauty of this lavish mausoleum, which took 20,000 labourers 22 years to complete. Be sure to show your kids the intricate detail in the walls, which are inlaid with malachite, turquoise, lapis lazuli, coral, jasper

and other precious stones. Just 40 km from Agra lies another Mughal masterpiece – Fatehpur Sikri, an ancient royal city guarded by massive gates. Around 15 km further to the west is Bharatpur, the eastern gateway town to Rajasthan, where you'll find Keoladeo Ghana Bird Sanctuary. A former royal hunting reserve, this small park is now a haven for 300 species of birds, including migratory Siberian cranes (September to February) and nesting populations of painted storks, herons and pelicans (July and August).

Jaipur

Located 260 km from Delhi and 240 km from Agra, the Pink City of Jaipur completes the popular 'Golden Triangle' route of northern India. Painted pink to commemorate a visit by the Prince of Wales in 1876, Jaipur's centrepiece is the City Palace which has exhibits of regal costumes, weaponry and art, as well as private quarters for the royal family. Don't miss the Palace of the Winds with its extraordinary honeycombed façade of 953 pink sandstone windows. In the rugged hills surrounding Jaipur, you can explore several forts – none more spectacular than the Amber Fort which can be reached on elephant-back.

Kerala Backwaters houseboat

Converted from rice barges, these elegant vessels offer a comfortable base from which to cruise the labyrinthine network of channels and lakes that seep through the coastal hinterland of southern Kerala.

🔍 Golden extras

Embellish your Golden Triangle tour with a tiger safari (see box) and a visit to Pushkar, a sacred lakeside town that hosts a famous camel fair each November. North of Delhi, hill stations like Naini Tal offer tantalizing glimpses of the Indian Himalayas, cool respite from the lowlands and family-friendly walking. With time you could also visit the Golden Temple at Amritsar and Mcleod Ganj – home of the Dalai Lama. Adventurous families will be lured to remote Ladakh where pony-supported treks in the Zanskar Range can reach altitudes of over 5000 m.

Taj Mahal

☸ **Tiger** trail

They say tigers make the orchestra of the forest play. When the lord of the jungle is on the prowl, sambar and spotted deer whistle and snort, while langur monkeys, magpies and babblers pitch in with coughs, grunts and chatters. Any one of these alarm calls is enough to transform a long, dusty tiger-spotting safari into an edge-of-seat drama, snapping your senses taut as you strain for a glimpse of smouldering orange fur, the black and white tufts of twitching ears or the flick of a tail.

A 2010 census carried out in India (home to half the world's wild tigers) revealed a population increase from 1411 cats (in 2007) to 1706 – good news for the beleaguered big cat, but no guarantee you'll see one. Tigers are still spread thin across India's spattering of reserves and national parks. They're secretive, solitary hunters with vast territories and impeccable camouflage.

To boost your chances of a sighting, visit between October and April when leaves fall and grasses wither (improving visibility) and water sources recede, concentrating tigers – and their prey – around waterholes.

Tiger numbers in Ranthambhore – Rajasthan's premier wildlife reserve – are not what they used to be, but the national park can still feel overrun by jeep safaris. Focus instead on quieter Pench, Kanha and Bandhavgarh. They're easily combined into a manageable safari circuit, and each one offers elephant-back rides, allowing you to delve off-track and listen for those all-important telltale alarm calls. Bandhavgarh has one of India's highest tiger densities, and you also have a good chance of spotting sloth bear, wild dog and leopard. Kanha is renowned for its swamp deer and avian beauties like the Malabar pied hornbill, while Pench National Park (inspiration for Kipling's *Jungle Book*) is studded with dry-season river pools, framed by teak forest – ideal spots for tigers to spring an ambush. For something even more adventurous, make tracks for Satpura National Park where, in addition to game drives, you can explore tiger country on walking safaris and boat trips.

Mumbai

There's no shortage of important buildings and landmarks in Mumbai, the Gateway of India being a prime example. However, you may well find your kids are more fascinated by the general swirl of life going on around them. Give them time to soak it all up by hopping on a red double-decker bus or taking a boat trip in the harbour. For broader-minded children, Reality Tours and Travel (realitytoursandtravel.com) takes guided groups into Dharavi, Asia's largest slum, for an insight into the area's enterprising industries, such as leather tanning and plastic recycling. Mumbai's museums include Chhatrapati Shivaji Maharaj Vastu Sanghralaya (also known as the Prince of Wales Museum) which houses thousands of ancient artefacts and an interesting natural history section. Interactive exhibits can be found at Nehru Science Centre. When it all gets too much, seek refuge in the Horniman Circle Garden and along the nature trails of Maharashtra Nature Park. Located opposite the Hanging Gardens, Kamal Nehru Park has shady gardens, a giant shoe-shaped slide and views of Marine Drive. Popular at weekends with locals and tourists, Juhu Beach has fairground rides, snack vendors and pony rides, while the combined theme parks of EsselWorld and Water Kingdom (esselworld.com), reached via a short ferry ride, boast around 100 ways (dry or wet) to get your heart thumping.

Goa

An almost continuous 130-km swathe of palm-fringed beaches, Goa's coastline has obvious family appeal. There are the inevitable overdeveloped spots, just as there are peaceful wildlife sanctuaries and authentic temples to be explored inland. Accommodation ranges from simple budget hotels to five-star resorts. Some of the most popular beaches include Calangute (for watersports), Anjuna (for its party atmosphere and flea market), Morjim (a turtle nesting site) and Colva (Goa's longest beach).

Kerala

Like Goa, the sandy beaches of Kerala's Malabar Coast (keralatourism.org) have several resorts offering family accommodation. But it's what lies behind the palm-fringed shore that will really captivate your children. The Kerala Backwaters, a maze of canals and rivers, are easily explored on a houseboat. These converted rice barges offer both a gentle pace of travel and a superb vantage point from which to watch rural life glide by. Other highlights in the region include the fishing boats and Portuguese fort at Cochin, walking trails in the Salim Ali Bird Sanctuary, the tame elephants at Kodanad and the wild elephants at Periya National Park in the cool Cardamom Hills – the perfect place to discover how India's spices are grown.

Inside info

▸▸ One of India's most popular tourist circuits links Delhi with Agra, Bharatpur, Ranthambore National Park and Jaipur; allow a minimum of 10 days.
▸▸ Join an organized tour, or travel independently using a combination of sleeper train, car with driver/guide, jeep and camel.
▸▸ Visit between late November and early February when it is relatively cool.
▸▸ Brace yourself for general mayhem in Mumbai, particularly during the Ganesh Chaturthi festival (August/September) when images of the elephant god Ganesh are paraded through the streets before being dunked in the sea at Chowpatty Beach.

🔍 Offbeat Asia Six less-trodden destinations

① Oman

Explore the dunes and canyons of Wahiba Sands by jeep and camel and then visit a Bedouin camp and the 17th-century stronghold of Jabrin Fort. Ras Al Hadd is renowned for its nesting green turtles, while humpback whales and dolphins can be spotted offshore. Elsewhere along the coast, you can visit dhow-building yards and fishing villages or peruse the mosques, forts and palaces of Muscat.

When Anytime except summer when it's too hot.

How long Allow at least a week.

② Japan

Scale skyscrapers in modern Tokyo, visit temples in ancient Kyoto and explore the incredible marine life of the Pacific Rim at Osaka's aquarium – linking all three cities by high-speed Bullet Train. Away from the urban centres, you can climb to the 3776-m summit of sacred Mount Fuji, visit the mountain Buddhist retreat at Nikko or relax on the beaches of the Izu Peninsula.

When May to September.

How long Allow two weeks.

③ Indonesia

Combine beach days on Bali with exciting adventures in the island's interior, climbing the volcano of Mount Batur, canoeing on Lake Bratan and exploring the Monkey Forest and Hindu temples at Ubud. Alternatively, combine Bali with a Javan odyssey, witnessing sunrise from the crater rim of Mount Bromo and visiting the coastal rainforest and turtle-nesting beaches of Meru Beriti National Park.

When April to October is the driest period.

How long Allow at least two weeks.

④ Cambodia

The ruins of Angkor Wat will fire your children's imagination – even if they haven't seen *Tomb Raider* or any of the other films made there. The 800-year-old 'Lost Cities' of Angkor have enough temples to explore and story-telling bas-reliefs to decipher to keep you enthralled for days. Take along a copy of *Angkat: The Cambodian Cinderella* for an extra dose of fairy-tale magic.

When Year round, but December and January are best.

How long Allow at least two weeks.

⑤ Vietnam

Vietnam has that irresistible family-friendly mix of adventure and beaches. The journey from Hanoi to Ho Chi Minh by road and rail is not only a classic adventure, but you can stop en route to enjoy Hoi An's beaches and sandwich the easy-going journey with boat trips on Halong Bay in the north and the Mekong Delta in the south.

When Year round, but April, May and October are best.

How long Allow at least two weeks.

⑥ Mongolia

Take the kids to Mongolia? Yeah, right – might as well fly them to the moon! Actually, a family holiday to Mongolia is not as daft as it might sound. The capital, Ulaan Baatar, not only has plenty to interest kids, such as the Natural History Museum with its stunning collection of dinosaur fossils, but it is also a perfect base for exciting and safe forays into two of Asia's last great wilderness areas.

Jalman Meadows A three- to four-hour bus drive to the northeast of Ulaan Baatar takes you across treeless steppes and through larch and birch forests to reach the upper Tuul River Valley. The autumn and winter pastures for nomadic herders, Jalman Meadows is also the summer location of a camp for just 20 tourists. Based on traditional gers, the camp has composting toilets, solar-powered electricity and leaves little trace when it's packed away at the end of each season. Activities include hiking, horse riding and yak-cart rafting where an inflatable raft is towed upstream by bovine power.

Arburd Sands Another low-impact ger camp has been set up on the Gobi steppes, a four-hour drive from Ulaan Baatar. Arburd Sands is just 35 km from the Zorgol Hairhan Uul, a gigantic rock formation that's home to Argali sheep and Siberian ibex. You can camp out in the sands, stake out a wolf hide and ride horses or camels.

When July and August.

How long Allow at least two weeks.

Contact the expert Nomadic Journeys (nomadicjourneys.com).

🐾 Dragon quest

★ Imagine cruising through the islands of eastern Indonesia aboard a sailing schooner, stopping to explore volcanoes, crater lakes and coral reefs before embarking on a search for Komodo dragons. A nine-day family voyage is available from Explore (explore.co.uk). The world's largest lizards, Komodo dragons can reach lengths in excess of 3 m. They prey mainly on Timor deer and water buffalo, using their toxic saliva to deliver a fatal bite.

With an enticing blend of palm-fringed beaches, rich wildlife and ancient monuments, Sri Lanka is a great family destination – particularly for those with school-age children who might appreciate the island's cultural and natural highlights more than toddlers. Split your time between exploring the Cultural Triangle, visiting a national park and relaxing on the coast. Sri Lanka has a peaceful, friendly, laid-back atmosphere, and foreigners – particularly children – are made very welcome.

Cultural Triangle

Allow four hours to drive from Colombo to the extraordinary cave temples at Dambulla. You will need to climb 200 or so steps to reach the first cave where a 14-m-long reclining Buddha has been carved from the rock. If anything, the second cave is even more spectacular, containing over 150 life-size statues of gods and a ceiling fresco depicting the Buddha's life. To the north, Anuradhapura, Sri Lanka's sprawling ancient capital, has plenty to interest budding archaeologists, including the bell-shaped dagobas of Thuparama and Ruwanweli. However, Polonnaruwa is more compact and can be easily explored by bicycle. Don't miss Gal Vihara, a group of enormous Buddha carvings hewn from granite. Sri Lanka's undisputed 'rock star' is Sigiriya rock fortress, a 370-m-high monolith crowned by a palace and surrounded by an elaborate complex of water gardens, moats and ramparts. Dating from the 5th century AD, Sigiriya can be scaled by anyone with stamina and a head for heights. A stone stairway leads past wall frescoes to the Lion Gate where a huge head with open jaws once served as the entrance to the palace. Now all that remains is a pair of massive paws. Gone, too, is the final section of original steps; to continue to the summit you'll need to use a rickety metal stairway.

Hill country

Spread around a lake at 500 m above sea level, Kandy (the capital of Sri Lanka's hill country) is renowned for its Tooth Temple where the sacred tooth of the Lord Buddha is enshrined. Three times daily, the magnificent temple reverberates to the drumming and conch-shell blasts of ceremonial *poojas* as clouds of incense fill the air and devotees make offerings of flowers. Elsewhere in Kandy, you can watch traditional dancing and drumming performances, take a boat ride on the lake, visit the railway museum or have a picnic in nearby Peradeniya's Royal Botanical Gardens.

Reclining Buddha, Anuradhapura

In the Matale Hills to the north of Kandy, children can sniff-test cinnamon, cloves, nutmeg, pepper and cardamom at various spice gardens. Continuing south to Nuwara Eliya there are several opportunities to visit tea estates, while the Horton Plains offers an easy 4-km hike to World's End, a sheer escarpment with a dizzying 880-m drop. There are more dramatic views at Ella Gap where an adventure centre offers activities such as canoeing, mountain biking and abseiling.

The coast

West coast The main tourist beaches along the stretch of coast between Colombo and Galle are at Bentota, Beruwela and Hikkaduwa. Watersports, such as scuba diving and windsurfing, are widely available and many beaches have lifeguards on duty outside the main hotels. There are turtle hatcheries at Induruwa and Kosgoda, just south of Bentota. Visit between November and April and you might be allowed to help release the hatchlings. Inland from the coast, Sinharaja Biosphere Reserve provides a great opportunity to explore the rainforest.

South coast Founded in the 16th century by the Portuguese, the fortified city of Galle is worth a morning's exploration. Walk along the ramparts to the lighthouse and then delve into the museum where you can find out about everything from traditional fishing to gemstone polishing. South of Galle is Unawatuna, a beautiful curve of coral sand where you can build sandcastles under the shade of palm trees. For more wildlife, head to Yala National Park, home to elephants, leopards, sloth bears, jackals and buffalo. Herds of elephants can also be seen at Udawalawe National Park; however Sri Lanka's ultimate jumbo offering can be found further north at Minneriya National Park where, from June to September, an extraordinary 'gathering of the herds' takes place.

Inside info

▶▶ For flexibility hire a car and driver; for peace of mind book an organized tour, and for a taste of adventure try the local trains.
▶▶ The best time for visiting Cultural Triangle sites is January to April; the local pilgrimage season is May to June.
▶▶ Remember to dress modestly and remove footwear and headwear when entering Buddhist or Hindu shrines.
▶▶ Beaches with fishing villages, where you can watch the daily catch being landed, are fascinating to visit, but stick to the cleaner, safer tourist beaches for swimming.

The Nepalese Himalayas include eight peaks over 8000 m, but that doesn't mean you have to plan a three-week assault on Everest Base Camp to appreciate these mighty mountains (although teenagers might relish the challenge). There are several family-friendly treks that are not only shorter, but more crucially, avoid high passes and the inherent risks of altitude sickness. Kids may well surprise you with their trekking stamina, while porters are usually happy to carry young children in their baskets. Don't forget, there is a lot more to Nepal than trekking. You may come with high ideals, but remember to also set your sights lower on the steamy jungles of Chitwan National Park.

Kathmandu

With its profusion of temples, palaces and shrines, Durbar Square is the heart and soul of Kathmandu. Get there early in the morning before it seethes with curio vendors and other tourists. As you enter the square from New Road, look out for two stone lions guarding the home of the Kumari – Kathmandu's living goddess. Intricately carved lattice windows and balconies enable her to look out, but not be seen. Across the square, the towering pagoda of Maju Deval is a great spot to sit quietly and soak up the atmosphere. Nearby is the statue of Garuda – half-man, half-bird – on which the Hindu god Vishnu travels, and behind that lies Maru Tole, a small square where devotees can buy marigold garlands to lay at the shrine of Ganesh, the Hindu god of good fortune. Maru Tole is dominated by Kasthamandap, a three-storey wooden pagoda that, according to legend, was built from a single tree in the 12th century. There are viewing platforms on the first floor.

Walking in to Hanuman Dhoka Square, peep through the large lattice screen set into a wall of the old royal palace. Inside is a scary visage of Shiva – a gruesome mask with huge fangs designed to ward off evil. A little further on, you may wish to divert your children's scrutiny of the erotic carvings on the wooden roof struts of Jagannath Temple. Adjacent to this, however, is the statue of Hanuman, the much-beloved monkey king who rescued princess Sita from the evil Ravana and has come to symbolise devout loyalty. It is completely covered in orange paste left by worshippers. Nearby, the ornately decorated Golden Door leads inside Hanuman Dhoka, the former royal palace. As you walk inside, look out for the statue of Narsimha, half-man, half-lion, devouring the demon Haranyakashipu. Another sight that's sure to delight

most kids is Kal Bhairav, a 3-m-tall statue of the Lord of Destruction, complete with a crown of human skulls.

Sights worth seeing beyond Kathmandu city include the Buddhist stupas of Boudhanath and Swayambhunath, the Patan Museum and the pedestrian-friendly streets of Bhaktapur – Nepal's medieval capital.

Pokhara

A six-hour bus drive or 35-minute flight from Kathmandu, this lazy lakeside town may well offer your first glimpse of the Himalaya – a spectacular panorama of the Annapurnas dominated by Machhapuchare, the 6997-m 'Fish Tail Peak'. It's a great base from which to plan a trek, but before you head for the hills spend a few days enjoying Pokhara itself – browsing the handicraft stalls, boating on Phewa Lake and visiting the World Peace Pagoda with its all-seeing eyes of Buddha.

The Himalaya

From Pokhara, it's a short bus ride to trailheads leading into the Annapurna Conservation Area. Not only is this one of the world's best trekking areas, but it is also a haven for plants and animals, ranging from orchids and rhododendrons to blood pheasants and snow leopards. Treks can vary from a two-day taster, walking into the foothills and camping near a spectacular lookout, to a 16-day Annapurna Circuit crossing the 5416-m Thorung La pass. See the box, opposite, for suggestions of two family-friendly options, and remember to trek gently to minimize your impact on this fragile environment (ntnc.org.np).

The Annapurnas

There are moments on every Himalayan trek when you'll have difficulty convincing yourself, let alone your children, that the white flecks hovering above the horizon are not clouds but mountains. White and pristine, like tall ships under full sail, the snow-capped peaks of the Himalayas seem to float – aloof and unassailable – on a sea of haze rising from the lowlands.

Boudhanath

😊 Family treks Two five-day options from Pokhara

❶ Royal Trek

Day 1 Begnas Bazaar to Sundar Danda. A 30-minute drive from Pokhara leads to Begnas Bazaar from where a wide path leads between two lakes (1 hr).

Day 2 To Chisopani. A steep climb on stone steps leads to Chisopani from where there are amazing views of the Annapurna and Dhulagiri ranges, particularly from the hilltop temple above the village (5 hrs).

Day 3 To Shaklung. The trail descends to a river valley, then climbs to the Gurung village of Shaklung (3 hrs).

Day 4 To Kalikastan. A forested ridge links the villages of Naudanda, Mathi Thana and Thulokot before reaching Kalikastan where there are good views of Machhapuchhare and Annapurna (4 hrs).

Day 5 To Bijayapur, drive to Pokhara. The trail descends gently through Brahman and Chhetri villages towards the Pokhara roadhead (2 hrs).

❷ Ghorepani Trek

Day 1 Birethanti to Tikhedhunga. A wide trail follows the Bhurungdi Khola before climbing steadily to Hille at 1495 m. From there it's a short climb to Tikhedhunga (4 hrs).

Day 2 To Ghorepani. A stone stairway of 3767 steps leads to Ulleri – your efforts rewarded with fine views of Annapurna South and Hiunchuli. The trail ascends to Banthanti and Nangethanti before reaching Ghorepani at 2775 m (6 hrs).

Day 3 To Poon Hill and Tadapani. An early morning climb leads to Poon Hill (3210 m) from where there are stunning views of Machhapuchhare and the Annapurna and Dhaulagiri massifs. The trail continues to Tadapani (2590 m) (3 hrs).

Day 4 To Ghandruk. Leaving Tadapani, the trail winds through forests to Ghandruk (1950 m) where there is a visitor centre of the Annapurna Area Conservation Project (4 hrs).

Day 5 To Nayapul, drive to Pokhara. Gentle walking alongside the Modi Khola river (5 hrs).

There are dozens of trek outfitters in Kathmandu and Pokhara, although booking through an overseas family adventure specialist will ensure that your local operator is genuinely child-friendly. Accommodation can be anything from tents and teahouses to lodges.

Chitwan National Park

A popular haunt of aristocratic hunters in the 19th century, Chitwan National Park is now one of Asia's premier wildlife reserves, offering jeep and elephant-back safaris in search of tiger and Asian one-horned rhinoceros. Other wildlife in the national park includes spotted deer, leopard, sloth bear, wild boar, rhesus monkey, grey langur, wild dog, marsh crocodile, gharial (or Gangetic crocodile) and freshwater dolphin. Of the 450 bird species that have been recorded in Chitwan, look out for year-round residents like woodpeckers, hornbills and redheaded trogons. Brahminy ducks and bareheaded geese flock here in winter, while summer sees Chitwan's forests all-of-a-flutter with migrant parakeets and paradise flycatchers. The park has a good range of lodges and tented camps and can be reached by air, road or river.

Also in Nepal's lowlands, Koshi Tappu Wildlife Reserve is a large wetland area that will have keen birdwatchers ticking off a long list of egrets, herons, storks, ibises, gulls, terns and warblers. The rarely visited Bardia National Park protects a swathe of forest along the Karnali River, where rafting trips sometimes allow sightings of smooth otter and Ganges river dolphin.

🔌 Activities without trekking

Whitewater rafting The Trishuli is not the wildest river in Nepal, but it's close to Kathmandu and offers one- or two-day trips on mainly grade III rapids, making it the best option for families. Teenagers in search of something more awesome should consider the grade IV Bhote Kosi and Kali Gandaki Rivers. Whitewater Nepal (raftnepal.com) runs family trips, minimum age seven.

Mountain biking Hire bikes in Kathmandu and drive them out to Nagarkot from where it's downhill all the way to Bhaktapur. For serious biking expeditions, contact Dawn till Dusk (nepalbiking.com).

Ultralight flights Based in Pokhara, Avia Club Nepal (aviaclubnepal.com) offers a vulture's eye-view of Machhapuchare from an ultralight. Suitable for children aged seven and over.

🔍 Fossil hunting

★ Saligrams are black stones found in the Kali Gandaki Valley which, when broken open, reveal the fossils of 130-million-year-old ammonites. Hindus walking to pilgrimage sites in the Himalayas believe the fossils represent the god Vishnu. Palaeontologists, however, see the stones as proof that rocks in the Himalayas once formed the seabed of a prehistoric ocean. How else could the remains of extinct sea creatures find their way 4000 m above sea level?

Inside info ℹ️

▶▶ With pollution, construction, traffic and tourist hustle all on the rise in Kathmandu, consider basing yourself in Bhaktapur and making daytrips into the capital.

▶▶ On treks, porters carry all luggage and even small children if necessary.

▶▶ Be especially vigilant over hygiene issues in mountain villages.

Everything about China makes your head spin. Not only is it the world's third largest country (covering an area of 9.5 million sq km), but it is also home to over 1.3 billion people. There are a baffling number of native tongues and no less than 56,000 characters in its written language. Development is proceeding at breakneck speed. The Maglev train, for example, shifts travellers from Shangai's airport to the city at 430 km/h, while Shanghai itself is actually subsiding under the weight of its skyscrapers. China is nothing if not daunting, which is why many holidaymakers stick to a fairly well-trodden circuit in the northeast, combining the imperial highlights of Beijing and Xi'an with a visit to the Great Wall. If you have time, however, make a detour south to Yángshuò where you'll catch a glimpse of traditional rural life. From there, it's just a short flight back to the future with touchdown in Hong Kong (see page 258).

Beijing

The world's largest public square, Tiananmen Square has more than enough space for children to burn off excess energy, either by flying a kite or stomping across acres of paving stones. It shouldn't, however, be too difficult to lure them through the Gate of Heavenly Peace. Located on the northern side of the square, this symbolic portal leads to the entrance of the Forbidden City – home to no less than 24 emperors between 1420 and 1923. Cross a wide moat and walk beneath the massive Meridien Gate and you face yet another threshold – the Supreme Harmony Gate. Beyond lies a vast courtyard that once held imperial audiences of up to 100,000 people. The large building rearing before you on marbled terraces is the first of three great halls where the emperor ruled from his Dragon Throne. The inner court, meanwhile, contains three palaces – forbidden to all but the imperial family and the emperor's concubines and eunuchs. At its rear is a remarkable garden of ancient conifers, rockeries, walkways and pavilions, while to the east of the palace complex are various exhibitions of bronzes, ceramics and jewellery. See if you can track down the Well of the Pearl Concubine – a narrow cleft into which a 25-year-old favourite was dispatched for daring to defy the emperor.

Great Wall of China

Get an early start for a day exploring the Great Wall. Just 70 km to the northwest of Beijing, Badaling is

rainy days in Beijing

★ **Natural History Museum** (bmnh.org.cn) Little in the way of English captions, but the Chinese dinosaur exhibits on the ground floor will appeal to kids.

★ **Le Cool Ice Rink** Indoor skating fun at the China World Shopping Mall. Can get very busy at weekends.

★ **ExploraScience** Hands-on journey into a world of gadgets and technology, including everything from robotic dogs to soap bubble rings.

Great Wall of China

The busiest location is at Badaling where you'll battle crowds and fend off souvenir hawkers. More peaceful are the sections at Simatai and Jinshanling – around 100 km from Beijing, but worth the effort for the chance to stride along the top of the Wall, admiring the views.

one of the most popular sections – particularly during summer weekends when it can be swarming with tourists. Families with young children will appreciate the cable car that whisks you up to a wooded mountain ridge where the Great Wall, punctuated by watchtowers every 70 m, snakes off into the distance. Along its outer edge, crenellated battlements provide plenty of opportunities for your kids to fire imaginary arrows at advancing Mongol hordes – while at the same time preventing them from toppling off the 6-m-wide, 9-m-tall ramparts. At Badaling you will also find a museum, film theatre and souvenir stalls. Slightly further afield, the 19-km long Simatai section of the Great Wall undulates along a ridge with much steeper drops than those at Badaling. Older children may relish the challenge of a scramble, but there's also a cable car for the less stout of heart. An added attraction at

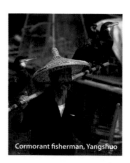

Cormorant fisherman, Yangshuo

Guilín

Forbidden City, Beijing

66 99 **In Guìlín we cycled along a rough track that meandered through a mêlée of conical fairy-tale hills. The sky was milky-white; fishponds flecked the rice paddies like squares of foil, and thickets of giant bamboo unfurled above our heads.** William Gray

Simatai is the 3-km downhill toboggan ride. If your children feel up to the challenge, head to Jinshanling from where you can hike along the Wall to Simatai. The 10-km trek takes around four hours, but be warned – there are several ruined sections of Wall to negotiate.

Zhengzhou

Around 520 km south of Beijing, the modern capital of Hénán province is the jumping off point for visits to Shaolin Temple, the birthplace of Kung Fu. Your kids will be bowled over by the regular martial arts performances where young monks spar with one another, delivering karate chops and side kicks that look as if they could bring an elephant to its knees. Also worth seeing are the Buddha carvings adorning the Longmen Caves, 13 km south of Luòyáng.

Xi'an

Arrayed like massed ranks of life-size toy soldiers, the 2000-year-old Army of Terracotta Warriors is, from a child's point of view, probably the most arresting sight in China. Some 6000 stony-faced warriors, along with their horses, face east in battle formation – ready to march into the afterworld at the eternal service of emperor Qin Shi Huang. Their weapons, which include crossbows, axes and swords, are now in storage, but you can see an impressive pair of bronze war chariots in the museum. Creepy, but captivating, no two

warrior's faces are exactly alike – and archaeologists believe there may be thousands more awaiting excavation at this extraordinary burial site.

Yángshuò

Located 65 km south of Guìlín, Yángshuò is well known to the backpacker fraternity and makes a laid-back base from which to explore the surreal karst landscape of limestone peaks that characterize this part of South China. Hire bikes and set off along tracks that lead through rice fields to nearby villages and caves. From Yángshuò you can also take a boat trip on the Li River – or paddle yourself in a canoe or raft. Don't miss the nightly cormorant fishing tours where the birds' fetch-and-return hunting skills are demonstrated by floodlight. If you have time, head north of Guìlín to the Dragon's Backbone where dramatic rice terraces scale a series of 800-m-high hills.

Terracotta Warriors

Inside info (i)

▸▸ The best time to visit Beijing is autumn (September to early November) after the summer heat has subsided and before the often bitterly cold winter sets in.
▸▸ Take the sleeper train from Beijing to Luòyáng and Xi'an, or from Guangzhou to Guìlín.
▸▸ Many attractions offer discounts, usually for children under 130 cm in height.

Hong Kong
Dim sum & Disney

Hong Kong and Singapore are two of Asia's most exciting and vibrant cities. Both are popular stopovers en route to and from Australia and New Zealand, and both are supremely child-friendly. So which do you choose? Hong Kong has Disneyland, but will that be enough to swing it in your favour? Don't forget Singapore's much-hyped Night Safari and the Sentosa 'island of fun'. Use the three-day action plans, below, to help you decide which Asian metropolis gets your vote.

City action plans

Day 1 If you've let slip that there is a Disneyland in Hong Kong you might as well take the kids there on day one to get it out of their systems. Actually, HK Disneyland (disney.com.hk) is excellent. It may be smaller than its sister parks, but it's friendly, immaculate and the food verges on the nutritious. As well as all the regular rides, like Space Mountain, Buzz Lightyear and Autopia, there's an arboreal adventure in Tarzan's treehouse and the jungle cruise has been spiced up with geysers and erupting volcanoes. Mickey opens the doors at 1000 and it's a piece of cheese to get there on the slick Mass Transit Railway (MTR) to Sunny Bay, followed by a ride on the Disney train.

If Disney doesn't appeal, hop on a fast ferry to Cheung Chau island – gawping at Hong Kong's towering skyline as you slip out of the harbour. For lunch, pick and mix from live seafood tanks at restaurants along Cheung Chau's waterfront, then enjoy a meal overlooking the tangle of junks in the harbour. Back in Hong Kong, ride the Central-Mid-Levels Escalator, a 792-m long conveyor belt that moves around 40,000 people through the city each day. For another 'moving' experience ride the tram up to the Peak (thepeak.com.hk) for spectacular views across the city. The Peak Tower has viewing platforms, shops, restaurants and even a Madame Tussaud's waxworks. Catch the Star Ferry across the harbour to Kowloon and haggle for knick-knacks at Temple Street Night Market, while snacking at the street stalls.

Day 2 For breakfast, try authentic dim sum at City Hall Maxim's Palace. With children aged 10 and over, head out of town on a full-day jolly with Fast Pursuit Craft Adventures (kayak-and-hike.com). Barely 20 km from Kowloon, the rugged Sai Kung Peninsula is fringed by a maze of islands and inlets that are inaccessible to all but the smallest craft. You'll spend the day careering through the archipelago in a speedboat and sea

View from The Peak

kayaking along a dramatic coast of sea caves, arches and deserted beaches. Hikes on nearby peaks are also possible. With younger children, take a three-hour boat trip off the coast of Lantau island in search of bubble gum-pink Indo-Pacific humpback dolphins. Hong Kong Dolphinwatch (hkdolphinwatch.com) operates trips every Wednesday, Friday and Sunday, with pick-ups in Hong Kong Central and Kowloon.

Day 3 Take the MTR to Tung Chung on Lantau island, from where the Ngong Ping 360 Skyrail (np360.com.hk) whisks you 5.7 km up to the giant Tian Tan Buddha statue on Lantau Peak. At 34 m high, it is the world's largest seated, outdoor, bronze statue of its kind. Climb the flight of 260 steps that leads to the great Buddha, then visit the nearby Po Lin monastery. The touristy Ngong Ping Village has several attractions, including 'Walking with Buddha', a multimedia exhibition where you can follow the path to enlightenment of Siddhartha Gautama – the man who became Buddha. Kids will love the shows at The Monkey's Tale Theatre, based on traditional Buddhist Jataka tales like *The jackal who saved the lion*. The streets of Ngong Ping, meanwhile, are patrolled by jugglers, Kung Fu experts and other entertainers. The Ngong Ping Tea House offers traditional Chinese tea ceremonies and copious cakes, while the Po Lin monastery has vegetarian meals.

In the afternoon, visit the Wetland Park (wetlandpark.com), a 64-hectare nature reserve where you can learn about conservation at the huge visitor centre, with its interactive computers, wildlife models and wetland simulations. Alternatively, head to Ocean Park (oceanpark.com.hk) which has everything from sharks, orcas and giant pandas to a Dragon Rollercoaster. Back in the city, watch the Symphony of Lights – a sound and light spectacular put on by skyscrapers on both sides of the harbour, then tuck into good-value Cantonese food at The Jade Garden.

Inside info ⓘ

▶▶ If you're planning to do a lot of travel to the Outlying Islands and New Territories it's worth getting an Octopus smart card (octopuscard.com).
▶▶ Some of the major events to look out for are Chinese New Year (January), Hong Kong Arts Festival (February) and the Dragon Boat Festival (June).
▶▶ For further info, visit discoverhongkong.com

Singapore skyline

Singapore
Zoo quests & islands of fun

City action plans

Day 1 For breakfast, try yam cakes and porridge served with *you tiao* (Chinese fried fritters) at the Tiong Bahru Market. Then head to Suntec City Mall to begin a 60-minute Duck Tour (ducktours.com.sg) – a light-hearted city tour and harbour cruise combo in a converted Vietnam War amphibious craft. Grab a quick snack at any of the plethora of food outlets at Suntec City, then allow 30 minutes by taxi or 75 minutes by MRT and bus to reach Singapore Zoo (zoo.com.sg). Spot free-roaming orang-utans from the Rainforest Walk before finding out about a day in the life of a working Asian elephant. Visit the walk-through Fragile Forest with its mouse deer and tree kangaroos, learn about big cat conservation at the interactive Tiger Trek exhibit and see the Hamadryas baboons in their spectacular Ethiopian Great Rift Valley setting. For dinner, enjoy an Asian buffet at the Safari Restaurant before taking a 3-km tram ride to spot nocturnal wildlife on the Night Safari (nightsafari.com.sg). During the 40-minute ride, you'll journey from the Himalayan foothills to Equatorial Africa, discovering the nocturnal antics of tigers, tapirs and numerous other species.

Day 2 Pop into Ya Kun Kaya Toast at Raffles City for toast with anything from cheese and ice cream to coconut-and-egg jam. Then head west on the MRT to Snow City (snowcity.com.sg) which is not only a great place to chill out if the heat is proving too much, but you can also ski, snowboard and build snowmen. Backtrack to HarbourFront Tower 2 (have lunch on the go) for the cable car ride to the playground island of Sentosa (sentosa.com.sg). Ask for the glass-bottomed cabin and then get an even better view of Singapore and the Southern Islands from the 110-m high Sky Tower – just one of the attractions at Imbriah Lookout. Brace yourself for the multi-sensory 4D Magix show where special effects ensure you get a lot more

than just a movie. Visit the Merlion, a larger-than-life recreation of Singapore's famous icon, then ride the 650-m luge run. Unwind at Coastes, a relaxed beach bar and grill overlooking Silosa Beach (the island has over 3 km of sandy shore), then take the Sentosa Express light rail back to HarbourFront Singapore.

Day 2 Explore Chinatown Heritage Centre on a motorized trishaw, pausing to sample local food. Get to grips with over 1000 interactive exhibits, an IMAX cinema and a huge outdoor Waterworks park at the Singapore Science Centre (science.edu.sg). Sample *char kway teow* (Singapore noodles) at any central food centre. Learn about ancient traditions at the Asian Civilisations Museum (acm.org.sg) at Empress Place. Don't miss the Singapore River Gallery which traces the city's fascinating story of colonization and trade. Bring the exhibit to life by viewing the modern-day metropolis on a bumboat ride (rivercruise.com.sg) along the Singapore River. Round off the day with some souvenir hunting along the streets of Chinatown or Little India. Dine at Lau Pa Sat Festival Market, the oldest Victorian filigree cast-iron building in Asia, or enjoy a seafood feast at Clarke Quay.

Buddha Tooth Relic Temple, Singapore

Inside info

▶▶ Other big attractions include Sentosa Island's Universal Studios Singapore (rwsentosa.com) and the Marina Bay Sands & Sky Park (marinabaysands.com) with its spectacular city observation platform.
▶▶ In addition to the zoo, natural highlights include Jurong Bird Park (birdpark.com.sg) and River Safari (riversafari.com.sg) – a journey through the world's greatest rivers in one park.
▶▶ For further info, visit yoursingapore.com

Thailand
Temples in the tropics

According to the Thai psyche, anything worth doing should involve an element of *sànùk* or 'fun' – something that fraught parents might question when cajoling overheated kids around manic Bangkok. Overwhelmingly, though, Thailand is bursting with excuses for having fun. You could start with some jetlag-recovery time on the tropical island of Koh Samet or take a sleeper train to the hill country around Chiang Mai – ideal if *sànùk* equates to some cool relief from the hot and humid lowlands. Elsewhere, children will be all smiles riding elephants, paddling sea kayaks and snorkelling on coral reefs.

Bangkok

Prepare to be dazzled by Bangkok's temple monasteries or Wats. These architectural gems with their gleaming orange-and-green roof tiles, mosaic-clad stupas and gilded ornamentation are a must-see. Head first to Wat Phra Kaew where the diminutive 66-cm tall Emerald Buddha resides in a lavishly decorated *bòt* (chapel) guarded by statues of mythical giants. Adjoining Wat Phra Kaew is The Grand Palace, another impressive monument, but only worth a quick look with kids in tow. Before they get 'templed out' or frazzled by the heat, you need to stroll along to nearby Wat Pho to show them the reclining Buddha. It measures an astounding 46 m in length and 15 m in height and is completely clad in gold leaf and mother-of-pearl. Next, hop on a long-tail boat for a refreshing zip around Bangkok's canals and river tributaries – a veritable 'Venice of the East'. If the kids are up for another temple, squeeze in a stop at Wat Arun with its impressive 82-m-tall central spire. That's the essential sightseeing stuff over with. So, how do you keep children entertained for the rest of the day? Older children may want to mingle with trendy Thai teens in MBK, a shopping centre crammed with shops and stalls selling cheap 'designer' clothing and just about everything else. For somewhere green, Lumphini Park has lawns to run about on, a lake to boat on and even a kite-flying season from February to April. For cooling down, slide over to Central World Ice Skating in the World Trade Centre. There's a Children's Discovery Museum at Chatuchak Park, a collection of rare indigenous wildlife at Dusit Zoo and a nest of vipers at the Queen Saovabha Memorial Institute where lethal snakes are milked in order to produce anti-venoms.

Out of town A 69-ha wildlife park located 45 km east of Bangkok, Safari World (safariworld.com) has a

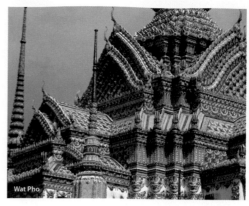
Wat Pho

drive-through safari experience with lions and tigers, while Muang Boran (ancientcity.com), 33 km from the city, is an open-air museum with scaled replicas of Thailand's famous monuments. Further afield, you can catch a train or bus to Kanchanaburi, visit the famous 'Bridge over the River Kwai' and take a dip in the natural pools fed by the seven-tiered waterfalls of Erawan National Park. To the south, meanwhile, the beachside resort of Hua Hin has calm waters, plenty of restaurants and pony rides on the beach.

Kids' top 10 Thailand

❶ **Float** on a bamboo raft down the Mai Pae River (and pray that it doesn't sink).
❷ **Explore** the ancient tropical rainforest of Khao Sok National Park by elephant-back, then discover the jungle's strange nocturnal wildlife during a night safari.
❸ **Ride** the sleeper train from Bangkok to Chiang Mai, scale the Dragon Staircase to Doi Suthep Temple and visit the elephant sanctuary at nearby Lampang.
❹ **Learn** to scuba dive on Ko Tao, see psychedelic coral reefs and (fingers crossed) spot a whale shark.
❺ **Taste** delicious Thai food, like *kaeng phèt kài nàw mái* (chicken and bamboo shoot curry) and *kuaytiaw plaa* (rice noodles with fish balls) – but steer clear of the really spicy stuff like *yam phrík chíi fáa*.
❻ **Trek** in the Hill Tribe region, sleeping in local villages and finding out how people live in this remote corner of northern Thailand.
❼ **Paddle** a kayak into the sea caves of Ao Phang-Nga Marine National Park.
❽ **Discover** beach bliss, lazing under coconut palms and snorkelling over coral reefs at islands like Ko Samet, Ko Samui, Ko Pha-Ngan, Ko Phi-Phi, Ko Lanta and Ko Hai.
❾ **Listen** out for the haunting cry of a gibbon during a dawn walk in the rainforest.
❿ **Shop** in markets for traditional souvenirs like Hill-Tribe embroidery, Thai silk and shadow puppets.

It may well start as just a vague idea for adding a few days to a stopover in Kuala Lumpur en route to or from Australia. Then it becomes a week once you realize that Peninsular Malaysia actually has a lot going for it in terms of family appeal – whether it's tropical islands like Langkawi or the rainforest reserve of Taman Negara. And then Malaysia plays its trump card – your mind wanders across the South China Sea to the East Malaysian states of Sarawak and Sabah and suddenly you're plotting a full-blown family adventure into the heart of Borneo (see pages 262-263). And who can blame you? With its headhunting legacy, giant bat-filled caves and endangered orang-utans, northern Borneo ranks as one of the world's most exciting destinations for children and adults alike.

Tioman Island

Malaysia
Peninsular hotspots

Kuala Lumpur

One of the world's tallest buildings, the 88-storey, 452-m-high Petronas Twin Towers has a Skybridge with stomach-lurching views of the city. The adjacent KLCC Park has shops, a science centre, children's playground, musical fountain and aquarium. More vertigo moments are available at the top of the KL Tower and from the 60-m-tall Eye on Malaysia big wheel. Back on street level, head to the peaceful Lake Gardens, a 92-ha green oasis with a lake, butterfly park and orchid garden. Upping the tempo, Central Market is a bustling hub for traditional arts and craft – the riverside amphitheatre has regular cultural shows, batik painting demonstrations and shadow puppet plays. Nearby is Chinatown where, on Petaling Street, you can browse the stalls and visit the elaborate Chan See Shu Yuen Temple.

By far the most popular city excursion, Batu Caves, 15 km north of KL, is a subterranean wonder of ornate Hindu shrines. You'll need to scale 272 steps to reach the main temple cave.

Taman Negara

Over 130 million years in the making, the ancient rainforest of Taman Negara (wildlife.gov.my) is teeming with life. See how many of the national park's 250 bird species you can spot from the canopy walkway, then take a river cruise in search of tapir, elephant and, if you're extremely lucky, leopard and tiger. Other activities available include jungle trekking and caving. South of Taman Negara, the Kuala Gandah Elephant Orphanage (myelephants.org) is a refuge for jumbos that have run out of space elsewhere in Peninsular

Malayasia – you can ride them and give them a bath. In the northern state of Kedah, the 950-m-long Tree Top Walk in the Sedim River Recreation Park is the longest in the world, while northern Perak's Kuala Gula Bird Sanctuary is full of feathered friends between September and March when 200,000 migrant birds descend on its mudflats and mangroves. If you only have time for a brief rainforest foray, make your way to the Forest Research Institute of Malaysia. Located just 16 km northwest of KL, the centre has four walking trails and a canopy walk.

Cameron Highlands

Escape the muggy lowlands with a visit to the Cameron Highlands where tea plantations mingle with honey farms. Trekking and birdwatching are popular activities – and useful for building up an appetite for the local ever-so-colonial tradition of tea and scones. Around 90 minutes drive to the south of KL, A'Famosa Water World (afamosa.com) has a children's adventure pool, a seven-storey high-speed waterslide, a wave pool and reputedly the longest lazy river ride in the world.

Islands

Peninsular Malaysia has tropical islands off both its east and west coasts. Langkawi, in the northwest, has arguably the country's most stunning beach – Tanjung Rhu – although there are dozens more in this cluster of 99 islands that will feel like sand made in heaven. Langkawi also has an international airport, modern resorts and plenty of activities and attractions to make family holidays a piece of cake. Don't miss out on a snorkelling excursion to the nearby Pulau Payar Marine Park. The most popular east-coast alternative to Langkawi is Tioman Island which, like lesser-developed Pulau Redang in the far north, is a paradise for scuba diving and jungle trekking.

Inside info ⓘ

▶▶ Allow around three hours to reach Taman Negara or the Cameron Highlands by road from KL..
▶▶ In Peninsular Malaysia the risk of malaria is confined to Taman Negara National Park, however malaria is widespread in Sabah and Sarawak on the island of Borneo.

Borneo

Visit a longhouse

Where Skrang River or Batang Ai National Park, Sarawak

Why Visiting a longhouse is the best way to learn about the customs of the Iban – Sarawak's largest indigenous group. You'll find out how a typical Iban community lives under one roof, how rice cultivation underpins their culture and – most intriguing of all – how they once gained a reputation as headhunters. Spend a night or more in a longhouse and you may be invited to take part in fast-and-furious drumming competitions, adorn feather headdresses for traditional dancing and purchase local handicrafts, such as wooden carvings of hornbills – the sacred bird of the Iban. Just remember to go easy on the *tuak* – the locally brewed and potent rice wine.

How Leaving Kuching by 4WD, you transfer to motorized longboat for a thrilling ride on the Skrang River. You may need to get out and help push the boat through shallow rapids. Remember to remove your shoes before entering a longhouse.

Go underground

Where Gunung Mulu National Park, Sarawak

Why It is only when you stand at the gaping maw of Deer Cave and try to envisage five St Paul's Cathedrals snug inside that the true enormity of Mulu's subterranean wonders strikes you. Deer Cave is the world's largest cave passage, 1600 m long by 120 m high – a fitting backdrop for the nightly exodus of two million wrinkle-lipped bats whose frenzied wingbeats sound like distant surf. Walking inside the cave you crunch over vast domes of bat guano, seething with cockroaches, centipedes and other minibeasts. Lovely.

How You can fly to Mulu from Miri or take a boat from Kuala Baram via Marudi. Try to get to the viewing platform in front of Deer Cave by 1800 to witness the bat exodus.

Also consider Gomantong Caves in Sabah are famous for their colonies of swiftlets. These tiny birds use saliva to construct their nests – the prized ingredient for bird's nest soup that is harvested (on a controlled basis between February and April) by locals using a gravity-defying system of rattan ladders, ropes and poles.

Climb a mountain

Where Mount Kinabalu, Sabah

Why At 4101 m, Mount Kinabalu is the tallest mountain between the Himalayas and New Guinea. Kinabalu is also a treat for naturalists. Mist-wrapped and shaggy with moss and lichen, its forests seem otherworldly. This is a place where worms grow to the length of your leg, frogs are as tiny as your fingernail and carnivorous pitcher plants feast on insects. The mountain's slopes run riot with 1200 different orchids, numerous indigenous rhododendrons and the rare, but unforgettable, Rafflesia – a parasite devoid of leaf, stem or root that produces a single, whiffy bloom measuring nearly a metre across.

Old man of the forest

The rehabilitation centre at the Kabili-Sepilok Forest Reserve is one of the best places in the world for a close encounter with orang-utans – most of which have been orphaned through hunting or deforestation.

Iban dancer

Rainforest in Sabah

How It's a knee-busting two-day slog to the summit and back. Allow at least five hours after setting out from the national park headquarters to reach Laban Rata, a hut at 3272 m where trekkers spend the night before tackling the summit. Well before dawn the following morning, you steal outside and grope your way upwards by torchlight. The forest soon succumbs to the altitude as you scramble across bare slopes of granite using fixed ropes and ladders to scale the steepest sections. The effort is more than worthwhile, however, when you reach the summit in time to witness the remarkable spectacle of Sabah spread beneath you – from the smooth sweep of the South China Sea to the crumpled mantel of the Crocker Range. Having conquered Kinabalu, most trekkers hobble to nearby Poring Hot Springs for a long soak.

Meet the Wild Man of Borneo
Where Kabili-Sepilok Forest Reserve, Sabah
Why Although orang-utans are sometimes glimpsed during boat trips along the Kinabatangan River, the best place to see them is this 5666-ha sanctuary near Sandakan. Sepilok is renowned for its rehabilitation centre – a kind of hospital and training camp for orang-utans that have been orphaned by hunting or deforestation. Once nursed to health, young orphans literally have to be taught all the skills essential to life in the jungle – everything from swinging to eating. A tedious diet of milk and fruit encourages them to forage in the wild and gradually gain independence.

How The best time to visit is at 1000 or 1430 when the apes emerge from the forest for their daily ration of bananas and milk at feeding platforms in the reserve.
Also consider Turtle Islands Park, a cluster of islands lying 40 km off the coast near Sandakan, puts the conservation focus on turtles. The marine reptiles come ashore to nest year-round on Pulau Selingan where it is possible to join rangers in their efforts to safeguard the vulnerable clutches from predators.

Probe the interior
Where Kinabatangan River, Sabah
Why River travel is the classic (and easiest) way to travel into the thickly forested heart of Borneo – or at least to explore the dwindling remnants that haven't been cleared for oil palm plantations. At 560 km, the Kinabatangan is Sabah's longest river, flowing east from the Crocker Range to spill into the mangrove-fringed Sulu Sea. Its lower reaches pulse through one of Southeast Asia's richest rainforests – a haven for elephants, monkeys, otters and other rare species.
How Join an organized tour from Sandankan or stay at a riverside lodge.
Also consider Located 83 km southwest of Lahad Datu, the 440 sq km Danum Valley Conservation Area is home to such rarities as the Sumatran rhinoceros, orang-utan and clouded leopard. You can stay at the Borneo Rainforest Lodge, a comfortable eco-resort offering jungle treks, river swimming, night safaris and excursions to nearby logging sites.

> **" "**
> Less than two hours into our river cruise, we encounter a troop of proboscis monkeys. A male is squatting on a branch, peering at us over the bulbous protrusion of one of nature's finest hooters – a wonderfully droopy red nose that looks like a flaccid party balloon.
> William Gray

When to go

The best time to visit **Jordan** is during spring or autumn. You'll bake in summer, while winter brings cold winds, rain and even snow. In **Dubai**, blue skies and sunshine are the norm. Not surprisingly, summer's sizzling highs of 45-48°C coincide with the best hotel deals, so be prepared to spend more on accommodation during cooler months. **India's** climate varies dramatically from north to south, but generally there are three seasons: hot and dry, hot and wet (monsoon) and cool and dry – the latter, most popular, period lasting from November to mid-February. Escape the brutal heat and humidity of May and June by heading for the cooler hill stations. The main monsoon sweeps in from the southwest during June and July, while the northwest monsoon douses Kerala and other parts of the southeast coast during October and November. Dodge the monsoons by visiting **Sri Lanka** either between December and late April or during August. The ideal months to visit **Nepal** are October and November when the air has been washed clean by the monsoon, the countryside is green and the weather is balmy. December and January are also good, but be prepared for snow and frigid temperatures on treks in the Himalayas. **China** is best visited during spring or autumn. Winters can be bitter in the northeast, while summers in the south are hot and humid. In **Hong Kong**, most rain falls between May and September. **Thailand**, **Malaysia** and **Singapore** are hot and humid all year, with fairly constant annual temperatures of around 24-31°C. Thailand's beaches are at their best during February and March, with the monsoon hitting between May and October. Try to avoid Peninsular Malaysia's east coast in November and December when the monsoon brings winds and tropical downpours. The rainy season occurs on the west coast during April and May and again from October to November.

Getting there

Asia's major airline hubs at Dubai, Mumbai, Colombo, Bangkok, Kuala Lumpur, Singapore, Jakarta and Hong Kong are like giant stepping-stones across the continent. National carriers serve numerous destinations throughout Europe, Africa, Australasia and North America and include Emirates (emirates.com), Singapore Airlines (singaporeair.com), Air China (airchina.co.uk), Air India (airindia.in), Gulf Air (gulfair.com), Malaysia Airlines (malaysiaairlines.com), Royal Jordanian (rja.com), Sri Lankan Airlines (srilankan.aero) and Thai Airways (thaiairways.com).

Getting around

Jordan has a good road network plied by modern, air-conditioned coaches, but you might also want to consider renting a car. Taxis are the easiest way of getting around in **Dubai**. Look out for the cream-coloured metered cabs from the Dubai Transport Corporation.

In **India**, the safest, least stressful way to travel independently is to hire a car with a driver/guide and use sleeper trains for longer journeys. Indian Railways (indianrail.gov.in or cleartrip.com) offers an extensive and efficient service throughout the country. If you need to keep internal travel times to a minimum, there are several domestic airlines, including Go Airlines (goair.in) and Jet Airways (jetairways.com).

Although some of the main routes are busy and occasionally hair-raising, road travel is still the best way to get around in **Sri Lanka**. Hiring a vehicle with a driver is also excellent value.

Domestic flights in **Nepal** are operated by several airlines, including Buddha Air (buddhaair.com).

To meet growing numbers of tourists, **China** has modernized its domestic air and rail systems. China Train Ticket (china-train-ticket.com) provides an online rail reservation system. Travelling around **Hong Kong** is a cinch with a choice of trains, buses, trams, taxis and ferries. The MTR (mtr.com.hk) shifts 2.5 million people every weekday, while Star Ferry (starferry.com.hk) and First Ferry (nwff.com.hk) serve nearby islands. **Singapore's** transport infrastructure is also efficient, thanks to taxis, buses and the MRT (smrt.com.sg).

In **Thailand**, local airlines include Bangkok Airways (bangkokair.com). The State Railway of Thailand (railway.co.th) can get you from Bangkok to Chiang Mai. In the capital, you can get around using the Bangkok Metro (bangkokmetro.co.th), metered taxis, river taxis or tuk-tuks.

Malaysia has an excellent transport system, with air-conditioned coaches and trains connecting Kuala Lumpur with all main towns. Driving in Malaysia is easy and safe as long as you steer clear of the capital.

Accommodation

In **Jordan**, Petra has dozens of hotels, including the Mövenpick (movenpick-petra.com). You can also stay at a Bedouin camp in Wadi Rum. **Dubai** has excellent city hotels and beach resorts, many with kids' clubs, such as Le Royal Meridien (leroyalmeridien-dubai.com) and the Jumeirah Beach Hotel (jumeirah.com). Out of town, try the Bab Al Shams Desert Resort.

In **India**, accommodation ranges from international city hotels to national park restcamps.

Delhi's LaLit (thelalit.com) has a swimming pool and is conveniently located on Connaught Square. The Jaypee Palace (jaypeehotels.com) is a comfortable hotel in Agra. For a spot of luxury on the Goa coast, the Park Hyatt Resort (goa.park.hyatt.com) has an Ayurvedic spa and a huge pool with waterslides.

Sri Lanka has an excellent range of family-friendly accommodation. In Kandy, try the Chaaya Citadel (chaayahotels.com) which has interconnecting rooms and a children's pool. A good base for exploring the Cultural Triangle, Hotel Sigiriya (serendibleisure.com) organizes children's activities, such as birdwatching walks and visits to local villages. Its sister property, Club Hotel Dolphin, is located on the coast at Waikkal.

In **Nepal**, hotels in Kathmandu and Pokhara usually have pools, while accommodation on treks can be anything from fully supported camping to local teahouses and more upmarket lodges. Temple Tiger Lodge (catmando.com) in Chitwan National Park has 33 en suite villas, each one raised on stilts with views across the grasslands.

China's main tourist centres offer a wide range of accommodation to suit all budgets. For a spot of indulgence, check out the Peninsula Beijing (beijing. peninsula.com) which is ideally located near the Forbidden City. A good mid-range bet in **Hong Kong's** Kowloon district is the BP International (bpih. com.hk). Family suites at Salisbury YMCA (ymcahk.org. hk) are also excellent value.

Top family picks in **Singapore** include Costa Sands Resort Downtown East (costasands.com.sg) which kids will be thrilled to discover is located next to the Escape Theme Park and Wild Wild Wet.

Thailand and **Malaysia** have a plethora of international city hotels and beach resorts, as well as apartments and guesthouses. In Bangkok, the Bel-Aire Princess (bel-aireprincess.com) is less pricey than other city hotels, but has a central location, swimming pool and Thai cookery school. In Kuala Lumpur, try the Hotel Equatorial (equatorial.com); in Langkawi, splash out on the Sheraton Beach Resort (sheraton.com) which has family rooms and a kids' club.

Food & drink

For a traditional meal in **Jordan**, expect appetizers like hummous, followed by *mansaf* (stewed lamb, rice and yoghurt) and a selection of syrup-drenched pastries. **Dubai** offers a cosmopolitan range of cuisine, from Indian and Thai to Filipino, Lebanese and Persian. If you want to sample truly authentic Emirati cuisine head to the souks where you will find everything from dates to camel meat. Concocted from stir-fried masalas of onion, garlic and freshly ground spices, authentic **Indian** curries are usually served with rice and flat breads. Yoghurt-based *lassi* drinks are a good way to cool taste buds, but most young children will find curries too spicy. There are usually blander alternatives on the menu and, of course, in popular tourist locations you will find a choice of eateries. Rice and curry (often made with fish and coconut milk) feature predominantly in **Sri Lanka**, but beach hotels will usually offer a range of other dishes as well. The staple meal in **Nepal** is *dal-bhat* (steamed rice with lentil soup), accompanied by curried vegetables and pickles. *Momos* (stuffed dumplings) and *rotis* are also popular. **China** has more than enough variety in its cuisine to satisfy even the most pernickety feeder – from fried rice and steamed chicken to soups and sweet-and-sour dishes. In **Thailand** and **Malaysia**, traditional food consists of delicious seafood, satays, coconut-based curries, noodles and boiled rice in banana leaves. Kids will love coconut milk straight from the nut or freshly squeezed sugarcane juice.

Health & safety

Malaria affects large areas of Asia, so you need to discuss malaria prevention with your doctor well before you travel. Malaria-free areas include Jordan, Dubai, Singapore and Hong Kong. Before visiting Asia you should plan an appropriate course of **vaccinations**, which may include hepatitis A, typhoid and yellow fever. Be wary of drinking tap **water** anywhere in Asia, with the exception of cities like Dubai, Hong Kong and Singapore. **Traffic** can be chaotic and random, so take care when crossing streets. Never let your children approach street **dogs** – a bite may carry a high risk of rabies. Other health precautions you need to take include avoiding overexposure to **sun** and **heat** and taking a sensible approach to trekking at **high altitude** with children.

Fast facts

Country	Time	Language*	Currency	Code	Tourist information
Jordan	GMT+2	Arabic	Dinar	+962	visitjordan.com
Dubai	GMT+4	Arabic	Dirham	+971	dubaitourism.ae
India	GMT+5½	Hindi	Indian rupee	+91	incredibleindia.org
Sri Lanka	GMT+6	Sinhala	Sri Lankan rupee	+94	srilankatourism.org
Nepal	GMT+6	Nepali	Nepalese rupee	+977	welcomenepal.com
China	GMT+8	Mandarin	Yuan Renminbi	+86	cnto.org
Hong Kong	GMT+8	Cantonese	Hong Kong dollar	+852	discoverhongkong.com
Singapore	GMT+8	Malay	Singapore dollar	+65	yoursingapore.com
Thailand	GMT+7	Thai	Baht	+26	tourismthailand.org
Malaysia	GMT+8	Malay	Ringgit	+60	tourism.gov.my

* Tamil also spoken in Sri Lanka; English widely spoken in Hong Kong and Singapore

Shangri-La's Rasa Sentosa Resort
Where? Singapore.
Why? The Rasa Sentosa is the only beachfront resort in Singapore. The powdery white sand of Siloso Beach is a short stroll through the hotel's immaculate gardens. If you can tear yourself away from the resort's swimming pools, clubs and leisure facilities, the attractions of Sentosa Island, including the Universal Studios theme park, are only a light railway ride away.
Contact Shangri-La, T+65 (0)6275-0100, shangri-la.com

Borneo Rainforest Lodge
Where? Danum Valley, Sabah, Eastern Malaysia.
Why? Occupying a magnificent setting next to the Danum River in Sabah's largest area of protected lowland rainforest, this comfortable lodge has chalets built on stilts and balconies looking straight out onto pristine jungle. Activities include spotting wildlife from the lodge's 300-m-long canopy walkway.
Contact Borneo Nature Tours, T+60 (0)88-267 637, borneonaturetours.com

King's Lodge
Where? Bandhavgarh National Park, India.
Why? Designed to blend into its surroundings, Kings Lodge has 18 rural-style cottages (some on stilts) with large verandas overlooking sal forest and grassland. Located 10 minutes from Bandhavgarh National Park, the lodge offers jeep and elephant-back safaris, as well as cycling, walks and village visits and workshops outside the park.
Contact Pugdundee Safaris, T+91 (0)124-422 2657, kingslodge.in

Banjaar Tola Kanha Tented Camp
Where? Kanha National Park, India
Why? Tucked into indigenous forest right beside the Banjaar River and looking across to the lush woodland and grassy meadows of Kanha National Park, the two intimate camps of Banjaar Tola Kanha each have nine tented suites, designed with a light footprint to protect the sensitive riverine environment. Each of the contemporary suites features bamboo floors, canvas roof and walls, and glass doors leading onto a riverside veranda. Both camps have a spacious open-air dining area and library. Activities include twice-daily jungle drives with expert naturalists, guided nature walks, birdwatching and tiger viewing from elephant back in Kanha National Park. Banjaar Tola Kanha is one of four luxury camps operated by &Beyond in Madhya Pradesh – the others are located near Bandhavgarh, Panna and Pench National Parks.
Contact &Beyond, T+91 (0)11-4626 9000, andbeyond.com

Jumeirah Beach Hotel
Where? Dubai.
Why? With its own private beach, water park and five swimming pools, families are never short of sun, sand and swimming opportunities at Dubai's leading five-star family hotel. You can also learn to dive, play tennis night and day on floodlit courts and even arrange to snorkel on a purpose-built coral reef 2 km offshore.
Contact Jumeirah Beach Hotel, T+971 (0)4-348 0000, jumeirah.com

Asia

Family favourites

Easy riders

Learning to surf on the Coromandel Peninsula, North Island, New Zealand. Right: rainbow lorikeet, Queensland.

Australia & New Zealand

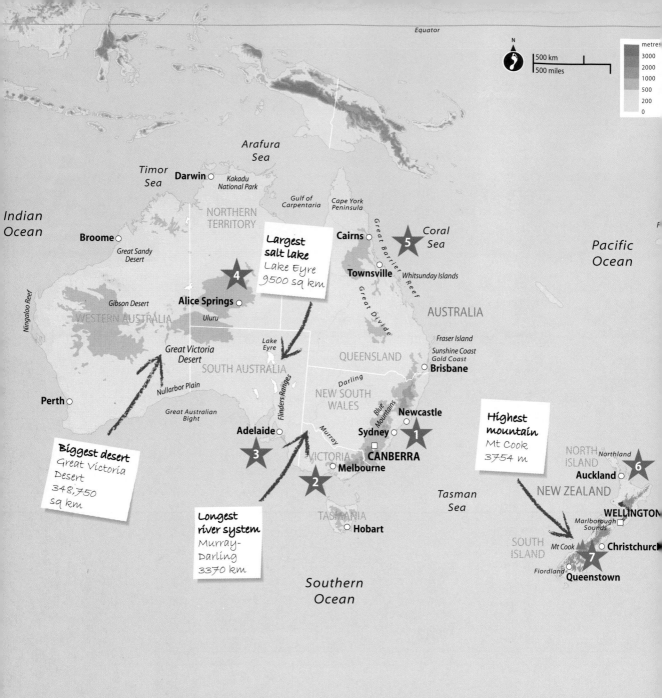

Equator

Indian
Ocean

Pacific
Ocean

Timor
Sea

Arafura
Sea

Darwin ○ *Kakadu
National Park*

NORTHERN
TERRITORY

Gulf of
Carpentaria

Cape York
Peninsula

Great Barrier Reef

Coral
Sea

Cairns ○

⭐ 5

Broome ○

*Great Sandy
Desert*

⭐ 4

Townsville ○

Whitsunday Islands

AUSTRALIA

Gibson Desert

WESTERN AUSTRALIA

Alice Springs ○

Uluru

*Great Victoria
Desert*

*Lake
Eyre*

SOUTH AUSTRALIA

QUEENSLAND

Darling

Fraser Island
Sunshine Coast
Gold Coast

Brisbane ○

NEW SOUTH
WALES

Ningaloo Reef

Nullarbor Plain

Flinders Ranges

*Blue
Mountains*

Newcastle ○

Perth ○

*Great Australian
Bight*

Adelaide ○

Murray

Sydney ○

□ ⭐ 1

⭐ 3

VICTORIA

CANBERRA

**Highest
mountain**
Mt Cook
3754 m

Biggest desert
Great Victoria
Desert
348,750
sq km

⭐ 2

○ **Melbourne**

**Largest
salt lake**
Lake Eyre
9500 sq km

**Longest
river system**
Murray-
Darling
3370 km

TASMANIA

○ **Hobart**

Tasman
Sea

NORTH
ISLAND

Northland

⭐ 6

Auckland ○

NEW ZEALAND

WELLINGTON

*Marlborough
Sounds*

SOUTH
ISLAND

Mt Cook

○ **Christchurch**

⭐ 7

Fiordland

Queenstown

Southern
Ocean

metres
3000
2000
1000
500
200
0

N

500 km
500 miles

Introduction Australia & New Zealand

1 Take a boat trip around Sydney Harbour

» New South Wales, page 276

2 Roam the Great Ocean Road

» Victoria, page 279

3 See Aussie wildlife on Kangaroo Island

» South Australia, page 280

4 Explore the Red Centre

» Northern Territory, page 282

5 Snorkel on the Great Barrier Reef

» Queensland, page 284

6 Learn to surf in Coromandel

» North Island, page 286

7 Follow in Frodo's footsteps

» South Island, page 288

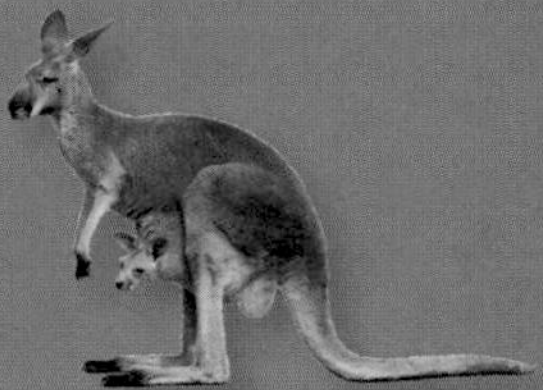

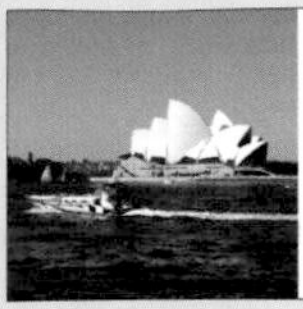

It's a long, long way to go, but don't ever let distance or jetlag stand in the way of two of the world's best family holiday destinations. The beaches alone more than justify the long haul to Australia and New Zealand – not that you're going to fly Down Under just to build sandcastles and splash in the sea. This is a region ripe for adventure, whether you take tots on a motorhome odyssey around South Island or tempt teens with a taste of Aussie surf culture. From camping in the Outback and snorkelling on the Great Barrier Reef to swimming with dolphins and searching for Mordor, kids will relish the non-stop action. Along the way, they'll pick up nuggets of Aboriginal and Maori lore, encounter some of the world's most endearing and fascinating wildlife and witness scenery ranging from glaciated peaks to tropical rainforest. Going hand-in-hand with this big bundle of fun is the constant reassurance that everything is supremely family-friendly, easy-going and affordable. But first, you just need to get there.

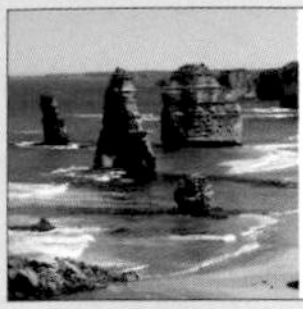

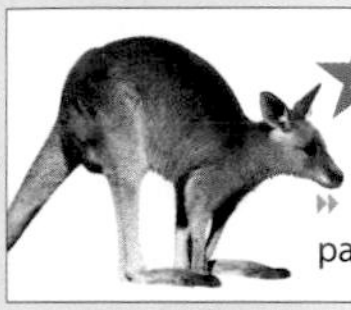

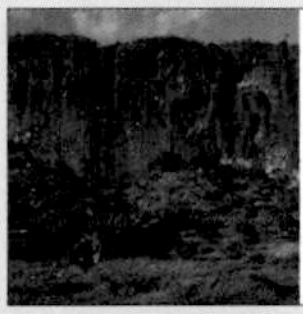

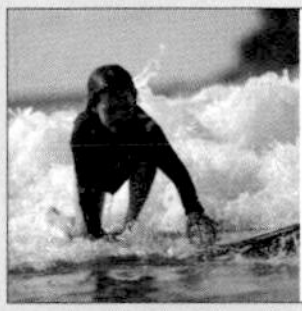

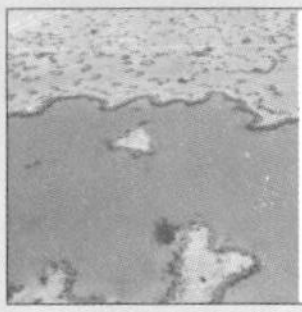

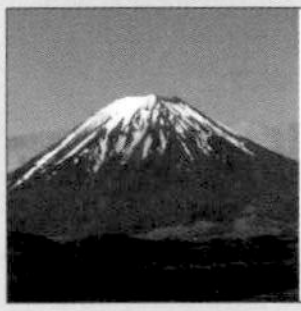

"Simply grappling with the sheer distance involved in travelling to New Zealand and Australia fired the imagination of our five-year-old twins. Judging by the looks on their faces it was almost as if they had become privy to some great secret when we explained that when they're awake people in Australia are asleep."

William Gray

Star rating

Wow factor ★★★★★

Worry factor ★

Value for money ★★★

Keeping teacher happy ★★★★★

Family accommodation ★★★★★

Babies & toddlers ★★★★

Cool for teenagers ★★★★★

id you know?

Anna Creek Station in South Australia is the orld's largest cattle station, which at around 4,000 sq km covers an area the size of Belgium.

★ The fact that kangaroos break wind considerably less than cows or sheep has intrigued scientists studying the effects of methane gas on global warming.

★ According to Maori lore, when the goddess of the underworld, Tuhinenuitepo, saw how beautiful Fiordland was she became so concerned that people would want to live there forever that she introduced the sandfly to ...f their mortality.

How to throw a boomerang

➤ Find a large grassy area, clear of trees, lamp posts and crystal vases.
➤ Hold the end of your boomerang between thumb and forefinger, making sure the curved side faces towards you.
➤ Scatter some leaves, noting which way the wind blows them. Face directly into the wind, then turn about 60 degrees to your right. This is the direction you should throw your boomerang.
➤ Always throw overhand, never side-arm. Snap your wrist at the end of the throw to create spin.
➤ Practise varying the degree of spin and the strength and direction of throw until your boomerang returns.
➤ Catch a returning boomerang by 'clapping' it between your hands.
➤ Remember, a miss-thrown boomerang can be dangerous. Always be ready to shout a warning to others – or to duck.

Taste of Australia bush tucker

➤ **Honey ants** Sweet, sugar-packed treats, these insects store honeydew in their swollen abdomens. But you need to know where to look for their underground nests.

➤ **Witchetty grubs** These large beetle larvae are found in the stems and trunks of certain wattle bushes. They can be eaten raw, made into soup or barbequed with or without their heads. Delicious with peanut sauce – just like chicken satay.

➤ **Macadamia nuts** These native Australian nuts are scrummy on their own, but taste even better chopped into pieces and smothered with freshly-made hot toffee. Allow to cool and harden, then smash into pieces with a hammer.

Warning! Many wild foods are unsafe to eat. If in doubt, leave well alone.

Deadly creatures in Australia

Box jellyfish 80-cm-long tentacles; sting can kill a human within a few minutes.

Saltwater crocodile World's largest reptile, up to 7 m in length.

Blue ring octopus Only the size of a golf ball, but venom is lethal.

★ Aussie lingo

Ankle biter: Small child
Bush telly: campfire
Corker: excellent
Don't spit the dummy: Don't get upset
Fair dinkum: True, real, genuine
Holy dooley: Good heavens
It's gone walkabout: It's lost
Rip snorter: Something fantastic
Shark biscuit: Someone new to surfing
Tell a porky: Lie

The Maori name for Hawkes Bay,
Taumatawhakatangihangakoauauotamateaturipukakapimaungahoronukupokaiwhenuaakitanarahu
reputedly translates to 'the place where Tamatea, the man with big knees, who slid, climbed and swallowed mountains, played his flute to his loved one.'

Kids' stuff
Australia & New Zealand

Great reads ◄ • • • • • • • •
5 children's books

Early years

One Woolly Wombat
Rod Trinca and Kerry Argent (Kane/Miller)
A superbly illustrated first counting book using zany Australian animal characters, from one woolly wombat to 14 slick seals.

Ages 6+

Land of the Long White Cloud
Kiri Te Kanawa (Chrysalis Children's Books)
Opera singer Kiri Te Kanawa retells the intriguing folk-histories of her people, the Maori of New Zealand, in this collection of 19 short stories. Beautiful watercolour illustrations add to the vibrancy of the tales.

Ages 7+

The Drovers Road Collection
Joyce West (Bethlehem Budget Books)
Three adventure stories seen through the eyes of a child as she grows up on a sheep station in New Zealand during the 1920s and 1930s paint a vivid portrait of Maori culture and rural life.

Jack Stalwart: The Search for the Sunken Treasure
Elizabeth Singer Hunt (Red Fox)
Off the coast of Australia, a diver has vanished along with treasure from the wreck of the *HMS Pandora*. Can Secret Agent Jack Stalwart find the diver and defeat a band of pirates before they escape with the treasure?

Ages 8+

Australia, the People
(Prentice Hall)
Discover all things Australian from the Aboriginal Dreamtime to Aussie rules football and from surfing to the Flying Doctor Service.

Kids' top 10
Lord of the Rings filming locations

❶ **Hobbiton** Sam and Frodo's home, the Shire, was filmed near Matamata. Take a guided tour to Bag End with Hobbiton Tours (hobbitontours.com).
❷ **Mordor** Pictured below, the volcano, Mount Ruapehu in Tongariro National Park was just the place for Sauron to plot his domination over Middle Earth.
❸ **Dimholt Road** Closed to all but the Army of the Dead and the heir of Isildur, this haunted passageway was filmed at the Putangirua Pinnacles near Martinborough.
❹ **Pelennor Fields** The wide shots for the epic Battle of Pelennor Fields were filmed near Twizel. Guided tours with local Orcs and Rohirrim are available.
❺ **Rivendell** A popular spot for picnics and walking, Kaitoke Regional Park in the Tararua Ranges was the site of Elrond's tranquil forest refuge.
❻ **Ford of Bruinen** The shallow river where Arwen narrowly escaped the Nazgûl is 200 m upstream from Arrowtown.
❼ **Rohan** The rolling hills of the Ida Valley near remote Poolburn Reservoir in Central Otago were used to portray the realm of the Riddermark.
❽ **Lothlórien** Queenstown's Dart River Safaris (dartriver.co.nz) and Dart Stables (dartstables.com) can transport you into Galadriel's enchanted forest.
❾ **Dimrill Dale** When the Fellowship escaped from the Mines of Moria they emerged on the lunar-like slopes of Mount Owen, Kahurangi National Park.
❿ **Fanghorn Forest** Look carefully and you may spot an Ent in the dense forests around Marova Lakes, near Te Anau.

🐾 Places to cuddle
a cute koala

Sydney: Koala Park Sanctuary (koalaparksanctuary.com.au)

Brisbane: Lone Pine Koala Sanctuary (koala.net)

Cairns: Kuranda Koala Gardens (koalagardens.com)

Flying the family to Australia or New Zealand will be expensive. And there may well be moments on that long haul across Asia or the Pacific when boredom and jetlag transform your children into something quite unpleasant. And there may even be times when you gaze wistfully out of the aircraft window and yearn to be back in the 1980s – a footloose, child-free backpacker on your first global odyssey. But get a grip. This could well be the start of the most exciting, bonding, eye-opening family adventure you've ever had.

Babies

They might bawl occasionally, but eventually they'll sleep – and at least they can't move around. It's when babies develop an insatiable desire to crawl that those flights Down Under are going to seem like the longest 20 hours of your life. Should you consider a stopover in somewhere like Singapore or Tahiti? You may well be desperate to escape the confines of the plane and the mutterings from fellow passengers. However, do you really want to go through the rigmarole of immigration and check-in twice before reaching Australia or New Zealand? And is it worth subjecting your infant to a double dose of jetlag, moving on to a new time zone just as he or she is starting to adapt to Asia or South Pacific time? A lot will depend on the stopovers themselves – and let's face it, they are all pretty irresistible destinations. But whatever route you take to reach Australia or New Zealand, and however gruelling the journey may be, you can be confident that once Down Under, travel with babies is about as stress-free as it gets. You'll find all the gear, food and supplies you need are readily available (so you can travel light and buy stuff out there). The locals are friendly and laid-back, getting around with a buggy is generally hassle-free, and the beaches are clean and safe – although you do need to be extra-vigilant about sun protection.

Toddlers/pre-school

A flight to the Antipodes with children of this age requires a deep breath, infinite patience and a daypack stuffed with toys, colouring books and anything else that's likely to help pass the time. It also makes a difference if you choose an airline that's as toddler-friendly as possible and try to go for a minimum of three weeks. A motorhome touring holiday suits this age group perfectly. You can get them used to one bed (rather than hopping between a succession of hotels) and you can prepare meals they like, when they like. Another great option is a city-based holiday, staying in aparthotels with fully equipped kitchens. Just about every major city in Australia and New Zealand is close to a spectacular coastline, so when you're not visiting the aquariums, museums, zoos, parks and other city attractions you can easily escape for a day on the beach.

A paddle in the South Pacific

Perfect for a few days' stopover en route to New Zealand and Australia, Fiji (fijime.com) has no shortage of all-inclusive resorts and many, like Castaway Island (castawayisland.com), have kids' clubs. For exclusive pampering, splash out on Dolphin Island (dolphinislandfiji.com) and for something more adventurous, sign up for a week's sea kayaking with Tamarillo (tamarillo.co.nz) which offers special family departures featuring school visits and snorkelling tuition. Another great slice of jetlag purging, family-friendly paradise can be found in French Polynesia (tahiti-tourisme.com). The best way to dovetail the South Pacific into your itinerary Down Under is to arrange everything through a specialist operator like Bridge & Wickers (bridgeandwickers.co.uk).

Special needs

Several operators in Australia offer tours for travellers with special needs, including Wheelie Easy (wheelieeasy.com.au) and Wheelchair Tours Australia (wheeltours.com.au). In New Zealand, try Accessible Kiwi Tours (toursnz.com) and Rest New Zealand Tours (restnztours.co.nz). Based in Auckland, Accessible Motorhomes (accessiblemotorhomes.co.nz) provides vehicles with wheelchair lifts, while Weka (weka.net.nz) offers general information and advice for people with disabilities.

Single parents

Holidays with Kids (holidayswithkids.com.au) has an excellent section on single parent travel in Australia and beyond – you can even subscribe to a special newsletter for single parents.

> 66 99 **On the first night of our motorhome holiday in New South Wales I remember lying awake thinking, 'What have we done? Why aren't we in a lovely beach house somewhere?' But after that it was a great success. Not only did the motorhome give us freedom to explore the coast (we managed to fit in everything from sand boarding to dolphin watching), but our three kids loved the challenge of turning the seats into beds every evening.**
>
> Mark Pougatch, BBC Sports presenter

Kids/school age

Whereas tots and toddlers are too young for many of the more exciting adventures Down Under, by the time kids reach school age they'll be chafing at the bit to try everything from jetboating to body boarding. In New Zealand, those four magic words – Lord of the Rings – will have them double-taking every gnarled tree and snowy peak, while Aboriginal and Maori-led tours will open their eyes to fascinating indigenous cultures. Everywhere you go, the guides are outstanding – whether you're learning to pinpoint the Southern Cross, track wildlife in the Outback, decipher Aboriginal art or surf on Bondi Beach. The get-up-and-go mentality of the Aussies and Kiwis is infectious, so fill your trip with as much as possible, from cuddling koalas to paddling kayaks.

Teenagers

Bring it on! Australia and New Zealand are *ripa* for teenagers. The outdoor life, the sporting culture, the adrenaline activities, the trendy cities… it all adds up to one seriously cool holiday. Although pretty much anywhere will meet with their approval, a two- or three-centre trip is often the best way to go. If your mind is set on New Zealand, consider splitting your time between Auckland (for city buzz), the Coromandel Peninsula (for surfing) and Queenstown (for just about every daredevil pursuit teens could imagine – no matter how warped their minds). In Australia, combine Sydney with the coast of northern New South Wales or Queensland for the best of city chic and beach bliss.

Telling tales David Gower
Former England cricket captain

When I'm in Australia for the Ashes, whatever happens with the cricket the best part for me is when the family get on the plane and come and join me. It might only be for three or four weeks, but there is a lot you can cram into your time Down Under – once you've got over the jet lag. Alex (13) and Sammi (10) loved Bondi – particularly the surf, the buzzy restaurants and the shops. Next we headed for Melbourne with its great restaurants and yet more shops! Imagine the contest: it's a hot Saturday prior to New Year and I'm thinking, let's go to Black Rock Beach, half an hour out of town, and enjoy the sun. But I'm outnumbered by three girls who want to check out the sales on Chapel Street. Sorry, did I say contest? We got to the beach at about 4.30 that afternoon. Back in Sydney we stayed in the city close to the harbour and the Botanical Gardens which are full of the most gorgeous cockatoos and enormous fruit bats. Time ran out all too quickly and the girls were making notes of the things they would have to do next time. One day we might take them on the train from east to west, a trip I once made from Adelaide to Kalgoorlie. It is just mind-boggling how much red earth one can see in one day…

L ots of cities claim to be great for kids – and Sydney is no exception. In fact, it could well come out on top of the pile. Not only does it have instant 'wow' factor, courtesy of its stunning harbour, but it also boasts a bewildering range of attractions, from bridge climbs to walk-through aquariums. Bright, clean, sunny and fun, Sydney doesn't simply have suburbs it has suburbs with surfing beaches. Hop on a train and within a couple of hours you could be gazing across the Blue Mountains. Head north or south and the coast unfurls in a dreamy-eyed succession of bays, coves and World-Heritage listed national parks – each one oozing with the promise of adventure.

Sydney

Day 1 Start with a cruise. It's the best introduction to one of the world's most spectacular natural harbours. Tour boats depart regularly from Circular Quay, passing classic sights like the Sydney Opera House and Harbour Bridge. Disembark at Darling Harbour (darlingharbour.com) – home to dozens of shops, eating places and an IMAX cinema, as well as several leading family attractions. Pick of the bunch is the Sydney Aquarium (sydneyaquarium.com.au) where kids' favourites include the fairy penguins and duck-billed platypus. Tunnels get you on intimate terms with large sharks and rays and also delve beneath a wonderful seal sanctuary where you can watch fur seals and sea lions whizzing past.

For a double whammy of Aussie wildlife, buy a combo ticket that includes entry to both the aquarium and Sydney Wildlife World (sydneywildlifeworld.com.au), a breathtaking biome inhabited by wallabies, parrots, koalas, frilled lizards and other native species.

If, however, you prefer warships to wombats, head for the Australian National Maritime Museum (anmm.gov.au) an indoor/outdoor nautical feast that includes a replica of Captain Cook's *Endeavour* and the destroyer, *HMAS Vampire*. Hands-on science fun at the Powerhouse Museum (powerhousemuseum.com) is another option.

Day two Time to raise the stakes. If your kids are aged 10 or over, test their steel (and yours) on a Harbour Bridge Climb (bridgeclimb.com) where a clamber on the Coathanger will get you 134 m above the harbour for the ultimate Sydney photo opportunity. Back at ground level, bag some local souvenirs in the weekend craft market at The Rocks (a good spot for lunch) before hopping on a ferry from Circular

Quay for the 12-minute ride to Taronga Zoo (taronga. org.au). Star species include the orang-utan, snow leopard, komodo dragon and leopard seal. If, however, you've peaked on wildlife from day one, head instead to Luna Park (lunaparksydney.com) for some traditional fairground fun.

For a different twist to day two, start by getting your city views from the 305-m Sydney Tower (sydneytowereye.com.au) which has an observation deck, Skywalk and 4D cinema. Next, stroll through Hyde Park to the Australian Museum (austmus.gov. au) – the nation's showcase for natural history where under-fives can explore their own mini-museum while older kids grapple with bugs and bones in the Search & Discover section. Round off the day spotting fruit bats in the Royal Botanic Gardens (rbgsyd.nsw.gov.au).

Best days out

The beach has got to be top of your list. Sydney has 37 of them, but Manly (manlyaustralia.com.au) is the most popular. Easily reached by ferry from Circular Quay, it has all the tourist trappings of a seaside holiday resort, including a lively waterfront fringed with cafés, restaurants, souvenir and surf shops and, of course, some gorgeous sandy beaches. If you didn't get a chance to visit Sydney Aquarium, catch the rays at Manly's Oceanworld (oceanworld.com.au) where you can also dive with sharks if you're over 14.

For an equally active day out, Sydney Olympic Park (sydneyolympicpark.com.au) has loads to keep kids happy. Hire a bike and cycle one of three circuits, develop your archery skills, swing out on the flying trapeze, doggy paddle in the pool of Olympic champions, spot wildlife from the Badu Mangroves boardwalk and tour the famous Telstra Stadium. Superb transport links (another legacy of the Sydney 2000 Olympics) make it a doddle to get there.

Sydney rocks

The Opera House and Coathanger bridge, with the historic Rocks district in the foreground. Below: A replica of Cook's *Endeavour* at the Australian National Maritime Museum.

Jamison's Lookout, Blue Mountains

Kids' top 10 Beyond Sydney

❶ **Ride** the world's steepest incline railway at Scenic World (scenicworld.com.au) before hiking in the Blue Mountains with Auswalk (auswalk.com.au). Trek through lush rainforest, listening out for lyrebirds (which can impersonate anything from chainsaws to car alarms) and then scale or descend the Giant Stairway next to the famous Three Sisters, pictured below.

❷ **Slip** and slide at The Big Banana (bigbanana.com), Coffs Harbour, where a day pass gets you two rides on the 600-m Wild Banana toboggan ride, entry to the ice-skating rink and a free banana split. Alternatively, swim with dolphins (minimum age six) at the nearby Dolphin Marine Magic (dolphinmarinemagic.com.au). For thrills and spills south of Sydney, splash out on Jamberoo Action Park (jamberoo.net) near Kiama which has water slides, race tracks and toboggan runs.

❸ **Dare** to stroll the Skywalk at Dorrigo National Park (nationalparks.nsw.gov.au) where you'll feel like an eagle soaring above the rainforest.

❹ **Spot** dolphins on a boat trip, zooming through a network of coastal waterways with Port Macquarie's Cruise Adventures (cruiseadventures.com.au).

❺ **Experience** the past at Timbertown (timbertown.com.au) near Wauchope where steam trains and horse-drawn carriages take you back to the pioneer days.

❻ **See** humpback whales (June-November) from the whale-watching platform at Iluka (ilukansw.com.au), reached by walking the World Heritage Rainforest Walk. Alternatively, take a boat trip with one of the many operators along the New South Wales coast, such as Whale Watching Byron Bay (whalewatchingbyronbay.com.au).

❼ **Learn** to surf with the Byron Bay Surf School (byronbaysurfschool.com). A one-day course teaches you basic surf awareness, paddling, catching waves and, all importantly, how to stand up and ride them.

❽ **Check** out the capital, Canberra, where a '3 in Fun' ticket provides entry to the miniature village of Cockington Green (cockingtongreen.com.au), The Australian Institute of Sport (ausport.gov.au/tours) and Questacon – The National Science & Technology Centre (questacon.edu.au).

❾ **Strike** out south of Sydney to Jervis Bay where activities range from sea kayaking with the Jervis Bay Kayak Co (jervisbaykayaks.com) to learning about Aboriginal traditions with Barry's Bush Tucker Tours.

❿ **Wander** west of Sydney, crossing the Great Dividing Range to Dubbo where the Western Plains Zoo (zoo.nsw.gov.au) operates Roar and Snore (minimum age five) – an exciting opportunity to spend the night at this free-roaming wildlife park.

Left: Jervis Bay. Right: Byron Bay

New South Wales
A perfect state to find

> **"** **It began with a gentle stroll to Echo Point, overlooking the Three Sisters. Then it took a downward turn on the tendon-twanging Giant Stairway – 862 stone and metal steps chiselled into the cliff face during the early 1900s.**
> William Gray

Inside info ⓘ

▶▶ The See Sydney Pass (seesydneypass.iventurecard.com) offers free entry to over 40 top Sydney attractions, tours, and things to do.
▶▶ Sydney Harbour tours are offered by Captain Cook Cruises (captaincook.com.au) and Oz Jet Boating (ozjetboating.com).
▶▶ For further informtion, log on to sydney.com.au and visitnsw.com.au.

B e warned. Victoria will almost certainly throw a spanner in the works when you plan a trip Down Under. Just when you've cajoled Sydney, the Red Centre and the Great Barrier Reef into a comfortable three-week itinerary, Melbourne catches your eye and suddenly your plans start unravelling in a tempest of fresh possibilities. Not only are Melbourne's family attractions on a par with those in Sydney, but the coastline either side is nothing short of irresistible – the Mornington Peninsula and Phillip Island to the east and the Great Ocean Road to the west. Inland, Victoria unfurls in a panoply of fertile valleys, eucalypt forests and rugged mountains – a green and palatable land dotted with vineyards and historic gold rush towns. By the time you start contemplating the natural wonders of Tasmania, New South Wales might – just might – have become a distant memory.

Melbourne

Officially rated one of the world's most liveable cities, Melbourne has fine Victorian architecture (best appreciated from a ride on one of the burgundy and gold City Circle trams), child-friendly food (plenty of Italian and Greek restaurants) and some excellent parks and beaches. To see it all from a heady height, the Melbourne Observation Deck (melbourne360rialto.com.au) offers far-reaching views from the Rialto Towers.

A superb, non-stuffy introduction to Australian natural history and culture, the Melbourne Museum (melbourne.museum.vic.gov.au) explores everything from dinosaurs and the human brain to the traditions of the Aborigines and Pacific islanders. It's trump cards for families, however, are the Children's Gallery for three- to eight-year-olds, the 3D IMAX theatre and the Forest Gallery which contains living trees up to 20 m tall. Equally captivating is Melbourne Aquarium (melbourneaquarium.com.au) where one of the highlights is a behind-the-scenes glass-bottom boat trip over the 2.2-million-litre Oceanarium – home to sharks, stingrays, turtles and over 3000 fish from the Southern Ocean. Kids will also enjoy getting face-to-face with giant spider crabs, blood-sucking leeches and other delightful critters at the Creepy Creatures exhibit. For more wild encounters, hop on Tram 55 to Melbourne Zoo (zoo.org.au) which has a treetop boardwalk at its Orang-utan Sanctuary.

Sports enthusiasts, meanwhile, should make a dash for the National Sports Museum (nsm.org.au), a super-charged celebration of Australian football,

cricket, the Olympics, soccer and many other sports. Budding superstars should make for the Game on! gallery where they can test their goal-kicking skills, play on a virtual cricket pitch and kick, throw, shoot, ride, race and run to their heart's content. Interaction is also the name of the game at Scienceworks (scienceworks.museum.vic.gov.au) which incorporates the Melbourne Planetarium and the Lightning Room – a vivid (and thankfully non-interactive) demonstration of the power of lightning. If you have three- to eight-year-olds, unleash them at Nitty Gritty Super City where they can construct a building, steer a ship and record their own weather reports.

Best days out

A 25-minute tram ride south takes you to the seaside suburb of St Kilda – a great place to enjoy the beach or walk, cycle and skate along the palm-fringed waterfront. It's also where you will find Luna Park (lunapark.com.au) with plenty of thrill rides.

Steaming through the fern gullies and mountain ash forests of the Dandenong Ranges (east of Melbourne), the Puffing Billy (puffingbilly.com.au) makes a fun outing for kids – especially when you combine the steam train with a visit to the Healesville Sanctuary (zoo.org.au) – one of Australia's premier native wildlife parks and probably your best chance of seeing a platypus. Children will also be enthralled by Healesville's birds of prey flight show and a tour of the animal hospital.

Jutting out into Port Phillip Bay and just an hour's drive from Melbourne, the Mornington Peninsula

Urban seaside

There are some great beaches close to Melbourne. Below: little penguin – the big star of Phillip Island.

Coast with the most

★ **The Great Ocean Road** in southwest Victoria hugs one of the world's most dramatic coastlines where waves have sculpted 45-m-high limestone cliffs into a gallery of mighty sea stacks, arches and caves. Nowhere are these features more striking than at the Twelve Apostles in Port Campbell National Park. Other highlights of the notorious Shipwreck Coast (shipwreckcoast.com) include spotting southern right whales at Warrnambool between June and late September, discovering the region's seafaring past at Flagstaff Hill Maritime Village (flagstaffhill.com) and surfing, swimming or simply jumping waves at the many superb beaches.

has sheltered sandy beaches and every kind of water activity, from sailing and surfing to fishing and dolphin swims. One of the most popular family beaches, Rosebud is protected by offshore sandbars and has picnic, barbecue and play facilities. Polperro Dolphin Swims (polperro.com.au) operate from Sorrento between October to April.

Further east along the coast, Phillip Island (penguins.org.au) hosts one of Australia's most famous and endearing wildlife spectacles when, each dusk, a steady parade of little penguins (the world's smallest at just 33 cm in height) bumbles ashore. There are several viewing options, although some have rather stringent age restrictions. Best for families is Penguins Plus (minimum age four) where you can view the penguins from a platform and boardwalk. On the Private Penguin Parade Experience (minimum age 12) you stake out the beach with your own personal ranger, while the Ultimate Penguin Tour takes groups of just 10 people to a secluded bay far from the tourist masses – and any children under 16. Other highlights on Phillip Island include the seals and rock pools at the Nobbies, the koalas and birds at the treetops boardwalk and the farm animals and heritage buildings at Churchill Island.

Further afield Popular for fishing, camping and hiking, the wild and spectacular coastline of Gippsland in Eastern Victoria encompasses Wilsons Promontory National Park and Ninety Mile Beach. Between two- and three-hours' drive north of Melbourne, the historic Port of Echuca (portofechuca.org.au) offers paddlesteamer cruises on the Murray River.

A 90-minute drive west of Melbourne, Sovereign Hill (sovereignhill.com.au), on the outskirts of Ballarat, keeps alive the gold rush days of the 1850s. Stroll down Main Street and you'll rub shoulders with prospectors, blacksmiths and other characters in period dress. Underground gold mine tours are also available, along with gold panning.

🔍 Let's go to Tasmania

Tasmanian devils have attitude, but don't expect the slavering, tree-felling whirlwind of fur and gnashing teeth that Warner Bros would have you believe. In fact, this carnivorous marsupial inhabits a rather peaceful wilderness of mountains, forests and deserted beaches where numerous other native Australian species have found sanctuary. At Hobart's Tasmanian Museum, you can learn about one that didn't make it – the thylacine or Tasmanian tiger. But just an hour's drive southeast to Taranna, you can eyeball devils, along with quolls and golden possums, at the Tasmanian Devil Conservation Park. Continue south to the Tinderbox Marine Reserve and a sheltered snorkelling trail trains your gaze on pipefish and leafy sea dragons. More marine marvels await at Bruny Island where albatrosses, gannets, sea eagles, dolphins, penguins and fur seals guarantee a riveting boat trip. No trip to Tasmania is complete without a visit to Cradle Mountain-Lake St Clair National Park where the Enchanted Forest Walk, suitable for all ages, probes a magical old-growth rainforest and even turns up the odd wombat burrow. Bennett's wallabies and pademelons can be seen during the day around the visitor centre, while Tasmanian devils, quolls and eastern pygmy possums emerge at dusk.

▶▶ Further information: discovertasmania.com.au

South Australia
Hop to Kangaroo Island

South Australia has two very contrasting faces. To the north and west lies a stark expanse of the Outback where huge salt lakes shimmer beneath ancient, heat-shattered mountains and the Great Victoria Desert merges relentlessly with the flat, arid Nullarbor Plain. And then there's Adelaide and the southeast, a verdant blend of manicured city parks and vineyards, gentle rivers, sandy bays and islands teeming with wildlife. No prizes for guessing where you'll be taking the kids. Notwithstanding South Australia's Outback attractions (such as the opal-mining community of Coober Pedy), the Adelaide area makes for a varied and manageable family holiday.

Adelaide

A fun way to see Adelaide is to hire a paddleboat on the River Torrens, which flows through the heart of the city. You will find Riverside Bike and Paddle Boat Hire by the Festival Centre (adelaidefestivalcentre. com.au) – a great place to take kids, either for a picnic or to browse the arts and crafts at the Sunday market. On North Terrace, the South Australia Museum (samuseum.sa.gov.au) has permanent exhibits on local natural history, deep sea life, Ancient Egypt, the cultures of Pacific islanders and Aboriginal people, the exploits of Antarctic explorer Douglas Mawson and the extraordinary opal fossils discovered at Coober Pedy. A short walk to the east lie the riverside Botanic Gardens and Adelaide Zoo (adelaidezoo.com.au) which offers a range of exciting behind-the-scenes encounters with giant pandas, orang-utans, sun bears and Sumatran tigers.

Best beaches Easily reached on the City-to-Bay tram, Glenelg is Adelaide's most popular beach destination. Its waterfront is buzzing with shops and cafés, while the Town Hall contains the Bay Discovery Centre and the Rodney Fox Shark Experience. The Beachouse (thebeachouse.com.au) has waterslides, dodgems, mini golf and other amusements, while nearby Holdfast Shores Marina is the departure point for joy rides with Hel-a-Va-Jet Boat (helava.com.au) and dolphin cruises with Temptation Sailing (dolphinboat. com.au). About 5 km south along the Esplanade, Brighton is another favourite beach playground. Continue on towards the Fleurieu Peninsula to reach the popular seaside towns of Victor Harbour and Goolwa or strike out north of Adelaide to explore the Yorke Peninsula where water sports include surfing, kayaking, beach fishing and sailing.

Inside info

▶▶ The Adelaide Metro (adelaidemetro.com. au) serves the greater metropolitan region with trains, buses and the Glenelg tram; look out for the bright yellow Adelaide Free buses – the 99B and 99C – which go to the main attractions in the city.
▶▶ For River Murray houseboat rental, try houseboats.com.au.
▶▶ For further information, log on to southaustralia.com.

River Torrens, Adelaide

Best days out

One of the highlights of a family visit to the Adelaide region is a trip to Kangaroo Island (tourkangarooisland.com.au) – although you really need more than a single day to fully appreciate this wildlife haven. Children will love sharing the beach with a large colony of sea lions at Seal Bay and watching the nightly procession of little penguins at Kingscote and Penneshaw. Be sure to also arrange a guided nocturnal tour since many species are only active at night. In addition to wildlife, Kangaroo Island offers safe swimming at Penneshaw Beach and sandboarding in the giant dunes at Little Sahara.

For messing about on the Murray River, head east of Adelaide to Renmark where cruises are available on historic paddlesteamers. You can also water ski, canoe and fish at several riverside towns, while a houseboat holiday is sure to get a thumbs-up from the kids.

Wildlife ticklist

Eight animals to find on Kangaroo Island:

- ✓ **Fur seal** 7000 breed at Cape du Couedic
- ✓ **Heath goanna** Basking on sunny days
- ✓ **Kangaroo** Flinders Chase National Park Visitor Centre
- ✓ **Koala** Large gum trees
- ✓ **Platypus** Flinders Chase Platypus Waterholes Walk
- ✓ **Sea lion** Sandy beach at Seal Bay
- ✓ **Short-beaked echidna** Digging for ants and termites
- ✓ **Tammar wallaby** Roadsides at night

Western Australia
Big beaches, big skies, big fish

With over 12,000 km of pristine coastline, Western Australia shouldn't pose any problems when it comes to finding a beach – whether your kids are into surfing, snorkelling or building sandcastles. Perth, a compact, modern city with skyscrapers rising like giant crystals above the Swan River, makes an easy-going base for exploring highlights in the southwest like Fremantle and Rottnest Island. Venture further afield and you'll quickly appreciate the vast size of Western Australia, but those long drives will be more than compensated by some truly inspiring natural wonders – from the surreal Wave Rock to Monkey Mia's dolphins and the whale sharks of Ningaloo Reef.

Beach on the Ningaloo coast

Perth

Base yourself north of Perth on the 30-km swathe of the Sunset Coast and you get the best of everything: superb beaches, top attractions and easy access to the city when you need it. Located at Hillarys Boat Harbour, the Aquarium of Western Australia (aqwa.com.au) transports you through the state's major marine habitats. Children over 15 can join a guided snorkelling adventure with 4-m-long sharks in the huge Indian Ocean tank, while Ocean Safaris, in search of dolphins and humpback whales, are organized by the aquarium between October and December.

A short distance inland from Hillarys, the bushland reserve of Whiteman Park (whitemanpark.com.au) makes a great family outing, offering everything from camel and steam train rides to sheep-shearing demonstrations and native wildlife displays. You'll find more Aussie critters at Perth Zoo (perthzoo.wa.gov.au) just five minutes from the city centre, while Adventure World (adventureworld.net.au) is the place to go for roller coasters and other wild rides.

Best beaches Whether you want to swim, surf or snorkel, Cottesloe Beach is perfect for all ages. The sheltered turquoise lagoon of The Basin on Rottnest Island (see right) is a prime spot for goggling at colourful fish, while Scarborough Beach with its surf breaks and trendy vibe is teen heaven. Experienced surfies will want to ride the more challenging waves at Trigg. If you've got toddlers take them for a paddle at Mettams Pool.

Best days out

Founded in 1829 at the mouth of the Swan River, Fremantle (fremantlewesternaustralia.com) can be easily reached by boat from Perth. Spend some time soaking up the atmosphere of the busy harbour and marketplace, then focus on the Western Australian Maritime Museum (museum.wa.gov.au/maritime). Split into three sections, the main museum provides an overview of all things nautical and also houses impressive vessels such as the America's Cup racing yacht *Australia II*. On Cliff Street, the Shipwreck Galleries contain the haunting remains of the VOC ship *Batavia*, wrecked off Western Australia's coast in 1629. However, it's the submarine, *HMAS Ovens*, high and dry on Victoria Quay that will enthral kids most.

Fremantle is also one of the departure points for boat trips to Rottnest Island (rottnestisland.com) – perfect for exploring by bike. Keep an eye out for quokkas (cute little wallabies) and don't forget your cossies – the beaches here are stunning.

A three-hour drive south of the city, Margaret River is not only one of Australia's premium wine-growing regions, it's also a corker for sensational white sand beaches. Hamelin Bay is a great family all-rounder, while Ocean Beach further along the coast at Denmark is big on surf. Whale watching is possible from Dunsborough and Albany, while the 600-m Valley of the Giants Treetops Walk (valleyofthegiants.com.au) at Walpole elevates you 40 m into the canopy of a tingle forest. A four-hour drive east of Perth, the enormous granite 'breaker' of Wave Rock (waverock.com.au) is awesome, but remote.

★ Kids' top 5 WA

❶ **Wade** with dolphins at Monkey Mia.
❷ **Ride** a camel along Cable Beach, Broome.
❸ **Spot** a dugong in Shark Bay.
❹ **Peer** at the Pinnacles in Nambung National Park.
❺ **Snorkel** with a whale shark off Ningaloo Reef.

Inside info ⓘ

▶▶ Perth is way out west – a three-hour flight from Adelaide, the nearest big city.
▶▶ Ferries to Rottnest Island are operated by Rottnest Fast Ferries (rottnestfastferries.com.au) and Rottnest Express (rottnestexpress.com.au).
▶▶ For further info, log on to perthtourism.com.au, and westernaustralia.com.

Uluru

Kids' top 10 The Red Centre

1 Learn about life in the Outback, past and present, by visiting the Telegraph Station (nt.gov.au/nreta/parks), the School of the Air (assoa.nt.edu.au) and the Royal Flying Doctor Service (flyingdoctor.net) in Alice Springs.

2 Ride a camel along the dry riverbed of the Todd River in Alice Springs, spotting cockatoos, galahs and other colourful parrots in the gum trees before enjoying breakfast in the bush. Take a Camel to Breakfast tours are run by Anangu Waai! (ananguwaai.com.au).

3 See rock wallabies, bilbies, lizards and other Outback wildlife at the brilliant Alice Springs Desert Park (alicespringsdesertpark.com.au) and discover how Aboriginal people use the region's plants and animals for food and medicine.

4 Hear amazing didgeridoo music at Sounds of Starlight (soundsofstarlight.com), a spectacular evening show held in Alice Springs on Tuesdays, Fridays and Saturdays, April to November (recommended for children over five).

5 Learn the MacDonnell Ranges west of Alice Springs, visiting scenic hotspots at Simpsons Gap, Standley Chasm, Serpentine Gorge and Ormiston Gorge. Spot rock wallabies and parrots – and take a cooling dip in one of the freshwater pools.

6 Experience life on a working cattle and camel farm at Kings Creek Station (kingscreekstation.com.au) 36 km from the magnificent Kings Canyon. Explore the Outback by quad bike, camel or helicopter, camp in the bush and try a camel burger.

7 Visit the magnificent monolith of Uluru, starting with the Uluru-Kata Tjuta Cultural Centre (environment.gov.au/parks/uluru) to learn about the national park from its traditional Aboriginal owners, the Anangu. Delve into the display of indigenous paintings and carvings at Maruku Arts (maruku.com.au) – a great place to buy an authentic

boomerang – and then join a Dot Painting Workshop (ananguwaai.com.au) with local artists. Don't miss the spectacle of Uluru glowing red at sunset, then stay up late for some stargazing at the observatory.

8 Hike around the base of Uluru – an easy 10-km loop that takes around four hours, pausing to read the interpretive signs that tell the Dreamtime stories of Kuniya and Liru. Guided tours can be booked at the Cultural Centre (see above).

9 Discover the weird and wonderful landscape of Kata Tjuta, a cluster of 36 giant domes rising from the desert to the west of Uluru. For a magical walk, set off into Walpa Gorge (the mythical home of the corkwood-tree women) that weaves between two of the rocky outcrops.

10 Fossick at Moonlight Rockhole near Tennant Creek (500 km north of Alice Springs). Gems and minerals found in the Northern Territory include agate, amethyst, apatite, epidote, beryl, garnet, gold and jasper. You don't need a permit to fossick, however you will need obtain consent to fossick from the landowner.

▶▶ Further information: alicesprings.nt.gov.au

Aboriginal art

> **Many of the plants are deeply rooted in Aboriginal bushlore. Bark from the gnarled old corkwoods, for example, can be burnt and ground to produce a soothing powder for sores, while sap from the sticky hopbush is effective against toothache. This 'pick-your-own chemist' is part of a much bigger bush-superstore which offers juicy witchetty grubs and thirst-quenching nectar, as well as poisons and spear shafts.**
>
> William Gray

West MacDonnell Ranges

The Northern Territory is textbook Australia. It's home to some of the country's most enigmatic landmarks and wildlife, from the mesmerizing monolith of Uluru to the bustling billabongs of Kakadu. Underlying everything is the Dreamtime – the cultural bedrock of Aboriginal belief that children will be able to grasp by visiting the region's museums and rock art sites or by joining bush walks and workshops led by local guides. Darwin makes a great base from which to explore the tropical Top End where a trio of national parks offers everything from crocodile safaris to canoeing trips. Uluru-Kata Tjuta National Park, meanwhile, is the heart and soul of Australia's Red Centre where activities include bush tucker walks and camel riding.

Kakadu National Park

Darwin & the Top End

Always a winner with children, Aquascene (aquascene.com.au) at Doctor's Gully (a short walk from the city centre) allows them to feed thousands of milkfish, mullet, catfish, bream and other slithery scroungers as they gather in the shallows at high tide. At Stokes Hill Wharf you'll find more fish – battered and served with chips at the excellent harbourside restaurants or swirling in technicolour splendour at the Indo-Pacific Marine coral reef aquarium. While you're there, take the plunge into Darwin's pearling heritage at the Australian Pearling Exhibition. More historical jewels can be found at the Museum and Art Gallery of the Northern Territory (nt.gov.au/nreta/museums) which contains some of the world's finest Aboriginal paintings. Don't miss the Cyclone Tracy Gallery – a chilling display on the tropical storm that flattened Darwin in 1974 – and be sure to say g'day to Sweetheart, a 5-m-long stuffed saltwater crocodile.

To see live salties, head to Crocodylus Park (crocodyluspark.com) on Darwin's outskirts or join a Crocodile Jumping Cruise (jumpingcrocodile.com.au) on the Adelaide River (about an hour's drive from Darwin) where crocs are teased with hunks of suspended bait. A 45-minute drive south of the city, Territory Wildlife Park (territorywildlifepark.com.au) provides a wonderful introduction to the diverse habitats of Australia's Top End, from billabongs squirming with longneck turtles and monitor lizards to monsoon forests dripping with birds and bats. Special features, such as the walk-through aviary, aquarium tunnel and nocturnal house get you up-close and personal to wildlife that is often hard to spot in the wild. More wet wonders can be found at the Window on the Wetlands Visitor Centre.

Litchfield National Park Located 100 km southwest of Darwin, this beautiful park encompasses a sandstone plateau riven with forest-edged creeks and waterfalls that lead to idyllic (and safe) swimming holes. One of the most popular spots for a dip is at Florence Falls where you will also find a shady picnic spot and a couple of easy walking trails.

Nitmiluk (Katherine) Gorge National Park

A thriving town located 300 km south of Darwin, Katherine is the gateway to a spectacular series of gorges where adventurous families can paddle Canadian-style canoes beneath looming cliffs of red sandstone, pausing for a refreshing swim or a picnic on a sandbank. Canoes can be hired from Nitmiluk Tours (nitmiluktours.com.au) which also organizes boat trips – a better option for families with young children. Remember hats, sunscreen and water.

Kakadu National Park Around 250 km east of Darwin, Kakadu is one of Australia's finest sites for wildlife and indigenous culture. Don't go for less than three days. Arriving at Jabiru, visit the Bowali Visitor Centre for an overview of Kakadu's heritage and habitats and then join a ranger-guided walk at Ubirr admiring the Aboriginal art – some of which is over 20,000 years old. The following morning, explore Nourlangie Rock, another famous Aboriginal rock art site, before taking an afternoon cruise on Yellow Water Billabong in search of magpie geese, jabiru and other bird species. Return to the water at night for a boat trip spotting crocodiles by torchlight. The next day, join a cultural cruise on the East Alligator River with local Aboriginal guides. If it's the dry season (May to September), try to squeeze in a 4WD adventure to Jim Jim and Twin Falls.

Daintree rainforest; right: flying fox at O'Reilly's Rainforest Retreat

Kids' top 10 reef & rainforest

① **Feel** the sand squeak between your toes on Whitehaven Beach, a dazzling 9-km stretch of pure white silica grains on Whitsunday Island.

② **Ride** the Skyrail Rainforest Cableway (skyrail.com. au), skimming over treetops to Kuranda where you can explore the rainforest on an amphibious Duck tour before returning to Cairns on the gorge-clinging Kuranda Scenic Railway (ksr.com.au).

③ **Wade** through the shallows of the coral lagoon at Heron Island (heronisland.com), where the Junior Ranger Programme helps seven- to 12-year-olds uncover the secrets of the Great Barrier Reef.

④ **Shoot** the grade II-III rapids on the Barron River, near Cairns, with Raging Thunder (ragingthunder.com.au) or up the adrenaline levels with a whitewater frenzy on the Tully (grade III-IV rapids) near Mission Beach. Minimum age 13.

⑤ **Swoop** through the trees like a sugar glider on the 25-m-high flying fox at O'Reilly's Rainforest Retreat (oreillys. com.au) in Lamington National Park.

⑥ **Discover** a tropical adventure paradise on Dunk Island (dunk-island.com) where you can learn how to snorkel, de-husk a coconut and throw a boomerang. Check the website for latest opening information.

⑦ **Explore** the tropical rainforest and Aboriginal culture of the Cape York Peninsula on a 4WD safari – only serious adventurers need apply.

⑧ **Choose** from 17 white-sand beaches and a host of activities (from bush walks to banana boat rides) on Great Keppel Island near Rockhampton.

⑨ **Spot** saltwater crocodiles on a river cruise in Daintree National Park and then discover where the rainforest meets the sea at Cape Tribulation.

⑩ **Learn** to scuba dive (minimum age 12) at one of the many dive centres in Cairns and Townsville.

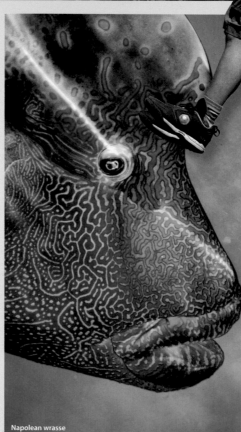

Napolean wrasse

> 66 99
> We went snorkelling and we saw lots of stripy fish and bright blue fish and yellow fish and very big black fish. It was good fun. There was lots of fish.
> Ellie Gray (age 6)

Crimson rosella

Beautiful one day, perfect the next, Australia's Sunshine State is heaven-on-earth for kids. Its beaches will blow their minds, whether they're clutching a surfboard, a mask and snorkel or a bucket and spade. There are riveting resorts along the Gold Coast where children of all ages will get a thrill out of Australia's best theme parks. The Sunshine Coast is more relaxed, while a liberal scattering of tropical islands provides a mixture of pampered paradise and Aussie adventure. Several resorts in Queensland organize special activities for kids, whether it's exploring world heritage rainforest in Lamington National Park or searching for Nemo on the Great Barrier Reef. Nowhere does the three R's – reef, rainforest and recreation – better than Queensland.

Whitsunday Islands

Queensland
Australia's tropical playground

Brisbane & the Queensland coast

Chances are you'll be staying on the coast north or south of Brisbane, but if you have a day or two to spare in the city you'll find plenty to do. The South Bank Parklands is the place to go. Not only does it have a leisurely mix of cafés, play areas, riverside walks, open-air markets and even a pristine swimming lagoon, but it's also close to several child-friendly attractions. At the northwestern end of the park, the Queensland Museum (qm.qld.gov.au) has impressive prehistoric exhibits and lots of interactive science stuff for budding Einsteins, while at the opposite end of the park, the Queensland Maritime Museum (maritimemuseum.com.au) has various historic vessels including the Second World War frigate *HMAS Diamantina*. Nearby, you can nip across the Brisbane River on the Goodwill Bridge and explore the Botanical Gardens or hit the shops on Queen Street.

Gold Coast With its irresistible blend of sand, sea and 300 sunny days a year, the Gold Coast is one of Australia's most popular holiday destinations. Around two hours' drive south of Brisbane, it boasts a huge range of accommodation, from motels and apartments to luxurious resorts. Although dining out and shopping are major tourist activities (particularly at Surfers Paradise), it's the theme parks that are more likely to wow kids. Wet 'n' Wild Water World (wetnwild.com.au) has something for all ages, from the Extreme H2O Zone (featuring rides like Kamikaze, Tornado, Black Hole and Mach 5 for those with bottle) to an eight-lane racing slide and special play area for children aged 10 or less. Dreamworld (dreamworld. com.au) is actually several worlds in one – a kind of 'theme park chocolate box' of daredevil rides, wildlife

encounters, water slides and cartoon characters. Sea World (seaworld.com.au) has animal shows, thrill rides, dolphin encounters and an impressive Shark Bay lagoon and a penguin exhibit. Known as 'Hollywood on the Coast', Movie World (movieworld.com.au) has a cast of Warner Bros characters, as well as some serious white-knuckle rides like the Lethal Weapon and Green Lantern roller coasters. If all that sounds too brash and boisterous, escape the Gold Coast crowds by staying on unspoiled South Stradbroke Island.

Sunshine Coast Located north of Brisbane, the Sunshine Coast is more restrained than the Gold Coast – not that children will find it dull. The beaches are just as spectacular, while the sun beams down on average seven hours a day. There are also plenty of non-beach attractions, such as the late Steve Irwin's Australia Zoo (australiazoo.com.au) and the theme park Aussie World (aussieworld.com.au). The southern gateway to the region, Caloundra (caloundratourism.com.au) makes an excellent family-friendly base.

Hervey Bay & Fraser Island Renowned as one of the best centres for whale watching in Australia, Hervey Bay is a resting site for humpback whales migrating south towards Antarctica between August and October. The largest sand island in the world, Fraser Island has shipwreck-strewn beaches, dense rainforest and idyllic lakes. It's the perfect 4WD camping escape for adventurous families.

Whitsunday Islands If it's pampered holiday bliss you're after, look no further than the Whitsundays – 70-odd islands scattered off the coast near Airlie Beach. Hamilton Island (hamiltonisland.com.au) is Australia's best-loved family beach resort (see page 292).

Inside info

▶▶ Tours to Fraser or Moreton Island can be booked with Sunrover Expeditions (sunrover.com.au) and Coastal Island Safaris (coastalislandsafaris.com).
▶▶ Manly Harbour Village, Brisbane's gateway to Moreton Bay Marine Park, has restaurants, shops, playgrounds, cycle tracks and walking paths.
▶▶ For further info, visit queenslandholidays. com.au.

Northland protrudes from the top of New Zealand's North Island like a giant thumbs up – and that's precisely the reaction you'll get from your kids when they discover this far-flung adventure paradise, offering everything from sandboarding and kayaking to swimming with dolphins and spotting kiwis in a forest of giant kauri trees. Endowed with excellent museums, Auckland and Wellington provide fascinating introductions to North Island's wildlife, culture and history, while Rotorua and Tongariro are the ultimate New Zealand hotspots for turbo-charged adventure, Maori traditions and volcanic shenanigans. Basically, North Island has it all – whether you're a Lord of the Rings location-spotter or a surf dude catching the waves on the Coromandel Peninsula.

Auckland

At 328 m high, the Sky Tower (skytower.co.nz) not only provides buttock-clenching views of New Zealand's largest city, but also gives you the option of taking the quick route down – by jumping. With a minimum age of just 11, Sky Jump (skyjump.co.nz) provides elastic-cord-assisted descents where you reach speeds of 85 km/h for 11 seconds before slowing in the last few metres for a gentle landing. Unlike bungee jumping, there is no hanging upside down or bouncing around. So, no worries there then. More teeth-clattering moments are available at Rainbow's End (rainbowsend.co.nz), a theme park boasting New Zealand's only corkscrew roller coaster, and Snowplanet (snowplanet.co.nz), an indoor winter resort with three lifts and a snowboarding park.

Of course, there's much more to Auckland than adrenaline abuse. The sea features prominently in some of the city's top family attractions, such as the New Zealand National Maritime Museum (nzmaritime.org) with its seafaring exhibits and harbour cruises, and Kelly Tarlton's Antarctic Encounter and Underwater World (kellytarltons.co.nz) where you can see penguins, sharks and stingrays and explore a life-sized replica of Captain's Scott's hut. Native and exotic wildlife, from kiwis and tuataras to orang-utans and zebras, are always a big hit with kids at Auckland Zoo (aucklandzoo.co.nz), while the Museum of Transport and Technology (motat.org.nz) provides endless opportunities for fiddling, twiddling and experimenting. For shopping, head to Champions of the World (champions.co.nz) for authentic All Blacks merchandise, The Fairy Shop (thefairyshop.co.nz) for wands, wings and things, and Aotea Square Markets (the-edge.co.nz) for Pacific arts and crafts, traditional Maori carvings and contemporary jewellery.

Best city escapes A short drive across Harbour Bridge, or a 10-minute ferry ride from downtown Auckland, the suburbs of North Shore (northshorenz. com) have more than 20 beaches, including the 1-km sandy stretch of Takapuna (takapunabeach.co.nz) – Auckland's best urban beach with safe swimming, cracking harbour views and lots to do. Both Auckland and North Shore are perfectly placed for boat trips in the Hauraki Gulf – whether you opt for a yacht or a sea kayak. Just 40 minutes by ferry from downtown Auckland, Waiheke Island (waiheke.co.nz) has gorgeous beaches, bush walks and plenty of family restaurants and cafés.

Wellington

Unusually for New Zealand, the capital's top family attraction is not a wilderness excursion, Lord of the Rings tour or daredevil activity – but a museum. Te Papa (tepapa.govt.nz), the country's national museum, is easily worth a full morning or afternoon. You'll find all kinds of bold and imaginative exhibits on geography, wildlife and culture, but it's the Discovery Centres and StoryPlace that captivate children. StoryPlace offers 45-minute storytelling, song and art sessions for under-fives, while the Discovery Centres are split into four themes for older children. In NatureSpace, they can step inside a dinosaur footprint, inspect an insect under a microscope and find a fossil; Inspiration Station encourages them to get creative

Bay of Islands

Northland's choicest slice of seaside, the Bay of Islands is brimming with activities. Take the ferry across to the historic, cutesy settlement of Russell – once bemoaned by 19th-century sailors and whalers as the 'hellhole of the Pacific'.

Surf lessons

★ Head for Whangamata on the Coromandel Peninsula and ask for Ricky Parker who runs the Whangamata Surf School (whangamatasurfschool.co.nz). He's great with kids and can provide an hour's one-to-one introductory lesson – 20 minutes on the beach and 40 minutes in the sea. You'll learn everything from how to position your feet correctly to how to fall off safely. Early in the summer, you will need a shortie wetsuit, while later in the season a rash shirt will do.

Fumaroles and Maori culture at Te Puia, Rotorua

Kids' top 10 North Island

1 Learn about New Zealand's icon at Rainbow Springs (rainbowsprings.co.nz), a hatchery and nursery where you can see eggs being incubated and chicks weighed and fed.

2 Feel the heat on a White Island Tours (whiteisland.co.nz) boat trip to New Zealand's only active marine volcano, cruising to White Island in the Bay of Plenty before venturing to the crater's edge.

3 Zorb like you've never zorbed before. It's bouncy, it's barmy – it's a big inflatable ball bounding down a hill with you strapped inside. Try it wet or dry with Zorb (zorb.co.nz) in Rotorua. There's even a kids' Zorb for under 6's.

4 Paddle over the edge of a 9-m high dam with Taranaki Outdoor Adventures (toa.co.nz).

5 Glimpse glow worms by night on a Lake McLaren Glow Worm Kayak Tour (kayaks.co.nz), paddling stable two-person sea kayaks into a twinkling canyon.

6 Watch a traditional Maori haka at Te Puia (tepuia.com), practise posturing, feet stamping and sticking your tongue out at your parents and then experience some of Rotorua's other highlights, like the Skylines Luge (skylineskyrides. co.nz/rotorua) and Agrodome (agrodome.co.nz).

7 Experience the magic of the Waipoua Forest at night, when the cries of kiwis echo amongst the world's tallest kauri trees. Feel a tingle along your spine as Maori guides from Footprints Waipoua (footprintswaipoua.com) recount ancient legends and sing spiritual songs as you venture deep into the forest.

8 Discover the legacy of pioneer mining days on a tour with Kiwi Dundee (kiwidundee.co.nz) where guides will show you how prospectors toiled for gold and silver in the hills of the Coromandel Peninsula during the late 1890s.

9 Snorkel or kayak around Goat Island Marine Reserve (goatislanddive.co.nz) where snapper, blue cod, red moki and other fish will swim right up to you.

10 Poach yourself at Hot Water Beach on the Coromandel Peninsula where, at low tide, geothermal water bubbles up through the sand. Bring a shovel, dig a hole, check the temperature, then lie back and relax.

with cartoons and puppets; PlaNet Pasifika celebrates Pacific Island cultures, while Te Huka ā Tai brings Maori traditions to life. Children will also love Te Papa's Bush City, a living exhibit with a rainforest rope-bridge and a crawl-through glowworm cave.

Having given their brains such a workout at Te Papa, your kids may well need to release some physical energy. Waitangi Park on Wellington's waterfront has a fantastic playground and skateboard park, while Ferg's Kayaks (fergskayaks.co.nz) offers kayaking trips, inline skating and New Zealand's largest indoor rock-climbing wall. For wildlife, catch the Number 10 or 23 bus to Wellington Zoo (wellingtonzoo.com) or spend the evening at the Karori Wildlife Sanctuary (sanctuary.org.nz) where you can experience the dusk chorus, see native birds and try your luck at spotting a nocturnal kiwi.

Best city escapes Explore the South Coast and visit a fur seal colony on an exciting 4WD adventure with Seal Coast Safari (sealcoast.com). For gentle walks and a chance to feed animals, visit Staglands Wildlife Reserve (staglands.co.nz) in the Akatarawa Valley.

⊙ Let's go to the top

The most exciting way to reach Cape Reinga at the tip of North Island is on a flying safari with Salt Air (saltair. co.nz). Departing from Pahia, you climb above the Bay of Islands before tracking north across Doubtless Bay and the dazzling silica sands of Rarawa Beach. Landing near the cape, a minibus takes you to a lighthouse presiding over the whitewater hurly-burly between Tasman Sea and Pacific. Then it's off for a paddle at Tapotupotu Bay and sandboarding in an area of giant dunes.

Inside info

▶▶ The Discover New Zealand Centre at 180 Quay Street can arrange transport, tours and accommodation in Auckland and beyond.
▶▶ Ferries to Waiheke Island and other destinations in Hauraki Gulf are operated by Fullers (fullers.co.nz) and SeaLink (sealink.co.nz).
▶▶ Wellington's compact city centre is easily explored on foot.
▶▶ The Wellington Cable Car operates between Lambton Quay and the Lookout where you'll find the Carter Observatory (carterobservatory.org).
▶▶ For further information, log on to aucklandnz.com and wellingtonnz.com.

Classic South Island tour

Days 1-2 Wellington With its superb museum, Wellington in North Island (see page 286) makes a fascinating start to this epic journey and cuts out a lot of potential backtracking in South Island. And, of course, it also makes it easy to add on a North Island extension should you have the luxury of a four- or five-week holiday!

Days 3-5 Marlborough Sounds Sauvignon Blanc heaven to parents, this enticing region of inlets, coves and vineyards is easily reached by ferry across Cook Strait. Spend your days walking, kayaking and boating. Cruises are operated by the Maori-owned Myths and Legends Eco Tours (eco-tours.co.nz) and Beachcomber Fun Cruises (mailboat.co.nz) where you help deliver mail and groceries to families living in remote bays. The Marlborough Adventure Company (marlboroughsounds.co.nz) offers half-day guided kayaking trips for families with children aged 13 and over, or you could swap paddles for saddles and go horse riding with High Country Horse Trek (high-horse.co.nz). Before you get too carried away with the Marlborough Sounds area, however, spare a thought for Abel Tasman National Park where sandy beaches, turquoise waters and lush native forest conspire to form one of New Zealand's most luxuriant adventure playgrounds. Getting around is easy – just hop on the Abel Tasman Aqua Taxi (aquataxis.co.nz) which shuttles back and forth to all the park's main beaches and walking trailheads. Kaiteriteri Kayak (seakayak.co.nz) can kit you out for paddling.

Days 6-7 Kaikoura New Zealand's 'cetacean central', Kaikoura is one of the world's best marine wildlife destinations. The traditional sperm whale tour with Whale Watch Kaikoura (whalewatch.co.nz) is exciting enough, but children may well find the smaller, more intimate Albatross Encounter (oceanwings.co.nz) more enthralling. To be surrounded by dozens of squawking, hissing seabirds with 3-m wingspans is one thing, but add to that a pod of 600 acrobatic dusky dolphins and you have a wildlife spectacle to rival anything on earth. With Dolphin Encounter (dolphinencounter.co.nz), children aged eight and over can don wetsuits and swim with the dolphins. On dry land, Maori Tours (maoritours.co.nz) offers one of South Island's most enlightening cultural tours, visiting fortified villages and learning about bush medicines. Continuing south from Kaikoura, a diversion inland leads to Hanmer Springs (hanmersprings.co.nz) where a thermal spa and children's pool complete with water slides should keep the entire family happy.

Days 8-9 Aoraki/Mount Cook Bypassing Christchurch, continue towards Geraldine where a Lord of the Rings tour (lordoftheringstours.co.nz) takes you in search of the Misty Mountains, Helms Deep, Edoras and other big-screen locations. Nowhere in New Zealand does the scenery reach more epic proportions than in Mount Cook National Park where kids can hike beneath giant saw-tooth peaks and skim stones across spearmint-coloured glacial tarns. Glacier Sea Kayaking (mtcook.com) organizes paddling trips in iceberg-strewn lakes, while Mount Cook Ski Planes (mtcookskiplanes.com) whisks you past Aoraki's 3764-m summit for a sensational landing on the Tasman Glacier.

Days 10-11 Wanaka A fine spot to spend a couple of days experiencing farm life at a hill station, Wanaka is also within easy range of the Cardrona Valley where Backcountry Saddle Expeditions (backcountrysaddles.co.nz) offers horse treks across hillsides of wind-combed tussock grass and alongside streams where prospectors toiled during the gold-rush days of the 1860s. Nearby Arrowtown is the area's best-preserved gold-mining settlement where you can visit the Lakes District Museum and try your hand at gold panning. To up the pace, sign up for a jetboat ride with Clutha River Jet (lakelandadventures.co.nz) on Lake Wanaka.

Days 12-14 Queenstown From its humble beginnings as a gold-rush town, Queenstown began its bid for adventure capital of the world in 1970 when Bill Hamilton invented a highly manoeuvrable, shallow draft, jet-powered boat to reach inaccessible parts of his land. Hamilton's idea was given the tourist spin when Shotover Jetboat rides were launched in Queenstown. Following in their wake came whitewater rafting. Then someone thought it would be fun to jump off a bridge on a long elastic rope. Once bungee jumping took off, there was no looking back. Queenstown became awash with adrenaline. Nowadays, the lakeside town offers at least 70 activities, from skydiving to underground rafting. More mellow activities include cruises aboard the *TSS Earnslaw* (a 1912 paddle steamer) and riding the Skyline Gondola up Bob's Peak, from where there are eye-popping views of Lake Wakatipu, snug beneath the snow-dusted Remarkables. See opposite for some of the best child-friendly activities.

Days 15-17 Te Anau Gateway to the majestic wilderness of the 21,000-sq-km Fiordland National Park, Te Anau's essential excursions include the glowworm caves and a cruise on either Milford Sound or Doubtful Sound – all possible with Real Journeys (realjourneys.co.nz).

Days 18-20 Southeast coast Keep an eye out for Hector's dolphins cavorting in the surf at Curio Bay on the beautiful Catlins Coast between Balclutha and Invercargill. Further north, the Royal Albatross Centre (albatross.org.nz) on the Otago Peninsula provides more close encounters with rare wildlife. This beautiful headland is also fringed with wild, sandy beaches – mostly deserted except for the odd dozing sea lion. Don't miss Penguin Place (penguinplace.co.nz), home of the Yellow-Eyed Penguin Conservation Reserve, or the chance to kayak in sheltered Otago Harbour with Wild Earth Adventures (wildearth.co.nz). In Dunedin, stop for a sweet treat at Cadbury World (cadbury.co.nz) before heading north to Christchurch, via the intriguing Moeraki Boulders.

Day 21 Christchurch See opposite.

Wanaka

> **“ ”**
> **Part of the fun of driving across South Island is planning your route. With little more than a map and a pencil you can indulge in the ultimate dot-to-dot.**
> William Gray

🔍 **Let's go to** Stewart Is

At the southern tip of South Island, Bluff is the departure point for Stewart Island (stewartislandexperience.co.nz) where you can visit tiny Ulva Island to glimpse kakas, wekas, tuis and other avian rarities in the moss-clad splendour of one of New Zealand's most pristine forests. Night trips in search of kiwis on surf-pummelled Ocean Beach a also possible

Have you ever wondered why Gandalf never spurred his white charger across a deserted beach? Or why Frodo was never confronted by a wild, surf-gnawed headland on his way to Mount Doom? It's a pity Tolkein never sought inspiration in New Zealand because its coast is every bit as dramatic as the mountains, plains and forests popularized in *The Lord of the Rings*. South Island's shore ranges from brooding fiords in the southwest to turquoise coves in the north; from sandy bays on the Catlins Coast to wildlife honeypots at Kaikoura and the Otago Peninsula. Combine with inland highlights like adrenaline-pumping Queenstown and the sawtooth peaks of the Southern Alps and you have something quite irresistible. Just don't tell Gollum.

Christchurch

On 22 February 2011, Christchurch, New Zealand's second-largest city, was hit by a magnitude 6.3 earthquake. While parts of the city were badly affected and will take time to rebuild, the city as a whole continues to operate.

Ensnared by a loop of the River Avon, the Christchurch Botanic Gardens (ccc.govt.nz/parks) has sweeping lawns, impressive trees, a rose garden, children's play area and paddling pool – the perfect place to shrug off jetlag if you have just arrived in New Zealand. On the edge of the gardens, the Canterbury Museum (canterburymuseum.com) features a 'Discovery' natural history centre where children can dig for fossils and learn about wildlife. From there, it's a short stroll along Worcester Boulevard to the Arts Centre (artscentre.org.nz) and Cathedral Square – both badly damaged in the earthquake.

Located on the city's outskirts, the International Antarctic Centre (iceberg.co.nz) is the base for the New Zealand, United States and Italian Antarctic programmes. People are kitted out here before being flown to the great white continent in huge Hercules aircraft fitted with skis. But it's also a fascinating interactive museum where kids (large and small) can discover what life is like in Antarctica. The Hagglund ride, in which an all-terrain vehicle hurls you around an assault course sculpted with crevasses and precipices, is positively genteel compared to the Antarctic storm simulation in which you are shut in a giant freezer and pummelled with gale-force winds. Other highlights 15-20 minutes' drive from downtown Christchurch include the Air Force Museum (airforcemuseum. co.nz), Ferrymead Heritage Park (ferrymead.org.nz) and Willowbank Wildlife Reserve (willowbank.co.nz).

Mount Cook Skiplanes

Queenstown adventures

1 Dart River Safaris (dartriver.co.nz) Jetboat ride along the Dart River deep into Mount Aspiring National Park.
2 Dart Stables (dartstables.com) Horse ride through the golden woods of Lothlórien, with views over Isengard.
3 Family Adventures (familyadventures.co.nz) Gentle whitewater rafting on the Shotover River.
4 Goldfields Mining Centre (goldfieldsmining.co.nz) Visit a gold mining ghost town and try your hand at gold panning in Kawarau Gorge.
5 Kawarau Bridge Bungy (bungy.co.nz) The original 43-m bungee jump. The 134-m Nevis Highwire Bungy is for 13-year-olds and over.
6 Kingston Flyer (kingstonflyer.co.nz) Steam train journey along 14 km of countryside between Kingston and Fairlight.
7 Off Road Adventures (offroad.co.nz) Quad bike tours tailored to suit different age children.
8 Serious Fun Riversurfing (riversurfing.co.nz) Whitewater bodyboarding on the Kawarau River.
9 Shotover Stables Gentle horseback ride along the banks of the Shotover River.
10 Shotover Jet (shotoverjet.com) Thrilling jetboat ride through the narrow canyons of the Shotover River.
11 Skyline Gondola & Luge (skyline.co.nz) Take the gondola up Bob's Peak and ride either the Scenic or Advanced luge tracks.
12 TSS Earnslaw (realjourneys.co.nz) Cruise on a vintage steamship across Lake Wakatipu to Walter Peak farm where you can feed the animals.

To get above it all, the Christchurch Gondola (gondola. co.nz) provides panoramic views of the city, Lyttelton Harbour, Banks Peninsula, Canterbury Plains and the distant peaks of the Southern Alps.

Inside info

▶▶ The Christchurch Tramway (tram.co.nz) links key attractions such as Cathedral Square, The Arts Centre, Botanic Gardens and Canterbury Museum.
▶▶ Punts operate from various landings along the river, including Worcester Bridge.
▶▶ For further information, log on to christchurchnz.net or christchurch.org.nz.

Welcome to New Zealand

When to go
Australia can be visited year round. The southern half of the country is best from October to April, while the more tropical north is less humid and wet from May to September. The coolest months for exploring the Outback are from April to September, while Queensland's Gold Coast and Sunshine Coast have pleasant temperatures and reliable sunshine all year. The peak season for visiting Australia is mid-December to the end of January when it is essential to book accommodation, tours, and transport well in advance. The best months to visit **New Zealand** are from September to April. During mid-summer (December to February) temperatures average 22-26°C, but this is also the peak tourist season when accommodation is at a premium. For less crowds and better deals, travel in spring and autumn when the weather is still generally fine, particularly in North Island. May to August can be wet and cold, although don't forget that some destinations, like Queenstown, switch to skiing during the winter.

Getting there
Several airlines serve Australia and New Zealand. Flying time is generally around 24 hours, but you can easily break the long trek Down Under with a stopover in a US or Asian city or on a South Pacific island. Stick to the most popular routes and you may find that a round-the-world ticket is as cheap, if not cheaper, than a standard return. The national carriers, Qantas (qantas.com.au) and Air New Zealand (airnewzealand.com) have extensive global networks. Qantas flies to Sydney from London, Frankfurt, Johannesburg, New York, Los Angeles, San Francisco and Vancouver, as well as from several Asian cities. There is also a service to Melbourne from London, Los Angeles and Singapore; to Brisbane from Los Angeles and to Adelaide and Perth from Singapore. Air New Zealand (airnewzealand.com) flies daily from London to Auckland via Los Angeles, and also has frequent connections from Los Angeles to Christchurch. Asian routes go via Hong Kong. Other airlines serving the region include Emirates (emirates. com) which flies via Dubai to Melbourne from several UK airports, including Birmingham, Glasgow, London and Manchester. Virgin Atlantic (virgin-atlantic.com) has direct flights from Heathrow to Sydney.

Getting around
Distances are huge in Australia – and even in New Zealand you shouldn't underestimate travel times or petrol costs if planning a major road trip. All the major **car hire** companies are represented in airports and cities. A popular option for families, motorhomes can be rented from numerous companies, including Britz (britz.com), Maui (maui-rentals.com) and United Campervans (campervan.co.nz). Although main roads and tourist routes are generally of a very high standard in Australia and New Zealand, some remote areas have gravel roads which you may not be insured to drive on. Check the small print on your rental agreement.

Australia has an excellent **coach** network with operators like Greyhound Australia (greyhound.com.au) offering a range of excellent value passes. However, bear in mind that journeys can be unbearably long for children, with few stops.

Internal flights may well be your best bet for covering large distances. There are several regional airlines servicing Australia and some international ticket deals include free internal flights. Try Jetstar Airways (jetstar.com), Virgin Australia (virginaustralia.com) and Skywest (skywest.com.au), as well as Qantas and Air New Zealand.

Getting between North Island and South Island in New Zealand is straightforward with Interislander (interislander.co.nz) which offers three-hour **ferry** crossings (for vehicles and passengers) between Wellington and Picton. Cook Strait ferry crossings are also operated by Blue Bridge (bluebridge.co.nz).

Accommodation
Wherever you stay in Australia and New Zealand you can expect good value for money and a great range of options. Accommodation includes everything from campsites, hostels and farmstays to luxury resorts, eco-lodges and yacht charters. In Australia, apartment-style hotels, consisting of a couple of bedrooms and a kitchen, offer a practical solution for families, although motorhomes (see Getting around) will generally work out cheaper. Try to make room in your itinerary for a family farmstay. You'll appreciate the occasional break from your campervan and kids love helping out on the farm. In New Zealand, self-catering seaside holiday homes, or baches, are as popular with locals as they are with tourists. Rental is usually for a minimum of three nights. Kiwi Bach and Holiday Homes (kiwibachandholidayhomes.co.nz) has a selection of properties at Ohope Beach on North Island's Bay of Plenty; Holiday Houses (holidayhouses.co.nz) rents out baches on the popular Coromandel Peninsula, while Book a Bach (bookabach.co.nz) provides a letting service for hundreds of baches throughout New Zealand. For a spot of luxury, Australia and

New Zealand have no shortage of special places to stay. UK-based Bridge & Wickers (bridgeandwickers. co.uk) offers a range of largely upmarket family accommodation, including mouthwatering properties in Australia like Chocolate Gannets (stylish two-bedroom villas overlooking the Great Ocean Road, Victoria), Dunk Island (tropical paradise in North Queensland with a World Heritage listed rainforest, boat trips to the Reef and a kids' club) and Quay West Suites (spectacular apartments overlooking Sydney Harbour). Whatever type of accommodation you go for, book well in advance during school holidays. Try regional tourist office websites for online directories.

Food & drink

Whether you believe in the Aussie or Kiwi version of the origins of pavlova, kids will be pleased to discover that it is readily available in both countries, along with other sweet treats like Hokey Pokey ice-cream (a calorific concoction of ice cream, strawberries, golden syrup and sugar) and Rocky Road (a chocolate, marshmallow, biscuit and nut extravaganza). Parents, meanwhile, will be happy to learn that Australia and New Zealand have a bountiful cuisine with plenty of less tooth-rotting options. In New Zealand, national specialities range from kiwi fruit to lamb – both juicy and delicious in their own way. Expect to eat pumpkin and *kumara* (sweet potatoes) with a traditional roast. During a Maori cultural tour you may be invited to try food cooked in an earth oven, or *hangi*. As you'd expect, New Zealand's seafood is excellent, while grown-ups will no doubt be keen to sample the fine Chardonnays and Sauvignon Blanc from prime wine regions like Marlborough and Hawkes Bay. Australian food and drink is equally palatable. Children with big appetites will enjoy getting to grips with authentic Aussie barbecues of chicken, steak and seafood. Fresh fruits and vegetables are abundant, particularly in subtropical and tropical regions, while coastal areas are renowned for their varied seafood. Cities offer a rich blend of flavours, with influences from Europe, Asia and the Pacific. From pies and pizza to Chinese *yum cha* and Thai green curry, kids can be as adventurous as they like.

Health & safety

Australia and New Zealand are generally very safe countries to visit. As with travel anywhere, it's wise to be up to date with regular vaccinations, especially tetanus. Take extra care when driving long distances or trying out adrenaline-charged adventure activities. Be especially wary

of exposure to heat and sun, particularly in desert and coastal regions of Australia. Wear hats and sunblock and drink plenty of water. In New Zealand, be prepared for sudden changes in the weather, especially if you are planning outdoor activities in remote regions like Fiordland. Sandflies can be a nuisance in some areas, so remember to take repellent. There are several potentially dangerous animals in Australia, ranging from snakes and spiders to saltwater crocodiles. However, as long as you take precautions and follow the advice of your guide in national parks and other wild areas, you're unlikely to be bothered by them. Box jellyfish and the Irukandji jellyfish (collectively known as marine stingers) affect beaches in northern Australia between October and June. Remember to always seek advice from local lifeguards before swimming and wear wetsuits or lycra swimsuits. Stinger nets protect certain beaches at Port Douglas, Cairns, Mission Beach and Townsville.

Feeding the lambs at a farmstay (that's not really New Zealand Chardonnay in the bottle)

Fast facts

Country	Time	Language	Currency	Code	Tourist information
Australia	GMT+8-10	English	Australian dollar	+61	australia.com
New Zealand	GMT+12	English	NZ dollar	+64	newzealand.com

Sal Salis

Where? Cape Range National Park, Western Australia.

Why? A little bit of bush luxury, this wilderness dune camp has nine safari tents (including one for families) just metres from the Ningaloo shore, renowned for its annual gathering of whale sharks. Turtles are seen daily in front of the camp, while snorkellers only have to drift a few metres offshore to find coral gardens squirming with fish.

Contact Sal Salis, T+61 (0)2-9571 6399, salsalis.com

O'Reilly's Rainforest Retreat

Where? Lamington National Park, Queensland.

Why? Explore subtropical rainforest from the comfort of this beautiful ecolodge with its tree-top walkway, jungle hikes, glowworm walks, evening spotlighting and canopy zip-wiring. Hand feed wild parrots and look out for red-necked pademelons (relatives of wallabies) feeding on the lodge's lawns at dawn and dusk.

Contact O'Reilly's, T+61 (0)7-5502 4911, oreillys.com.au

Arthur's Pass Wilderness Lodge

Where? Southern Alps, South Island.

Why? Tucked into beech forest on its own 3000-ha nature reserve and Merino sheep farm, this idyllic lodge has 20 mountain-view rooms and four luxurious lodges. A programme of guided nature walks, canoeing and star-gazing is available, as well as farm activities, such as sheep mustering.

Contact New Zealand Wilderness Lodges, T+64 (0)3-750 0881, wildernesslodge.co.nz

Wildman Wilderness

Where? Kakadu National Park, Northern Territory.

Why? Camp out in luxury on the Mary River floodplains at this fabulous lodge with its cabins and tents on raised decks. Local Aboriginal guides take you birdwatching and crocodile-spotting, while 4WD safaris explore paper bark forests and pandanus swamps in search of sea eagles and other wildlife.

Contact Wildman Wilderness Lodge, T+61 (0)8-8978 8955, wildman wildernesslodge.com.au

Great Ocean Ecolodge

Where? Apollo Bay, Victoria.

Why? Children are welcome at this superb lodge where all profits are reinvested into wildlife conservation. Located just off the Great Ocean Road and Great Ocean Walk, the five-room guesthouse has lawns grazed by wild kangaroos. During your visit, naturalists will lead you on twilight bush walks in search of koalas.

Contact Great Ocean Ecolodge, T+61 (0)3-5237 9297, greatoceanecolodge.com

Hamilton Island

Where? Whitsunday Islands, Queensland.

Why? This stunning self-sufficient resort has an airport, marina, restaurants, shops and a wide choice of accommodation. Kids love whizzing around on the island's golf buggies, visiting the koala sanctuary, snorkelling, kayaking or taking part in activities at the Clownfish Club. Popular excursions include boat trips to Whitehaven Beach and the Great Barrier Reef.

Contact Hamilton Island, hamiltonisland.com.au

> **A popular holiday bolthole on the North Island's Pacific coast, Tairua's population more than quadruples during the summer months when Aucklanders take up residence in traditional beach houses known as baches. Ours was a typical single-storey clapboard building with open-plan lounge-diner and 'wrap-around' verandah.** William Gray

Farmstays are becoming an increasingly popular way of experiencing the 'real' New Zealand. Not only are they located amidst some of the country's most spectacular scenery, but your hosts can provide fascinating insights into farming history and rural life – and you won't get that by staying in a hotel or touring in a campervan. You can expect few other guests, a relaxed atmosphere and genuinely warm hospitality from people who are proud of their country and want to share it with you. Some farmstays operate year-round, while others open only for the summer tourist season, October-March. The main sheep-shearing period is June-August (with lambs sheared March-May); lambing and calving can start as early as September, while livestock numbers reach their peak between December and February.

Lake Hawea Station
Where? Wanaka, Central Otago, South Island.
Why? Stay in a converted musterer's hut, refurbished with comfortable lounges and modern kitchens and sleeping between five and eight. Decks provide wonderful views of Lake Hawea and surrounding mountains. Walking, fishing and horse riding are available on the farm, while Queenstown's adventure activities are all within an hour's drive.
Contact Lake Hawea, T+64 (0)3-443 1744, lakehaweastation.co.nz

Tasman Downs Station
Where? Lake Pukaki, Mount Cook, South Island.
Why? A peaceful and remote cattle station with two guest bedrooms that are reminiscent of a comfortable, old-fashioned B&B. A farm tour is not to be missed. Not only are there incredible views of Lake Pukaki and Mount Cook, but the farmsheds reek of settler ingenuity and memorabilia – from a blacksmith's forge and 1944 tractor to a handmade watermill.
Contact Tasman Downs Station, bnb.co.nz

North America

The Great Outdoors

Taking in the views from the South Rim of the Grand Canyon. Right: Statue of Liberty.

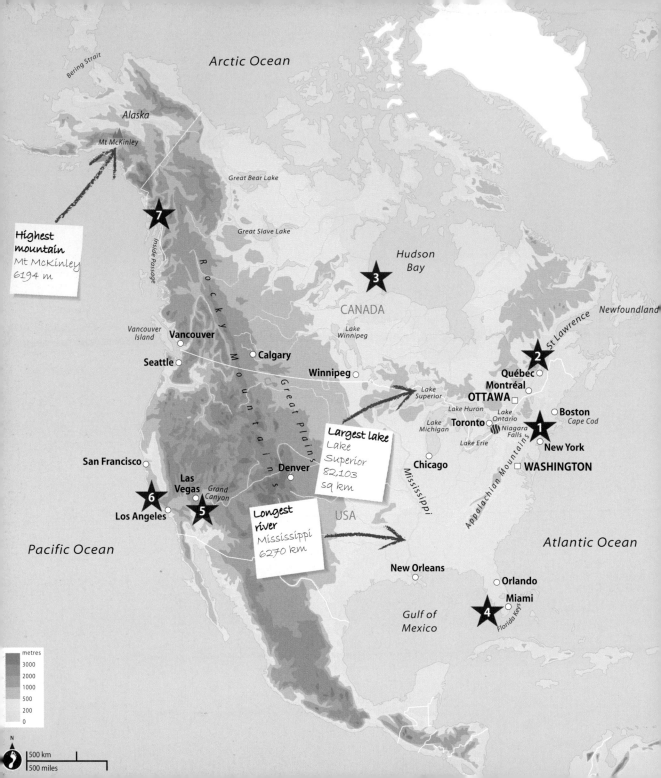

Arctic Ocean

Bering Strait

Alaska

Mt McKinley

Highest mountain
Mt McKinley
6194 m

★7

Great Bear Lake

Great Slave Lake

Hudson Bay

★3

CANADA

Newfoundland

St Lawrence

Inside Passage

Vancouver Island

○ **Vancouver**

Seattle ○

Calgary ○

Winnipeg ○

Lake Winnipeg

Lake Superior

Lake Huron

Lake Michigan

Québec ○ ★2

Montréal ○

OTTAWA ☐

Toronto ○

Lake Ontario

Niagara Falls

Lake Erie

Boston ○

Cape Cod

★1

New York ○

Largest lake
Lake Superior
82,103 sq km

San Francisco ○

Las Vegas ○

Grand Canyon

Denver ○

Chicago ○

Mississippi

Appalachian Mountains

☐ **WASHINGTON**

★6

Los Angeles ○

★5

USA

Longest river
Mississippi
6270 km

Rocky Mountains

Great Plains

New Orleans ○

Atlantic Ocean

Pacific Ocean

Gulf of Mexico

Orlando ○

Miami ○

★4

Florida Keys

metres
3000
2000
1000
500
200
0

N

500 km
500 miles

Did you know?

★ Around 38% of North America is wilderness.
★ The Pentagon in Washington DC has over 28 km of corridors.
★ A Boeing 747's wingspan is longer than the Wright brothers' first flight in 1903, North Carolina.
★ The oldest known living tree, about 4600 years old, is a bristlecone pine in California's White Mountains.
★ Less than 1% of visitors to Yellowstone National Park ever get more than 400 m from

Introduction
North America

Let's face it – given half a chance, most kids would happily trade a sibling or possibly even a parent for the chance to go on holiday to North America! And the reason can be summed up in three simple letters: wow. It's not simply the fact that Canada and the United States offer spectacular wilderness, epic adventures, engaging cities, cutting-edge theme parks and idyllic beaches – lots of places in the world have those. Rather, it's the continent's flare for combining these attributes into an irresistible family-friendly package, where you know that everything from transport and food to the park ranger talk and the waitress saying 'Have a nice day' will make you feel welcome and relaxed. In a child's mind, North America's 'wow' factor is also borne from the sheer scale of everything – from California's redwoods to Orlando's roller coasters. But somehow, it never seems overwhelming – there's usually an option for any age, whether you're searching for orcas off Vancouver Island, delving into the Everglades or getting a taste of the Big Apple. North America's stringent (and inevitably protracted) airport security might put some parents off – but once you're through immigration there's no denying that this is a supremely family-friendly destination.

Star rating

Wow factor
★★★★★

Worry factor
★

Value for money
★★★

Keeping teacher happy
★★★★★

Family accommodation
★★★★★

Babies & toddlers
★★★★

Cool for teenagers
★★★★★

How to
be a dinosaur
hunter ▶▶
see opposite

How to make a dreamcatcher

Traditionally made of willow and hide, Native American dreamcatchers are traditionally hung above sleeping children (or grown-ups) to trap bad dreams and let the good ones filter through.

What you need
▶▶ A bendy twig about 30 cm long
▶▶ Thin wire
▶▶ String
▶▶ Beads
▶▶ Feathers

What to do
▶▶ Carefully bend the twig into a circle and tie the two ends together using wire.
▶▶ Take a long piece of string and tie one end to the twig hoop.
▶▶ Thread a few of the beads onto the string.
▶▶ Wrap the string around the opposite side of the hoop.
▶▶ Thread some more beads and repeat the process, creating a web design.
▶▶ Tie some smaller pieces of string to the bottom of the hoop and attach the feathers.
▶▶ Hang the dreamcatcher above your bed and sleep well.

🜚 How to pan for gold

Panning is easy – it's finding the gold that's the hard part! First, get hold of a pan – anything with sloping sides will do, but don't use a Teflon-coated one. Next, find a likely location. The best places are along creeks, particularly behind boulders where eddies form. Black sand containing magnetite is also a good indicator that you're in the right spot. Scoop up some sand and gravel from the creek. Fill the rest of the pan with water and start shaking it gently from side to side. After a couple of minutes (adding more water when necessary), pick out and discard the bigger stones that are becoming separated – but make sure you don't throw away any nuggets! Now start adding a circular motion to your panning, swirling the soupy mixture of water and grit around so that gravel starts to slop over the side. Keep the rim of the pan higher than the base, otherwise you may lose the gold that settles to the bottom. Take care and slow down when you get to the last traces of sediment. See any gold? 'Bonanza!' is the traditional declaration of success.

Kids' stuff
North America

North American Dreams for kids

Junior Ranger
A fun way to learn about history, culture and the environment, the Junior Ranger Program operates in about 286 US national parks (nps.gov). To qualify as Junior Rangers, children aged 5-14 must complete a series of activities, games and puzzles during their park visit. Different parks offer different programmes, so in the Everglades, for example, wannabee 'JRs' might investigate bird diversity or the importance of water conservation, while in Yellowstone they might tackle the basics of geothermal geology. Simply pick up a Junior Ranger activity pack at the park visitor centre, complete it at your own pace and then share your findings with a ranger to receive an official Junior Ranger badge and certificate. There's also an online programme called Web Rangers (nps.gov/webrangers) that contains puzzles, games and stories based on America's natural and cultural heritage.

Cowboy (or girl)
There are numerous dude ranches throughout the western states and provinces of North America. Riding along well-marked trails through the foothills of the Rocky Mountains is just part of the experience. You'll also toast marshmallows around the campfire, sleep in cosy log cabins and take part in other activities, from fly-fishing and float trips to roping lessons and square dancing. Many ranches cater for horse-riding novices, while others have a separate programme for children.

Dinosaur hunter
North America is big on dinosaurs. Chicago's Field Museum (fieldmuseum.org) has Sue – the world's largest, most complete and best-preserved *Tyrannosaurus rex* skeleton, named after the palaeontologist who discovered it in 1990 in South Dakota. Sue's 58 teeth measure a knee-trembling 19-30 cm in length. For other great dinosaur exhibits, check out the National Museum of Natural History in Washington DC and New York's American Museum of Natural History. However, you can't call yourself a real dinosaur hunter unless you get out in the field. The most famous site is Dinosaur National Monument (nps.gov/dino) in Colorado where Allosaurus, Apatosaurus, Diplodocus, Stegosaurus and other Jurassic giants once roamed. Their bones lie exposed in a fossil-filled cliff in Dinosaur Quarry. Just to the south lies the town of Dinosaur which has street names like Brontosaurus Boulevard and Diplodocus Drive. In Canada, Dinosaur Provincial Park (tpr.alberta.ca/parks/dinosaur) in Alberta is the place to prowl. Not only can you see skeletons of Cretaceous beasts like Albertosaurus and Triceratops in the Royal Tyrrell Museum of Palaeontology (tyrrellmuseum.com), but you can also take guided hikes through the Alberta Badlands where discoveries are still being made.

Great reads ◀ ·········
6 children's books

Ages 4-8
Bear and Turtle and the Great Lake Race
Fusek Peters (Child's Play)
Based on a traditional Native American trickster tale, turtle attempts to outsmart a grumpy old bear.

A Tree for All Seasons
Robin Bernard (National Geographic)
See how a maple tree changes through the year; discover the wildlife of America's maple forests and find out where maple syrup comes from.

M is for Majestic
Pam Carroll (Sleeping Bear Press)
A is for Acadia, where the mountains meet the shore, and the forest stands silent beside the ocean's roar. Explore the national parks of the United States from A to Z in this evocative picture book.

Ages 6+
Gold Fever!
Rosalyn Schanzer (National Geographic)
Well researched and illustrated, this absorbing book uses journals and letters from the forty-niners to evoke a colourful chapter in American history.

Ages 7+
The Escape of the Deadly Dinosaur
Elizabeth Singer Hunt (Random House)
An Allosaurus is on the rampage through the streets of New York. Can Secret Agent Jack Stalwart save the day? Over 100 pages of non-stop action.

Ages 9-12
Little House on the Prairie
Laura Ingalls Wilder (HarperTrophy)
Laura Ingalls Wilder's classic 1935 tale, based on her family's life in the 19th-century American west.

Taste of USA *pecan pie*

What you need
» 23-cm ready-made pie case
» 3 eggs
» 110 g sugar
» 4 tbsp golden syrup
» 50 g butter
» Pinch of salt
» Vanilla extract
» 175 g pecan halves

What to do
» Preheat oven to 200°C.
» Beat the eggs in a mixing bowl.
» Mix in remaining ingredients.
» Pour mixture into pastry case, bake for 10 minutes, then reduce the oven temperature to 180°C and bake for another 30 minutes.

From a family travel perspective, North America is rather like an inside-out sandwich – all the tasty, interesting bits seem to be on the outside – the east and west coasts – rather than in the middle. Florida is bound to be the first place kids set their hungry eyes on, followed by California. The vast space in between becomes a blur as they bounce back and forth between Orlando and San Francisco, New York and Vancouver. However, while there's no denying the immense appeal of North America's coastal states and provinces, don't overlook Yellowstone, the Grand Canyon and other inland natural wonders.

Babies

Logistically, once you're there, travelling with a baby in North America presents no major headaches. Shops selling baby supplies are open 24/7, baby-changing facilities are widespread and there's rarely a problem finding a hotel or restaurant with a cot or highchair. One of the big issues for parents travelling from Europe is going to be the trans-Atlantic flight. It takes at least nine hours to fly from London to Orlando and around eight to reach New York or Toronto. And that's before you've factored in airport time and the gruelling queues that go hand in hand with increased security measures. Putting the journey (and jetlag) aside, you also need to consider North America's 'baby appeal'. Tiny tots will no doubt love Florida's beaches,

but will get very little from its theme parks. Similarly, they might enjoy a good crawl in Central Park, but will be oblivious to the other delights of New York. There are some amazing things to see and do in North America – the big question is whether you can wait until your kids are old enough to appreciate them.

Toddlers/pre-school

With everything from Disney to Wet 'n Wild, Florida is one giant playground. However, many parents are wary of taking toddlers, claiming that 'they won't appreciate the magic' or 'they'll be too small for the rides'. While it's true that kids will get more from Orlando's attractions when they're five-plus (see page 308), remember that it's not compulsory to spend a week trail-blazing every roller coaster and waterslide in the state. A good option with young children is to pick a couple of parks (Magic Kingdom and SeaWorld, for example, have plenty to interest even toddlers) and combine these with the fantastic beaches. You might want to give the Everglades a miss with toddlers – or at the very least restrain them with reins to prevent them from nose-diving into all those alligator-infested creeks. Stressful moments could also be envisaged at precipitous attractions, like Niagara Falls or the Grand Canyon. That's not to say kids of this age group are barred from anything adventurous in the USA or Canada. Far from it. There are family-friendly guest ranches in the Rockies where

Beach on the Bay

Building sandcastles in San Francisco.

Special needs

Easter Seals (easterseals.com) operates 140 accessible camping and recreation facilities for children and adults; Alpenglow Adventures (alpenglowadventures.org) offers challenging trips for people with physical disabilities, including expeditions into the Grand Canyon, and Accessible Journeys (disabilitytravel.com) offers wheelchair-accessible tours in Wyoming, South Dakota and the Canadian Rockies. Also try Adaptive Adventures (adaptiveadventures.org) and World on Wheelz (worldonwheelz.com).

Single parents

The most comprehensive resource, Single Parent Tours (singleparenttravel.net) offers advice and tips for single parents, as well as a selection of tours. Neilson (neilson.co.uk) offers discounts for single parents on skiing trips to the Rockies.

> **" Killer whales sometimes swim past our house,** one girl has written in a display at the local visitor centre in Petersburg, Southeast Alaska. **Sometimes you can see moose at the park,** mentions another. **They get their antlers caught up in the swings.** William Gray

you can give them a taster of the Wild West and even plonk them on a horse for a gentle ride. You could also go whale watching, hiking, canoeing, skiing or base yourself in a family-friendly city like San Francisco or Vancouver from where you can make brief forays into the Great Outdoors.

Kids/school age

At this age, most kids will be boggle-eyed over the prospect of a holiday in North America. Take them to Florida and they'll be able to live the magic, feel the adrenaline rush and get the autographs of all their favourite characters. You'll also get 'added value' from the state in the form of educational excursions to the Kennedy Space Center and the Everglades. If you're looking to expand your kids' minds, you won't find anywhere in North America more 'brainy' than Washington DC with its superb museum complex showcasing everything from dinosaurs to space shuttles. British Columbia's First Nations heritage also offers great scope for an educational odyssey – as do Québec and New England with their vivid tales of early settler life. When it comes to stimulating young minds, however, the real jewel in the crown is the US National Park Service. Parks like Yosemite, Acadia and Zion not only offer access to landscapes oozing with the 'wow' factor, but they also provide outstanding interpretation for children – whether it's a ranger-led walk or the highly acclaimed Junior Ranger Program

(see page 299). Of course, national parks are also some of the best places for embarking on adventures – from paddling a canoe in Banff to riding a mule into the Grand Canyon.

Teenagers

With its shops, shows and happening vibe, New York has immense appeal to teenagers. So too do other cool cities like San Francisco, Las Vegas and Miami. If your teen is less of an urban beast and more of an adrenaline monster, let them loose on the big rides in Florida and California, or challenge them to a backcountry expedition, horse riding through the Rockies, trekking in the Appalachians or kayaking in Alaska. Classic road journeys, like the Pacific Coast Highway and Route 66, will also appeal to older children, particularly if you let them help plan the journey and choose the cruising music.

Universal Orlando Resort

Visiting the world's largest museum complex might seem like anathema to kids. But don't let that put you off going to Washington DC. Far from being dusty, dingy and dull, the Smithsonian Institution Museums are utterly riveting and could easily consume three or more days of your holiday with barely a yawn or a shuffle of feet. Combine the US Capital with some free-spirited roaming in Virginia's Blue Ridge Mountains and then head north for a good drenching at mighty Niagara Falls. From there, either loop south to New York for a head-spinning finale of shopping and sightseeing, or strike east towards New England where the beaches of Cape Cod and Maine beckon.

Washington DC

Lying at the heart of Washington DC, the National Mall is the epicentre for sightseeing in the capital. At one end, you've got the US Capitol (aoc.gov) and at the other, the Washington Monument and White House. While all three landmarks are worth at least a walk-past, it's the treasure trove of museums lining each side of the Mall that will fascinate children. Pick two or three that particularly appeal, and intersperse them with less brain-curdling stuff, like a visit to the National Zoological Park (nationalzoo.si.edu) with its giant pandas, gorillas and tigers, an outing to the National Theatre (nationaltheatre.org) which holds free shows on Saturday mornings, or a day trip to Rock Creek Park and Nature Center (nps.gov) which has trails for walking, cycling and horse riding.

Best Museums No visit to Washington DC is complete without experiencing at least one of the Smithsonian Institution's 14 museums (open daily from 1000-1730, admission free). The National Air and Space Museum (nasm.si.edu) is a head-spinning, neck-craning shrine to flying. Exhibits range from the original 1903 *Wright Flyer* to the command module of *Apollo 11*. You can handle a lump of moon rock, take a virtual journey through space and race paper darts. If your kids want more, a separate branch of the museum, the Udvar-Hazy Center near Washington Dulles International Airport, has a vast hangar where pride of place goes to the Space

Shuttle *Enterprise*. More winged wonders can be seen in the butterfly garden outside the National Museum of Natural History (mnh.si.edu). Inside you'll find a 'natural selection' that would have made Darwin go weak at the knees. Must-sees include the imposing African elephant in the Rotunda, the 15-m-long northern right whale suspended in the Ocean Hall and the wonderful dioramas in the Hall of Mammals – where you can experience a thunderstorm and crawl through an arctic snow tunnel. Dinosaur nuts won't be disappointed either. As well as Allosaurus, Diplodocus and a digitally restored Triceratops, you'll find a life-size model of a pterosaur with a 12-m wingspan and the jaws of a prehistoric shark, *Carcharodon megalodon*, with 15-cm-long teeth. Have a peep at the palaeontologists at work in the glass-enclosed FossilLab, then do a spot of detective work yourself in the hands-on Discovery Room. Other museums with stimulating children's programmes include the National Museum of the American Indian (nmai.si.edu) and the National Gallery of Art (nga.gov).

City escapes From Washington DC, head 120 km westbound on I-66 and you'll reach Front Royal – starting point for the spectacular Skyline Drive. This 170-km route undulates across the forested ridges of the Appalachian Mountains in Shenandoah National Park. Be sure to take a walk in the woods, even if it's just on the Limberlost Trail (milepost 43), a gentle 2-km stroll that's accessible to all. At Waynesboro, the road continues south on the 755-km Blue Ridge Parkway through the Great Smoky Mountains.

Niagara Falls

Tourism is in free-flow at Niagara Falls, where both Canada and the United States have splashed out on

High flyers

The Boeing Aviation Hangar at the National Air and Space Museum in Washington DC. Below left: The *Apollo 11* Command Module *Columbia*; below: *Maid of the Mist* at Niagara Falls.

Kids' top 10 New York

❶ **See** the classic sights of Manhattan. The best view is from the top of the Empire State Building (esbnyc. com) where elevators whisk you up to an observation deck on the 80th floor. The neon razzmatazz of Times Square is another must-see, as is the Rockefeller Center (rockefellercenter.com).

❷ **Shop** at mega toy stores like Fifth Avenue's FAO Schwarz and Toys 'R' Us in Times Square.

❸ **Run** free in Central Park, NYC's 340-ha green oasis where you can cycle, fly kites, throw Frisbees, ride on a vintage carousel or visit the Wildlife Center.

❹ **Cower** beneath dinosaurs at the American Museum of Natural History (amnh.org) where you'll find T Rex, Apatosaurus and Stegosaurus.

❺ **Cruise** to the Statue of Liberty (nps.gov/stli) and gaze in awe at the 225-tonne icon with the 140-cm-long nose, before continuing to Ellis Island (ellisisland.org) where the Immigration Museum brings history to life.

❻ **Catch** a show on Broadway. Long-running children's favourites include *The Lion King,* while the New Victory Theatre (newvictory.org) stages shows and dance performances exclusively for family audiences.

❼ **Kayak** on the Hudson River with the Manhattan Kayak Company (manhattankayak.com). Or, if you prefer something zippier, board the *Beast* (circleline42.com) for a 70-km/h speedboat ride around the harbour.

❽ **Board** the *USS Intrepid*, a Second World War aircraft carrier moored at Pier 86 ((intrepidmuseum.org)

❾ **Learn** how to make a movie or animate a cartoon at the American Museum of the Moving Image (ammi.org).

❿ **Ride** in style on a stretch limo over Brooklyn Bridge or flit over the Big Apple with New York Helicopters (newyorkhelicopter.com).

added attractions ranging from fireworks shows to a wax museum and haunted house. However, the 800-m-wide and 50-m-high Horseshoe Falls, together with its smaller sibling, the 30-m wide American Falls, still manage to steal the thunder. The Canadian shore has panoramic views of both cataracts, while the US side has lookouts over American Falls from Prospect Point, and Horseshoe Falls from Terrapin Point. But don't stop there. You can also look down on the Falls from the 160-m-tall Skylon Tower (skylon.com), circle them in a chopper with Niagara Helicopters (niagarahelicopters.com) and skim over rapids beneath them with Whirlpool Jet Boat Tours (whirlpooljet.com). However, the best way

to guarantee that Niagara Falls leaves an indelible impression on your children is for them to get well and truly soaked. The classic way to do this is with Maid of the Mist (maidofthemist.com), a plucky fleet of sightseeing boats that conveys its passengers (clad in blue rain ponchos) to the base of the Falls. If you prefer something firmer under your feet, the Cave of Winds Tour (niagarafallsstatepark.com) takes you down into Niagara Gorge by elevator where you follow a guide on boardwalks to the Hurricane Deck, within 6 m of American Falls. Perhaps the most unusual perspective of Niagara, however, is from the Journey Behind the Falls (niagaraparks.com) where tunnels take you to portals that look out through the plumes of water at Horseshoe Falls. As you peer through the blur of water, try to imagine three million litres of the stuff passing before your eyes every second.

New England

Boston A fun way to introduce kids to the major sights, Boston Duck Tours (bostonducktours.com) operates a fleet of amphibious landing craft. As well as splashing into the Charles River for a duck's eye view of the city, you'll visit Boston Common (the oldest public park in the United States, established in 1634), the Public Garden (a more manicured landscape, famous for its Swan Boats) and the *USS Constitution* (ussconstitution.navy.mil) – a magnificent 18th-century frigate that earned the nickname 'Old Ironsides' after it shrugged off a broadside from British warships during the War of 1812.

Cape Cod The spectacular Cape Cod National Seashore (nps.gov/caco) preserves a 50-km stretch of sandy coastline, pimpled with historic lighthouses and easily explored by bike along the Cape Cod Rail Trail. The walks at Salt Pond Visitor Center are also worth exploring, but take care if you're tempted to take a dip in the ocean – it's cold and prone to surf and strong currents. It was on this dune-backed shore, in 1620, that the Pilgrims first set foot on American soil having voyaged from England aboard the *Mayflower* – a full-scale replica of which can be seen at Plimoth Plantation (plimoth.org).

Rhode Island There's no shortage of sandy beaches along Rhode Island's 650-km coastline, but don't forget to coax the kids away from their sandcastles for a boat trip in search of humpback, fin and minke whales. Providence has a children's museum and a pleasant park, while Newport County is renowned for its decadent mansions (newportmansions.org).

Inside info

▶▶ Children's Concierge (childrensconcierge. com) offers city tours that are tailor-made to the ages and interests of your children.

▶▶ If you don't fancy walking, Bike the Sites (bikethesites.com) and DC Ducks (dcducks. com) offer interesting alternatives.

▶▶ Contact Big Apple Greeters (bigapple greeter.org) for free tours by locals who love NYC.

▶▶ The Boston City Pass (citypass.com) includes admission to the New England Aquarium and other attractions.

A more enticing river would be hard to imagine. The mouth of the St Lawrence seems to gulp at the North Atlantic, its 1200-km gullet framed in the wolf-head profile of Québec. There's even a tongue, the Gaspé Peninsula, drooping above the dimpled chin of New Brunswick. The St Lawrence River is a hungry invitation to the heart of a continent. Along its length you'll encounter everything from whale sanctuaries to historic cities. Further west, Montréal, Toronto, Ottawa and the Great Lakes beckon, while to the north, vast swathes of forest-clad wilderness promise the ultimate initiation to Canada's Great Outdoors.

Québec

Montréal Founded in 1642 as a fur-trading centre, Québec's largest city has a fascinating historical district. You can easily explore Vieux-Montréal and its adjacent port on foot or by bike. Star sights in the old town include the richly adorned interior of the Basilique Notre-Dame (one of North America's finest churches) and the collection of early-settler artefacts in Château Ramezay. Keep these attractions short and sweet, however, since it's the old port (quaysoftheoldport.com) that really appeals to families. As well as cycling, skating or simply strolling through the riverside recreational park, you can take to the water on anything from an amphibious vehicle (amphitours.ca) to a jet boat (jetboatingmontreal.com). Don't miss the Montréal Science Centre (centredessciencesdemontreal.com) with its IMAX theatre and interactive exhibits on computers, robotics and physical phenomena. Almost as perplexing is Montréal's Underground City – a vast subterranean maze of passageways and plazas lined with 1500 shops, 200 restaurants and 30 cinemas. Probing this parallel universe is the city's Métro, which can also whisk you to Olympic Park – site of the 1976 Olympic Games. Attractions here include the Olympic Stadium (used today for concerts, exhibitions and major-league baseball matches) and the 175-m-tall Montreal Tower. Nearby, the Biodome (biodome.qc.ca) recreates four ecosystems (tropical rainforest, polar, Laurentian Mountains and St Lawrence river) with superb attention to detail.

Québec City Overlooking the St Lawrence River, Terrasse Dufferin, a wide boardwalk beneath the copper-roofed landmark of the 1893 Château Frontenac, could almost have been purpose-built for families. Not only is the vast expanse of decking supremely buggy-friendly, but it is also riddled with street performers and ice-cream vendors. A long flight of steps (or a short funicular railway) leads to the Lower Town, or Basse-Ville, where you can wander among 18th- and 19th-century houses, browse in curio shops, watch street performers or relax in cafés. Just outside the old city walls, the historic battlefield of the Plains of Abraham is now a beautiful urban park with lots of space for picnics and hyperactive kids. Alternatively, drive 20 minutes out of town to Village Vacances Valcartier (valcartier.com) – Canada's largest water park with 35 slides, a Pirates' Hideout and two themed river rides, as well as whitewater rafting and hydrospeed tours on the Jacques-Cartier River.

Tadoussac A relaxed holiday village at the confluence of the Saguenay and St Lawrence rivers, Tadoussac is steeped in history. Inside the reconstruction of the 1600 Chauvin Trading Post (tadoussac.com), kids (especially those who have seen Disney's *Pocahontas*) will be intrigued by the displays of Montagnais peace pipes, pelt scrapers and birch-frame snowshoes alongside European trade goods like rifles, metal knives and blankets – a time capsule that reflects some of the earliest meetings between settlers and Native Americans. The big reason for visiting Tadoussac, however, is what lurks beneath the St Lawrence. At the Sea Mammals Interpretation Center (baleinesendirect.net) you can learn about the 11 species of whales – from diminutive minkes to mighty blues – that migrate each summer into the river's estuary to feed on krill. A resident pod of white belugas is also present, and you have an excellent chance of spotting them on a three-hour whale-watching cruise with Croisières 2001 (croisieres2001.com), available May to October.

Québec City

Fairmont Le Château Frontenac looms over the old town.

Polar bears

Polar bears can weigh 600 kg and sprint at over 40 km/h. They are fearless, powerful hunters that can smell you coming from over 30 km away. That's why you're in a tundra buggy – a giant-wheeled 'snow b[...] that provides a safe vantage from which observe these magnificent beasts. Timi[...] is crucial for an encounter. The peak per[...] is October to early November when the[...] congregate near Churchill on the coast [...] Hudson Bay. Contact Discover the Wor[...] (discover-the-world.co.uk) for details.

Toronto

Gaspé Peninsula The Appalachian Mountains fizzle out on this rugged peninsula of sea cliffs, brooding forests and 18th-century fishing villages. Highlights include the unexpectedly exotic Reford Gardens (jardinsmetis.com) and the exuberant (and whiffy) gannet colony on Bonaventure Island – reached by boat from the holiday centre of Percé. At Parc National Forillon (pc.gc.ca), the Grand-Grave National Historic Site bears witness to the hardships faced by early cod-fishing communities. Watch your kids' faces when they learn of the traditional recipe for soap: 'Take water and mix with beef or pork suet, cod liver oil and sifted ashes from the woodstove'.

Ontario

Toronto At 553 m in height, the CN Tower (cntower. ca) is one of the world's tallest buildings. Rising like a colossal exclamation mark above Toronto's Harborfront, it offers views of up to 160 km on a clear day. With 1769 steps, the internal staircase is the longest in the world, but don't worry – the exterior, glass-fronted elevators will whisk you up the tower at ear-popping speed. The main lookout (that's the bulgy bit two-thirds of the way up) has a glass floor offering heart-in-mouth views of the city 342 m below, while above this there's an open viewing area with steel safety grills. But that's not the highest point for visitors. Just when you think you've controlled your vertigo, the kids will be dragging you towards another elevator bound for the Sky Pod at a dizzying 447 m. Serious adrenaline addicts aged 13 and over should try the Edgewalk (edgewalkcntower.ca). Back on ground level, height becomes an issue again at the Tower's Himalamazon motion theatre and 3D cinema.

After the CN Tower, Toronto's other big family attraction requires a subway ride to the northeastern suburbs where Toronto Zoo (torontozoo.com) sprawls

across a mighty 287-ha chunk of recreated African savannah, tropical rainforest, Canadian wilderness and Australian Outback. Other more central highlights include the Royal Ontario Museum (rom.on.ca) which has no less than 18 complete dinosaur skeletons on display in the James and Louise Temerty Galleries, as well as a walk-through bat cave and a hands-on discovery centre.

Ottawa It's probably fair to say that Canada's capital has less to interest kids than Toronto, but you could easily spend a pleasant few hours in Ottawa exploring the cycling and walking paths along the banks of the Rideau Canal while ogling the Gothic pile of the Parliament Buildings. Nearby, you can pet livestock at the Central Experimental Farm or get to grips with exhibits at the National Museum of Science and Technology (sciencetech.technomuses.ca). South of the city, at Kingston, boat tours weave through the maze of The Thousand Islands. Boldt Castle, a millionaire's folly on one of the islands, has a quirky claim-to-fame as the birthplace of Thousand Island salad dressing.

Algonquin Provincial Park Quintessentially Canadian, this 7725-sq-km patchwork of forests and lakes stretches to the west of Ottawa. Take your pick from some 1500 km of canoe trails, ranging from child-friendly paddles of just 6 km to epic 70-km camping expeditions. Keep your eyes peeled for beaver, moose and bear, and your ears open for the haunting cry of the loon. During August, nightly 'howls' are organized in Algonquin Provincial Park in an attempt to elicit a response from native wolf packs. Find out more at the Algonquin Visitor Center (algonquinpark.on.ca).

The Great Lakes In addition to Niagara Falls (page 302) other highlights of the Great Lakes that lie within easy striking distance of Toronto, include Point Pelee National Park (pc.gc.ca) on Lake Eerie where you can rent bikes or canoes and spot birds from the Marsh Boardwalk. North of Toronto, Georgian Bay on Lake Huron is a popular holiday spot with attractions ranging from the world's longest freshwater beach – a 14-km stretch of sand at Wasaga Beach – to Discovery Harbour (discoveryharbour.on.ca), a reconstruction of a 19th-century British naval base. Also on a historical vein, Sainte-Marie among the Hurons (saintemarieamongthehurons.on.ca) recreates a 17th-century French Jesuit mission. Don't miss the Bruce Peninsula – a great excuse for a day-out with its sandy beaches, fishing villages and bizarre sea stacks.

Inside info

▶▶ Although cities are geared up for winter tourism, with all kinds of snowy capers, it's best to avoid the annual big freeze if you want to venture further afield.
▶▶ Rue de Petit Champlain in Québec City is a good spot for souvenir hunting.
▶▶ The Toronto City Pass (citypass.com) includes entry to the CN Tower and other attractions.
▶▶ Regional tourist office websites include bonjourquebec.com, ottawatourism.ca and ontariotravel.net.

Florida is the number-one family destination in the United States – if not the entire universe. And it's small wonder. Not only is it home to Disney, Universal, SeaWorld and other dream parks, but Florida also has 3000 km of sun-kissed coastline, and natural wonders ranging from the 'gator-filled Everglades to the coral reefs of the Florida Keys. Where else can you get face-to-face with Mickey Mouse, Cinderella and a real-life astronaut all within a few days? Or swim with gentle manatees one morning, and plunge down a death-defying waterslide the next? Whether your idea of fun is to paddle a canoe to a deserted island or take a simulated mission to Mars, Florida will always leave you wanting more. And more is exactly what you get – more water parks, more theme parks, more wildlife encounters, more quirky attractions. So be warned – one visit to the Sunshine State will rarely be enough.

Miami

Perfect if you don't want to rent a car, many of Miami's attractions are within easy walking or cycling distance. With its Latin-American vibe, this is a particularly cool city for teenagers who will appreciate its Art Deco buildings, buzzing nightlife and serious shopping potential, particularly at Aventura Mall, Dolphin Mall and the boutiques along Ocean Drive. As well as great beaches, Miami has numerous family attractions, including animal antics at Jungle Island (jungleisland. com), Seaquarium (miamiseaquarium.com) and Metrozoo (miamimetrozoo.com) where there is an excellent zookeeper programme for children. The Miami Children's Museum (miamichildrensmuseum. org) has interactive exhibits ranging from a television studio to a mini cruise ship, while Gator Park (gatorpark.com) offers airboat rides into the Everglades National Park (see right). To the north of Miami, chic Fort Lauderdale has beaches, sidewalk cafés and the vast Sawgrass Mills – one of America's largest outlet malls.

Florida Keys

A 260-km chain of stepping-stones extending into the Gulf of Mexico, the Florida Keys consists of around 800 islands, 42 of which are linked by bridges. The entire archipelago lies within the Florida Keys National Marine Sanctuary (floridakeys.noaa.gov), while Key Largo provides access to the John Pennekamp Coral Reef State Park (pennekamppark.com) and Biscayne National Park (nps.gov/bisc), both of which offer

snorkelling, diving and glass-bottom-boat tours. Heading west along the Keys, Islamorada's Theatre of the Sea (theaterofthesea.com) provides opportunities for swimming with dolphins, sea lions and stingrays. At Marathon, in the heart of the Keys, you can hike through a tropical hardwood grove and visit the home of an early settler family before crossing Seven Mile Bridge to Bahia Honda – a great spot for kayaking or simply lazing about on some of the Keys' best beaches. Next is Big Pine Key with its National Key Deer Refuge, while at the end of the chain lies Key West, renowned for its watersports and sunsets – the latter of which are celebrated by street performers in Mallory Square.

Everglades National Park

A refuge to endangered species like the American crocodile, Florida panther and West Indian manatee, this vast subtropical wetland sprawls over 600,000 ha of southern Florida. Stop at one of the park's four visitor centres (nps.gov/ever) for an introduction to the area's fascinating ecology and for details of independent and ranger-led activities. A short distance from the Ernest F Coe Visitor Center (the nearest to Miami), the 800-m Anhinga Trail offers one of the best opportunities for close-up views of birds and alligators. Continuing south towards Flamingo there are several short, well-interpreted trails (many of which are buggy-friendly) leading from parking areas along the 61-km Park Road. At Flamingo Visitor Center, boat tours explore Florida Bay

Whipper snapper

Baby American alligator at the Corkscrew Swamp Sanctuary.

🐾 **Manatee** swims

Endangered West Indian manatees migrate to the Crystal River National Wildlife Refuge (fws.gov/crystalriver) each winter – the best time to snorkel with them is December to March when the weather is at its coolest and manatees are concentrated around warm-water springs.

Shell seeker's rewards on the Gulf Coast

and the backcountry. There are also several canoe and walking trails nearby (canoes can be rented from the marina). At Shark Valley Visitor Centre, off the Tamiami Trail, a tram tour leads to an observation tower providing superb views across the sawgrass prairie. The Gulf Coast Visitor Center at Everglades City is the jumping-off point for canoe trips along the Wilderness Waterway or Ten Thousand Islands. North American Canoe Tours (evergladesadventures.com) offer guided trips or, if you're up for a wilderness challenge, rent a canoe and set off on your own, paddling out to a deserted island or *chickee* (a wooden platform on stilts) where you can spend the night with nothing but manatees, ospreys and raccoons for company.

Naples

Style-central for western Florida, Naples goes to town with boutique shops and gourmet restaurants. At the pier, kids will enjoy watching pelicans belly-flop on scraps tossed by fishermen. The Gulf Coast entrance to the Everglades is nearby, and so too is Corkscrew Swamp Sanctuary (audubon.org) where a 3.6-km boardwalk weaves through pinewoods, prairie and a stand of 40-m-tall bald cypress. As well as alligators, the 4455-ha reserve is renowned for its birdlife, including a colony of endangered wood storks. To the south of Naples, Marco Island has gorgeous Gulf Coast beaches, like Sand Dollar Bay, where children will wile away hours shelling, kayaking, snorkelling and building sandcastles. To the north of Naples are the equally laid-back islands of Sanibel and Captiva and the more lively mainland resort of Fort Myers.

Tampa Bay

Two of the best-known Gulf Coast beach resorts in this area are Clearwater Beach and St Pete Beach. There's plenty to keep families happy here, from long sandy beaches to fishing trips and dolphin encounters. To the south lies Sarasota – another beach beauty. The big attraction in the Tampa Bay area, however, is Busch Gardens (buschgardens.com), a heady mix of exotic wildlife and pulse-pounding rides. One moment you'll be hand-feeding giraffes on the Serengeti Safari, the next you'll be clutching your stomach on SheiKra, North America's first dive coaster that sends riders on a 60-m vertical drop at speeds of over 110 km/h. Other highlights include the Pirates 4D show and Congo River Rapids. Just across the street, Busch Gardens' water park, Adventure Island, is awash with slippery slides, wave pools and adventure lagoons, but it's Riptide – Florida's original four-lane mat-slide – that kids will make a beeline for.

Orlando

Home to Walt Disney World Resort, Universal Studios and SeaWorld, Orlando is theme-park heaven. See pages 308-309 for tips on how to plan the ultimate fantasy escape in Florida's number-one holiday destination. From Orlando, it's also possible to arrange excursions to east-coast highlights, including Kennedy Space Center – see below – and Daytona International Speedway (daytonainternationalspeedway.com).

🔍 See spacemen

It's just one of the 'other-worldly' experiences on offer at the superb Kennedy Space Center (kennedyspacecenter.com). Start with a tour of the LC-39 observation gantry for a bird's eye view of the shuttle launch pads, then gawk at the huge *Saturn V* moon rocket and explore a mock-up of the International Space Station. You can then experience lift-off yourself with the Shuttle Launch Experience, a motion simulator that brings to life the sights, sounds and sensations of an actual launch. Equally riveting is the *Space Station 3D* IMAX presentation and the Astronaut Hall of Fame with its hands-on exhibits and collection of astronaut memorabilia. As for meeting a real-life astronaut, there are daily Astronaut Encounters where you can question a member of NASA's Astronaut Corps. Alternatively, sign up for Lunch with an Astronaut. If that inspires you to greater things, you can always enrol for Family ATX – an Astronaut Training Experience where families (with children aged 8-14) spend a half-day immersed in a special programme, riding simulators, building and launching rockets and performing a shuttle mission to the International Space Station in a full-scale orbiter mock-up.

See pages 308-309 for tips on how to plan the ultimate fantasy escape

Inside info

▶▶ Shop around for special deals, like free kids' places, rental car upgrades, twin centre discounts and multi-theme-park passes.
▶▶ Rent a car at the airport – it will give you flexibility to roam at your own pace.
▶▶ Accommodation ranges from camping and self-catering apartments to resorts.
▶▶ For further info go to visitflorida.com.

Florida How to do Orlando

How to fit everything in

It's not going to be easy. Your six-year-old daughter is desperate to meet Cinderella, your 10-year-old son wants to see The Wizarding World of Harry Potter and your teenager is obsessed with roller coasters. To make the most of a family holiday in Orlando you need to plan each day with military precision. Once you've made a list of everyone's top five priorities you can start to shortlist which parks and attractions are 'must-dos' and which are 'maybes'. Then look critically at your itinerary and, if it's wall-to-wall theme parks, try to free up at least one day for a water park, one for Daytona Beach and another for Kennedy Space Center (see page 307). It's also useful to have a 'free' day where you can return to one of your favourite theme parks to see and do the things you didn't have time for first time around.

How to pick the right park

There's something for all ages at every park. Having said that, however, certain parks appeal more to specific age groups, and many rides have height restrictions. If you have young children start by looking at Magic Kingdom and Animal Kingdom. With older children set your sights on Epcot and Disney-MGM. If you have children of widely mixed ages, SeaWorld and Universal's Islands of Adventure have a good range of attractions. Of course, even with teenagers in tow, you might think it inconceivable to visit Orlando and not see the Magic Kingdom – a bit like flying to Cairo and skipping the Pyramids. It's largely a matter of personal preferences, although special multi-park ticket offers (see below) may well be the deciding factor in which parks you end up visiting.

How to save money

Available for pre-purchase in the UK only, Disney's Ultimate Tickets provide unlimited admission to all Disney attractions for either two- or three-week periods. Better suited for shorter visits, five- or seven-day Premium Tickets allow unlimited entry to all four Disney theme parks and either four or six admissions to water parks and other attractions depending on which version you purchase. The Orlando Flexticket (orlandoflexticket.co.uk) gives you 14 consecutive days of unlimited admission to five or six theme parks, including Universal Studios, Universal's Islands of Adventure, SeaWorld, Wet 'n Wild and Busch Gardens. You can also pre-book one- or two-week Universal Holiday Tickets for unlimited entry to Universal Studios, Universal's Islands of Adventure and Universal CityWalk venues.

How to save time

A useful and fun planning tool, personalized maps of any of Disney's four parks can be created online at disneyworld. disney.go.com/maps. Simply select your favourite attractions, dining options and special events, and a customized map is generated which you can print out and take with you. Several of your must-dos are bound to have a FastPass facility. This is essentially a polite way of queue jumping – just insert your entrance ticket into a FastPass machine and you'll receive a designated time when you can board the ride by a special, often queue-free, entrance. The catch, of course, is that you can only FastPass one ride at a time. Still, it's worth doing as

Theme park thrills

From top: meeting Mickey and Cinderella at Magic Kingdom, roller coaster and Revenge of the Mummies at Islands of Adventure.

often as you can – as is Parent Switch, which allows parents with young children to take turns on adult rides, without having to queue a second time.

Walt Disney World Resort

disneyworld.disney.go.com

Magic Kingdom features six lands radiating out from Cinderella Castle. As well as thrill rides like Space Mountain (see right), popular attractions include Mickey's PhilharMagic (spectacular 3D animation), Buzz Lightyear's Space Ranger Spin (zap aliens with a laser cannon), Pirates of the Caribbean (action-packed voyage with rowdy pirates), Space Mountain (roller coaster in the dark), Splash Mountain (log flume ride), the Haunted Mansion, Jungle Cruise, Peter Pan's Flight, Swiss Family Treehouse, Tom Sawyer Island and Tomorrowland Speedway. Fantasyland is being doubled in size during 2012.

Animal Kingdom's centrepiece is a huge, exquisitely carved Tree of Life, from which six themed lands spread out. The attention to detail in the African and Asian villages is remarkable. Must-see attractions include Kilimanjaro Safaris (open-air vehicle ride through an African savannah roamed by elephants, rhinos and lions), Maharajah Jungle Trek (walk-through ruined palace inhabited by tigers, tapirs and fruit bats), It's Tough to be a Bug! (3D animation inspired by *A Bug's Life*), Finding Nemo (musical puppet show), Festival of the Lion King (Broadway-style song and dance), Kali River Rapids and the Wildlife Express Train.

Epcot is probably the one park you'll want to return to more than any other. There is simply so much to see and do. World Showcase transports you to 11 nations, each one depicted by an authentic pavilion. Future World focuses on science and discovery with big rides and interactive exhibits. Don't miss Soarin' – a virtual hang-gliding adventure over California's natural wonders where you can feel the wind in your face and smell the scent of the pine trees. Other attractions include Test Track (95 km/h speedway ride), Turtle Talk with Crush (interactive digital show) and Mission: SPACE (realistic space flight to Mars).

Disney's Hollywood Studios brings movie-making to life with special effects shows like Lights, Motors, Action! and Indiana Jones Epic Stunt Spectacular. You can also learn about animation and see live performances of *Beauty and the Beast*. Thrill rides include the Star Tours flight simulator, the Rock 'n' Roller Coaster Starring Aerosmith and The Twilight Zone Tower of Terror.

Blizzard Beach water park boasts one of the world's tallest, fastest, free-fall speed slides – Summit Plummet. Open year-round, other highlights include the Downhill Double Dipper (inner-tube speed slide on parallel flumes), Teamboat Springs (family raft ride) and Tike's Peak ('snow-covered' play area for tots).

Typhoon Lagoon water park has roaring rapids, relaxing rivers and even a wave pool where you can hone your body-surfing skills.

Universal Orlando Resort

universalorlando.com

Universal Studios Florida takes you beyond the screen and puts you in the thick of the movie action. Brave the storm in

Thrill rides
good reasons to have a growth spurt

park	The ride	The thrill	The catch Min height
Magic Kingdom	Space Mountain	High speed coaster through the blackness of space.	112 cm
	Big Thunder Mountain Railroad	Runaway train through the Old West, mild but wild.	102 cm
Epcot	Mission: SPACE	Extreme motion simulator; don't forget your sick bag.	113 cm
	Test Track	100-km/h test-drive through hairpins and banked turns.	102 cm
MGM Studios	Tower of Terror	Elevator from hell, random drops of up to 13 storeys.	102 cm
	Rock 'n' Roller Coaster	Twists, turns and loops to the beat of Aerosmith.	122 cm
Animal Kingdom	Dinosaur	Mad dash back in time, plenty of dino-surprises.	102 cm
	Expedition Everest	High-speed train, forwards and backwards; scary yeti.	113 cm
Blizzard Beach	Summit Plummet	90-km/h, 110-m-long freefall water slide from 37 m up.	122 cm
	Slush Gusher	27-m-high water slide with bumps and a big splash.	122 cm
Typhoon Lagoon	Crush 'n' Gusher	Water coaster with gravity-defying ups and downs.	122 cm
	Humunga Kowabunga	Choice of three 65-m enclosed speed slides.	122 cm
Universal Studios	Men in Black Alien Attack	Zap aliens in mad dash through New York's streets.	107 cm
	Revenge of the Mummy	Psychological thrill ride at 70-km/h – and it's dark.	122 cm
Islands of Adventure	Dragon Challenge	Harry Potter-themed duelling roller coasters.	137 cm
	The Incredible Hulk Coaster	0-60 in two seconds, 108 km/h max, seven inversions.	137 cm
Sea World	Kraken	Dangling feet on floorless, 105-km/h monster coaster.	137 cm
	Journey to Atlantis	High speed, spooky ride with 18-m splash drop finale.	107 cm
Busch Gardens	SheKra	Floorless dive coaster, 90-degree drop to 110 km/h.	137 cm
	Kumba coaster	33-m drop, three seconds of weightlessness.	137 cm

Twister… Ride it Out; trot along with your favourite ogre and donkey in Shrek 4-D and battle the supernatural in Revenge of the Mummy. Other top attractions include The Simpsons Ride (shambolic ride through Krustyland), Hollywood Rip Ride Rockit (a roller coaster where you choose the soundtrack) and Despicable Me (3D adventure). Then there are the long-established kids' favourites like ET Adventure (take to the skies on flying bikes) and Earthquake (collapsing ceilings and exploding gasoline trucks in an authentic simulation of a 'quake registering 8.3 on the Richter Scale). Younger children will enjoy Jimmy Neutron's Nicktoon Blast where you meet SpongeBob SquarePants and the Rugrats, and Woody Woodpecker's KidZone which has a gentle coaster and a sing-along Barney show.

Islands of Adventure gives myths, legends and comic-book heroes a high-tech spin with attractions like The Amazing Adventures of Spider-Man, The Incredible Hulk coaster and The High in the Sky Seuss Trolley Train Ride. The big highlight here, however, is the Wizarding World of Harry Potter where you can visit the shops of Hogsmeade (like Honeydukes, Zonko's Joke Shop and Ollivanders), dine at the Three Broomsticks and get your pulse pounding on rides such as Dragon Challenge (two high-speed, intertwining roller coasters), Flight of the Hippogriff (a more gentle coaster) and Harry Potter and the Forbidden Journey (a spectacular ride through Hogwarts, visiting iconic locations like the Gryffindor common room and Defence against the Dark Arts classroom).

SeaWorld Parks & Entertainment
seaworldparksblog.com
SeaWorld Orlando (seaworld.com) is famous for its live mammal shows starring Shamu the orca. You can also see beluga whales, penguins, manatees, dolphins, sharks, turtles and rays. The Pacific Point Preserve is a clever recreation of a rocky cove, complete with Californian sea lions, harbour seals and herons. Thrill rides range from the floorless Kraken roller coaster to kiddie's stuff at Shamu's Happy Harbour play area. For details of Busch Gardens and Adventure Island Tampa Bay, see page 307.

Wet 'n Wild
wetnwildorlando.com
Experience a rush of adrenaline and a surge of water on rides like Brain Wash (16-m drop into a giant funnel), The Black Hole (two-person ride in dark tunnel) and Der Stuka (six-storey speed slide). There is also a surf lagoon and numerous water-play areas for younger children.

Early morning light

Grand Canyon for kids

There are plenty of ways to make the Grand Canyon more child-friendly. The big-screen production of *Grand Canyon* at the National Geographic IMAX Theater (explorethecanyon.com) in nearby Tusayan is both thrilling and informative. And a sightseeing flight over the Canyon (grandcanyonairlines.com or papillon.com) is another adrenaline-charged, if pricey, way to experience the natural world wonder.

Essentially, though, to get the most from the Grand Canyon you need to walk. Obviously, age and ability play a crucial role in what you can do. Some parents reach the brink of nervous breakdowns as they struggle to restrain high-energy offspring from climbing on viewpoint railings along the popular South Rim. That's not to say the Canyon is a no-go zone for very young children – just make sure you've got a firm harness-hold at the very least.

Older children can join hikes into the Canyon, even if it's just for a day walk on either the South Kaibab or Bright Angel Trail. For overnight trips to Phantom Ranch, consider joining a mule-assisted hike. Kids aged 4-14 who make it to this cluster of cabins at the Canyon's base can qualify as Phantom Rattler Junior Rangers with the National Park Service. The Grand Canyon Field Institute (grandcanyon.org/fieldinstitute) arranges excellent family tours where you'll learn about wildlife and geology on short hikes.

For something different, head to the Grand Canyon Skywalk (grandcanyonskywalk.com), a glass walkway suspended 1200 m above the Colorado River at Grand Canyon West.

Mule train in the Canyon

“ ”

Our guide knew how to make rocks sound cool. Instead of droning on about the Grand Canyon's 1.7 billion years of geological shenanigans, she got the children in our group to act it out, role-playing thrusting mountains, invading seas and eroding rivers. She succeeded in getting across the basic principles of Grand Canyon tectonics to children aged six to eleven.
William Gray

Bighorn sheep

Two weeks to explore the highlights of Southwest USA? It's going be fast and furious, just like the Wild West ought to be. But what a ride! In just a fortnight you can combine a tour of some of North America's most famous natural wonders, including the Grand Canyon, Monument Valley and Bryce Canyon, with three of its cultural icons – Las Vegas, Route 66 and the Navajo Reservation. Casting a huge lasso across Nevada, Arizona and Utah, your grand circuit will inevitably involve some long driving days, but there are also plenty of opportunities for hiking and even inner-tube floats and helicopter flights. And it wouldn't be the Wild West without saddling up for a spot of horse riding. Yee-ha!

Wild West tour

Days 1-2: Las Vegas It's brash, bewildering and brilliant fun. Las Vegas (visitlasvegas.com) has a 'Sin City' image, but there's still plenty to appeal to kids in this outrageous desert metropolis. Nowhere in the world will you find a more imaginative, bizarre and neon-clad array of themed hotels than along Las Vegas Boulevard South (the Strip). Watch a volcano explode at the Mirage and pirates battle at Treasure Island; ride a roller coaster through the faux-Manhattan façade of New York-New York and drift in a gondola through 'virtual Venice' at the Venetian.

Day 3: Drive to Grand Canyon Allow five to six hours for the drive from Las Vegas to the Grand Canyon – or make a full day of it by stopping en route at Hoover Dam (usbr.gov/lc/hooverdam) where the Discovery Tour takes you 150 m down into the Black Canyon to see eight colossal power generators. Back on the road, take Route 66 (historic66.com) at Kingman to get a taste of the Mother Road (and Disney-Pixar's *Cars* movie). You'll pass historic stores with rusty old trucks, wagons and other Wild-West kitsch parked outside. Rejoin I40 East at Ash Fork from where it's another two hours to the Grand Canyon.

Days 4-5: Grand Canyon Get up early to watch sunrise over this mighty chasm – 445 km long, up to 24 km wide and plunging to more than 1800 m at its deepest point. The visitor infrastructure in Grand Canyon Village on the South Rim is excellent. Orientate yourself at the Canyon View Information Plaza and see opposite for child-friendly activities in Grand Canyon National Park (nps.gov/grca).

Day 6: Drive to Lake Powell Continuing north on Highway 89, you enter the 70,000-sq-km Navajo Reservation (discovernavajo.com). Stop at the Cameron Visitor Center for an insight into the history

and culture of the Navajo Nation and a chance to shop for Native American arts and crafts, before continuing on to Lake Powell.

Day 7: Lake Powell Swimming, canoeing and other watersports are available at this dazzling man-made lake, but try to squeeze in a visit to nearby Antelope Canyon (navajonationparks.org). Known to the Navajo as Tse' bighanilini (the place where water runs through rocks), this narrow cleft is only 37 m deep, but has been sculpted by flash floods into a surreal masterpiece of curvaceous amber-hued sandstone.

Day 8: Monument Valley Few landscapes are as iconic of the Wild West as the huge sandstone towers and spires that soar from the desert of Monument Valley Navajo Tribal Park. A favourite location for moviemakers, the best way to get your own take on the Mittens, Three Sisters, Camel Butte and other famous landmarks is to join a jeep tour with a local Navajo guide. On the way to Monument Valley, stop at Navajo National Monument (nps.gov/nava) where you can see the remains of lofty cliff dwellings once inhabited by the Ancestral Puebloan people.

Day 9: To Capitol Reef Another long drive north brings you to Capitol Reef (nps.gov/care), a spectacular, 160-km-long wrinkle in the earth's crust where kids can learn about geology as part of the park's Junior Ranger Program.

Days 10-11: Bryce Canyon Named after Mormon settler, Ebenezer Bryce (who declared it "a hell of a place to lose a cow"), Bryce Canyon National Park (nps.gov/brca) is yet another weird and wonderful landscape – this time an amphitheatre riddled with a giant maze of rocky pillars known as hoodoos. You can walk to four viewpoints along the 8-km Rim Trail (an incredible spectacle at dawn or dusk when the hoodoos seem to glow like embers), but be sure to hike (or ride a pony) into the Canyon itself. Although you need to take similar precautions against overexposure to sun and heat, it's nothing like as epic an undertaking as venturing on foot into the Grand Canyon. Try the Navajo Loop and Queen's Garden Trail (5 km in total) or, if your kids are good walkers, take them on the 13-km Fairyland Loop Trail.

Days 12-13: Zion National Park Around 140 km to the south, Zion National Park (nps.gov/zion) with its cathedral-like canyon of sandstone cliffs, waterfalls and hanging gardens, is a fitting finale to your two-week tour. As well as several family-friendly hikes, such as the Emerald Pool Trails, activities include horse rides alongside the Virgin River (for children as young as seven) and an excellent Junior Ranger Program.

Day 14: To Las Vegas Zion is around 250 km from Las Vegas.

▸▸ Join an organized tour or rent a car in Las Vegas and self-drive.
▸▸ With another week or more, why not add on California (page 312) to create the ultimate Wild West tour? Allow around eight hours to drive from Zion to Yosemite.
▸▸ For further tourist info visit travelnevada.com, arizonaguide.com and utah.com.

The fun begins the moment you board a cable car in San Francisco, whirring and clanking its way up and down the city's slow-motion roller coaster of streets; the two-man teams working the brakes, traffic weaving around you as skyscrapers frame tantalizing views of the Bay. 'Frisco is a great place to spend a few days with kids, but sooner or later you'll feel the need for some good old California cruisin'. Two of the most exciting options are the Pacific Coast Highway – an ocean odyssey that will transform your kids into beach connoisseurs – and the inland Sierra Nevada route, which reaches its peak, both spiritually and physically, at Yosemite National Park.

San Francisco

A ride on a cable car (sfcablecar.com) is an essential San Francisco experience. The best route is Powell-Hyde, which begins at the Powell/Market turntable and ends near Fisherman's Wharf. On the way you can hop off at Union Square (where you'll find shops ranging from Macy's to Disney) and Lombard Street – America's most bendy, with no less than eight hairpin turns. Try to allow a full day at Fisherman's Wharf. Fortunately, the Powell-Hyde cable car stops at the opposite end to Pier 39 so you'll be able to enjoy the waterfront's many and varied attractions before your kids are lured like zombies into the vast Riptide Arcade. The first must-see is the San Francisco Maritime Historic Park (nps.gov/safr) where you can stand at the helm of the 1886 three-masted square-rigger, *Balclutha*, and board a variety of other old-timer boats ranging from schooners to tugboats. Servicing a 300-strong fishing fleet, Pier 45 is dominated by seafood-processing plants, but it's also the mooring for two Second World War vessels – the *SS Jeremiah O'Brien* Liberty ship and the *USS Pampanito* submarine.

Have a quick peep at the busy bakers in Boudin Sourdough Bakery, grab a lunchtime snack of freshly steamed Dungeness crab from a kerbside stand, then book a sightseeing cruise with Blue & Gold Fleet (blueandgoldfleet.com) at the kiosk near Pier 39. The one-hour trip features both of San Francisco Bay's classic landmarks. First you'll cruise right under Golden Gate Bridge (with onboard commentary from Captain Nemo recounting yarns about everything from bolt riveters and humpback whales to the devastating earthquake and firestorm of 1906). Then you'll circle Alcatraz Island (nps.gov/alcatraz). If you want to go ashore and tour the infamous federal

penitentiary, you need to book with Alcatraz Cruises (alcatrazcruises.com). The Walk-in Prison Experience, suitable for ages eight and above, takes you behind bars to where prisoners ate, slept, exercised, or did solitary time in the notorious Hole. Alcatraz Kidz Tourz (parksconservancy.org) offers family programmes.

Back at Fisherman's Wharf, the Californian sea lions at Pier 39 (pier39.com) are free to come and go as they please – however, numbers reach a winter high of around 900. In addition to 110 shops and 13 restaurants, Pier 39 is home to the excellent Aquarium of the Bay (aquariumofthebay.com) where you can see medium-sized sharks in a 92-m-long walk-through tunnel, stroke small ones in a touch pool and see what a very large one (a great white) can do to a surfboard.

On the subject of marine hazards, do not be tempted to swim or wade at Ocean Beach on the west side of San Francisco – the surf and currents are too dangerous. You're far safer at Crissy Field, a recreational park on the Bay side of Golden Gate Bridge with a sheltered beach and great views. The nearby Exploratorium (exploratorium.edu) invites hands-on science investigation.

Yosemite National Park

Half Dome is one of the most celebrated icons of America's Great Outdoors. A glacier-scalped mountain in the Sierra Nevada of Yosemite National Park (nps.gov/yose) it can be climbed by anyone prepared to hike for 27 km and use cables to haul themselves up the final very steep section.

Needless to say, most families will set their sights lower. Sentinel Bridge, a short stroll from Valley Visitor Centre, offers a classic view of Half Dome, while paved trails to Mirror Lake, Lower Yosemite Falls and Bridalveil Falls are also easy – although remember

Rock star

Half Dome, Yosemite National Park. Below: San Francisco's Golden Gate Bridge – 1900 m in length, 600,000 rivets per tower and designed to flex 8 m during an earthquake.

★ State capital

Wooden sidewalks, horse-drawn carriages and Mississippi-style riverboats offer a hands-on introduction to American pioneer days in Old Sacramento (discovergold.org), an 11-ha historic district in California's state capital. At the California State Railroad Museum, kids can clamber aboard enormous steam locos, like the 500-tonne *Southern Pacific 4929*. The Discovery Museum's Gold Rush History Center has dressing-up and role play areas, while the Schoolhouse Museum has costumed 'schoolmarms' teaching lessons.

that waterfalls in Yosemite usually run dry by August. Keep your eyes and ears open for mule deer, squirrels and blue jays and try to visit one of the park's giant redwood groves.

Pacific Coast Highway

Long road journeys and family travel are not always easy partners, but if there's one drive guaranteed to banish boredom, this is it. It doesn't matter which direction you drive California State Route 1, you will have a spectacular ocean view most of the way. Hugging the Pacific coastline from Leggett in the north to San Juan Capistrano in the south, the entire route covers nearly 900 km. However, unless you plan to tack on visits to Legoland (legoland.com) in Carlsbad and Disneyland (disneyland.disney.go.com) in Anaheim, you would be wise to skip the southernmost part of the drive, avoiding LA's congestion, and start or finish at Santa Monica (which has the added incentive of a glorious beach).

Allow at least three days to complete the drive, stopping wherever a beach or viewpoint takes your fancy. Don't pass Monterey without visiting the mesmerizing Monterey Bay Aquarium (montereybayaquarium.org) with its towering three-storey kelp forest display, sea otter habitat, jellyfish exhibit and gargantuan 3.8-million-litre Outer Bay tank – home to sharks, turtles, giant tuna and barracuda. Another must-do, Monterey Bay Whale Watch (gowhales.com) offers three- to five-hour boat trips in search of the region's outstanding marine life. Orcas, sea lions, sea otters, harbour seals and no less than six species of dolphins are seen year-round; grey whales are present from mid-December through April, while humpback and blue whales arrive to feed during the summer and autumn.

Alcatraz

Kids' top 10 Fisherman's Wharf

① **Scoff** freshly made chocolates at Ghirardelli Square.
② **Count** the sea lions hauled out at Pier 39.
③ **Explore** the submarine, *USS Pampanito*.
④ **Watch** the fishing fleet come in along Jefferson Street.
⑤ **Dunk** warm sourdough in a bowl of seafood chowder.
⑥ **Cruise** under Golden Gate Bridge.
⑦ **Feel** what it's like to be locked up on Alcatraz.
⑧ **Touch** sharks at the Aquarium of the Bay.
⑨ **Meet** Hollywood celebrities at the wax museum.
⑩ **Shop** for souvenirs at Pier 39.

★ Theme parks

▶▶ **Legoland** has the Pirate Shores water play area and a miniature Lego-brick version of the Strip in Las Vegas.
▶▶ **Disneyland** has all the regulars (Space Mountain, Splash Mountain etc), plus a *Finding Nemo* submarine ride.
Universal Studios Hollywood is packed with movie-themed attractions, including Shrek-4D and Jurassic Park.

★ Hawaii hotstuff

Hawaii (gohawaii.com) is a five-hour flight from San Francisco and has a time difference of GMT-10. That might seem like a long way to go for a beach holiday, but there's a lot more to this far-flung Pacific archipelago than the sun, sand and surf of Waikiki. The tips of huge volcanoes rising from the floor of the Pacific, the islands of Hawaii are one of the best places in the world to see molten lava, steam vents and other volcanic bedlam. In contrast to the smouldering desolation of calderas like Kilauea, other parts of Hawaii run riot with verdant tropical forests. There are towering sea cliffs and waterfalls, while on Kauai you'll even find a kilometre-deep 'Grand Canyon of the Pacific'. The surrounding seas teem with life, whether you want to watch humpback whales breaching off Maui or peer into the aquarium-like tidal pools of Hulopoe Bay on Lanai. Hawaii's Polynesian culture is just as exuberant and fascinating, while the Second World War monuments in Pearl Harbour provide a more sobering insight into the islands' history.
▶▶ Get an eyeful of one of the world's most active volcanoes at the Kilauea Visitor Center in Hawai'i Volcanoes National Park. If it's spewing lava, take a sightseeing flight to watch the bright ribbons of molten rock flowing into the sea amid great clouds of steam.
▶▶ Watch the sunrise over Haleakala – a dormant volcano on Maui that's big enough to swallow Manhattan.

California
Seaside cities to high sierras

Inside info

▶▶ In San Francisco, a free shuttle links the international airport with the car rental centre or BART station, from where trains take you downtown.
▶▶ The San Francisco City Pass (citypass.com) includes admission to the Aquarium of the Bay and Exploratorium.
▶▶ For further tourist information visit onlyinsanfrancisco.com and visitcalifornia.com.

Extending some 4800 km from New Mexico to British Columbia, the Rockies are the great backbone of North America. The tallest peak, Mount Elbert, soars to 4399 m, while the range varies in width from 120-650 km. A towering wilderness of ice fields, alpine meadows and forests, the Rockies are a stronghold for all of America's big critters, from elk, moose and bighorn sheep to grizzly bear and mountain lion. Your best chance of seeing them is in one of the national parks established to protect this fragile high ground. Popular activities in the Rockies include hiking, biking, whitewater rafting and horse riding.

US Rockies

Denver Colorado's big city, Denver (denver.com) has plenty to keep families occupied for a day or two. Pick of the museums goes to Wings over the Rockies (wingsmuseum.org) which has exhibits ranging from a B-52 Stratofortress to a Star Wars X-Wing fighter. Also worth a look are the Denver Museum of Nature & Science (dmns.org) and Colorado Railroad Museum (coloradorailroadmuseum.org).

Ultimately, though, Denver is all about the Great Outdoors and you'll be chafing at the bit to get stuck into an adventure or two. Start by swinging yourself into the saddle at a horse-riding ranch in the Rocky Mountain foothills. There are several family-friendly options to choose from, including the American Safari Ranch (americansafariranch.com) near Fairplay, Triple B Ranch (triplebranch.com) near Colorado Springs and North Fork Ranch (northforkranch.com), about a 90-minute drive south of Denver.

Next, swap reins for paddles. Based near Buena Vista, Wilderness Aware (inaraft.com) offers whitewater rafting trips on the Upper Colorado River and Upper Bighorn Sheep Canyon for families with children as young as four.

National parks Located just 105 km from Denver, Rocky Mountain National Park (nps.gov/romo) gets very busy in July and August. The best way to escape the summer crowds is to take a hike. Child-friendly options range from paved paths around Bear and Sprague Lakes to more ambitious hikes across alpine tundra starting from various points along Trail Ridge Road. Families with children aged at least 10 can pedal in the park with Colorado Bicycling Adventures (coloradobicycling.com), while horse riding is available at Moraine Park for children as young as six. Rocky Mountain's Junior Ranger Program is considered one

of the best in the park system.

Tucked into a corner of Wyoming, Grand Teton National Park (nps.gov/grte) and Yellowstone National Park (nps.gov/yell) make a truly spectacular combination – the former an awesome jumble of jagged peaks; the latter a vast mountain plateau roamed by bison and wolves and pockmarked by geysers. As well as hiking, horse riding and biking, Grand Teton offers canoeing on Jackson Lake and gentle rafting on the Snake River (the rougher whitewater sections are south of the park). In Yellowstone, brave the crowds to watch Old Faithful perform (the famous geyser spurts water 55 m into the air roughly every 90 minutes), and then get a taste for the backcountry on the nearby 8-km Lone Star Geyser Trail. Other highlights include the multihued limestone terraces of Mammoth Hot Springs and the 10-km round-trip hike up Mount Washburn. Horse riding (minimum age eight) is available through Yellowstone National Park Lodges (yellowstonenationalparklodges.com) at Canyon Village, Mammoth Hot Springs and Roosevelt Lodge.

Snug against the Canadian border where it merges with Waterton Lakes National Park, Montana's Glacier National Park (nps.gov/glac) is a rugged mélange of jutting granite peaks, U-shaped valleys and azure lakes (experts predict that the park's remaining glaciers will have vanished by 2030 due to global warming). As well as sightseeing from the Going-to-the-Sun Road, which traverses the heart of the park, you can hike, ride horses and cruise on various lakes.

Canadian Rockies

Driving west from Calgary on the Trans Canada Highway, you should reach Banff National Park

Great Outdoors

Rocky Mountain National Park. Below: Old Faithful in Yellowstone National Park.

(pc.gc.ca) in around two hours. The town of Banff (banfflakelouise.com) makes a comfortable base – whether you're there for winter skiing or summer hiking. Don't miss the Banff Gondola (banffgondola. com) which transports you to 2281 m on Mount Sulphur where an elevated boardwalk leads to an old weather observatory. Back down in the valley, Lake Minnewanka Boat Tours (minnewankaboattours.com) offers 90-minute cruises between May and October, but most kids will get more of a buzz from paddling a canoe. You can rent Canadian-style canoes (with middle seats for young children) from Blue Canoe Rentals (banfftours.com).

The highlight of any visit to the Canadian Rockies, however, is a journey along the Icefields Parkway (icefieldsparkway.ca), a 288-km scenic route linking Banff, Lake Louise and Jasper that twists and turns through a crystal kingdom of ice-fluted peaks, sparkling glaciers and turquoise lakes. On the way, stop at the Columbia Icefield (columbiaicefield.com) which, at 325 sq km, is the world's largest non-polar icecap. This vast dome of snow and ice feeds no less than eight major glaciers. You can walk on one of them – the 6-km-long Athabasca – after scaling its frozen snout in a 56-seater all-terrain Ice Explorer bus on Brewster's Ice Age Adventure (brewster.ca).

⟩ **Calgary** Stampede

Held annually in July, the Calgary Stampede (calgarystampede.com) has events ranging from chuckwagon racing and steer wrestling to calf roping and wild cow milking (a blood-curdling sport if ever there was one). Calgary whips itself into a frenzy of clinking spurs, square dancing and pancake breakfasts at least a week before the Stampede's opening parade. It's best to book well in advance if you want to stay at one of the popular ranches in the area. These include Kananaskis Guest Ranch (brewsteradventures.com), which has a prime spot on the Bow River between Banff and Calgary and offers overnight horse trips and 'ride and raft' packages. The Lazy M Guest Ranch (lazymcanada. com) in Caroline is a working ranch specializing in horsemanship – ideal for brushing up on your riding skills – while the Homeplace Guest Ranch (homeplaceranch. com) in Priddis offers family-style meals, riding lessons and horseback trips into the Rockies.

☸ **Bear** necessities

Stories abound of tourists in US national parks offering bears a slurp of ice cream or even urging their children to pose for photos alongside them. Needless to say, bears demand the same high levels of respect and space as any wild animal you might encounter on holiday. The most dangerous bear is a surprised bear. If you do encounter one make plenty of noise to let it know you're there. Don't approach it and never offer food. Avoid attracting bears by placing garbage in bear-proof boxes.

Canadian Rockies

Inside info

▶▶ The Yellowstone Association (yellowstone association.org) offers summer or winter 'ed-ventures' in Yellowstone National Park where families can learn about anything from wolves to volcanoes.
▶▶ Don't forget sun hats, sunblock and sunglasses for high elevations.
▶▶ The stylish Rocky Mountaineer (rockymountaineer.com) offers train journeys between Vancouver and Banff or Jasper.
▶▶ For further tourist info try colorado.com, wyomingtourism. org and visitmt.com, discoveralberta.com and hellobc.com.

It's quite possibly the ultimate fusion of America's Great Outdoors – the rainforest-cloaked Coast Ranges and the spectacular crinkle-cut Pacific shore. Base yourself in either Vancouver or Seattle, and you'll find wilderness right on your doorstep, whether you plan to hike, kayak or simply admire it from the deck of a ferry. Both cities have loads to keep kids occupied, from sandy beaches and sprawling parks to learning about totem poles and the fascinating culture of the First Nations. Not to be missed is a visit to Vancouver Island where picture-perfect Victoria is the jumping-off point for whale-watching adventures and some of the world's wildest and most exciting beaches.

Seattle

For a rainy day, top of your list should be the Pacific Science Center (pacsci.org) which has everything from animatronic dinosaurs to a Puget Sound tide pool. There's also The Children's Museum (thechildrensmuseum.org) and Woodland Park Zoo (zoo.org). If the sun is shining, head south to Long Beach – 18 km of sandcastle-building, kite-flying and birdwatching heaven. Alternatively, nip across to the Olympic Peninsula where Olympic National Park (nps.gov/olym) transports you into a mysterious forest of giant, moss-strewn hemlock and spruce.

Vancouver

It's hard to imagine a more family-friendly city park than Vancouver's Stanley Park – a 400-ha peninsula with walking trails, cycle tracks, a miniature train, horse-drawn carriage rides, a children's farm, totem poles, a water park and fantastic views of big ships coming and going. But it's the Vancouver Aquarium (vanaqua.org) that is the park's real crowd-puller. In addition to habitat-themed displays ranging from the walk-through Amazon gallery (with piranhas, crocs and sloths) to rocky coves inhabited by sea lions, sea otters and beluga whales, you can learn about Marine Mammal Rescue and other conservation programmes. Two of the best museums for children in Vancouver are Science World (scienceworld.bc.ca) and the Vancouver Museum (museumofvancouver.ca). Located about 10 minutes from downtown Vancouver, Kitsilano Beach is a favourite with locals, while Grouse Mountain (accessible by cable car) has great views and hiking potential.

Vancouver Island

Situated at the southern tip of Vancouver Island, Victoria is renowned for its historic buildings and formal gardens. It's worth spending a few hours soaking up the atmosphere around the Inner Harbour and seeing the natural history and First Nations exhibits in the Royal British Columbia Museum (royalbcmuseum.bc.ca). However, you could easily spend a week or more exploring the natural wonders of this beautiful island. Start by heading north to Qualicum Beach, a laid-back east-coast village with safe, sandy beaches and lots of child-friendly activities, including easy walking trails to waterfalls and old-growth forest. Next, strike across the island to the more invigorating Pacific-coast settlement of Tofino – gateway to a spectacular wilderness of surf-swept beaches, teeming rock pools and ancient cedar forest. Activities here include whale watching, surfing, kayaking and beachcombing. Families with younger children will enjoy exploring the boardwalks at the Tofino Royal Botanical Gardens.

Backtracking to the east coast, continue north to Telegraph Cove. This popular ecotourism destination is well known for its whale-watching tours – either by boat or sea kayak – in search of Johnstone Strait's famous orcas which come in search of salmon during the summer months. You can also visit Alert Bay on Cormorant Island where ceremonial masks, totem poles and other artefacts provide a vivid insight into Namgis First Nation culture.

Near the tip of Vancouver Island, Port Hardy is the embarkation point for ferries bound for the Inside Passage and Alaska (see opposite). For a taster of this epic maritime journey, take a 15-hour cruise from Port Hardy to Prince Rupert with BC Ferries (bcferries.com). From there, you can take a fabulous two-day, 1160-km rail trip on the Skeena (viarail.ca) to Jasper National Park in the heart of the Canadian Rockies (see page 315). Then, either return to Vancouver or push on towards Calgary.

(see page 315)

Inside info

» The Victoria Clipper ferry (victoriaclipper.com) from Seattle takes around three hours to reach Vancouver Island.
» In Vancouver, pick up a free copy of Kids Guide Vancouver, available at tourist info centres.
» For further tourist info visit experiencewa.com, seattle.gov, hellobc.com, tourismvancouver.com, vancouverisland.travel.

Sea kayaking in Johnstone Strait

Alaska
Call of the wild

They called it the last grand adventure. In July 1897, the streets of Seattle echoed with the wild cries of 'Gold!' and over 100,000 people surged north. The Klondike Gold Rush promised escape and quick wealth during a time of depression and poverty. But to reach the gold fields of the interior the prospectors had to haul their supplies over mountain passes and along rapid-strewn rivers. And all this was only possible once they had voyaged in crowded steamers along North America's vast marine highway – the 1600-km Inside Passage. Today, the lure of the north is as strong as ever. Each summer, luxury cruise ships slip sedately through a maze of forested islands, probing inlets, straits and sounds to reach the old Alaskan gold rush town of Skagway. They share these convoluted waters with fishing boats, timber barges, floatplanes and, best of all for independent travellers, a fleet of public ferries.

Bald eagle

Southeast Alaska

The Southeast Alaska Discovery Centre in Ketchikan (visit-ketchikan.com) provides an excellent introduction to the region, while nearby Saxman Village boasts the world's largest collection of standing totem poles and a chance to watch modern-day carvers at work. Ketchikan is a gateway to the Misty Fjords National Monument – a rugged, brooding wilderness that's perfect for hiking, kayaking or fishing. At Wrangell (wrangell.com) you can search for ancient petroglyph rock carvings on the beach or venture by kayak into the mouth of the Stikine River. Petersburg (petersburg.org) offers the chance to appreciate the workings of a busy Alaskan fishing port. Facing the open Pacific and built in the shadow of an extinct volcano, Sitka (sitka.org) has several attractions, including the Russian Orthodox St Michael's Cathedral, Sitka National Historic Park, the Sheldon Jackson Museum (containing one of Alaska's best collections of indigenous culture) and the Alaska Raptor Rehabilitation Centre.

At Juneau (juneau.com), stretch your legs by hiking to the Mendenhall Glacier, take a boat trip to Tracy Arm Fjord and visit Admiralty Island (the 'Fortress of the Bears'). Juneau is also the starting point for cruises into Glacier Bay National Park (nps.gov/glba), while Skagway (skagway.com) offers a nostalgic and captivating glimpse into the gold rush days. The more adventurous can hike the five-day Chilkoot Trail in the prospectors' footsteps or ride the White Pass & Yukon scenic railway (wpyr.com).

Denali National Park

Denali's 'big five' (moose, caribou, Dall sheep, wolf and grizzly bear) can often be seen on a bus ride along the 137-km park road – the sole vehicle access into the heart of the park. This provides a better chance of seeing wildlife than hiking, as you have a higher vantage point and the benefit of many eyes. If you plan to explore Denali on foot, be sure to take bear safety precautions (see page 315).

There are approximately 1800 moose in the park, with bulls weighing up to 630 kg. The Denali caribou herd has similar numbers; calves are born mid-May to early June. Keeping to ridges and steep slopes to avoid predators, Dall sheep are found in mountain regions in the east and west of the park. Denali's wolf numbers fluctuate at around 100. Roaming large areas, the packs feed primarily on caribou, moose and Dall sheep. Grizzly bears, meanwhile, eat everything from caribou calves and carrion to roots and salmon.

Kids' top 10 Alaskan adventures

1. **See** tidewater glaciers and whales in Kenai Fjords.
2. **Raft** the Class II-IV rapids of the Nenana River.
3. **Speed** along in a jetboat on the Susitna River.
4. **Travel** on the legendary Alaska Railroad.
5. **Spot** a grizzly bear in Denali National Park.
6. **Paddle** a sea kayak on Prince William Sound.
7. **Pan** for gold or fish for salmon in an Alaskan creek.
8. **Fly** in a floatplane to a lakeside wilderness cabin.
9. **Ride** a horse or bike in Chugach National Forest.
10. **Hike** or husky sled across a glacier.

Inside info

▶▶ Bellingham, 140 km north of Seattle, is the southernmost terminal for Alaska Marine Highway Ferries.
▶▶ Route maps, ferry schedules and online reservations can be made through the Alaska Marine Highway System (akferry.org).
▶▶ Keep watch on deck for sightings of orcas and humpback whales.
▶▶ For further tourist information visit travelalaska.com.

Holiday operators

When to go

North America's climate covers every extreme. Some parts offer year-round sunshine, while others become inaccessible during winter. Although **Québec** is geared up as a year-round destination with a spectacular carnival of snow slides, parades and ice sculpting during early February, it is best to avoid winter if you want to venture off the beaten track. With over 3 m of snowfall and temperatures plunging as low as –25°C, many tourist attractions outside the city close down during winter months. By contrast, summers are warm, with temperatures up to 30°C. Autumn is crisp and favoured by those in search of flamboyant fall colours.

If you want to see a polar bear, visit **Churchill** from October to early November – but wrap up warm. June to October is best for sightings of humpback, minke and fin whales along the **Atlantic Coast**, while May to September is prime time for spotting orcas off **Vancouver Island**.

It is no coincidence that the Pacific Coast of **British Columbia** and **Southeast Alaska** is cloaked in lush forest – the region's climate is generally mild and wet. Temperatures average 20°C in summer, the driest and most popular time to travel. Ferries and accommodation can become heavily booked from June to August, so it's worth considering a visit in May or early September.

Spring and autumn are also the best seasons for visiting **Southwest USA**. Summer can be insanely hot in the desert canyons – take plenty of water if you are planning to hike or bike. Many of the big national parks such as Yellowstone and Yosemite become crowded in the height of summer – another good reason for travelling in the shoulder seasons. The best period to visit **Florida** is from late November to the end of April when it is drier and cooler with daytime temperatures reaching 29°C. The hurricane season is officially from 1 June to 30 November.

Getting there

There is no shortage of scheduled non-stop and direct flights from the UK to various cities throughout the USA and Canada, with onward connections to hundreds of other destinations. There are also a number of charter flights from the UK to destinations such as Orlando and Las Vegas. Major airlines include Air Canada (aircanada.ca), American Airlines (aa.com), British Airways (britishairways.com), Continental Airlines

Alaska Marine Highway ferry

(continental.com), Delta Airlines (delta.com), United Airlines (united.com) and Virgin (virginatlantic.com).

Getting around

Despite the American love affair with the car, there are plenty of alternatives for getting around. Due to competition on domestic routes, internal flights in the USA are a relatively cheap way to cover large distances. Try JetBlue (jetblue.com) or Ted (flyted.com). In Canada, internal flights are a little more expensive, but you can get good deals on budget carriers like WestJet (westjet.com).

For rail travel, Amtrak (amtrak.com) covers most major US destinations, while The Canadian (viarail.ca) can whisk you, in 1950s style, from Toronto to Vancouver, with stopovers along the way.

Canada's east and west coasts are well served by fast, frequent and reasonably-priced ferries. The St Lawrence Seaway provides passage from the Atlantic Ocean to the Great Lakes, while BC Ferries (bcferries.com) operates services linking British Columbia's mainland with Vancouver Island and towns along the Inside Passage.

Major international car rental companies have offices at all gateway airports and in most cities. You can often save money by arranging a fly-drive deal or by booking a car in advance. The American Automobile Association (aaa.com) and Canadian Automobile Association (caa.ca) offer touring services and travel advice to affiliate auto club members. Hiring a motorhome, or 'recreational vehicle' (RV), is a supremely family-friendly option for getting around. Cruise America (cruiseamerica.com) is one of the best-known RV hire specialists.

Accommodation

It is possible to find family-friendly accommodation in every region you visit – some hotels lavish goodie bags on your children or provide kids' programmes and babysitting, while others have games consoles in children's rooms or fantastic locations in wonderful natural playgrounds.

From camping to five-star luxury, there is something for every budget and taste. Kampgrounds of America (koa.com) have sites across the USA and Canada with tent pitches, RV hook-ups and cabins. For the ultimate camping adventure, Canadian Adventure Rentals (canadian-adventure-rentals.com) in Vancouver will kit you out with everything you need, from car hire to tent, cooking equipment and bedding – they'll even throw in some bikes or kayaks on request.

If you are planning to stay in one of the more popular national parks during peak season, you will need to book well in advance (up to a year for some parks). Log on to recreation.gov for information and reservations. Bookings in Yellowstone, Zion and Grand Canyon are covered by Xanterra Parks and Resorts (xanterra.com). Yosemite has a collection of affordable and family-friendly resorts and lodges that can be booked through Yosemite Resorts (yosemiteresorts.us). Located a few kilometres from the El Portal entrance to the park, Yosemite View Lodge, for example, has kitchenettes, restaurant and shop. In Banff, The Sunshine Village (skibanff.com) is well placed for adventure activities, summer and winter.

For playing at cowboys and cowgirls, search for the ranch that suits your family's needs through the Dude Rancher's Association (duderanch.org). For the all-out Disney experience, stay at a Disney Resort like Animal Kingdom Lodge (disneyworld.disney.go.com) where you will be surrounded by an African savannah roamed by giraffes, zebras and kudus. Other Orlando family favourites include Disney's All Star Movies Resort, the Nickelodeon Suites Resort (nickhotel.com), Universal's Hard Rock Hotel (universalorlando.com) and the Hyatt Regency Grand Cypress Resort (grandcypress.hyatt.com) which features 'dive-in' movies over the pool area. For a budget, family-friendly option, pitch a tent in one of Florida's State Parks (floridastateparks.org). Many, like St Andrews, have well-equipped campgrounds.

Food & drink
Your family will certainly not go hungry on a trip to North America. Your biggest problem will probably be finding that you keep ordering too much food, as portions tend to be larger than you're used to back home. You can order any type of coffee, any size of pizza or steak and any style of eggs. That's before you've even had a chance to ponder the fries, burgers, shakes, ice-creams and doughnuts. But it's not all junk food, there's a mouthwatering spread of nutritious regional specialities, such as key lime pie (Florida), clam chowder (New England), fresh Florida orange juice, Winnipeg goldeye trout and juicy steaks from Alberta's cattle ranches. And no trip to Canada would be complete without sampling buttermilk pancakes doused in maple syrup.

Health & safety
Health care in the USA and Canada is not cheap. Be well-insured with medical cover up to US$1 million which includes hospital treatment and medical evacuation. Always check that your travel insurance covers you for any activities that you plan to do. As with travel anywhere in the world, it's wise to be up to date with your regular vaccinations, especially tetanus. Some summer camps require proof of inoculation. Accidents pose the greatest risk to your health and safety when holidaying in North America, so take care when driving or trying out new adventure activities. Potentially dangerous animals include bears, scorpions and bats – the last of which may transmit rabies. There is also a small risk of contracting the tick-borne Lyme disease when walking in forested areas. Be sure to apply insect repellent and check your body for ticks, removing them gently with tweezers.

Crime rates are high in some of the major cities, so take sensible precautions such as not leaving valuables visible in your car. For the latest advice on potential terrorist activity, visit the website of the Department of Homeland Security (dhs.gov).

Country	Time	Language	Currency	Code	Tourist information
Canada	GMT-3.5 to -8	English, French	Canadian dollar	+1	canada.travel
USA	GMT-5 to -10	English	US dollar	+1	visitusa.org.uk

Fast facts

Hard Rock Hotel
Where? Orlando, Florida.
Why? With its California mission-style façades, palm-lined swimming pool (with underwater music) and sumptuous rooms kitted out with all the latest entertainment gizmos, this has to be one of the coolest places to stay in the world. Throughout the hotel you'll find rock memorabilia from such legendary icons as Elvis Presley, Elton John, Jimi Hendrix and Madonna.
Contact Hard Rock Hotel, T+1 (0)888-832 7155, hardrockhotelorlando.com

Yosemite Lodge at the Falls
Where? Yosemite National Park, California.
Why? Accommodation in Yosemite ranges from the upmarket Ahwahnee Hotel to the more basic High Sierra Camps (accessible only by foot or on horseback). Yosemite Lodge at the Falls is a good mid-range option, with 249 rooms. Numerous activities are available, from cycling, rafting and horse riding to cross-country skiing.
Contact Yosemite Park, T801-559 4884, yosemitepark.com

Tweedsmuir Park Lodge
Where? Bella Coola Valley, British Columbia.
Why? This 10-chalet ecolodge has bears frequently wandering across its lawns. Tucked into the heart of the Great Bear Rainforest, it's perfectly placed for observing grizzlies feeding on salmon during the autumn. Other activities include guided forest walks, river drifts and storytelling by First Nations Nuxalk.
Contact Tweedsmuir, T+1 (0)250-982 2407, tweedsmuirparklodge.com

Cathedral Mountain Lodge
Where? Yoho National Park, British Columbia.
Why? These stylish cabins have fireplaces and hot tubs, while the main lodge building offers fine cuisine with views of the glacier-fed Kicking Horse River. An onsite adventure specialist can recommend the best places to view wildlife, or organize activities ranging from hiking and canoeing to paragliding and climbing.
Contact Cathedral Mtn, T+1 (0)250-343 6442, cathedralmountain.com

Echo Valley Ranch & Spa
Where? British Columbia.
Why? Located in the heart of the wild and beautiful Cariboo region, a few hours northeast of Vancouver, Echo Valley Ranch & Spa provides a comfortable base from which to explore the backcountry. Activities – many tailored for children – range from horse riding and 4WD safaris to fly fishing, gold panning and horse-shoe throwing.
Contact Echo Valley Ranch & Spa, T+1 (0)604-988 3230, evranch.com or audleytravel.com

Sadie Cove Wilderness Lodge

" " **The ultimate wilderness family adventure, Sadie Cove in Kachemak State Park is accessible only by seaplane, helicopter or boat. Stay in handcrafted eco-cabins with delicious home-cooked Alaskan fare – often caught by yourselves. Activities include hiking and kayaking in search of bears, sea otters, whales and eagles.** William Gray

Backcountry camping in the Everglades

New York-New York Hotel, Las Vegas

Latin America

Eye to eye with iguanas

Wildlife encounters don't get any closer or more memorable than on the Galápagos Islands. Right: Hummingbirds will often come within centimetres of your face in the Andean cloudforest.

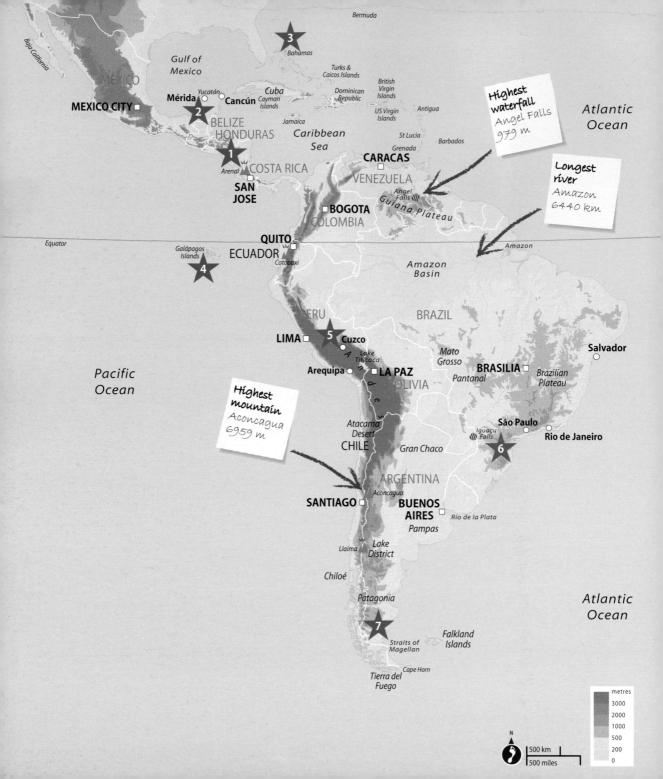

Bermuda

Baja California

★ 3

Bahamas

MEXICO

Gulf of
Mexico

Yucatán

Mérida ○ ○ Cancún

★ 2

Cuba

Cayman
Islands

Turks &
Caicos Islands

Dominican
Republic

British
Virgin
Islands

US Virgin
Islands

Antigua

MEXICO CITY □

BELIZE

HONDURAS

Jamaica

Caribbean
Sea

St Lucia

Barbados

Grenada

★ 1

Arenal

COSTA RICA

**SAN
JOSE** □

CARACAS

VENEZUELA

Angel
Falls

Guiana Plateau

*Highest
waterfall*
Angel Falls
979 m

Atlantic
Ocean

BOGOTA □

COLOMBIA

*Longest
river*
Amazon
6440 km

Equator

QUITO □

ECUADOR

Galápagos
Islands

Cotopaxi

★ 4

Amazon

Amazon
Basin

PERU

BRAZIL

LIMA ○

★ 5

Cuzco ○

Lake
Titicaca

A
n
d
e
s

Salvador ○

BRASILIA □

Mato
Grosso

Arequipa ○

LA PAZ □

BOLIVIA

Pantanal

Brazilian
Plateau

Pacific
Ocean

*Highest
mountain*
Aconcagua
6959 m

Atacama
Desert

CHILE

Gran Chaco

Iguaçu
Falls

São Paulo ○

Rio de Janeiro

★ 6

ARGENTINA

SANTIAGO □

Aconcagua

**BUENOS
AIRES** □

Río de la Plata

Pampas

Llaima

Lake
District

Chiloé

Patagonia

★ 7

Straits of
Magellan

Falkland
Islands

Atlantic
Ocean

Tierra del
Fuego

Cape Horn

metres

3000
2000
1000
500
200
0

N

500 km
500 miles

Did you know?

★ The cardón cactus of Baja California can reach 21 m in height.
★ The world's smallest bird, the Cuban bee hummingbird, measures 5 cm in length.
★ The Atacama Desert is the driest place on earth. Rain has never been recorded in some parts.
★ Originally from South America, potatoes still grow wild in the Andean highlands.
★ When *The Sound of Music* was released in Mexico, it appeared under a different title *The Rebel Novice Nun*.

Introduction
Latin America

Latin America might strike you as a rather exotic and impractical place to take children, but it's easier than you think. Not only have basics, like transport and accommodation, been greatly improved in recent years, but many of the key sites – from Mayan ruins to Patagonian glaciers – are surprisingly accessible. If you don't feel you're quite ready for an Amazonian adventure, focus instead on the family-friendly Brazilian coast or the Caribbean, where you can combine a beach holiday with daytrips to the forested interior. But if it's all-out action you're after, Latin America is unrivalled. From sea kayaking in Mexico and horse riding in Argentina to trekking in Peru and snorkelling in the Galápagos Islands, you'll find professionally organized activities to suit all levels. Your children's minds will be equally stimulated as they learn about ancient civilizations and vibrant cultures. And don't forget that Latin Americans adore children, so your kids can expect a friendly welcome and plenty of cheek-squidging and hair-ruffling wherever you go.

" I never thought I'd be lucky enough to visit Ecuador with my family, but here we are: a wide-eyed, giggling posse riding horses through the Andes. All of a sudden we're hushed. Two Andean condors have appeared in the forest-clad maw of the canyon ahead. Black specks, like swirling flakes of ash from a bonfire, they drift lazily down the valley towards us. William Gray

Star rating

Wow factor
★★★★★
Worry factor
★★★
Value for money
★★★
Keeping teacher happy
★★★★★
Family accommodation
★★★
Babies & toddlers
★★★★
Cool for teenagers
★★★★

☠ Scary sightings

Anaconda 10-m-long snake that squeezes its prey to death and then swallows it whole, head first.
Vampire bat Pesky bloodsuckers that hunt at night, nipping sleeping mammals (usually cattle).
Tarantula A group of about 800 hairy, sometimes very large, spiders. In Peru, the chicken-eating tarantula measures up to 25 cm and has a fowl reputation.

⚽ Football superstars

Pelé
Date of birth: 1940
Country: Brazil
Goals/international appearances: 77/92

Garrincha
Date of birth: 1933
Country: Brazil
Goals/international appearances: 12/50

Mario Kempes
Date of birth: 1954
Country: Argentina
Goals/international appearances: 20/43

Maradona
Date of birth: 1960
Country: Brazil
Goals/international appearances: 34/91

How to make a piñata

A centrepiece of traditional Hispanic celebrations, a piñata is a bright container that is filled with sweets and toys and suspended from a tree or ceiling. Children, blindfolded and wielding a stick, take turns to break it open.

What you need
- Old newspapers
- Flour and water paste
- Mixing bowl
- Large balloon
- Coloured crepe paper, paints, stickers and decorations
- Glue, pin, coat hanger, thick string
- Sweets and small toys

What to do
- Tear newspaper into strips.
- Mix flour and water in bowl to make a sticky paste.
- Inflate balloon and smear a little cooking oil over it.
- Dip the strips of paper into the paste and stick them in layers around the balloon and allow to dry.
- Burst the balloon at the top and pull it out.
- Paint and decorate your piñata.
- Make a small hole in the top of the piñata and fill with sweets and toys.
- Make a hook in the top using the coat hanger. Suspend the piñata using string, tied firmly to the hanger.

⑨ Weirdlife the stink bird

Also known as: hoatzin
Vital statistics: about the size and weight of a chicken.
Found in: swamps and flooded forests of the Amazon.
What's so weird? The punky head crest and blue eye shadow are pretty wacky, but what really elevates this feathered freak into the realms of the super-weird is that the chicks have a prehistoric-like claw on each wing. When danger threatens (in the form of a hungry capuchin monkey) the chick clambers to safety using its claws to grip branches. If that fails, it dives underwater (hoatzins always nest in trees overhanging lakes or rivers) until the danger has passed. Local people call hoatzins 'stink birds' because the aromatic oils in their diet of leaves gives them a distinctive whiff.

Great reads
5 children's books

Ages 3-8
Caribbean Animals
Dawne Allette (Tamarind)
From his tree house, Ned spots animals ranging from an agouti to a zandoli. Exquisite illustrations linked by rhyming text, plus extra facts on each creature.

From Beans to Batteries
Steve Brace (Child's Play)
In Peru, Aldomero and Amerita go to the market and try to sell the beans they have picked, hoping to make enough money to buy batteries for their radio.

Ages 5-12
The Shaman's Apprentice: A Tale of the Amazon Rain Forest
Lynne Cherry (Harcourt Brace)
A richly illustrated and vividly told story of a child's belief in the medicinal properties of plants and his aspiration to become a healer for his people.

Ages 6+
Butter-finger
Bob Cattell (Frances Lincoln)
Riccardo Small lives on a Caribbean island. He loves cricket and can tell you the averages of every West Indian test match player in history. But when he is dropped from the cricket team after missing a vital catch, Riccardo wanders the island, taking refuge in his poems.

Ages 8+
Angry Aztecs & Incredible Incas
Terry Deary (Random House)
A 'Horrible History' of the Incan and Aztec Empires with gory details, such as how to predict your future with inflated llama lungs and how to make a shaker bracelet using llama toenails.

Kids' stuff
Latin America

Taste of Mexico quesadilla

Quesadilla (pronounced 'kay-suh-dee-uh') literally means 'little cheesy thing' and, traditionally, that's exactly what you get – a tortilla or dough wrap stuffed with melted cheese. However, they work just as well filled with potato, sausage, chicken, mushrooms, onions and anything else you fancy adding!

What you need
» 4 cups of harina flour (to make your own *masa* dough) or 4 readymade flour tortillas
» 2 large potatoes
» Chorizo sausage
» Can of refried beans
» Butter and cooking oil
» Salt and pepper
» Guacamole, salsa & sour cream

What to do
» Boil and mash the potatoes with salt, pepper and butter.
» Heat the beans; slice the chorizo and gently fry.
» Mix the mashed potatoes, beans and chorizo together; set aside and keep warm.
» To make masa dough, mix the flour with warm water, kneading until dough is firm.
» Make small balls of dough about 5 cm in diameter and roll them out into flat tortillas
» Add the filling, fold in half and seal edges with your fingers.
» Place in a frying pan over a medium heat and cook both sides until golden brown.
» Cut into triangles and serve with guacamole, salsa and sour cream.

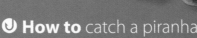

☝ How to catch a piranha

❶ First, you need to get to the Amazon and hire a boat with an experienced guide.
❷ Find a quiet backwater with overhanging branches where piranhas like to lurk.
❸ Make yourself a fishing pole – a straight wooden stick from the jungle will do.
❹ Tie some fishing line and a hook to one end; bait with a chunk of raw, juicy chicken.
❺ Toss your hook into the water and splash your pole on the surface – these feisty nippers are often attracted to anything that sounds like a floundering animal.
❻ Keep feet, hands and other body parts inside the boat!

❼ Yank hard and sideways as soon as you feel a bite (wait too long and they'll eat your bait and be gone).
❽ Haul your catch aboard and let your guide remove the hook. Warning! A piranha out of water is still dangerous enough to inflict a powerful bite, as your guide will no doubt demonstrate by holding a stick to its mouth.
❾ Traditionally, piranha teeth are used to make tools and weapons. Grilled, they taste rather like trout.

The Caribbean is a well-established family destination, but would you consider taking your kids to Peru? Or Patagonia? What's the minimum age you should contemplate a Galápagos cruise or a trip to the Amazon? And what about more fundamental issues, like health and safety?

Babies

You've endured months of sleepless nights, the kitchen has been doused in baby vomit more times than you can remember and you've strained your back lifting the stroller out of the car. There had better be a good reason for hauling the little monster halfway around the world on holiday – particularly if it means potentially undoing what little feeding and sleeping routine you've managed to install. In the Caribbean and Bahamas, of course, there are plenty of excellent reasons for a holiday with babies, and they all have one thing in common: parent pampering. Your baby will no doubt love splashing in the warm sheltered sea, shovelling clean white sand into his mouth and making friends at the resort's crèche, but ultimately a Caribbean holiday with tiny tots has as much, if not more, to do with parents' facilities than those for children. This is the ideal time and place to snatch a couple of weeks of well-earned rest at an all-inclusive, no-effort-required, family-friendly resort where you can nurse that bad back at the onsite wellbeing centre. Don't forget – with a baby on your lap during the flight and sharing your hotel room – it might also be the only time you can afford a family holiday in the Caribbean! To ease the journey time, choose an island with direct flights and short transfers. You will need to be extra-vigilant to prevent sunburn and heat exposure, but (apart from the Dominican Republic) there is no risk from malaria.

Toddlers/pre-school

The Caribbean also scores highly for this age range. As well as toddler-friendly beaches, guaranteed sunshine and a wide choice of food, you'll find a friendly and laid-back atmosphere on just about any island you choose. There's also a wide choice of family resorts with kids' clubs, children's pools and toddler-tempting food. Another option for a beach holiday is to head for the Brazilian coast. Bahia is renowned for its string of family-friendly eco-resorts, while the stretch of coast south of Rio de Janeiro has some wonderful family villas. It's all malaria-free and has the added bonus of some great city-sightseeing potential. Kids will love riding the cable car in Rio or exploring the old town of Salvador. Latin America's other top beach destination is Mexico, where you will find no shortage of resorts.

Kids/school age

If you still have a yearning for the Caribbean, boost the excitement levels by visiting Cuba or the

Holiday souvenirs

Trying on a bead necklace at Otavalo Market in Ecuador. Below: Walking a fine balance along the Equator.

Special needs

Several resorts and villas in the Caribbean and Bahamas are wheelchair accessible, as are many cruise ships. Méxíco Accesíble (accesiblemexico.com) offers trips to Puerto Vallarta with special facilities, such as roll-in showers. Go with Wheelchairs (gowithwheelchairs.com) offers wheelchair travellers a safe and reliable means of visiting Costa Rica or Panama, while Experience Belize Tours (experiencebelizetours.com) offers wheelchair-friendly tours to the Mayan site of Altun-Ha. Apumayo Expeditions (apumayo.com) can arrange trips to Peruvian highlights, such as Machu Picchu, Pisac and the Amazon.

Single parents

With their small size and well-equipped resorts, the Caribbean Islands are the best bet for single-parent families who want minimal logistical fuss. Generally, though, most of the information in this chapter applies equally to single-parent families as two-parent ones.

> " " **Chile is, in my view, particularly suited to children's activity holidays. It is developed and safe, yet not at the theme-park stage of its evolution. We were there for three weeks and I felt that Wilf (my eight-year-old son) had a genuine wilderness experience within a totally safe framework.**
>
> Sara Wheeler, Author of *Chile: Travels in a thin country*

Dominican Republic where there's a greater choice of adventure and sightseeing opportunities. By the time your children reach the age of five, however, you may be feeling more comfortable with the idea of giving them anti-malarial pills. If that's the case, skip the Caribbean and head instead to Costa Rica. It's one of the safest and friendliest countries in Latin America; the transport system is excellent and, best of all, there are enough national parks in this little green nation to satisfy all budding creepy-crawly experts. Belize and Honduras are also excellent choices, particularly if you combine jungle escapades with time-out on the offshore coral islands. Ecuador, Peru and Chile are equally well suited to overland adventures. Family operators offer various organized tours (usually for ages six and above), with all kinds of enticing combinations. In Peru, for example, you can travel from the coast high into the Andes before taking a dip in the Amazon basin. In Ecuador, perhaps the ultimate Latin American feast is served up in the form of the Andes, Amazon and Galápagos Islands, while in Chile you can head north to south, taking in the Atacama Desert, Lakes District and Patagonia. Which option you choose depends on a range of factors – not least your budget. Galápagos cruises don't come cheap, but you could save money by staying on the main island and taking day excursions. Similarly, a visit to the more accessible cloudforest regions of the Andes will work out cheaper than a full-blown Amazon

adventure. You may also have safety concerns over young children climbing in and out of boats in the Galápagos – or being bitten by mosquitoes in the Amazon (don't forget this is a malarial region). Other health factors to be aware of include high altitude and sun exposure in the Andes. Ultimately, though, with a few sensible precautions and a healthy bank balance, any of these countries promises a superb family adventure. Educationally, they will have your kids' eyes popping, while adventure hotspots, like Cusco in Peru or Pucón in Chile, offer numerous activities, such as whitewater rafting and horse riding.

Teenagers

Latin America has huge appeal for teens. Several of its cities are super-cool – tango in Buenos Aires, beach life in Rio, shopping in Nassau, classic cars in Havana – while the whole continent is pervaded by lively rhythms, sassy fashion and a love of sport. You can also take adventure to new levels. So, instead of a sea kayaking daytrip in Baja California (suitable for younger children), you can set off on a weeklong paddling odyssey. There are also dozens of trekking opportunities in the Andes, including the classic Inca Trail to Machu Picchu and camping trips in Patagonia. If that sounds too much like hard work, there's always the Caribbean. A laid-back resort with watersports, a bit of nightlife and other teens to mix with could well be the ultimate place to chill.

Mexico can be as adventurous as you want it to be. You can play it safe at fly 'n' flop mega-resorts like Cancún and Acapulco, or you can play at being Indiana Jones by exploring the jungles and Mayan ruins of the Yucatán Peninsula. Mexico City can be overwhelming for children, but nearby archaeological ruins are well worth visiting. Further north, the vast Copper Canyon is the setting for a dramatic rail journey, while Baja California – Mexico's desert peninsula – is a prime spot for whale watching and sea kayaking.

Mexico City

Built on the site of the Aztec capital of Tenochitlán, Mexico City is a somewhat manic metropolis that's home to over 20 million people. But take a deep breath and focus on one or two highlights and you will discover a city rich in heritage.

Plaza de la Constitucion Also known as the Zócalo, Mexico City's historical square is dominated by the Catedral Metropolitana, a Baroque giant that took 250 years to complete. Like much of the city, it is built on an ancient lakebed and needs frequent reinforcement to prevent it from sinking. For a quick visual guide to Mexico's history, take a look inside the Palacio Nacional where the Diego Rivera murals recount scenes ranging from the Aztec empire to the revolutionary hero of Francisco Villa. On most days in the Zócalo, indigenous dancers dressed in flamboyant costumes and feathered headdresses re-enact Aztec ceremonies, while a short walk away you can see the excavated ruins of Templo Mayor – the Great Temple that was once the sacred centre of the Aztec universe.

Museums The Museo Nacional de Anthropologia houses an enormous collection of pre-Hispanic artefacts, including all the best bits excavated from the ruins of ancient civilizations, such as the Aztec, Maya, Olmec, Toltec and Zapotec. You would need at least two days to see everything, so instead set your sights on the Aztec calendar, the Mayan Chacmool from Chichén Itzá and the jade mask from Palenque. Another museum worth visiting is the Papalote Museo del Niño, a children's museum with hands-on science and cultural exhibits and an IMAX cinema.

City getaways Escape the smog and mayhem by taking a day trip to the mysterious ceremonial site of Teotihuacán (pronounced 'the-oh-tee-wa-khan'). While parents contemplate the ghost of a once great

city (abandoned around AD 700), children will be eager to climb all 248 steps to the top of the Pyramid of the Sun – the third largest in the world. Further afield you can reach Oaxaca by luxury inter-city coach or a short flight. This handsome colonial city has a tree-shaded central plaza surrounded by cafés and a cathedral. Peruse the local market for colourful textiles and handicrafts, sample the traditional *mole* dishes (meat smothered in a chocolate and chilli sauce) and visit the ancient Zapotec capital of Monte Albán.

Yucatán Peninsula

On the Yucatán you're never far from an idyllic sandy beach, so there's no excuse for not making those hot and sweaty archaeological jaunts into the interior.

Chichén Itzá Kids may always remember it as Chicken Pizza, but the fact remains that this magnificent Mayan site (pronounced 'chee-chen eet-zah') is a must-see for anyone visiting Mexico. The imposing El Castillo pyramid is a magnet to children, but once they tire of counting the 91 steps in its four stairways and romping across the ruined city's wide-open plazas they will begin to discover some fascinating, often gory, clues to Chichén Itzá's past. The Juego de Pelota, for example, was where the Maya played a killer ballgame (see Copán, page 333) in which contestants sometimes received a fate far worse than a red card. See if you can spot the carving on the ball court wall depicting a beheaded player, blood spurting from his neck, while an opponent holds the severed head aloft – an early form of 'sudden death' perhaps? In the Temple of the Skulls, meanwhile, youngsters will go pop-eyed over scenes of eagles ripping hearts from human victims.

Step to it

The magnificent Mayan temple of Chichén Itzá on the Yucatán Peninsula.

🐋 **Baja** spouts

Blue whale (max length: 34 m) Produces a tall column of spray rising to 9 m or more.

Grey whale (max length: 15 m) Blow is often heart shaped, reaching 4.5 m tall. Pictured above.

Humpback whale (max length: 19 m) A dense and bushy blow that can rise to 3 m.

Pacific coast of Baja California

Tulum Within daytrip range of Cancún and perched right on the edge of the Caribbean, the clifftop ruins of Tulum can become clogged with visitors, so stay nearby and visit in the early morning when sunlight rakes the walls of this coastal Mayan city. Tulum is smaller than Chichén Itzá and the carvings aren't as gruesome, so it's a better bet for younger children.

Xel-Ha Just 13 km from Tulum, Xel-Ha (xel-ha.com) is a Mayan-themed water park. Based around natural creeks, lagoons, caves and forests, it offers everything from swimming with dolphins and snorkelling to jungle walks and a 5-m cliff jump.

Baja California

A gnarled peninsula of desert mountains and cactus-stubbled plains, Baja probes the Pacific like a skeletal finger. But where barren land meets cobalt sea, this 1300-km-long Mexican frontier teems with life. Each winter, over 20,000 grey whales visit Magdalena Bay and other sheltered lagoons along the Pacific coast to give birth and mate before resuming their epic 8000-km migration to the Bering Sea. Pioneered by local fisherman Francisco 'Pachico' Mayoral in the 1970s, whale watching in Ignacio Lagoon is best between January and mid-April (pachicosecotours. com), allowing the grey whales time to recover from their long migration and nurse newborn calves. Exploring the lagoon in small, open pangas, you'll often experience close encounters with the whales and observe other wildlife such as sea lions, dolphins and turtles.

The Sea of Cortez, meanwhile, is a cetacean hotspot where you can encounter anything from the mighty blue, humpback and fin whale to more diminutive species such as minke, Bryde's and orca. Dolphins can be found in pods occasionally

numbering a thousand strong, while sea lions, turtles and manta rays add to the marine bonanza. You can either kayak here or take a boat trip. For another, possibly even greater thrill visit Los Islotes where you can snorkel with playful sea lions.

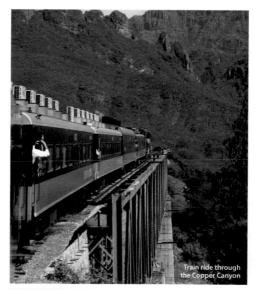
Train ride through the Copper Canyon

Copper Canyon

For adventurous families, Baja combines well with one of the world's great train rides. Simply take the ferry from La Paz to Topolobampo and on to Los Mochis, from where the Chihuahua-Pacific Railway rattles inland for 655 km, stopping at several points in the Copper Canyon – a vast axe-stroke through the Sierra Madre that could swallow four Grand Canyons. It's a straight-through 14-hour ride to Chihuahua, but spread this epic journey over three or four days to take advantage of the hiking, biking and horse-riding opportunities en route.

Inside info ⓘ

▶▶ Explore the historical centre of Mexico City on a traditional tram.
▶▶ Avoid the crowds and midday heat by aiming to reach Chichén Itzá early morning – or better still spend the night and enjoy the sound and light show.
▶▶ Boat trips to see grey whales in Baja's Pacific lagoons (December to April) operate from Guerrero Negro and Lopez Mateos.
▶▶ Sea kayaking is available at Espíritu Santo island in the Sea of Cortez.

It's not surprising that Costa Rica was chosen as one of the filming locations for Spielberg's epic dinosaur fantasy. Trekking deep in one of the country's cloudforests or canoeing through one of its mangrove swamps you can almost sense the velociraptors skulking in the shadows, ready to execute their deadly pincer movement. Perfect for the nature-loving family, this Central American beauty has jungles, active volcanoes, Pacific and Caribbean beaches, plus lots of opportunities for adventure. But probably no dinosaurs (sorry kids).

Costa Rica

No less than 25% of Costa Rica is protected as national parks and reserves. A fifth the size of the UK it boasts 1200 species of orchids, 850 varieties of birds and more types of butterfly than Africa. Binoculars ready? Then let's begin…

San José and the Central Highlands Costa Rica's capital has a few interesting museums, but you haven't come all this way to be stuck inside. Instead, spend a day or two exploring the Central Highlands. The Lankester Botanical Gardens provide a gentle and informative introduction to Costa Rica's dazzling flora (and you'll probably spy your first hummingbird here). With spectacular lake-filled craters that you can drive to within a few hundred metres of, Poás and Irazú are the two volcanoes closest to San José. For peak perfection, however, aim for Arenal, a classic cone rising above the town of La Fortuna. One of the world's most active volcanoes, it erupts almost daily and on clear nights you can see (from a safe distance) the incandescent lava spewing from the crater.

Monteverde Cloudforest Reserve This misty, high-altitude, moss-drizzled forest looks like it's sprouted straight from the pages of *The Lord of the Rings*. Top tick is the resplendent quetzel, a secretive bird that was sacred to the Maya. The male has an iridescent green head and back, scarlet belly and long tail streamers. Get on level-beak terms by strolling the Sky Walk (skyadventures.travel) – a series of suspended walkways in the canopy (all with strong wire mesh from floor to handrail) – or for something a little more exhilarating take a canopy zip-line ride.

Pacific coast Manuel Antonio National Park has an easy 1-km forest trail leading to a pristine sandy beach. Take your time and you may spot squirrel monkeys, coatis, racoons, sloths, iguanas, toucans and parrots. Reached by boat from Sierpe, the more remote Corcovado National Park offers sea kayaking, snorkelling and whale watching.

Caribbean coast For a country rich in wildlife Tortuguero National Park is Costa Rica's biodiversity honey pot. Most of the excursions here are by boat, allowing you to cruise beneath trees festooned with everything from howler monkeys and sloths to parrots and poison-dart frogs. Don't forget to keep an eye on the water's edge where you may spot herons, otters or an emerald-coloured basilisk – also known as the Jesus Christ lizard for its ability to run on water.

Best beaches If you're a turtle it has to be Tortuguero; if you're a surfer Jacó on the central Pacific coast is where the action is (but beware of rip tides). The Nicoya Peninsula has quiet coves sheltered from the Pacific surf by reefs and forested headlands. There are also fine beaches at Manuel Antonio and Gandoca-Manzanillo. For something more off-the-beaten-track, nip into Panama for a few days of desert-island-living on the coral cays of Bocas del Toro.

Best action Spice up your wildlife watching with a whitewater rafting trip (adventurecostarica.com). Costa Rica has three wild and wonderful rivers: the Pacuare (class III-IV rapids, minimum age 12), Sarapiquí (class III rapids, minimum age 10) and Corobicí (class II rapids, minimum age eight).

Natural beauties

Arenal volcano rises above Costa Rica's rainforest. Below left: one of the country's stunning beaches.

Turtle watching

Five varieties of sea turtle nest on Costa Rica's beaches, ranging from modest olive ridleys to mammoth leatherbacks (weighing a hefty 550 kg). Head to Tortuguero and Santa Rosa National Parks where, at night, it's possible to observe these marine reptiles hauling themselves onto beaches to lay their eggs. Leatherbacks nest from February to July and green turtles from June to October.

Belize Barrier Reef

Copán

Belize

Wildlife sanctuaries A great introduction to the country's wildlife, the Belize Zoo (belizezoo.org) is home to a wide range of native species. Located on a 34-ha swathe of tropical savannah, the adjacent Tropical Education Centre offers walking trails and a half-day canoe trip on the Sibun River. Stay at one of the centre's forest cabanas and you'll be able to join a nocturnal tour of the zoo. Once you've honed your wildlife-watching skills, put them into practice at some of Belize's renowned wildlife reserves (belizeaudubon.org). Crooked Tree Wildlife Sanctuary is a good spot for birds, crocodiles and howler monkeys, while Cockscomb Basin Wildlife Sanctuary is a vast area of rugged, forest-clad mountains where you may be lucky enough to spot the elusive tapir or jaguar.

Belize Barrier Reef Measuring nearly 300 km in length, the world's second longest barrier reef is scattered with thousands of coral islands, ranging from desert-island specks to Ambergris Caye (ambergriscaye.com) – a large island in the north with a wide choice of places to stay and things to do.

Mayan ruins Altun Ha is the most easily accessible site from Belize City. However, if you're in the mood for some Mayan ruins, they don't get more impressive than Tikal – a daytrip across the border into Guatemala. One of the great Mayan cities, Tikal flourished between 600 BC and AD 900. Today, its pyramids rise majestically above the rainforest, providing views across the canopy and the bonus of spotting monkeys and toucans. The Temple of the Double-Headed Serpent is the tallest – an exquisitely forged pyramid looming 65 m above the city's plazas.

Adventure activities In addition to canoeing, biking and snorkelling, one of the more daredevil pursuits in

Belize is tubing along the subterranean rivers of the Caves Branch system (cavesbranch.com). Sitting in an inflated inner tube with just your headlamp to light the way, it's not for the faint-hearted…

Honduras

Not only does Honduras boast the region's largest tract of virgin jungle (La Mosquitia), but it also has the coral-fringed Bay Islands and the ruined city of Copán – the crowning glory of Mayan achievement.

Copán Sprouting from a forest clearing, tall stone pillars (or stellae) depicting great Mayan rulers like 18-Rabbit are the trademarks of these enigmatic ruins. There are also temples beneath temples – the compressed 400-year dynasty of 16 kings through which archaeologists have burrowed to reveal intricate hieroglyphs and elaborate façades. Look out for the Ballcourt, a narrow alley hemmed in by sloping walls on which six upright macaw heads were mounted – the equivalent of goalposts. Over one thousand years ago, this was where Copán's sporting heroes refined the art of ball control. The game was called *pok-a-tok*, the rubber ball weighed 3 kg and full-time usually resulted in a sacrifice or two.

Rainforest reserves Take your pick from the mangrove channels of Punta Izopo (perfect for canoeing), Punta Sal (one of your best chances for spotting howler monkeys) and Pico Bonito (for birdwatching, hiking and whitewater rafting).

Bay Islands For the perfect way to round off a tour of mainland Honduras, rent a beach house in the laid-back settlement of West End on the island of Roatán. The snorkelling is superb and you can also rent sea kayaks, go horse riding, glass-bottom boating, learn how to scuba dive or simply chill out on the beach.

Inside info ⓘ

▶▶ In Costa Rica, join a guided tour or plan a self-drive. Distances are short and there are plenty of guesthouses, ecolodges and beach retreats; a 4WD vehicle is recommended.
▶▶ Accommodation in Belize ranges from jungle ecolodges to beach resorts on Ambergris Caye.
▶▶ Roatán in the Bay Islands, Honduras, offers a wide range of accommodation and is an excellent place to learn scuba diving.

If you're looking for an island adventure with lots to see and do, try Barbados, Cuba, Jamaica or the Dominican Republic where you can hike in mountains one day and flop on a beach the next. If island hopping is more your thing, think about joining a cruise or visiting the Bahamas (see page 347) where you can easily combine two or three islands. Some Caribbean islands are renowned for particular activities (for example, scuba diving on Grand Cayman or sailing in the British Virgin Islands), while others tend to attract couples seeking luxury and privacy (such as St Martin and St Kitts).

▶▶ **How do we get there?**
Several islands, like Barbados, Jamaica, the Cayman Islands and St Lucia, have non-stop flights from Europe or the United States (a real boon if you have a fractious toddler on your lap). Remember to factor in the transfer time to your hotel. Caribbean islands are GMT-4 or -5.

▶▶ **What accommodation do we need?**
Teenagers will appreciate full-on resorts where they can hang out with other teens and do stuff as and when they feel like it. For older teenagers a villa within a resort is ideal since it gives them the option to laze around like they might do at home without irritating other guests! You'll find good options in the British Virgin Islands and Antigua. For younger children look for a dedicated pool and kids' club, plus a gently shelving sandy beach that's sheltered from the wind. Tots, of course, will need childcare facilities like babysitting and crèches if you want any adult time for watersports or a romantic meal. At the other extreme, a self-catering villa will give you independence and put you in touch with locals.

Now here's a pleasant dilemma: there are thousands of islands in the Caribbean, ranging from chunky Cuba to the sandy slivers of the Exuma Cays. Take it as granted that most, if not all, will have idyllic beaches and warm sea, so how do you begin to zone in on your perfect piece of family paradise? Start by asking yourself the three questions in the box, left, then dive in to the following reviews.

Antigua

Family appeal Very laid-back with safe reef-fringed waters and beaches galore.
Best beaches Half Moon Bay on the east coast is an all-round gem, while Darkwood Beach and Long Bay are perfect for snorkelling and reef walks.
Best days out Take a boat trip to Barbuda to see the frigatebird sanctuary. English Harbour on Antigua is home to Nelson's Dockyard where you can visit forts, museums and the restored Admiral's House, while St Johns has a lively market.
Find out more antigua-barbuda.com

Barbados

Family appeal Something for everyone, from lively to totally chilled, plus a great choice of accommodation, from all-inclusive resorts to self-catering.
Best beaches The west coast has sandy beaches with gentle waves, while those along the south coast are a bit livelier and attract surfers and boogie boarders.
Best days out Spend a day exploring colonial Bridgetown then strike out on an island safari in search of some of old plantation houses. Don't miss the train ride into Harrisons Caves or ziplining above Jack-in-the-Box Gully.
Find out more visitbarbados.org

British Virgin Islands

Family appeal Islands made in heaven for families keen on sailing. Peaceful, relaxed and unspoilt with a good range of accommodation.
Best beaches On Tortola, Cane Garden Bay has fine sand and clear water, while Apple Bay is best for surf.
Best days out Take a boat trip to find your own deserted cove. Visit the more lively US Virgin Islands.
Find out more bvitourism.com

Cayman Islands

Family appeal A Holy Grail to divers, the Caymans

Toddler heaven

also offer plenty for families. There's a wide choice of accommodation, from self-catering to five-star luxury, while watersports, from snorkelling to submersible rides, will appeal to most ages.
Best beaches Seven-Mile Beach is where you'll find most of the resorts, as well as plenty of cafés, restaurants and watersports. Boatswains Beach has a turtle conservation project.
Best days out Spot a prehistoric-looking blue iguana in the Botanic Park, interact with stingrays at Stingray City (a shallow sandbank off the coast of Grand Cayman) or hone your board skills at the Black Pearl Skate & Surf Park.
Find out more caymanislands.co.uk

Cuba

Family appeal All the sun, sea, sand and laid-back vibe of the Caribbean, but with a unique cultural twist.
Best beaches Mile upon mile of pristine sand and lots of amenities make Varadero numero uno on the beach stakes, while Playa Paraíso and Playa Sirenas are quieter and less developed.
Best days out Admire the faded grandeur of Havana's Spanish colonial architecture and classic 1950s American cars, learn how to dance the salsa and visit the Museum of the Revolution. Other historical hotspots include the Bay of Pigs and the Mausoleum of Ché Guevara at Santa Clara. For adventure head to Vinales for biking trips into a dramatic landscape of limestone peaks, to Trinidad for snorkelling on the reef at Cayo Blanco and to Topes de Collantes National Park for hiking and birdwatching.
Find out more travel2cuba.co.uk

Dominican Republic

Family appeal Superb beaches, a good range of accommodation and lots of adventure activities.
Best beaches Cabarete offers kitesurfing and windsurfing, and is also a base for excursions into the

Caribbean reef fish

mountains. All-inclusive resorts can be found at the beaches of Bayahibe, Punta Cana and Playa Dorada, whereas the stunning beaches on the Samana peninsula have more limited accommodation.
Best days out Take a 4WD safari into the mountains to visit rural villages and to witness coffee and sugar cane farming in action. The mountain town of Jarabacoa is a base for whitewater rafting, parasailing, hiking and horse riding, while Ocean World is a large marine park with dolphin and shark encounters.
Find out more godominicanrepublic.com

Grenada

Family appeal Low key and eco-friendly, with a mixture of sandy beaches and jungle interior; accommodation options range from luxury resorts to self-catering cottages.
Best beaches Grand Anse has a lovely sweep of white sand shaded by palms.
Best days out St Georges has the most beautiful harbour in the Caribbean where you can browse market stalls piled with nutmeg, cinnamon and other local spices. Take a walk in Grand Etang National Park to spot monkeys and cool off under waterfalls. Keen snorkellers should take a boat ride to Carriacou island.
Find out more grenadagrenadines.com

Jamaica

Family appeal Beautiful beaches, spectacular mountain scenery and legendary reggae beat.
Best beaches Negril Beach, Frenchman's Cove, Long Beach, Hellshire Beach, Dragon Bay, the list goes on...
Best days out For the ultimate induction to Jamaican culture, visit the Bob Marley Museum in Port Royal, take in a reggae session and then visit the beach shacks at Blue Lagoon or Boston Bay for the island's famous jerked chicken. Adventure activities include walking and biking in the Blue Mountains, exploring the caves and waterfalls near Port Antonio and

floating on a bamboo raft down the Rio Grande.
Find out more visitjamaica.com

St Lucia

Family appeal A stunning island ripe for exploration; good range of accommodation.
Best beaches The windward (east) coast is wildly spectacular – look, but don't swim. The quirky volcanic, black-sand beaches will wow kids, but you'll also find plenty of the more traditional white stuff at idyllic beaches like Reduit at Rodney Bay.
Best days out See flatulent mud pits and jets of steam at the 'drive-in' volcano; explore the lush interior by horseback or mountain bike, visit the famous Pitons, explore the ruins at Pigeon Island National Park and go humpback whale watching.
Find out more stlucia.org

Turks & Caicos

Family appeal Miles of deserted beaches, impressive coral reefs, perfect for a Robinson Crusoe experience.
Best beaches You're spoilt for choice. On Providenciales, Grace Bay is an 18 km ribbon of powder-soft sand with snorkelling trails in the lagoon. Accessible only by boat, East Caicos has a 27-km beach on its north coast. Governor's Beach on Grand Turk is perfect for all ages with its talcum sand, shallow, calm waters and shady casuarina trees. Shell-seekers, meanwhile, should comb the strandline of Little Bluff Point Beach near the lighthouse.
Best days out Pack a picnic and find yourself a desert island. Humpback whale watching is possible between January and March.
Find out more turksandcaicostourism.com

US Virgin Islands

Family appeal The ultimate Caribbean playground, rivalling even the Bahamas for its choice of accommodation and activities.
Best beaches Lively, popular Magens Bay on St Thomas has a long crescent of sand and calm, sheltered waters. On St John, Cinnamon Bay Beach has good watersport facilities, while Trunk Bay has an underwater snorkel trail, ideal for beginners.
Best days out Children will enjoy Coral World Marine Park with its underwater observatory and touch pool, while keen shoppers will want to browse the duty-free shops in Charlotte Amalie. Adventure activities include everything from sailing to horse riding.
Find out more usvitourism.vi

Land blubbers at Gardner Bay, Española

Galápagos Islands for kids

The wildlife on these volcanic islands has not only evolved along peculiar lines, but it is also largely unfazed by humans, making this an exciting opportunity for children to learn about ecology, evolution and conservation.

Santa Cruz The most populated of the islands, around 6000 people live in Puerto Ayora. Not to be missed is the Charles Darwin Research Station (darwinfoundation.org) where you can gen up on the islands' geology, natural history and conservation. There is also a breeding centre for giant tortoises – including poor old Lonesome George, last of the Pinta Island subspecies. Other highlights on Santa Cruz include a pair of large volcanic craters known as Los Gemelos (The Twins) and several lava tubes, some of which are big enough to walk through.

Seymour An easy day trip from Santa Cruz this tiny island offers a perfect introduction to Galápagos wildlife. The moment you step from your panga on to the rocky shore you'll notice marine iguanas, sea lions and a variety of birds, including blue-footed boobies, lava gulls, swallow-tailed gulls, noddy terns and pelicans.

Española Special even by Galápagos' standards, Española hosts the entire world population of waved albatrosses between April and December when these great ocean wanderers arrive to nest. You may also see the Hood mocking bird and the Española lava lizard – both endemic to the island. Blue-footed boobies, tropicbirds and marine iguanas are also present, while the sandy strip of Gardner Bay is a favourite haunt of sea lions and nesting turtles.

Fernandina Westernmost and youngest of the islands, Fernandina is also the most volcanically active. The contorted lava flows and large colony of marine iguanas make a primeval combination. Brightly coloured Sally-lightfoot crabs are everywhere and you can also see flightless cormorants and sea lions.

Floreana Interesting for its history as much as its natural history, Floreana was one of the first islands to be inhabited. In the late 18th century, whaling ships called by to stock up on water and giant tortoises (for food).

At Post Office Bay the sailors left letters in a barrel for homeward-bound ships to collect and deliver – a tradition that continues to this day, only now it's tourists leaving postcards. Check to see if there are any you can post once you get home. A short walk inland from Punta Cormorant, a lagoon is home to a large population of flamingos.

Genovesa Also known as the Tower, Genovesa is renowned for its seabird colonies, including storm petrels that are preyed upon by daytime-hunting short-eared owls.

Isabela The largest of the islands in the archipelago, Isabela has several sites of interest, including the Mariela Islands (penguins), Tagus Cove (marine iguanas) and Urvina Bay (flightless cormorants).

San Cristóbal Home to Puerto Baquerizo, the capital of the Galápagos, San Cristóbal also has a naval base and airport. Head to Frigatebird Hill for nesting colonies of both great and magnificent frigatebirds, to Punta Pitt for three species of boobies (red-footed, blue-footed and masked) and to Isla Lobos for sea lions.

Santa Fé You may well find yourself weaving between dozing sea lions when you wade ashore to Barrington Bay on the northeast side of Santa Fé. The island is also renowned for its endemic land iguana.

Santiago Tidal pools at Puerto Egas are squirming with fur seals, while overhead you should spot the Galápagos hawk. Buccaneer Cove has a large sea lion population, while a trail leading from Espumilla Beach should reward you with sightings of several species of Darwin's finches.

▸▸ The Galápagos are a 90-minute flight from the mainland.
▸▸ Several boats in the Galápagos offer family departures featuring special lectures, activities and children's meals; cruises from three to seven days are available.
▸▸ As an alternative to a cruise, stay in a hotel on Santa Cruz and take daytrips to surrounding islands – a better option for children aged five and under.
▸▸ Visit year-round, although the water is warmer for snorkelling between January and April. Boat landings are either wet (wading to a beach) and dry (stepping on to a rocky shore).

> **❝❞** You couldn't dream up a cast of creatures with more child appeal – from marine iguanas that snort water from their nostrils to frigatebirds shaking bright red, party-balloon throat pouches – and it's all there, right at your feet. The magic continues underwater. During a snorkel off Isabela Island, we count 26 green turtles, but sea lions steal the show in surging swim-pasts, with penguins zipping along at the surface like overwound bath toys. William Gray

Frigatebird

Size isn't everything. Although dwarfed by neighbouring Peru and Colombia, Ecuador (about the size of New Zealand) is neatly sliced into Amazon rainforest, Andean mountains and Pacific coast – with an irresistible side order in the form of the Galápagos Islands lying 1000 km to the west. In just a couple of weeks, you could sample all of these South American icons. It's not a cheap option for a family holiday (particularly once you've splashed out on a Galápagos cruise), but if you're looking for that once-in-a-lifetime experience, few countries can match Ecuador for jaw-dropping scenery, vibrant culture and unforgettable wildlife encounters.

Horse riding in the Andes

The mainland

Quito Ecuador's capital lies at an altitude of 2800 m so it's worth taking it easy for the first few days while you adapt to the thin air. The flip side to Quito's lofty location is that the high altitude tempers the searing equatorial heat, creating pleasant temperatures more reminiscent of the Mediterranean. Spend an afternoon wandering the cobbled streets of Quito's old town – a World Heritage site containing several impressive colonial buildings, such as the Jesuit church of La Compañía with its elaborately carved and gilded altar. For fantastic views of the city and surrounding peaks take the Teleferiqo cable car up Pichincha or a taxi to Cerro Panecillo, site of a 45-m-tall statue of the Winged Virgin.

Mitad del Mundo About 25 km north of Quito, Mitad del Mundo marks the location where Charles Marie de la Condamine pinpointed zero degrees of latitude in 1736. Children will enjoy straddling the equator and jumping from one hemisphere to the other. The nearby Inti-Ñan museum explores the astronomical knowledge of the region's pre-Hispanic people who used solar observatories and temples to determine Quito's position at the 'centre of the earth' long before Europeans arrived.

Cotopaxi National Park At 5897 m, Cotopaxi is not only the world's highest continuously active volcano, but its appearance is just as a volcano should be – a perfect cone shape neatly topped with snow. It is the most dramatic and alluring of the peaks lining Ecuador's fabled Avenue of the Volcanoes. On a day trip from Quito it's possible to drive as high as 4500 m on Cotopaxi's lava-scoured flanks, then walk about 45 minutes to the refugio at 4723 m. Be warned though that the air is very thin at this altitude and you should

not attempt this unless you've spent a couple of days acclimatizing in Quito. If you're feeling light-headed due to the altitude, there's great cycling and horse-riding country at haciendas near the base of the mountain. In fact, a couple of nights at one of these traditional ranches, helping out with daily chores like collecting eggs, milking cows, planting crops and feeding guinea pigs, is a great option for all ages.

Mindo cloudforests Just two hours' drive from Quito the seaward slopes of the western mountains are draped with cloudforest. If you're short on time, this rich habitat, teeming with over 350 species of birds, makes a good alternative to an Amazon excursion. Bring your binoculars and see how many kinds of hummingbird you can spot.

Otovalo Another two-hour drive from Quito, this time to the north, Otovalo is a shopper's paradise. The town's market (held every day, but biggest and most colourful on Saturday) is crammed with textiles, handicrafts, musical instruments, jewellery and clothing. This is the place to find those panpipes and the alpaca sweater you've always wanted.

Ecuadorian Amazon The most popular region is centred on the Río Napo where the small town of Coca (reached by road or air) is the starting point for jungle jollies. There are several lodges downstream of Coca, including Napo Wildlife Centre, La Selva and Sacha Lodge. All provide comfortable accommodation, excellent guides and various means of watching wildlife, from forest trails and dugout canoes to canopy towers. You'll also get a chance to go fishing for piranhas at night.

Best beaches Many of Ecuador's Pacific beaches have white sand, good surf and excellent seafood. Two of the finest are at Canoa and Bahía de Caráquez. And if you're on a tight schedule or find the Galápagos Islands simply too expensive, stick to mainland Ecuador where you can see albatrosses, boobies, frigatebirds and sea lions at Isla de la Plata and, between June and October, humpback whales on boat trips from Puerto López.

 Inside info

▸▸ Quito makes a convenient base for exploring some of Ecuador's highlights.
▸▸ Self-drive is possible, but most people arrange tours. Metropolitan Touring (metropolitan-touring. com) are recommended.
▸▸ Accommodation ranges from city hotels to highland haciendas (countryside ranches).
▸▸ Allow a minimum of three nights to visit an Amazonian lodge.

Lost and found

A trekker surveys the fabled Lost City of the Incas, Machu Picchu.

Peru makes an exciting and unusual destination for adventurous families – and your children will no doubt have always wondered what Paddington Bear's home was like. The Inca ruins of Machu Picchu are a must, whether you take the train from Cusco to Aguas Calientes and hike for a day, or embark on the four-day Inca Trail. Children will also be enthralled by the mysterious Nasca Lines – giant desert etchings best viewed from a light aircraft. Other highlights include searching for condors at Colca Canyon, taking a boat trip to the famous floating reed islands on Lake Titicaca and exploring the steamy jungles of the Peruvian Amazon.

Andes

Nasca Get airborne in a light aircraft to gaze down on these huge and mysterious designs, which include a 100-m-wide monkey and a 50-m-long spider, as well as a killer whale, a hummingbird and various geometrical shapes, etched into the stony desert about 22 km north of Nasca. There's even one of a humanlike figure, its hand raised in greeting, which has been dubbed 'the Astronaut'. For decades scientists have pondered the meaning of these spectacular desert doodles. Some believe that the Nasca Lines were an astronomical calendar, while other theories point to giant running tracks, weaving designs, fertility rights, the map of a vanished empire or the spiritual journey of ancient shamans. It's still open to debate, so hop on a plane, take a peek and see if you can crack the Nasca code.

Arequipa Located in a valley at the foot of the evocatively named El Misti volcano (a perfect snow-capped cone, 5822 m high), Arequipa is a beautiful colonial city adorned with fine churches and mansions. The jewel in the crown is the Santa Catalina convent (santacatalina.org.pe) – a colourful contrast to the 'White City's' predominantly pale, volcanic stonework. Join a 90-minute tour to explore the convent's maze of cobbled streets, cloisters, flower-speckled plazas and brightly painted houses. The nearby Plaza de Armas has peaceful gardens, attractive buildings and a good selection of handicraft shops and restaurants.

Colca Canyon Twice as deep as the Grand Canyon (and only 163 m shy of being the deepest canyon in the world – nearby Cotahuasi Canyon snatches that title), Colca Canyon offers spectacular views of pre-Inca terracing, precipitous rock faces, traditional Andean villages – and Andean condors. In fact, these giant vultures (with a wingspan up to 320 cm) steal the show at Cruz del Cóndor, a mirador located at the deepest point in the canyon, where people flock to watch them swooping past. Get there by 0900 when

On the trail to Machu Picchu

Lake Titicaca

Manú Biosphere Reserve

the condors are riding morning thermals. They spend the middle of the day scouring the upper slopes for carrion before returning to the canyon late afternoon.

Lake Titicaca Like a sliver of lapis lazuli slipped into the high Andes, the startlingly blue waters of Lake Titicaca are awash with intrigue. For starters, Titicaca is the highest navigable lake in the world – a breathless 3856 m above sea level. But it's the floating Uros Islands (reached by boat tours from Puno) that will really fire the imagination of your children. The Uros have lived on these islets (fashioned entirely from totora reeds) since Inca times. Tourists visit around 15 of the 32 islands. You can walk on their springy, spongy surfaces and buy straw handicrafts from local women and children – a supplement to the more traditional fishing and hunting lifestyle of the Uros.

Cusco A lively and comfortable city in which to spend a few days, Cusco stands at the head of the Sacred Valley of the Incas. Its popularity stems mainly from the fact that Machu Picchu lies only a train ride or four-day hike away. However, it's well worth scheduling some extra time in and around Cusco to visit other key sites and to take advantage of the wide range of activities on offer. A 30-minute walk or short taxi ride from the city centre, the ruined ceremonial site of Sacsayhuaman is an impressive introduction to the Inca's mastery of masonry. Some of the rocks in the perfectly sutured walls weigh over 120 tonnes. There are more outstanding Inca ruins at Pisac, 30 km north of Cusco, although it's the famous local market here that draws the crowds. In Cusco there are dozens of tour operators offering rafting, mountain biking, walking and horse-riding trips. The gentlest rafting option for children is the Huambutio-Pisac.

Machu Picchu The easiest way to reach the fabled Lost City of the Incas is to take a four-hour train ride from Cusco to Aguas Calientes and a bus from there to the ruins. However, you should really use your feet

if you want to sense some of the magic and majesty surrounding Machu Picchu. That doesn't mean you have to slog it out on the four-day 43-km Inca Trail. From Kilometre 104 (on the railway line from Cusco) it's a short, one or two-day trek to Machu Picchu via the beautiful ruins of Wiñay-Wayna (Forever Young) – an ideal option for families. But for those up to the challenge there's no denying that the Inca Trail is a superb and immensely satisfying adventure.

Peruvian Amazon

Manú Biosphere Reserve This vast chunk of Peruvian Amazon probably has more species of plants and animals than anywhere else on earth, including 1000 different birds and 13 varieties of monkey. You will literally be surrounded by thousands of yet-to-be-discovered species. Fly in or take the three-day overland journey from Cusco, crossing the Andes and delving into cloudforest en route. Once in Manu explore the jungle on foot and by canoe, staying in simple but comfortable lodges.

Tambopata National Reserve Renowned for its clay licks (attracting up to 260 macaws and a dozen species of parrots), Tambopata's Heath River and Sandoval Lake are rich in wildlife. Heath River Wildlife Centre (inkanatura.com) is close to a floating hide overlooking a clay lick and also runs night-time caiman-spotting trips.

 Inca Trail tips

▶▶ You can only trek with a registered agency which will arrange permits, guide, porters, camping gear, food and transport to and from trailheads.
▶▶ Dry season is from May to October.
▶▶ It's camping all the way, except at Wiñay-Wayna where there's a hostel.
▶▶ Take trekking poles with rubber tips or buy bamboo ones.
▶▶ Don't take short cuts – the vegetation at high altitude may take years to recover from careless trampling.

Brazil is vast. Only four countries – Canada, China, Russia and the United States – are larger. And it's not all Amazon jungle. There are iconic cities, like Rio de Janeiro, São Paulo and Salvador; there's the watery wilderness of the Pantanal, the ground-shaking Iguaçu Falls, a spectacular coastline, carnival, samba, football… Clearly you are going to have to make a few hard choices when it comes to taking the kids to Brazil. Few families will have the time, energy or money to see it all in one go. The good news is that local air passes link many of the main attractions, making it possible to visit two or three in a single holiday. A great option is to combine a few active days in the Amazon, the Pantanal or Iguaçu Falls, followed by time-out in Rio or at one of the family-friendly resorts along the Atlantic coast near Salvador.

Rio de Janeiro

Sugar Loaf The cable car ride to the 396-m summit of Sugar Loaf Mountain (bondinho.com.br) is Rio's essential attraction. Spread out in panoramic perfection you'll see Copacabana and Ipanema beaches, the Christ statue, the Bay of Guanabara, Tijuca Forest and other city highlights. The cable car leaves every half-hour from 0800. It's a two-stage journey, stopping at Morro de Urca where there is a café and children's play area.

Corcovado For more heavenly views of Rio, a narrow-gauge railway winds its way up 710-m Corcovado (corcovado.com.br) to the foot (or feet) of the huge Christ the Redeemer statue. For the best views sit on the right-hand side of the train.

Best beaches On Sundays, the waterfronts at Copacabana, Flamengo, Ipanema, and Leblon beaches are closed to traffic and instead you'll find all kinds of street performers, from musicians to fire-eaters. Leblon also has a play area for toddlers, while Copacabana has plenty of kiosks selling snacks.

Iguaçu Falls

Straddling the border between Brazil and Argentina, Iguaçu Falls are about 4 km wide and consist of 275 cascades ranging from 62 to 84 m in height. Try to allow at least three days here so that you can view the falls from both sides, take a river safari and explore the surrounding forest. The Guaraní people weren't exaggerating when they named these falls

South American beauty

Copacabana beach, Rio de Janeiro.

🗨 Local tips

▸▸ Take a jeep trip to Tijuca Forest, the world's largest urban rainforest.

▸▸ Witness a classic 'Fla-Flu' showdown between Flamengo and Fluminense at Maracanã football stadium.

▸▸ Sample the ice creams at Mil Frutas (Ipanema) – cinnamon and ginger flavour is highly recommended.

Iguaçu (Great Water). At the peak of the wet season (January to February), some 12 million litres of water surge over the cataracts every second. Niagara can manage a relatively paltry peak flow of just eight million litres per second (upon seeing Iguaçu, First Lady Eleanor Roosevelt reportedly exclaimed, "Poor Niagara!"). The most spectacular cataract is Garganta del Diablo (Devil's Throat), a narrow horseshoe canyon. Helicopter flights provide a wonderful perspective of Iguaçu Falls, but for pure exhilaration take a boat ride to the very base of the cataracts. You'll battle upstream through rapids in a large inflatable dinghy until you are surrounded on all sides by curtains of water. Be warned, however, that the boat drivers like to nose the dinghies under one or two of the smaller cascades. Older kids will love the pummelling. Younger kids might not.

Bahia coast

Caiman

Iguaçu Falls

A guided walk along one of the trails in the subtropical rainforest that surrounds Iguaçu Falls is a real treat. You might hear howler monkeys or glimpse an agouti, but it's the 250 species of butterflies that will enchant children. Look out for the metallic blue morphos flitting about on hand-sized wings. Keep your eyes peeled, too, for some of Iguaçu's 448 bird species. Toucans are the most conspicuous.

Brazilian Amazon

It's sometimes a case in the Amazon of not being able to see the animals for the trees. Immersing yourself in this immense tropical forest, however, still ranks as one of the world's most exciting and rewarding wildlife travel experiences. Simply being there, staying in a jungle lodge or cruising upstream in a small riverboat, will give you a strong sense of the forest's vibrant biodiversity. With patience, you'll glimpse tapirs, monkeys and otters by the water's edge, macaws flashing scarlet and blue over the forest canopy or caiman skulking in the backwaters, just their eyes and nostrils protruding above the surface.

Boost your chances of wildlife sightings by staying at places like Uakari Lodge and Cristalino Jungle Lodge which have canopy towers, hides and trails. A 60-km river trip from Manaus, the Anavilhanas Archipelago is also a good base. The forest floods here in April and May, allowing canoe trips through the treetops in search of giant, air-gulping pirarucu fish and – if you are very lucky – river dolphins and manatees too.

Bahia Atlantic Coast

For a beach holiday with a twist, Brazil's Bahia region mixes family essentials, like soft sand and safe swimming, with some unusual excursions. Praia do Forte EcoResort (one of the most popular along this stretch of coast) is next to the Tamar sea turtle conservation project (tamar.org.br). No less than five turtle species nest along Brazil's coast and Praia do Forte is one of the most important egg-laying sites. You can see various turtles, from adults to hatchlings, at the visitor centre, while guided turtle-spotting walks along the beaches are available between December and February.

Just 50 km south of the Praia do Forte lies the city of Salvador. Head for the traffic-free historic district (Pelourinho) where capoeira dancers demonstrate their acrobatic and martial art skills. And don't miss Igreja de São Francisco, a Baroque church adorned with some 100 kg of gold.

✪ Pantanal safari

In this huge wetland (about half the size of France), you have a better chance of seeing wildlife than in the rainforest. Top ticks include anaconda, caiman, giant anteater, hyacinth macaw, jabiru stork and jaguar. Ecolodges in the area offer activities ranging from caiman-feeding and canoeing to horse riding and night-time safaris. Visit any time, although the land dries out between May and September, concentrating wildlife around pools and making it easier to see. Temperatures are also cooler during this period.

Inside info

▶▶ Rio is a year-round destination, but it's hot between January and March, wet during December and chaotic in the build-up to the Carnival (February)
▶▶ Locals take their kids everywhere – including restaurants and dances.
▶▶ The Bahia region is malaria-free and GMT-3.
▶▶ Trade winds bring rain mainly from December to April.

Argentina
Tango to Tierra del Fuego

Most kids will feel right at home in Argentina. There's plenty they can relate to, from football and dancehall fever in Buenos Aires to a day on the farm rounding up sheep. But don't imagine for one minute that Argentina is dull or predictable. Far from it. Stretching from the subtropical rainforest at Iguaçu Falls in the north to the ice-scoured wilderness of Patagonia in the south, this huge country can put you in touch with some extraordinary landscapes. Brace yourself for towering glaciers, jagged peaks, vast windswept plains and ancient brooding forests.

Buenos Aires

Argentina's capital makes a great launch pad for kids visiting South America. The locals love 'em (children are welcome everywhere except nightclubs), while the city itself has plenty of attractions. A good way to spend a day is to combine a visit to the central Plaza de Mayo area and the converted docks at Puerto Madero with a trip 32 km north to El Tigre where you can take a boat trip on the Paraná Delta – perfect if you need to escape the city heat. Other Buenos Aires highlights include Recoleta Cemetery. Not many cities can boast a graveyard as a tourist trap, but Recoleta's macabre maze of extravagant tombs is worth a visit. Challenge your kids to find the grave of Eva Perón. For security reasons, La Boca (a lively neighbourhood renowned for its colourful houses and street artists) should only be visited during the day and with a local driver and guide to show you around. It's also probably wise to avoid the area on match days when Boca Juniors are playing at home in their famous Bombonera stadium – unless you're a football fan and going to the game of course.

Argentinian Patagonia

Covering almost a third of Argentina, this vast, empty and hauntingly beautiful region is ripe for adventure. If you only have time for visiting one part of Argentinian Patagonia (don't forget, there's more of it in Chile) set your sights on Los Glaciares National Park, a rugged melange of Andean peaks and giant glaciers that oozes wilderness – yet has enough tourist infrastructure to keep families happy. The lakeside resort of El Calafate makes an ideal base for icy escapades to the creaking, groaning snout of the 60-m-tall Perito Moreno Glacier. You can also go hiking, horse riding and fishing.

Although rather far-flung, Tierra del Fuego is also

Tierra del Fuego

> ### 🎯 Local obsessions
>
> ▶▶ **Meat** Argentineans love their steaks. They eat more meat than any other nation in the world. Try a succulent *bife de chorizo* at a parrilla (grill restaurant).
> ▶▶ **Football** It's more than simply a beautiful game in Argentina. Feel the passion for *futbol* during a match at River Plate stadium.
> ▶▶ **Tango** Don't miss out on a tango show in Buenos Aries where this exotic dance was invented.

an excellent place to travel with kids. You arrive at a small city called Ushuaia where, each Austral summer, a steady trickle of tourists join cruise ships bound for the Antarctic Peninsula – just two days' voyage across Drake's Passage. But there's plenty to do in and around Ushuaia itself. Excellent museums trace the city's history, from the hardships faced by shipwreck survivors and the indigenous Yámana people to the settlement's early role as a prison. You can also hike in the ancient and mysterious beech forests of Tierra del Fuego National Park and take boat trips on the Beagle Channel to spot rare wildlife, such as the flightless steamer duck which propels itself across the surface on stubby wings.

Finally, there's Península Valdés, a spectacular wildlife haven jutting from the Patagonian mainland near the town of Puerto Madryn. Southern right whales congregate here between June and mid-December to mate and give birth, while Magellanic penguins congregate in large colonies. The beaches are positively squirming with elephant seals, sea lions and fur seals. Pups born between August and November add to the beach hullaballoo, but things reach fever pitch in March when orca whales surf onto the beach to seize unsuspecting youngsters.

Inside info ⓘ

▶▶ Buenos Aires can be visited year-round, although temperatures are more pleasant during spring (September to November) and autumn (March to May).
▶▶ Patagonia is big – it takes four hours, for example, to fly from Buenos Aires to Tierra del Fuego. Aim to spend at least three nights in any one location.
▶▶ Iguaçu Falls (see page 340) is accessible from Puerto Iguazú.

Chile
Fat rewards in a skinny land

For a thin slip of a country, Chile certainly packs a lot in. From the lofty Atacama Desert in the north it's like one long thrill ride all the way to wave-scoured Tierra del Fuego in the south. Along the way you'll find everything from coastal resorts and vineyards to sheltered fiords and austere Andean wilderness. Travel in Chile can be as pampered or as hardcore as you like. Families with young children may want to plump for the country's gentle midriff where the Lakes District has none of the extreme altitude or climate often associated with Patagonia or the Atacama Desert. Wherever you go, however, you'll find travel reassuringly straightforward. And even though it's Chile you'll still get a warm welcome…

Torres del Paine

Santiago

Chile's capital has enough to keep children occupied for a day or two. The walk up Cerro Santa Lucia, for example, provides great views of the city and – if it's clear – the Andes, while the Museo de Santiago portrays local history through some imaginative displays. If you're not in the mood for cities, however, Cascades de las Animas (cascada.net) just 60 km southeast of Santiago, offers easy walking, horse riding and whitewater rafting (minimum age eight) on an old horse ranch in the Andean foothills. Between June and September, there's excellent skiing at several resorts to the east of Santiago. El Colorado (elcolorado. cl) and Farellones (farellones.cl) both offer a good range of facilities, including ski classes for kids.

Atacama Desert

San Pedro de Atacama is the staging point for forays into the driest desert on earth – and a pretty weird and wonderful place it is too. Your kids will feel like lunar explorers when they 'touch down' in the Valley of the Moon with its otherworldly rock formations. Then there are eggs to boil in the steaming geysers at El Tatio and flamingos to spy in the giant salt flats of Salar de Atacama.

Lakes District

Moving south from the Atacama, Chile gets wetter but no less magical. The Lakes District has smouldering volcanoes, forests of araucaria (monkey puzzle) trees and a serene patchwork of lakes and fiords. At Parque Nacional Conguillio you can take a nature trail through an araucaria forest, while just to the south, Pucón is a centre for whitewater rafting,

canyoning, horse riding, cycling and walking, as well as swimming and watersports on Lago Villarrica. Further south still, Puerto Montt is the gateway to the Chilean fiords. Boat trips here range from a one-day affair to see the rainforest at Parque Nacional Alerce Andino to a four-day cruise to Puerto Natales, gliding through a truly spectacular wilderness of mountains, glaciers and forests. Alternatively, you could simply nip across to tranquil Chiloé Island, a verdant time capsule of traditional villages and ancient forests where kids can run free on deserted sandy beaches, explore hidden creeks and enjoy life on a farm.

Chilean Patagonia

Torres del Paine is the showcase national park on the Chilean side of Patagonia (see opposite for what Argentina can offer). The iconic, cloud-snagging towers of Torres del Paine are a magnet to walkers, while exciting places to stay, like Ecocamp Patagonia and Remota, offer a range of excursions, from horse riding and boat trips to estancia visits and exploring the Milodon Cave – the object of Bruce Chatwin's quest in his classic travelogue, *In Patagonia*.

 ## Let's go to Cape Horn

Few passport stamps evoke that 'ends of the earth' feeling more than the one you get upon making landfall at Cape Horn. However, the southernmost point of the Americas is surprisingly easy to reach. Departing on four-day voyages between Ushuaia and Punta Arenas, the cruise ship, *Mare Australis* (australis.com) makes weekly visits throughout the summer. This weather-beaten outpost, notorious for its ship-swallowing gales and distinctly unfriendly seas, has a permanently manned lighthouse, a chapel and boardwalks. Other highlights of the cruise include the Beagle Channel and Pia Glacier.

Inside info

▶▶ Chile is less than 180 km wide, but it's long (4270 km), so you'll find it easiest and quickest to use internal flights to get around. However, also consider renting a car or using the efficient long-distance buses.
▶▶ High season is December to March (Chile's summertime).
▶▶ Don't forget Easter Island. It's full of big heads and can be reached by flights from Santiago.

When to go

The most comfortable time to visit **Mexico** is from December to February when the Yucatán Peninsula is at its coolest and least humid. The desert heat of Baja California is often tempered by a sea breeze, while the highlands of the Sierra Madre offer cool respite from the muggy lowlands.

Affecting the **Caribbean**, the **Bahamas** and **Central America**, as well as Mexico, the hurricane season runs roughly from May/June to October/November. The National Weather Service (nws.noaa.gov) provides daily updates. Costa Rica, Belize, Honduras, Cuba and other islands are sunny and dry from December to April, although even in the wet season rain tends to be short-lived – if torrential.

Ecuador and **Peru** are year-round destinations, with climate varying more with altitude than time of year. One of the best times to visit the mountains is during the dry, sunny period between June and September. Coastal areas can be wet from January to April – although this is the driest time for the jungle. The Galápagos Islands are sunny, hot and humid from December to June and cooler, with the chance of mist or drizzle, between June and November.

Amazonian **Brazil** is hot and humid all year with temperatures ranging from 25-35°C. Visit between June and November, however, and you can expect less rain and fewer mosquitoes. Head to the coast for cooling sea breezes and book well in advance if you want to visit during the local holiday periods of July and December to February.

Argentina and **Chile** are generally best visited between October and April when the days are longer, there's more chance of sun and Patagonia is at its most accessible – however, the further south you go, the more unpredictable the weather becomes.

Getting there

Several airlines have flights to Latin America, including Aerolineas Argentinas (aerolineas.com.ar), Air France (airfrance.com), British Airways (britishairways.com), Continental Airlines (continental.com), Iberia (iberia.com), KLM (klm.com), LAN (lan.com) and Lufthansa (lufthansa.com).

Getting around

If you want to cover large distances or combine several countries, an **airpass** is convenient and good value. The South America Airpass from LAN (lan.com), for example, allows you to purchase one-way tickets to multiple destinations in Argentina, Brazil, Chile, Ecuador and Peru.

Several South American countries, including Brazil, Mexico and Peru, have good road networks served by comfortable intercity **coaches**. You could also consider **self-drive**, although car rental can be expensive and distances huge. Latin America specialists, Geodyssey (geodyssey.co.uk) can arrange self-drive itineraries in Costa Rica – ideal for adventurous families who want the freedom of independent touring, but the security of prebooked accommodation every night. Don't attempt to drive in any major South American city – book a tour or use public transport instead.

There are several tourist-orientated **train** services in South America, two of the most popular being from Cusco to Machu Picchu and Lake Titicaca (perurail.com). Ferries can also be useful, particularly in southern Chile and Baja California, while there's no shortage of operators offering cruises around the Caribbean, the Galápagos Islands and, to a lesser extent, Patagonia and Tierra del Fuego.

Accommodation

Mexico has a wide range of accommodation, from boutique hotels and rural haciendas to beach resorts on both the Caribbean and Pacific coasts.

In the **Caribbean** you are also spoilt for choice. However, if you had to make a shortlist of the best family resorts, it would have to include Almond Beach Village, Barbados (almondresorts.com), Beaches Turks & Caicos Resort (beaches.com), Club Med Punta Cana, Dominican Republic (clubmed.com), Windjammer Landing Villa Beach Resort, St Lucia (windjammer-landing.com), Four Seasons Resort Nevis (fourseasons.com) and Westin Casuarina Resort & Spa, Grand Cayman (starwoodhotels.com). All have imaginative kids' clubs, extensive child-care facilities, children's menus and other extra touches.

In **Central America**, you will find a good range of beach resorts and jungle lodges. Costa Rica's Corcovado Camp (corcovado.com) has 20 twin-bedded tents on raised platforms overlooking the Pacific, while Chaa Creek (chaacreek.com) in Belize has its own butterfly farm and spa. On Roatán, largest of the Bay Islands, Palmetto Bay Plantation (palmettobayplantation.com) has thatched villas, each with a living room and kitchen.

Ecuador's accommodation options are as diverse as its scenery. In the highlands, try to spend a few nights in a hacienda. Home of the former Ecuadorian president Galo Plaza Lasso, Hacienda Zuleta (zuleta.com) is now a 16-room hotel on a working farm with a stable of Andalucian crossbreds. In the Ecuadorian Amazon, Kapawi Lodge (kapawi.com) is run in partnership with members of the local Achuar community who will lead you on hikes through the rainforest, identifying medicinal plants and some of the 400 varieties of birds.

Perfect for a land-based stay in the Galápagos Islands, Hotel Finch Bay (finchbayhotel.com) on Santa Cruz has a beach, swimming pool and activities such as sea kayaking, mountain biking, guided hikes and, of course, day cruises to other islands.

For a gentle introduction to the Amazon rainforest, Reserva Amazonica (reserva-amazonica.info) in **Peru** is just 45 minutes by boat from Puerto Maldonado. In Cusco, meanwhile, you can choose from budget hostels to top-end hotels.

South of Rio de Janeiro, **Brazil's** Costa Verde has a Mediterranean feel with numerous villas for rent, while the Bahia coast to the north has resorts like Praia do Forte (praiadoforte.org.br). An hour's drive from Salvador, this supremely child-friendly property hugs a sheltered beach and has everything from a kids' club and children's pool to a resident population of cheeky marmosets that launch daily raids on the breakfast buffet. Another excellent family option along this stretch of coast is Costa do Sauipe (superclubs.org).

To fully appreciate the ranching lifestyle of rural **Argentina** you should spend at least one night in a traditional homestead. Just 20 km from El Calafate (gateway to the Perito Moreno Glacier) Galpón del Glaciar (estanciaalice.com.ar) will allow you to witness the daily workings of a Patagonian sheep farm – from shearing and mustering to enjoying a lamb barbecue.

Like Argentina, **Chile** has several farmstay opportunities. If you want to experience some of Chile's more extreme environments (without sacrificing creature comforts), you can't go wrong with explora (explora.com). This pioneering company has properties in the Atacama Desert, Torres del Paine National Park and Easter Island, and can tailor a programme of activities to suit different ages and energy levels. Be sure to also check out the equally cutting-edge Remota (remota.cl) in Patagonia.

Food & drink
If your kids will eat potatoes and beans at home they won't go hungry in Latin America. Along with corn, tomatoes, cocoa and vanilla, these child-friendly staples all have their origins in Latin America and still form the basis of many traditional menus. In **Mexico**, for example, children will enjoy chomping through corn *tamales* (stuffed dumplings), tortillas, beans and chilli con carne, while those with more adventurous appetites can sample *mole poblano* (meat covered in a sauce of chocolate and chillies).

In **Central American** countries, a typical meal consists of beef, rice, beans, fried plantain, sour cream and a stack of tortillas on the side. Fried chicken is also common, while grilled fish and lobster (often with coconut) is available along the coast. Not surprisingly, local seafood dishes feature predominantly on menus throughout the **Caribbean**. Local specialities include peas 'n' rice and grouper fingers.

Andean food is a wholesome spread of potatoes, rice, pork, chicken and lamb. Guinea pig is a local delicacy, but you won't get many kids willing to eat something they've always regarded as the family pet.

One of **Brazil's** best-known dishes is a black bean and pork stew known as *feijoada*, but you'll also find everything from seafood and steak to pasta and salad. On the northeast coast you should sample the exotic African-Brazilian fusion cuisine.

In **Argentina** they like their beef, so barbecue fans will be in heaven here. Also try the savoury *empanada* pasties. **Chile**, meanwhile, is renowned for its seafood (*curanto* is a typical shellfish stew served with potato bread), rich pastries and wines.

Health & safety
Malaria is present in parts of Latin America, so be sure to discuss malaria prevention with your doctor well before you travel. You should plan an appropriate course of vaccinations. In general, stick to bottled or purified drinking water. Only eat properly prepared food (peeled fruit, salad washed in treated water etc). Also be aware of the potential effects of exposure to high altitude and severe sunlight in the Andes. Rabies is widespread, so never let your children approach dogs. Similarly, leave all the poking around in the rainforest to your professional guide – those hairy caterpillars may look cute to hold, but they are loaded with noxious irritants. Major cities have a reputation for being unsafe, but as long as you use common sense, your visit should be trouble-free.

Grown-ups' stuff
Latin America

Fast facts

Country	Time	Language*	Currency	Code	Tourist information
Mexico	GMT-6	Spanish	Mexican peso	+52	visitmexico.com
Costa Rica	GMT-6	Spanish	Colón	+506	visitcostarica.com
Belize	GMT-6	English	Belize dollar	+501	travelbelize.org
Honduras	GMT-6	Spanish	Lempira	+504	honduras.com
Ecuador	GMT-5 to -8	Spanish	US dollar	+593	ecuador.travel
Peru	GMT-5	Spanish	Nuevo sol	+51	peru.info
Brazil	GMT-3 to -5	Portuguese	Real	+55	turismo.gov.br
Argentina	GMT-3	Spanish	Argentine peso	+54	turismo.gov.ar
Chile	GMT-4	Spanish	Chilean peso	+56	chile.travel

* English widely spoken in Costa Rica and Honduras; Quecua in Ecuador and Peru.

Isabela II
Where? Galápagos Islands.
Why? Cramped with 70 crew on the *Beagle*, Darwin would no doubt have appreciated the stable bearing of the *Isabela II*, her library and lounge, spacious cabins, fine dining and little extras like the jacuzzi and sun deck. The 40-berth ship has kayaks, zodiacs, snorkelling gear and glass-bottom boat – everything you need for the ultimate Galápagos voyage.
Contact Metropolitan Touring, T+55(0)11-3588 0818, metropolitan-touring.com

Lapa Ríos Ecolodge
Where? Osa Peninsula, Costa Rica.
Why? Set in a 376-ha private nature reserve with dreamy views across pristine rainforest to the Pacific coast, Lapa Ríos offers naturalist-led day hikes, birdwatching walks, boat trips in the mangrove forest, whale watching and kayaking. You can also spend a night even closer to nature by sleeping on a special outdoor platform.
Contact Lapa Ríos, T+1 (0)506-2735 5281, laparios.com

Ecocamp Patagonia
Where? Torres del Paine National Park, Chile.
Why? Inspired by the traditional huts of the nomadic Kawesqar of Patagonia, this minimal impact camp consists of spacious dome-shaped tents, sleeping four and built on raised platforms linked by walkways to avoid damaging the ground. Expert local guides arrange treks and horse riding. An exciting adventure base where children are welcome.
Contact Ecocamp Patagonia, T+56 (0)2-923 5950, ecocamp.travel

Araras Ecolodge
Where? Pantanal, Brazil.
Why? Located right in the heart of the Pantanal, 19-room Araras Ecolodge frequently has capybara wandering through its grounds. Two tree-top lookouts provide a wonderful view across the wildlife-rich wetlands and a chance to spot hyacinth macaws (over 40 nest in the lodge area). Canoeing, horse riding, trekking, jeep safaris and piranha fishing are also available.
Contact Araras Ecolodge, T+55 (0)65-3682 2800, araraslodge.com.br

Bellavista Cloud Forest
Where? Ecuador
Why? This peaceful lodge almost feels like an organic part of the forest, its thatched roofs smothered in epiphytes. Imaginative rooms include the dome with spiral staircase and ladders climbing to a den overlooking the canopy (great for kids). The lodge is a paradise for hummingbirds, while numerous child-friendly trails probe the surrounding cloud forest.
Contact Bellavista Lodge, T+593 (0)2-290 3166, bellavistacloudforest.com

» Mexico
A good choice for families visiting the Yucatán Peninsula, **Omni Puerto Aventuras** (omnihotels.com) is a small resort with just 30 rooms on a palm-fringed beach near Playa del Carmen. As well as a children's pool and kids' club, the resort is well located for visiting the Mayan ruins at Tulum and Xel-Ha water park. On Mexico's Pacific coast, **Fiesta Americana Puerto Vallarta** (fiestamericana.com) also has a kids' club and plenty of watersports. Away from the beach, you can go cycling, horse riding and birdwatching in the Sierra Madre.

Atlantis, Bahamas

> ❝❞ **The Bahamas excel in family-friendly accommodation, boasting everything from self-catering villas, such as those offered by Hope Town Hideaways on Abaco (hopetown.com) to all-inclusive resorts, like the legendary Atlantis (atlantis.com) on Paradise Island with its spectacular marine lagoons and aquarium (pictured above).** William Gray

▶▶ Caribbean

Carlisle Bay (totstoo.com) ticks all the right boxes for a supremely relaxing, indulgent family holiday in the Caribbean. Parents get a fabulous spa, fine dining and luxury accommodation; children get activities galore and their own special kids' clubs. Add two-room suites, safe beach and spectacular setting on Antigua's south coast and this might well be family paradise found.

Family friendly almost seems too mundane a term for **Beaches'** sensational Caribbean resorts (beachesresorts.co.uk). Each one is right on a dazzling stretch of powder-sand beach, water sports are unlimited and accommodation includes spacious family suites. A couple even have their own waterparks.

For further options, visit 101familyholidays.co.uk.

Index

WE KNOW THE LATIN AMERICA YOU'LL LOVE

For family travel recommendations and unrivalled insight,
speak to the UK's Nº1 specialist in travel to Latin America

JOURNEY
LATIN
AMERICA

www.journeylatinamerica.co.uk ☎ 020 8622 8464

Picture credits

William Gray (author): 1, 2-3, 6-7, 10, 12, 18, 19, 20, 21, 22, 26-27, 29, 30, 31, 32, 33, 34, 35, 36, 37, 38, 39, 40, 41, 42, 43, 44, 45, 46, 47, 48, 49, 52, 53, 54, 55, 56-57, 59, 60, 62, 64, 65, 69, 70, 72, 76, 80-81, 83, 84, 88, 99, 100, 104-105, 107, 110, 114, 116, 117, 118, 121, 122, 131, 137, 141, 148-149, 151, 154, 160, 167, 169, 172, 174, 175, 190-191, 193, 195, 196, 200, 202, 204, 205, 206, 207, 210, 211, 212-213, 215, 216, 217, 218, 221, 222, 223, 224, 225, 226, 227, 228, 229, 230, 231, 232, 233, 234, 235, 238, 239, 240-241, 242, 243, 244, 246, 247, 250, 254, 255, 256, 257, 258, 260, 261, 262, 263, 268-269, 271, 274, 276, 277, 281, 282, 284, 285, 286, 287, 288, 289, 290, 291, 293, 294-295, 297, 300, 304, 306, 310, 312, 313, 316, 317, 318, 319, 321, 322-323, 325, 328, 330, 331, 333, 334, 336, 337, 338, 339, 340, 342, 346, 347

Shutterstock: 7, 16, 22, 31, 33, 35, 40, 41, 48, 50, 51, 52, 59, 60, 61, 64, 66, 70, 71, 74, 75, 76, 83, 84, 85, 88, 89, 90, 92, 93, 94, 96, 97, 98, 105, 107, 108, 109, 112, 113, 114, 115, 117, 118, 119, 120, 122, 123, 124, 125, 127, 129, 131, 132, 133, 134, 137, 138, 139, 140, 142, 143, 144, 145, 146, 147, 151, 152, 153, 155, 156, 157, 158, 159, 161, 163, 164, 168, 169, 170, 171, 174, 176, 177, 178, 179, 180, 181, 182, 183, 185, 191, 194, 195, 199, 200, 201, 205, 213, 215, 216, 217, 220, 225, 234, 235, 241, 242, 244, 245, 248, 249, 251, 252, 253, 254, 256, 257, 259, 260, 271, 272, 273, 276, 277, 278, 279, 280, 282, 283, 284, 295, 297, 298, 299, 302, 303, 305, 306, 307, 314-315, 323, 325, 326, 327, 330, 331, 332, 335, 339, 340, 341, 343

&Beyond: 266
Abama Golf Resort: 103
Adventure Company: 215
Atlantis: 347
Cachet Travel: 1
Cape Grace Hotel: 238
Casa Olea: 102
Center Parcs: 79
Club Med: 79, 126, 189
Completely Croatia: 165
Corsican Places: 79
CV Travel: 188
Discover the World: 206, 210, 211, 320

Disney: 66, 67, 78, 308
The Dolphin Connection: 86
Echo Valley Ranch: 320
Esprit Holidays: 59, 73, 146
Eurocamp: 78, 126, 146
Exodus: 166-167, 184
French Affair: 79
GIC Villa Collection: 189
Great Ocean Ecolodge: 292
Heritage Hotels: 238
Inntravel: 103, 126, 146
Jumeirah: 267
Keycamp: 78, 102, 126, 165
Kinderhotels: 146
Kontiki Museum: 203
Mallorca Farmhouses: 102
La Manga Club: 103
Mark Warner: 188
NASM: 302
Wilderness Lodges: 292
Powder Byrne: 127
Sadie Cove Wilderness Lodge: 321
Sal Salis: 292
Shangri-La: 266
Sheraton: 102
Siblu: 78
Sovereign: 103, 188
Switzerland Tourism: 128-129, 131, 134, 140
Universal Studios: 301, 308, 309
Visit Denmark: 193, 198
Western & Oriental: 188

Publishing credits & acknowledgements

Acknowledgements

Travel with Kids has been very much a family effort. It wouldn't have been possible without the tremendous support of my wife, Sally, who is not only a brilliant mother to our twins, Joseph and Eleanor, but has also been the calming, super-efficient mastermind behind the extensive family trips we've undertaken for this book. As for Joe and Ellie, now 11, they have both responded superbly to every weird and wonderful travel experience their parents have hauled them off on. They are fantastic little travellers, always happy to confront new challenges, whether it's learning to surf or coping with jetlag. I feel privileged and immensely proud to have shared so many wonderful experiences with them around the world – and I hope this book will be the inspiration for many more to come.

I must also say a huge thank you to family and friends for their help, advice, constant encouragement and for putting up with my antisocial behaviour during the writing of this book; particular thanks to my parents, parents-in-law, Simon Gray and Adam Gray.

I owe a huge debt of gratitude to the many people who have taken the time to share their family travel experiences and supply quotes for the book. My apologies to those whose quotes could not be squeezed in. Matt Berna, Chris Breen, Maxine Browning, Emma Bunce, Simon Calder, Katie Derham, Judith Escribano & Steen Eriksson, Emily Gage, Judith & John Gage, Sarah & Philip Gale, Lottie Gale, Tina Gandy, David Gower, David Gray, Kerrina Gray, Robert Gray, Sanka Guha, Martin Henderson, Sarah & Duncan Hetherington, Charlotte Hindle, Jason Hobbins, Rachel Hosier, Charlotte & Huw Jenkins, Samuel Jenkins, Dan Linstead, Celia & Alan Littlefield, The Mason family, Caroline & Robin Mewes, Chris McIntyre, Lori & John Oestreich, Charlie Panton, Victoria & Mark Pougatch, Sir Steve Redgrave, Alison & Alex Rippon, Ben Roseveare, Sharon Ryan, India Seely, David Shepherd, Magdalena Slawecka-Williams, Jennifer Stevens, The Stockwell family, Sally & Chris Sugg, Su & Carl Taylor, Olivia Titmuss, Sarah Tucker, Mike Unwin, Antonia Vaquero, Sara Wheeler, David Wickers, The Williams Family, Alison & David Williams, Emma Woollacott, Hannah Wright, Mark Wright and Mike Wynne. I am also grateful to Dr Jane Wilson-Howarth for checking the main health and safety section of the book.

Far too numerous to list, but grateful thanks must go to the hundreds of tour operators, tourist boards, travel PR companies, airlines etc who have supplied invaluable information and practical support for the research of this book. Thanks, also, to *Wanderlust* magazine and *The Sunday Times Travel* magazine for supporting my obsession with family travel.

Finally, I am immensely grateful to the team at Footprint for sharing my vision for *Travel with Kids* and for their support and patience as I effortlessly managed to sail past every deadline they gently imposed. They are without doubt the friendliest and most dedicated team I've had the pleasure of working with. Very special thanks to Alan Murphy and Patrick Dawson for their calming influence.

William Gray

Footprint credits

Project Editor: Alan Murphy
Layout & design: William Gray
Picture Editor: William Gray
Proofreader: Beverley Jollands

Managing Director: Andy Riddle
Publisher: Alan Murphy
Commercial Director: Patrick Dawson
Editorial: Felicity Laughton, Nicola Gibbs Jo Williams
Digital: Tom Mellors
Marketing: Liz Harper
Sales: Di McEntee
Advertising: Renu Sibal
Finance & administration: Elizabeth Taylor

Photography

Images © William Gray/william-gray.co.uk, unless otherwise credited on page 351.

Print

Manufactured in India by Replika Press Pvt Ltd

Publishing information

Footprint *Travel with Kids*, 2nd edition
© Footprint Handbooks Ltd, February 2012

ISBN 978-1-907263-56-9
CIP DATA: A catalogue record for this book is available from the British Library.

® Footprint Handbooks and the Footprint mark are a registered trademark of Footprint Handbooks Ltd.

Published by Footprint

6 Riverside Court, Lower Bristol Road
Bath BA2 3DZ, UK
T +44 (0)1225 469141
F +44 (0)1225 469461
footprinttravelguides.com

Distributed in the USA by
Globe Pequot Press, Guilford, Connecticut